TOWARD
a
PHILOSOPHY
of
EDUCATION

TOWARD

a

PHILOSOPHY

of

EDUCATION

Thomas O. Buford

HOLT, RINEHART AND WINSTON, INC.
New York • Chicago • San Francisco • Atlanta • Dallas
Montreal • Toronto • London • Sydney

Copyright © 1969 by Holt, Rinehart and Winston, Inc.
All rights reserved
Library of Congress Catalog Card Number: 69-13556
03-074540-3
Printed in the United States of America
1 2 3 4 5 6 7 8 9

Preface

The ideas which permeate this book have been formed in an effort to think through a philosophy of education for a small, independent, liberal arts college. Kentucky Southern College was conceived by a few visionary and energetic men in Louisville, Kentucky, to provide a kind of education which was to their way of thinking lacking in most other institutions of higher learning. The core of this educational program and, indeed, the *raison d'etre* of the institution was the interdisciplinary studies program. My responsibility for the first six years of the college's existence was to think through such a program and to articulate those thoughts in a core curriculum. Like others who try to teach students and to develop educational programs in both small colleges and large multiversities, I searched for an educational philosophy which could be defended and which could guide in the realization of this interesting educational vision. In this search, questions of a universal, philosophical character arose which required not only careful articulation but also sound philosophical investigation. To do otherwise was to allow the program to develop under less than rational guidance. The questions which I raised for myself in the course of developing an educational philosophy undergirding the interdisciplinary studies program at Kentucky Southern College were for the most part the same questions which are raised in this text.

The intent of this book is to guide students in educational philosophy courses to see how issues in the philosophy of education can arise and to think philosophically about those issues. No attempt is made in this text to present or develop any one position. On the contrary, it makes clear some of the main issues in the field and distinguishes the important theories which deal with those issues. Also, it allows each philosopher to make his case for the particular theory he defends. The book is organized systematically, but historically important essays are included. However, because philosophy of education as a distinct discipline has arisen only recently and because many of the great strides in the field have taken place in the twentieth century, most of the material is taken from the writings of contemporary philosophers and philosophers of education.

The essays are organized into four chapters. The first chapter deals with the context in which questions in the philosophy of education arise, and the other three chapters deal with specific issues for educational philosophy. In order to understand the context in which the last three chapters are cast, the first chapter should be read first. The order in which the remaining chapters are read is left to the discretion of the instructor. Each chapter is introduced with a brief discussion of the issues the authors deal with and the general outlines of their positions. The purpose of each introduction is to provide the student with a map to follow while working through the selections. At the end of each chapter an annotated bibliography is given to aid the student in further reading.

Most of the essays are intelligible to the beginning reader. However, a few difficult ones have been included. These were required because of the need to include a particular author whose writings are uniformly difficult and/or to include a statement of a position which raises the issues better or deals with them in a more cogent manner. The student may proceed effectively to a later essay without having mastered the ones before it; each essay is intelligible on its own, and the student may return to the more difficult essay and find that his other reading has put him in a better position to understand it. A glossary of major terms undefined in the selections in which they appear is included to aid the student in working through the more technical passages.

For their tough-minded but congenial criticism I am most grateful to Professors R. Freeman Butts of Columbia University and Wayne E. Bell of Kentucky Southern College. Miss Becky Baker and Mrs. Betty Jane Davis were helpful beyond expectation in the preparation of the manuscript.

Thomas O. Buford

Denton, Texas
November 1968

Contents

vii

4
CULTURAL POSTURES
AND EDUCATIONAL AIMS   415

INTRODUCTION

THE term "philosophy of education," like most labels or names which are in frequent use, has a broad range of possible meanings. Some philosophers of education have adopted a philosophical system such as idealism, realism, or pragmatism and have worked out the implications of that philosophy for education. Although many contemporary educational philosophers no longer accept such metaphysical and epistemological systems, they do adopt a methodology such as that employed by linguistic analysts or by phenomenologists and use that method as a way of investigating the field of education. Whether the systems approach or the methodological approach is taken, there is a tendency to make philosophical commitments outside the field of education and to bring those commitments to the philosophical study of educational problems. The choice of the data to be investigated, the way the problems are stated, and the answers advanced are significantly influenced, if not completely determined, by the methodological stance or the system orientation taken by the educational philosopher. That one cannot completely bracket one's preconceptions when one begins the philosophical study of education is granted. However, it is important that one be aware of these presuppositions and not let them unduly influence one's investigations. Furthermore, if one is to investigate educational questions in a philosophical manner, it is important that the questions arise out of the educational experience itself. For these reasons the approach to the philosophy of education which guided both the organization of this anthology and the choice of the selections included centers on problems which arise when the transmission of culture is critically examined. How these problems arise and what it means to approach them in a philosophical manner can be spelled out through a discussion of philosophy, culture, and education.

1

The attempt to define philosophy has been one of the thorniest problems philosophers have faced since the beginning of their inquiry. It should be no surprise that those who give themselves to understanding the assumptions underlying the thoughts and actions of men should turn their critical gaze on themselves. This spirit of critical inquiry, which is deeply rooted in the philosophical tradition of the West, suggests the following definition: Philosophy is the attempt to interpret rationally the totality of man's experience. As it stands, this statement provides little understanding of the meaning of philosophy as a critically reflective discipline. However, each word is packed with meaning and through an analysis or "unpacking" of each term the view of philosophy couched therein can be clarified.

The word "attempt" points to the searching character of the philosophical enterprise. It may seem strange to those who are beginning the study of philosophy that final answers are rarely if ever given to the questions philosophers raise. It is not in finding so called "final answers" that the vitality of philosophy is based. Rather it is the search, the creative attempt to understand, that invigorates philosophers to continue their work. In a society in which security is a primary concern, particularly economic and political security, it is noteworthy that some people find their security neither in final answers nor in an economic or political system. Rather, security for them is found in searching, in seeking defensible answers to ultimate questions. To what end should men be educated? What does it mean to learn? What method should one use in the search for philosophical understanding? In this anthology, for example, no attempt is made to guide the reader to accept a set of preconceived "final answers" to the questions raised. On the contrary, the search motif is present in setting up the cultural problems men face in contemporary American society, in outlining the major philosophical methods available for investigating the educational issues which arise from the problems, in examining the major theories of learning developed in the Western philosophical tradition, and in setting up alternative educational goals for a society whose culture is in conflict. Indeed, part of the search is present in the attempt to outline the problems.

The philosophical search for understanding is carried on in a rational manner. The history of Western philosophy has been conducted on the belief that man through his rational powers is able to understand whatever he considers important to understand. Although some philosophers, such as the sceptic Sextus Empiricus, questioned whether man could know either through sense or through reason, most philosophers remained confident in the capacity of reason to know. Since the beginning of the modern period of philosophy, the nature of reason has been a topic of philosophical investigation. The apex of this philosophical study was achieved by

Immanuel Kant in his works, *The Critique of Pure Reason, The Critique of Practical Reason,* and *The Critique of Judgment.* Even though "reason" has come under the critical investigation of men such as Kant, it has been through a belief in the capacity of reason to know that those conducting the investigations were confident that they could articulate questions and search for defensible answers. This belief also pervades this anthology.

The attempt to understand in a rational manner is to go about the philosophical search in a particular way. Feelings, intuitions, insights, although important as data for reason in its search, do not *guide* the search. One could follow their lead if one wanted to do so, but there is nothing in them that is self-corrective, that would allow one to determine the best or the correct answer. To allow reason to guide the search is to proceed in an analytic and a synoptic manner. Reason proceeding analytically divides the data under investigation into parts. But reason does not rest with the data broken into discrete units. It then seeks to put the pieces back together again, to interrelate them, to establish some kind of connectedness within experience. This attempt to view the data of experience from the point of view of the whole is reason operating synoptically. Furthermore, to follow reason in the search is to apply standards of consistency to determine the adequacy of one's analytic and synoptic understanding. In the chapters to follow, the attempt is made to divide the field of philosophy of education into areas, to examine the areas carefully, and to establish interconnections among them.

When the philosophical search is conducted in a rational manner, an attempt is made to interpret the area under investigation. To interpret an area of investigation is to uncover the assumptions and beliefs which underlie the area, to evaluate critically the assumptions, and to promulgate new ones or retread the old ones. For example, in Section 3 the question is asked, "What does it mean to learn?" All of us have some notion of what it means to learn, but few of us attempt to bring to the surface of our attention our assumptions about learning and to evaluate them. To interpret "learning" is to investigate the beliefs and assumptions which are held about learning, to evaluate the beliefs, and to attempt to advance a defensible learning theory. Philosophers since Plato have investigated the learning experience and have developed theories which to them were acceptable. Through such investigatory activities an understanding may be gained of areas of experience which are the most direct and immediate experiences persons have. What is learned about these experiences are the assumptions which underlie them and the physical, social, and cultural forces which have contributed to their development. Such achievement of critical self-awareness is a liberating experience.

Once one is aware of his assumptions and has critically evaluated them, he is then able to exert some control over his decisions or, at least, to understand the forces influencing him.

Finally, the philosophical search is to be conducted in every area of experience. Nothing is sacrosanct to the critical evaluation of the philosopher's roving eye whether it is learning, values, existence, or art. Philosophy has as its province for investigation all of man's life and asks ultimate questions about every aspect of human existence. Of course, the areas of human experience under investigation here are limited to those which could be placed under the general heading of education. Within this area, however, every aspect of experience is liable to critical study. Without a willingness to examine all relevant data how else could an adequate understanding be achieved?

A final comment about philosophy must be made. The rational search for understanding in all areas of human life is a paradoxical endeavor. On the one hand, philosophy is the most concrete, "down to earth," personal study one can pursue. Indeed, what is more immediate to us than existing, valuing, learning? On the other hand, philosophy is one of the most abstract studies in which one can become involved. To think about existence, learning, and valuing is to deal with a subject matter which seems distant, obscure, and strange. To become involved in the philosophical quest is to ask questions which drive to the core of the personal dimensions of life, to learn that we often do not really understand ourselves, and to discover that the attempt to understand philosophically is a difficult but liberating task.

It may be a truism to say that persons involved in the philosophical search live in societies, but this should not blind us to the truth and importance of the observation. The philosopher may perceive that most other members of society are not involved, and will not join him in his search. In this sense the philosophical quest is often a lonely endeavor. The philosopher is nevertheless a member of a society and shares its culture. Whatever he understands as a result of his search will be conditioned by the culture of the society of which he is part. This point can be clarified through a discussion of what "culture" means and the implications of this meaning for philosophical investigation.

The eminent anthropologist Ralph Linton defined culture as " . . . the configuration of learned behavior and results of behavior whose component elements are shared and transmitted by the members of a particular society."[1] Included under "learned behavior" would be meanings, patterns of thinking, ways of achieving what the society thinks is impor-

[1]Ralph Linton, *The Cultural Background of Personality* (New York: Appleton-Century-Crofts, Inc., 1945), p. 32.

tant, the material employed by the society, the language which conveys the meanings of the society, and social groupings. A person growing up in a particular society would be incorporated into the society by achieving status and role. He would also be enculturated by the society. Enculturation refers to that process by which society transmits to its members the patterns of behavior the society thinks are important. Through its language the social group conditions the child to fundamentals such as habits of personal cleanliness, dress, speech, interpersonal relations. As the child grows older, the more complex dimensions of the culture are transmitted to him, such as the intricacies of the language; behavioral patterns expected of adults; society's self-understandings as articulated through its art, literature, philosophy; and society's methods for understanding nature, such as the scientific method. As the person progresses through the stages of physical and psychological growth, he continues to learn and is continually conditioned by the culture in which he lives. From this point of view, then, enculturation continues from birth until death.

A person engaged in the philosophical quest lives in a society and is being enculturated by that society. The language, meanings, understandings, knowledge, and ways of gaining new knowledge which he employs in the philosophical quest have been given to him by his society. Although he may be able to look objectively at himself as being culturally conditioned, his cultural conditioning is present in all of his observations. For example, Plato in *The Republic* sought to give a rational interpretation of Greek social life and to give the *polis* a foundation based on the nature of the soul. However, in his investigation of this topic, his Greek cultural heritage is revealed. Plato's understanding of what social life meant was the Greek *polis* and his investigations took that turn. Further in his study of the ends toward which the *polis* ought to move, he became involved in a discussion of the nature of *physis,* that which underlies all things and which is self-dependent, that is, reality. This datum, *physis,* has its origins in the earliest religious experiences of the Greek people and is taken as the primary object of investigation by most Greek philosophers. One could enumerate other ideas central to Plato's thought which were part of his Greek cultural heritage, but one more should suffice to make the point. Plato along with most other Greeks disliked excess. To them moderation in all things was of obvious value. Nowhere does Plato critically reflect on the intelligibility of this belief. He simply assumes its importance and conducts his philosophical search on the basis of it. Hence, the philosophical search takes place under the conditions set by the culture in which the philosopher lives. The philosopher may be conscious of the framework in which he thinks, but that framework nevertheless permeates all that he does.

One final comment must be made about culture and the philosopher's place within it. Cultures are not static; on the contrary, they are constantly in change. Even though a primitive culture may appear to remain generally intact through many generations, some changes do take place. Change is particularly prevalent in highly developed cultures such as the American culture. How social change takes place is a complex question. It is important, however, to point out some of the elements which may contribute to changes in a society. The older generation through the home, mass media, the schools, and the churches calls for various kinds of behavior on the part of the young. When the younger generation hears often discordant voices along with its own, conflict and change are the result. Such conflict often provides the stimulus to begin the philosophical quest for self and social awareness and for defensible answers to ultimate questions. For example, conflicting racial attitudes raise such questions as what actions are right in interpersonal relationships, what character traits are praiseworthy or blameworthy, what is the good toward which men ought to direct their lives. These questions, distinctly ethical in character, are among those which philosophers raise when they find themselves faced both with the desire to live life intelligently and with conflicting cultural beliefs about the life most worth living. Problems of an ethical nature arise when a culture is in change; but what is more important for those of us who are attempting to study the philosophy of education, problems of an educational nature arise when a society's culture is in conflict and change.

We have seen that each member of a society is experiencing the processes of socialization and enculturation from birth until death. Furthermore, we have seen that in the process of transmission of culture conflicts arise and change occurs. If these conflicts force us to consider ultimate questions about ethics, they also force us to consider ultimate questions about the process of transmitting culture. Education in its broadest sense is the process of transmission of culture from one generation to the next. This process may take place formally through a school with a clearly defined curriculum or it may take place informally through the home, the peer group, mass media, or the church. Whether it is formal or informal in setting, the process of cultural transmission is open to the cultural conflicts and changes experienced by the rest of society. The ultimate questions which the philosopher of education asks are those which arise from his critically investigating this vital dimension of social life. In his attempt to give a rational interpretation he raises questions. How should one proceed in the investigation of the educative process? What does it mean to learn? What posture ought one to take toward the crisis-culture in which one finds oneself and what specific goals are implied by that posture? Such ultimate questions as these arise when one carries the philosophical quest into the area of enculturation.

In conclusion, philosophy of education is the attempt to investigate in a philosophical manner ultimate questions which persons who are experiencing their culture in conflict ask about the process of cultural transmission. Furthermore, these questions are not brought to the educative process from philosophical disciplines such as ethics or epistemology and then dealt with from the point of view of a preconceived philosophical position. Rather the problems arise out of a critical reflection on the educative experience itself. Of course, any insight which can be found in the best that is known from other fields of knowledge is valuable. But such aid must always enhance the prospects of understanding the educative process and must never prejudge it. In the chapters to follow, the attempt is made to consider philosophically the educational problems developing out of a culture in conflict, to articulate clearly the questions, and to make available to the reader the best work of philosophers in the West who have come to grips with some of the central issues arising from a critical reflection on the process of cultural transmission.

THE SPIRIT OF MODERN
AMERICAN CULTURE*

Issues in the philosophy of education grow out of a critical investigation of a society's transmission and acquisition of its culture. When a culture is stable, the cultural values to be transmitted and the process of transmission and acquisition are usually well defined. However, when a culture changes and tends toward disorientation and disorganization, what is at stake is at least a questioning if not in fact an overthrowing of major traditional values. When this takes place, issues arise regarding the whole educative process. Let us examine a value basic to contemporary American culture to see not only the tendencies which are threatening to overthrow it, but also the issues which are being raised for philosophy of education by these tendencies. This analysis will set the context in which and about which the authors in this chapter are speaking.

It has long been a human goal, whether conscious or unconscious, to find meaning in life through the analytic-synoptic method of specifying areas of experience and then attempting to interrelate them from the point of view of the whole. If in the search either the analytic or the synoptic aspect of the method is exclusively employed, then meaning is difficult, if not impossible, to find. The part may be clearly delineated, yet it has no meaning for us until we know what it is a part of and how it is related to the whole to which it belongs. On the other hand, wholes without content are meaningless abstractions. The parts of a jigsaw puzzle would have no meaning unless we knew to what puzzle they belonged and how they fitted into the overall picture, and a jigsaw puzzle without parts would not be meaningful. The creative search for meaning demands that one cannot

*Sections of the introduction are taken from "Towards a Philosophy of General Education," by Thomas O. Buford. Reprinted by permission of *The Personalist*, Vol. 48, No. 4 (Autumn 1967), pp. 474-480.

follow *either* one method *or* the other exclusively. Both methods must be employed, one illumining and completing the other. During the last 700 years, Western man has increasingly employed the analytic method and decreasingly employed the synoptic method, and the contempory result is a spirit which can be called "the analytic temperament." There are at least four manifestations in Western society of this spirit: intellectual specialization and compartmentalization, social estrangement, spiritual anxiety over values, and the knowledge explosion. These issues, we shall see, clearly point to the need for developing an adequate and defensible philosophy of education.

That there is a strong tendency to overspecialize in our society is obvious. The intricacies of each field of knowledge increase daily and society needs highly skilled minds to fathom them. This tendency is fed by the demands for goods and services in an industrial, urban society which only an increase in specialization seems to be able to meet. In order to meet these requirements, and to advance in one's field, one finds that he has to be more and more proficient in highly specialized areas. Societal necessities point up the immediate occasion of specialization and compart-mentalization, but one must go back to the demise of the Middle Ages and the birth of the Renaissance to find the modern origins of the analytic temperament, the concern over one area of knowledge to the exclusion of its whole context.

The High Middle Ages was characterized by a cultural synthesis brought about in part through the balanced tension between the Church's Christian values and Greek metaphysics. In the High Middle Ages Scholastics under Aristotle's influence believed that philosophy was the study of man and nature. It was the province of the Church and theology to examine God. This did not mean that reason and faith were separated into two distinct, watertight compartments. Rather, reason could give evidence where faith needed it and faith could correct and guide reason. With the tool of reason and the guide of faith Scholastic thinkers attempted to synthesize all knowledge. Following Aristotle, the Schoolmen organized revealed knowledge into theology and philosophical knowledge into the theoretical (first philosophy, mathematics, and physics) and the practical (ethics, economics, and politics). In the grand scheme of St. Thomas Aquinas' *Summa Theologiae* and in the literary cultural synthesis of Dante's *Divine Comedy* the Medievalist truly believed he had achieved an adequate and defensible world view which explained all of man's experience. However, with the attacks on the Great Chain of Being by nominalists such as Occam and Scotus and with the scientific findings of Copernicus and Galileo, the grand synthesis which filled the Scholastic with awe began to be suspect. The world of Renaissance man was not subject to the neat packaging the Medievalist supplied. Social and intellectual structures were undergoing changes which were in no small degree the expression of a new dominant spirit, the spirit of analysis. Although the spirit of synopsis was not done away with, to the center of man's attention ascended the spirit of analysis manifesting itself particularly in the scientific method.

It is not hard to see the effects of the modern analytic spirit in the sciences. Since the Renaissance the physical sciences have become more and more divided as new areas of experience have been investigated by means of the scientific method. With the tool of the scientific method in their hands scientists began to understand old areas of concern better and new areas were opened up. Among these were physics, under such men as Newton, chemistry under Boyle and Lavoisier, mathematics under Newton and Leibniz, biology under John Ray and Linnaeus. Today these are subdivided into many diverse areas of study. Though the physical sciences were the first to break from the bond of Aristotelianism, the social sciences soon followed. Especially in the nineteenth century do we find thinkers becoming concerned with society. Though thinkers had been writing about politics and economics for centuries, not until the late eighteenth century and early nineteenth century did they use the scientific method. Enamored with the dazzling success of the methods of the physical sciences and beset with the societal problems brought on by the Industrial and French Revolutions, thinkers began to apply the scientific method to society. Sociology developed under such men as Auguste Comte; psychology under Wundt and Freud; economics under Adam Smith, Ricardo, Malthus and Karl Marx; history under Hegel and Vico; and political science under Mill and Bentham. (Parsons traces the development of the disciplines since the Renaissance, the attempts to unify them, and the growth and legitimacy of the social sciences. That Parsons traces the attempts to unify the disciplines is evidence not only of a lingering synoptic spirit but also of the tendency toward overspecialization within the disciplines.)

The effects of the modern analytic spirit are found not only in the sciences but also in the humanities. Literary analysis, a process which showed great promise when Lorenzo Valla used it to refute the credibility of the Donation of Constantine, was widely used by Renaissance scholars in evaluating newly discovered Greek and Roman literature. Quickly this process was taken up for use in Biblical interpretation by Erasmus, Zwingli, Calvin, Luther, and others. Biblical scholars since the sixteenth century have developed the technique into the reliable methods of higher and lower criticism. However, literary analysis has not been the sole possession of Biblical students. Contemporary humanists have used it in an effort to determine the authorship and date of writing of works of great men of letters such as Shakespeare and Plato.

The analytic spirit is seen not only in study of literary works but also in the method and style of writers. Although it is found in writers of all ages, one has only to examine the satire and critical cultural analyses in the writings of Dante, Erasmus, Voltaire, Swift, Flaubert, Ibsen, and Samuel Beckett to find the critical aspect of the spirit of analysis in literature. In the arts one can detect the spirit of analysis in the movement from dominance of the church and of architecture into individual disciplines. Painting and sculpture in the Renaissance were freed from church architecture and considered meaningful in and for themselves. Drama moved from the church to the courtyard of the church and finally into the towns. Music during the Renaissance was no longer the possession of the church. It was widely used to express secular values such as romantic love. Thus, from the Renaissance to the twentieth century, painting, sculpture, drama, and music have constituted themselves as individual means of expressing values and no longer derive their meaning from the world view of the church. Each possesses its own world view and seeks to be viewed as a significant way of seeking and expressing meaning.

Thus, the spirit of analysis which developed in the Renaissance has permeated every aspect of contemporary life. When the Renaissance man began to see that values could be found outside the church and that the world was a marvelous place filled with interesting and satisfying experiences, he discovered new ways of dealing with his world and of controlling it, and he began a mood which persists as the dominant force in contemporary culture. The mood, though scandalized by the evil of two world wars, is that men through science and its techniques of studying and controlling the "part" can develop a view of man and his environment which is ultimately satisfying. (Cassirer speaks to this point in his search for an adequate philosophy of man.) Thus, the analytic temperament has occasioned an intellectual specialization and compartmentalization in the contemporary world; it has also occasioned social estrangement.

The breakdown in interpersonal and intergroup relations is not new to the twentieth century. Though it is to some extent part and parcel of any society, the contemporary estrangement of persons and groups and of American society from its traditional values is a manifestation of the analytic temperament begun in the Renaissance. That temperament is expressed as an individualism which may be defined as a seeking to escape from restriction of traditional authority and an urge to develop potentialities of man and groups to their fullest degree. Such a Faustian view of man manifested itself during the Renaissance in the rise of a humanism stripped of its religious trappings, the modern secular state, capitalism, and the right to make private judgments in the realm of religion. Heirs to this individualism, filtered through the French and Industrial Revolutions, are contemporary movements such as nationalism, racism, and collectivism.

Collectivism, explicit in totalitarianism, and implicit in business organization and economic planning, tends to make man an object to be manipulated and to separate men from one another: the ruler from the ruled, the owner from the laborer, the planner from the recipient of the planning. Besides estrangement resulting from collectivism, there is also estrangement resulting from emphasis on race. Because of his color and regardless of his economic and educational background, the black, the brown, or the yellow man has at times been made to feel that he is intellectually and biologically inferior to men of other races. The growth of nations in Africa and southeast Asia points up another area of estrangement among people. The nationalistic spirit that received a strong impetus in the French Revolution and has spread throughout the world has tended to separate people. Pride of nation and heritage have made people look inward and ignore or depreciate that which is not a part of their heritage. That there is all too little understanding between East and West, American and Russian, Chinese and Russian, French and English is obvious. Finally, the differentiation that takes place in a society when men began to compare themselves with others and to stratify themselves often results in social estrangement. The rich consider the poor lazy, the poor consider the rich crooked, the educated consider the uneducated unfortunate, and the uneducated consider the educated impractical, unrealistic, and snobbish. In the midst of this social estrangement men look for meaningful interpersonal relationships. What is my relation to my neighbor? What ought it to be? In the light of the social gulfs separating people, how and where are men to find meaning? (The nature of social estrangement or alienation is discussed by Seeman. Whyte investigates business organizations as one example of alienation in contemporary American society. Marcuse, from the viewpoint of the New Left, suggests that American society is experiencing an advanced stage of alienation in the "one-dimensional society.")

The third manifestation of the analytic temperament is the anxious concern over values. Although this problem was not conspicuous from the Renaissance through the close of the Second World War, it has become a dominant characteristic since that time. When in the Renaissance men began to throw off the shackles of religious authoritarianism and assert themselves religiously, intellectually, socially, politically, and economically, they opened themselves to the fundamental issue of what is the good and the right. Intellectuals before the twentieth century raised the issue, but the majority of Western society held to the teachings of the Judeo-Christian religion. However, the demonic as manifested in two world wars has touched off the sceptical spirit of man, and the writings of Nietzsche, Heidegger, Sartre, and Ayer are no longer the sole possession of the intellectuals. People, especially college students, are seriously questioning if there are any values which are valid for all people.

The proliferation of choices given to people in a highly industrial and urban society has added to the anxiety over the good and the right. Indeed, is there an ultimate right and wrong to which people ought to adjust their lives, or are right and wrong mere conventions to be settled by each person for himself? By society alone? By the individual and society in dialogue? Or what? The questions about the nature of values, which values to accept, why they should be accepted, and what happens if they are accepted face us as forcefully as they did Socrates and Plato in fourth and fifth century B.C. Athens, and Augustine in fifth century A.D. Rome. The obvious result of such anxious questioning is that persons are being thrown into a maze of values and are finding it difficult indeed to work their way to any principles for living, to "wisdom." (Sartre speaks to these issues in the selection in this chapter and offers his own solution. Jung, taking a different approach from Sartre, examines the psychical dimension of the modern anxiety over values.)

Finally, the analytic spirit has contributed to what is being called in this century the knowledge explosion. (See the selection from Bell for an excellent treatment of this and related phenomena.) When Renaissance men found the joys of the search in the natural world and the demanding but fulfilling artistic subjects beyond the walls of the church and below the heavens, new understandings began to be made available. No doubt the major invention contributing to the knowledge explosion of the Renaissance was the printing press. Books, pamphlets, pictures, newspapers were now available to more people than ever before. With this instrument at their disposal scholars could and did write their findings and musings for others to read. The development of the individual disciplines, the scientific method, the expansion of literary forms, the growing literacy of people in the West contributed to an increasing fund of information and knowledge. However, the twentieth century has witnessed an increase in knowledge far beyond the vision of any man of the Renaissance. The technological impact on mass media, the increased emphasis on the natural and social sciences, the growth of the public school system and the university systems, the almost unbelievable emphasis put on research just for sake of research have all contributed to a fund of knowledge that stretches the imagination of any man.

One of the major results of the knowledge explosion is the greater understanding we have of our social and physical environment and, indeed, of ourselves. Disease, social problems, mental illness, physical deformity, and mental retardation are all being dealt with in varying degrees of success. That they are being controlled even partially is evidence of the new knowledge at our disposal. However, the increase in knowledge makes it evident that no man can ever expect to know all there is to know about any area of knowledge. Since one cannot know all there is to know, then what should he know, what areas of knowledge should he gain an understanding and a mastery of? With competing perspectives clamoring for one's allegiance, which perspectives should one accept and why? Furthermore, the unparalleled diversity of information available to persons today raises the question of whether and to what extent any order can be brought out of it. How could anyone in the face of such a knowledge explosion expect to achieve unity amid such diversity?

To summarize a present crisis in the West and especially in America, then, we find ourselves in an age of analysis uncovering and amassing the facts of the parts of our world and hoping thereby to understand its meaning. We have divided our intellectual world into a multitude of areas so that we can get a clear view of them and find meaning through controlling them to suit our desires. We have divided our social world into many parts and have so distinguished groups and individuals that we have left little hope of getting them together again. Further, in our search for meaning through the tools of science we have never gotten hold of that something which will give our lives significance. The multitude of value opportunities almost overwhelms us and leaves us reeling with the question: What ought I to do and why? Finally, the knowledge explosion seriously threatens the possibility of achieving a defensible integrating order or perspective.

These issues force upon us the responsibility of rethinking the educative process, the process of transmitting and of acquiring culture. If we are faced with these issues resulting in part if not completely from the analytic temperament, then *how* are we to go about the job of rethinking education, *on what grounds* can we claim that knowledge is acquired, to what *ends* should one educate? Indeed, if the above analysis is correct, then the questions just raised must be dealt with carefully and rationally. The alternative is to allow the whole socialization activity of our society to proceed without even the attempt to evaluate it and control it on a rational basis. In the following chapters each of these questions will be investigated in turn. In Section 2 the methodological question will be considered, the philosophy of learning will be investigated in Section 3, and, finally, in Section 4, the question of the aims of education will be investigated.

Intellectual Specialization and Compartmentalization

Unity and Diversity in the Modern Intellectual Disciplines: The Role of the Social Sciences *

TALCOTT PARSONS

This essay will discuss the intellectual disciplines as one major aspect of contemporary culture. Roughly, I conceive their scope as comparable to that of the German term *Wissenschaft*. Perhaps their best criterion is general recognition in this country as main subjects for teaching and research in the central university faculties of Arts and Sciences. Thus, for most purposes, the "applied" fields that predominate in professional schools are excluded,[1] as are the creative and performing arts. Typically, the included disciplines are also organized in professional associations, both national and international, though the networks of such associations are extremely complex.

I will particularly address the problem of understanding the unity and diversity exhibited by these disciplines: the principles on which they are organized, the principles from which distinctions among them derive, and the principles they hold sufficiently in common that their common placement in typical "pure discipline" faculties is justified. That the intellectual

[1]There are, however, some difficult borderline problems, such as the status of law as an intellectual discipline.

*Reprinted by permission from *Daedalus*, Journal of the American Academy of Arts and Sciences, Boston, Mass., Vol. 94 (1965), pp. 39–65.

disciplines can be treated as belonging together requires an explanation salient to problems of both the conjunction of cultural disciplines and the social organization of the university system. When, in so many respects, our society steadily becomes more specialized, why do our universities not specialize in one field, the humanities, the natural sciences, or the social sciences, leaving the other two for other universities? Why do such technical schools as the Massachusetts Institute of Technology tend to "round out" by strengthening their humanities and social sciences instead of specializing in the natural sciences with increasing rigor? Similarly, the Brookings Institution, originally conceived as a graduate school of the social sciences, did not long survive on that specialized basis except as a research organization.

When conceived broadly enough, all the disciplines seem to share certain normative elements, that is, standards, or values and norms that derive from their common grounding in man's quest for knowledge. Whether the subject materials are natural phenomena, human behavior, or documents of the cultural heritage, in language or in stone, it is agreed that assertions about them should be solidly grounded in objective evidence accessible, if at all possible, to the relevant scholarly public. Similarly, inferences from factual statements should follow standard canons of logic, concepts should be precise and clear, and different statements claiming objective grounding should be logically consistent with each other. In social terms, scholars' assertions and evidence should be public and exposed to the criticism of professional peers. These standards apply no less to the humanistic disciplines than to the sciences. It is not necessarily required that a poet be logically consistent. But a scholarly critic of poetry must face the negative criticism of colleagues if his statements *about* his subject are not consistent.

These common standards of the intellectual disciplines, in which commitment to specific convictions other than procedural beliefs in their own importance and their own methodological standards is inherently tentative, suggest that a convenient distinction separates them from structures in which *commitment* takes precedence over further investigation, which necessarily places questions of how and why particular bases of commitment should be accepted above action on the bases of commitment.

Four basic areas of the latter type of commitment may be distinguished. Where empirical scientific knowledge is the primary focus, members of the applied professions must act with what knowledge is immediately available. Thus a surgeon responsible for a patient with cancer will operate to remove the malignant tissue to the best of his ability, *not* stopping for further investigation into the causes of even this particular cancer except insofar as he can improve his knowledge of the particular case within the available time. There seems to be a parallel line between humanistic scholarship and the "creative" arts. Like the good applied scientist, the good artist is certainly concerned with knowledge of the traditions and history of his art and with "theories" about it, but in the actual process of creation he is a practitioner, not an historical scholar or theorist. He must act upon his commitments and convictions, not primarily consider on what bases they are justified or not.

In the field of religious activity, the central concern is faith, which is a matter of commitment, not of posing a problem for investigation. The religious believer, including the clergyman, is not in the first instance a theologian or philosopher, but a practitioner, no matter how important the theological traditions of his faith may be. Finally, the distinction between investigator and practitioner has a special application, which will be more fully discussed presently, to the relation between moral culture or "values" and social action. The responsible social activist, whether high official or ordinary citizen, defender of the *status quo* or revolutionist, is not as such a moral philosopher or social scientist, but once again a practitioner.

Contrary to much received opinion, I shall base my discussion on the fact that the proper classification of disciplines now seems to be broadly *tripartite* rather than dichotomous; we have the humanities, the natural sciences, and the social sciences. The last are the latest comers and are considerably more prominent in the United States than in Great Britain, or, indeed, France. The relatively late emergence of the social sciences as a "third force" seems to be a particularly important phenomenon—a deserving focus for the following discussion.

THE PHILOSOPHICAL BACKGROUND

The modern form of the intellectual disciplines originated during the Renaissance. In that early phase, they were, variously, *secular* studies not rigidly bound to *specific* religious premises like the theological-philosophical and literary-artistic endeavors of the Middle Ages. Stimulated by their encounter with texts long since lost to them, the humanists of the West eagerly undertook to recapture the civilization of the past, its religion, philosophy, art, science, even its social organization. Beyond this, it served as a point of departure not only for new and independent creation of their own in imitation of the ancients, but for such use of the riches of antiquity as Aquinas' theological appropriation of Aristotelian philosophy.

The humanities were thus the oldest and generally most prestigeful of the intellectual disciplines. With important components of theology, philosophy, and, eventually, mathematics, they comprised the core of higher learning throughout the Western world for a very long time, maintaining a virtual monopoly which was not really broken before the middle of the nineteenth century. They thereby constituted the principal common culture of the educated classes of Europe, with history, philosophy, language, and literature gradually assuming more prominent places within the same basic framework.

The natural sciences developed notably only in the late Renaissance, after the humanistic studies had been deeply absorbed. But despite the great achievements of such figures as Galileo and Newton—and the impact of their ideas on philosophy—the natural sciences did not effectually rival the humanities in higher education and the culture of the most influential social classes until well into the nineteenth century. Thus President Charles Eliot of Harvard, the most eminent modernizer of the American university system, was "only" a chemist, and his appointment was viewed very much askance because of the relatively low repute of scientists even at that late day.

It is often said that a most distinctive feature of modern Western philosophy has been its concern with the epistemological problem, the grounding of the validity of cognitive enterprises. The great seventeenth century synthesis certainly established a frame of reference that gave primacy to the problem in Descartes' sharp formulation of a subject-object dichotomy. This tended toward a metaphysical dualism of the knowing mind and the known external world.

Interestingly, such conceptions as Hobbes's "passions" and power or Locke's "sensations" and the association of ideas contained the germs of many outstanding later developments in psychology and the social sciences. Yet their prototype of the external world was the physical world as understood by the new physical science.[2] Thus, during its first stage, modern philosophy, as "philosophy of knowledge," concentrated on knowledge of the physical world. This comprised only part of philosophy, which was also concerned, above all, with metaphysics and its relation to theology. But with reference to empirical knowledge, the internal world of "experience," the subjective side of Descartes' dichotomy, was generally understood to be only a "position of the observer" for studying physical objects, not a category of objects for study.

It is curious—and would merit investigation in terms of the sociology and psychology of knowledge—that the priority given to knowledge of the physical world in the development of modern philosophy reverses the

[2]This is extremely clear, for instance, in Hobbes's deliberate construction of his social science on the model of "geometry." See the opening chapters of Thomas Hobbes, *Leviathan*, Blackwell, Oxford, 1946.

priorities applying to the development of the human individual's knowledge of his own environment and, it seems, the formation of empirical knowledge in early cultural evolution.

Since Freud, it has been known that the child's first structured orientation to his world occurs in the field of his *social* relationships. The "objects" involved in Freud's fundamental concept of object relations are "social" objects: persons in roles, particularly parents, and the collectivities of which they are parts and into which the child is socialized. This orientation includes an empirical cognitive component which is the foundation on which a child builds his later capacity for the scientific understanding of the empirical world. What is often interpreted as the child's "magical" thinking about the physical world probably evidences a lack of capacity to differentiate between physical and social objects.[3]

Similar things appear true of cultural evolution more generally, though, coming under the general principle that ontogeny repeats phylogeny only very broadly; the parallels are far from exact. Perhaps the best single reference on the problem is the old article by Durkheim and Mauss on the forms of primitive classification.[4] This emphasizes, with special but not exclusive reference to the Australian aborigines, the priority of the social aspect of primitive categorization of the world, notably in the conception of spatial relations in terms of the arrangement of social units in the camp.

THE TWO PRINCIPAL CONCEPTIONS OF THE INTELLECTUAL DISCIPLINES

That these problems are crucial in an underlying sense is perhaps evidenced by the fact that the great British empiricist philosophers who most sharply crystallized the basic problems of epistemology were also greatly interested in human behavior and social phenomena—especially Hobbes and Locke in the seventeenth century and Hume in the eighteenth. Hume's essays, for example, contain outstanding insights into many fields of social analysis.[5]

This concern with both the physical and social worlds was the source of

[3]On this aspect of Freud, see my article, "Social Structure and the Development of Personality," reprinted as Chapter 4 of my volume, *Social Structure and Personality,* Free Press, 1964.

[4]Emile Durkheim and Marcel Mauss, *Primitive Classification,* The University of Chicago Press, 1963; French edition, 1903.

[5]Just to give examples, cf. "Of Superstition and Enthusiasm," which is a kind of charter for the sociology of religion, and the essays on commerce, money, trade, public credit, interest, and taxes, which are landmarks in economics. David Hume: *Essays and Treatises,* vol. I, Cadell, London, 1793.

s tended to emerge in the contention that each "realm" func-
·ding to its own unique necessities and in the failure to
·rly how the "realms" interacted with each other. The dialect-
n of the ultimate unity of conflict and integration was a third
· which, however, may be considered secondary.

x set of variations on the theme of Cartesian dualism seems to
ped. We have not stressed the common philosophical concern
fference between mind and matter, but rather the problems
· issues of the development of social science. The social terms
'itarian tradition evidently emerged from what, contrary to
·, were the inherently open boundaries of the physical world as
by early modern science and philosophy. The utilitarian ten-
to assimilate analysis of human behavior as closely to that of
bjects as seemed feasible. The case of the logical structure of
bmic theory is paradigmatic. The consequence was the exten-
e behavioral realm of conceptions of the scientific treatment of
· objects in a way which left the status of knowing subjects
ivocal in this context.

ntian statement cut off this tendency to extension sharply. It
shifted the problem to the field of the noumenal, which we can
ith essentially humanistic concerns, in German terminology, of
·re the crucial questions concerned whether and in what sense the
cience, conceived roughly as a compromise between the Western
s on physical science and the broader German conception of
·chaft (roughly equivalent to "discipline" in English), could find an
·tion in the intellectual world of the idealistic movement. That it did
st be interpreted in terms of the operation of the imperatives of
·ctual discipline, the general values of integrity in intellectual objec-
· and generality, in the subject-matters of subjectively meaningful
·an concerns. Another process of "extension," parallel to the utilitarian
extension of the paradigm of physical science, occurred here.

The sharpness of the Kantian dichotomy could not be expected to
endure without modification. One reason lay in the fact that each of the
two great traditions issued in an extremism having a profound bearing on
the future structure of the intellectual disciplines. On the utilitarian side, it
took the form of the pervasive physicalist reductionism that tended to hold
that only the natural sciences, on the model of classical mechanics, could
yield valid empirical knowledge in any sense. On the idealistic side, there
was a corresponding radicalism that in a sense considered Hegel too
"rationalistic" in attempting to formulate laws of the development of the
Weltgeist. In the Germany of the later nineteenth century, Hegelianism
thus gave way to radical "historicism," the conception of the universe as

one of the most important movements from which modern social science
has derived. It seems best to call the movement "utilitarian" in a sense
close to Halévy's term, "philosophical radicalism,"[6] applying to the early
nineteenth century. From it grew, first and perhaps with the most solid
grounding, the main outline of the science of economics, in the line
running from Locke to Adam Smith to Ricardo and his successors. It is no
accident that economics could be relatively easily related to a viewpoint
particularly concerned with the physical world. As a practical field
economics is the sphere of social action most directly concerned with
articulating the social and physical worlds, especially regarding technology's place in physical production and the psychological significance of
physical goods in consumption contexts. The fact that money, the generalized medium of economic transaction, is quantified in a linear continuum
having a logical pattern identical with that of the principal variables of
classical mechanics is particularly significant in this connection.

Social science's other principal point of emergence from a utilitarian
base was in psychology. Here the problem involved bridging the gap
between concepts of the sheer givenness of the consumption wants of
individuals, a cardinal reference point for economic theory, and the
problem of explaining the genesis of wants or motives.[7] Insofar as handling this problem went beyond just postulating the association of inherently discrete elements (e.g., in the "association" psychology of James Mill),
this frame of reference contained very strong pressures to "reduce" its
psychological phenomena to more or less physical terms and lead directly
into the heredity-environment dichotomy which came to dominate its
biological thought. This has broadly produced the dichotomy between the
"instinct" psychology of the Anglo-American tradition and "behaviorism,"
with its environmentalist emphasis and, hence, concern with the mechanisms of learning. The crucial point for present purposes is that the
differences between the social and physical aspects of the actor's environment were not considered problematical for the purposes of this
type of psychology.

Like perhaps all great intellectual movements, utilitarianism had its
"revolutionary underground" subverting the neat, orderly schemes of the
main trend. The greatest of its representatives were probably Hobbes, one
of its chief founders, and Malthus. Both were deeply concerned with the
problem of the grounding of elementary social order, something which
Locke took for granted.[8] The problems they posed were destined to play
in various ways a critical part in breaking the closed system which gave

---

[6]Halevy, *The Growth of Philosophical Radicalism,* Beacon Paperbacks, 1960.
[7]James Olds, *The Growth and Structure of Motives,* The Free Press, 1954.
[8]Talcott Parsons, *The Structure of Social Action,* McGraw-Hill, New York, 1937

the physical world, as conceived by early modern science, essential priority in the whole theory of possible empirical knowledge.

It will be remembered that this basically epistemological phase of modern philosophy took its departure from the Cartesian dichotomy of knowing subject and known object, and the attempt to relate them to each other. The empiricist-utilitarian phase of the movement seems to have retained a relatively simple version of this frame of reference, essentially treating its "subjective" side *only* as a point of reference and then concerning itself with objects treatable as involved *only* on the objective side. For the physical world this seemed quite appropriate, but it presented difficulties for the study of human behavior. It seems that the economists' insistence on the *givenness* of wants, involving *de facto* assumptions of their randomness, was in the first instance a way of avoiding the apparently hopeless complications of considering the knowing, wanting subject as also belonging to the objective category and requiring analysis on its merits. The complications derived from the fact that the Cartesian dichotomy had then to be conceived as being not singly but doubly salient. There were, concretely, no longer only knowing subjects on the one hand and known or observed objects on the other hand, but there were also entities in both positions at the same time. Insofar as they were both, how could specific structured properties of their different aspects relate to each other? It does not seem too harsh to say that the history of utilitarian thought has involved an elaborate evasion of this problem. The favorite device has been to hold, implicitly if not explicitly, that the subject-as-object in fact has no determinate structure. Insofar as it exists empirically at all, it consists only of given wants which, so far as they do not reflect physical realities, may safely be treated as random.

KANT, HEGEL, AND GERMAN IDEALISM

The alternative treatment of the problem was embarked upon, with all its enormous hazards, by the idealistic movement. The first step was taken by Kant. He focused in the first instance on the skeptical consequences which Hume drew from the conception of an uncontrolled impact of sense impressions from all phases of the action situation impinging on a knowing subject as equally valid "experience." Kant's answer was that order could be grounded in the field of what he called empirical knowledge only by a sharp *restriction* of the conception of empirical knowledge to what he called the field of phenomena, which in effect meant the physical world in the sense of the relevance of Newtonian theory. This world could be ordered in terms of the combination of the forms of intuition, namely Euclidean space and linear time, and the categories of the Understanding—among which causality appeared with special prominence.

This realm constituted only a small part of the legitimat[e] human interest. Kant, however, threw everything else into o[...] the realm of phenomenal determinism, he contrasted the r[...] dom. To that of theoretical understanding, he contrasted th[e] Reason. In this connection, one of his principal concerns status of theology, which he radically denied could be a rati[o] cal discipline. Thus the realms of theoretical understanding commitment were radically dissociated, the latter h[...] precedence for all realms of human concern other than natur[e]

Important as this was in setting the whole frame of ref[e] modern intellectual world, it was very substantially modifie[d] quent development. The next major step was introduced [...] cessor, Hegel, and consisted in a highly ambitious attemp[t] subjective side of the dichotomy in terms of the conceptio[n] *Geist,* or spirit, as it can sometimes be translated. The imp[...] here is in the objective element—i.e., that what are no[w] cultural patterns, namely ideas, norms, or, more diffusely, [...] are treatable as *objects* of observation and rigorous analy[sis] merely as ways of locating the ultimate reference point for phenomenal objects in Kant's sense.

Although he reintroduced the conception that the worl[d] longed to that of objects, Hegel did not simply assimilate it world, but rather formulated its characteristics in a spec[...] greatest importance for the future. "Ideal" objects were [...] thentically objects, but they were to be treated conceptuall[y] "historical" terms. The conception historical contained tw[o] ponents. One was that the historical object stood in a sequence cognizance of which was essential to knowledge [...] asserted the object's uniqueness and, hence, in certain resp[...] parability with other empirical entities.

Hegel himself built this into a grand scheme of the history, interpreted as a process of the "unfolding" of t[he] (*Weltgeist*) through the agency of human action. This h[...] importance as one of the principal early versions of the [...] evolution, antedating Darwin by nearly half a century. It the ideas of conflict and progress through the conception process in the famous formula of thesis-antithesis-synthesis.

Two themes involved in the aftermath, however, especi[...] The first is the insistence that the field of human "subjecti[ve] meanings, must be conceptualized in ideographic as dist[...] generalized and analytical terms. Secondly, the implicatio[n] ation between the realms of the physical (and in Kant's s[...] al) and of the "ideal" were pressed so radically that a c[...]

one of the most important movements from which modern social science has derived. It seems best to call the movement "utilitarian" in a sense close to Halévy's term, "philosophical radicalism,"[6] applying to the early nineteenth century. From it grew, first and perhaps with the most solid grounding, the main outline of the science of economics, in the line running from Locke to Adam Smith to Ricardo and his successors. It is no accident that economics could be relatively easily related to a viewpoint particularly concerned with the physical world. As a practical field economics is the sphere of social action most directly concerned with articulating the social and physical worlds, especially regarding technology's place in physical production and the psychological significance of physical goods in consumption contexts. The fact that money, the generalized medium of economic transaction, is quantified in a linear continuum having a logical pattern identical with that of the principal variables of classical mechanics is particularly significant in this connection.

Social science's other principal point of emergence from a utilitarian base was in psychology. Here the problem involved bridging the gap between concepts of the sheer givenness of the consumption wants of individuals, a cardinal reference point for economic theory, and the problem of explaining the genesis of wants or motives.[7] Insofar as handling this problem went beyond just postulating the association of inherently discrete elements (e.g., in the "association" psychology of James Mill), this frame of reference contained very strong pressures to "reduce" its psychological phenomena to more or less physical terms and lead directly into the heredity-environment dichotomy which came to dominate its biological thought. This has broadly produced the dichotomy between the "instinct" psychology of the Anglo-American tradition and "behaviorism," with its environmentalist emphasis and, hence, concern with the mechanisms of learning. The crucial point for present purposes is that the differences between the social and physical aspects of the actor's environment were not considered problematical for the purposes of this type of psychology.

Like perhaps all great intellectual movements, utilitarianism had its "revolutionary underground" subverting the neat, orderly schemes of the main trend. The greatest of its representatives were probably Hobbes, one of its chief founders, and Malthus. Both were deeply concerned with the problem of the grounding of elementary social order, something which Locke took for granted.[8] The problems they posed were destined to play in various ways a critical part in breaking the closed system which gave

---

[6]Halevy, *The Growth of Philosophical Radicalism,* Beacon Paperbacks, 1960.
[7]James Olds, *The Growth and Structure of Motives,* The Free Press, 1954.
[8]Talcott Parsons, *The Structure of Social Action,* McGraw-Hill, New York, 1937

the physical world, as conceived by early modern science, essential priority in the whole theory of possible empirical knowledge.

It will be remembered that this basically epistemological phase of modern philosophy took its departure from the Cartesian dichotomy of knowing subject and known object, and the attempt to relate them to each other. The empiricist-utilitarian phase of the movement seems to have retained a relatively simple version of this frame of reference, essentially treating its "subjective" side *only* as a point of reference and then concerning itself with objects treatable as involved *only* on the objective side. For the physical world this seemed quite appropriate, but it presented difficulties for the study of human behavior. It seems that the economists' insistence on the *givenness* of wants, involving *de facto* assumptions of their randomness, was in the first instance a way of avoiding the apparently hopeless complications of considering the knowing, wanting subject as also belonging to the objective category and requiring analysis on its merits. The complications derived from the fact that the Cartesian dichotomy had then to be conceived as being not singly but doubly salient. There were, concretely, no longer only knowing subjects on the one hand and known or observed objects on the other hand, but there were also entities in both positions at the same time. Insofar as they were both, how could specific structured properties of their different aspects relate to each other? It does not seem too harsh to say that the history of utilitarian thought has involved an elaborate evasion of this problem. The favorite device has been to hold, implicitly if not explicitly, that the subject-as-object in fact has no determinate structure. Insofar as it exists empirically at all, it consists only of given wants which, so far as they do not reflect physical realities, may safely be treated as random.

KANT, HEGEL, AND GERMAN IDEALISM

The alternative treatment of the problem was embarked upon, with all its enormous hazards, by the idealistic movement. The first step was taken by Kant. He focused in the first instance on the skeptical consequences which Hume drew from the conception of an uncontrolled impact of sense impressions from all phases of the action situation impinging on a knowing subject as equally valid "experience." Kant's answer was that order could be grounded in the field of what he called empirical knowledge only by a sharp *restriction* of the conception of empirical knowledge to what he called the field of phenomena, which in effect meant the physical world in the sense of the relevance of Newtonian theory. This world could be ordered in terms of the combination of the forms of intuition, namely Euclidean space and linear time, and the categories of the Understanding— among which causality appeared with special prominence.

This realm constituted only a small part of the legitimate concerns of human interest. Kant, however, threw everything else into one basket. To the realm of phenomenal determinism, he contrasted the realm of freedom. To that of theoretical understanding, he contrasted that of *Practical Reason.* In this connection, one of his principal concerns was with the status of theology, which he radically denied could be a rational, theoretical discipline. Thus the realms of theoretical understanding and practical commitment were radically dissociated, the latter having radical precedence for all realms of human concern other than natural science.

Important as this was in setting the whole frame of reference for the modern intellectual world, it was very substantially modified in its subsequent development. The next major step was introduced by Kant's successor, Hegel, and consisted in a highly ambitious attempt to order the subjective side of the dichotomy in terms of the conception of *objectiver Geist,* or spirit, as it can sometimes be translated. The important concept here is in the objective element—i.e., that what are now often called cultural patterns, namely ideas, norms, or, more diffusely, "orientations," are treatable as *objects* of observation and rigorous analysis rather than merely as ways of locating the ultimate reference point for knowledge of phenomenal objects in Kant's sense.

Although he reintroduced the conception that the world of *Geist* belonged to that of objects, Hegel did not simply assimilate it to the physical world, but rather formulated its characteristics in a special way of the greatest importance for the future. "Ideal" objects were considered authentically objects, but they were to be treated conceptually in exclusively "historical" terms. The conception historical contained two primary components. One was that the historical object stood in a developmental sequence cognizance of which was essential to knowledge of it. The other asserted the object's uniqueness and, hence, in certain respects, its incomparability with other empirical entities.

Hegel himself built this into a grand scheme of the philosophy of history, interpreted as a process of the "unfolding" of the world spirit (*Weltgeist*) through the agency of human action. This had the greatest importance as one of the principal early versions of the general idea of evolution, antedating Darwin by nearly half a century. It also integrated the ideas of conflict and progress through the conception of the dialectic process in the famous formula of thesis-antithesis-synthesis.

Two themes involved in the aftermath, however, especially concern us. The first is the insistence that the field of human "subjective" concerns, of meanings, must be conceptualized in ideographic as distinguished from generalized and analytical terms. Secondly, the implications of the dissociation between the realms of the physical (and in Kant's sense phenomenal) and of the "ideal" were pressed so radically that a certain duality of determinisms tended to emerge in the contention that each "realm" functioned according to its own unique necessities and in the failure to consider clearly how the "realms" interacted with each other. The dialectic conception of the ultimate unity of conflict and integration was a third major theme which, however, may be considered secondary.

A complex set of variations on the theme of Cartesian dualism seems to have developed. We have not stressed the common philosophical concern with the difference between mind and matter, but rather the problems close to the issues of the development of social science. The social terms of the utilitarian tradition evidently emerged from what, contrary to Kant's view, were the inherently open boundaries of the physical world as conceived by early modern science and philosophy. The utilitarian tendency was to assimilate analysis of human behavior as closely to that of physical objects as seemed feasible. The case of the logical structure of early economic theory is paradigmatic. The consequence was the extension into the behavioral realm of conceptions of the scientific treatment of a world of objects in a way which left the status of knowing subjects highly equivocal in this context.

The Kantian statement cut off this tendency to extension sharply. It radically shifted the problem to the field of the noumenal, which we can equate with essentially humanistic concerns, in German terminology, of *Geist.* Here the crucial questions concerned whether and in what sense the idea of science, conceived roughly as a compromise between the Western emphasis on physical science and the broader German conception of *Wissenschaft* (roughly equivalent to "discipline" in English), could find an application in the intellectual world of the idealistic movement. That it did so must be interpreted in terms of the operation of the imperatives of intellectual discipline, the general values of integrity in intellectual objectivity and generality, in the subject-matters of subjectively meaningful human concerns. Another process of "extension," parallel to the utilitarian extension of the paradigm of physical science, occurred here.

The sharpness of the Kantian dichotomy could not be expected to endure without modification. One reason lay in the fact that each of the two great traditions issued in an extremism having a profound bearing on the future structure of the intellectual disciplines. On the utilitarian side, it took the form of the pervasive physicalist reductionism that tended to hold that only the natural sciences, on the model of classical mechanics, could yield valid empirical knowledge in any sense. On the idealistic side, there was a corresponding radicalism that in a sense considered Hegel too "rationalistic" in attempting to formulate laws of the development of the *Weltgeist.* In the Germany of the later nineteenth century, Hegelianism thus gave way to radical "historicism," the conception of the universe as comprised of discrete, empirically observable "historical individuals" which were, however, in principle incomparable. The sharpest formulation of the philosophical position of historicism in this sense was probably in the work of Wilhelm Dilthey.[9]

The emergence of this radically empirical trend was associated with a major intellectual movement in Germany, namely, the rise of the "historical schools" in a whole range of disciplines concerning human affairs, not only in history itself, but also in law, economics, and the cultural fields. This in turn involved a great deal of meticulous and detailed scholarship. The pull of this scholarship, as contrasted with the tendency to generalize, seems to have been responsible for a major division which appeared within this tradition and formed an exceedingly important background for the work, among others, of Max Weber.

This was the division between the atomistic and holistic trends within historicism. The first tended to break down the phenomena into minimum units and treat each as maximally independent of all others. The second tended to treat whole civilizations or epochs of history as unified entities. For the latter, the untranslatable German word *Gestalt* seems to be the best single characterization.

Very clearly, this entire mode of thinking tended to assimilate the whole sphere of human concerns to the model of the humanities. Indeed, it carried this emphasis to an extreme comparable in certain respects to the extremism of physical reductionism. The attempt to relate the two main conceptions of knowledge to each other systematically was perhaps carried farthest by Heinrich Rickert, who discussed the basic distinction between the problems of knowledge in the natural sciences and those in the *Kulturwissenschaften*.[10] Contrary to the generalizing, analytical characteristics of conceptualization in the former, the latter were characterized by emphasizing the individuality of each phenomenon and therefore its inherent incomparability with others.

MOVEMENTS TOWARD SYNTHESIS

The two patterns of extremism, physical reductionism and historicist uniqueness and ultimate givenness, could not completely dominate the field for long, however prominently their theses still reverberate. Three main movements toward a synthesis soon appeared and have played an important part in the intellectual history of the last century.

[9]Wilhelm Dilthey, *Einleitung in die Geisteswissenschaften* (Duncker und Humblat, Leipzig, 1883).

[10]Heinrich Rickert, *Über die Grenzen der Naturwissenschaftlichen Begriffsbildung*, 5th edition, J. C. B. Mohr, Tübingen, 1929.

The first of these can hardly be called a movement at all. Yet it has certainly contributed importantly to the present definition of the situation. On the Western, more "empiricist" side, it has involved a combination of biological and "humanistic" emphases. Its essential keynote is a concern with the phenomena of organization—and the fact that this emphasis directs attention to patterns of relationship rather than to units in the sense of the individual particle. The trend sketched above which united physics and classical economics generally gave primary consideration to units, that is, the wants of individuals were the particles of the economic system. Biology, however, with its concern for organization and structure, tends to emphasize "forms" or patterns, in the first instance as anatomical traits. Seen in this context, the emergence of Darwinism was a culmination rather than an origin—these emphases were "in the air."

From this viewpoint, "human biology," the concern with organizational traits, can move very readily from anatomy and physiology to the behavioral and cultural levels. Indeed, there is a long tradition connecting "natural history" with an historical approach to the study of human artifacts and "ways of doing things," viewed in terms of their meanings and functions, and social institutions.

This seems to be the origin of the predominantly Anglo-American discipline of anthropology. Its self-definition, the "science of man," was conceived in a biological frame of reference as comparable to branches of biology, such as ornithology or ichthyology, which studied other sectors of the organic world. In this respect, there was nothing unusual in the specialization on humanity, except that biologically it was very limited in time and variety, there being only one human species. Such study, however, inevitably led into the human traits which were separable from man's genetically organic constitution, which anthropologists have designated generically as his "culture." Anthropology then had to define its concern as the "environmental" side of the human equation, with reference to distinctively human behavioral phenomena, if "culture" could be considered to characterize these.

Within this definition, however, the anthropological concern was with "traits," not with particles. This was a radically different focus from that of the utilitarian economists, because traits were elements in the organization of human relationships, not properties of the individual human being. There was a much less direct correspondence with the logical structure of the physical theory of the day. In fact, the crucial point for present purposes is that this background of anthropology permitted a direct convergence with the trait particularism of the German historical tradition. This convergence was most directly mediated by Franz Boas, the most influential figure in American anthropology in the first part of this century. It is significant both that Boas was a biologist before becoming an anthropologist and that he was German. In the light of this connection, it is not surprising that anthropology also developed the alternative position within ideographic historicism in the idea of a total "culture" as a unified *Gestalt.* This occurred most prominently in the work of Ruth Benedict, whose book title, *Patterns of Culture,* gave a classic expression to this viewpoint.

The second, largely contemporaneous, though somewhat earlier, synthesis was developed by Karl Marx. It involved building a bridge between the pre-historicist Hegelian works and the utilitarian aspect of the empiricist tradition.

All the emphasis in Marxian theory on "materialism" refers primarily to a contrast with "ideal" in the Hegelian sense, not to matter in the more primitive Cartesian sense. The theory does not seriously treat the physical world at all, and has had severe difficulties in the biological sphere. It is primarily an attempt to redress the imbalance created by Hegelianism in its idealistic emphasis by "setting Hegel on his head," as Marx said. The significant thing here is that Marx went rather directly to theory developed from a utilitarian base, namely, classical economics in a modified Ricardian form. As we have noted, this conceptual scheme had special connections with the physical sphere, but clearly was not itself a part of physical science—and it wholly by-passed the biological level.

The crucial Marxian concept here is "material interests." These are clearly economic in the utilitarian sense, which includes the assumption of the *unproblematical* character of individuals' wants. The concept attempts to introduce determinism into the system by postulating that, in the situation of the individual in a market economy, basically only *one* line of action is open.[11] For the "Capitalist," this is maximization of profit. For the "worker," it is staving off disaster by the acceptance of employment on the available terms.

Any serious student of modern industrial societies recognizes the tremendous oversimplification inherent in this scheme—no Western society has ever been that deterministic in precisely such narrow terms. Marx and, by and large, his followers have met this problem primarily by supplementing the economic element, which had the virtue of its special articulation with the physical sphere, with one which we · would call political today. That is, Marx interpreted the structure of the situation in which interests in the economic sense were defined and pursued in terms of a socially structured conflict—which he construed as class conflict. This, however, involved the use of coercive sanctions by those occupying positions of superior power, the individual capitalist vis-à-vis his workers

[11]Michel Crozier, *The Bureaucratic Phenomenon,* University of Chicago Press, 1964.

at the level of the firm, the capitalist class conceived as basically controlling the state at the macro-social level. The Hegelian dialectic of ideas was thus translated into a dialectic of interests which were both economic and political; the two categories were not clearly differentiated from each other.

It may be said that Marx took over Hegel's conception of the pattern of historical development, but replaced the *Weltgeist* with a modified version of Ricardo, and the periphery[12] of Ricardian theory in the broad utilitarian tradition. The content of this scheme was formulated in terms of human interests in "want-satisfaction" or goal-attainment, mainly at the individual level. But the paradigm of the Hegelian historical process, activated by dialectic conflict and moving through a series of stages, gave it a quite different meaning. This aspect is crucially significant because Marxian theory has never taken, with all its materialism, many steps toward giving human social behavior a generalized analytical treatment, but, on the basis of certain broad assumptions about "human nature," has relativized all problems to particular systems and historical stages of their development. For Marxians, Ricardian economic theory has been *only* the theory of capitalist economics and not an early stage of a general economic theory applicable, with others and with appropriate qualifications, to socialist societies.

Thus the Marxian synthesis, though certainly a genuine one, was incomplete in not breaking with the basic assumptions of the idealistic tradition in three respects. First, though it formulated, with heavy borrowing from utilitarian sources, the conception of material interests and gave it priority in analyzing the causal historical process, it remained historical in the ideographic sense and did not extend the conception of generalized analytical theory from the natural sphere to that of human behavior. In this respect it represents a retrogressive step relative to the great traditions of English economics from Ricardo through J. S. Mill and Marshall to Keynes.

Secondly, though repudiating the specifically Hegelian conception of the determination of human behavior by the unfolding *Geist,* Marxism retained the "ideal"—"real" dichotomy of "factors," so that explanation was couched in either-or terms rather than terms of interdependence. Since Hegel's ideal factors could not explain "history," Marx tended to propound an explanation totally in terms of material factors as the only alternative. The logical resemblance of this dilemma to that between heredity and environment in biology is too patent to need further discussion.

---

[12]In these respects, Marx was more Hobbesian and Malthusian than Lockean in stressing the potentials for disorder and conflict.

Third and most basically, Marxian theory, by accepting, largely implicitly, the utilitarian formula of the givenness of wants, tended to cut itself off from the most important problems leading toward a synthesis of the two sides of the Kantian dichotomy. The basic question is why, having freedom of choice, people in fact opt for one, not some other, personal goal and means of attaining it. The "ideal" component is postulated as given in Marxian theory, in a sense directly comparable to that in which the wants of individuals were assumed to be given in utilitarian theory. In other words, this is the area of an intellectual "neutrality pact," which in the nature of the subject-matter is suspect of inherent instability.

The period including the turn of the last century and the early decades of this century saw extraordinary ferment in all the fields of this discussion. A critically important development was the philosophical criticism of older views concerning the status of physical theory, strongly influenced by internal developments within physics itself. This was classically stated by Whitehead, who attributed a new level of abstraction to this type of theory, the ignoring of which involved the fallacy of misplaced concreteness.[13] This was clearly a more radical conception of the relativity of references to the physical world than that formulated by Kant. It demonstrated the validity of considering the same concrete empirical phenomena from the viewpoint of various different modes of cognitive interest, not just that of understanding in the Kantian sense.

A second major trend of the period developed interests in organizational conceptions in the biological sphere at the more physiological level, as well as at the more anatomical level. This extended the conception of organization involved in the original emergence of anthropology to dynamic levels. Perhaps the most eminent figure here is W. B. Cannon,[14] the physiologist. With *homeostasis,* he conceived of a spontaneous built-in control within the organism which maintained an equilibrium state within boundaries; this concept referred more to a "pattern of functioning" like that of behavior than to an "inert" anatomical structure.

Still later, this trend of thinking established contact with that of cybernetics and information theory, which originated in the physical field of engineering more than in physics itself, but which has nevertheless grounded conceptions of an organized system maintained by integrative control mechanisms much more solidly in the *general* theory of science. This trend in the fields closest to the physical sciences has been most important to the development of a new status for the social disciplines. However, its primary references have been outside the latter field.

[13]A. N. Whitehead, *Science and the Modern World,* Macmillan Company, 1925.
[14]W. B. Cannon, *The Wisdom of the Body.* A comparable view with reference to genetics is stated by H. S. Jennings, *The Biological Basis of Human Nature.*

Another substantive field tending to bridge the traditional gap between the humanities and the natural sciences in a way directly involving the social sciences has been the science of linguistics. Language has been the citadel of humanistic studies. Indeed, German humanists in general have tended to call themselves "philologists." This is understandable, since language has been the primary medium of symbolic process and cultural communication. However, increasingly language has been subjected to analytical rather than merely historical study. Also, this trend has connected very directly with theoretical developments in the natural science field, notably information theory. Linguistics has also had important contact with the social sciences. First there was the older French work of de Saussure and Meillet. In American anthropology in particular, Edward Sapir and Benjamin Whorf have treated linguistic evidence as a main keynote of the idea of cultural relativity. More recently, Claude Levi-Strauss has been attempting to develop general social theory from linguistic models. It is perhaps not too much to say that linguistics is becoming a discipline that is concurrently a natural science, a branch of the humanities, and a social science.

A very significant methodological convergence should be added to these substantive convergences. First, logic itself is a general resource of all intellectual disciplines—as it has become refined technically, its general relevance has become increasingly evident. Secondly, logic has tended to merge increasingly with mathematics as a preeminent tool of analysis. Then statistics, from having been an empirical art, has increasingly gained mathematical foundations and extended its range of application, even into the humanistic disciplines, particularly via linguistic studies. The recent rapid development of computer techniques is a latest phase involving an application of a complex combination of these elements. The essential point is that these technical innovations cut clean across traditional divisions between disciplines. Their recent invasion of the humanities is the clearest sign that the latter cannot be regarded as inherently isolated from their "scientific" sister disciplines.

After this digression, however, we may return to the more specifically social and behavioral reference. Somewhat antedating most of the movements just sketched has been a third major synthetic development, following the anthropological and the Marxian. This, the emergence of the modern phase of sociological theory, may be considered synthesis of a higher order than either of the other two because it has included the principal components of the other syntheses and because it has avoided the extremism of the either-or dichotomies which have plagued the other syntheses, namely, heredity-environment in the one case and ideal-material in the other.

MAX WEBER AND EMILE DURKHEIM

Two great figures were mainly responsible for this development, namely Max Weber, starting in Germany from a critique of the idealist-historicist tradition, and Emile Durkheim, developing in France a corresponding critique of the utilitarian tradition.[15] These two converged very significantly on a common, though broad, conceptual scheme. Let us start with Weber.

Because of the relation to the humanistic tradition, it may be illuminating to note that Weber began his intellectual career in jurisprudence under the aegis of the historical school then dominant in Germany. This is significant because, in a very important sense, the law stands squarely between the two poles of the Hegelian-Marxian spectrum so far as human behavior is concerned. Though, as noted above, legal norms, as rules and institutions, are essentially cultural in structure, they are relational patterns. As such, they are the first-line mechanisms regulating the pursuit of the type of interests which predominate in Marxian theory. Furthermore, so far as a society is concerned, law has a reference to the system as a whole, to the "public" interest, which is not shared with the "self-interest" of businesses or political "interest groups." It may also be noted that the Marxian attitude toward law has been exceedingly ambiguous. By grounding the conception of capitalistic interest in the concrete structure of the family firm, certain property institutions, and market structures regulated by institutions of contract, Marxians have generally tended to *include* basic legal institutions within the famous material factors, the relations of production. At other times, however, they have treated law as a component of the "superstructure," and thus as "determined by," rather than as a *part of,* the relations of production. The historicist pattern of thinking facilitates this ambiguity by denying the legitmacy of the abstract analytical procedures required to straighten out the problem.

From his juristic start, Weber embarked on an ambitious study of the "material" base underlying and interacting with legal institutions, mostly through various historical studies in economic organization after the genre of the historical school of economics of the time. He did so reacting against the "formalism" of much of the jurisprudence of the time, notably

15See Talcott Parsons, *The Structure of Social Action,* McGraw-Hill, New York, 1937, and H. Stuart Hughes, *Consciousness and Society,* Knopf, New York, 1958, for more detailed analyses of the theoretical positions surveyed in the following: Vilfredo Pareto in sociology, Freud in psychology and the American development of social psychology, related to Pragmatism and involving James, Dewey, C. H. Cooley, G. H. Mead and W. I. Thomas.

Rudolf Stammler's work. In his excursions into economic history, Weber did not, however, abandon the basic idea that legal norms *control* action in pursuit of interests, both economic and political.[16] Here he was very much concerned with Marxian ideas, but the retention of this fundamental position is a prime index of his refusal to become a Marxist.

A major reorientation in Weber's thought occurred after he had recovered from an incapacitating mental illness in about 1904, and was expressed in writings on a new front. Substantively the first important new work was the famous essay on the *Protestant Ethic and the Spirit of Capitalism.*[17] This dealt directly with an "ideal factor" in reference to its significance for a specific process of historical development, indeed, the one Marxian theory had spotlighted. It was undoubtedly meant to challenge the Marxian view, but *not* in the sense of "setting Hegel back on his feet." Rather, it put the problem in a frame of reference neither Hegelian nor Marxian nor historicist in Dilthey's sense.

The crucial point is that Weber's analysis, the core of which is the Protestant Ethic thesis, bridged the theoretical gap between "want" in the economic-psychological sense and "cultural patterns" in the idealistic senses. To put it simply and radically, Weber's solution was that, once cultural patterns of meaning have been internalized in the personality of an individual, they define the situation for the structuring of motives. Therefore questions of how action (including the acceptance of the goals toward which it is oriented) makes sense must be answered by reference to the meaning-system defining the situation of action. Weber then postulated, not given wants, but given cultural definitions of the situation (the human condition) which make commitment to the satisfaction of certain classes of wants intelligible. These meaning-systems, however, were the very subject-matter of humanistic-cultural study.

Did this, however, constitute only a step along a line of regression which merely put the discreteness of cultural patterns, within which particular wants became meaningful, in the place of the givenness of discrete wants of individuals? At the very least, the discrimination of two levels in the want system, the concrete, satisfaction-oriented want itself and the cultural grounding of its meaning, would be a gain. But Weber's analysis went a step farther. He treated these as independently variable factors in the determination of action, which, in their mutual inter-relations and in relation to other factors, could be treated as interdependent in a system. This view basically broke through the ideal-material dichotomy of idealistic thinking about human action. The answer, analogous to that of modern

---

[16]Max Weber, *Max Weber on Law in Economy and Society*, Harvard University Press, 1954.

[17]Max Weber, *The Protestant Ethic and the Spirit of Capitalism*, C. Scribner's Sons, New York, 1930; German original, 1905.

biology regarding the heredity-environment problem, is that *both* sets of factors are crucial, standing in complex relations of interdependence with each other.

Before Weber, the "cement" which had been holding the parts of the dichotomy in their rigid relationship was the postulate of *historical* connection in its Hegelian-Marxian version. Thus, either the ideal constellation or that of material interests constituted a *Gestalt,* which either existed or did not, as a totality. A second focus of Weber's break with the tradition was salient there. He assumed as a matter of principle that the components of such a *Gestalt* should be treated as independently variable. He set out to analyze certain of these relations by the *comparative* method, which in terms of the logic of science is the nearest empirical equivalent to the experimental method that is accessible to this subject-matter.

In treating the problem of Protestantism's role in the development of capitalism, any historicist, idealist, or Marxist would have treated the problems entirely as one of the sequences in Western history from the Reformation, and its immediate antecedents, to the Industrial Revolution. But Weber, in adopting the comparative method, studied the negative cases especially. Along with the question of why modern "capitalism" developed in Europe, Weber investigated its *non*-development in other advanced civilizations. He completed extensive monographs on China and India in this connection.[18] Again, the substantive question, how far he progressed toward the empiricial demonstration of his case, is not our concern here. The point is that his *method* involved an *analytical* isolation of classes of variables by comparing cases in which they demonstrably varied independently of each other.[19] In the subject matter of cultural *Gestalten* this was a very new departure.

Concurrently, in a series of essays which, in the first instance, were polemically oriented, Weber attempted a principled grounding of this new orientation in the conception of empirical knowledge as such, but particularly in the context of the social sciences.[20] As noted he anticipated

[18]Max Weber, *The Religion of China,* The Free Press, Glencoe, 1951; *The Religion of India,* The Free Press, Glencoe, 1958; the original German editions of both, posthumous.

[19]Here it should be noted that the comprehensive survey of religious structures recently translated as *The Sociology of Religion,* Beacon Press, Boston, 1962 (originally published as *Religionssoziologie* in *Wirtschaft und Gesellschaft,* 1922), unparalleled at the time in the analytical qualities of its approach, was written as a relatively independent section of a larger work on the relationships between the economy and other aspects of social structure.

[20]Max Weber, *Gesammelte Aufsätze zur Wissenschaftslehre,* 2nd edition, Johannes Winckelmann, editor, Mohr, Tubingen, 1951. Selections from this work have been translated and edited by Edward A. Shils and Henry K. Finch, *The Methodology of the Social Sciences,* The Free Press, Glencoe, 1949.

writers like Whitehead in establishing that analytical abstraction was essential even to physical science. By no means does its theory, for example, in the case of classical mechanics, simply "reflect" the reality of the external world. It is selective and hence in important degrees evaluative in its concern for empirical problems and facts. Thus it is partly determined by the interests and values of the scientist, among which possibilities of controlling natural events figure prominently, but by no means exclusively. This dependence on the evaluative concerns of the investigator (which Weber called *Wertbeziehung*) had to be matched in whatever field, natural, social, or humanistic, by a favorable evaluative orientation to problems of the empirical disciplines centering about the canons of intellectual discipline, above all for objectivity in empirical observation and for logical, clear, and precise theoretical statement and inference. This is the focus of Weber's famous doctrine of the "value-freedom" of social science (*Wertfreiheit*). It does not mean, as so many have erroneously believed, that the scientist or scholar should be free of *any* values, but rather that in his professional role, he must be free to give the discipline's values priority over others, notably in Weber's mind over political commitments. In contemporary terminology, I believe he meant that the values of the intellectual disciplines must be *differentiated* from other types of values constitutive of the culture. Only on such a basis can science and scholarship be institutionalized.

As a matter of course, however, Weber also insisted on the central importance of the "empathic" understanding (*Verstehen*) of motives and patterns of meaning as this had been emphasized in the humanistic and idealistic tradition, namely, the "subjective" side of the Cartesian dichotomy. These entities, however, were now also given the full status of objects, as regards both their own internal structure and the relevance to them of analytical abstraction and abstract generalized conceptualization. In certain senses the utilitarians had prepared the way for this, but had shied away from its full consequences. They had preferred to limit this whole realm to the status of givenness under a set of restrictive assumptions, and to follow the problems of variability only in the other direction.

The *Verstehen* conception, however, was crucial to the new position because the impact of the "ideal" factors as *variables* was to be systematically studied precisely in the definite, specific structures of cultural patterns, including legal norms, and motives. Both the utilitarian and the behavioristic positions simply foreclosed this possibility with bland philosophical assumptions.

On the background of these three essential doctrines of social science methodology, Weber thus culminated his argument by asserting that the social disciplines required generalized analytical concepts and propositions. Indeed, when Weber wrote, such theory-building had already advanced considerably in economics and parts of psychology. He, however, stated this requirement very sharply and clearly while discussing the idealist and humanistic tradition. Weber's own attempts at formulation in this field primarily took the form of ideal types. Though legitimate, they have certain limitations and constitute only one of a number of the necessary theoretical components of the social sciences.

Weber thus broke cleanly with the dogma that cultural and historical materials were subject only to ideographic conceptualization as forming unique historical individuals. His most important contention was that the more advanced analytical methods of the natural sciences must be adopted in the realm of the cultural disciplines—which meant primarily the humanities, but the bridge between the natural sciences and humanities was constituted by the new social disciplines. In Weber's case, above all, economics could not be allowed to remain caught between the imperatives of a "Western" analytical definition of its scope and a German "historical" one. Indeed, it can be said that the main rationale of Weber's venture into sociology was that he saw this as the only way out of the dilemma, the only path to a synthesis of the best in the two traditions of economics that could relate both to the essentials of the "cultural" sciences.

Weber's views in this respect cannot be said to have fully prevailed as yet. They do, however, constitute a break of such magnitude that a return to the positions of Hegel or Marx, or of Dilthey or Sombart on the idealistic side is clearly out of the question. Similarly, Weber's capacity to handle the relations between cultural movements and social organization in an historical and comparative context was such that a return to utilitarian modes of thought seems equally out of the question.

This conviction is strongly reinforced by Durkheim's striking convergence with Weber, even though they were of different nationality, did not communicate with each other, and knew little of each other's work. Significant to the convergence is the fact that Durkheim also was trained in jurisprudence. In his first major work, *De la division du travail social,*[21] 1893, he used law as a principal index of the structure of societies.

Durkheim's critical point of departure was a devastating critique of the utilitarian position, couched in terms of Herbert Spencer's conception of "contractual relations," but covering the whole frame of reference back to Hobbes.[22] The crucial thesis was that, from a strictly utilitarian viewpoint, it was impossible to account for *order* in social systems, which

[21]Emile Durkheim: *The Division of Labor in Society,* The Free Press, Glencoe, 1949; French original, 1893.
[22]*Ibid.* Book I, Chap. VII.

Durkheim, using a Kantian pattern of analysis, treated as a *fact,* not a possibility. Paralleling Kant's famous question about empirical knowledge, Durkheim stated that social order, in the sense contrary to a Hobbesian state of nature, in fact exists. Given this fact, how is it possible?

Durkheim thus, from the other side, came to essentially the same basic conclusion as Weber. He established a connection between the wants of individuals, as conceived in the utilitarian tradition, and the normative patterning of the social structure, particularly as analyzed in law. The institution of contract was treated as analytically independent of the interests of contracting parties, but the former constituted an indispensable set of conditions for the effective satisfaction of the latter.

The basic theme of internalization of the normative patterns defining situations had, as noted, been partially worked out by Weber. It was considerably further analyzed by Durkheim in his studies of suicide and education—his famous concept of *anomie* was a name for the failure of this relation to become stabilized in the relation of a normative system to the personality of the individual. In this basic respect Durkheim converged impressively with Freud and the American social psychologists mentioned above, particularly George Herbert Mead.

CONCLUSION

In outlining this intellectual history, I have attempted to trace a principal path by which the intellectual disciplines, institutionalized in the central faculties of American universities, acquired the foundation of a basic unity which is nevertheless compatible with their inherent diversity. In a sense it was natural that, as modern intellectual culture emerged, the humanities and sciences should hold radically different patterns of orientation, and that the social disciplines should be substantially less well crystallized.

The growth of knowledge itself, accompanied by generalization and sophistication on both sides, exerted pressure for firmer methodological and, eventually, philosophical groundings. Indeed, this pressure may well have been an important factor in the emphasis modern philosophy has placed on epistemological concerns.

In the movement emerging from philosophical empiricism, which included the physical sciences, utilitarianism, and eventually Darwinian biology, these problems were not generally brought into sharp focus. The social disciplines developed slowly on the basis of a rather empirical, common-sense view of the task of history, utilitarian theorizing in economics and psychology, and the extension of Darwinian biology into the behavioral fields.

This history clearly illustrates the difficulty of drawing sharp boundaries to the domain of natural science within this frame of reference. One mode of extension into the social field, of which classical economics is the type case, could be stabilized only by a "walling off" against further extension by assuming the givenness of wants and their purely individual character. The development of biological thinking, however, presented still greater difficulties, since it introduced, particularly in its extension through anthropology to the human behavioral field, the especially important conceptions of organization and relational pattern. This, in its environmental reference, eventuated in the concept of culture, which, on a utilitarian background, was a truly revolutionary concept. This too tended to be "walled off" through the trait atomist doctrine of the so-called "historical" school of British-American anthropology.

The relevant intellectual history on the background of empiricism and utilitarianism involved a gradually increasing strain in the direction of giving a more independent status to the human cultural-behavioral fields, but attended by a continuing anxiety that doing so would imply abandoning the attempt to be scientific. Kant introduced a clean break in these respects, explicitly confining science to the field of physical phenomena— only this limited area was accessible to the methods of "pure reason." Problems of how the areas of human behavior excluded from science could be treated as objects of observation and analysis thereby became acute. The idealistic movement, especially with Hegel, solved this by focusing on the conception of *Geist* as itself objectively observable through a rather different kind of "understanding" than the Kantian, namely, that conveyed by later uses of the German term *Verstehen*. The problem here was the obverse of the one posed for the utilitarian tradition, namely, not how to treat human motives or wants as independent of their conditioning substratum in the physical world or the organism, but how to relate the imperatives of ideal patterns to the exigencies of the real world in a way accounting for the realistically effective qualities of such entities in actual behavior. This orientation went through two stages: the Hegelian grand philosophy of history and the historicist particularism which keynoted the conception of the isolated historical individual.

Beginning with this orientation, Marx developed the first major bridge toward the phenomenal world, to use Kant's term. By setting Hegel on his head, he conceived of a dialectic of "material interests" which directly matched Hegel's dialectic of the *Geist* in form. This venture directly complemented the anthropological introduction of cultural pattern as a discrete elementary particle in the human field. Each intellectual movement had, in a peculiar sense, undercut the ground of the other. The anthropologists, from a naturalistic base, had come to see the "essence" of the human behavioral world in cultural-humanistic terms, whereas the Marxians, from an idealistic base, had located its essence in the interest formulated by the utilitarians. In each case, the dominant category was the one which had figured most prominently in the history of the other tradition.

Surely this was an intellectual impasse. It is in this setting that I place the movement of which the Weber-Durkheim convergence may be regarded as the core. Its most important feature was its capacity to synthesize the two great sets of intermediate categories, wants or interests on the one side and organization and relational pattern on the other side. Culture, as well as the organism and the physical world, had become inherently involved in the human behavioral sphere. This concurrently becomes the subject of an autonomous set of intellectual disciplines, neither humanities nor natural sciences. They are cultural in that they study the cultural productions of human experience, but they are at the same time analytical, oriented to empirical understanding in the sense of science.

This chapter of intellectual history has been sketchily analyzed to help make intelligible the *three*-fold structure of the intellectual disciplines in modern academic organization. It is my contention that neither the implicit empiricist-utilitarian monistic structure, in which basically all such disciplines were conceived as monolithic, nor the idealistic dualism is tenable as a frame of reference for the modern level of sophistication in this area. The social sciences must be treated as a fully autonomous category. They are not natural sciences in the sense of excluding the categories of subjective meaning, that is, they must consider knowing subjects as objects. Nor are they humanistic-cultural in the sense that the individuality of particular meanings must take complete precedence over analytical generality and such categories as causality. The emergence of sociological theorizing in the sense outlined crystallized this synthesis more sharply than any other intellectual event of recent times.

On this basis it has at last become clear that the analytical and historical components of knowledge are just that—components, not concrete classes. First, this means specifically that generalized analytical methods have become crucial, not only to economics and behavioristic psychology, but also to the social disciplines extending much farther into the "humanistic" range, such as sociology, anthropology, law, political science, and certain aspects of history itself. Conversely, however, historical perspectives have been extended far into the normal domains of natural science. Perhaps the original crystallization of this perspective lay in "natural history's" exceedingly important role in biology. A particularly important extension of this conception went toward paleontology as the historical perspective on the whole process of organic evolution. This in turn is most intimately related to the historical aspect of geology, the "story" of the planet earth. Extension to still further ranges has become very prominent in recent times, through the historical aspect of astronomy, the history of planets, suns, and indeed galaxies.

Finally, all three sets of disciplines have their practical aspects as knowledge applied to the implementation of human values and interests, not only as fields of knowledge for its own sake. The concept of "practical reason" is not confined to any one branch of learning, but is relevant to all of them. There is, however, the essential proviso that it is exceedingly important not to confuse the two references.[23] Increasingly, this distinction seems to be becoming institutionalized in the distinction between arts and sciences faculties and the applied "professional" faculties. Equally, the underlying premises of all the intellectual disciplines require grounding at levels which are not problematic simply for the development of the individual sets of disciplines. Thus the philosophy of science is not itself a science in the sense of physics or chemistry. All the members of the triad of intellectual disciplines look both downward to the fields applying their "pure" patterns of knowledge and upward to the grounding of their premises in the more ultimate problems of the meaning of the human condition. No basic distinction can be drawn among them on either of these two accounts.

[23]The fields of engineering technology and somatic medicine, as applications of natural science knowledge, and of economic policy and of the use of psychological testing in personnel selection, as applications of social science, are relatively obvious. Sometimes, however, humanists make a virtue of their claim that the humanities are completely free of any taint of practicality—that they are fields of the pursuit of learning solely for its own sake. This claim may be doubted on one ground in particular. This is that for a considerable period in European history a humanistic education constituted the principal basis of the common culture of the elite classes of European Society—and indeed still does to a considerable extent. We may suggest that the "use" of the humanistic disciplines in giving its principal cultural character to the elite of a great civilization was just as much a "social" application as any of engineering or medicine. Far from being simply the erudite scholar whose studies had no relevance beyond his own esoteric self-gratification, the typical humanist has been par excellence the educator of men of understanding and character.

The Crisis in Man's Knowledge of Himself*
ERNST CASSIRER

―――――――――

1

That self-knowledge is the highest aim of philosophical inquiry appears to be generally acknowledged. In all the conflicts between the different philosophical schools this objective remained invariable and unshaken: it proved to be the Archimedean point, the fixed and immovable center, of all thought. Nor did the most sceptical thinkers deny the possibility and necessity of self-knowledge. They distrusted all general principles concerning the nature of things, but this distrust was only meant to open a new and more reliable mode of investigation. In the history of philosophy scepticism has very often been simply the counterpart of a resolute *humanism.* By the denial and destruction of the objective certainty of the external world the sceptic hopes to throw all the thoughts of man back upon his own being. Self-knowledge—he declares—is the first prerequisite of self-realization. We must try to break the chain connecting us with the outer world in order to enjoy our true freedom. "La plus grande chose du monde c'est de scavoir être à soy," writes Montaigne.

Yet even this approach to the problem—the method of introspection— is not secure against sceptical doubts. Modern philosophy began with the principle that the evidence of our own being is impregnable and unassailable. But the advance of psychological knowledge has hardly confirmed this Cartesian principle. The general tendency of thought is nowadays again directed toward the opposite pole. Few modern psychologists would admit or recommend a mere method of introspection. In general they tell us that such a method is very precarious. They are convinced that a strictly objective behavioristic attitude is the only possible approach to a scientific psychology. But a consistent and radical behaviorism fails to attain its end. It can warn us against possible methodological errors, but it cannot solve all the problems of human psychology. We may criticize or suspect the purely introspective view, but we cannot suppress or eliminate it. Without introspection, without an immediate awareness of feelings, emotions, perceptions, thoughts, we could not even define the field of human psychology. Yet it must be admitted that by following this way alone we can never arrive at a comprehensive view of human nature. Introspection reveals to us only that small sector of human life which is accessible to our individual experience. It can never cover the whole field

*Reprinted by permission of Yale University Press from *An Essay on Man* by Ernst Cassirer, pp. 1–22. Copyright © 1944 by Yale University Press.

of human phenomena. Even if we should succeed in collecting and combining all the data, we should still have a very meager and fragmentary picture—a mere torso—of human nature.

Aristotle declares that all human knowledge originates from a basic tendency of human nature manifesting itself in man's most elementary actions and reactions. The whole extent of the life of the senses is determined by and impregnated with this tendency.

> All men by nature desire to know. An indication of this is the delight we take in our senses; for even apart from their usefulness they are loved for themselves; and above all others the sense of sight. For not only with a view to action, but even when we are not going to do anything we prefer seeing to everything else. The reason is that this, most of all senses, makes us know and brings to light many differences between things.[1]

This passage is highly characteristic of Aristotle's conception of knowledge as distinguished from Plato's. Such a philosophical eulogy of man's sensuous life would be impossible in the work of Plato. He could never compare the desire for knowledge with the delight we take in our senses. In Plato the life of the senses is separated from the life of the intellect by a broad and insurmountable gulf. Knowledge and truth belong to a transcendental order—to the realm of pure and eternal ideas. Even Aristotle is convinced that scientific knowledge is not possible through the act of perception alone. But he speaks as a biologist when he denies this Platonic severance between the ideal and the empirical world. He attempts to explain the ideal world, the world of knowledge, in terms of life. In both realms, according to Aristotle, we find the same unbroken continuity. In nature as well as in human knowledge the higher forms develop from the lower forms. Sense perception, memory, experience, imagination, and reason are all linked together by a common bond; they are merely different stages and different expressions of one and the same fundamental activity, which attains its highest perfection in man, but which in a way is shared by the animals and all the forms of organic life.

If we were to adopt this biological view we should expect that the first stages of human knowledge would deal exclusively with the external world. For all his immediate needs and practical interests man is dependent on his physical environment. He cannot live without constantly adapting himself to the conditions of the surrounding world. The initial steps toward man's intellectual and cultural life may be described as acts which involve a sort of mental adjustment to the immediate environment. But as human culture progresses we very soon meet with an opposite tendency of human life. From the earliest glimmering of human con-

---

[1]Aristotle, *Metaphysics*, Book A. 1 980^{a}21. English trans. by W. D. Ross, *The Works of Aristotle* (Oxford, Clarendon Press, 1924), Vol. VIII.

sciousness we find an introvert view of life accompanying and complementing this extrovert view. The farther we trace the development of human culture from these beginnings the more this introvert view seems to come to the fore. Man's natural curiosity begins slowly to change its direction. We can study this growth in almost all the forms of the cultural life of man. In the first mythological explanations of the universe we always find a primitive *anthropology* side by side with a primitive *cosmology*. The question of the origin of the world is inextricably interwoven with the question of the origin of man. Religion does not destroy these first mythological explanations. On the contrary, it preserves the mythological cosmology and anthropology by giving them new shape and new depth. Henceforth self-knowledge is not conceived as a merely theoretical interest. It is not simply a subject of curiosity or speculation; it is declared to be the fundamental obligation of man. The great religious thinkers were the first to inculcate this moral requirement. In all the higher forms of religious life the maxim "Know thyself" is regarded as a categorical imperative, as an ultimate moral and religious law. In this imperative we feel, as it were, a sudden reversal of the first natural instinct to know—we perceive a transvaluation of all values. In the histories of all the religions of the world—in Judaism, Buddhism, Confucianism, and Christianity—we can observe the individual steps of this development.

The same principle holds good in the general evolution of philosophical thought. In its earliest stages Greek philosophy seems exclusively concerned with the physical universe. Cosmology clearly predominates over all the other branches of philosophical investigation. It is, however, characteristic of the depth and comprehensiveness of the Greek mind that almost every individual thinker represents at the same time a new general *type* of thought. Beyond the physical philosophy of the Milesian School the Pythagoreans discover a mathematical philosophy, while the Eleatic thinkers are the first to conceive the ideal of a logical philosophy. Heraclitus stands on the border line between cosmological and anthropological thought. Although he still speaks as a natural philosopher, and he belongs to the "ancient physiologists," yet he is convinced that it is impossible to penetrate into the secret of nature without having studied the secret of man. We must fulfil the demand of self-reflection if we wish to keep hold of reality and to understand its meaning. Hence it was possible for Heraclitus to characterize the whole of his philosophy by the two words ἐδιζησάμην ἐμεωτόν ("I have sought for myself").[2] But this new tendency of thought, although in a sense inherent in early Greek philosophy, did not come to its full maturity until the time of Socrates. Thus it is in the

[2]Fragment 101, in Diels, *Die Fragmente der Vorsokratiker*, ed. by W. Krantz (5th ed. Berlin, 1934), I, 173.

problem of man that we find the landmark separating Socratic from pre-Socratic thought. Socrates never attacks or criticizes the theories of his predecessors. He does not intend to introduce a new philosophical doctrine. Yet in him all the former problems are seen in a new light because they are referred to a new intellectual center. The problems of Greek natural philosophy and of Greek metaphysics are suddenly eclipsed by a new question which seems henceforth to absorb man's whole theoretical interest. In Socrates we no longer have an independent theory of nature or an independent logical theory. We do not even have a coherent and systematic ethical theory—in that sense in which it was developed in the later ethical systems. Only one question remains: What is man? Socrates always maintains and defends the ideal of an objective, absolute, universal truth. But the only universe he knows, and to which all his inquiries refer, is the universe of man. His philosophy—if he possesses a philosophy—is strictly anthropological. In one of the Platonic dialogues Socrates is described as being engaged in a conversation with his pupil Phaedrus. They are walking, and after a short time they come to a place outside the gates of Athens. Socrates bursts into admiration for the beauty of the spot. He is delighted with the landscape, which he praises highly. But Phaedrus interrupts. He is surprised that Socrates behaves like a stranger who is being shown about by a guide. "Do you ever cross the border?" he asks. Socrates puts symbolic meaning into his reply. "Very true, my good friend," he replies, "and I hope that you will excuse me when you hear the reason, which is, that I am a lover of knowledge, and the men who dwell in the city are my teachers, and not the trees, or the country."[3]

Yet when we study Plato's Socratic dialogues nowhere do we find a direct solution of the new problem. Socrates gives us a detailed and meticulous analysis of individual human qualities and virtues. He seeks to determine the nature of these qualities and to define them: goodness, justice, temperance, courage, and so on. But he never ventures a definition of man. How is this seeming deficiency to be accounted for? Did Socrates deliberately adopt a roundabout approach—one that allowed him only to scratch the surface of his problem without ever penetrating into its depth and its real core? But here, more than anywhere else, we should suspect Socratic irony. It is precisely the negative answer of Socrates which throws new and unexpected light on the question, and which gives us the positive insight into the Socratic conception of man. We cannot discover the nature of man in the same way that we can detect the nature of physical things. Physical things may be described in terms of their objective properties, but man may be described and defined only in terms of his consciousness. This fact poses an entirely new problem which cannot be solved by our

[3]Plato, *Phaedrus* 230A (Jowett trans.).

usual modes of investigation. Empirical observation and logical analysis, in the sense in which these terms were used in pre-Socratic philosophy, here proved inefficient and inadequate. For it is only in our immediate intercourse with human beings that we have insight into the character of man. We must actually confront man, we must meet him squarely face to face, in order to understand him. Hence it is not a new objective content, but a new activity and function of thought which is the distinctive feature of the philosophy of Socrates. Philosophy, which had hitherto been conceived as an intellectual monologue, is transformed into a dialogue. Only by way of dialogical or dialectic thought can we approach the knowledge of human nature. Previously truth might have been conceived to be a sort of ready-made thing which could be grasped by an effort of the individual thinker, and readily transferred and communicated to others. But Socrates could no longer subscribe to this view. It is as impossible—says Plato in the *Republic*—to implant truth in the soul of a man as it is to give the power of seeing to a man born blind. Truth is by nature the offspring of dialectic thought. It cannot be gained, therefore, except through a constant cooperation of the subjects in mutual interrogation and reply. It is not therefore like an empirical object; it must be understood as the outgrowth of a social act. Here we have the new, indirect answer to the question "What is man?" Man is declared to be that creature who is constantly in search of himself—a creature who in every moment of his existence must examine and scrutinize the conditions of his existence. In this scrutiny, in this critical attitude toward human life, consists the real value of human life. "A life which is unexamined," says Socrates in his *Apology,* "is not worth living."[4] We may epitomize the thought of Socrates by saying that man is defined by him as that being who, when asked a rational question, can give a rational answer. Both his knowledge and his morality are comprehended in this circle. It is by this fundamental faculty, by this faculty of giving a response to himself and to others, that man becomes a "responsible" being, a moral subject.

2

This first answer has, in a sense, always remained the classical answer. The Socratic problem and the Socratic method can never be forgotten or obliterated. Through the medium of Platonic thought it has left its mark[5]

[4]Plato, *Apology* 37E (Jowett trans.).

[5]In the following pages I shall not attempt to give a survey of the historical development of anthropological philosophy. I shall merely select a few typical stages in order to illustrate the general line of thought. The history of the philosophy of man is still a desideratum. Whereas the history of metaphysics, of natural philosophy, of ethical and scientific thought has been studied in all detail, we are here still at the beginning. During the last century the importance of this problem has been felt more and more vividly. Wilhelm Dilthey has concentrated all his efforts upon its solution. But

on the whole future development of human civilization. There is perhaps no surer or shorter way of convincing ourselves of the deep unity and perfect continuity of ancient philosophic thought than by comparing these first stages in Greek philosophy with one of the latest and noblest products of Graeco-Roman culture, the book *To Himself* written by the Emperor Marcus Aurelius Antoninus. At first sight such a comparison may appear arbitrary; for Marcus Aurelius was not an original thinker, nor did he follow a strictly logical method. He himself thanks the gods that when he had set his heart on philosophy he did not become a writer of philosophy or a solver of syllogisms.[6] But Socrates and Marcus Aurelius have in common the conviction that in order to find the true nature or essence of man we must first of all remove from his being all external and incidental traits.

> Call none of those things a man's that do not fall to him as a man. They cannot be claimed of a man; the man's nature does not guarantee them; they are no consummations of that nature. Consequently neither is the end for which man lives placed in these things, nor yet that which is perfective of the end, namely the Good. Moreover, if any of these things did fall to a man, it would not fall to him to contemn them and set his face against them, . . . but as it is, the more a man can cut himself free, . . . from these and other such things with equanimity, by so much the more is he good.[7]

All that which befalls man from without is null and void. His essence does not depend on external circumstances; it depends exclusively on the value he gives to himself. Riches, rank, social distinction, even health or intellectual gifts—all this becomes indifferent (ἀδιάφορον). What matters alone is the tendency, the inner attitude of the soul; and this inner principle cannot be disturbed. "That which does not make a man himself worse than before cannot make his life worse either, nor injure it whether from without or within."[8]

The requirement of self-questioning appears, therefore, in Stoicism, as in the conception of Socrates, as man's privilege and his fundamental

---

Dilthey's work, however rich and suggestive, remained incomplete. One of the pupils of Dilthey, Bernhard Groethuysen, has given an excellent description of the general development of anthropological philosophy. But unfortunately even this description stops short of the last and decisive step—that of our modern era. See Bernhard Groethuysen, "Philosophische Anthropologie," *Handbuch der Philosophie* (Munich and Berlin, 1931), III, 1–207. See also Groethuysen's article, "Towards an Anthropological Philosophy," *Philosophy and History, Essays Presented to Ernst Cassirer* (Oxford, Clarendon Press, 1936), pp. 77–89.

[6]Marcus Aurelius Antoninus, *Ad se ipsum* (εἰς ἑαυτόν), Bk. I, par. 8. In most of the following passages I quote the English version of C. R. Haines, *The Communings with Himself of Marcus Aurelius Antoninus* (Cambridge, Mass., Harvard University Press, 1916), Loeb Classical Library.

[7]Marcus Aurelius, *op. cit.*, Bk. V, par. 15.

[8]*Idem*, Bk. IV, par. 8.

duty.[9] But this duty is now understood in a broader sense; it has not only a moral but also a universal and metaphysical background. "Never fail to ask thyself this question and to cross-examine thyself thus: What relation have I to this part of me which they call the ruling Reason (τὸ ἡγεμονικόν)?"[10]   He who lives in harmony with his own self, his demon, lives in harmony with the universe; for both the universal order and the personal order are nothing but different expressions and manifestations of a common underlying principle. Man proves his inherent power of criticism, of judgment and discernment, by conceiving that in this correlation the Self, not the Universe, has the leading part. Once the Self has won its inner form, this form remains unalterable and imperturbable. "A sphere once formed continues round and true."[11] That is, so to speak, the last word of Greek philosophy—a word that once more contains and explains the spirit in which it was originally conceived. This spirit was a spirit of judgment, of critical discernment between Being and Non-Being, between truth and illusion, between good and evil. Life in itself is changing and fluctuating, but the true value of life is to be sought in an eternal order that admits of no change. It is not in the world of our senses, it is only by the power of our judgment that we can grasp this order. Judgment is the central power in man, the common source of truth and morality. For it is the only thing in which man entirely depends on himself; it is free, autonomous, self-sufficing.[12] "Distract not thyself," says Marcus Aurelius,

> be not too eager, but be thine own master, and look upon life as a man, as a human being, as a citizen, as a mortal creature. . . . Things do not touch the soul, for they are external and remain immovable, but our disturbance comes only of that judgment that we form in ourselves. All these things, which thou seest, change immediately, and will no longer be; and constantly bear in mind how many of these changes thou hast already witnessed. The Universe—mutation, Life—affirmation.[13]

The greatest merit of this Stoic conception of man lies in the fact that this conception gives to man both a deep feeling of his harmony with

---

[9]*Idem,* Bk. III, par. 6.

[10]*Idem,* Bk. V, par. 11.

[11]*Idem,* Bk. VIII, par. 41.

[12]Cf. *idem,* Bk. V, par. 14. Ὁ λόγος καὶ ἡ λογικὴ τέχνη δυνάμεις εἰσὶν ἑαυταῖς ἀρκούμεναι καὶ τοῖς καθ' ἑαυτὰς ἔργοις.

[13]Ὁ κόσμος ἀλλοίωσις' ὁ βίος ὑπόληψις Bk. IV, par. 3. The term "affirmation" or "judgment" seems to me a much more adequate expression of the thought of Marcus Aurelius than "opinion," which I find in all the English versions I have consulted. "Opinion" (the Platonic δόξα) contains an element of change and uncertainty which is not intended by Marcus Aurelius. As equivalent terms for ὑπόληψις we find in Marcus Aurelius κρίσις, κρῖμα, διάκρισις. Cf. Bk. III, par. 2; VI, par. 52; VIII, pars. 28, 47.

nature and of his moral independence of nature. In the mind of the Stoic philosopher these assertions do not conflict; they are correlated with one another. Man finds himself in perfect equipoise with the universe, and he knows that this equipoise must not be disturbed by any external force. Such is the dual character of Stoic "imperturbability" (ἀταραξία). This Stoic theory proved to be one of the strongest formative powers of ancient culture. But it found itself suddenly in the presence of a new, and hitherto unknown, force. The conflict with this new force shook the classical ideal of man to its very foundations. The Stoic and the Christian theories of man are not necessarily hostile to one another. In the history of ideas they work in conjunction, and we often find them in close connection in one and the same individual thinker. Nevertheless, there always remains one point on which the antagonism between the Christian and the Stoic ideals proves irreconcilable. The asserted absolute independence of man, which in the Stoic theory was regarded as man's fundamental virtue, is turned in the Christian theory into his fundamental vice and error. As long as man perseveres in this error there is no possible road to salvation. The struggle between these two conflicting views has lasted for many centuries, and at the beginning of the modern era—at the time of the Renaissance and in the seventeenth century—we still feel its full strength.[14]

Here we can grasp one of the most characteristic features of anthropological philosophy. This philosophy is not, like other branches of philosophical investigation, a slow and continuous development of general ideas. Even in the history of logic, metaphysics, and natural philosophy we find the sharpest oppositions. This history may be described in Hegelian terms as a dialectic process in which each thesis is followed by its antithesis. Nevertheless there is an inner consistency, a clear logical order, connecting the different stages of this dialectic process. Anthropological philosophy, on the other hand, exhibits a quite different character. If we wish to grasp its real meaning and import, we must choose not the epic manner of description but the dramatic. For we are confronted, not with a peaceful development of concepts or theories, but with a clash between conflicting spiritual powers. The history of anthropological philosophy is fraught with the deepest human passions and emotions. It is not concerned with a single theoretical problem, however general its scope; here the whole destiny of man is at stake and clamoring for an ultimate decision.

This character of the problem has found its clearest expression in the work of Augustine. Augustine stands at the frontier of two ages. Living in the fourth century of the Christian era, he has grown up in the tradition of Greek philosophy, and it is especially the system of Neo-Platonism which has left its mark on his whole philosophy. But, on the other hand, he is

[14]For a detailed account see Cassirer, *Descartes* (Stockholm, 1939), pp. 215 ff.

the pioneer of medieval thought; he is the founder of medieval philosophy and of Christian dogmatics. In his *Confessions* we can follow every step of his way from Greek philosophy to Christian revelation. According to Augustine all philosophy prior to the appearance of Christ was liable to one fundamental error, and was infected with one and the same heresy. The power of reason was extolled as the highest power of man. But what man could never know until he was enlightened with a special divine revelation is that reason itself is one of the most questionable and ambiguous things in the world. Reason cannot show us the way to clarity, to truth and wisdom. For it is itself obscure in its meaning, and its origin is wrapped in mystery—in a mystery soluble only by Christian revelation. Reason for Augustine does not have a simple and unique but rather a double and divided nature. Man was created in the image of God; and in his original state, in which he went out from the hands of God, he was equal to his archetype. But all this has been lost through the fall of Adam. From that time on all the original power of reason has been obscured. And reason alone, when left to itself and its own faculties, never can find the way back. It cannot reconstruct itself; it cannot, by its own efforts, return to its former pure essence. If such a reformation is ever possible, it is only by supernatural aid, by the power of divine grace. Such is the new anthropology, as it is understood by Augustine, and maintained in all the great systems of medieval thought. Even Thomas Aquinas, the disciple of Aristotle, who goes back to the sources of Greek philosophy, does not venture to deviate from this fundamental dogma. He concedes to human reason a much higher power than Augustine did; but he is convinced that reason cannot make the right use of these powers unless it is guided and illuminated by the grace of God. Here we have come to a complete reversal of all the values upheld by Greek philosophy. What once seemed to be the highest privilege of man proves to be his peril and his temptation; what appeared as his pride becomes his deepest humiliation. The Stoic precept that man has to obey and revere his inner principle, the "demon" within himself, is now regarded as dangerous idolatry.

It is not practicable here to describe further the character of this new anthropology, to analyze its fundamental motives and to follow up its development. But in order to understand its purport we may choose a different and shorter way. At the beginning of modern times there appeared a thinker who gave to this anthropology a new vigor and a new splendor. In the work of Pascal it found its last and perhaps most impressive expression. Pascal was prepared for this task as no other writer had been. He possessed an incomparable gift for elucidating the most obscure questions and condensing and concentrating complex and scattered systems of thought. Nothing seems to be impermeable to the keenness of his thought and the lucidity of his style. In him are united all the advantages of modern literature and modern philosophy. But he uses them as weapons against the modern spirit, the spirit of Descartes and his philosophy. At first sight Pascal seems to accept all the presuppositions of Cartesianism and of modern science. There is nothing in nature that can resist the effort of scientific reason; for there is nothing that can resist geometry. It is a curious event in the history of ideas that it was one of the greatest and profoundest geometers who became the belated champion of the philosophical anthropology of the Middle Ages. When sixteen years old, Pascal wrote the treatise on conic sections that opened a new and a very rich and fertile field of geometrical thought. But he was not only a great geometer, he was a philosopher; and as a philosopher he was not merely absorbed in geometrical problems but he wished to understand the true use, the extent, and the limits of geometry. He was thus led to make that fundamental distinction between the "geometrical spirit" and the "acute or subtle spirit." The geometrical spirit excels in all these subjects that are capable of a perfect analysis—that may be divided into their first elements.[15] It starts with certain axioms and from them it draws inferences the truth of which can be demonstrated by universal logical rules. The advantage of this spirit consists in the clarity of its principles and in the necessity of its deductions. But not all objects are capable of such treatment. There are things which because of their subtlety and their infinite variety defy every attempt at logical analysis. And if there is anything in the world that we have to treat in this second way, it is the mind of man. What characterizes man is the richness and subtlety, the variety and versatility of his nature. Hence mathematics can never become the instrument of a true doctrine of man, of a philosophical anthropology. It is ridiculous to speak of man as if he were a geometrical proposition. A moral philosophy in terms of a system of geometry—an *Ethica more geometrico demonstrata*—is to the mind of Pascal an absurdity, a philosophical dream. Traditional logic and metaphysics are themselves in no better position to understand and solve the riddle of man. Their first and supreme law is the law of contradiction. Rational thought, logical and metaphysical thought can comprehend only those objects which are free from contradiction, and which have a consistent nature and truth. It is, however, just this homogeneity which we never find in man. The philosopher is not permitted to construct an artificial man; he must describe a real one. All the so-called definitions of man are nothing but

[15]For the distinction between *l'esprit géométrique* and *l'esprit de finesse* compare Pascal's treatise "De l'esprit géométrique" and Pascal's *Pensées*, ed. by Charles Louandre (Paris, 1858), chap. ix, p. 231. In the passages which follow I quote the English translation of O. W. Wight (New York, 1861).

airy speculation so long as they are not based upon and confirmed by our experience of man. There is no other way to know man than to understand his life and conduct. But what we find here defies every attempt at inclusion within a single and simple formula. Contradiction is the very element of human existence. Man has no "nature"—no simple or homogeneous being. He is a strange mixture of being and nonbeing. His place is between these two opposite poles.

There is, therefore, only one approach to the secret of human nature: that of religion. Religion shows us that there is a double man—the man before and after the fall. Man was destined for the highest goal, but he forfeited his position. By the fall he lost his power, and his reason and will were perverted. The classical maxim, "Know thyself," when understood in its philosophic sense, in the sense of Socrates, Epictetus, or Marcus Aurelius, is therefore not only ineffectual, it is misleading and erroneous. Man cannot confide in himself and listen to himself. He has to silence himself in order to hear a higher and truer voice. "What shall become of you, then, O man! you who search out what is your true condition by your natural reason? . . . Know, then, haughty man, what a paradox you are to yourself. Humble yourself, impotent reason; be silent, imbecile nature; learn that man infinitely surpasses man, and hear from your master your true condition, which you are ignorant of. Listen to God."[16]

What is given here is not meant to be a theoretical solution of the problem of man. Religion cannot offer such a solution. By its adversaries religion has always been accused of darkness and incomprehensibility. But this blame becomes the highest praise as soon as we consider its true aim. Religion cannot be clear and rational. What it relates is an obscure and somber story: the story of the sin and the fall of man. It reveals a fact of which no rational explanation is possible. We cannot account for the sin of man; for it is not produced or necessitated by any natural cause. Nor can we account for man's salvation; for this salvation depends on an inscrutable act of divine grace. It is freely given and freely denied; there is no human action and no human merit that can deserve it. Religion, therefore, never pretends to clarify the mystery of man. It confirms and deepens this mystery. The God of whom it speaks is a *Deus absconditus,* a hidden God. Hence even his image, man, cannot be other than mysterious. Man also remains a *homo absconditus.* Religion is no "theory" of God and man and of their mutual relation. The only answer that we receive from religion is that it is the will of God to conceal himself. "Thus, God being concealed, every religion that does not say that God is concealed is not true; and every religion which does not render a reason for this, is not instructive. Ours does all this: *Vere tu es Deus absconditus.*[17]

[16]*Pensees*, chap. x, sec. 1.
[17]*Idem*, chap. xii, sec. 5.

. . . For nature is such, that it everywhere indicates a God lost, both in man and out of man."[18] Religion is, therefore, so to speak, a logic of absurdity; for only thus can it grasp the absurdity, the inner contradiction, the chimerical being of man. "Certainly, nothing strikes us more rudely than this doctrine; and yet, without this mystery, the most incomprehensible of all, we are imcomprehensible to ourselves. The knot of our condition takes its twists and turns in this abyss; so that man is more inconceivable without this mystery, than this mystery is inconceivable to man."[19]

3

What we learn from Pascal's example is that at the beginning of modern times the old problem was still felt in its full strength. Even after the appearance of Descartes' *Discours de la méthode* the modern mind was still wrestling with the same difficulties. It was divided between two entirely imcompatible solutions. But at the same time there begins a slow intellectual development by which the question What is man? is transformed and, so to speak, raised to a higher level. The important thing here is not so much the discovery of new facts as the discovery of a new instrument of thought. Now for the first time the scientific spirit, in the modern sense of the word, enters the lists. The quest now is for a general theory of man based on empirical observations and on general logical principles. The first postulate of this new and scientific spirit was the removal of all the artificial barriers that had hitherto separated the human world from the rest of nature. In order to understand the order of human things we must begin with a study of the cosmic order. And this cosmic order now appears in a wholly new light. The new cosmology, the heliocentric system introduced in the work of Copernicus, is the only sound and scientific basis for a new *anthropology*.

Neither classical metaphysics nor medieval religion and theology were prepared for this task. Both of these bodies of doctrine, however different in their methods and aims, are grounded in a common principle. They both conceive the universe as a hierarchic order in which man occupies the highest place. In Stoic philosophy and in Christian theology man was described as the end of the universe. Both doctrines are convinced that there is a general providence ruling over the world and the destiny of man. This concept is one of the basic presuppositions of Stoic and Christian thought.[20] All this is suddenly called into question by the new cosmology. Man's claim to being the center of the universe has lost its founda-

[18]*Idem*, chap. xiii, sec. 3.
[19]*Idem*, chap. x, sec. 1.
[20]For the Stoic concept of providence (πρόνοια) see, for instance, Marcus Aurelius, *op. cit.*, Bk. II, par. 3.

tion. Man is placed in an infinite space in which his being seems to be a single and vanishing point. He is surrounded by a mute universe, by a world that is silent to his religious feelings and to his deepest moral demands.

It is understandable, and it was indeed necessary, that the first reaction to this new conception of the world could only be a negative one—a reaction of doubt and fear. Even the greatest thinkers could not free themselves from this feeling. "Le silence éternel des ces espaces infinis m'effraye," says Pascal. [21] The Copernican system became one of the strongest instruments of that philosophical agnosticism and scepticism which developed in the sixteenth century. In his criticism of human reason Montaigne uses all the well-known traditional arguments of the systems of Greek scepticism. But he adds a new weapon which in his hands proves to be of the greatest strength and of paramount importance. Nothing is more apt to humiliate us and to break the pride of human reason than an unprejudiced view of the physical universe. Let man, he says in a famous passage of his *Apologie de Raimond Sebond,*

> make me understand by the force of his reason, upon what foundations he has built those great advantages he thinks he has over other creatures. Who has made him believe that this admirable motion of the celestial arch, the eternal light of those luminaries that roll so high over his head, the wondrous and fearful motions of that infinite ocean, should be established and continue so many ages for his service and convenience? Can anything be imagined so ridiculous, that this miserable and wretched creature, who is not so much as master of himself, but subject to the injuries of all things, should call himself master and emperor of the world, of which he has not power to know the least part, much less to command the whole? [22]

Man is always inclined to regard the small circle in which he lives as the center of the world and to make his particular, private life the standard of the universe. But he must give up this vain pretense, this petty provincial way of thinking and judging.

> When the vines of our village are nipped with the frost, the parish-priest presently concludes that the indignation of God is gone out against all the human race. . . . Who is it that, seeing these civil wars of ours, does not cry out, That the machine of the whole world is upsetting, and that the day of judgment is at hand! . . . But whoever shall represent to his fancy, as in a picture, the great image of our mother nature, portrayed in her full majesty and lustre; whoever in her face shall read so general and so constant a variety, whoever shall observe himself in that figure, and not

[21]Pascal, *op. cit.,* chap. xxv, sec. 18.
[22]Montaigne, *Essais,* II, chap. xii. English trans. by William Hazlitt, *The Works of Michael de Montaigne* (2d ed. London, 1845), p. 205.

himself but a whole kingdom, no bigger than the least touch of a pencil, in comparison of the whole, that man alone is able to value things according to their true estimate and grandeur.[23]

Montaigne's words give us the clue to the whole subsequent development of the modern theory of man. Modern philosophy and modern science had to accept the challenge contained in these words. They had to prove that the new cosmology, far from enfeebling or obstructing the power of human reason, establishes and confirms this power. Such was the task of the combined efforts of the metaphysical systems of the sixteenth and seventeenth centuries. These systems go different ways, but they are all directed toward one and the same end. They strive, so to speak, to turn the apparent curse of the new cosmology into a blessing. Giordano Bruno was the first thinker to enter upon this path, which in a sense became the path of all modern metaphysics. What is characteristic of the philosophy of Giordano Bruno is that here the term "infinity" changes its meaning. In Greek classical thought infinity is a negative concept. The infinite is the boundless or indeterminate. It has no limit and no form, and it is, therefore, inaccessible to human reason, which lives in the realm of form and can understand nothing but forms. In this sense the finite and infinite, πέρας and ἄπειρον, are declared by Plato in the *Philebus* to be the two fundamental principles which are necessarily opposed to one another. In Bruno's doctrine infinity no longer means a mere negation or limitation. On the contrary, it means the immeasurable and inexhaustible abundance of reality and the unrestricted power of the human intellect. It is in this sense that Bruno understands and interprets the Copernican doctrine. This doctrine, according to Bruno, was the first and decisive step toward man's self-liberation. Man no longer lives in the world as a prisoner enclosed within the narrow walls of a finite physical universe. He can traverse the air and break through all the imaginary boundaries of the celestial spheres which have been erected by a false metaphysics and cosmology.[24] The infinite universe sets no limits to human reason; on the contrary, it is the great incentive of human reason. The human intellect becomes aware of its own infinity through measuring its powers by the infinite universe.

All this is expressed in the work of Bruno in a poetical, not in a scientific language. The new world of modern science, the mathematical theory of nature, was still unknown to Bruno. He could not, therefore, pursue his way to its logical conclusion. It took the combined efforts of all the metaphysicians and scientists of the seventeenth century to overcome the intellectual crisis brought about by the discovery of the Copernican system. Every great thinker—Galileo, Descartes, Leibniz, Spinoza—has

---

[23]*Idem*, I, chap. xxv. English trans., pp. 65 f.
[24]For further details see Cassirer, *Individuum und Kosmos in der Philosophie der Renaissance* (Leipzig, 1927), pp. 197 ff.

his special share in the solution of this problem. Galileo asserts that in the field of mathematics man reaches the climax of all possible knowledge—a knowledge which is not inferior to that of the divine intellect. Of course the divine intellect knows and conceives an infinitely greater number of mathematical truths than we do, but with regard to objective certainty the few verities known by the human mind are known as perfectly by man as they are by God.[25] Descartes begins with his universal doubt which seems to enclose man within the limits of his own consciousness. There seems to be no way out of this magic circle—no approach to reality. But even here the idea of the infinite turns out to be the only instrument for the overthrow of universal doubt. By means of this concept alone we can demonstrate the reality of God and, in an indirect way, the reality of the material world. Leibniz combines this metaphysical proof with a new scientific proof. He discovers a new instrument of mathematical thought— the infinitesimal calculus. By the rules of this calculus the physical universe becomes intelligible; the laws of nature are seen to be nothing but special cases of the general laws of reason. It is Spinoza who ventures to make the last and decisive step in this mathematical theory of the world and of the human mind. Spinoza constructs a new ethics, a theory of the passions and affections, a mathematical theory of the moral world. By this theory alone, he is convinced, can we attain our end: the goal of a "philosophy of man," of an anthropological philosophy, which is free from the errors and prejudices of a merely anthropocentric system. This is the topic, the general theme, which in its various forms permeates all the great metaphysical systems of the seventeenth century. It is the rationalistic solution of the problem of man. Mathematical reason is the bond between man and the universe; it permits us to pass freely from the one to the other. Mathematical reason is the key to a true understanding of the cosmic and the moral order.

4

In 1754 Denis Diderot published a series of aphorisms entitled *Pensées sur l'interprétation de la nature.* In this essay he declared that the superiority of mathematics in the realm of science is no longer uncontested. Mathematics, he asserted, has reached such a high degree of perfection that no further progress is possible; henceforth mathematics will remain stationary.

> Nous touchons au moment d'une grande révolution dans les sciences. Au penchant que les esprits me paroissént avoir à la morale, aux belles lettres, à l'histoire de la nature et à la physique expérimentale j'oserois presque

[25]Galileo, *Dialogo dei due massimi sistemi del mondo,* I (Edizione nazionale), VII, 129.

assurer qu'avant qu'il soit cent ans on ne comptera pas trois grands géomètres en Europe. Cette science s'arrêtera tout court où l'auront laissé les Bernoulli, les Euler, les Maupertuis et les d'Alembert. Ils auront posés les colonnes d'Hercule, on n'ira point au delà.[26]

Diderot is one of the great representatives of the philosophy of the Enlightenment. As the editor of the *Encyclopédie* he stands at the very center of all the great intellectual movements of his time. No one had a clearer perspective of the general development of scientific thought; no one had a keener feeling for all the tendencies of the eighteenth century. It is all the more characteristic and remarkable of Diderot that, representing all the ideals of the Enlightenment, he began to doubt the absolute right of these ideals. He expects the rise of a new form of science—a science of a more concrete character, based rather on the observation of facts than on the assumption of general principles. According to Diderot, we have highly overrated our logical and rational methods. We know how to compare, to organize, and systematize the known facts; but we have not cultivated those methods by which alone it would be possible to discover new facts. We are under the delusion that the man who does not know how to count his fortune is in no better position than the man who has no fortune at all. But the time is near when we shall overcome this prejudice, and then we shall have reached a new and culminating point in the history of natural science.

Has Diderot's prophecy been fulfilled? Did the development of scientific ideas in the nineteenth century confirm his view? On one point, to be sure, his error is obvious. His expectation that mathematical thought would come to a standstill, that the great mathematicians of the eighteenth century had reached the Pillars of Hercules, proved to be entirely untrue. To that eighteenth-century galaxy we must now add the names of Gauss, of Riemann, of Weierstrass, of Poincaré. Everywhere in the science of the nineteenth century we meet with the triumphal march of new mathematical ideas and concepts. Nevertheless, Diderot's prediction contained an element of truth. For the innovation of the intellectual structure of the nineteenth century lies in the place that mathematical thought occupies in the scientific hierarchy. A new force begins to appear. Biological thought takes precedence over mathematical thought. In the first half of the nineteenth century there are still some metaphysicians, such as Herbart, or some psychologists, such as G. Th. Fechner, who cherish the hope of founding a mathematical psychology. But these projects rapidly disappear after the publication of Darwin's work *On the Origin of Species*. Henceforth the true character of anthropological philosophy appears to be fixed once and for all. After innumerable fruitless attempts the philosophy of man stands at last on firm ground. We no longer need indulge in airy speculations, for we are not in search of a general definition of the nature

[26] Diderot, *Pensées sur l'interprétation de la nature*, sec. 4; cf. secs. 17, 21.

or essence of man. Our problem is simply to collect the empirical evidence which the general theory of evolution has put at our disposal in a rich and abundant measure.

Such was the conviction shared by the scientists and philosophers of the nineteenth century. But what became more important for the general history of ideas and for the development of philosophical thought was not the empirical facts of evolution but the theoretical *interpretation* of these facts. This interpretation was not determined, in an unambiguous sense, by the empirical evidence itself, but rather by certain fundamental principles which had a definite metaphysical character. Though rarely acknowledged, this metaphysical cast of evolutionary thinking was a latent motivating force. The theory of evolution in a general philosophical sense was by no means a recent achievement. It had received its classical expression in Aristotle's psychology and in his general view of organic life. The characteristic and fundamental distinction between the Aristotelean and the modern version of evolution consisted in the fact that Aristotle gave a formal interpretation whereas the moderns attempted a material interpretation. Aristotle was convinced that in order to understand the general plan of nature, the origins of life, the lower forms must be interpreted in the light of the higher forms. In his metaphysics, in his definition of the soul as "the first actualization of a natural body potentially having life," organic life is conceived and interpreted in terms of human life. The teleological character of human life is projected upon the whole realm of natural phenomena. In modern theory this order is reversed. Aristotle's final causes are characterized as a mere *"asylum ignorantiae."* One of the principle aims of Darwin's work was to free modern thought from this illusion of final causes. We must seek to understand the structure of organic nature by material causes alone, or we cannot understand it at all. But material causes are in Aristotle's terminology "accidental" causes. Aristotle had emphatically asserted the impossibility of understanding the phenomenon of life by such accidental causes. Modern theory takes up this challenge. Modern thinkers have held that, after the innumerable fruitless attempts of former times, they have definitely succeeded in accounting for organic life as a mere product of chance. The accidental changes that take place in the life of every organism are sufficient to explain the gradual transformation that leads us from the simplest forms of life in a protozoon to the highest and most complicated forms. We find one of the most striking expressions of this view in Darwin himself, who is usually so very reticent with regard to his philosophical conceptions. "Not only the various domestic races," observes Darwin at the end of his book, *The Variation of Animals and Plants under Domestication,* but the most distinct genera and orders within the same great class—for instance, mammals, birds, reptiles, and fishes—are all the descendants of one common progenitor, and we must admit that the whole vast amount of difference between these forms has primarily arisen from simple variability. To consider the subject under this point of view is enough to strike one dumb with amazement. But our amazement ought to be lessened when we reflect that beings almost infinite in number, during an almost infinite lapse of time, have often had their whole organization rendered in some degree plastic, and that each slight modification of structure which was in any way beneficial under excessively complex conditions of life has been preserved, whilst each which was in any way injurious has been rigorously destroyed. And the long-continued accumulation of beneficial variations will infallibly have led to structures as diversified, as beautifully adapted for various purposes and as excellently co-ordinated as we see in the plants and animals around us. Hence I have spoken of selection as the paramount power, whether applied by man to the formation of domestic breeds, or by nature to the production of species . . . If an architect were to rear a noble and commodious edifice, without the use of cut stone, by selecting from the fragments at the base of a precipice wedge-formed stones for his arches, elongated stones for his lintels, and flat stones for his roof, we should admire his skill and regard him as the paramount power. Now, the fragments of stone, thought indispensable to the architect, bear to the edifice built by him the same relation which the fluctuating variations of organic beings bear to the varied and admirable structures ultimately acquired by their modified descendents.[27]

But still another, and perhaps the most important, step had to be taken before a real anthropological philosophy could develop. The theory of evolution had destroyed the arbitrary limits between the different forms of organic life. There are no separate species; there is just one continuous and uninterrupted stream of life. But can we apply the same principle to human life and human *culture?* Is the cultural world, like the organic world, made up of accidental changes?—Does it not possess a definite and undeniable teleological structure? Herewith a new problem presented itself to all philosophers whose starting point was the general theory of evolution. They had to prove that the cultural world, the world of human civilization, is reducible to a few general causes which are the same for the physical as for the so-called spiritual phenomena. Such was the new type of philosophy of culture introduced by Hippolyte Taine in his *Philosophy of Art* and in his *History of English Literature.* "Here as elsewhere," said Taine,

[27]Darwin, *The Variation of Animals and Plants under Domestication* (New York, D. Appleton & Co., 1897), II, chap. xxviii, 425 f.

we have but a mechanical problem; the total effect is a result, depending entirely on magnitude and direction of the producing causes . . . Though the means of notation are not the same in the moral and physical sciences, yet as in both the matter is the same, equally made up of forces, magnitudes, and directions, we may say that in both the final result is produced after the same method.[28]

It is the same iron ring of necessity that encloses both our physical and our cultural life. In his feelings, his inclinations, his ideas, his thoughts, and in his production of works of art, man never breaks out of this magic circle. We may consider man as an animal of superior species which produces philosophies and poems in the same way as silkworms produce their cocoons or bees build their cells. In the preface to his great work, *Les origines de la France contemporaine,* Taine states that he is going to study the transformation of France as a result of the French Revolution as he would the "metamorphosis of an insect."

But here another question arises. Can we be content with counting up in a merely empirical manner the different impulses that we find in human nature? For a really scientific insight these impulses would have to be classified and systematized. Obviously, not all of them are on the same level. We must suppose them to have a definite structure—and one of the first and most important tasks of our psychology and theory of culture is to discover this structure. In the complicated wheelwork of human life we must find the hidden driving force which sets the whole mechanism of our thought and will in motion. The principal aim of all these theories was to prove the unity and homogeneity of human nature. But if we examine the explanations which these theories were designed to give, the unity of human nature appears extremely doubtful. Every philosopher believes he has found the mainspring and master-faculty—*l'idée maîtresse,* as it was called by Taine. But as to the character of this master-faculty all the explanations differ widely from, and contradict, one another. Each individual thinker gives us his own picture of human nature. All these philosophers are determined empiricists: they would show us the facts and nothing but the facts. But their interpretation of the empirical evidence contains from the very outset an arbitrary assumption—and this arbitrariness becomes more and more obvious as the theory proceeds and takes on a more elaborate and sophisticated aspect. Nietzsche proclaims the will to power, Freud signalizes the sexual instinct, Marx enthrones the economic instinct. Each theory becomes a Procrustean bed on which the empirical facts are stretched to fit a preconceived pattern.

[28]Taine, *Histoire de la littérature anglaise*, Intro. English trans. by H. van Laun (New York, Holt & Co., 1872), I, 12 ff.

Owing to this development our modern theory of man lost its intellectual center. We acquired instead a complete anarchy of thought. Even in the former times to be sure there was a great discrepancy of opinions and theories relating to this problem. But there remained at least a general orientation, a frame of reference, to which all individual differences might be referred. Metaphysics, theology, mathematics, and biology successively assumed the guidance for thought on the problem of man and determined the line of investigation. The real crisis of this problem manifested itself when such a central power capable of directing all individual efforts ceased to exist. The paramount importance of the problem was still felt in all the different branches of knowledge and inquiry. But an established authority to which one might appeal no longer existed. Theologians, scientists, politicians, sociologists, biologists, psychologists, ethnologists, economists all approached the problem from their own viewpoints. To combine or unify all these particular aspects and perspectives was impossible. And even within the special fields there was no generally accepted scientific principle. The personal factor became more and more prevalent, and the temperament of the individual writer tended to play a decisive role. *Trahit sua quemque voluptas*: every author seems in the last count to be led by his own conception and evaluation of human life.

That this antagonism of ideas is not merely a grave theoretical problem but an imminent threat to the whole extent of our ethical and cultural life admits of no doubt. In recent philosophical thought Max Scheler was one of the first to become aware of and to signalize this danger. "In no other period of human knowledge," declares Scheler,

> has man ever become more problematic to himself than in our own days. We have a scientific, a philosophical, and a theological anthropology that know nothing of each other. Therefore we no longer possess any clear and consistent idea of man. The ever-growing multiplicity of the particular sciences that are engaged in the study of men has much more confused and obscured than elucidated our concept of man.[29]

Such is the strange situation in which modern philosophy finds itself. No former age was ever in such a favorable position with regard to the sources of our knowledge of human nature. Psychology, ethnology, anthropology, and history have amassed an astoundingly rich and constantly increasing body of facts. Our technical instruments for observation and experimentation have been immensely improved, and our analyses have become sharper and more penetrating. We appear, nevertheless, not yet to have found a method for the mastery and organization of this material.

[29]Max Scheler, *Die Stellung des Menschen im Kosmos* (Darmstadt, Reichl, 1928), pp. 13 f.

When compared with our own abundance the past may seem very poor. But our wealth of facts is not necessarily a wealth of thoughts. Unless we succeed in finding a clue of Ariadne to lead us out of this labyrinth, we can have no real insight into the general character of human culture; we shall remain lost in a mass of disconnected and disintegrated data which seem to lack all conceptual unity.

Social Estrangement

On the Meaning of Alienation *

MELVIN SEEMAN

At the present time, in all the social sciences, the various synonyms of alienation have a foremost place in studies of human relations. Investigations of the "unattached," the "marginal," the "obsessive," the "normless," and the "isolated" individual all testify to the central place occupied by the hypothesis of alienation in contemporary social science.

So writes Robert Nisbet in *The Quest for Community;*[1] and there would seem to be little doubt that his estimate is correct. In one form or another, the concept of alienation dominates both the contemporary literature and the history of sociological thought. It is a central theme in the classics of Marx, Weber, and Durkheim; and in contemporary work, the consequences that have been said to flow from the fact of alienation have been diverse, indeed.

*Reprinted by permission of the author and the American Sociological Association from *American Sociological Review*, Vol. 24, No. 6 (Dec. 1959), pp. 783-791. This paper is based in part on work done while the author was in attendance at the Behavioral Sciences Conference at the University of New Mexico, in the summer of 1958. The conference was supported by the Behavioral Sciences Division, Air Force Office of Scientific Research, under contract AF 49(638)-33. The work on alienation was carried out in close conjunction with Julian B. Rotter and Shephard Liverant of The Ohio State University. I gratefully acknowledge their very considerable help, while absolving them of any commitment to the viewpoints herein expressed.

[1] New York: Oxford, 1953, p. 15.

Ethnic prejudice, for example, has been described as a response to alienation—as an ideology which makes an incomprehensible world intelligible by imposing upon that world a simplified and categorical "answer system" (for example, the Jews cause international war).[2] In this examination of the persuasion process in the Kate Smith bond drive, Merton emphasizes the significance of pervasive distrust: "The very same society that produces this sense of alienation and estrangement generates in many a craving for reassurance, an acute need to believe, a flight into faith"[3]— in this case, faith in the sincerity of the persuader. In short, the idea of alienation is a popular vehicle for virtually every kind of analysis, from the prediction of voting behavior to the search for *The Sane Society*.[4] This inclusivness, in both its historical and its contemporary import, is expressed in Erich Kahler's remark: "The history of man could very well be written as a history of the alienation of man."[5]

A concept that is so central in sociological work, and so clearly laden with value implications, demands special clarity. There are, it seems to me, five basic ways in which the concept of alienation has been used. The purpose of this paper is to examine these logically distinguishable usages, and to propose what seems a workable view of these five meanings of alienation. Thus, the task is a dual one: to make more organized sense of one of the great traditions in sociological thought; and to make the traditional interest in alienation more amenable to sharp empirical statement.*

I propose, in what follows, to treat alienation from the personal standpoint of the actor—that is, alienation is here taken from the social-psychological point of view. Presumably, a task for subsequent experimental or analytical research is to determine (a) the social conditions that produce these five variants of alienation, or (b) their behavioral consequences. In each of the five instances, I begin with a review of where and how that usage is found in traditional sociological thought; subsequently, in each case, I seek a more researchable statement of meaning. In these latter statements, I focus chiefly upon the ideas of expectation and value.[6]

[2]T. W. Adorno *et al.*, *The Authoritarian Personality*, New York: Harper, 1950, pp. 617ff.

[3]R. K. Merton, *Mass Persuasion*, New York: Harper, 1946, p. 143.

[4]Erich Fromm, *The Sane Society*, New York: Rinehart, 1955.

[5]*The Tower and the Abyss*, New York: Braziller, 1957, p. 43.

*An effort in this direction is reported by John P. Clark in "Measuring Alienation Within a Social System," pp. 849-852 of this issue of the *Review*. —*The Editor*.

[6]The concepts of expectancy and reward, or reinforcement value, are the central elements in J. B. Rotter's "social learning theory"; see *Social Learning and Clinical Psychology*, New York: Prentice Hall, 1954. My discussion seeks to cast the various meanings of alienation in a form that is roughly consistent with this theory, though not formally expressed in terms of it.

POWERLESSNESS

The first of these uses refers to alienation in the sense of *powerlessness*. This is the notion of alienation as it originated in the Marxian view of the worker's condition in capitalist society: the worker is alienated to the extent that the prerogative and means of decision are expropriated by the ruling entrepreneurs. Marx, to be sure, was interested in other alienative aspects of the industrial system; indeed, one might say that his interest in the powerlessness of the worker flowed from his interest in the consequences of such alienation in the work place—for example, the alienation of man from man, and the degradation of men into commodities.

In Weber's work, we find an extension beyond the industrial sphere of the Marxian notion of powerlessness. Of this extension, Gerth and Mills remark:

> Marx's emphasis upon the wage worker as being 'separated' from the means of production becomes, in Weber's perspective, merely one special case of a universal trend. The modern soldier is equally 'separated' from the means of violence; and the civil servant from the means of administration.[7]

The idea of alienation as powerlessness is, perhaps, the most frequent usage in current literature. The contributors to Gouldner's volume on leadership, for example, make heavy use of this idea; as does the work of C. Wright Mills—and, I suppose, any analysis of the human condition that takes the Marxist tradition with any seriousness. This variant of alienation can be conceived as *the expectancy or probability held by the individual that his own behavior cannot determine the occurrence of the outcomes, or reinforcements, he seeks.*

Let us be clear about what this conception does and does not imply. First, it is a distinctly social-psychological view. It does not treat powerlessness from the standpoint of the objective conditions in society; but this does not mean that these conditions need be ignored in research dealing with this variety of alienation. These objective conditions are relevant, for example, in determining the degree of realism involved in the individual's response to his situation. The objective features of the situations are to be handled like any other situational aspect of behavior—to be analyzed, measured, ignored, experimentally controlled or varied, as the research question demands.

[7]H. H. Gerth and C. W. Mills, *From Max Weber: Essays in Sociology*, New York: Oxford, 1946, p. 50.

Second, this construction of "powerlessness" clearly departs from the Marxian tradition by removing the critical, polemic element in the idea of alienation. Likewise, this version of powerlessness does not take into account, as a definitional matter, the frustration an individual may feel as a consequence of the discrepancy between the control he may expect and the degree of control that he desires—that is, it takes no direct account of the value of control to the person.

In this version of alienation, then, the individual's expectancy for control of events is clearly distinguished from (a) the *objective* situation of powerlessness as some observer sees it, (b) the observer's *judgment* of that situation against some ethical standard, and (c) the individual's sense of a *discrepancy* between his expectations for control and his desire for control.

The issues in the philosophy of science, or in the history of science, on which these distinctions and decisions touch cannot be debated here. Two remarks must suffice: (1) In any given research, any or all of the elements discussed above—expectancies, objective conditions, deviation from a moral standard, deviation from the actor's standards—may well be involved, and I see little profit in arguing about which is "really" alienation so long as what is going on at each point in the effort is clear. I have chosen to focus on expectancies since I believe that this is consistent with what follows, while it avoids building ethical or adjustmental features into the concept. (2) I do not think that the expectancy usage is as radical a departure from the Marxian legacy as it may appear. No one would deny the editorial character of the Marxian judgment, but it was a judgment about a state of affairs—the elimination of individual freedom and control. My version of alienation refers to the counterpart, in the individual's expectations, of that state of affairs.

Finally, the use of powerlessness as an expectancy means that this version of alienation is very closely related to the notion (developed by Rotter) of "internal *versus* external control of reinforcements." The latter construct refers to the individual's sense of personal control over the reinforcement situation, as contrasted with his view that the occurrence of reinforcements is dependent upon external conditions, such as chance, luck, or the manipulation of others. The congruence in these formulations leaves the way open for the development of a closer bond between two languages of analysis—that of learning theory and that of alienation— that have long histories in psychology and sociology. But the congruence also poses a problem—the problem of recognizing that these two con-

[8]Cf. W. H. James and J. B. Rotter, "Partial and One Hundred Percent Reinforcement under Chance and Skill Conditions," *Journal of Experimental Psychology*, 55 (May, 1958), pp. 397–403. Rotter and his students have shown that the distinction

structs, though intimately related, are not generally used to understand the same things.[8]

In the case of alienation, I would limit the applicability of the concept to expectancies that have to do with the individual's sense of influence over socio-political events (control over the political system, the industrial economy, international affairs, and the like). Accordingly, I would initially limit the applicability of this first meaning of alienation to the arena for which the concept was originally intended, namely, the depiction of man's relation to the larger social order. Whether or not such an operational concept of alienation is related to expectancies for control in more intimate need areas (for example, love and affection; status-recognition,) is a matter for empirical determination. The need for the restriction lies in the following convictions: First, the concept of alienation, initially, should not be so global as to make the *generality* of powerlessness a matter of fiat rather than fact. Second, the concept should not be dangerously close to merely an index of personality *adjustment*—equivalent, that is, to a statement that the individual is maladjusted in the sense that he has a generally low expectation that he can, through his own behavior, achieve any of the personal rewards he seeks.[9]

---

between internal and external control (a distinction which is also cast in expectancy terms) has an important bearing on learning theory. The propositions in that theory, they argue, are based too exclusively on experimental studies which simulate conditions of "external control," where the subject "is likely to perceive reinforcements as being beyond his control and primarily contingent upon external conditions" (p. 397). Compare this use of what is essentially a notion of powerlessness with, for example, Norman Podheretz's discussion of the "Beat Generation": "Being apathetic about the Cold War is to admit that you have a sense of utter helplessness in the face of forces apparently beyond the control of man." "Where is the Beat Generation Going?" *Esquire*, 50 (December, 1958), p. 148.

[9]It seems best, in regard to the adjustment question, to follow Gwynn Nettler's view. He points out that the concepts of alienation and anomie should not "be equated, as they so often are, with personal disorganization defined as intrapersonal goallessness, or lack of 'internal coherence' . . . [their] bearing on emotional sickness must be independently investigated." "A Measure of Alienation," *American Sociological Review*, 22 (December, 1957), p. 672. For a contrasting view, see Nathan Glazer's "The Alienation of Modern Man," *Commentary*, 3 (April, 1947), p. 380, in which he comments: "If we approach alienation in this way, it becomes less a description of a single specific symptom than an omnibus of psychological disturbances having a similar root cause—in this case, modern social organization."

With regard to the question of the generality of powerlessness, I assume that high or low expectancies for the control of outcomes through one's own behavior will (a) vary with the behavior involved—e.g., control over academic achievement or grades, as against control over unemployment; and (b) will be differentially realistic in different areas (it is one thing to feel powerless with regard to war and quite another, presumably, to feel powerless in making friends). My chief point is that these are matters that can be empirically rather than conceptually solved; we should not, therefore, build either "generality" or "adjustment" into our concept of alienation. This same view is applied in the discussion of the other four types of alienation.

MEANINGLESSNESS

A second major usage of the alienation concept may be summarized under the idea of *meaninglessness.* The clearest contemporary examples of this usage are found in Adorno's treatment of prejudice; in Cantril's *The Psychology of Social Movements,* in which the "search for meaning" is used as part of the interpretive scheme in analyzing such diverse phenomena as lynchings, the Father Divine movement, and German fascism; and in Hoffer's portrait of the "true believer" as one who finds, and needs to find, in the doctrines of a mass movement "a master key to all the world's problems."[10]

This variant of alienation is involved in Mannheim's description of the increase of "functional rationality" and the concomitant decline of "substantial rationality." Mannheim argues that as society increasingly organizes its members with reference to the most efficient realization of ends (that is, as functional rationality increases), there is a parallel decline in the "capacity to act intelligently in a given situation on the basis of one's own insight into the interrelations of events."[11]

This second type of alienation, then, refers to the individual's sense of understanding the events in which he is engaged. We may speak of high alienation, in the meaninglessness usage, when *the individual is unclear as to what he ought to believe—when the individual's minimal standards for clarity in decision-making are not met.* Thus, the post-war German situation described by Adorno was "meaningless" in the sense that the individual could not choose with confidence among alternative explanations of the inflationary disasters of the time (and, it is argued, substituted the "Jews" as a simplified solution for this unclarity). In Mannheim's depiction, the individual cannot choose appropriately among alternative interpretations (cannot "act intelligently" or "with insight") because the increase in functional rationality, with its emphasis on specialization and production, makes such choice impossible.

It would seem, for the present at least, a matter of no consequence what the beliefs in question are. They may, as in the above instance, be simply descriptive beliefs (interpretations); or they may be beliefs involving moral standards (norms for behavior). In either case, the individual's choice among alternative beliefs has low "confidence limits": he cannot

[10]See, respectively, Adorno *et al., op. cit.;* Hadley Cantril, *The Psychology of Social Movements,* New York: Wiley, 1941; and Eric Hoffer, *The True Believer,* New York: Harper, 1950, p. 90.

[11]Karl Mannheim, *Man and Society in an Age of Reconstruction,* New York: Harcourt, Brace, 1940, p. 59.

predict with confidence the consequences of acting on a given belief. One might operationalize this aspect of alienation by focusing upon the fact that it is characterized by a *low expectancy that satisfactory predictions about future outcomes of behavior can be made*. Put more simply, where the first meaning of alienation refers to the sensed ability to control outcomes, this second meaning refers essentially to the sensed ability to predict behavioral outcomes.

This second version of alienation is logically independent of the first, for, under some circumstances, expectancies for personal control of events may not coincide with the understanding of these events, as in the popular depiction of the alienation of the intellectual.[12] Still, there are obvious connections between these two forms of alienation: in some important degree, the view that one lives in an intelligible world may be a prerequisite to expectancies for control; and the unintelligibility of complex affairs is presumably conducive to the development of high expectancies for external control (that is, high powerlessness).[13]

NORMLESSNESS

The third variant of the alienation theme is derived from Durkheim's description of "anomie," and refers to a condition of *normlessness*. In the traditional usage, anomie denoted a situation in which the social norms regulating individual conduct have broken down or are no longer effective as rules for behavior. As noted above, Merton emphasizes this kind of rulelessness in his interpretation of the importance of the "sincerity" theme in Kate Smith's war bond drive:

> The emphasis on this theme reflects a social disorder—"anomie" is the sociological term—in which common values have been submerged in the welter of private interests seeking satisfaction by virtually any means

[12]C. Wright Mills' description reflects this view: "The intellectual who remains free may continue to learn more and more about modern society, but he finds the centers of political initiative less and less accessible. . . . He comes to feel helpless in the fundamental sense that he cannot control what he is able to foresee." *White Collar*, New York: Oxford, 1951, p. 157. The same distinction is found in F. L. Strodtbeck's empirical comparison of Italian and Jewish values affecting mobility: "For the Jew, there was always the expectation that everything could be understood, if perhaps not controlled." "Family Interaction, Values and Achievement," in D. C. McClelland *et al.*, *Talent and Society*, New York: Van Nostrand, 1958, p. 155.

[13]Thorstein Veblen argues the same point, in his own inimitable style, in a discussion of "The Belief in Luck" : ". . . the extra-causal propensity or agent has a very high utility as a recourse in perplexity" [providing the individual] "a means of escape from the difficulty of accounting for phenomena in terms of causal sequences." *The Theory of the Leisure Class*, New York: Macmillan, 1899; Modern Library Edition, 1934, p. 386.

which are effective. Drawn from a highly competitive, segmented urban society, our informants live in a climate of reciprocal distrust which, to say the least, is not conducive to stable human relationships. . . . The very same society that produces this sense of alienation and estrangement generates in many a craving for reassurance. . . .[14]

Elsewhere, in his well-known paper "Social Structure and Anomie," Merton describes the "adaptations" (the kinds of conformity and deviance) that may occur where the disciplining effect of collective standards has been weakened. He takes as his case in point the situation in which culturally prescribed goals (in America, the emphasis upon success goals) are not congruent with the available means for their attainment. In such a situation, he argues, anomie or normlessness will develop to the extent that "the technically most effective procedure, whether culturally legitimate or not, becomes typically perferred to institutionally prescribed conduct."[15]

Merton's comments on this kind of anomic situation serve to renew the discussion of the expectancy constructs developed above—the idea of meaninglessness, and the idea of powerlessness or internal-external control. For Merton notes, first, that the anomic situation leads to low predictability in behavior, and second, that the anomic situation may well lead to the belief in luck:

Whatever the sentiments of the reader concerning the moral desirability of coordinating the goals-and-means phases of the social structure, it is clear that imperfect coordination of the two leads to anomie. Insofar as one of the most general functions of the social structure is to provide a basis for predictability and regularity of social behavior, it becomes increasingly limited in effectiveness as these elements of the social structure become dissociated. . . . The victims of this contradiction between the cultural emphasis on pecuniary ambition and the social bars to full opportunity are not always aware of the structural sources of their thwarted aspirations. To be sure, they are typically aware of discrepancy between individual worth and social rewards. But they do not necessarily see how this comes about. Those who do find its source in the social structure may become alienated from that structure and become ready candidates for Adaptation V [rebellion]. But others, and this appears to include the great majority, may attribute their difficulties to more mystical and less sociological sources. . . . in such a society [a society suffering from anomie] people tend to put stress on mysticism: the workings of Fortune, Chance, Luck.[16]

[14]Merton, *op. cit.*, p. 143.
[15]R. K. Merton, *Social Theory and Social Structure*, Glencoe, Ill.: Free Press, 1949, p. 128.
[16]*Ibid.*, pp. 138, 148–149.

It is clear that the general idea of anomie is both an integral part of the alienation literature, and that it bears upon our expectancy notions. What is not so clear is the matter of how precisely to conceptualize the events to which "anomie" is intended to point. Unfortunately, the idea of normlessness has been over-extended to include a wide variety of both social conditions and psychic states: personal disorganization, cultural breakdown, reciprocal distrust, and so on.

Those who employ the anomie version of alienation are chiefly concerned with the elaboration of the "means" emphasis in society—for example, the loss of commonly held standards and consequent individualism, or the development of instrumental, manipulative attitudes. This interest represents our third variant of alienation, the key idea of which, again, may be cast in terms of expectancies. Following Merton's lead, the anomic situation, from the individual point of view, may be defined as one in which there is a *high expectancy that socially unapproved behaviors are required to achieve given goals.* This third meaning of alienation is logically independent of the two versions discussed above. Expectancies concerning unapproved means, presumably, can vary independently of the individual's expectancy that his own behavior will determine his success in reaching a goal (what I have called "powerlessness") or his belief that he operates in an intellectually comprehensible world ("meaninglessness"). Such a view of anomie, to be sure, narrows the evocative character of the concept, but it provides a more likely way of developing its research potential. This view, I believe, makes possible the discovery of the extent to which such expectancies are held, the conditions for their development, and their consequences either for the individual or for a given social system (for example, the generation of widespread distrust).

The foregoing discussion implies that the means and goals in question have to do with such relatively broad social demands as the demand for success or for political ends. However, in his interesting essay, "Alienation from Interaction," Erving Goffman presents a more or less parallel illustration in which the focus is on the smallest of social systems, the simple conversation:

> If we take conjoint spontaneous involvement in a topic of conversation as a point of reference, we shall find that alienation from it is common indeed. Conjoint involvement appears to be a fragile thing, with standard points of weakness and decay, a precarious unsteady state that is likely at any time to lead the individual into some form of alienation. Since we are dealing with obligatory involvement, forms of alienation will constitute *misbehavior of a kind that can be called mis-involvement.* [17]

[17] *Human Relations,* 10 (February, 1957), p. 49 (italics added).

Goffman describes four such "mis-involvements" (for example, being too self-conscious in interaction), and concludes: "By looking at the ways in which individuals can be thrown out of step with the sociable moment, perhaps we can learn something about the way in which he can become alienated from things that take much more of his time."[18] In speaking of "misbehavior" or "mis-involvement," Goffman is treating the problem of alienation in terms not far removed from the anomic feature I have described, that is, the expectancy for socially unapproved behavior. His analysis of the social microcosm in these terms calls attention once more to the fact that the five variants of alienation discussed here can be applied to as broad or as narrow a range of social behavior as seems useful.

ISOLATION

The fourth type of alienation refers to *isolation*. This usage is most common in descriptions of the intellectual role, where writers refer to the detachment of the intellectual from popular cultural standards—one who, in Nettler's language, has become estranged from his society and the culture it carries.[19] Clearly, this usage does not refer to isolation as a lack of "social adjustment"—of the warmth, security, or intensity of an individual's social contacts.

In the present context, in which we seek to maintain a consistent focus on the individual's expectations or values, this brand of alienation may be usefully defined in terms of reward values: The alienated in the isolation sense are those who, like the intellectual, *assign low reward value to goals or beliefs that are typically highly valued in the given society.* This, in effect, is the definition of alienation in Nettler's scale, for as a measure of "apartness from society" the scale consists (largely though not exclusively) of items that reflect the individual's degree of commitment to popular culture. Included, for example, is the question "Do you read *Reader's*

[18]*Ibid.*, p. 59. Obviously, the distinction (discussed above under "powerlessness") between objective condition and individual expectancy applies in the case of anomie. For a recent treatment of this point, see R. K. Merton, *Social Theory and Social Structure*, Glencoe, Ill.: Free Press, 1957 (revised edition), pp. 161–194. It is clear that Srole's well-known anomie scale refers to individual experience (and that it embodies a heavy adjustment component). It is not so clear how the metaphorical language of "normative breakdown" and "structural strain" associated with the conception of anomie as a social condition is to be made empirically useful. It may be further noted that the idea of rulelessness has often been used to refer to situations in which norms are unclear as well as to those in which norms lose their regulative force. I focused on the latter case in this section; but the former aspect of anomie is contained in the idea of "meaninglessness." The idea of meaninglessness, as defined above, surely includes situations involving uncertainty resulting from obscurity of rules, the absence of clear criteria for resolving ambiguities, and the like.

[19]Nettler, *op. cit.*, p. 672.

Digest?" a magazine that was selected "as a symbol of popular magazine appeal and folkish thoughtways."[20]

The "isolation" version of alienation clearly carries a meaning different from the three versions discussed above. Still, these alternative meanings can be profitably applied in conjunction with one another in the analysis of a given state of affairs. Thus, Merton's paper on social structure and anomie makes use of both "normlessness" and "isolation" in depicting the adaptations that individuals may make to the situation in which goals and means are not well coordinated. One of these adaptations—that of the "innovator"—is the prototype of alienation in the sense of normlessness, in which the individual innovates culturally disapproved means to achieve the goals in question. But another adjustment pattern—that of "rebellion"—more closely approximates what I have called "isolation." "This adaptation [rebellion] leads men outside the environing social structure to envisage and seek to bring into being a new, that is to say, a greatly modified, social structure. It presupposes alienation from reigning goals and standards."[21]

SELF-ESTRANGEMENT

The final variant distinguishable in the literature is alienation in the sense of *self-estrangement.* The most extended treatment of this version of alienation is found in *The Sane Society,* where Fromm writes:

[20]*Ibid.,* p. 675. A scale to measure social isolation (as well as powerlessness and meaninglessness) has been developed by Dean, but the meanings are not the same as those given here; the "social isolation" measure, for example, deals with the individual's friendship status. (See Dwight Dean, "Alienation and Political Apathy," Ph.D. thesis, Ohio State University, 1956.) It seems to me now, however, that this is not a very useful meaning, for two reasons. First, it comes very close to being a statement of either social adjustment or of simple differences in associational styles (i.e., some people are sociable and some are not), and as such seems irrelevant to the root historical notion of alienation. Second, the crucial part of this "social isolation" component in alienation—what Nisbet, for example, calls the "unattached" or the "isolated"—is better captured for analytical purposes, I believe, in the ideas of meaninglessness, normlessness, or isolation, as defined in expectancy or reward terms. That is to say, what remains, after sheer sociability is removed, is the kind of tenuousness of social ties that may be described as value uniqueness (isolation), deviation from approved means (normlessness), or the like.

[21]Merton, "Social Structure and Anomie," *op. cit.,* pp. 144–145. Merton is describing a radical estrangement from societal values (often typified in the case of the intellectual)—i.e., the alienation is from reigning *central* features of the society, and what is sought is a "greatly" modified society. Presumably, the "isolation" mode of alienation, like the other versions, can be applied on the intimate or the grand scale, as noted above in the discussion of Goffman's analysis. Clearly, the person who rejects certain commonly held values in a given society, but who values the society's tolerance for such differences, is expressing a fundamental commitment to societal values and in this degree he is not alienated in the isolation sense.

In the following analysis I have chosen the concept of alienation as the central point from which I am going to develop the analysis of the contemporary social character. . . . By alienation is meant a mode of experience in which the person experiences himself as an alien. He has become, one might say, estranged from himself.[22]

In much the same way, C. Wright Mills comments: "In the normal course of her work, because her personality becomes the instrument of an alien purpose, the salesgirl becomes self-alienated;" and, later, "Men are estranged from one another as each secretly tries to make an instrument of the other, and in time a full circle is made: One makes an instrument of himself and is estranged from It also."[23]

There are two interesting features of this popular doctrine of alienation as self-estrangement. The first of these is the fact that where the usage does not overlap with the other four meanings (and it often does), it is difficult to specify what the alienation is *from*. To speak of "alienation from the self" is after all simply a metaphor, in a way that "alienation from popular culture," for example, need not be. The latter can be reasonably specified, as I have tried to do above; but what is intended when Fromm, Mills, Hoffer, and the others speak of self-estrangement?

Apparently, what is being postulated here is some ideal human condition from which the individual is estranged. This is, perhaps, clearest in Fromm's treatment, for example, in his description of production and consumption excesses in capitalist society: "The *human* way of acquiring would be to make an effort qualitatively commensurate with what I acquire.·. . . But our craving for consumption has lost all connection with the real needs of man."[24] To be self-alienated, in the final analysis, means to be something less than one might ideally be if the circumstances in society were otherwise—to be insecure, given to appearances, conformist. Riesman's discussion of other-direction falls within this meaning of alienation; for what is at stake is that the child learns "that nothing in his character, no possession he owns, no inheritance of name or talent, no work he has done, is valued for itself, but only for its effect on others.[25]

Riesman's comment brings us to the second feature of special interest in the idea of self-alienation. I have noted that this idea invokes some explicit or implicit human ideal. And I have implied that such comparisons of modern man with some idealized human condition should be

[22]Fromm, *op. cit.,* pp. 110, 120.

[23]Mills, *op. cit.,* pp. 184, 188.

[24]Fromm, *op. cit.,* pp. 131, 134 (italics in original).

[25]David Riesman, *The Lonely Crowd,* New Haven: Yale University Press, 1950, p. 49. Although the idea of self-estrangement, when used in the alienation literature, usually carries the notion of a generally applicable human standard, it is sometimes the individual's standard that is at issue: to be alienated in this sense is to be aware of a discrepancy between one's ideal self and one's actual self-image.

viewed simply as rhetorical appeals to nature—an important rhetoric for some purposes, though not very useful in the non-analytical form it generally takes. But Riesman's assertion contains, it seems to me, one of the key elements of this rhetoric—one, indeed, that not only reflects the original interest of Marx in alienation but also one that may be specifiable in a language consistant with our other uses of alienation.

I refer to that aspect of self-alienation which is generally characterized as the loss of intrinsic meaning or pride in work, a loss which Marx and others have held to be an essential feature of modern alienation. This notion of the loss of intrinsically meaningful satisfaction is embodied in a number of ways in current discussions of alienation. Glazer, for example, contrasts the alienated society with simpler societies characterized by "spontaneous acts of work and play which were their own reward."[26]

Although this meaning of alienation is difficult to specify, the basic idea contained in the rhetoric of self-estrangement—the idea of intrinsically meaningful activity—can, perhaps, be recast into more manageable social learning terms. One way to state such a meaning is to see alienation as *the degree of dependence of the given behavior upon anticipated future rewards,* that is, upon rewards that lie outside the activity itself. In these terms, the worker who works merely for his salary, the housewife who cooks simply to get it over with, or the other-directed type who acts "only for its effect on others"—all these (at different levels, again) are instances of self-estrangement. In this view, what has been called self-estrangement refers essentially to the inability of the individual to find self-rewarding— or in Dewey's phrase, self-consummatory—activities that engage him.[27]

CONCLUSION

I am aware that there are unclarities and difficulties of considerable importance in these five varieties of alienation (especially, I believe, in the attempted solution of "self-estrangement" and the idea of "mean-

[26]Glazer, *op. cit.,* p. 379.

[27]The difficulty of providing intrinsically satisfying work in industrial society, of course, has been the subject of extensive comment; see, for example, Daniel Bell, *Work and Its Discontents,* Boston: Beacon Press, 1956. A similar idea has been applied by Tumin to the definition of creativity: "I would follow Dewey's lead and view 'creativity' as the esthetic experience, which is distinguished from other experiences by the fact that it is self-consummatory in nature. This is to say, the esthetic experience is enjoyed for the actions which define and constitute the experience, whatever it may be, rather than for its instrumental results of social accompaniments in the form of social relations with others." Melvin M. Tumin, "Obstacles to Creativity," *Etc.: A Review of General Semantics,* II (Summer 1954), p. 261. For a more psychological view of the problem of "instrinsically" governed behavior, see S. Koch, "Behavior as 'Intrinsically' Regulated: Work Notes Toward a Pre-Theory of Phenomena Called 'Motivational,'" in M. R. Jones, editor, *Nebraska Symposium on Motivation,* Lincoln: University of Nebraska Press, 1956, pp. 42–87.

inglessness"). But I have attempted, first, to distinguish the meanings that have been given to alienation, and second, to work toward a more useful conception of each of these meanings.

It may seem, at first reading, that the language employed—the language of expectations and rewards—is somewhat strange, if not misguided. But I would urge that the language is more traditional than it may seem. Nathan Glazer certainly is well within that tradition when, in a summary essay on alienation, he speaks of our modern ". . . sense of the splitting asunder of what was once together, the breaking of the seamless mold in which *values, behavior,* and *expectations* were once cast into interlocking forms."[28] These same three concepts—reward value, behavior, and expectancy—are key elements in the theory that underlies the present characterization of alienation. Perhaps, on closer inspection, the reader will find only that initial strangeness which is often experienced when we translate what was sentimentally understood into a secular question.

[28]Glazer, *op. cit.*, p. 378 (italics added).

The Organization Man*
WILLIAM H. WHYTE, JR.

Officially, we are a people who hold to the Protestant Ethic. Because of the denominational implications of the term many would deny its relevance to them, but let them eulogize the American Dream, however, and they virtually define the Protestant Ethic. Whatever the embroidery, there is almost always the thought that pursuit of individual salvation through hard work, thrift, and competitive struggle is the heart of the American achievement.

But the harsh facts of organization life simply do not jibe with these precepts. This conflict is certainly not a peculiarly American development. In their own countries such Europeans as Max Weber and Durkheim many years ago foretold the change, and though Europeans now like to see their troubles as an American export, the problems they speak of stem from a bureaucratization of society that has affected every Western country.

It is in America, however, that the contrast between the old ethic and current reality has been most apparent—and most poignant. Of all peoples it is we who have led in the public worship of individualism. One

*Reprinted by permission of Simon and Schuster, Inc., and Laurence Pollinger Ltd., from *The Organization Man,* pp. 5-24. Copyright, ©, by William H. Whyte, Jr.

hundred years ago De Tocqueville was noting that though our special genius—and failing—lay in co-operative action, we talked more than others of personal independence and freedom. We kept on, and as late as the twenties, when big organization was long since a fact, affirmed the old faith as if nothing had really changed at all.

Today many still try, and it is the members of the kind of organization most responsible for the change, the corporation, who try the hardest. It is the corporation man whose institutional ads protest so much that Americans speak up in town meeting, that Americans are the best inventors because Americans don't care that other people scoff, that Americans are the best soldiers because they have so much initiative and native ingenuity, that the boy selling papers on the street corner is the prototype of our business society. Collectivism? He abhors it, and when he makes his ritualistic attack on Welfare Statism, it is in terms of a Protestant Ethic undefiled by change—the sacredness of property, the enervating effect of security, the virtues of thrift, of hard work and independence. Thanks be, he says, that there are some people left—e.g., businessmen—to defend the American Dream.

He is not being hypocritical, only compulsive. He honestly wants to believe he follows the tenets he extols, and if he extols them so frequently it is, perhaps, to shut out a nagging suspicion that he, too, the last defender of the faith, is no longer pure. Only by using the language of individualism to describe the collective can he stave off the thought that he himself is in a collective as pervading as any ever dreamed of by the reformers, the intellectuals and the utopian visionaries he so regularly warns against.

The older generation may still convince themselves, the younger generation does not. When a young man says that to make a living these days you must do what somebody else wants you to do, he states it not only as a fact of life that must be accepted but as an inherently good proposition. If the American Dream deprecates this for him, it is the American Dream that is going to have to give, whatever its more elderly guardians may think. People grow restive with a mythology that is too distant from the way things actually are, and as more and more lives have been encompassed by the organization way of life, the pressures for an accompanying ideological shift have been mounting. The pressures of the group, the frustrations of individual creativity, the anonymity of achievement: are these defects to struggle against—or are they virtues in disguise? The organization man seeks a redefinition of his place on earth—a faith that will satisfy him that what he must endure has a deeper meaning than appears on the surface. He needs, in short, something that will do for him what the Protestant Ethic did once. And slowly, almost imperceptibly, a body of thought has been coalescing that does that.

I am going to call it a Social Ethic. With reason it could be called an organization ethic, or a bureaucratic ethic; more than anything else it rationalizes the organization's demands for fealty and gives those who offer it wholeheartedly a sense of dedication in doing so—*in extremis,* you might say, it converts what would seem in other times a bill of no rights into a restatement of individualism.

But there is a real moral imperative behind it, and whether one inclines to its beliefs or not he must acknowledge that this moral basis, not mere expediency, is the source of its power. Nor is it simply an opiate for those who must work in big organizations. The search for a secular faith that it represents can be found throughout our society—and among those who swear they would never set foot in a corporation or a government bureau. Though it has its greatest applicability to the organization man, its ideological underpinnings have been provided not by the organization man but by intellectuals he knows little of and toward whom, indeed, he tends to be rather suspicious.

Any groove of abstraction, Whitehead once remarked, is bound to be an inadequate way of describing reality, and so with the concept of the Social Ethic. It is an attempt to illustrate an underlying consistency in what in actuality is by no means an orderly system of thought. No one says, "I believe in the social ethic," and though many would subscribe wholeheartedly to the separate ideas that make it up, these ideas have yet to be put together in the final, harmonious synthesis. But the unity is there.

In looking at what might seem dissimilar aspects of organization society, it is this unity I wish to underscore. The "professionalization" of the manager, for example, and the drive for a more practical education are parts of the same phenomenon; just as the student now feels technique more vital than content, so the trainee believes managing an end in itself, an *expertise* relatively independent of the content of what is being managed. And the reasons are the same. So too in other sectors of our society; for all the differences in particulars, dominant is a growing accommodation to the needs of society—and a growing urge to justify it.

Let me now define my terms. By Social Ethic I mean that contemporary body of thought which makes morally legitimate the pressures of society against the individual. Its major propositions are three: a belief in the group as the source of creativity; a belief in "belongingness" as the ultimate need of the individual; and a belief in the application of science to achieve the belongingness.

In subsequent chapters I will explore these ideas more thoroughly, but for the moment I think the gist can be paraphrased thus: Man exists as a unit of society. Of himself, he is isolated, meaningless; only as he collaborates with others does he become worth while, for by sublimating himself in the group, he helps produce a whole that is greater than the sum of its parts. There should be, then, no conflict between man and society. What we think are conflicts are misunderstandings, breakdowns in communication. By applying the methods of science to human relations we can eliminate these obstacles to consensus and create an equilibrium in which society's needs and the needs of the individual are one and the same.

Essentially, it is a utopian faith. Superficially, it seems dedicated to the practical problems of organization life, and its proponents often use the word *hard* (versus *soft*) to describe their approach. But it is the long-range promise that animates its followers, for it relates techniques to the vision of a finite, achievable harmony. It is quite reminiscent of the beliefs of utopian communities of the 1840s. As in the Owen communities, there is the same idea that man's character is decided, almost irretrievably, by his environment. As in the Fourier communities, there is the same faith that there need be no conflict between the individual's aspirations and the community's wishes, because it is the natural order of things that the two be synonymous.

Like the utopian communities, it interprets society in a fairly narrow, immediate sense. One can believe man has a social obligation and that the individual must ultimately contribute to the community without believing that group harmony is the test of it. In the Social Ethic I am describing, however, man's obligation is in the here and now; his duty is not so much to the community in a broad sense but to the actual, physical one about him, and the idea that in isolation from it—or active rebellion against it—he might eventually discharge the greater service is little considered. In practice, those who most eagerly subscribe to the Social Ethic worry very little over the long-range problems of society. It is not that they don't care but rather that they tend to assume that the ends of organization and morality coincide, and on such matters as social welfare they give their proxy to the organization.

It is possible that I am attaching too much weight to what, after all, is something of a mythology. Those more sanguine than I have argued that this faith is betrayed by reality in some key respects and that because it cannot long hide from organization man that life is still essentially competitive the faith must fall of its own weight. They also maintain that the Social Ethic is only one trend in a society which is a prolific breeder of counter-trends. The farther the pendulum swings, they believe, the more it must eventually swing back.

I am not persuaded. We are indeed a flexible people, but society is not a clock and to stake so much on counter-trends is to put a rather heavy burden on providence. Let me get ahead of my story a bit with two examples of trend vs. counter-trend. One is the long-term swing to the highly vocational business-administration courses. Each year for seven years I have collected all the speeches by businessmen, educators, and others on the subject, and invariably each year the gist of them is that this particular pendulum has swung much too far and that there will shortly be a reversal. Similarly sanguine, many academic people have been announcing that they discern the beginnings of a popular swing back to the humanities. Another index is the growth of personality testing. Regularly year after year many social scientists have assured me that this bowdlerization of psychology is a contemporary aberration soon to be laughed out of court.

Meanwhile, the organization world grinds on. Each year the number of business-administration majors has increased over the last year—until, in 1954, they together made up the largest single field of undergraduate instruction outside of the field of education itself. Personality testing? Again, each year the number of people subjected to it has grown, and the criticism has served mainly to make organizations more adept in sugar-coating their purpose. No one can say whether these trends will continue to outpace the counter-trends, but neither can we trust that an equilibrium-minded providence will see to it that excesses will cancel each other out. Counter-trends there are. There always have been, and in the sweep of ideas ineffectual many have proved to be.

It is also true that the Social Ethic is something of a mythology, and there is a great difference between mythology and practice. An individualism as stringent, as selfish as that often preached in the name of the Protestant Ethic would never have been tolerated, and in reality our predecessors co-operated with one another far more skillfully than nineteenth-century oratory would suggest. Something of the obverse is true of the Social Ethic; so complete a denial of individual will won't work either, and even the most willing believers in the group harbor some secret misgivings, some latent antagonism toward the pressures they seek to deify.

But the Social Ethic is no less powerful for that, and though it can never produce the peace of mind it seems to offer, it will help shape the nature of the quest in the years to come. The old dogma of individualism betrayed reality too, yet few would argue, I dare say, that it was not an immensely powerful influence in the time of its dominance. So I argue of the Social Ethic; call it mythology, if you will, but it is becoming the dominant one.

. . .

While the burden of this book is reportorial, I take a position and, in fairness to the reader, I would like to make plain the assumptions on which I base it. To that end, let me first say what I am *not* talking about.

This book is not a plea for nonconformity. Such pleas have an occasional therapeutic value, but as an abstraction, nonconformity is an empty goal, and rebellion against prevailing opinion merely because it is prevailing should no more be praised than acquiescence to it. Indeed, it is often a mask for cowardice, and few are more pathetic than those who flaunt outer differences to expiate their inner surrender.

I am not, accordingly, addressing myself to the surface uniformities of U.S. life. There will be no strictures in this book against "Mass Man"—a person the author has never met—nor will there be any strictures against ranch wagons, or television sets, or gray flannel suits. They are irrelevant to the main problem, and, furthermore, there's no harm in them. I would not wish to go to the other extreme and suggest that these uniformities per se are good, but the spectacle of people following current custom for lack of will or imagination to do anything else is hardly a new failing, and I am not convinced that there has been any significant change in this respect except in the nature of the things we conform to. Unless one believes poverty ennobling, it is difficult to see the three-button suit as more of a strait jacket than overalls, or the ranch-type house than old law tenements.

And how important, really, are these uniformities to the central issue of individualism? We must not let the outward forms deceive us. If individualism involves following one's destiny as one's own conscience directs, it must for most of us be a realizable destiny, and a sensible awareness of the rules of the game can be a condition of individualism as well as a constraint upon it. The man who drives a Buick Special and lives in a ranch-type house just like hundreds of other ranch-type houses can assert himself as effectively and courageously against his particular society as the bohemian against his particular society. He usually does not, it is true, but if he does, the surface uniformities can serve quite well as protective coloration. The organization people who are best able to control their environment rather than be controlled by it are well aware that they are not too easily distinguishable from the others in the outward obeisances paid to the good opinions of others. And that is one of the reasons they do control. They disarm society.

I do not equate the Social Ethic with conformity, nor do I believe those who urge it wish it to be, for most of them believe deeply that their work will help, rather than harm, the individual. I think their ideas are out of joint with the needs of the times they invoke, but it is their ideas, and not their good will, I wish to question. As for the lackeys of organization and the charlatans, they are not worth talking about.

Neither do I intend this book as a censure of the fact of organization society. We have quite enough problems today without muddying the issue with misplaced nostalgia, and in contrasting the old ideology with the new I mean no contrast of paradise with paradise lost, an idyllic eighteenth century with a dehumanized twentieth. Whether or not our own era is worse than former ones in the climate of freedom is a matter that can be left to later historians, but for the purposes of this book I write with the optimistic premise that individualism is as possible in our times as in others.

I speak of individualism *within* organization life. This is not the only kind, and someday it may be that the mystics and philosophers more distant from it may prove the crucial figures. But they are affected too by the center of society, and they can be of no help unless they grasp the nature of the main stream. Intellectual scoldings based on an impossibly lofty ideal may be of some service in upbraiding organization man with his failures, but they can give him no guidance. The organization man may agree that industrialism has destroyed the moral fabric of society and that we need to return to the agrarian virtues, or that business needs to be broken up into a series of smaller organizations, or that it's government that needs to be broken up, and so on. But he will go his way with his own dilemmas left untouched.

I am going to argue that he should fight the organization. But not self-destructively. He may tell the boss to go to hell, but he is going to have another boss, and, unlike the heroes of popular fiction, he cannot find surcease by leaving the arena to be a husbandman. If he chafes at the pressures of his particular organization, either he must succumb, resist them, try to change them, or move to yet another organization.

Every decision he faces on the problem of the individual versus authority is something of a dilemma. It is not a case of whether he should fight against black tyranny or blaze a new trail against patent stupidity. That would be easy—intellectually, at least. The real issue is far more subtle. For it is not the evils of organization life that puzzle him, *but its very beneficence.* He is imprisoned in brotherhood. Because his area of maneuver seems so small and because the trapping so mundane, his fight lacks the heroic cast, but it is for all this as tough a fight as ever his predecessors had to fight.

Thus to my thesis. I believe the emphasis of the Social Ethic is wrong for him. People do have to work with others, yes; the well-functioning team is a whole greater than the sum of its parts, yes—all this is indeed true. But is it the truth that now needs belaboring? Precisely because it *is* an age of organization, it is the other side of the coin that needs emphasis. We do need to know how to co-operate with The Organization but, more than ever, so do we need to know how to resist it. Out of context this would be an irresponsible statement. Time and place are critical, and history has taught us that a philosophical individualism can venerate conflict too much and co-operation too little. But what is the context today? The tide has swung far enough the other way, I submit, that we need not worry that a counteremphasis will stimulate people to an excess of individualism.

The energies Americans have devoted to the co-operative, to the social, are not to be demeaned; we would not, after all, have such a problem to discuss unless we had learned to adapt ourselves to an increasingly collective society as well as we have. An ideal of individualism which denies the obligations of man to others is manifestly impossible in a society such as ours, and it is a credit to our wisdom that while we preached it, we never fully practiced it.

But in searching for that elusive middle of the road, we have gone very far afield, and in our attention to making organization work we have come close to deifying it. We are describing its defects as virtues and denying that there is—or should be—a conflict between the individual and organization. This denial is bad for the organization. It is worse for the individual. What it does, in soothing him, is to rob him of the intellectual armor he so badly needs. For the more power organization has over him, the more he needs to recognize the area where he must assert himself against it. And this, almost because we have made organization life so equable, has become excruciatingly difficult.

To say that we must recognize the dilemmas of organization society is not to be consistent with the hopeful premise that organization society can be as compatible for the individual as any previous society. We are not hapless beings caught in the grip of forces we can do little about, and wholesale damnations of our society only lend a further mystique to organization. Organization has been made by man; it can be changed by man. It has not been the immutable course of history that has produced such constrictions on the individual as personality tests. It is organization man who has brought them to pass and it is he who can stop them.

The fault is not in organization, in short; it is in our worship of it. It is in our vain quest for a utopian equilibrium, which would be horrible if it ever did come to pass; it is in the soft-minded denial that there is a conflict between the individual and society. There must always be, and it is the price of being an individual that he must face these conflicts. He cannot evade them, and in seeking an ethic that offers a spurious peace of mind, thus does he tyrannize himself.

There are only a few times in organization life when he can wrench his destiny into his own hands—and if he does not fight then, he will make a surrender that will later mock him. But when is that time? Will he know the time when he sees it? By what standards is he to judge? He does feel an obligation to the group; he does sense moral constraints on his free will. If he goes against the group, is he being courageous—or just stubborn? Helpful—or selfish? Is he, as he so oftens wonders, right after all? It is in the resolution of a multitude of such dilemmas, I submit, that the real issue of individualism lies today.

Let us go back a moment to the turn of the century. If we pick up the Protestant Ethic as it was then expressed we will find it apparently in full flower. We will also find, however, an ethic that already had been strained by reality. The country had changed. The ethic had not.

Here, in the words of banker Henry Clews as he gave some fatherly advice to Yale students in 1908, is the Protestant Ethic in purest form:

> Survival of Fittest: *You may start in business, or the professions, with your feet on the bottom rung of the ladder; it rests with you to acquire the strength to climb to the top. You can do so if you have the will and the force to back you. There is always plenty of room at the top. . . . Success comes to the man who tries to compel success to yield to him. Cassius spoke well to Brutus when he said, "The Fault is not in our stars, dear Brutus, that we are underlings, but in our natures."*
>
> Thrift: *Form the habit as soon as you become a money-earner, or money-maker, of saving a part of your salary, or profits. Put away one dollar out of every ten you earn. The time will come in your lives when, if you have a little money, you can control circumstances; otherwise circumstances will control you. . . .*

Note the use of such active words as *climb, force, compel, control*. As stringently as ever before, the Protestant Ethic still counseled struggle against one's environment—the kind of practical, here and now struggle that paid off in material rewards. And spiritually too. The hard-boiled part of the Protestant Ethic was incomplete, of course, without the companion assurance that such success was moral as well as practical. To continue with Mr. Clews:

> *Under this free system of government, whereby individuals are free to get a living or to pursue wealth as each chooses, the usual result is competition. Obviously, then, competition really means industrial freedom. Thus, anyone may choose his own trade or profession, or, if he does not like it, he may change. He is free to work hard or not; he may make his own bargains and set his price upon his labor or his products. He is free to acquire property to any extent, or to part with it. By dint of greater effort or superior skill, or by intelligence, if he can make better wages, he is free to live better, just as his neighbor is free to follow his example and to learn to excel him in turn. If anyone has a genius for making and managing money, he is free to exercise his genius, just as another is free to handle his tools. . . . If an individual enjoys his money, gained by energy and successful effort, his neighbors are urged to work the harder, that they and their children may have the same enjoyment.*

It was an exuberantly optimistic ethic. If everyone could believe that seeking his self-interest automatically improves the lot of all, then the application of hard work should eventually produce a heaven on earth. Some, like the garrulous Mr. Clews, felt it already had.

> *America is the true field for the human race. It is the hope and the asylum for the oppressed and downtrodden of every clime. It is the inspiring example of America—peerless among the nations of the earth, the brightest star in the political firmament—that is leavening the hard lump of aristocracy and promoting a democratic spirit throughout the world. It is indeed the gem of the ocean to which the world may well offer homage. Here merit is the sole test. Birth is nothing. The fittest survive. Merit is the supreme and only qualification essential to success. Intelligence rules worlds and systems of worlds. It is the dread monarch of illimitable space, and in human society, especially in America, it shines as a diadem on the foreheads of those who stand in the foremost ranks of human enterprise. Here only a natural order of nobility is recognized, and its motto, without coat of arms or boast of heraldry, is "Intelligence and integrity."* [1]

Without this ethic capitalism would have been impossible. Whether the Protestant Ethic preceded capitalism, as Max Weber argued, or whether it grew up as a consequence, in either event it provided a degree of unity between the way people wanted to behave and the way they thought they *ought* to behave, and without this ideology, society would have been hostile to the entrepreneur. Without the comfort of the Protestant Ethic, he couldn't have gotten away with his acquisitions—not merely because other people wouldn't have allowed him, but because his own conscience would not have. But now he was fortified by the assurance that he was pursuing his obligation to God, and before long, what for centuries had been looked on as the meanest greed, a rising middle class would interpret as the earthly manifestation of God's will.

But the very industrial revolution which this highly serviceable ethic begot in time began to confound it. The inconsistencies were a long while in making themselves apparent. The nineteenth-century inheritors of the ethic were creating an increasingly collective society but steadfastly they denied the implications of it. In current retrospect the turn of the century seems a golden age of individualism, yet by the 1880s the corporation had already shown the eventual bureaucratic direction it was going to take. As institutions grew in size and became more stratified, they made all too apparent inconsistencies which formerly could be ignored. One of the key assumptions of the Protestant Ethic had been that success was due neither

[1] Henry Clews, *Fifty Years in Wall Street* (New York: Irving Publishing Company, 1908).

to luck nor to the environment but only to one's natural qualities—if men grew rich it was because they deserved to. But the big organization became a standing taunt to this dream of individual success. Quite obviously to anyone who worked in a big organization, those who survived best were not necessarily the fittest but, in more cases than not, those who by birth and personal connections had the breaks.

As organizations continued to expand, the Protestant Ethic became more and more divergent from the reality The Organization was itself creating. The managers steadfastly denied the change, but they, as much as those they led, were affected by it. Today, some still deny the inconsistency or blame it on creeping socialism; for the younger generation of managers, however, the inconsistencies have become importuning.

Thrift, for example. How can the organization man be thrifty? Other people are thrifty *for* him. He still buys most of his own life insurance, but for the bulk of his rainy-day saving, he gives his proxy to the financial and personnel departments of his organization. In his professional capacity also thrift is becoming a little un-American. The same man who will quote from Benjamin Franklin on thrift for the house organ would be horrified if consumers took these maxims to heart and started putting more money into savings and less into installment purchases. No longer can he afford the luxury of damning the profligacy of the public; not in public, at any rate. He not only has to persuade people to buy more but persuade them out of any guilt feelings they might have for following his advice. Few talents are more commercially sought today than the knack of describing departures from the Protestant Ethic as reaffirmations of it.[2]

In an advertisement that should go down in social history, the J. Walter Thompson agency has hit the problem of absolution head-on. It quotes Benjamin Franklin on the benefits of spending. "Is not the hope of being one day able to purchase and enjoy luxuries a great spur to labor and industry? . . . May not luxury therefore produce more than it consumes, if, without such a spur, people would be, as they are naturally enough inclined to be, lazy and indolent?" This thought, the ad says, in a meaningful aside, "appears to be a mature afterthought, qualifying his earlier and more familiar writings on the importance of thrift."

[2]Helping in this task is what a good part of "motivation research" is all about. Motivation researcher Dr. Ernest Dichter, in a bulletin to business, says, "We are now confronted with the problem of permitting the average American to feel moral even when he is flirting, even when he is spending, even when he is not saving, even when he is taking two vacations a year and buying a second or third car. One of the basic problems of this prosperity, then, is to give people the sanction and justification to enjoy it and to demonstrate that the hedonistic approach to his life is a moral, not an immoral one."

"Hard work?" What price capitalism, the question is now so frequently asked, unless we turn our productivity into more leisure, more of the good life? To the organization man this makes abundant sense, and he is as sensitive to the bogy of overwork and ulcers as his forebears were to the bogy of slothfulness. But he is split. He believes in leisure, but so does he believe in the Puritan insistence on hard, self-denying work—and there are, alas, only twenty-four hours a day. How, then, to be "broad gauge"? The "broad-gauge" model we hear so much about these days is the man who keeps his work separate from leisure and the rest of his life. Any organization man who managed to accomplish this feat wouldn't get very far. He still works hard, in short, but now he has to feel somewhat guilty about it.

Self-reliance? The corporation estates have been expanding so dynamically of late that until about now the management man could suppress the thought that he was a bureaucrat—bureaucrats, as every businessman knew, were those people down in Washington who preferred safety to adventure. Just when the recognition began to dawn, no one can say, but since the war the younger generation of management haven't been talking of self-reliance and adventure with quite the straight face of their elders.

That upward path toward the rainbow of achievement leads smack through the conference room. No matter what name the process is called— permissive management, multiple management, the art of administration— the committee way simply can't be equated with the "rugged" individualism that is supposed to be the business of business. Not for lack of ambition do the younger men dream so moderately; what they lack is the illusion that they will carry on in the great entrepreneurial spirit. Although they cannot bring themselves to use the word bureaucrat, the approved term—the "administrator"—is not signally different in its implications. The man of the future, as junior executives see him, is not the individualist but the man who works through others for others.

Let me pause for a moment to emphasize a necessary distinction. Within business there are still many who cling resolutely to the Protestant Ethic, and some with as much rapacity as drove any nineteenth-century buccaneer. But only rarely are they of The Organization. Save for a small, and spectacular, group of financial operators, most who adhere to the old creed are small businessmen, and to group them as part of the "business community," while convenient, implies a degree of ideological kinship with big business that does not exist.

Out of inertia, the small business is praised as the acorn from which a great oak may grow, the shadow of one man that may lengthen into a large enterprise. Examine businesses with fifty or less employees, however, and it becomes apparent the sentimentality obscures some profound differences. You will find some entrepreneurs in the classic sense—men who develop new products, new appetites, or new systems of distribution— and some of these enterprises may mature into self-perpetuating institutions. But very few.

The great majority of small business firms cannot be placed on any continuum with the corporation. For one thing, they are rarely engaged in primary industry; for the most part they are the laundries, the insurance agencies, the restaurants, the drugstores, the bottling plants, the lumber yards, the automobile dealers. They are vital, to be sure, but essentially they service an economy; they do not create new money within their area and they are dependent ultimately on the business and agriculture that does.

In this dependency they react more as antagonists than allies with the corporation. The corporation, it has become clear, is expansionist—a force for change that is forever a threat to the economics of the small businessman. By instinct he inclines to the monopolistic and the restrictive. When the druggists got the "Fair Trade" laws passed it was not only the manufacturers (and customers) they were rebelling against but the whole mass economy movement of the twentieth century.

The tail wagged the dog in this case and it still often does. That it can, in the face of the growing power of the corporation, illustrates again the dominance mythology can have over reality. Economically, many a small businessman is a counterrevolutionist and the revolution he is fighting is that of the corporation as much as the New or Fair Deal. But the corporation man still clings to the idea that the two are firm allies, and on some particulars, such as fair trade, he often makes policy on this basis when in fact it is against the corporation's interests to do so.

But the revolution is not to be stopped by sentiment. Many anachronisms do remain; in personal income, for example, the corporation man who runs a branch plant on which a whole town depends is lucky to make half the income of the local car dealer or the man with the Coca-Cola franchise. The economy has a way of attending to these discrepancies, however, and the local businessman can smell the future as well as anyone else. The bland young man The Organization sent to town to manage the plant is almost damnably inoffensive; he didn't rent the old place on the hill but a smaller house, he drives an Olds instead of a Caddy, and when he comes to the Thursday luncheons he listens more than he talks. But he's the future just the same.

I have been talking of the impact of organization on the Protestant Ethic; just as important, however, was the intellectual assault. In the great revolt against traditionalism that began around the turn of the century, William James, John Dewey, Charles Beard, Thorstein Veblen, the muckrakers and a host of reformers brought the anachronisms of the

Protestant Ethic under relentless fire, and in so doing helped lay the groundwork for the Social Ethic. It would be a long time before organization men would grasp the relevance of these new ideas, and to this day many of the most thorough-going pragmatists in business would recoil at being grouped with the intellectuals. (And vice versa.) But the two movements were intimately related. To what degree the intellectuals were a cause of change, or a manifestation, no one can say for certain, but more presciently than those in organization they grasped the antithesis between the old concept of the rational, unbeholden individual and the world one had to live in. They were not rebels against society; what they fought was the denial of society's power, and they provided an intellectual framework that would complement, rather than inhibit, the further growth of big organization.

It is not in the province of this book to go into a diagnosis of the ideas of Dewey and James and the other pragmatists. But there is one point of history I think very much needs making at this time. Many people still look on the decline of the Protestant Ethic as our fall from grace, a detour from Americanism for which we can blame pragmatism, ethical relativism, Freudianism and other such developments. These movements have contributed much to the Social Ethic, and many of their presuppositions are as shaky as those they replaced. To criticize them on this score is in order; to criticize them as having subverted the American temper, however, is highly misleading.

Critics of pragmatism, and followers too, should remember the context of the times in which the pragmatists made their case. The pragmatists' emphasis on social utility may be redundant for today's needs, but when they made their case it was not a time when psychology or adjustment or social living were popular topics but at a time when the weight of conservative opinion denied that there was anything much that needed adjusting. Quite clearly, revolt was in order. The growth of the organization society did demand a recognition that man was not entirely a product of his free will; the country did need an educational plant more responsive to the need of the people. It did need a new breeze, and if there had been no James or no Dewey, some form of pragmatism would probably have been invented anyway. Nonphilosophical Americans sensed that changes were in order too; what the philosophers of pragmatism did was to give them guidance and tell them in intellectually responsible terms that they were right in feeling that way.

Pragmatism's emphasis on the social and the practical, furthermore, was thoroughly in the American tradition. From the beginning, Americans had always been impatient with doctrines and systems; like the Puritans, many came here because of a doctrine, but what they came to was a new enviroment that required some powerful adapting to, and whenever the doctrine got in the way of practicality, the doctrine lost out. Few people have had such a genius for bending ideals to the demands of the times, and the construction of fundamental theory, theological or scientific, has never excited Americans overmuch. Long before James, *Does it work?* was a respectable question to ask. If impatience at abstract thought was a defeat, it was the defeat of a virtue, and the virtue, call it what you will, has always been very close to pragmatism as Dewey and James defined it. By defining it they gave it coherence and power at a time when it needed assertion, but the inclination to the practical antedated the philosophy; it was not the product of it.

Reform was everywhere in the air. By the time of the First World War the Protestant Ethic had taken a shellacking from which it would not recover; rugged individualism and hard work had done wonders for the people to whom God in his infinite wisdom, as one put it, had given control of society. But it hadn't done so well for everyone else and now they, as well as the intellectuals, were all too aware of the fact.

The ground, in short, was ready, and though the conservative opinion that drew the fire of the rebels seemed entrenched, the basic temper of the country was so inclined in the other direction that emphasis on the social became the dominant current of U.S. thought. In a great outburst of curiosity, people became fascinated with the discovering of all the environmental pressures on the individual that previous philosophies had denied. As with Freud's discoveries, the findings of such inquiries were deeply disillusioning at first, but with characteristic exuberance Americans found a rainbow. Man might not be perfectible after all, but there was another dream and now at last it seemed practical: the perfectibility of *society*.

One-Dimensional Man*
HERBERT MARCUSE

A comfortable, smooth, reasonable, democratic unfreedom prevails in advanced industrial civilization, a token of technical progress. Indeed, what could be more rational than the suppression of individuality in the mechanization of socially necessary but painful performances; the concentration of individual enterprises in more effective, more productive corporations; the regulation of free competition among unequally equipped economic subjects; the curtailment of prerogatives and national sovereignties which impede the international organization of resources. That this technological order also involves a political and intellectual coordination may be a regrettable and yet promising development.

The rights and liberties which were such vital factors in the origins and earlier stages of industrial society yield to a higher stage of this society: they are losing their traditional rationale and content. Freedom of thought, speech, and conscience were—just as free enterprise, which they served to premote and protect—essentially *critical* ideas, designed to replace an obsolescent material and intellectual culture by a more productive and rational one. Once institutionalized, these rights and liberties shared the fate of the society of which they had become an integral part. The achievement cancels the premises.

To the degree to which freedom from want, the concrete substance of all freedom, is becoming a real possibility, the liberties which pertain to a state of lower productivity are losing their former content. Independence of thought, autonomy, and the right to political opposition are being deprived of their basic critical function in a society which seems increasingly capable of satisfying the needs of the individuals through the way in which it is organized. Such a society may justly demand acceptance of its principles and institutions, and reduce the opposition to the discussion and promotion of alternative policies *within* the status quo. In this respect, it seems to make little difference whether the increasing satisfaction of needs is accomplished by an authoritarian or a non-authoritarian system. Under the conditions of a rising standard of living, non-conformity with the system itself appears to be socially useless, and the more so when it entails tangible economic and political disadvantages and threatens the smooth operation of the whole. Indeed, at least in so far as the necessities of life are involved, there seems to be no reason why the production and distribution of goods and services should proceed through the competitive concurrence of individual liberties.

Freedom of enterprise was from the beginning not altogether a blessing. As the liberty to work or to starve, it spelled toil, insecurity, and fear for the vast majority of the population. If the individual were no longer compelled to prove himself on the market, as a free economic subject, the disappearance of this kind of freedom would be one of the greatest achievements of civilization. The technological processes of mechanization and standardization might release individual energy into a yet uncharted realm of freedom beyond necessity. The very structure of human existence would be altered; the individual would be liberated from the work world's imposing upon him alien needs and alien possibilities. The individual would be free to exert autonomy over a life that would be his own. If the productive apparatus could be organized and directed toward the satisfaction of the vital needs, its control might well be centralized; such control would not prevent individual autonomy, but render it possible.

This is a goal within the capabilities of advanced industrial civilization, the "end" of technological rationality. In actual fact, however, the contrary trend operates: the apparatus imposes its economic and political requirements for defense and expansion on labor time and free time, on the material and intellectual culture. By virtue of the way it has organized its technological base, contemporary industrial society tends to be totalitarian. For "totalitarian" is not only a terroristic political coordination of society, but also a nonterroristic economic-technical coordination which operates through the manipulation of needs by vested interests. It thus precludes the emergence of an effective opposition against the whole. Not only a specific form of government or party rule makes for totalitarianism, but also a specific system of production and distribution which may well be compatible with a "pluralism" of parties, newspapers, "countervailing powers," etc.

Today political power asserts itself through its power over the machine process and over the technical organization of the apparatus. The government of advanced and advancing industrial societies can maintain and secure itself only when it succeeds in mobilizing, organizing, and exploiting the technical, scientific, and mechanical productivity available to industrial civilization. And this productivity mobilizes society as a whole, above and beyond any particular individual or group interests. The brute fact that the machine's physical (only physical?) power surpasses that of the individual, and of any particular group of individuals, makes the machine the most effective political instrument in any society whose basic organization is that of the machine process. But the political trend may be reversed; essentially the power of the machine is only the stored-up and projected power of man. To the extent to which the work world is conceived of as a machine and mechanized accordingly, it becomes the *potential* basis of a new freedom for man.

Contemporary industrial civilization demonstrates that it has reached the stage at which "the free society" can no longer be adequately defined in the traditional terms of economic, political, and intellectual liberties, not because these liberties have become insignificant, but because they are too significant to be confined within the traditional forms. New modes of realization are needed, corresponding to the new capabilities of society.

Such new modes can be indicated only in negative terms because they would amount to the negation of the prevailing modes. Thus economic freedom would mean freedom *from* the economy—from being controlled by economic forces and relationships; freedom from the daily struggle for existence, from earning a living. Political freedom would mean liberation of the individuals *from* politics over which they have no effective control. Similarly, intellectual freedom would mean the restoration of individual thought now absorbed by mass communication and indoctrination, abolition of "public opinion" together with its makers. The unrealistic sound of these propositions is indicative, not of their utopian character, but of the strength of the forces which prevent their realization. The most effective and enduring form of warfare against liberation is the implanting of material and intellectual needs that perpetuate obsolete forms of the struggle for existence.

The intensity, the satisfaction and even the character of human needs, beyond the biological level, have always been preconditioned. Whether or not the possibility of doing or leaving, enjoying or destroying, possessing or rejecting something is seized as a *need* depends on whether or not it can be seen as desirable and necessary for the prevailing societal institutions and interests. In this sense, human needs are historical needs and, to the extent to which the society demands the repressive development of the individual, his needs themselves and their claim for satisfaction are subject to overriding critical standards.

We may distinguish both true and false needs. "False" are those which are superimposed upon the individual by particular social interests in his repression: the needs which perpetuate toil, aggressiveness, misery, and injustice. Their satisfaction might be most gratifying to the individual, but this happiness is not a condition which has to be maintained and protected if it serves to arrest the development of the ability (his own and others) to recognize the disease of the whole and grasp the chances of curing the disease. The result then is euphoria in unhappiness. Most of the prevailing needs to relax, to have fun, to behave and consume in accordance with the advertisements, to love and hate what others love and hate, belong to this category of false needs.

Such needs have a societal content and function which are determined by external powers over which the individual has no control; the development and satisfaction of these needs is heteronomous. No matter how much such needs may have become the individual's own, reproduced and fortified by the conditions of his existence; no matter how much he identifies himself with them and finds himself in their satisfaction, they continue to be what they were from the beginning—products of a society whose dominant interest demands repression.

The prevalence of repressive needs is an accomplished fact, accepted in ignorance and defeat, but a fact that must be undone in the interest of the happy individual as well as all those whose misery is the price of his satisfaction. The only needs that have an unqualified claim for satisfaction are the vital ones—nourishment, clothing, lodging at the attainable level of culture. The satisfaction of these needs is the prerequisite for the realization of *all* needs, of the unsublimated as well as the sublimated ones.

For any consciousness and conscience, for any experience which does not accept the prevailing societal interest as the supreme law of thought and behavior, the established universe of needs and satisfactions is a fact to be questioned—questioned in terms of truth and falsehood. These terms are historical throughout, and their objectivity is historical. The judgment of needs and their satisfaction, under the given conditions, involves standards of *priority*—standards which refer to the optimal development of the individual, of all individuals, under the optimal utilization of the material and intellectual resources available to man. The resources are calculable. "Truth" and "falsehood" of needs designate objective conditions to the extent to which the universal satisfaction of vital needs and, beyond it, the progressive alleviation of toil and poverty, are universally valid standards. But as historical standards, they do not only vary according to area and stage of development, they also can be defined only in (greater or lesser) *contradiction* to the prevailing ones. What tribunal can possibly claim the authority of decision?

In the last analysis, the question of what are true and false needs must be answered by the individuals themselves, but only in the last analysis; that is, if and when they are free to give their own answer. As long as they are kept incapable of being autonomous, as long as they are indoctrinated and manipulated (down to their very instincts), their answer to this question cannot be taken as their own. By the same token, however, no tribunal can justly arrogate to itself the right to decide which needs should be developed and satisfied. Any such tribunal is reprehensible, although our revulsion does not do away with the question: how can the people who have been the object of effective and productive domination by themselves create the conditions of freedom?

The more rational, productive, technical, and total the repressive administration of society becomes, the more unimaginable the means and ways by which the administered individuals might break their servitude and seize their own liberation. To be sure, to impose Reason upon an entire society is a paradoxical and scandalous idea—although one might dispute the righteousness of a society which ridicules this idea while making its own population into objects of total administration. All liberation depends on the consciousness of servitude, and the emergence of this consciousness is always hampered by the predominance of needs and satisfactions which, to a great extent, have become the individual's own. The process always replaces one system of preconditioning by another; the optimal goal is the replacement of false needs by true ones, the abandonment of repressive satisfaction.

The distinguishing feature of advanced industrial society is its effective suffocation of those needs which demand liberation—liberation also from that which is tolerable and rewarding and comfortable—while it sustains and absolves the destructive power and repressive function of the affluent society. Here, the social controls exact the overwhelming need for the production and consumption of waste; the need for stupefying work where it is no longer a real necessity; the need for modes of relaxation which soothe and prolong this stupefication; the need for maintaining such deceptive liberties as free competition at administered prices, a free press which censors itself, free choice between brands and gadgets.

Under the rule of a repressive whole, liberty can be made into a powerful instrument of domination. The range of choice open to the individual is not the decisive factor in determining the degree of human freedom, but *what* can be chosen and what *is* chosen by the individual. The criterion for free choice can never be an absolute one, but neither is it entirely relative. Free election of masters does not abolish the masters or the slaves. Free choice among a wide variety of goods and services does not signify freedom if these goods and services sustain social controls over a life of toil and fear—that is, if they sustain alienation. And the spontaneous reproduction of superimposed needs by the individual does not establish autonomy; it only testifies to the efficacy of the controls.

Our insistence on the depth and efficacy of these controls is open to the objection that we overrate greatly the indoctrinating power of the "media," and that by themselves the people would feel and satisfy the needs which are now imposed upon them. The objection misses the point. The preconditioning does not start with the mass production of radio and television and with the centralization of their control. The people enter this stage as preconditioned receptacles of long standing; the decisive difference is in the flattening out of the contrast (or conflict) between the given and the possible, between the satisfied and the unsatisfied needs. Here, the so-called equalization of class distinctions reveals its ideological function. If the worker and his boss enjoy the same television program and visit the same resort places, if the typist is as attractively made up as the daughter of her employer, if the Negro owns a Cadillac, if they all read the same newspaper, then this assimilation indicates not the disappearance of classes, but the extent to which the needs and satisfactions that serve the preservation of the Establishment are shared by the underlying population.

Indeed, in the most highly developed areas of contemporary society, the transplantation of social into individual needs is so effective that the difference between them seems to be purely theoretical. Can one really distinguish between the mass media as instruments of information and entertainment, and as agents of manipulation and indoctrination? Between the automobile as nuisance and as convenience? Between the horrors and the comforts of functional architecture? Between the work for national defense and the work for corporate gain? Between the private pleasure and the commercial and political utility involved in increasing the birth rate?

We are again confronted with one of the most vexing aspects of advanced industrial civilization: the rational character of its irrationality. Its productivity and efficiency, its capacity to increase and spread comforts, to turn waste into need, and destruction into construction, the extent to which this civilization transforms the object world into an extension of man's mind and body makes the very notion of alienation questionable. The people recognize themselves in their commodities; they find their soul in their automobile, hi-fi set, split-level home, kitchen equipment. The very mechanism which ties the individual to his society has changed, and social control is anchored in the new needs which it has produced.

The prevailing forms of social control are technological in a new sense. To be sure, the technical structure and efficacy of the productive and destructive apparatus has been a major instrumentality for subjecting the population to the established social division of labor throughout the modern period. Moreover, such integration has always been accompanied by more obvious forms of compulsion: loss of livelihood, the administration of justice, the police, the armed forces. It still is. But in the contemporary period, the technological controls appear to be the very embodiment of Reason for the benefit of all social groups and interests—to such an extent that all contradiction seems irrational and all counteraction impossible.

No wonder then that, in the most advanced areas of this civilization, the social controls have been introjected to the point where even individual protests is affected at its roots. The intellectual and emotional refusal "to go along" appears neurotic and impotent. This is the socio-psychological aspect of the political event that marks the contemporary period: the passing of the historical forces which, at the preceding stage of industrial society, seemed to represent the possibility of new forms of existence.

But the term "introjection" perhaps no longer describes the way in which the individual by himself reproduces and perpetuates the external controls exercised by his society. Introjection suggests a variety of relatively spontaneous processes by which a Self (Ego) transposes the "outer" into the "inner." Thus introjection implies the existence of an inner dimension distinguished from and even antagonistic to the external exigencies—an individual consciousness and an individual unconscious *apart from* public opinion and behavior.[1] The idea of "inner freedom" here has its reality: it designates the private space in which man may become and remain "himself."

Today this private space has been invaded and whittled down by technological reality. Mass production and mass distribution claim the *entire* individual, and industrial psychology has long since ceased to be confined to the factory. The manifold processes of introjection seem to be ossified in almost mechanical reactions. The result is, not adjustment but *mimesis*: an immediate identification of the individual with *his* society and, through it, with the society as a whole.

This immediate, automatic identification (which may have been characteristic of primitive forms of association) reappears in high industrial civilization; its new "immediacy," however, is the product of a sophisticated, scientific management and organization. In this process, the "inner" dimension of the mind in which opposition to the status quo can take root is whittled down. The loss of this dimension, in which the power of negative thinking—the critical power of Reason—is at home, is the ideological counterpart to the very material process in which advanced industrial society silences and reconciles the opposition. The impact of progress turns Reason into submission to the facts of life, and to the dynamic capability of producing more and bigger facts of the same sort of life. The efficiency of the system blunts the individuals' recognition that it contains no facts which do not communicate the repressive power of the whole. If the individuals find themselves in the things which shape their life, they do so, not by giving, but by accepting the law of things—not the law of physics but the law of their society.

I have just suggested that the concept of alienation seems to become questionable when the individuals identify themselves with the existence which is imposed upon them and have in it their own development and satisfaction. This identification is not illusion but reality. However, the reality constitutes a more progressive stage of alienation. The latter has become entirely objective; the subject which is alienated is swallowed up

[1]The change in the function of the family here plays a decisive role: its "socializing" functions are increasingly taken over by outside groups and media. See my *Eros and Civilization* (Boston: Beacon Press, 1955), p. 96 ff.

by its alienated existence. There is only one dimension, and it is every-where and in all forms. The achievements of progress defy ideological indictment as well as justification; before their tribunal, the "false con-sciousness" of their rationality becomes the true consciousness.

This absorption of ideology into reality does not, however, signify the "end of ideology." On the contrary, in a specific sense advanced industrial culture is *more* ideological than its predecessor, inasmuch as today the ideology is in the process of production itself.[2] In a provocative forum, this proposition reveals the political aspects of the prevailing technological rationality. The productive apparatus and the goods and services which it produces "sell" or impose the social system as a whole. The means of mass transportation and communication, the commodities of lodging, food, and clothing, the irresistible output of the entertainment and in-formation industry carry with them prescribed attitudes and habits, certain intellectual and emotional reactions which bind the consumers more or less pleasantly to the producers and, through the latter, to the whole. The products indoctrinate and manipulate; they promote a false consciousness which is immune against its falsehood. And as these beneficial products become available to more individuals in more social classes, the indoc-trination they carry ceases to be publicity; it becomes a way of life. It is a good way of life—much better than before—and as a good way of life, it militates against qualitative change. Thus emerges a pattern of *one-dimensional thought and behavior* in which ideas, aspirations, and objec-tives that, by their content, transcend the established universe of discourse and action are either repelled or reduced to terms of this universe. They are redefined by the rationality of the given system and of its quantitative extension.

The trend may be related to a development in scientific method: operationalism in the physical, behaviorism in the social sciences. The common feature is a total empiricism in the treatment of concepts; their meaning is restricted to the representation of particular operations and behavior. The operational point of view is well illustrated by P. W. Bridgman's analysis of the concept of length:[3]

> We evidently know what we mean by length if we can tell what the
> length of any and every object is, and for the physicist nothing more is

[2]Theodor W. Adorno, *Prismen. Kulturkritik und Gesellschaft.* (Frankfurt: Suhrkamp, 1955), p. 24 f.

[3]P. W. Bridgman, *The Logic of Modern Physics* (New York: Macmillan, 1928), p. 5. The operational doctrine has since been refined and qualified. Bridgman himself has extended the concept of "operation" to include the "paper-and-pencil" operations of the theorist (in Philipp J. Frank, *The Validation of Scientific Theories* [Boston: Beacon Press, 1954], Chap. II). The main impetus remains the same: it is "desirable" that the paper-and-pencil operations "be capable of eventual contact, although perhaps indirect-ly, with instrumental operations."

required. To find the length of an object, we have to perform certain physical operations. The concept of length is therefore fixed when the operations by which length is measured are fixed: that is, the concept of length involves as much and nothing more than the set of operations by which length is determined. In general, we mean by any concept nothing more than a set of operations; *the concept is synonymous with the corresponding set of operations.*

Bridgman has seen the wide implications of this mode of thought for the society at large.[4]

To adopt the operational point of view involves much more than a mere restriction of the sense in which we understand "concept," but means a far-reaching change in all our habits of thought, in that we shall no longer permit ourselves to use as tools in our thinking concepts of which we cannot give an adequate account in terms of operations.

Bridgman's prediction has come true. The new mode of thought is today the predominant tendency in philosophy, psychology, sociology, and other fields. Many of the most seriously troublesome concepts are being "eliminated" by showing that no adequate account of them in terms of operations or behavior can be given. The radical empiricist onslaught thus provides the methodological justification for the debunking of the mind by the intellectuals—a positivism which, in its denial of the transcending elements of Reason, forms the academic counterpart of the socially required behavior.

Outside the academic establishment, the "far-reaching change in all our habits of thought" is more serious. It serves to coordinate ideas and goals with those exacted by the prevailing system, to enclose them in the system, and to repel those which are irreconcilable with the system. The reign of such a one-dimensional reality does not mean that materialism rules, and that the spiritual, metaphysical, and bohemian occupations are petering out. On the contrary, there is a great deal of "Worship together this week," "Why not try God," Zen, existentialism, and beat ways of life, etc. But such modes of protest and transcendence are no longer contradictory to the status quo and no longer negative. They are rather the ceremonial part of practical behaviorism, its harmless negation, and are quickly digested by the status quo as part of its healthy diet.

One-dimensional thought is systematically promoted by the makers of politics and their purveyors of mass information. Their universe of discourse is populated by self-validating hypotheses which, incessantly and monopolistically repeated, become hypnotic definitions or dictations. For example, "free" are the institutions which operate (and are operated on)

[4]P. W. Bridgman, *The Logic of Modern Physics,* loc. cit., p. 31.

in the countries of the Free World; other transcending modes of freedom are by definition either anarchism, communism, or propaganda. "Socialistic" are all encroachments on private enterprises not undertaken by private enterprise itself (or by government contracts), such as universal and comprehensive health insurance, or the protection of nature from all too sweeping commercialization, or the establishment of public services which may hurt private profit. This totalitarian logic of accomplished facts has its Eastern counterpart. There, freedom is the way of life instituted by a communist regime, and all other transcending modes of freedom are either capitalistic, or revisionist, or leftist sectarianism. In both camps, non-operational ideas are non-behavioral and subversive. The movement of thought is stopped at barriers which appear as the limits of Reason itself.

Such limitation of thought is certainly not new. Ascending modern rationalism, in its speculative as well as empirical form, shows a striking contrast between extreme critical radicalism in scientific and philosophic method on the one hand, and an uncritical quietism in the attitude toward established and functioning social institutions. Thus Descartes' *ego cogitans* was to leave the "great public bodies" untouched, and Hobbes held that "the present ought always to be preferred, maintained, and accounted best." Kant agreed with Locke in justifying revolution *if and when* it has succeeded in organizing the whole and in preventing subversion.

However, these accommodating concepts of Reason were always contradicted by the evident misery and injustice of the "great public bodies" and the effective, more or less conscious rebellion against them. Societal conditions existed which provoked and permitted real dissociation from the established state of affairs; a private as well as political dimension was present in which dissociation could develop into effective opposition, testing its strength and the validity of its objectives.

With the gradual closing of this dimension by the society, the self-limitation of thought assumes a larger significance. The interrelation between scientific-philosophical and societal processes, between theoretical and practical Reason, asserts itself "behind the back" of the scientists and philosophers. The society bars a whole type of oppositional operations and behavior; consequently, the concepts pertaining to them are rendered illusory or meaningless. Historical transcendence appears as metaphysical transcendence, not acceptable to science and scientific thought. The operational and behavioral point of view, practiced as a "habit of thought" at large, becomes the view of the established universe of discourse and action, needs and aspirations. The "cunning of Reason" works, as it so often did, in the interest of the powers that be. The insistence on operational and behavioral concepts turns against the efforts to free thought and behavior *from* the given reality and *for* the suppressed alternatives.

Theoretical and practical Reason, academic and social behaviorism meet on common ground: that of an advanced society which makes scientific and technical progress into an instrument of domination.

"Progress" is not a neutral term; it moves toward specific ends, and these ends are defined by the possibilities of ameliorating the human condition. Advanced industrial society is approaching the stage where continued progress would demand the radical subversion of the prevailing direction and organization of progress. This stage would be reached when material production (including the necessary services) becomes automated to the extent that all vital needs can be satisfied while necessary labor time is reduced to marginal time. From this point on, technical progress would transcend the realm of necessity, where it served as the instrument of domination and exploitation which thereby limited its rationality; technology would become subject to the free play of faculties in the struggle for the pacification of nature and of society.

Such a state is envisioned in Marx's notion of the "abolition of labor." The term "pacification of existence" seems better suited to designate the historical alternative of a world which—through an international conflict which transforms and suspends the contradictions within the established societies—advances on the brink of a global war. "Pacification of existence" means the development of man's struggle with man and with nature, under conditions where the competing needs, desires, and aspirations are no longer organized by vested interests in domination and scarcity—an organization which perpetuates the destructive forms of this struggle.

Today's fight against this historical alternative finds a firm mass basis in the underlying population, and finds its ideology in the rigid orientation of thought and behavior to the given universe of facts. Validated by the accomplishments of science and technology, justified by its growing productivity, the status quo defies all transcendence. Faced with the possibility of pacification on the grounds of its technical and intellectual achievements, the mature industrial society closes itself against this alternative. Operationalism, in theory and practice, becomes the theory and practice of *containment*. Underneath its obvious dynamics, this society is a thoroughly static system of life: self-propelling in its oppressive productivity and in its beneficial coordination. Containment of technical progress goes hand in hand with its growth in the established direction. In spite of the political fetters imposed by the status quo, the more technology appears capable of creating the conditions for pacification, the more are the minds and bodies of man organized against this alternative.

The most advanced areas of industrial society exhibit throughout these two features: a trend toward consummation of technological rationality, and intensive efforts to contain this trend within the established institutions. Here is the internal contradiction of this civilization: the irrational element in its rationality. It is the token of its achievements. The industrial society which makes technology and science its own is organized for the ever-more-effective domination of man and nature, for the ever-more-effective utilization of its resources. It becomes irrational when the success of these efforts opens dimensions of human realization. Organization for peace is different from organization for war; the institutions which served the struggle for existence cannot serve the pacification of existence. Life as an end is qualitatively different from life as a means.

Such a qualitatively new mode of existence can never be envisaged as the mere by-product of economic and political changes, as the more or less spontaneous effect of the new institutions which constitute the necessary prerequisite. Qualitative change also involves a change in the *technical* basis on which this society rests—one which sustains the economic and political institutions through which the "second nature" of man as an aggressive object of administration is stabilized. The techniques of industrialization are political techniques; as such, they prejudge the possibilities of Reason and Freedom.

To be sure, labor must precede the reduction of labor, and industrialization must precede the development of human needs and satisfactions. But as all freedom depends on the conquest of alien necessity, the realization of freedom depends on the *techniques* of this conquest. The highest productivity of labor can be used for the perpetuation of labor, and the most efficient industrialization can serve the restriction and manipulation of needs.

When this point is reached, domination—in the guise of affluence and liberty—extends to all spheres of private and public existence, integrates all authentic opposition, absorbs all alternatives. Technological rationality reveals its political character as it becomes the great vehicle of better domination, creating a truly totalitarian universe in which society and nature, mind and body are kept in a state of permanent mobilization for the defense of this universe.

Spiritual Anxiety over Values

The Spiritual Problem of Modern Man*

C. G. JUNG

The spiritual problem of modern man is one of those questions which belong so intimately to the present in which we are living that we cannot judge of them fully. The modern man is a newly formed human being; a modern problem is a question which has just arisen and whose answer lies in the future. In speaking, therefore, of the spiritual problem of modern man we can at most state a question—and we should perhaps put this statement in different terms if we had but the faintest inkling of the answer. The question, moreover, seems rather vague; but the truth is that it has to do with something so universal that it exceeds the grasp of any single human being. We have reason enough, therefore, to approach such a problem with true moderation and with the greatest caution. I am deeply convinced of this, and wish it stressed the more because it is just such problems which tempt us to use high-sounding words—and because I shall myself be forced to say certain things which may sound immoderate and incautious.

To begin at once with an example of such apparent lack of caution, I must say that the man we call modern, the man who is aware of the

*From *Modern Man in Search of a Soul* by C. G. Jung, translated by W. S. Dell and Cary F. Baynes, pp. 196–220. Reprinted by permission of Harcourt, Brace and World, Inc., and Routledge and Kegan Paul, Ltd. The author has made some changes in this essay since its publication in German. (*Trans.*)

immediate present, is by no means the average man. He is rather the man who stands upon a peak, or at the very edge of the world, the abyss of the future before him, above him the heavens, and below him the whole of mankind with a history that disappears in primeval mists. The modern man—or, let us say again, the man of the immediate present—is rarely met with. There are few who live up to the name, for they must be conscious to a superlative degree. Since to be wholly of the present means to be fully conscious of one's existence as a man, it requires the most intensive and extensive consciousness, with a minimum of unconsciousness. It must be clearly understood that the mere fact of living in the present does not make a man modern, for in that case everyone at present alive would be so. He alone is modern who is fully conscious of the present.

The man whom we can with justice call "modern" is solitary. He is so of necessity and at all times, for every step towards a fuller consciousness of the present removes him further from his original *"participation mystique"* with the mass of men—from submersion in a common unconsciousness. Every step forward means an act of tearing himself loose from that all-embracing, pristine unconsciousness which claims the bulk of mankind almost entirely. Even in our civilizations the people who form, psychologically speaking, the lowest stratum, live almost as unconsciously as primitive races. Those of the succeeding stratum manifest a level of consciousness which corresponds to the beginnings of human culture, while those of the highest stratum have a consciousness capable of keeping step with the life of the last few centuries. Only the man who is modern in our meaning of the term really lives in the present; he alone has a present-day consciousness, and he alone finds that the ways of life which correspond to earlier levels pall upon him. The values and strivings of those past worlds no longer interest him save from the historical standpoint. Thus he has become "unhistorical" in the deepest sense and has estranged himself from the mass of men who live entirely within the bounds of tradition. Indeed, he is completely modern only when he has come to the very edge of the world, leaving behind him all that has been discarded and outgrown, and acknowledging that he stands before a void out of which all things may grow.

These words may be thought to be but empty sound, and their meaning reduced to mere banality. Nothing is easier than to affect a consciousness of the present. As a matter of fact, a great horde of worthless people give themselves the air of being modern by overleaping the various stages of development and the tasks of life they represent. They appear suddenly by the side of the truly modern man as uprooted human beings, blood-sucking ghosts, whose emptiness is taken for the unenviable loneliness of the modern man and casts discredit upon him. He and his kind, few in number as they are, are hidden from the undiscerning eyes of mass-men by those clouds of ghosts, the pseudo-moderns. It cannot be helped; the "modern" man is questionable and suspect, and has always been so, even in the past.

An honest profession of modernity means voluntarily declaring bank-ruptcy, taking the vows of poverty and chastity in a new sense, and—what is still more painful—renouncing the halo which history bestows as a mark of its sanction. To be "unhistorical" is the Promethean sin, and in this sense modern man lives in sin. A higher level of consciousness is like a burden of guilt. But, as I have said, only the man who has outgrown the stages of consciousness belonging to the past and has amply fulfilled the duties appointed for him by his world, can achieve a full consciousness of the present. To do this he must be sound and proficient in the best sense—a man who has achieved as much as other people, and even a little more. It is these qualities which enable him to gain the next highest level of consciousness.

I know that the idea of proficiency is especially repugnant to the pseudo-moderns, for it reminds them unpleasantly of their deceits. This, however, cannot prevent us from taking it as our criterion of the modern man. We are even forced to do so, for unless he is proficient, the man who claims to be modern is nothing but an unscrupulous gambler. He must be proficient in the highest degree, for unless he can atone by creative ability for his break with tradition, he is merely disloyal to the past. It is sheer juggling to look upon a denial of the past as the same thing as conscious-ness of the present. "Today" stands between "yesterday" and "tomor-row," and forms a link between past and future; it has no other meaning. The present represents a process of transition, and that man may account himself modern who is conscious of it in this sense.

Many people call themselves modern—especially the pseudo-moderns. Therefore the really modern man is often to be found among those who call themselves old-fashioned. He takes this stand for sufficient reasons. On the one hand he emphasizes the past in order to hold the scales against his break with tradition and that effect of guilt of which I have spoken. On the other hand he wishes to avoid being taken for a pseudo-modern.

Every good quality has its bad side, and nothing that is good can come into the world without directly producing a corresponding evil. This is a painful fact. Now there is the danger that consciousness of the present may lead to an elation based upon illusion: the illusion, namely, that we are the culmination of the history of mankind, the fulfilment and the end-product of countless centuries. If we grant this, we should understand that it is no more than the proud acknowledgement of our destitution: we are also the disappointment of the hopes and expectations of the ages. Think of nearly two thousand years of Christian ideals followed, instead of by the return of the Messiah and the heavenly millennium, by the World War among Christian nations and its barbed-wire and poison-gas. What a catastrophe in heaven and on earth!

In the face of such a picture we may well grow humble again. It is true that modern man is a culmination, but tomorrow he will be surpassed; he is indeed the end-product of an age-old development, but he is at the same time the worst conceivable disappointment of the hopes of mankind. The modern man is aware of this. He has seen how beneficent are science, technology and organization, but also how catastrophic they can be. He has likewise seen that well-meaning governments have so thoroughly paved the way for peace on the principle "in time of peace prepare for war," that Europe has nearly gone to rack and ruin. And as for ideals, the Christian church, the brotherhood of man, international social democracy and the "solidarity" of economic interests have failed to stand the baptism of fire—the test of reality. Today, fifteen years after the war, we observe once more the same optimism, the same organization, the same political aspirations, the same phrases and catch-words at work. How can we but fear that they will inevitably lead to further catastrophes? Agreements to outlaw war leave us sceptical, even while we wish them all possible success. At bottom, behind every such palliative measure, there is a gnawing doubt. On the whole, I believe I am not exaggerating when I say that modern man has suffered an almost fatal shock, psychologically speaking, and as a result has fallen into profound uncertainty.

These statements, I believe, make it clear enough that my being a physician has coloured my views. A doctor always spies out diseases, and I cannot cease to be a doctor. But it is essential to the physician's art that he should not discover diseases where none exists. I will therefore not make the assertion that the white races in general, and occidental nations in particular, are diseased, or that the Western world is on the verge of collapse. I am in no way competent to pass such a judgment.

It is of course only from my own experience with other persons and with myself that I draw my knowledge of the spiritual problem of modern man. I know something of the intimate psychic life of many hundreds of educated persons, both sick and healthy, coming from every quarter of the civilized, white world; and upon this experience I base my statements. No doubt I can draw only a one-sided picture, for the things I have observed are events of psychic life; they lie within us—on the *inner side,* if I may use the expression. I must point out that this is not always true of psychic life; the psyche is not always and everywhere to be found on the inner side. It is to be found on the *outside* in whole races or periods of history which take no account of psychic life as such. As examples we may choose any of the ancient cultures, but especially that of Egypt with its imposing objectivity and its naive confession of sins that have not been committed.[1] We can no more feel the Pyramids and the Apis tombs of Sakkara to be expressions of personal problems or personal emotions, than we can feel this of the music of Bach.

Whenever there is established an external form, be it ritual or spiritual, by which all the yearnings and hopes of the soul are adequately expressed—as for instance in some living religion—then we may say that the psyche is outside, and no spiritual problem, strictly speaking, exists. In consonance with this truth, the development of psychology falls entirely within the last decades, although long before that man was introspective and intelligent enough to recognize the facts that are the subject matter of psychology. The same was the case with technical knowledge. The Romans were familiar with all the mechanical principles and physical facts on the basis of which they could have constructed the steam engine, but all that came of it was the toy made by Hero of Alexandria. There was no urgent necessity to go further. It was the division of labour and specialization in the nineteenth century which gave rise to the need to apply all available knowledge. So also a spiritual need has produced in our time our "discovery" of psychology. There has never, of course, been a time when the psyche did not manifest itself, but formerly it attracted no attention—no one noticed it. People got along without heeding it. But today we can no longer get along unless we give our best attention to the ways of the psyche.

It was men of the medical profession who were the first to notice this; for the priest is concerned only to establish an undisturbed functioning of the psyche within a recognized system of belief. As long as this system gives true expression to life, psychology can be nothing but a technical adjuvant to healthy living, and the psyche cannot be regarded as a problem in itself. While man still lives as a herd-being he has no "things of the spirit" of his own; nor does he need any, save the usual belief in the immortality of the soul. But as soon as he has outgrown whatever local form of religion he was born to—as soon as this religion can no longer embrace his life in all its fulness—then the psyche becomes something in its own right which cannot be dealt with by the measures of the Church alone. It is for this reason that we of today have a psychology founded on experience, and not upon articles of faith or the postulates of any philo-

[1]According to Egyptian tradition, when the dead man meets his judges in the underworld, he makes a detailed confession of the crimes he has not committed, but leaves unmentioned his actual sins. (*Trans.*)

sophical system. The very fact that we have such a psychology is to me symptomatic of a profound convulsion of spiritual life. Disruption in the spiritual life of an age shows the same pattern as radical change in an individual. As long as all goes well and psychic energy finds its application in adequate and well-regulated ways, we are disturbed by nothing from within. No uncertainty or doubt besets us, and we *cannot* be divided against ourselves. But no sooner are one or two of the channels of psychic activity blocked, than we are reminded of a stream that is dammed up. The current flows backward to its source; the inner man wants something which the visible man does not want, and we are at war with ourselves. Only then, in this distress, do we discover the psyche; or, more precisely, we come upon something which thwarts our will, which is strange and even hostile to us, or which is incompatible with our conscious standpoint. Freud's psychoanalytic labors show this process in the clearest way. The very first thing he discovered was the existence of sexually perverse and criminal fantasies which at their face value are wholly incompatible with the conscious outlook of a civilized man. A person who was activated by them would be nothing less than a mutineer, a criminal or a madman.

We cannot suppose that this aspect of the unconscious or of the hinterland of man's mind is something totally new. Probably it has always been there, in every culture. Each culture gave birth to its destructive opposite, but no culture or civilization before our own was ever forced to take these psychic undercurrents in deadly earnest. Psychic life always found expression in a metaphysical system of some sort. But the conscious, modern man, despite his strenuous and dogged efforts to do so, can no longer refrain from acknowledging the might of psychic forces. This distinguishes our time from all others. We can no longer deny that the dark stirrings of the unconscious are effective powers—that psychic forces exist which cannot, for the present at least, be fitted in with our rational world-order. We have even enlarged our study of these forces to a science—one more proof of the earnest attention we bring to them. Previous centuries could throw them aside unnoticed; for us they are a shirt of Nessus which we cannot strip off.

The revolution in our conscious outlook, brought about by the catastrophic results of the World War, shows itself in our inner life by the shattering of our faith in ourselves and our own worth. We used to regard foreigners—the other side—as political and moral reprobates; but the modern man is forced to recognize that he is politically and morally just like anyone else. Whereas I formerly believed it to be my bounden duty to call other persons to order, I now admit that I need calling to order myself. I admit this the more readily because I realize only too well that I am losing my faith in the possibility of a rational organization of the world, that old dream of the millennium, in which peace and harmony should rule, has grown pale. The modern man's scepticism regarding all such matters has chilled his enthusiasm for politics and world-reform; more than that, it does not favor any smooth application of psychic energies to the outer world. Through his scepticism the modern man is thrown back upon himself; his energies flow towards their source and wash to the surface those psychic contents which are at all times there, but lie hidden in the silt as long as the stream flows smoothly in its course. How totally different did the world appear to mediaeval man! For him the earth was eternally fixed and at rest in the centre of the universe, encircled by the course of a sun that solicitously bestowed its warmth. Men were all children of God under the loving care of the Most High, who prepared them for eternal blessedness; and all knew exactly what they should do and how they should conduct themselves in order to rise from a corruptible world to an incorruptible and joyous existence. Such a life no longer seems real to us, even in our dreams. Natural science has long ago torn this lovely veil to shreds. That age lies as far behind as childhood, when one's own father was unquestionably the handsomest and strongest man on earth.

The modern man has lost all the metaphysical certainties of his mediaeval brother, and set up in their place the ideals of material security, general welfare and humaneness. But it takes more than an ordinary dose of optimism to make it appear that these ideals are still unshaken. Material security, even, has gone by the board, for the modern man begins to see that every step in material "progress" adds just so much force to the threat of a more stupendous catastrophe. The very picture terrorizes the imagination. What are we to imagine when cities today perfect measures of defense against poison-gas attacks, and practice them in "dress rehearsals"? We cannot but suppose that such attacks have been planned and provided for—again on the principle "in time of peace prepare for war." Let man but accumulate his materials of destruction and the devil within him will soon be unable to resist putting them to their fated use. It is well known that fire-arms go off of themselves if only enough of them are together.

An intimation of the law that governs blind contingency, which Heraclitus called the rule of *enantiodromia* (conversion into the opposite), now steals upon the modern man through the by-ways of his mind, chilling him with fear and paralysing his faith in the lasting effectiveness of social and political measures in the face of these monstrous forces. If he turns away from the terrifying prospect of a blind world in which building and destroying successively tip the scale, and if he then turns his gaze inward upon the recesses of his own mind, he will discover a chaos and a darkness there which he would gladly ignore. Science has destroyed even the refuge of the inner life. What was once a sheltering haven has become a place of terror.

And yet it is almost a relief for us to come upon so much evil in the depths of our own minds. We are able to believe, at least, that we have discovered the root of the evil in mankind. Even though we are shocked and disillusioned at first, we yet feel, because these things are manifestations of our own minds, that we hold them more or less in our own hands and can therefore correct or at least effectively suppress them. We like to assume that, if we succeeded in this, we should have rooted out some fraction of the evil in the world. We like to think that, on the basis of a widespread knowledge of the unconscious and its ways, no one could be deceived by a statesman who was unaware of his own bad motives; the very newspapers would pull him up: "Please have yourself analyzed; you are suffering from a repressed father-complex."

I have purposely chosen this grotesque example to show to what absurdities we are led by the illusion that because something is psychic it is under our control. It is, however, true that much of the evil in the world is due to the fact that man in general is hopelessly unconscious, as it is also true that with increasing insight we can combat this evil at its source in ourselves. As science enables us to deal with injuries inflicted from without, so it helps us to treat those arising from within.

The rapid and world-wide growth of a "psychological" interest over the last two decades shows unmistakably that modern man has to some extent turned his attention from material things to his own subjective processes. Should we call this mere curiosity? At any rate, art has a way of anticipating future changes in man's fundamental outlook, and expressionist art has taken this subjective turn well in advance of the more general change.

This "psychological" interest of the present time shows that man expects something from psychic life which he has not received from the outer world: something which our religions, doubtless, ought to contain, but no longer do contain—at least for the modern man. The various forms of religion no longer appear to the modern man to come from within—to be expressions of his own psychic life; for him they are to be classed with the things of the outer world. He is vouchsafed no revelation of a spirit that is not of this world; but he tries on a number of religions and convictions as if they were Sunday attire, only to lay them aside again like worn-out clothes.

Yet he is somehow fascinated by the almost pathological manifestations of the unconscious mind. We must admit the fact, however difficult it is for us to understand, that something which previous ages have discarded should suddenly command our attention. That there is a general interest in these matters is a truth which cannot be denied. Their offense to good taste notwithstanding. I am not thinking merely of the interest taken in psychology as a science, or of the still narrower interest in the psychoanalysis of Freud, but of the widespread interest in all sorts of psychic phenomena as manifested in the growth of spiritualism, astrology, theosophy, and so forth. The world has seen nothing like it since the end of the seventeenth century. We can compare it only to the flowering of Gnostic thought in the first and second centuries after Christ. The spiritual currents of the present have, in fact, a deep affinity with Gnosticism. There is even a Gnostic church in France today, and I know of two schools in Germany which openly declare themselves Gnostic. The modern movement which is numerically most impressive is undoubtedly Theosophy, together with its continental sister, Anthroposophy; these are pure Gnosticism in a Hindu dress. Compared with these movements the interest in scientific psychology is negligible. What is striking about Gnostic systems is that they are based exclusively upon the manifestations of the unconscious, and that their moral teachings do not balk at the shadow-side of life. Even in the form of its European revival, the Hindu *Kundalini-Yoga* shows this clearly. And as every person informed on the subject of occultism will testify, the statement holds true in this field as well.

The passionate interest in these movements arises undoubtedly from psychic energy which can no longer be invested in obsolete forms of religion. For this reason such movements have a truly religious character, even when they pretend to be scientific. It changes nothing when Rudolf Steiner calls his Anthroposophy "spiritual science," or Mrs. Eddy discovers a "Christian Science." These attempts at concealment merely show that religion has grown suspect—almost as suspect as politics and world-reform.

I do not believe that I am going too far when I say that modern man, in contrast to his nineteenth-century brother, turns his attention to the psyche with very great expectations; and that he does so without reference to any traditional creed, but rather in the Gnostic sense of religious experience. We should be wrong in seeing mere caricature or masquerade when the movements already mentioned try to give themselves scientific airs; their doing so is rather an indication that they are actually pursuing "science" or knowledge instead of the *faith* which is the essence of Western religions. The modern man abhors dogmatic postulates taken on faith and the religions based upon them. He holds them valid only in so far as their knowledge-content seems to accord with his own experience of the deeps of psychic life. He wants to know—to experience for himself. Dean Inge of St. Paul's has called attention to a movement in the Anglican Church with similar objectives.

The age of discovery has only just come to a close in our day when no part of the earth remains unexplored; it began when men would no longer *believe* that the Hyperboreans inhabited the land of eternal sunshine, but wanted to find out and to see with their own eyes what existed beyond the boundaries of the known world. Our age is apparently bent on discovering what exists in the psyche outside of consciousness. The question asked in every spiritualistic circle is: What happens when the medium has lost consciousness? Every Theosophist asks: What shall I experience at higher levels of consciousness? The question which every astrologer puts is this: What are the effective forces and determinants of my fate beyond the reach of my conscious intention? And every psychoanalyst wants to know: What are the unconscious drives behind the neurosis?

Our age wishes to have actual experiences in psychic life. It wants to experience for itself, and not to make assumptions based on the experience of other ages. Yet this does not preclude its trying anything in a hypothetical way—for instance, the recognized religions and the genuine sciences. The European of yesterday will feel a slight shudder run down his spine when he gazes at all deeply into these delvings. Not only does he consider the subject of this research all too obscure and uncanny, but even the methods employed seem to him a shocking misuse of man's finest intellectual attainments. What can we expect an astronomer to say when he is told that at least a thousand horoscopes are drawn today to one three hundred years ago? What will the educator and the advocate of philosophyical enlightenment say to the fact that the world has not been freed of one single superstition since Greek antiquity? Freud himself, the founder of psychoanalysis, has thrown a glaring light upon the dirt, darkness and evil of the psychic hinterland, and has presented these things as so much refuse and slag; he has thus taken the utmost pains to discourage people from seeking anything behind them. He did not succeed, and his warning has even brought about the very thing he wished to prevent: it has awakened in many people an admiration for all this filth. We are tempted to call this sheer perversity; and we could hardly explain it save on the ground that it is not a love of dirt, but the fascination of the psyche, which draws these people.

There can be no doubt that from the beginning of the nineteenth century—from the memorable years of the French Revolution onwards—man has given a more and more prominent place to the psyche, his increasing attentiveness to it being the measure of its growing attraction for him. The enthronement of the Goddess of Reason ın Nôtre Dame seems to have been a symbolic gesture of great significance to the Western world—rather like the hewing down of Wotan's oak by the Christian missionaries. For then, as at the Revolution, no avenging bolt from heaven struck the blasphemer down.

It is certainly more than an amusing coincidence that just at that time a Frenchman, Anquetil du Perron, was living in India, and, in the early eighteen-hundreds, brought back with him a translation of the *Oupnek-hat*—a collection of fifty *Upanishads*—which gave the Western world its first deep insight into the baffling mind of the East. To the historian this is mere chance without any factors of cause and effect. But in view of my medical experience I cannot take it as accident. It seems to me rather to satisfy a psychological law whose validity in personal life, at least, is complete. For every piece of conscious life that loses its importance and value—so runs the law—there arises a compensation in the unconscious. We may see in this an analogy to the conservation of energy in the physical world, for our psychic processes have a quantitative aspect also. No psychic value can disappear without being replaced by another of equivalent intensity. This is a rule which finds its pragmatic sanction in the daily practice of the psychotherapist; it is repeatedly verified and never fails. Now the doctor in me refuses point blank to consider the life of a people as something that does not conform to psychological law. A people, in the doctor's eyes, presents only a somewhat more complex picture of psychic life than the individual. Moreover, taking it the other way round, has not a poet spoken of the "nations" of his soul? And quite correctly, as it seems to me, for in one of its aspects the psyche is not individual, but is derived from the nation, from collectivity, or from humanity even. In some way or other we are part of an all-embracing psychic life, of a single "greatest" man, to quote Swedenborg.

And so we can draw a parallel: just as in me, a single human being, the darkness calls forth the helpful light, so does it also in the psychic life of a people. In the crowds that poured into Notre Dame, bent on destruction, dark and nameless forces were at work that swept the individual off his feet; these forces worked also upon Anquetil du Perron, and provoked an answer which has come down in history. For he brought the Eastern mind to the West, and its influence upon us we cannot as yet measure. Let us beware of underestimating it! So far, indeed, there is little of it to be seen in Europe on the intellectual surface: some orientalists, one or two Buddhist enthusiasts, and a few sombre celebrities like Madame Blavatsky and Annie Besant. These manifestations make us think of tiny, scattered islands in the ocean of mankind; in reality they are like the peaks of submarine mountain-ranges of considerable size. The Philistine believed until recently that astrology had been disposed of long since, and was something that could be safely laughed at. But today, rising out of the social deeps, it knocks at the doors of the universities from which it was banished some three hundred years ago. The same is true of the thought of the East; it takes root in the lower social levels and slowly grows to the surface. Where did the five or six million Swiss francs for the Anthroposophist temple at Dornach come from? Certainly not from one individual. Unfortunately there are no statistics to tell us the exact number of avowed Theosophists today, not to mention the unavowed. But we can be sure that there are several millions of them. To this number we must add a few million Spiritualists of Christian or Theosophic leanings.

Great innovations never come from above; they come invariably from below; just as trees never grow from the sky downward, but upward from the earth, however true it is that their seeds have fallen from above. The upheaval of our world and the upheaval in consciousness is one and the same. Everything becomes relative and therefore doubtful. And while man, hesitant and questioning, contemplates a world that is distracted with treaties of peace and pacts of friendship, democracy and dictatorship, capitalism and Bolshevism, his spirit yearns for an answer that will allay the turmoil of doubt and uncertainty. And it is just people of the lower social levels who follow the unconscious forces of the psychic; it is the much-derided, silent folk of the land—those who are less infected with academic prejudices than great celebrities are wont to be. All these people, looked at from above, present mostly a dreary or laughable comedy; and yet they are as impressively simple as those Galileans who were once called blessed. Is it not touching to see the refuse of man's psyche gathered together in compendia a foot thick? We find recorded in *Anthropophyteia* with scrupulous care the merest babblings, the most absurd actions and the wildest fantasies, while men like Havelock Ellis and Freud have dealt with the like matters in serious treatises which have been accorded all scientific honors. Their reading public is scattered over the breadth of the civilized, white world. How are we to explain this zeal, this almost fanatical worship of repellent things? In this way: the repellent things belong to the psyche, they are of the substance of the psyche and therefore as precious as fragments of manuscript salvaged from ancient ruins. Even the secret and noisome things of the inner life are valuable to modern man because they serve his purpose. But what purpose?

Freud has prefixed to his *Interpretation of Dreams* the citation: *Flectere si nequeo superos Acheronta movebo*—"If I cannot bend the gods on high, I will at least set Acheron in uproar." But to what purpose?

The gods whom *we* are called to dethrone are the idolized values of our conscious world. It is well known that it was the love-scandals of the ancient deities which contributed most to their discredit; and now history is repeating itself. People are laying bare the dubious foundations of our belauded virtues and incomparable ideals, and are calling out to us in triumph: "There are your man-made gods, mere snares and delusions tainted with human baseness—whited sepulchres full of dead men's bones and of all uncleanness." We recognize a familiar strain, and the Gospel words, which we never could make our own, now come to life again.

I am deeply convinced that these are not vague analogies. There are too many persons to whom Freudian psychology is dearer than the Gospels, and to whom the Russian Terror means more than civic virtue. And yet all these people are our brothers, and in each of us there is at least *one* voice which seconds them—for in the end there is a psychic life which embraces us all.

The unexpected result of this spiritual change is that an uglier face is put upon the world. It becomes so ugly that no one can love it any longer—we cannot even love ourselves—and in the end there is nothing in the outer world to draw us away from the reality of the life within. Here, no doubt, we have the true significance of this spiritual change. After all, what does Theosophy, with its doctrines of *karma* and reincarnation, seek to teach except that this world of appearance is but a temporary health-resort for the morally unperfected? It depreciates the present-day world no less radically than does the modern outlook, but with the help of a different technique; it does not vilify our world, but grants it only a relative meaning in that it promises other and higher worlds. The result is in either case the same.

I grant that all these ideas are extremely "unacademic," the truth being that they touch modern man on the side where he is least conscious. Is it again a mere coincidence that modern thought has had to come to terms with Einstein's relativity theory and with ideas about the structure of the atom which lead us away from determinism and visual representation? Even physics volatilizes our material world. It is no wonder, then, in my opinion, if the modern man falls back upon the reality of psychic life and expects from it that certainty which the world denies him.

But spiritually the Western world is in a precarious situation—and the danger is greater the more we blind ourselves to the merciless truth with illusions about our beauty of soul. The Occidental burns incense to himself, and his own countenance is veiled from him in the smoke. But how do we strike men of another color? What do China and India think of us? What feelings do we arouse in the black man? And what is the opinion of all those whom we deprive of their lands and exterminate with rum and venereal disease?

I have a Red Indian friend who is the governor of a pueblo. When we were once speaking confidentially about the white man, he said to me: "We don't understand the whites; they are always wanting something—always restless—always looking for something. What is it? We don't know. We can't understand them. They have such sharp noses, such thin, cruel lips, such lines in their faces. We think they are all crazy."

My friend had recognized, without being able to name it, the Aryan bird of prey with his insatiable lust to lord it in every land—even those that concern him not at all. And he had also noted that megalomania of ours which leads us to suppose, among other things, that Christianity is the only truth, and the white Christ the only Redeemer. After setting the whole East in turmoil with our science and technology, and exacting tribute from it, we send our missionaries even to China. The stamping out of polygamy by the African missions has given rise to prostitution on such a scale that in Uganda alone twenty thousand pounds sterling is spent yearly on preventatives of venereal infection, not to speak of the moral consequences, which have been of the worst. And the good European pays his missionaries for these edifying achievements! No need to mention also the story of suffering in Polynesia and the blessings of the opium trade.

That is how the European looks when he is extricated from the cloud of his own moral incense. No wonder that to unearth buried fragments of psychic life we have first to drain a miasmal swamp. Only a great idealist like Freud could devote a lifetime to the unclean work. This is the beginning of our psychology. For us acquaintance with the realities of psychic life could start only at this end, with all that repels us and that we do not wish to see.

But if the psyche consisted for us only of evil and worthless things, no power in the world could induce a normal man to pretend to find it attractive. This is why people who see in Theosophy nothing but regrettable intellectual superficiality, and in Freudian psychology nothing but sensationalism, prophesy an early and inglorious end for these movements. They overlook the fact that they derive their force from the fascination of psychic life. No doubt the passionate interest that is aroused by them may find other expressions; but it will certainly show itself in these forms until they are replaced by something better. Superstition and perversity are after all one and the same. They are transitional or embryonic stages from which new and riper forms will emerge.

Whether from the intellectual, the moral or the aesthetic viewpoint, the undercurrents of the psychic life of the West present an uninviting picture. We have built a monumental world round about us, and have slaved for it with unequalled energy. But it is so imposing only because we have spent upon the outside all that is imposing in our natures—and what we find when we look within must necessarily be as it is, shabby and insufficient.

I am aware in saying this I somewhat anticipate the actual growth of consciousness. There is as yet no general insight into these facts of psychic life. Westerners are only on the way to a recognition of these facts, and for quite understandable reasons they struggle violently against it. Of course Spengler's pessimism has exerted some influence, but this has been safely confined to academic circles. As for psychological insight, it always trespasses upon personal life, and therefore meets with personal resistances and denials. I am far from considering these resistances meaningless; on the contrary, I see in them a healthy reaction to something which threatens destruction. Whenever relativism is taken as a fundamental and final principle it has a destructive effect. When, therefore, I call attention to the dismal undercurrents of the psyche, it is not in order to sound a pessimistic note; I wish rather to emphasize the fact that the unconscious has a strong attraction not only for the sick, but for healthy, constructive minds as well—and this in spite of its alarming aspect. The psychic depths are nature, and nature is creative life. It is true that nature tears down what she has herself built up—yet she builds it once again. Whatever values in the visible world are destroyed by modern relativism, the psyche will produce their equivalents. At first we cannot see beyond the path that leads downward to dark and hateful things—but no light or beauty will ever come from the man who cannot bear this sight. Light is always born of darkness, and the sun never yet stood still in heaven to satisfy man's longing or to still his fears. Does not the example of Anquetil du Perron show us how psychic life survives its own eclipse? China hardly believes that European science and technology are preparing her ruin. Why should we believe that we must be destroyed by the secret, spiritual influence of the East?

But I forget that we do not yet realize that while we are turning upside down the material world of the East with our technical proficiency, the East with its psychic proficiency is throwing our spiritual world into confusion. We have never yet hit upon the thought that while we are overpowering the Orient from without, it may be fastening its hold upon us from within. Such an idea strikes us as almost insane, because we have eyes only for gross material connections, and fail to see that we must lay the blame for the intellectual confusion of our middle class at the doors of Max Müller, Oldenberg, Neumann, Deussen, Wilhelm and others like them. What does the example of the Roman Empire teach us? After the conquest of Asia Minor, Rome became Asiatic; even Europe was infected by Asia, and remains so today. Out of Cilicia came the Mithraic cult—the religion of the Roman army—and it spread from Egypt to fog-bound Britain. Need I point to the Asiatic origin of Christianity?

We have not yet clearly grasped the fact that Western Theosophy is an amateurish imitation of the East. We are just taking up astrology again, and that to the Oriental is his daily bread. Our studies of sexual life, originating in Vienna and in England, are matched or surpassed by Hindu teachings on this subject. Oriental texts ten centuries old introduce us to philosophical relativism, while the idea of indetermination, newly broached in the West, furnishes the very basis of Chinese science. Richard Wilhelm has even shown me that certain complicated processes discovered by analytical psychology are recognizably described in ancient Chinese texts. Psychoanalysis itself and the lines of thought to which it gives rise—surely a distinctly Western development—are only a beginner's attempt compared to what is an immemorial art in the East. It should be mentioned that the parallels between psychoanalysis and yoga have already been traced by Oskar A. H. Schmitz.

The Theosophists have an amusing idea that certain Mahatmas, seated somewhere in the Himalayas or Tibet, inspire or direct every mind in the world. So strong, in fact, can be the influence of the Eastern belief in magic upon Europeans of a sound mind, that some of them have assured me that I am unwittingly inspired by the Mahatmas with every good thing I say, my own inspirations being of no account whatever. This myth of the Mahatmas, widely circulated and firmly believed in the West, far from being nonsense, is—like every myth—an important psychological truth. It seems to be quite true that the East is at the bottom of the spiritual change we are passing through today. Only this East is not a Tibetan monastery full of Mahatmas, but in a sense lies within us. It is from the depths of our own psychic life that new spiritual forms will arise; they will be expressions of psychic forces which may help to subdue the boundless lust for prey of Aryan man. We shall perhaps come to know something of that circumscription of life which has grown in the East into a dubious quietism; also something of that stability which human existence acquires when the claims of the spirit become as imperative as the necessities of social life. Yet in this age of Americanization we are still far from anything of the sort, and it seems to me that we are only at the threshold of a new spiritual epoch. I do not wish to pass myself off as a prophet, but I cannot outline the spiritual problem of modern man without giving emphasis to the yearning for rest that arises in a period of unrest, or to the longing for security that is bred of insecurity. It is from need and distress that new forms of life take their rise, and not from mere wishes or from the requirements of our ideals.

To me, the crux of the spiritual problem of today is to be found in the fascination which psychic life exerts upon modern man. If we are pessimists, we shall call it a sign of decadence; if we are optimistically inclined, we shall see in it the promise of a far-reaching spiritual change in the Western world. At all events, it is a significant manifestation. It is the more noteworthy because it shows itself in broad sections of every people; and it is the more important because it is a matter of those imponderable psychic forces which transform human life in ways that are unforeseen and—as history shows—unforeseeable. These are the forces, still invisible to many persons today, which are at the bottom of the present "psychological" interest. When the attractive power of psychic life is so strong that man is neither repelled nor dismayed by what he is sure to find, then it has nothing of sickliness or perversion about it.

Along the great highroads of the world everything seems desolate and outworn. Instinctively the modern man leaves the trodden ways to explore the by-paths and lanes, just as the man of the Graeco-Roman world cast off his defunct Olympian gods and turned to the mystery-cults of Asia. The force within us that impels us to the search, turning outward, annexes Eastern Theosophy and magic; but it also turns inward and leads us to give our thoughtful attention to the unconscious psyche. It inspires in us the self-same scepticism and relentlessness with which a Buddha swept aside his two million gods that he might come to the pristine experience which alone is convincing.

And now we must ask a final question. Is what I have said of the modern man really true, or is it perhaps the result of an optical illusion? There can be no doubt whatever that the facts I have cited are wholly irrelevant contingencies in the eyes of many millions of Westerners, and seem only regrettable errors to a large number of educated persons. But I may ask: What did a cultivated Roman think of Christianity when he saw it spreading among the people of the lowest classes? The biblical God is still a living person in the Western world—as living as Allah beyond the Mediterranean. One kind of believer holds the other an ignoble heretic, to be pitied and tolerated if he cannot be changed. What is more, a clever European is convinced that religion and such things are good enough for the masses and for women, but are of little weight compared to economic and political affairs.

So I am refuted all along the line, like a man who predicts a thunderstorm when there is not a cloud in the sky. Perhaps it is a storm beneath the horizon that he senses—and it may never reach us. But what is significant in psychic life is always below the horizon of consciousness, and when we speak of the spiritual problem of modern man we are dealing with things that are barely visible—with the most intimate and fragile things—with bowers that open only in the night. In daylight everything is clear and tangible; but the night lasts as long as the day, and we live in the night-time also. There are persons who have bad dreams which even spoil their days for them. And the day's life is for many people such a bad dream that they long for the night when the spirit awakes. I even believe that there are nowadays a great many such people, and this is why I maintain that the spiritual problem of modern man is much as I have presented it. I must plead guilty, indeed, to the charge of one-sidedness, for I have not mentioned the modern spirit of commitment to a practical world about which everyone has much to say because it lies in such full view. We find it in the ideal of internationalism or supernationalism which is embodied in the League of Nations and the like; and we find it also in sport and, very expressively, in the cinema and in jazz music.

These are certainly characteristic symptoms of our time; they show unmistakably how the ideal of humanism is made to embrace the body also. Sport represents an exceptional valuation of the human body, as does also modern dancing. The cinema, on the other hand, like the detective story, makes it possible to experience without danger all the excitement, passion and desirousness which must be repressed in a humanitarian ordering of life. It is not difficult to see how these symptoms are connected with the psychic situation. The attractive power of the psyche brings about a new self-estimation—a re-estimation of the basic facts of human nature. We can hardly be surprised if this leads to the rediscovery of the body after its long depreciation in the name of the spirit. We are even tempted to speak of the body's revenge upon the spirit. When Keyserling sarcastically singles out the chauffeur as the culture-hero of our time, he has struck, as he often does, close to the mark. The body lays claim to equal recognition; like the psyche, it also exerts a fascination. If we are still caught by the old idea of an antithesis between mind and matter, the present state of affairs means an unbearable contradiction; it may even divide us against ourselves. But if we can reconcile ourselves with the mysterious truth that spirit is the living body seen from within, and the body the outer manifestation of the living spirit—the two being really one—then we can understand why it is that the attempt to transcend the present level of consciousness must give its due to the body. We shall also see that belief in the body cannot tolerate an outlook that denies the body in the name of the spirit. These claims of physical and psychic life are so pressing compared to similar claims in the past, that we may be tempted to see in this a sign of decadence. Yet it may also signify a rejuvenation, for as Hölderlin says:

> Danger itself
> Fosters the rescuing power.[2]

What we actually see is that the Western world strikes up a still more rapid tempo—the American tempo—the very opposite of quietism and resigned aloofness. An enormous tension arises between the opposite poles of outer and inner life, between objective and subjective reality. Perhaps it is a final race between ageing Europe and young America; perhaps it is a desperate or a wholesome effort of conscious man to cheat the laws of nature of their hidden might and to wrest a yet greater, more heroic

[2] *Wo Gefahr ist,*
Wächst das Rettende auch. (Hölderlin.)

victory from the sleep of the nations. This is a question which history will answer.

In coming to a close after so many bold assertions, I would like to return to the promise made at the outset to be mindful of the need for moderation and caution. Indeed, I do not forget that my voice is but one voice, my experience a mere drop in the sea, my knowledge no greater than the visual field in a microscope, my mind's eye a mirror that reflects a small corner of the world, and my ideas—a subjective confession.

Existentialism *

JEAN-PAUL SARTRE

I should like on this occasion to defend existentialism against some charges which have been brought against it.

First, it has been charged with inviting people to remain in a kind of desperate quietism because, since no solutions are possible, we should have to consider action in this world as quite impossible. We should then end up in a philosophy of contemplation; and since contemplation is a luxury, we come in the end to a bourgeois philosophy. The communists in particular have made these charges.

On the other hand, we have been charged with dwelling on human degradation, with pointing up everywhere the sordid, shady, and slimy, and neglecting the gracious and beautiful, the bright side of human nature; for example, according to Mlle. Mercier, a Catholic critic, with forgetting the smile of the child. Both sides charge us with having ignored human solidarity, with considering man as an isolated being. The communists say that the main reason for this is that we take pure subjectivity, the *Cartesian I think,* as our starting point; in other words, the moment in which man becomes fully aware of what it means to him to be an isolated being; as a result, we are unable to return to a state of solidarity with the men who are not ourselves, a state which we can never reach in the *cogito.*

From the Christian standpoint, we are charged with denying the reality and seriousness of human undertakings, since, if we reject God's commandments and the eternal verities, there no longer remains anything but pure caprice, with everyone permitted to do as he pleases and incapable, from his own point of view, of condemning the points of view and acts of others.

*Reprinted by permission of Philosophical Library, Inc. from *Existentialism and Human Emotions*, by Jean-Paul Sartre, pp. 9–35.

I shall try today to answer these different charges. Many people are going to be surprised at what is said here about humanism. We shall try to see in what sense it is to be understood. In any case, what can be said from the very beginning is that by existentialism we mean a doctrine which makes human life possible and, in addition, declares that every truth and every action implies a human setting and a human subjectivity.

As is generally known, the basic charge against us is that we put the emphasis on the dark side of human life. Someone recently told me of a lady who, when she let slip a vulgar word in a moment of irritation, excused herself by saying, "I guess I'm becoming an existentialist." Consequently, existentialism is regarded as something ugly; that is why we are said to be naturalists; and if we are, it is rather surprising that in this day and age we cause so much more alarm and scandal than does naturalism, properly so called. The kind of person who can take in his stride such a novel as Zola's *The Earth* is disgusted as soon as he starts reading an existentialist novel; the kind of person who is resigned to the wisdom of the ages—which is pretty sad—finds us even sadder. Yet, what can be more disillusioning than saying "true charity begins at home" or "a scoundrel will always return evil for good"?

We know the commonplace remarks made when this subject comes up, remarks which always add up to the same thing: we shouldn't struggle against the powers-that-be; we shouldn't resist authority; we shouldn't try to rise above our station; any action which doesn't conform to authority is romantic; any effort not based on past experience is doomed to failure; experience shows that man's bent is always toward trouble, that there must be a strong hand to hold him in check; if not, there will be anarchy. There are still people who go on mumbling these melancholy old saws, the people who say, "It's only human!" whenever a more or less repugnant act is pointed out to them, the people who glut themselves on *chansons realistes*; these are the people who accuse existentialism of being too gloomy, and to such an extent that I wonder whether they are complaining about it, not for its pessimism, but much rather its optimism. Can it be that what really scares them in the doctrine I shall try to present here is that it leaves to man a possibility of choice? To answer this question, we must re-examine it on a strictly philosophical plane. What is meant by the term *existentialism*?

Most people who use the word would be rather embarrassed if they had to explain it, since, now that the word is all the rage, even the work of a musician or painter is being called existentialist. A gossip columnist in *Clarté's* signs himself *The Existentialist,* so that by this time the word has been so stretched and has taken on so broad a meaning, that it no longer means anything at all. It seems that for want of an advance-guard doctrine analogous to surrealism, the kind of people who are eager for scandal and flurry turn to this philosophy which in other respects does not at all serve their purposes in this sphere.

Actually, it is the least scandalous, the most austere of doctrines. It is intended strictly for specialists and philosophers. Yet it can be defined easily. What complicates matters is that there are two kinds of existentialist: first, those who are Christian, among whom I would include Jaspers and Gabriel Marcel, both Catholic; and on the other hand the atheistic existentialists, among whom I class Heidegger, and then the French existentialists and myself. What they have in common is that they think that existence precedes essence, or, if you prefer, that subjectivity must be the starting point.

Just what does that mean? Let us consider some object that is manufactured, for example, a book or a paper-cutter: here is an object which has been made by an artisan whose inspiration came from a concept. He referred to the concept of what a paper-cutter is and likewise to a known method of production, which is part of the concept, something which is, by and large, a routine. Thus, the paper-cutter is at once an object produced in a certain way and, on the other hand, one having a specific use; and one can not postulate a man who produces a paper-cutter but does not know what it is used for. Therefore, let us say that, for the paper-cutter, essence—that is, the ensemble of both the production routines and the properties which enable it to be both produced and defined—precedes existence. Thus, the presence of the paper-cutter or book in front of me is determined. Therefore, we have here a technical view of the world whereby it can be said that production precedes existence.

When we conceive God as the Creator, He is generally thought of as a superior sort of artisan. Whatever doctrine we may be considering, whether one like that of Descartes or that of Leibnitz, we always grant that will more or less follows understanding or, at the very least, accompanies it, and that when God creates He knows exactly what He is creating. Thus, the concept of man in the mind of God is comparable to the concept of paper-cutter in the mind of the manufacturer, and, following certain techniques and a conception, God produces man, just as the artisan, following a definition and a technique, makes a paper-cutter. Thus, the individual man is the realization of a certain concept in the divine intelligence.

In the eighteenth century, the atheism of the *philosophes* discarded the idea of God, but not so much for the notion that essence precedes existence. To a certain extent, this idea is found everywhere; we find it in Diderot, in Voltaire, and even in Kant. Man has a human nature; this human nature, which is the concept of the human, is found in all men, which means that each man is a particular example of a universal concept, man. In Kant, the result of this universality is that the wild-man, the natural man, as well as the bourgeois, are circumscribed by the same definition and have the same basic qualities. Thus, here too the essence of man precedes the historical existence that we find in nature.

Atheistic existentialism, which I represent, is more coherent. It states that if God does not exist, there is at least one being in whom existence precedes essence, a being who exists before he can be defined by any concept, and that this being is man, or, as Heidegger says, human reality. What is meant here by saying that existence precedes essence? It means that, first of all, man exists, turns up, appears on the scene, and, only afterwards, defines himself. If man, as the existentialist conceives him, is indefinable, it is because at first he is nothing. Only afterward will he be something, and he himself will have made what he will be. Thus, there is no human nature, since there is no God to conceive it. Not only is man what he conceives himself to be, but he is also only what he wills himself to be after this thrust toward existence.

Man is nothing else but what he makes of himself. Such is the first principle of existentialism. It is also what is called subjectivity, the name we are labeled with when charges are brought against us. But what do we mean by this, if not that man has a greater dignity than a stone or table? For we mean that man first exists, that is, that man first of all is the being who hurls himself toward a future and who is conscious of imagining himself as being in the future. Man is at the start a plan which is aware of itself, rather than a patch of moss, a piece of garbage, or a cauliflower; nothing exists prior to this plan; there is nothing in heaven; man will be what he will have planned to be. Not what he will want to be. Because by the word "will" we generally mean a conscious decision, which is subsequent to what we have already made of ourselves. I may want to belong to a political party, write a book, get married; but all that is only a manifestation of an earlier, more spontaneous choice that is called "will." But if existence really does precede essence, man is responsible for what he is. Thus, existentialism's first move is to make every man aware of what he is and to make the full responsibility of his existence rest on him. And when we say that a man is responsible for himself, we do not only mean that he is responsible for his own individuality, but that he is responsible for all men.

The word subjectivism has two meanings, and our opponents play on the two. Subjectivism means, on the one hand, that an individual chooses and makes himself; and, on the other, that it is impossible for man to transcend human subjectivity. The second of these is the essential meaning of existentialism. When we say that man chooses his own self, we mean that every one of us does likewise; but we also mean by that that in making this choice he also chooses all men. In fact, in creating the man that we want to be, there is not a single one of our acts which does not at the same time create an image of man as we think he ought to be. To choose to be this or that is to affirm at the same time the value of what we choose, because we can never choose evil. We always choose the good, and nothing can be good for us without being good for all.

If, on the other hand, existence precedes essence, and if we grant that we exist and fashion our image at one and the same time, the image is valid for everybody and for our whole age. Thus, our responsibility is much greater than we might have supposed, because it involves all mankind. If I am a workingman and choose to join a Christian trade-union rather than be a communist, and if by being a member I want to show that the best thing for man is resignation, that the kingdom of man is not of this world, I am not only involving my own case—I want to be resigned for everyone. As a result, my action has involved all humanity. To take a more individual matter, if I want to marry, to have children; even if this marriage depends solely on my own circumstances or passion or wish, I am involving all humanity in monogamy and not merely myself. Therefore, I am responsible for myself and for everyone else. I am creating a certain image of man of my own choosing. In choosing myself, I choose man.

This helps us understand what the actual content is of such rather grandiloquent words as anguish, forlornness, despair. As you will see, it's all quite simple.

First, what is meant by anguish? The existentialists say at once that man is anguish. What that means is this: the man who involves himself and who realizes that he is not only the person he chooses to be, but also a lawmaker who is, at the same time, choosing all mankind as well as himself, can not help escape the feeling of his total and deep responsibility. Of course, there are many people who are not anxious; but we claim that they are hiding their anxiety, that they are fleeing from it. Certainly, many people believe that when they do something, they themselves are the only ones involved, and when someone says to them, "What if everyone acted that way?" they shrug their shoulders and answer, "Everyone doesn't act that way." But really, one should always ask himself, "What would happen if everybody looked at things that way?" There is no escaping this disturbing thought except by a kind of double-dealing. A man who lies and makes excuses for himself by saying "not everybody does that," is someone with an uneasy conscience, because the act of lying implies that a universal value is conferred upon the lie.

Anguish is evident even when it conceals itself. This is the anguish that Kierkegaard called the anguish of Abraham. You know the story: an angel has ordered Abraham to sacrifice his son; if it really were an angel who has come and said, "You are Abraham, you shall sacrifice your son," everything would be all right. But everyone might first wonder, "Is it really an angel, and am I really Abraham? What proof do I have?"

There was a madwoman who had hallucinations; someone used to speak to her on the telephone and give her orders. Her doctor asked her, "Who is it who talks to you?" She answered, "He says it's God." What proof did she really have that it was God? If an angel comes to me, what proof is there that it's an angel? And if I hear voices, what proof is there that they come from heaven and not from hell, or from the subconscious, or a pathological condition? What proves that they are addressed to me? What proof is there that I have been appointed to impose my choice and my conception of man on humanity? I'll never find any proof or sign to convince me of that. If a voice addresses me, it is always for me to decide that this is the angel's voice; if I consider that such an act is a good one, it is I who will choose to say that it is good rather than bad.

Now, I'm not being singled out as an Abraham, and yet at every moment I'm obliged to perform exemplary acts. For every man, everything happens as if all mankind had its eyes fixed on him and were guiding itself by what he does. And every man ought to say to himself, "Am I really the kind of man who has the right to act in such a way that humanity might guide itself by my actions?" And if he does not say that to himself, he is masking his anguish.

There is no question here of the kind of anguish which would lead to quietism, to inaction. It is a matter of a simple sort of anguish that anybody who has had responsibilities is familiar with. For example, when a military officer takes the responsibility for an attack and sends a certain number of men to death, he chooses to do so, and in the main he alone makes the choice. Doubtless, orders come from above, but they are too broad; he interprets them, and on this interpretation depend the lives of ten or fourteen or twenty men. In making a decision he can not help having a certain anguish. All leaders know this anguish. That doesn't keep them from acting; on the contrary, it is the very condition of their action. For it implies that they envisage a number of possibilities, and when they choose one, they realize that it has value only because it is chosen. We shall see that this kind of anguish, which is the kind that existentialism describes, is explained, in addition, by a direct responsibility to the other men whom it involves. It is not a curtain separating us from action, but is part of action itself.

When we speak of forlornness, a term Heidegger was fond of, we mean only that God does not exist and that we have to face all the consequences of this. The existentialist is strongly opposed to a certain kind of secular ethics which would like to abolish God with the least possible expense. About 1880, some French teachers tried to set up a secular ethics which went something like this: God is a useless and costly hypothesis; we are discarding it; but, meanwhile, in order for there to be an ethics, a society, a civilization, it is essential that certain values be taken seriously and that they be considered as having an *a priori* existence. It must be obligatory, *a priori,* to be honest, not to lie, not to beat your wife, to have children, etc., etc. So we're going to try a little device which will make it possible to show that values exist all the same, inscribed in a heaven of ideas, though otherwise God does not exist. In other words—and this, I believe, is the tendency of everything called reformism in France—nothing will be changed if God does not exist. We shall find ourselves with the same norms of honesty, progress, and humanism, and we shall have made of God an outdated hypothesis which will peacefully die off by itself.

The existentialist, on the contrary, thinks it very distressing that God does not exist, because all possibility of finding values in a heaven of ideas disappears along with Him; there can no longer be an *a priori* Good, since there is no infinite and perfect consciousness to think it. Nowhere is it written that the Good exists, that we must be honest, that we must not lie; because the fact is we are on a plane where there are only men. Dostoievsky said, "If God didn't exist, everything would be possible." That is the very starting point of existentialism. Indeed, everything is permissible if God does not exist, and as a result man is forlorn, because neither within him nor without does he find anything to cling to. He can't start making excuses for himself.

If existence really does precede essence, there is no explaining things away by reference to a fixed and given human nature. In other words, there is no determinism, man is free, man is freedom. On the other hand, if God does not exist, we find no values or commands to turn to which legitimize our conduct. So, in the bright realm of values, we have no excuse behind us, nor justification before us. We are alone, with no excuses.

That is the idea I shall try to convey when I say that man is condemned to be free. Condemned, because he did not create himself, yet, in other respects is free; because, once thrown into the world, he is responsible for everything he does. The existentialist does not believe in the power of passion. He will never agree that a sweeping passion is a ravaging torrent which fatally leads a man to certain acts and is therefore an excuse. He thinks that man is responsible for his passion.

The existentialist does not think that man is going to help himself by finding in the world some omen by which to orient himself. Because he thinks that man will interpret the omen to suit himself. Therefore, he thinks that man, with no support and no aid, is condemned every moment to invent man. Ponge, in a very fine article, has said, "Man is the future of man." That's exactly it. But if it is taken to mean that this future is recorded in heaven, that God sees it, then it is false, because it would really no longer be a future. If it is taken to mean that, whatever a man may be, there is a future to be forged, a virgin future before him, then this remark is sound. But then we are forlorn.

To give you an example which will enable you to understand forlornness better, I shall cite the case of one of my students who came to see me under the following circumstances: his father was on bad terms with his mother, and, moreover, was inclined to be a collaborationist; his older brother had been killed in the German offensive of 1940, and the young man, with somewhat immature but generous feelings, wanted to avenge him. His mother lived alone with him, very much upset by the half-treason of her husband and the death of her older son; the boy was her only consolation.

The boy was faced with the choice of leaving for England and joining the Free French Forces—that is, leaving his mother behind—or remaining with his mother and helping her to carry on. He was fully aware that the woman lived only for him and that his going-off—and perhaps his death—would plunge her into despair. He was also aware that every act that he did for his mother's sake was a sure thing, in the sense that it was helping her to carry on, whereas every effort he made toward going off and fighting was an uncertain move which might run aground and prove completely useless; for example, on his way to England he might, while passing through Spain, be detained indefinitely in a Spanish camp; he might reach England or Algiers and be stuck in an office at a desk job. As a result, he was faced with two very different kinds of action: one, concrete, immediate, but concerning only one individual; the other concerned an incomparably vaster group, a national collectivity, but for that very reason was dubious, and might be interrupted en route. And, at the same time, he was wavering between two kinds of ethics. On the one hand, an ethics of sympathy, of personal devotion; on the other, a broader ethics, but one whose efficacy was more dubious. He had to choose between the two.

Who could help him choose? Christian doctrine? No. Christian doctrine says, "Be charitable, love your neighbor, take the more rugged path, etc., etc." But which is the more rugged path? Whom should he love as a brother? The fighting man or his mother? Which does the greater good, the vague act of fighting in a group, or the concrete one of helping a particular human being to go on living? Who can decide *a priori?* Nobody. No book of ethics can tell him. The Kantian ethics says, "Never treat any person as a means, but as an end." Very well, if I stay with my mother, I'll treat her as an end and not as a means; but by virtue of this very fact, I'm running the risk of treating the people around me who are fighting, as means; and, conversely, if I go to join those who are fighting, I'll be treating them as an end, and, by doing that, I run the risk of treating my mother as a means.

If values are vague, and if they are always too broad for the concrete and specific case that we are considering, the only thing left for us is to trust our instincts. That's what this young man tried to do; and when I saw him, he said, "In the end, feeling is what counts. I ought to choose whichever pushes me in one direction. If I feel that I love my mother enough to sacrifice everything else for her—my desire for vengeance, for action, for adventure—then I'll stay with her. If, on the contrary, I feel that my love for my mother isn't enough, I'll leave."

But how is the value of a feeling determined? What gives his feeling for his mother value? Precisely the fact that he remained with her. I may say that I like so-and-so well enough to sacrifice a certain amount of money for him, but I may say so only if I've done it. I may say "I love my mother well enough to remain with her" if I have remained with her. The only way to determine the value of this affection is, precisely, to perform an act which confirms and defines it. But, since I require this affection to justify my act, I find myself caught in a vicious circle.

On the other hand, Gide has well said that a mock feeling and a true feeling are almost indistinguishable; to decide that I love my mother and will remain with her, or to remain with her by putting on an act, amount somewhat to the same thing. In other words, the feeling is formed by the acts one performs; so, I can not refer to it in order to act upon it. Which means that I can neither seek within myself the true condition which will impel me to act, nor apply to a system of ethics for concepts which will permit me to act. You will say, "At least, he did go to a teacher for advice." But if you seek advice from a priest, for example, you have chosen this priest; you already knew, more or less, just about what advice he was going to give you. In other words, choosing your adviser is involving yourself. The proof of this is that if you are a Christian, you will say, "Consult a priest." But some priests are collaborating, some are just marking time, some are resisting. Which to choose? If the young man chooses a priest who is resisting or collaborating, he has already decided on the kind of advice he's going to get. Therefore, in coming to see me he knew the answer I was going to give him, and I had only one answer to give: "You're free, choose, that is, invent." No general ethics can show you what is to be done; there are no omens in the world. The Catholics will reply, "But there are." Granted—but, in any case, I myself choose the meaning they have.

When I was a prisoner, I knew a rather remarkable young man who was a Jesuit. He had entered the Jesuit order in the following way: he had had a number of very bad breaks; in childhood, his father died, leaving him in poverty, and he was a scholarship student at a religious institution where he was constantly made to feel that he was being kept out of charity; then, he failed to get any of the honors and distinctions that children like; later on, at about eighteen, he bungled a love affair; finally, at twenty-two, he failed in military training, a childish enough matter, but it was the last straw.

This young fellow might well have felt that he had botched everything. It was a sign of something, but of what? He might have taken refuge in bitterness or despair. But he very wisely looked upon all this as a sign that he was not made for secular triumphs, and that only the triumphs of religion, holiness, and faith were open to him. He saw the hand of God in all this, and so he entered the order. Who can help seeing that he alone decided what the sign meant?

Some other interpretation might have been drawn from this series of setbacks; for example, that he might have done better to turn carpenter or revolutionist. Therefore, he is fully responsible for the interpretation. Forlornness implies that we ourselves choose our being. Forlornness and anguish go together.

As for despair, the term has a very simple meaning. It means that we shall confine ourselves to reckoning only with what depends upon our will, or on the ensemble of probabilities which make our action possible. When we want something, we always have to reckon with probabilities. I may be counting on the arrival of a friend. The friend is coming by rail or street-car; this supposes that the train will arrive on schedule, or that the street-car will not jump the track. I am left in the realm of possibility; but possibilities are to be reckoned with only to the point where my action comports with the ensemble of these possibilities, and no further. The moment the possibilities I am considering are not rigorously involved by my action, I ought to disengage myself from them, because no God, no scheme, can adapt the world and its possibilities to my will. When Descartes said, "Conquer yourself rather than the world," he meant essentially the same thing.

The Marxists to whom I have spoken reply, "You can rely on the support of others in your action, which obviously has certain limits because you're not going to live forever. That means: rely on both what others are doing elsewhere to help you, in China, in Russia, and what they will do later on, after your death, to carry on the action and lead it to its fulfillment, which will be the revolution. You even *have* to rely upon that, otherwise you're immoral." I reply at once that I will always rely on fellow-fighters insofar as these comrades are involved with me in a common struggle, in the unity of a party or a group in which I can more or less make my weight felt; that is, one whose ranks I am in as a fighter and whose movements I am aware of at every moment. In such a situation, relying on the unity and will of the party is exactly like counting on the fact that the train will arrive on time or that the car won't jump the track. But, given that man is free and that there is no human nature for me to depend on, I can not count on men whom I do not know by relying on human goodness or man's concern for the good of society. I don't know what will become of the Russian revolution; I may make an example of it to the extent that at the present time it is apparent that the proletariat plays a part in Russia that it plays in no other nation. But I can't swear that this will inevitably lead to a triumph of the proletariat. I've got to limit myself to what I see.

Given that men are free and that tomorrow they will freely decide what man will be, I can not be sure that, after my death, fellow-fighters will carry on my work to bring it to its maximum perfection. Tomorrow, after my death, some men may decide to set up Fascism, and the others may be cowardly and muddled enough to let them do it. Fascism will then be the human reality, so much the worse for us.

Actually, things will be as man will have decided they are to be. Does that mean that I should abandon myself to quietism? No. First, I should involve myself; then, act on the old saw, "Nothing ventured, nothing gained." Nor does it mean that I shouldn't belong to a party, but rather that I shall have no illusions and shall do what I can. For example, suppose I ask myself, "Will socialization, as such, ever come about?" I know nothing about it. All I know is that I'm going to do everything in my power to bring it about. Beyond that, I can't count on anything. Quietism is the attitude of people who say, "Let others do what I can't do." The doctrine I am presenting is the very opposite of quietism, since it declares, "There is no reality except in action." Moreover, it goes further, since it adds, "Man is nothing else than his plan; he exists only to the extent that he fulfills himself; he is therefore nothing else than the ensemble of his acts, nothing else than his life."

According to this, we can understand why our doctrine horrifies certain people. Because often the only way they can bear their wretchedness is to think, "Circumstances have been against me. What I've been and done doesn't show my true worth. To be sure, I've had no great love, no great friendship, but that's because I haven't met a man or woman who was worthy. The books I've written haven't been very good because I haven't had the proper leisure. I haven't had children to devote myself to because I didn't find a man with whom I could have spent my life. So there remains within me, unused and quite viable, a host of propensities, inclinations, possibilities, that one wouldn't guess from the mere series of things I've done."

Now, for the existentialist there is really no love other than one which manifests itself in a person's being in love. There is no genius other than one which is expressed in works of art; the genius of Proust is the sum of Proust's works; the genius of Racine is his series of tragedies. Outside of that, there is nothing. Why say that Racine could have written another tragedy, when he didn't write it? A man is involved in life, leaves his impress on it, and outside of that there is nothing. To be sure, this may seem a harsh thought to someone whose life hasn't been a success. But, on the other hand, it prompts people to understand that reality alone is what counts, that dreams, expectations, and hopes warrant no more than to define a man as a disappointed dream, as miscarried hopes, as vain expectations. In other words, to define him negatively and not positively. However, when we say, "You are nothing else than your life," that does not imply that the artist will be judged solely on the basis of his works of art; a thousand other things will contribute toward summing him up. What we mean is that a man is nothing else than a series of undertakings, that he is the sum, the organization, the ensemble of the relationships which make up these undertakings.

When all is said and done, what we are accused of, at bottom, is not our pessimism, but an optimistic toughness. If people throw up to us our works of fiction in which we write about people who are soft, weak, cowardly, and sometimes even downright bad, it's not because these people are soft, weak, cowardly, or bad; because if we were to say, as Zola did, that they are that way because of heredity, the workings of environment, society, because of biological or psychological determinism, people would be reassured. They would say, "Well, that's what we're like, no one can do anything about it." But when the existentialist writes about a coward, he says that this coward is responsible for his cowardice. He's not like that because he has a cowardly heart or lung or brain; he's not like that on account of his physiological make-up; but he's like that because he has made himself a coward by his acts. There's no such thing as a cowardly constitution; there are nervous constitutions; there is poor blood, as the common people say, or strong constitutions. But the man whose blood is poor is not a coward on that account, for what makes cowardice is the act of renouncing or yielding. A constitution is not an act; the coward is defined on the basis of the acts he performs. People feel, in a vague sort of way, that this coward we're talking about is guilty of being a coward, and the thought frightens them. What people would like is that a coward or a hero be born that way.

One of the complaints most frequently made about *The Ways of Freedom* can be summed up as follows: "After all, these people are so spineless, how are you going to make heroes out of them?" This objection almost makes me laugh, for it assumes that people are born heroes. That's what people really want to think. If you're born cowardly, you may set your mind perfectly at rest; there's nothing you can do about it; you'll be cowardly all your life, whatever you may do. If you're born a hero, you may set your mind just as much at rest; you'll be a hero all your life; you'll drink like a hero and eat like a hero. What the existentialist says is that the coward makes himself cowardly, that the hero makes himself heroic. There's always a possibility for the coward not to be cowardly any more and for the hero to stop being heroic. What counts is total involvement; some one particular action or set of circumstances is not total involvement.

Knowledge Explosion

The Knowledge Revolution*
DANIEL BELL

In describing the broad social changes that have been refashioning the United States, one axis of change . . . which has great implications for all modern industrial societies, is the new impact of "knowledge"—its organization through systematic research guided by theory, and its mass dissemination through schools, publishing houses, and mass media.

Where it concerns the educational system, the nature of this "knowledge revolution" can be explored from four angles: the "exponential growth" of knowledge, the "branching" of new fields of knowledge, the rise of a new intellectual technology, and the rapid expansion of research and development as an organized activity of government.

The "exponential growth" of knowledge is now a prosaic idea. Derek Price, who popularized it, has estimated (in *Science Since Babylon*) that the total research effort in Great Britain since the time of Newton has doubled every ten to fifteen years (or about three times during the working life of a scientist). A major indicator of this expansion has been the scientific journal. The learned paper and the scientific journal were innovations of the scientific revolution in the late seventeenth century. It allowed for the relatively rapid communication of new ideas to a growing circle of men interested in science. From the first few journals, beginning

*Reprinted by permission of Columbia University Press from Daniel Bell, *The Reforming of General Education* (New York: Columbia University Press, 1966), pp. 73–87.

with the *Transactions of the Royal Society of London* in 1665, the number grew until by the beginning of the nineteenth century there were a hundred, by the middle of the nineteenth century a thousand, and by 1900 some ten thousand such journals.

Since 1750, when there were about ten scientific journals in the world, the number has increased by a factor of ten every half-century. By 1830, when about three hundred journals were being published in the world, it became obvious that the cultivated man of science could no longer keep abreast of new knowledge, and a new device—the abstract journal— appeared. It summarized each article in many journals, and the interested individual could then decide what to read in full. But as Price points out, even the number of abstract journals increased, following the same logistic curve, by a factor of ten in every century. Thus by 1950 the number of abstract journals had attained a critical magnitude of about three hundred. Moreover, each abstract journal itself has sizably increased. A journal devoted to publishing the abstracts of new papers in the chemical sciences now runs to some 13,000 pages annually, exclusive of indexes and cross-references; ten years ago it was only half this size.

The output of sheer words today is staggering. In 1964, nearly 320,000 separate book titles—nearly 1,000 works every day—were published throughout the world. Columbia University's new acquisitions, for example, take up two miles of bookshelves a year. In a single field, medicine, it is estimated that some 200,000 journal articles and 10,000 monographs are published annually, while in the physical and life sciences the number of books add up to about 60,000 annually, the number of research reports to about 100,000, and the number of articles in scientific and technical journals to about 1.2 million each year. Consider what will happen when writers, scholars, scientists, and professionals in the new states begin to produce in great number in these fields!

But it is not the prodigious accumulation alone that is creating a distinctive change in the structure of intellectual life. It is the fact that new discoveries bring their own differentiation, or "branching," so that as a field expands subdivision and subspecialties multiply within each field. Contrary to the nineteenth-century notion of science as a bounded or exhaustible field of knowledge whose full dimensions can ultimately be explored, each advance opens up, in its own way, new fields that in turn sprout their own branches.

To give an example: the field of shock waves, initiated in 1848 by the British mathematician and physicist G. G. Stokes and the astronomer J. Challis (who set up theoretical equations of motion in gases), led not only to significant contributions in mathematics and physics along this general line (by Mach, Bethe, and von Neumann, among others) but to the branching off of shock tube, aerodynamics, detonations, and magnetohydrodynamics as four distinct fields. Or, Nobel Laureate I. I. Rabi's success at Columbia, in 1929, in sending molecular beams through a magnetic field—a breakthrough in pure physics—gave rise to branching in several different directions: optics, solid state masers, atomic structures, and half a dozen other fields.

Sometimes a stasis is reached, and then a field spurts ahead. In 1895, Roentgen seemed to have exhausted all the major aspects of X rays, but in 1912 the discovery of X-ray diffraction in crystals by von Laue, Friedrich, and Knipping transformed two separate fields—X ray and crystallography. Similarly, the discovery in 1934 of artificial radioactivity by the Joliot-Curies created a qualitative change that gave rise at one branching point to the work of Hahn and Strassman, which Lise Meitner correctly interpreted as the splitting of the uranium atom, and to Fermi's work on the increased radioactivity of metals bombarded with "slow" neutrons—which led directly to controlled atomic fission and the bomb.[1]

One can see this extraordinary proliferation of fields in the specializations listed in the National Register of Scientific and Technical Personnel, a government-sponsored inventory of all competent persons engaged in scientific work.[2] The Register classifies over 900 distinct scientific and technical specializations (outside the social sciences and humanities), compared with 54 listed twenty years ago. Thus physics is broken down into 10 basic divisions—acoustics, atomic and molecular, electromagnetic waves and electron, mechanics, nuclear, optics, physics of fluids, solid state, theoretical, and thermal phenomena—and each of these has subspecialties, making a total of 81 distinct specializations in physics alone. The life sciences are divided into 17 fields (e.g., anatomy, pharmacology, nutrition and metabolism, genetics, phytopathology) and each of these contains at least 10 or more subdivisions. In the newer interdisciplinary subjects, biophysics has 18 subspecialties, biochemistry 17, physical chemistry 26, geochemistry 7, oceanography 13, and hydrology and hydrography 12, while computer technology already has 7 subspecialties and the "mathematics of resource use" (operations research, information theory, and the like) has 13.

---

[1] I have drawn these examples largely from Gerald Holton's "Scientific Research and Scholarship: Notes toward the Design of Proper Scales," *Daedalus* (Spring 1962), pp. 362–99.

[2] The National Register is a cooperative undertaking of the National Science Foundation and nine professional scientific societies which in turn work with about 200 specialized societies to produce full listings. Scientists are considered eligible for registration if they have attained the Ph.D. or an equivalent degree in a field of science, or have similar qualifications gained in professional experience. A review of the nation's scientific personnel in 1960 brought forth a listing of some 237,000 persons. See the National Science Foundation's *Scientific Manpower Bulletin*, No. 12, 1960; and the descriptive brochure on the National Register, NSF publication 61–46.

To the proliferation and branching of knowledge one can add the creation in recent years of what might be called a new "intellectual technology": the development of game theory, decision theory, simulation, linear programing, cybernetics, and operations research, many of which are tooled, as it were, by the computer. What makes the burgeoning of these fields significant is the effort, through novel intellectual techniques, to provide new and comprehensive theories of "rational choice" and to transform the social sciences in an unprecedented way.

Paradoxically, though this new intellectual revolution seeks "perfect" information, it starts out in vast linguistic disorder. Any eruptive change makes for great confusion, the more so in the new intellectual technology, since its innovators and practitioners are a motley pack of mathematicians, physicists, engineers (of all varieties), statisticians, biologists, neurophysiologists, economists, management consultants, sociologists, and each man brings to the new field his own perspectives, terminology, and concepts.

Thus, operations research, linear programing, systems analysis, and decision theory often overlap in technique and subject matter, yet, depending upon the occupational origins of the practitioner, one or another label will be used insistently to designate a distinctive approach. Information theory, for some writers, is a technical set of propositions, enunciated originally by the electrical engineer Claude Shannon, on switching circuits and channel capacity; for others it is a general field covering all problems of interaction, and it is then called "communication theory." Cybernetics is regarded by some writers as the design of self-regulating control mechanisms (such as the automatic pilot on an airplane, which adjusts speed and direction in response to wind variation in order to stay on a plotted course); others call it the new "queen of science," embracing all self-regulating behavior from mechanical devices to biological organisms.

Whatever the final clarification of terminology will be, it is clear that the computer and these new techniques open up vast new possibilities for the social sciences. It is an equal corollary that all future work in the social sciences will require a high degree of mathematical training and sophistication. One area is the refinement of knowledge—the handling of many variables. Warren Weaver once said that an effective social science was almost impossible because as a mathematician he could handle a three-variable problem or, through statistical probability, a hundred-variable problem, but that most of the interesting questions in the social sciences fell between three and a hundred. Thus, in charting voting behavior one could say that the relevant determinants are age, sex, religion, occupation, education, and a dozen other variables; but it has been difficult to hold more than a few factors constant in order to see which combination of determinants was decisive in a voter's choice. With the computer, however, a matrix can be set up to handle a dozen or more variables.

One can go even further. With the computer, complex situations can be simulated, which might make possible "controlled" experiments in the social sciences. By "varying" the situations and introducing different "independent variables" one can see what new alignments and combinations of decisions might be made by groups in a simulated environment.

Simulation has been applied to a large variety of economic and sociological problems, such as simulating an entire economy, charting demographic changes, or predicting changes of attitudes in response to changed social environments. Professor Richard Stone, of Cambridge University, has created a simulation model of the British economy, and is thus in a position to state what changes in different sectors of the British economy are required to achieve different economic growth rates. A bold effort to simulate social environments through a computer program, and thus carry out a "controlled experiment" in the social sciences, has been made by James Coleman at Johns Hopkins. In his book *The Adolescent Society,* Coleman showed how students deliberately "choose" to stress popularity or scholastic achievement at the unspoken behest of the cliques they belong to, or by identifying with a teacher. To see how these students would alter their behavior, Coleman subsequently worked out a computer model in which the degree of identification of the adolescent with his clique (as expressed in the actual sociometric tests) was tested by varying the rewards from parents, teachers, or peer group influencing the adolescent. (Technically, Coleman established different "gambles" for the individual's "preference scales.") In this fashion he sought to specify, for example, at what exact points a student might be willing to sacrifice scholastic achievement for social popularity, and vice versa. While an experiment of this sort would normally be made with a small number of students, using only a few variables, Coleman was able, by creating "fictional" students (though using actual preference scales), to chart the different choices of thousands of "students" as they responded to a half-dozen or so different variables, in numerous manipulated environments.

In the field of economics, various aspects of "decision theory" and "game theory" have already changed its dimensions. Linear programing, primarily an "ordering" technique to achieve optimal solutions where many alternative combinations confront a decision maker, is already widely used in business.[3] Statistical decision theory, as pioneered by the

[3]These are used principally in so-called "queuing" problems, such as the question, in a factory, whether to handle orders on a first-come first-served basis, or wait until different combinations of order will be built up; or the question of how to plot the best routes and combinations in the shipping of bulk commodities from a wide variety of sources to a large number of different destinations, etc.

late Abraham Wald of Columbia University, sets forth strategies in "games against nature"—i.e., in situations partly subject to chance and only partly controlled by the individual. With these techniques one can minimize risks and reduce uncertainty. And in the theory of games, initiated by the late John von Neumann, a revolution has begun in the definition of economics itself. An economic problem, as it is classically defined in general equilibrium theory, is one in which individuals and firms try to achieve "maximum" or optimal results. But the outcome of a man's actions depends not only on himself but on the actions of others as well. If two competitors follow a pure "maximizing" strategy it would lead, in the extreme, to a total victory or total defeat—the so-called zero-sum game. Von Newmann's theory of games, as Oskar Morgenstern has argued, signified a clear break in the development of economic thought, since under the conditions of competition or conflict the bent of "rational behavior" is to follow a so-called minimax strategy, which seeks to minimize losses, rather than the economic principle of seeking to maximize gains. "The structure of this theory," Morgenstern writes, "is, consequently, quite different from the current neo-classical one of general economic equilibrium. Lacking a new specific calculus, one has to fall back essentially on the fundamental, combinatorial elements of mathematical reasoning. Eventually, a new calculus may have to be invented or discovered, as specifically suited to economic-social problems as the differential calculus was to classical mechanics."[4]

If decision theory attempts to specify the best choices for a given premise, systems theory seeks to spell out the unified consequences of any choice for all the units in the system. The word "system" by now has the widest and most varied use of all the terms in the new intellectual vocabulary. It is used by engineers to denote complex devices like computing machines. ("Systems engineer" initially meant someone who can design or work on computers.) Military technologists talk about weapons systems, sociologists about kinship or social systems, and economists, of course, about the economic system. But despite this great diversity, the foundation for a common conceptual framework in what Norbert Wiener has called "organized complexity" does exist.

Now, the idea of a system is an obvious one. The human body is a system operating in homeostasis. The American economy, while not an "organism," is so interrelated that changes in a key variable (e.g., investment) will cause determinate changes in other variables (employment, consumption, etc.). Yet in most areas of our lives we do not think in "system" terms. In a city, for example, there will be considerable discus-

[4]Oskar Morgenstern, "Limits to the Use of Mathematics in Economics," in *Mathematics and the Social Sciences*, edited by James C. Charlesworth, a symposium sponsored by the American Academy of Political and Social Science (Philadelphia, June, 1963).

sion of the traffic problem, with only the dimmest realization that changes in traffic patterns will have important effects on industry locations, residential densities, and the like—one instance of how rarely we try to scrutinize a problem as a whole.

The Air Force has in the last ten years, for example, had the chastening experience of learning to think not about the production of bombers but about "weapons systems," and the difference is much more than a simple matter of terminology. In deciding what kinds of planes to produce, for example, the Air Force had to take into account such questions as target distances, cruise and dash speeds, bomb loads and yields, alternative ground bases or air refueling, enemy defense performance, enemy offense capabilities, and feasible production schedules; under each of these development variables there were four alternatives, each of which would have affected other aspects of the weapon—the length of landing strips, the size of crews, and so on. Designing a bomber therefore meant having a sense of the entire system in which the weapon was involved.[5]

In a similar way, one can think of transportation along the Eastern seaboard, from Boston to Washington, in "system" terms: instead of saving a dying railroad line or building more high-speed roads because more people have cars, the "system" approach calculates how many persons want to travel and how much freight has to be moved over what varying distances, and what combinations of rail, truck, bus, and air vehicles will best serve such diverse needs.

In short, behind all this is an ambitious revolution in conceptual thought. To put it most generally, we tend to think of *entities* but not of *relations, items* but not *contexts; dualities* rather than a *field.* Most of our vocabulary is rich in dualisms like "man and environment," "history and nature," "mind and body," "man and spirit," but we lack *process* terms, which see these relationships as interacting and interpenetrative. When we look at a problem in dualistic terms, we get questions like "How far does environment influence man?" or "How far does man modify his environment?" (the usual answer is "to some extent"), rather than an attempt to examine the question in the unified way of the ecologist—as a biotic community, or as a single analytical system that emphasizes interdependencies and patterned interchanges. By emphasizing relation of events (and not just classes of events), one goes beyond "classical" social analysis, just as modern logic has gone beyond its Aristotelian foundations.

The final item in this catalogue of the changing importance of "knowledge" is the recent emphasis on research and development. A simple set of figures makes this clear: in 1940, $377 million was spent by govern-

[5] I take my example from the study by Albert J. Wohlstetter for The RAND Corporation, Document P-1530 (October 1958).

ment, business, and the universities on research and development; by 1960 the total had risen to $14 billion; by 1964 the sum was well over $18 billion.

One can, however, overstate the magnitude of the change. The phrase "research and development" hides many ambiguities, and the customary division into basic research, applied research, and development does not always give a picture of the distribution of money or the value of work done. Thus, the complexity of modern weaponry accounts for much of the stupendous rise in "development" expenditures; and development costs make up more than two-thirds of the total of all research-and-development moneys. A change in accounting methods has also given a new look to what already existed. Thus changes made in 1960 in the budgetary procedures of the Defense Department, the single biggest source of research-and-development funds, greatly expanded the number of things classified under research and development. And in considering simple dollar figures, one has to remember the price inflation from 1940 to the present. Taking all these points into account, David Novick, an economist of the RAND Corporation, has stated that the estimated growth in research-and-development funds, in dollar terms, a sixty-fold increase from 1930 to 1958, in real terms should be deflated by half. Even so, the sums are impressive. And so is the number of persons now engaged in research and development. In 1940, about 37,000 persons were engaged in research and development; by 1960, the number had risen to 387,000, a growth rate of more than 10 percent a year.

In the expansion of research and development, a number of new social trends are evident. Before World War II, most of the research in the United States was underwritten by private industry, but today the basic source of funds is the American government. Given the increasing cost of research—a single experiment by Leon Lederman and Melvin Schwartz, a Columbia University team, which confirmed the existence of the neutrino, cost a million dollars—only the government would undertake such expenditures. Another crucial point is that while most of the research-and-development money goes into defense, a substantial sum—more than a billion and a half dollars a year for basic research alone—is being spent by the universities, under government contract. This financial fact is transforming the character of the universities as well.

The far-reaching consequences of these social changes are clear: society is becoming "future-oriented," and it is becoming more planned. Planning, in this instance, does not mean the centralized direction of the economy from a single source; it is doubtful whether such centralization is even possible in a complex economy. But in simpler and more differentiated ways, planning has already taken hold and will do so increasingly—among individuals planning for careers, corporations and organizations planning future growth and changes, and in a government that tries to anticipate new social needs and to identify future problems.

In step with all this is the growing need for professional and technical skills—and for the expansion of education facilities that train individuals in these skills. The professional and technical employees—the most highly educated of all workers—are, in fact, the fastest-growing occupational group in the United States (Table 1). In 1950, almost 5 million persons were employed as professionals and technicians. By 1960, the number rose 50 percent to 7.5 million. And by 1975 they will number 12.3 million, an increase of almost 65 percent.

These projections, given in absolute figures, mask some important changes. If we examine these figures for *relative proportions* (Table 2), some interesting perspectives emerge. For one, the semiskilled group, which from 1900 to 1960 went from 12.8 to 18.6 percent to become the largest

TABLE 1. *Employment by Occupational Groups: 1960 (actual) and 1975 (projected)*

	1960	1975	Percent Change, 1960–1975
Total	66,700,000	88,600,000	33 percent
Professional and technical	7,500,000	12,300,000	64
Managers and proprietors	7,100,000	9,600,000	35
Clerical	9,800,000	13,700,000	40
Sales	4,400,000	6,100,000	39
Craftsmen and foremen	8,600,000	11,900,000	38
Operatives (semiskilled)	12,000,000	15,500,000	29
Service workers	8,300,000	11,300,000	36
Laborers	3,700,000	3,800,000	3
Farmers and farm laborers	5,400,000	4,400,000	−18

TABLE 2. *Occupational Distribution of Labor Force as Percent of Total*

	1960	1975
Total	100 percent	100 percent
Professional and technical	10.8	13.8
Managers and proprietors	10.2	10.8
Clerical	14.5	15.2
Sales	6.5	6.8
Craftsmen and foremen	12.9	13.4
Operatives (semiskilled)	18.6	17.5
Service workers	12.6	12.7
Laborers	6.0	4.2
Farmers and farm laborers	7.9	4.9

single group in the labor force, will begin a relative decline. The proportion of laborers will show a sharp decline. Almost all other groups will
about hold their own or gain slightly, but as a proportion of the whole the
professional and technical groups will show an appreciably sharp rise.

It is the professional and technical class, therefore, which becomes the
base line for future needs—and educational demands—of the society, and
the bulk of these are in the scientific, teaching, and health fields (Table 3).

Given the direction of the economy and the weight of government
policy, it is quite clear that in the coming decades the demand for
professional and technical personnel will place a considerable burden on
the educational system. Take, as one example, the need for scientists and
engineers: while the rise of all professional employments will by 1975 be
almost *double* the average increase of the labor force, the demand for
scientists and engineers, as projected, is almost *triple* this average increase. It is estimated that by 1975 we may need as many as 650,000
scientists in the United States, or almost twice as many as in 1960; and
over the same period perhaps as many as 2 million engineers, compared
to the 850,000 in 1960.

And yet, startling as these projections may be, it is quite likely that by
1975—and perhaps by the year 2000—the need for scientists and engi-

TABLE 3.   *The Make-Up of Professional and Technical Occupations,* 1960

	Persons
Total	7,500,000
Scientific and technical	*1,860,000*
Engineers	850,000
Technicians and draftsmen	675,000
Scientists	335,000
Teaching	*1,775,000*
Elementary school	1,000,000
Secondary school	600,000
College and graduate	175,000
Health	*1,629,000*
Nurses	504,000
Physicians	235,000
Pharmacists	117,000
Dentists	97,000
Health technicians	330,000
Others	350,000
General	*2,160,000*
Accountants	400,000
Clergymen	250,000
Lawyers	230,000
Musicians and music teachers	175,000
Editors, writers, social workers, designers, etc.	1,000,000

neers can be fancifully looked at in another way. Harrison Brown has sought to demonstrate this by plotting the changing ratio of scientists and engineers to the total population. At the beginning of the century there was one scientist-engineer to about 1,800 persons in the United States. By 1960, the ratio was 1 to 200. (In India, there is one engineer or scientist to every 30,000 persons!) If one extrapolates these trends, by 1980 the ratio would be 1 to every 90 persons, and by the year 2000, 1 to every 40. By comparing this estimate of demand to the curve of supply, Brown concludes that we will need twice as many scientists and engineers as will be available in the year 2000. Or one can take, independently, the computations of the National Science Foundation. They have estimated that there is a 1:2 ratio between the number of engineers and scientists and the expenditures for research-and-development (e.g., from 1954 to 1960, the number of scientists rose 70 percent while research-and-development funds rose 140 per cent). So far, according to the Gilliland panel of the Science Advisory Committee, we are meeting the needs of the next decade, but the "fit" is a tight one.

In the health field, there are staggering needs for more physicians, nurses, and other technical personnel. The additional need for more professionals derives from three major factors: the fact that there is an increasing use of medical and hospital services; the change in the patterns of medical practice, as a growing number of doctors devote the greater portion of their time to research rather than to ministering to the sick; and the growth and the changing age distribution of the population. (Today, 17 million persons are between ages 55 and 65, and 18 million are 65 and over; by 1975, there will be 20 million persons between 55 and 65, and 21 million of 65 and over). There are today, in the United States, about 260,000 physicians, and we now graduate 7,500 physicians a year. But this number is not adequate to maintain the *present* physician-population ratio during the next fifteen years (in fact that ratio declined somewhat between 1950 and 1965), and with the increased demand for medical services the number of doctors will have to be expanded.

These projected gaps in scientific manpower suggest a new and unique dimension in social affairs: the economic growth rate in the future will be less dependent on physical capital (money) than it will be on "human capital." And this poses new problems for the society.

In the past, societies moving up the ladder of industrialization required huge sums of money to develop the "infrastructure" (i.e., highways, railroads, canals) and the basic physical plant of heavy industry (steel, energy resources, metals) in order to grow. Today the long-range expansion of the modern economy is limited by the impending shortages of technical and scientific manpower. (One can see this in such a growth area as computer technology, which employs about one-fourth of the 25,000 professional mathematicians in the United States).

The point is obvious. Physical, money capital can be generated rather quickly (as the Soviet Union has shown) by restricting consumption and "sweating" a population. But the planning of human capital is a much more difficult and arduous process. We need to know more about the genetic distribution of brainpower, the means of identifying talent, the procedures for raising I.Q.'s by reshaping home environments, the process of maintaining motivation, and the guidance and husbanding of talent over the long educational process. It means—given the length of schooling—vocational planning on a twenty-five-year cycle.

All of this points up the fact that we are entering a "post-industrial" society in which intellectual achievement will be the premium and in which the "new men" will be the research scientists, mathematicians, economists, et al. To say that the basic institutions of the new society will be intellectual is not to say that all or a majority of persons will be intellectuals, engineers, technicians, or scientists. The majority of individuals in contemporary society are not businessmen, yet one can say that this is a "business civilization." The basic values of the society have been embodied in the business institutions; the largest rewards are paid in business.

To say that the major institutions of the new society will be predominantly intellectual is to say, primarily, that the basic *innovative* features of the society will derive not from business as we know it today, principally the "product corporation," but from the research corporations, the industrial laboratories, the experimental stations, and the universities. The skeleton structure of that new society is already visible.

FOR FURTHER READING

Arendt, Hanna. *The Human Condition.* Garden City, New York: Doubleday & Company, Inc., 1959.

A phenomenological investigation of the most elementary dimensions of the human condition: work, labor, action. The final chapter is an attempt to analyze the effects of modern industrial scientific developments on Western man.

Bell, Daniel. *The Reforming of General Education.* New York: Columbia University Press, 1966. Chapter 4.

An examination of the place of General Education in the curriculum of Columbia College written with the support and encouragement of David Truman, Dean of the College. Investigation of the historical background of General Education, its place in the curriculum of Columbia College, the changing scene of American culture and its impact on education, and the directions in which General Education might go.

Berelson, Bernard, and Gary A. Steiner. *Human Behavior: An Inventory of Scientific Findings.* New York: Harcourt, Brace & World, Inc., 1964.

An inventory of scientific knowledge gained about human behavior.

Boulding, Kenneth E. *The Meaning of the Twentieth Century.* New York: Harper & Row, Publishers, 1964.

Argues that the twentieth century is a period of transition from civilization to postcivilization. However, whether or not the transition will be successful depends on avoiding a number of traps: war, economic development, population, entropy. Discusses the place of the social sciences and ideology in this transition and suggests attitudes toward it.

Cox, Harvey. *The Secular City.* New York: Crowell-Collier and Macmillan, Inc., 1965.

A controversial work investigating the rise of urban civilization and its impact on traditional values, especially religious ones. Cox argues that traditional religion is collapsing under the impact of secular values and calls for a new way of expressing the faith to modern American men.

Dewey, John. *Freedom and Culture.* New York: Capricorn Books, 1963.

An analysis of American culture. Investigates that kind of culture which is internally free enough to promote political freedom. Topics explored in an effort to answer this question are the impact on one another of culture and human nature, the background of American culture, totalitarian economics, science, and democracy.

Fromm, Erich. *Escape from Freedom.* New York: Avon Books, 1965.

A psychological, sociological, philosophical study of the significance of modern man's freedom. Modern man has been freed from the bonds of society, has found an individualism, and has experienced not only an isolation unknown in the preindividualistic society and the resulting anxiety and insecurity but also the independence and rationality that his newfound individualism has brought him. In this isolation he is confronted with the alternative of totalitarianism or of developing his human individuality and uniqueness.

Ginzberg, Eli (ed.). *Technology and Social Change.* New York: Columbia University Press, 1964.

A selection of essays edited for the Columbia University Seminar on Technology and Social Change. Essays discuss the impact of technology on society, the place of the intellectual in postindustrial society, the aerospace industry, economic growth, and issues and directions for a technological society.

Ginzberg, Eli, and Alfred S. Eichner. *The Troublesome Presence.* New York: The Free Press, 1964.

A history of the place of the Negro in American life. Excellent background material for understanding the racial conflicts today.

Graham, Saxon. *American Culture.* New York: Harper & Row, Publishers, 1957.

A descriptive, lucidly written study of American culture. Good background material for understanding social problems in America.

Harris, Raymond P. *American Education.* New York: Random House, 1961.

An analysis of American education carried out through a contrast of the schools as they are with what they are thought to be. Provocative and illuminating.

Heilbroner, Robert L. *The Limits of American Capitalism.* New York: Harper & Row, Publishers, 1966.

Written in a popular style, this book examines the place of capitalism in American life and the possibilities as well as impossibilities this economic system holds for life in this country.

May, Rollo. *Psychology and the Human Dilemma.* Princeton, New Jersey: D. Van Nostrand Company, Inc., 1967. Chapters 1, 2, 3.

Contends that all men are faced with a dilemma: to view themselves as objects or subjects. However, faced with this predicament men can suffer loss of identity and significance and feel alienated and anxious. Or they can see that within this predicament lie opportunities for the development of human consciousness. It takes courage to follow the latter approach, but to do so is to live creatively.

Moore, Wilbert E. *Social Change.* Englewood Cliffs, New Jersey: Prentice-Hall, Inc., 1963.

A short, concise discussion of social change written by a sociologist.

Pierce, John R. "Communications Technology and the Future," *Daedalus,* Vol. 94, No. 2 (Spring 1965), 506-517.

An examination of new developments and possibilities in communications technology and the kind of impact it can have on the future of American life.

Riesman, David. *The Lonely Crowd.* New Haven: Yale University Press, 1950.

A provocative interpretation of some trends in contemporary American society. Concerned with the implications of the confluence of persons who are "inner-directed" and those who are "other-directed." The former was characteristic of American people a generation or two ago while the latter type is growing in contemporary society.

Royce, Joseph R. *The Encapsulated Man.* New York: D. Van Nostrand Company, Inc. 1964.

Royce, a psychologist, argues that twentieth century Western man is searching for meaning and that the obstacle of undue specialization deters . him from achieving that goal. Calls for a multi-disciplinary approach to meaning, truth.

Snow, C. P. *The Two Cultures: and a Second Look.* New York: The New American Library of World Literature, Inc., 1964.

When first published, this work provoked widespread discussion about the bifurcation of the scientific and the literary cultures in the West. Argues that the two should establish communication and work together for the betterment of mankind.

Toffler, Alvin. *The Culture Consumer.* New York: St. Martin's Press, 1965.

Discusses the role of the arts in American society since World War II. Contends that healthy changes have occured and that Americans should no longer accept the image of being uncultured. Examines the so-called cultural explosion of the fifties and early sixties and evaluates its impact on American life.

2

METHODOLOGICAL OPTIONS FOR EDUCATIONAL PHILOSOPHY

The question of how one should proceed in investigating the philosophical problems issuing from the contemporary crisis in the transmission of Western values is in the final analysis a question of philosophical method. The educational philosopher must employ a method which will allow him to clarify specific problems in educational philosophy, to circumscribe the area of life which he thinks is important, to determine within that area which data are and are not relevant, and to interpret those relevant data through some kind of meaningful framework. In this search for a method the philosopher in education has many approaches from which to choose, and a major problem facing him is which method or methods should be employed to investigate adequately the topic he is interested in. If one can characterize Western philosophy from Plato through the nineteenth century, one could point to the strife of systems. Since the beginning of the twentieth century, however, the strife of systems has given way to the strife of methodologies. What separates most philosophers today, including those concerned with education, is not their systems. Most philosophy today is not of the system-building kind. Rather the methodology employed by a philosopher is what distinguishes his work from his colleagues. Educational philosophers in particular no longer find the system-building approaches of idealism, realism, and pragmatism useful in dealing with such topics as learning and the aims of education. They are now developing diverse methods which will allow them to deal effectively with the philosophical issues in education. Before proceeding to a discussion of four major methods open to philosophers of education, an investigation of what has happened in Western philosophy in the last sixty years to bring about this methodological strife is in order.

A. N. Whitehead once remarked that Western philosophy is but a series of footnotes to Plato. Though one can legitimately question this blanket statement, one cannot doubt that Plato epitomizes the philosophic ideal in the West from the fourth century B.C. through the nineteenth century A.D. What philosophy is about today is the rejection of this dominant ideal and the attempt to define for itself approaches to making intelligible this extremely perplexing age. If Whitehead is correct in his appraisal for philosophy until 1900, it is also correct to say that twentieth century philosophy is attempting to rewrite the book without even a footnote reference to Plato.

Plato was concerned with the permanent, the essential, the ideal and looked with disdain on the changing, the shadowy, the impermanent. Though he wanted "to save the appearances" and advanced the theory of ideas to render intelligible the world of sense and orderly change, he nevertheless deemed particular existence less real and less valuable than the universal. With a clearly drawn dualism running through his thought, he considered the eternal the real and the temporal the less than real, only a "moving image of eternity." In the development of this philosophy Plato, like the older Presocratics and his metaphysically minded contemporary Democritus, employed the deductive method. Starting with the assumption that the real is rational and the rational is real, Plato determined what was indubitably permanent and deduced the nature of reality from it. The result of his work, particularly that of his later period, was a view of reality which held that this is the best of all possible worlds; that the created cosmos possesses varying degrees of reality, ranging from the ideal, the permanent, and the good to the material, the changing, and the evil; and that it is being persuaded by God to become as much like the ideals as possible, that is, as good as possible. Such ideas as these form the guiding motif of the mainstream of Western philosophical thinking, including that of Aristotle, Augustine, Aquinas, Descartes, Leibniz, Berkeley, Spinoza, Hegel, Bradley. It can be accurately held that these thinkers emphasize the synoptic aspect of Western culture and that this spirit has been questioned progressively until its almost complete rejection in the twentieth century.

If contemporary philosophy is a rejection not only of the Platonic heritage in the West but also of F.H. Bradley, it is also an attempt to emphasize objects of investigation which have been rarely taken seriously until now and to develop methods of dealing with those objects. The four methods which are discussed in this chapter are attempts by philosophers concerned with educational problems to specify areas of investigation such as learning and educational goals and to develop techniques for investigating these areas. In the following selections the authors are more concerned, however, with the techniques of method and less with specifying the particular topics in education to be dealt with.

O'Connor represents the analytic approach to dealing with philosoph-ical problems, especially problems in the philosophy of education. In the search for meaning in a culture which seems to have lost direction and a sense of meaningfulness one must ask, where, if at all, is meaning to be found. A moment's reflection will indicate that it is language that carries whatever meanings a culture has and attempts to transmit through its educational processes. A society embodies in its words and in the words that are put together to form sentences the meanings which are the essentials of its culture. Furthermore, the educational goals and the mean-ings basic to a philosophy of learning held by a society are often confused, especially in the case of a society which is rejecting many of its traditions and searching for new ones. If one is interested in understanding the assumptions of the culture in which one participates and is concerned about the directions in which that culture may be moving, then one must be clear about the meaning of one's language. In the search for meaning, one must then concentrate one's attention on language and seek to clarify how it is being used by a particular society. And the way one goes about doing this is through analyzing language in use by a society to express its culture. This approach employed in the search for meaning is not new to the twentieth century. It is rather new to the investigation of philosophical problems in education, however.

The analytic method has its origins in the thought of David Hume and Immanuel Kant as well as in more recent figures such as G. E. Moore and Ludwig Wittgenstein. Hume held that all knowledge is acquired through the senses, and that there is nothing in the intellect which was not first in the senses. The mind with the mortar of the laws of association and the brick of ideas "builds" its objects and through these objects is able to make knowledge claims about the extra-mental world. Besides knowledge based on and limited to sense experience, Hume also believed that one could possess knowledge gained from valid deductions from assumed premises. All possible knowledge is circumscribed by these two kinds. Kant, being awakened from his dogmatic slumbers by Hume's attack on the traditional confidence in the mind to possess indubitable knowledge about the structure of reality, reworked his own philosophical position. In his attempt to develop adequate philosophical grounds for both the new science and mathematics, he contended that all knowledge claims are made either through analytic statements, through synthetic statements, or through synthetic a priori statements. A synthetic statement is any state-ment based on sense experience. For example, the interior of the house is blue. An analytic statement is a statement the denial of which is logically self-contradictory. "A bachelor is an unmarried male," is an example of this kind of statement. Finally, a synthetic a priori statement is a state-ment based on sense experience, but its truth value is dependent on tests other than that of appealing to sense experience. Kant believed that such a statement as $7 + 5 = 12$ is a synthetic a priori statement. That one can possess this kind of knowledge was evidence enough for Kant to believe that when one speaks mathematically about the phenomenal world one is grasping its internal structure. Contemporary analytic philosophers generally reject Kant's position that there are synthetic a priori statements by arguing that in fact any statement like $7 + 5 = 12$ is an analytic statement. What is important here is that Hume drew a distinction between two kinds of statements and two kinds of knowledge which Kant accepted and labeled. These distinctions among statements and among kinds of knowledge and particularly the setting of limits on the range of knowledge is generally accepted today among most philosophers in the analytic movement.

In G. E. Moore one finds an additional contribution to the analytic movement and a continuation of the empirical "bent" that is strong in British philosophical thinking. When he was a student, Moore was enamored with the work of F. H. Bradley. Under the influence of Bertrand Russell, however, the young Oxford student began to question Bradley's use of language and suggested that the way Bradley used words went against what every man knows simply by common sense. Indeed, how can one make a statement such as, "All is Spirit," and expect to make any sense out of it? Is it not the case that things other than "Spirit" exist? What about flowers, trees, rocks, and water? It is clear that they are somehow different from what I know as my mind. Bradley's statement is clearly nonsense. Through his concern with analyzing ordinary language and determining when it is used correctly, Moore not only dealt a heavy blow to the metaphysical excesses of some of his contemporaries but also became the great advocate of the "common sense" philosophy in Britain.

Wittgenstein stands alongside Hume, Kant, and Moore in shaping the analytic movement in contemporary philosophy. In his early works, especially the *Tractatus* (1921), Wittgenstein was concerned with establishing, if possible, the necessary conditions which must be met if language is to be used properly. Hume's and Kant's limitation of knowledge to that based on experience and that based on deduction from premises was adhered to rigorously. Furthermore, to justify any claim that language is being used meaningfully, one must submit it to rigorous tests. The truth value of statements must be verified in principle either through sense experience or through deduction from acceptable premises. A statement which is not open to verification through at least one of these two modes is a meaningless statement. However, in his *Philosophical Investigations* Wittgenstein acknowledges that language is used meaningfully and that there is no one set of conditions which must be met if language is to be used properly. Language is a social phenomenon, a cooperative achievement, a tool which men have in common and which is used in every area of their cultural experience. Furthermore, each universe of discourse in a culture has its own set of rules which language must follow. These sets of rules governing the use of language in each universe of discourse have ruling intents or purposes. Because of the different underlying intents each universe of discourse is clearly distinct from any other. This does not mean that they conflict. On the contrary, they complement one another by developing various perspectives on man's experience. The different but complementary character of universes of discourse is clearly illustrated by the views taken on a particular human act by a scientist, an educator, and a theologian. The scientist might ascribe the act to glands, the educator to miseducation, and the theologian to sin. One may argue that each thinker is at bottom attempting to find out what is happening and thus be able to find a coherent and comprehensive account of the event. But upon closer examination one finds that to resolve the differences one must eliminate the way each is using language. This cannot be done, however, because the language game being played in a given context is a live game with its own order and rules and is meaningful only in that context. There can be no question of dismissing language as used in any universe of discourse as improper. The three views on the event just mentioned do not have the same intent. Each man has a point of view which is meaningful in the universe of discourse in which he is talking. Thus, Wittgenstein contends that language is a social phenomenon, used in a relatively well-defined universe of discourse, shot through with many ruling perspectives or intents. Man's world is composed of numerous unrelated but complementary universes of discourse. The scientist as scientist cannot speak to the educator as educator; the humanist cannot speak to the theologian; and the theologian cannot speak to the scientist. With Wittgenstein the analytic temperament in the twentieth century is at its apex.

Some educational philosophers in the twentieth century, however, are not content with analyzing and clarifying language in use. They contend that men not only use language but also through the educational processes set up by society men learn to work toward goals. It is clearly the case that when decisions are made for or against seeking particular ends, those decisions are going to be heavily influenced by forces which are other than rational and are susceptible to being made on grounds which are indefensible. Since this is the case, philosophers must articulate goals toward which men and society ought to be educated and the grounds on which those goals can be justified. A society's or an individual's search for meaning is not going to be aided very much with only a clarification of the way one is using language, although it is a helpful part of the search. It must be understood that men are goal seekers and a great deal of the meaning they achieve is gained through learning what they expect of themselves and why. Philosophers then must be willing to propose how men ought to conduct themselves and to develop adequate grounds for those proposals. Dewey is an excellent representative of those members of the philosophical community who employ the normative method in their handling of philosophical issues in education.

In his use of the normative method, Dewey stands in the mainstream of Western philosophical tradition. Plato, speaking to Greeks who were experiencing the disintegration of the *polis,* advocated ends toward which the young ought to be educated. Most other ethical and social thinkers in Western philosophy have followed Plato in developing defensible patterns of conduct and in advocating that they be adopted by the members of their society. As one reads Dewey, however, one must be careful to grasp what he is and is not attempting to do. He is not resting his philosophical case when language has been clarified even though he believes that this is important. Neither is he developing a thoroughgoing world view and examining the place of man and his life in that context. Rather he believes that philosophers, in response to tensions in social behavior, should develop defensible ends and means which should be adhered to by all men in society. Though it is not a necessary characteristic of all normative philosophies of education, Dewey contends that goals of human life in society are not final, absolute, and otherworldly but are relative, this-worldly, within the educational process, and useful in guiding that process. It should be kept in mind, also, that these ends and means are not to be developed by a philosopher who sits in his comfortable study and merely examines alternative goals, purposes, values, and norms of education. The educational philosopher should also employ all that the social sciences have to say about man and his behavior. His view of the normative function of philosophy is that philosophers in education should use the best information available to them and advocate educational goals supported by that information.

A third approach taken by some contemporary philosophers of education is the "speculative" one. What these thinkers are advocating is a continuation of the metaphysical concern initiated by the Greeks. Although standing in the great metaphysical tradition of Plato in seeking an integrated view of reality, they do not advocate employing the deductive method of their predecessors. The classical and modern metaphysicians started with what is necessary, immutable, and eternal (like Plato's ideas) or with what is indubitable (like Descartes' *cogito ergo sum*) and proceeded to infer a thoroughly developed scheme of things and the place of man, learning, and educational goals within that scheme. Contemporary philosophers, in general, and educational philosophers, in particular, who are speculative in their approach, on the contrary, are more prone to be inductive in their general methodology. This means that they base their whole system on experience and constantly check their developing world scheme by its adequacy to experience. The selection included in this chapter from Whitehead's *Process and Reality* is an excellent example of the methodology of the contemporary speculative philosopher of education. Whitehead calls his particular articulation of the speculative approach "coherence."

Some of the major features of Whitehead's coherence method are these: analytical, inclusive, hypothetical, logical, and experimental. In every stage in the development and refinement of a synoptic understanding of reality and of the educative process, one must constantly analyze the data of experience. Each area of experience must be examined whether it is sensed, felt, or whatever. Any system or aspect of a system which is not rooted deeply in every part of the life-world of persons is an abstraction and not an understanding of what persons are experiencing. In the sense that one must always appeal to every part of experience in the articulation of a world-view, one can say that one must be inclusive in one's dealings with experience. Further, experience which is not interpreted is not meaningful and to give a general interpretation such as is required by any system-building one must advance hypotheses or visions which one hopes will render the data intelligible. This hypothesis is a kind of "root metaphor" or "conceptual model" which one uses to interpret one's experience not only by making statements about one's experiences but also by suggesting the possible interrelations of those statements. At the point of seeking interrelations among statements, one is employing logic, or the rules of inference, or simply attempting to be consistent. Finally, in the growth of a world-view a careful eye is always kept on the adequacy of the hypothesis or the adaptability of the hypothesis to the data. If the data are not rendered intelligible by the system as a whole or by any part of the system, then the system or part of the system must be recast. A constant checking must take place to see that the data are not *forced* into a preconceived framework and that the framework allows data full and proper meaning. In this sense the coherence method is experimental.

From what has been said so far, it is clear that Whitehead is primarily interested in doing metaphysics and that a philosophy of education must be seen as one aspect of the world-view he develops. At this point, however, one must be careful to see what Whitehead is attempting to do with his speculative method. He is attempting to obtain a vision of reality and to make it intelligible through developing the internal structure of that vision. His goal is primarily metaphysical understanding, and this includes what it means to learn and to what ends men ought to be educated. To the degree that he develops defensible educational goals and attempts to ground these on an individual's experience, on data from the social sciences, and on norms which he believes are significant one can say that Whitehead is both a speculative and a normative philosopher. However, one must note that a philosopher could employ a speculative approach in developing a philosophy of education without at the same time being normative. The goal could be simply to understand the nature and structure of reality and the place of man, learning, and educational values in that structure and not to prescribe what men ought to do and think.

The fourth major approach to dealing with philosophical issues arising from the contemporary crisis in the transmission of culture is existentialism. The existentialist movement has been strong on the European continent for most of the twentieth century. Only in the last twenty years, however, has it had much impact in the United States. Through the translation into English of the works of Kierkegaard, Sartre, Marcel, Heidegger, and others even the intelligent layman has felt the impact of its position. In calling existentialism a movement one must introduce a note of caution. In the first place, few men who are placed in this movement are eager to accept the label. Each is saying something which must be understood in and for itself and to attempt to place it under the umbrella of such an amorphous term as existentialism is to lean in the direction of distorting each position. Second, it is difficult to find many common themes running through their thought. About all one can hope for is to indicate what most of them seem to be fighting against.

Those thinkers who are frequently labeled as existentialists are usually concerned with the problems individual persons in the West have amid the strong scientific view of the twentieth century, the breakdown of values around which Western society tends to construct itself, and the loss of meaning which persons experience in their attempt to cope with their social and physical environment. Contemporary European and American culture is shot through with the belief that, by using the scientific method or some refinement of it, everything about man can be understood. Man is, after all, a reasoner and needs only to think correctly about his experiences in order to understand and possess meaning. Furthermore, with his understanding of technology and know-how, man can find ways to make, build, create a happy world. Unfortunately, in the process of creating this technological utopia, persons are often viewed as things to be manipulated, gadgets to be used both individually and collectively. In reacting against these tendencies in contemporary Western culture, thinkers of the existentialist stripe raise a significant group of questions and employ diverse methods in dealing with those questions.

It is generally recognized by existentialists that man is a social-cultural animal. He lives in societies, develops cultures, and transmits them through his schools. It is in this context that he must be understood if at all. But, what does it mean to exist in society? What is truth? Is truth exhausted by the rational, objective kind of truth which the scientist knows, or is there also a personal, subjective kind which those in love know? If persons are always persons-in-relation, what is the nature of interpersonal relationships? Further, where and how, if at all, is meaning to be found and achieved? In the learning situation, what are the conditions for the possibility of acquiring knowledge and behaving appropriately? To these and many other questions, thinkers in this movement take various approaches. Many, particularly German and French existentialists, employ the phenomenological method. This method developed by Husserl found its way into the thought of such men as Scheler, Sartre, Heidegger, Merleau-Ponty, and Marcel. Though one cannot characterize this method accurately in the space available here, one can indicate the direction in which they are moving. Through a suspension of one's preconceptions and metaphysical beliefs about experience, one attempts to "read" the structures essential to experience itself. Each thinker spins off this guiding motif and corrects the method to suit his own purposes. The other major methodology employed by existentialists is one which is difficult to characterize. Indeed, the thinkers who employ this method do not attempt to characterize it. Rather, they simply use it in their investigation of the experiences about which they are concerned. To understand how they proceed, it is best to follow them through an investigation of a significant question in education and see the method in operation. For now, however, some characterization of this method must be given.

First, it is introspective. A strong emphasis on the subjective aspect of persons is usually made. One should not infer that this limits them to an atomistic individualism or a solipsism. On the contrary, they are strongly concerned about interpersonal relations. They do not approach personal relations in an objective, scientific manner; they rely instead on what Augustine would call the "inward path" in their search for answers. Next, it is descriptive. At this point these thinkers have something in common with their more phenomenologically oriented colleagues. Further, they do not attempt to develop a consistent system in terms of which they claim to have exhausted the meaning of persons-in-relation. Rather, they are willing to live with paradox and with the unsystematic richness of experience. Finally, their way of expressing themselves tends to be poetic, imaginative, and elliptical.

In the selection in this chapter from the writings of Martin Buber one has an excellent example of a first-rate thinker employing the existentialist method. One must read Buber with the mind and attention which one would give to a poet and to a man with a great insight. To attempt to reduce either his method or his thought to a neat packaged system would be to distort him beyond recognition. To understand Buber, one must enter into his search with him. Only then will one "understand" what Buber is about and grasp the value of this method for investigating the basic questions in education.

In conclusion, the authors in this chapter, with the exception of Buber, are attempting to set forth as clearly and as precisely as possible the methodology which they employ to investigate the philosophical questions about which they are concerned. Because of this purpose, they do not directly relate their investigation to any particular problem of philosophy whether it be the nature of reality, the manner of acquiring knowledge, or the aims of education. One should not infer from this that the methods they develop are not useful in dealing with either general philosophical problems or the particular problems in philosophy of education. Rather, each is concerned at this point with setting out a perspective and a way of thinking within that perspective. It should be clear then that any one of these methods is useful in dealing with philosophical problems in the field of education. Of course, the degree of usefulness of each method will have to be determined by its fruitfulness in helping one to deal adequately with the problems being faced. In the selections in the following chapters all four methods will be employed in dealing with two major questions which arise when a society facing a breakdown in a major cultural value attempts to think through what it means to teach its young, what it means to learn, and to what ends the young should be educated.

Analytic

The Nature of Philosophy*

D. J. O'CONNER

I

The work of the philosopher has traditionally been supposed to consist of three connected tasks. In the first place, he has been expected to provide a compendious overall view of the universe and of man's place in it. Secondly, he has been expected to do this by rational procedures and not, for example, by intuition or poetic imagination. Lastly, men have looked to the philosopher to give them or at least justify for them, a religious point of view that would also be defensible by reason. Philosophers have thus been expected to combine the aims and achievements of scientists, moralists and theologians. But these expectations have proved far beyond what they have been able to accomplish. On rare occasions, a philosopher of genius like Aquinas[1] or Spinoza[2] has given us a map of the universe that many people have found both intellectually and spiritually satisfying. But in such cases it has proved only too easy for the philosopher's critics to attack the logic of his system or the truth of his premises. They have shown in this way that, however fascinating and persuasive his picture of the world may be, there is no good reason to believe that it is a true one.

At the present day, philosophers would state their aims very much more modestly though, naturally enough, a philosopher's view of the scope of

[1]St. Thomas Aquinas (1225–1274), a medieval theologian and philosopher.
[2]Baruch Spinoza (1632–1677), a Jewish philosopher who lived in Holland.

*Reprinted with the permission of Routledge and Kegan Paul, Ltd. and Philosophical Library from D.J. O'Conner, *An Introduction to the Philosophy of Education* (London: Routledge and Kegan Paul, Ltd., 1957), pp. 16–45.

his discipline will depend on his own philosophical opinions. A few of them might still want to maintain the traditional view. But most would agree that the traditional philosophers promised more than they were able to deliver and that their claims to interpret the universe on a grand scale must be rejected for just the same reason that the claims of alchemists, astrologers or magicians are now rejected. The reason is the simple and fundamental one that the results of any sort of enquiry are acceptable in so far as they are publicly testable, reliable and coherent with the rest of public knowledge. Traditional metaphysics,[3] like astrology and alchemy, cannot meet these requirements. It may perhaps be objected that the requirements themselves are arbitrary if they are applied to philosophy since these are standards by which we test scientific knowledge. We may return to this objection at the end of the chapter after we have looked at the way in which philosophy has developed.

The history of western philosophy started in fifth-century Greece. If we examine the doctrines of the Greek philosophers, we see that they cover an enormously wide field. We find discussions of characteristically philosophical problems like the existence of God, the nature of human knowledge and the good life for man. We also find interest in questions of mathematics and astronomy, physics and chemistry of a primitive kind, biology and the social sciences. Moreover we do not find that any clear distinction was made between those questions that we nowadays recognize as philosophical and those that we class as scientific. Not only was knowledge not departmentalized as it is today but it was not even divided into the main *logically distinct types of enquiry* that we now recognize. We distinguish

[3]The word "metaphysics" occurs here for the first time. As it will be used several times in the course of this book, it may be useful to explain the sense in which it will be understood. A statement is metaphysical if it assumes the existence of entities or facts which lie outside the range of human observation and experience. An argument is metaphysical if it purports to prove the existence of such entities or facts. Note that statements are not metaphysical because they cannot *in fact* be checked by observation, but because they cannot *in principle* be checked in this way. Compare the following statements: (1) On January 1st, 1567, there were 6537 crocodiles in the River Zambesi. (2) Some good actions are the result of divine grace. (3) Julius Caesar had blood belonging to group AB. (4) Julius Caesar had an immortal soul. (2) and (4) are metaphysical; (1) and (3) are not, because, although we do not know whether they are true and can never find out, the sort of evidence which would confirm them is within the range of human observation.

Examples of metaphysical statements of a more serious kind will be found on pages 41–42. This book will not intentionally contain metaphysical statements except as illustrative examples. But the reader should realize that not all metaphysical statements are as easy to recognize as (2) and (4) above and that the questions. "What is a metaphysical statement?" and "How far are such statements meaningful?" are still live and debatable issues in philosophy. The explanation of the term "metaphysical" given above is a very rough clarification which will serve our present purposes.

nowadays between physics, chemistry and zoology, for example, but this kind of distinction is largely a matter of administrative convenience, so to speak. The field of scientific knowledge has become far too detailed and complex for one man to deal effectively with more than a very small area. The division and subdivision of natural science into specialities is thus a practical device to meet the limitations of man's mind and the shortness of his life. There is however a more basic distinction between branches of knowledge. This depends not on the kind of material that we study but on the *sort of evidence* by which we advance our knowledge. Botanists study plants, geologists the history and structure of the earth's crust, astronomers the planets and stars. But all of them get their material by observing nature through the senses. Indeed this is one of the characteristic features of the sciences. Pure mathematics and formal logic on the other hand do not derive their material from observation of the world nor are the findings of these sciences proved or supported by this kind of evidence. Anyone who has taken a school course of elementary geometry is aware that we do not *prove* that the three angles of a plane triangle total two right angles by drawing a selection of triangles and measuring their angles. We prove such propositions by deductions from axioms or postulates conventionally accepted as a starting point. And when we turn to the problems of philosophy, it is easy to see that they cannot be decided either by the observational methods of the natural sciences or the deductive methods of mathematics and formal logic. For if they were decidable in this way, some of them at least would long since have been decided. (It is not merely a truism to say that *what is provable can be proved.* Indeed, we can read in this statement one reason for the failure of traditional metaphysics and natural religion.)

This very important logical point that different kinds of statement demand different kinds of evidence is not one that the Greek or medieval philosophers would have denied if it had been put to them. They were, in a sense, aware of the point but the presuppositions of their thinking and the state of knowledge in their time did not require them to bring it into focus and concede it any importance. But this situation was radically altered by the rise of natural science and the renaissance of mathematics during the seventeenth and eighteenth centuries.

All the sciences started as branches of philosophy in the sense that the Greek word "philosophia" was originally used in a very general sense to cover all investigations into the nature of man and of the universe. But in the sixteenth and seventeenth centuries a discovery was made about scientific method which seems to us nowadays trivial and obvious, perhaps because it is the unquestioned foundation of a civilization based on the achievements of natural science. This was the discovery that if you want to know what the world is like, you have to look and see. As a practical maxim, this was not always a commonplace. There have been long periods in the history of the world and no doubt there will be again, when people were discouraged from looking either by the intellectual fashions of their time or because the prevailing religious or political outlook might conflict with what observation would tell them. And of course mere observation of the world of nature was not enough to lay the foundations of science. The results of observation had to be refined by experiment and by measurement and the direction of observation controlled by hypothesis. But once men had learned the lesson of what has been called "respect for fact," natural science started on that brilliant epoch of development which has marked off the last three hundred years from all other periods of history. This lesson was first thoroughly, though slowly, learned by the scientists of western Europe during the seventeenth and eighteenth centuries.

Thus science became emancipated from philosophy by the discovery of its proper method; and the only relic of the long association between the two is the title of 'Professor of Natural Philosophy' which adorns the holders of chairs of physics in some of the older British universities. The method of observation and experiment had of course been practised in Greek and medieval times but in a half-hearted and sporadic way; and it had not usually been practised in conjunction with the language of mathematics, the language in which, in Galileo's famous epigram, the book of nature is written. But with the systematic adoption of the experimental method and the translation of natural laws into mathematical modes of expression, men were at last developing a large body of reliable and testable knowledge. They were moreover acquiring it with the aid of a method whose power they recognized and which they consciously applied to the solution of the problems of nature. Philosophers could now compare the uncertain powers of their own speculative methods with the method of hypothesis and experiment. Though it is a method that needs slow, laborious and piecemeal application, it gives answers that can be progressively corrected, tested and communicated and leads in the end to generally accepted results. Like many other important revolutions, this one did not take place overnight. Indeed its full impact has not been felt by all educated men even at the present day. But most philosophers since the seventeenth century, many of whom were also men of science, saw clearly enough what the new way of explaining the world meant for them. It was a challenge to find a method of tackling the problems of philosophy which would be appropriate to those problems and so would enable men to agree when a solution of them had been reached.

There is one important way in which the success of the natural scientists helped the philosophers to focus their difficulties more clearly. It became obvious with the rise of the scientific method that the attention of philosophers in ancient and medieval times sometimes had been taken up with questions that had not properly been matters for them at all, since they were questions decidable only by the methods of the scientists. Aristotle, for example, discussed not only philosophical questions such as origins of human knowledge, the nature of morality and the relations between mind and body but also scientific questions about the mechanism of sensation, the constitution of the physical universe, the nature and organization of the heavenly bodies and the like. There is no reason why a man should not be both a scientist and a philosopher but unless he clearly distinguishes his scientific questions from his philosophical ones, both his science and his philosophy are likely to suffer. Aristotle failed to make this distinction and in this he was followed by nearly all the medieval philosophers.

And so, in the seventeenth century, the physics of Aristotle were not corrected but rather replaced by the physics of Galileo and Newton. Philosophers were henceforth relieved of the duty of trying to solve problems about the observable facts and regularities of nature. But this restriction of their responsibilities was an embarrassment rather than a relief. If all questions of observable fact were questions for the scientist to answer, what questions remained for philosophy and how were they to be approached?

The upshot of the scientific revolution for philosophy is this: Some questions, characteristically those of the natural and social sciences, can be settled by empirical methods, by hypothesis arising out of observation and observation confirming hypothesis. Other questions, characteristic of logical and mathematical subject matters, can be settled by calculation in accordance with settled rules of deduction. But there are a very large number of questions that do not seem to fall into either of these categories and among these are the traditional problems of philosophy, of ethics and of natural religion. But if such questions cannot be decided either by empirical or by purely deductive methods, how are they to be answered? This is the problem that has been set to philosophy by the success of natural science. Of course, we see it more clearly at the present day than did the philosophers of the seventeenth and eighteenth centuries since we have the advantage of profiting by their work. But it was well understood by most of them that the first problem for the philosopher had become the problem of finding a method. Descartes[4] and Spinoza, impressed by the certainty and efficiency of mathematical methods of proof, tried to prove philosophical conclusions as they proved problems in geometry, and actually set out part of their work in the axiomatic form of Euclid's *Elements*

---

[4]René Descartes (1596–1650), a French mathematician, philosopher and scientist.

of Geometry. They were unsuccessful, as they misunderstood the nature of the axiomatic method that they were trying to use and overlooked the differences between mathematical symbolism and the language of philosophical arguments. Other philosophers, like Locke[5] and Kant,[6] did not raise the method so directly and preferred to ask: "What are the limits of human knowledge?" They tried to outline a sort of programme of possible discoveries based upon our knowledge of the powers of the human mind. Instead of speculating about the nature of the universe and man's place in it, as the Greeks and the medievals had done, they wanted, in Locke's words, first "to take a survey of our own understandings, examine our own powers and see to what things they were adapted."

This examination of the powers of the mind proved just as difficult and controversial a matter as any of the traditional problems of philosophy. It served a useful purpose, indeed, in directing the attention of philosophers to what has been called "the theory of knowledge," a group of important problems concerning the origin, nature and validity of human knowledge. Thus the moderate scepticism of the philosophers who tried in this way to solve the problem of philosophical method achieved only the incidental success of opening up a new field of enquiry. And as long as the problem of method was unsolved, this addition to the field of philosophy was rather like discovering new diseases without finding cures for the old ones. Nevertheless, though Locke's project of finding out the powers and limits of the human mind proved not to be the looked-for philosophical method, questions of this sort do offer a very good starting point for the search for such a method. Let us therefore look more closely at a variant of Locke's question: What kinds of problems can human reason solve for us?

II

Like many of the abstract words used in philosophy, the word "reason" is a vague one. There is no one "correct" definition by which we can pin down and fix its meaning. I shall take it to mean the capacity to solve problems, of whatever kind the problem may be; or, to put the same point in another way, reason is the ability to answer questions appropriately. We may defer for the present the obvious queries that arise from this: How do we know when a problem has been solved? How do we know what is an *appropriate* answer? The definition may seem perhaps a rather modest and restricted account of what we mean by "reason." But at least there is no doubt that human beings do have such a problem solving capacity as part of their make up. Some of us may have it to a greater

[5]John Locke (1632–1704), an English philosopher.
[6]Immanuel Kant (1724–1804) was Professor of Philosophy in Königsberg.

degree than others or have a specially good or specially poor capacity for solving some sorts of problems. (For example, those of mathematics or of administration.) But all human beings who are not very low grade mental defectives have this capacity in some degree, sufficient perhaps to justify us being described by the traditional epithet "rational animals." And of course, we should remember that the so-called brute animals, dogs, rats and the rest, have their own modest problem-solving capacities. This will remind us that rationality is a matter of degree and not a clear cut "all or nothing" affair.

We can expect too much of reason or again expect too little of it and it is easy to trace in the history of thought both of these mistaken attitudes. But of the people who have a wrong estimate of the powers of reason, those who over-value it are less at fault than those who despise it. Perhaps the best example of a large body of men who placed an exaggerated value on the powers of human reason is that of the medieval philosophers.

The defects of medieval thinking were not due to lack of talent or of intellectual curiosity. Many medieval philosophers were men of great intellectual gifts and a wide range of interests. What they lacked was a correct conception of what the human mind was capable of knowing and of how it should set about acquiring the knowledge that lay within its power. They were fully convinced that men could prove from ordinary commonsense knowledge plus a few so-called "self-evident principles" a large number of statements about the existence and nature of God, the nature and destiny of man, the constitution of the physical universe and so on. But unlike proofs in either mathematics or in natural science, their "proofs" on these subjects have not commanded any general assent among equally competent and well-informed philosophers. That is to say, the metaphysical findings of the medievals do not meet the criteria that we ordinarily apply to the theories offered to the world by scientists, mathematicians, scholars, economists and so on, namely the criteria of independent checking by experts in the same field and coherence with the established body of knowledge in that field. There is indeed no such established body of positive philosophical knowledge: and philosophy being the sort of enterprise that it is, there never could be. Any first-year undergraduate can point out the logical flaws in the scholastic "proofs" for the existence of God and the immortality of the soul and the like. The reason for the failure of the medieval philosophers seems to have been that they had not openly raised and settled the fundamental question: What kind of evidence would be appropriate to the sort of questions that we are asking? And that they had failed to do this was due not to any intellectual defects on their part but to the historical fact, which has already been noticed above, that they did not have at their command any large body of well-established knowledge which was public, testable and communicable. Such a body of knowledge would have served as a standard of comparison by providing them with at least one reliable example of what organized knowledge really was.

It is much better to trust reason too far than to trust it too little because by trusting it too far we learn through experience where its limits lie. We are thereby better armed for future attempts at solving our problems. We must give the philosophers and theologians of the middle ages the credit for having made for us the experiment of testing human reason beyond its utmost limits and showing, however inadvertently, to their successors where these limits may be found. But there is nevertheless a serious danger in this over-confidence about the powers of reason. If we consistently fail to reach definite and generally accepted results by rational methods, we may well come in time to mistrust the use of reason and to react against it. John Locke, writing in the seventeenth-century reaction against the methods of the medieval scholastics, put this point as follows:

> Thus men extending their enquiries beyond their capacities and letting their thoughts wander into those depths where they can find no sure footing, it is no wonder that they raise questions and multiply disputes, which, never coming to any clear resolution, are proper only to continue and increase their doubts and confirm them at last in perfect scepticism.

The second of the wrong attitudes to reason is the one which undervalues and mistrusts it. This attitude takes two forms, appealing to two quite different types of mind. On the one hand, there is what may be called the born irrationalist. He is the sort of man who shrinks from and distrusts any systematic use of reason. Confronted with a problem that calls for hard and careful thinking, he will either shirk it or turn to bogus substitute methods of solution. The irrationalist will decry what he calls "intellect" or "logic" and praise instead mysterious natural impulses and intuitions. It is a very widespread attitude and characterizes the intellectually lazy, the woolly minded, the fanatical and the superstitious. And it is the more pernicious in having supporters who enjoy some reputation—philosophers such as Nietzsche and Bergson, theologians like Kierkegaard and a great many artists and writers, to say nothing of well-known pretentious mystagogues like Rudolf Steiner and Ouspensky. Two contemporary examples of the effect of this attitude can be seen in the psychological theories (if they can so be called) of Carl Jung and the existentialist movement in Europe.

A second and very different type of mind that is prone to undervalue reason is that of the sceptic. The sceptic's distrust of reason arises paradoxically from a limited faith in it. He is prepared to justify and defend his attitude by offering reasons for it, by pointing to the general fallibility of the human mind and the untrustworthiness of all the sources of our knowledge from our senses and memory to our powers of deduction and our so-called intuitions. This is a much more healthy attitude and is indeed an excellent *preliminary* to philosophical thinking. The sceptic, unlike the irrationalist, does not avoid or decry rational processes of thought and behavior. He merely says that they are of very limited application. And in support of this (for he is rational enough to offer evidence for his statements) he points out that human beings are constantly making mistakes, endorsing and clinging to superstitions, taking dubieties for certainties and generally exhibiting in their behaviour the impotence of reason in action. This evidence that the sceptic offers is true enough but it does not justify his conclusion. If, indeed, we had no reliable standards whatever for distinguishing true statements from false ones and for assessing probabilities with success, the sceptic would be right. But we are not in that unfortunate position and if we were, we could not live successfully in the world at all. We may, perhaps somewhat fancifully, look upon our rational powers as a hand of cards to be played in a game like bridge or poker. To get the best out of them, they must neither be overplayed nor underplayed. We must neither grasp at knowledge that reason cannot ever give us nor ignore what it can successfully offer us. The scholastic metaphysicians (and, less excusably, other metaphysicians since their time) overplayed their hand. The irrationalists and the sceptics underplay it. What we have to do is to recognize what reason is capable of achieving and see that we use it only for those ends. But how are we to ensure that we do this?

It is easy enough to state in a general sort of way what reason and rational action consist in. Bertrand Russell once defined a reasonable or rational man as one who always proportioned the degree of intensity with which he held his various beliefs to the amount of evidence available for each belief. To strive after this degree of rationality is no doubt a counsel of perfection. None of us is so reasonable and most of us are very much less so. Nevertheless, if we are to use reason correctly this should be our aim. The use of reason consists in proportioning the degrees of conviction with which we hold our various beliefs to the strength of the evidence that we have to support them. The abuse of reason consists in holding beliefs on insufficient evidence or holding them with a degree of certainty that the evidence does not justify.

Such irrational conviction may of course be inappropriately weak or inappropriately strong, according as we ignore evidence available to us or presume upon evidence that we do not (and perhaps cannot) possess. But being human, we find that we all are very commonly prone to presuming upon absent evidence and not nearly so commonly prone to the fault of the other extreme (though we all are ready enough to ignore evidence that conflicts with some habitual or cherished belief). The holding of beliefs on insufficient evidence is superstition. We are not superstitious only when we put our faith in bogus sources of knowledge like astrology. We indulge in superstition every time that we repose a degree of belief in a statement that the evidence for the statement does not justify. A belief in the influence of the stars on human lives is only a gross and extreme form of a fault of which we are all guilty in greater or lesser degrees. Many of our moral, religious and political beliefs are superstitious in this sense; and so indeed are some of our scientific ones.

So far, it may seem that I have done nothing but repeat a number of platitudes well-known to us all, even if we ignore them. A critic may reply: "Of course, we ought to proportion our beliefs to our evidence. Everyone would agree to that. What people do *not* agree on is what constitutes evidence for different sorts of statements. And that is why men disagree on so many different things. They do not disagree on the principle of using appropriate evidence but on the standards by which we decide *what is evidence for what.* And that is what we would like to see decided."

This is a fair criticism. But it is not at all easy to give a final answer to the question: What sort of evidence is appropriate to the different sorts of questions that we ask? An important part of the work of philosophers in recent years has dealt with just this problem. And although we see both the question and part of the answer to it far more clearly than was previously seen, it cannot be said that there is yet any final agreement on the point. I do not want to suggest that nothing useful can be said on the matter. It is certain however that anything that can usefully be said will not be so platitudinous as what I have said so far. It is well to remember that in philosophy any statement that is not a truism is controversial. Nevertheless, even a truism may be true. Truisms are often worth reaffirming just because what is obvious to one man is not so to another. What we find "obvious" depends to a large extent on our training, knowledge and preconceptions.

III

I said above that I was going to take the word "reason" in the sense of a general capacity for problem solving, whether the problem arose from mathematics, from the natural or social sciences, from situations of everyday life, from philosophical or theological speculation or from any other source whatever. Now we can easily see, if we look at the historical facts referred to briefly at the beginning of this chapter, that men have been very much more successful at some kinds of problems that at others. The problems at which we have been most signally successful have been those of mathematics and those of the natural sciences. The extent to which we can nowadays understand and control the forces of nature is a measure of our success in this field. We have been notably less successful in dealing with questions of morals and politics and with those of metaphysics and religion. And we have been only moderately successful in tackling the problems of the social sciences. But it will not help us to try to use the same methods to deal with the intractable questions of philosophy that have worked so well in enabling us to understand the natural world. Questions of morals and metaphysics are simply not susceptible to this sort of treatment. The hope of a "scientific" philosophy or "scientific" morality is quite illusory if we mean by these phrases a philosophy or a morality that relies merely upon the methods of the sciences for its conclusions. We shall see later why this is so.

But we can gain some idea of the right approach to these problems by contrasting the spectacular success of the mathematicians and scientists in their own fields with the notable lack of success of the moralists, metaphysicians and theologians in theirs. If we ask ourselves for the reason why natural science suddenly burst into life in the sixteenth and seventeenth centuries, we can see the answer in the history of the subject. Physics became an independent and rapidly growing branch of learning when physicists discovered the method appropriate to their subject matter. It is indeed a complex historical question why the realization of the value of the experimental method should have occurred just when and where it did. But there is no doubt that the substitution of observation, experiment and measurement for the speculative methods of the medieval Aristotelians was a turning point in history. Mathematics also, though it has a much older lineage, takes its origin as an independent branch of knowledge from the development of the axiomatic method by the Greek geometers. We can learn this much at least from the successes of scientists and mathematicians that no set of problems is likely to yield its solutions until we find the right method of approaching it. The key to problem-solving of all sorts is first to find the general method of solution for the kind of problem in question. How does this help us here?

A quite superficial acquaintance with the history of philosophy will show us that the general method used by philosophers in the past has been deduction from what appeared to be "self-evident" premises. They believed, in other words, that it was possible to *prove* their conclusions about the existence of God, human destiny and the like by methods analogous to those used by mathematicians. The subject matter, to be sure, was very different from that of geometry but they supposed that the truth of their conclusions was guaranteed by the truth of the statements from which their arguments started and the logical validity of their deductions from these statements. This belief that philosophical discovery was essentially a process of proof took a long time to lose its plausibility even though none of the classical metaphysicians ever succeeded in proving anything and even though many of them did nevertheless make important philosophical discoveries. But these discoveries, like Columbus' discovery of America, were the by-product of a mistake. There can be no philosophical proofs because philosophy cannot proceed either by the axiomatic method of mathematics or by the experimental way of the scientist. And there are no other kinds of proof but formal deduction on the one hand and the establishment or refutation of hypotheses on the other. This is not to say that philosophy is not an exercise of reason; for reason does not consist only in giving proofs. But we are forced to conclude that questions which cannot be tackled by the deductive methods of mathematics or the observational and experimental methods of the natural and social sciences need a totally new method of approach. And we can get some sort of a lead to such a new approach by considering that scientists and mathematicians are relatively successful in their enquiries because they have a well-defined method of handling their problems. This means that they know in each case what evidence would settle the question that they are asking and that they usually know also how to set about collecting the evidence. Now this is just what we do not know in many questions relating to philosophy, morals, politics, religion and so on—all those questions that seem perennially controversial because there is no established, agreed and tested method of approaching them. The key question that we must ask as a preliminary to any sort of problem-solving procedure is this: What kind of evidence would have a bearing on this question?

If we have to admit, as well we may, that in some cases we simply do not know what the relevant evidence would be, then we should in all honesty admit that *for us* the question is not a meaningful one. This is a vitally important point for the proper use of reason. If you will consider for a moment some very simple examples of questions, you will see that they always presuppose some sort of knowledge about the answer. In other words, for a question to be a genuine one and capable of being answered, the questioner must have some idea of the terms in which the answer will be given. To take a trivial instance. If I say to someone: "What's the time?" and he replies "Tomorrow week" or "Four yards square," I shall think that either he has misunderstood my question or that he is making a silly joke. I shall know not that the answer is *wrong* but that it is *irrelevant*. I shall know this because in asking questions, we ourselves set the framework within which the answer must fall. For an answer to be right or wrong, it must fall within the framework set by the question. And for a question to be a genuine one, it must have a framework that will determine in advance the form that the answer must take and the terms in which it will be made. We have such a framework for a question when we know the *sort* of evidence that will give us the answer but are ignorant of *exactly what* the evidence will be.

For this reason it is often said of questions, both scientific and philosophical, that a question well put is already half answered or that the secret of success lies in asking the right questions. Now asking the right questions means, among other things, putting questions that specify implicitly *the type of evidence* appropriate to their solution.

A meaningful question cannot be quite neutral as to the answers it invites. The most precise kind of question would be one which took the form: "Which of these two answers is right, A_1, or A_2?" A vaguer question could be represented as asking: "Which of these possible answers is right, A_1, A_2 . . . or A_n?" The larger the number n of possible alternative replies the more general will be the question. And where a question is so general as not even to imply a set of alternative answers, it loses its interrogative function. Thus the answer to a vague or woolly question is to say: What sort of evidence would you accept as relevant to the answer? If the questioner cannot tell you what sort of evidence would be relevant to his answer, his query is a mere pseudo-question, having the grammatical form of a question but not its interrogative function. For if the questioner does not know what sort of evidence would be relevant to his problem, he is in no position to distinguish a relevant from an irrelevant answer, still less a true answer from a false one.

We can propose then as a minimum safeguard against the abuse of reason the use of the following query whenever we are confronted with a problem: What kind of evidence would be relevant to the solution? But it is important to notice that there are two types of situation in which we might be unable to meet this challenge by specifying the sort of evidence that we should accept as relevant. (1) It might merely be that we personally did not know what kind of evidence would answer the question for us. (2) It might be that there was not and never could be any such evidence. Let us look at these two cases separately.

1. Suppose that I know nothing of mathematics or of natural science. I may put questions to mathematicians or scientists that they can answer quite easily. For example: How is it known that squaring the circle is impossible? How is it known what the sun is made of? How do we know that the tide will be high at midnight on a certain place on January 1st next year? And so on. The experts could give me the answers easily

enough but these answers will necessarily presuppose a certain amount of knowledge if they are to be understood. Unless I know a good deal of mathematics I cannot understand the proof that it is impossible to square the circle. Unless I know a good deal of physics and chemistry, I cannot appreciate the spectroscopic evidence about the composition of the sun. Such questions—indeed, almost any question—may be *relatively* unanswerable, that is to say, unanswerable to those persons who do not have the necessary background of knowledge against which the question acquires a meaning. A question may, then, be a pseudo-question relatively to a given person who has not sufficient relevant knowledge to make the answer *meaningful for him.* (Many of the questions of young children are of this kind.) Such a person can always improve his knowledge if he wants to, with the consequence that questions that were once without meaning for him can subsequently acquire it.

2. But there is another sort of question, if it can so be called, that is not meaningless relatively to a particular set of persons but is meaningless in an absolute sense in that there is no framework of knowledge within which the question has a meaning and nobody can make any generally acceptable reply to the challenge: What sort of evidence would be relevant to the answer? The same point may be put in another way. Many questions can be converted into corresponding statements. (Obviously a question of the form "Is X, Y?" can be converted to "X is Y.") This statement, if it is to convey any information, must have a range of possible evidence that would be accepted as supporting it. If the person who makes the statement has not got the evidence that would establish it, he is acting irrationally in believing it. If, in addition to not possessing the evidence for the statement, he has not the faintest idea what sort of evidence would settle the question, he is making a merely empty statement. Now here we have the possibility of a very serious and dangerous kind of philosophical mistake, the making of statements or the asking of questions that have the outward appearance of genuine statements or questions but which, on examination, do not satisfy the criterion that their genuine counterparts must satisfy—namely, possessing a possible range of evidence that, *were it obtainable,* would verify the statement or answer the question. I say that we have the *possibility of this kind of mistake* for it is a matter of debate whether such errors have occurred in serious philosophizing and a matter of philosophical criticism to identify them. But it is easy enough to point to questions of this sort. Suppose that someone asks: When did time begin? Or: What color is an atom? An intelligent child or an unsophisticated adult might ask such questions because they seem analogous to

questions like: When did the Hundred Years' War begin? Or: What color is uranium? But they can be asked only because the questioner has not reflected on the subject matter of his question. He has not realized that a query of the form "When did X begin?" presupposes time in the sense of the existence of a convention for temporal measurement and that it makes no sense to ask such a question about time itself. He has not realized, in the second case, that questions of the form "What color is X?" presuppose that X is capable of reflecting light and that it makes no sense to ask the question about something like an atom which is too small to reflect any light. In other words, questions may very well be empty if they are asked by someone ignorant or careless of the meaning of terms contained in his question. Now it is perfectly possible to ask such questions and make the corresponding statements in philosophy without realizing that they are in fact empty of content. Indeed, some philosophers have suggested, perhaps unkindly, that all metaphysical statements and questions are of just this kind. Unfortunately, it is not possible to give any useful general rules that will enable us to proscribe such statements and questions in advance. We have to test each one and pass or fail it on its merits. The point of the question: What sort of evidence would be relevant? is to elucidate what are the logical merits of a given statement or question.

IV

It has become obvious to philosophers in the past fifty years that a great many of the unprofitable controversies of the past can take on a new and enlightening aspect if we look at them from this point of view. The metaphysicians who debated about God, morality, human destiny and so on were assuming that these problems were similar to scientific questions at least in being clear questions about definite matters of fact to which answers were in principle possible. Yet it is obvious from the history of philosophy that equally honest, intelligent and well-informed men may have all the supposedly relevant facts at their disposal and still disagree profoundly about such matters. This indicates that the facts which they supposed to be relevant were not really relevant at all. If they had been, it is incredible that generally acceptable answers on these matters should not by now have been reached. For it is important to notice that facts are never relevant in philosophy in the way that they are in history or in science. Historians and scientists may, and often do, disagree on the way in which the available facts are to be interpreted. But these disagreements can, in principle, always be resolved by the discovery of *further* relevant facts; and no historical or scientific disagreement could outlive the knowledge of *all* the facts, if these were ever obtainable. Yet this can and does happen in metaphysical disputes. It is indeed one sure way by which we may recognize that the dispute is metaphysical.

There are two ways of proceeding from this point. We can say that questions and statements of this sort to which no generally acceptable evidence seems at all relevant, are simply meaningless or nonsensical, that they are grammatically correct forms of words which carry no meaning whatever of an informative kind. This was the view of the logical positivists, a pre-war school of philosophy which no longer survives in its original hard-shelled form. Under this ruling, only two kinds of statements retain any cognitive meaning, statements of empirical fact that can be confirmed by sensory observation and statements of logic and mathematics that can be checked by calculation. Every other kind of statement is ruled out as lacking any kind of cognitive content. This is clearly a very rough way of dealing with the statements of ethics, politics, religion and criticism of literature and the arts as well as the writings of the metaphysicians. And it shows perhaps a rather cavalier and unsympathetic attitude to matters which have excited men of ability and integrity since the beginning of history.

A more tolerant point of view, which is now quite widely accepted among philosophers, may be expressed as follows: "These statements are certainly misleading in looking grammatically like statements of observable fact. But perhaps we are being misled by their linguistic form. After all, language has many uses and fact-stating is only one of them. Let us consider all the other possible uses of language to see if we can reinterpret such apparently empty propositions in such a way that we can see what they are really asserting and so come to some agreed decision about their value." This is one of the ways in which modern philosophers have come to be very interested in questions of language. And investigations of this kind have proved very fruitful in putting some of the oldest controversies of philosophy in quite a new light. Unfortunately, it is not easy to give in a summary way any adequate idea of the methods and results of the contemporary linguistic approach to philosophy. A general description of this work would be too vague to be informative. It can be appreciated only by seeing it in action.

All I can usefully do here is to give in illustration one or two of the more important discoveries about language and its workings that have been brought to light by these methods and show how they are philosophically enlightening. Perhaps the most basic of these notions (it is hardly recondite enough to be called a discovery) is a principle which derives chiefly from the work of G. E. Moore: [7] *The meaning of a word is created*

---

[7]Professor G. E. Moore (1873–   ) was Professor of Philosophy at Cambridge University from 1925 to 1939.

and controlled by the ways in which it is used. To say this is merely to say that the relations between a word or phrase and its meaning is not a part of nature independent of human wishes but rests upon social conventions. Words and phrases have those powers of communication that their habitual modes of use have endowed them with, *and no more.* This fact, obvious enough though it is, has important consequences for philosophy.

It follows from this that many words, and among them most of the key terms of philosophy, must be both vague and ambiguous *and irremediably so.* For it is clear that the abstract and uncommon terms of philosophy will be used much less often and in much less concrete contexts than the words describing the common features of our everyday experience. They will thus be much vaguer since the precedents for their use in some contexts will not have been clearly established or, indeed, established at all. And they will be ambiguous when divergent or incompatible speech customs have directed the occasions of their use. The philosopher faced with these natural debilities of language is often in the position of an English judge who has to give a judgment in a common law case for which the relevant precedents are either conflicting or fail to cover the circumstances at issue. But whereas the judge knows that his judgment must contain some arbitrary element, the classical philosopher, blind to the nature of language, too often assumed that he had given the only right answer to his problem.

The modern philosopher who is sensitive to this natural feature of language often looks to the ways in which we remedy vagueness when it troubles us in everyday speech. We commonly do so by pointing to examples and especially to borderline examples. If someone asks, for instance, "What colors do you include under the term 'violet'?" you can show him a range of samples, both of the shades you are prepared to call "violet" and also of those that are just too red or too blue to qualify for the term. Procedures of this kind will make your meaning much more precise, though still not perfectly so. In philosophy, the vagueness of such terms as "mind," "thought," "God," "free will," "cause," or "substance" is not so easily treated by this method. But where we can do something on these lines, the consequences may be important.

To take a concrete case, if we ask: "What do you mean by 'thinking'?," you might give a series of examples: I am thinking when I am daydreaming, when I am doing mathematics, when I am writing a letter, when I am playing chess, when I am talking with friends and so on. But are you thinking when you are dreaming as well as when you are daydreaming, when you are batting at cricket, as well as when you are playing chess, when you are playing the piano as well as when you are solving equations? And if you are thinking when you are solving your puzzles, does the rat think when he is solving his? Examples and counter-examples of this sort show how fuzzy this and similar concepts are round their edges and how there are no standard examples of them with a unitary set of properties that all genuine instances of the concept possess. Thinking is not an all-or-none affair but a matter of degree; and so too with the rest of those philosophical concepts whose vagueness can be elucidated in this way. The result of the elucidation is to show that these concepts are in no way like precise clear-cut technical terms. Thus a consideration of the workings of language has thrown new light on the nature of a concept and has gone a long way towards disposing of a philosophical problem that has been outstanding since Plato.

There is another important application of this principle that offers a useful way of deciding some philosophical questions. It has been called by a contemporary philosopher, Professor J. O. Urmson, the "appeal to the standard example." He instances a well-known application of this method by Susan Stebbing in her critique of Eddington in *Philosophy and the Physicists.* In *The Nature of the Physical World,* his popular exposition of twentieth-century advances in physics, Eddington tried to explain the scientist's view of material objects as follows. Solid objects, like tables and stones, were not really solid or substantial at all for the physicists had shown them to be clouds of tiny particles separated by distances that were very large in relation to the size of the particles. The floor that we tread upon, Eddington explained, was really much more like a swarm of flies than a plank of wood and had, as he put it, "no solidity of substance." It was really very remarkable that it supported the weight of anything placed upon it.

This piece of amateur philosophizing was decisively refuted by Stebbing in the following way. She pointed out that the word "solid" takes its meaning from its application to things like stones and tables and planks. If they are not solid, then nothing is, for it is by reference to such things that we learn to use the word "solid." If the word has no application to the standard cases of its use, it loses its meaning and has, in consequence, no application at all. Stebbing thus showed in this simple way that the language in which Eddington tried to explain physical discoveries, far from being enlightening, was simply misleading. This kind of appeal to the standard uses of words has had very wide application in contemporary philosophy and has proved a very effective logical weapon. It is particularly powerful in exposing the emptiness of those metaphysical theories whose point depends upon using ordinary words in very extraordinary senses. The well-known "first cause" argument[8] for the existence of God is an example of this sort.

[8]This argument, which purports to prove a "first cause" of the whole universe, uses the word "cause" in a sense entirely different from that conferred on it by ordinary usage.

A secondary important discovery about language that is philosophically important is that language is not a picture or map of the world and, in consequence, no conclusions can be drawn from the nature of language to the nature of reality. This is a very large subject, and in its details, still a controversial one. But briefly the position is that many of the classical philosophers assumed that our thinking about the world mirrored what we found there, at least when our thinking was not mistaken and that our language mirrored our thinking. It was believed that thinking, correct or mistaken, was a sort of mapping of the universe and that the map was a good one when our thinking was true and a bad or distorted or even totally misleading one when our beliefs were false. Moreover, language was a sort of externalized model of our internal cogitations, the map, as it were, in its published form. This view was first stated in an embryonic form by Aristotle and was later canonized into what was called the Correspondence Theory of Truth. There is just enough in this kind of metaphor to make it easy for us to press it too far. The real harm of this three-level view of knowledge, thinking mirroring fact and language mirroring thinking, is not so much in the metaphor of the mirror or the map, though this is a misleading way of explaining even very elementary kinds of knowledge. The danger lies rather in the supposed split between thinking and its expression as if thinking is some sort of mysterious inner process that can proceed apart from language or from any other kind of symbolism whatever. Both the sources of this error and its consequences are too complicated to dwell on here. One of its most damaging results is to make us suppose that the actual grammatical and syntactical structures of natural languages are a key to the nature of reality. For language, on this view, is a picture of the world, or rather, a picture of a picture. And what we find in the structure of languages may fairly be supposed to correspond to the structure of the world. Thus to take one example, some metaphysicians seem to have taken the grammatical distinction between subject and predicate as evidence for the philosophical theory that the world consisted of a number of substances characterized by different properties.

V

Let us consider how these views about language bear upon the work of the classical metaphysicians. We have seen that these philosophers, like contemporary philosophers, dealt with such questions as the following: What is the nature of the connection between the private "mental" events that occur in our consciousness and the physical events that occur in our sense organs and nervous systems? Are all mental events, including our choices, effects which can be completely explained and in principle predicted by an adequate knowledge of preceding events? What is the nature of the mind or self? That is to say, can we give an adequate account of it in terms of mental events or nervous events or both, or do we have to explain the facts of our mental life by supporting an unknown immaterial something which we can never experience but which we must postulate to make our experience logically coherent? What is the nature of the objects revealed to us by the senses? That is to say, how are we to describe them in order to allow for all the facts of normal and abnormal sense experience?

These particular philosophical questions look superficially like the problems of the psychologist because they deal with the subject matter of psychology. But they are not questions that can ever be answered by the psychologist as a scientist because no amount of factual evidence collected by the most careful observation and experiment could ever finally settle them. Now when the classical philosophers were faced with problems of this kind they were not bothered by the fact that observational evidence was not relevant to their solution. They assumed that as philosophers they had special methods of dealing with such problems which were perfectly logical and efficient although they were not the methods of natural science. We have seen that these supposedly philosophical methods of the classical philosophers have fallen into disrepute in recent years simply because they do not give the results that they promise. No alleged solution of any philosophical problem achieved by these methods has ever satisfied more than a small minority of philosophers. But our present interest in them is to see how they are connected with the mistakes about language discussed above. Such solutions usually consisted in showing how a certain view about the relation between mind and body, for example, followed as a logical consequence of a certain metaphysical system. These metaphysical systems were very general world pictures or, as it were, charts of the universe which were supposed to be established by a logical process of argument from statements which everyone would admit to be self-evidently true. And if we look at the methods of the philosophers who tried to work out such systems, it is easy to see why an examination of the powers and functions of language was a vital preliminary to their enterprise. They were trying to do for the universe as a whole what the natural scientists do for limited portions or aspects of the universe. They were trying to give a general ordered account of everything that exists in terms of abstract notions like existence, cause, substance, quality, space, time, matter, mind and so on just as the physicist gives such an account of certain aspects of the physical world in terms of energy, mass, velocity, and so on. But it is important to notice that the similarities between metaphysics and natural science are superficial and delusive while the differences between them are fundamental. There are two principal differences. In the first place, the physicists' theories about the world are based on controlled and accurate observation and can be checked by further observation. And if found substantially correct, they can be embodied in useful gadgets like dynamos and refrigerators which will be found to work efficiently. But the metaphysicians' theories about the world are never of this kind. No observations are relevant to the suggestions that time is unreal or that essence and existence are identical in God or that the human mind is immaterial. Nor can such suggestions be put to any practical use.

This, of itself, is no fatal criticism. But if these theories can neither be confirmed or refuted by observation, how are they to be established? This question points to a second difference between metaphysics and science. The metaphysician, unlike the scientist, derives his theories by tracing the logical connections between statements expressed in ordinary language enriched by the technical terms of his philosophical vocabulary. And by such tracing of logical connections, he claims to find out new, exciting and often paradoxical facts about the universe and man's relation to it. Now it is obvious that this procedure implies a great faith in the symbolic powers of ordinary language. It is true that mathematicians can make new and surprising discoveries by tracing the logical connections between symbolic expressions. But the symbols of mathematics are carefully and exactly defined and are totally different in nature and function from the words of our natural languages. Nor do the results of mathematics, *before they have been applied to the world,* yield us any new facts about the world. No one can trace the first beginnings of the systems of signs that make up our natural languages like English and French, but it is not unreasonable to suppose that in their early stages they were developed to express everyday emotions and communicate facts of common interest in a primitive society. The development of the abstract vocabulary that philosophers need is a very late stage in all languages and there are many languages at the present day which would be useless as media for philosophical writing merely because philosophical activities are not represented in the cultures in which these languages have developed.

The metaphysician has an answer to this charge of blind confidence in the symbolic powers of language. He would probably say something like this: "You are confusing the issue in stressing the limitations of language. All of us use language, whether in writing philosophy or in teatime gossip, only to express our thoughts. And though it is true that where thinking becomes very complex or abstract, the limitations of language act as a check on our *powers of expression,* they do not prevent us from thinking. Where we have no words adequate to express our thoughts, we invent new ones which are designed to express them. If this were not so, the civilized languages would never have developed from the uncouth dialects of illiterate peoples. In short, we think first and then clothe our thoughts in language. And when we do metaphysics and try to discover the general nature of the universe, we are relying not on tracing the logical connections between one linguistic expression and another but in tracing those connections between one thought or judgment and another. And because these judgments are judgments about reality, their logical consequences will give us new and often unexpected information about the universe we live in and our relation to it." If metaphysicians wish to defend their traditional methods they will be forced to reply to the charge of linguistic innocence outlined above in something like these terms. (Indeed, this sort of defence has been offered by some of them.) But it will be seen that this reply rests on the very assumptions about language that recently have been called in question: (1) that thinking is a process prior to and independent of language or any other kind of symbolization; (2) that words can have meanings that are to some degree independent of the way in which they are used. And there is very good reason to suppose that both these assumptions are false. If we consider the second assumption, in particular, it will be obvious that unless we believe that words have "natural meanings" independent of the contexts in which they have been used, abstract concepts of philosophy are far too vague and fluid to enable us to trace any logical connection between them that will enable us to make discoveries about reality. Philosophers who used this method have in fact been forced to supplement the inadequacies of conventional rules of usage by supplying rules of their own in the form of *definitions* of their basic terms. But, of course, no new information about the universe could ever be extracted from definitions.

I do not wish to suggest that traditional metaphysics must be rejected merely because of recent philosophical views about language. These views do indeed bring into focus some of the *reasons* for the failure of metaphysical speculation but the failure was obvious long before the attention of modern philosophers was directed to the nature of language. I suggested at the beginning of this chapter that no system of traditional metaphysics has ever proved to be publicly testable by experts in the same field and coherent with the rest of established knowledge; and that this, in itself, refuted the claims of such systems to be taken seriously. If it is objected that this is an unfair criterion to use because it has been developed by application to factual disciplines like science and history, we have to ask: How else is the truth of any theory, historical, scientific, mathematical or philosophical, to be established? We learn to recognize truth in the future by seeing how it has come to be recognized in the past. Public recognition by experts, progressive corrigibility and coherence with established knowledge are not indeed *infallible* guarantees of true beliefs. For truth has no such hall marks. But they are the best guarantees we have. And it would be absurd to accept any belief which lacked them as more than a tentative hypothesis. We cannot indeed even regard it as a hypothesis unless we know (*a*) what consequences would follow if it were true; and (*b*) how these consequences are to be established. The basic weakness of metaphysics has been that its practitioners claimed objective truth for their conclusions without recognizing objective tests by which their claim could be verified.

No doubt there will be metaphysical systems in the future which will take account of the way in which language works and even of the need for criteria of proof. Such systems will have to be judged on their merits. But the present state of philosophical knowledge and its past history cannot encourage us to look on philosophy as more than a laborious piecemeal effort to criticize and clarify the foundations of our beliefs. Such successes as philosophers can claim have all been of this kind. And this means that in the present condition of human knowledge we cannot hope for more from philosophy than occasional and fragmentary glimpses of enlightenment along with a reasonable confidence that its continuous practice will keep our minds free of nonsense. But this is something very valuable that only philosophy can give us.

Normative

Philosophy, Education, and Reflective Thinking*
JOHN DEWEY

1. PHILOSOPHY AND THE EDUCATION OF MAN

Philosophy has generally been defined in ways which imply a certain totality, generality, and ultimateness of both subject matter and method. With respect to subject matter, philosophy is an attempt to *comprehend*— that is, to gather the varied details of the world and of life into a single inclusive whole, which shall either be a unity, or, as in the dualistic systems, shall reduce the plural details to a small number of ultimate principles. On the side of the attitude of the philosopher and of those who accept his conclusions, there is the endeavor to attain as unified, consistent, and complete an outlook upon experience as is possible. This aspect is expressed in the word "philosophy"—love of wisdom. Whenever philosophy has been taken seriously, it has always been assumed that it signified achieving a wisdom which would influence the conduct of life. Witness the fact that almost all ancient schools of philosophy were also organized ways of living, those who accepted their tenets being committed to certain distinctive modes of conduct; witness the intimate connection of philosophy with the theology of the Roman church in the middle ages, its frequent association with religious interests, and, at national crises, its association with political struggles.

*Reprinted with the permission of The Modern Library from Joseph Ratner (ed.), *Intelligence and the Modern World: John Dewey's Philosophy* (New York: The Modern Library, 1939), pp. 255–274.

180

This direct and intimate connection of philosophy with an outlook upon life obviously differentiates philosophy from science. Particular facts and laws of science evidently influence conduct. They suggest things to do and not do, and provide means of execution. When science denotes not simply a report of the particular facts discovered about the world but a *general attitude* toward it—as distinct from special things to do—it merges into philosophy. For an underlying disposition represents an attitude not to this and that thing nor even to the aggregate of known things, but to the considerations which govern conduct.

Hence philosophy cannot be defined simply from the side of subject-matter. For this reason, the definition of such conceptions as generality, totality, and ultimateness is most readily reached from the side of the disposition toward the world which they connote. In any literal and quantitative sense, these terms do not apply to the subject-matter of knowledge, for completeness and finality are out of the question. The very nature of experience as an on-going, changing process forbids. In a less rigid sense, they apply to *science* rather than to philosophy. For obviously it is to mathematics, physics, chemistry, biology, anthropology, history, etc. that we must go, not to philosophy, to find out the facts of the world. It is for the sciences to say what generalizations are tenable about the world and what they specifically are. But when we ask what *sort* of permanent disposition of action toward the world the scientific disclosures exact of us we raising a philosophic question.

From this point of view, "totality" does not mean the hopeless task of a quantitative summation. It means rather *consistency* of mode of response in reference to the plurality of events which occur. Consistency does not mean literal identity; for since the same thing does not happen twice, an exact repetition of a reaction involves some maladjustment. Totality means continuity—the carrying on of a former habit of action with the readaptation necessary to keep it alive and growing. Instead of signifying a ready-made complete scheme of action, it means keeping the balance in a multitude of diverse actions, so that each borrows and gives significance to every other. Any person who is open-minded and sensitive to new perceptions, and who has concentration and responsibility in connecting them has, in so far, a philosophic disposition. One of the popular senses of philosophy is calm and endurance in the face of difficulty and loss; it is even supposed to be a power to bear pain without complaint. This meaning is a tribute to the influence of the Stoic philosophy rather than an attribute of philosophy in general. But in so far as it suggests that the wholeness characteristic of philosophy is a power to learn, or to extract meaning, from even the unpleasant vicissitudes of experience and to embody what is learned in an ability to go on learning, it is justified in any scheme. An analogous interpretation applies to the generality and ultimateness of philosophy. Taken literally, they are absurd pretensions; they indicate insanity. Finality does not mean, however, that experience is ended and exhausted, but means the disposition to penetrate to deeper levels of meaning—to go below the surface and find out the connections of any event or object, and to keep at it. In like manner the philosophic attitude is general in the sense that it is averse to taking anything as isolated; it tries to place an act in its context—which constitutes its significance.

More specifically, the demand for a "total" attitude arises because there is the need of integration in action of the conflicting various interests in life. Where interests are so superficial that they glide readily into one another, or where they are not sufficiently organized to come into conflict with one another, the need for philosophy is not perceptible. But when the scientific interest conflicts with, say, the religious, or the economic with the scientific or esthetic, or when the conservative concern for order is at odds with the progressive interest in freedom, or when institutionalism clashes with individuality, there is a stimulus to discover some more comprehensive point of view from which the divergencies may be brought together, and consistency or continuity of experience recovered. Often these clashes may be settled by an individual for himself; the area of the struggle of aims is limited and a person works out his own rough accommodations. Such homespun philosophies are genuine and often adequate. But they do not result in systems of philosophy. These arise when the discrepant claims of different ideals of conduct affect the community as a whole, and the need for readjustment is general.

The fact that philosophic problems arise because of widespread and widely felt difficulties in social practice is disguised because philosophers become a specialized class which uses a technical language, unlike the vocabulary in which the direct difficulties are stated. But where a system becomes influential, its connection with a conflict of interests calling for some program of social adjustment may always be discovered. At this point, the intimate connection between philosophy and education appears. In fact, education offers a vantage ground from which to penetrate to the human, as distinct from the technical, significance of philosophic discussions. The student of philosophy "in itself" is always in danger of taking it as so much nimble or severe intellectual exercise—as something said by philosophers and concerning them alone. But when philosophic issues are approached from the side of the kind of mental disposition to which they correspond, the life-situations which they formulate can never be far from view. If a theory makes no difference in educational endeavor, it must be artificial. The educational point of view enables one to envisage the philosophic problems where they arise and thrive, where they are at home, and where acceptance or rejection makes a difference in practice.

If we are willing to conceive education as the process of forming fundamental dispositions, intellectual and emotional, toward nature and fellow men, philosophy may even be defined as *the general theory of education.* Unless a philosophy is to remain symbolic—or verbal—or a sentimental indulgence for a few, or else mere arbitrary dogma, its auditing of past experience and its program of values must take effect in conduct. Public agitation, propaganda, legislative and administrative action are effective in producing the change of disposition which a philosophy indicates as desirable, but only in the degree in which they are educative—that is to say, in the degree in which they modify mental and moral attitudes. And at the best, such methods are compromised by the fact they are used with those whose habits are already largely set, while education of youth has a fairer and freer field of operation. On the other side, the business of schooling tends to become a routine empirical affair unless its aims and methods are animated by such a broad and sympathetic survey of its place in contemporary life as it is the business of philosophy to provide.

The reconstruction of philosophy, of education, and of social ideals and methods thus go hand in hand. If there is especial need of educational reconstruction at the present time, if this need makes urgent a reconsideration of the basic ideas of traditional philosophic systems, it is because of the thoroughgoing change in social life accompanying the advance of science, the industrial revolution, and the development of democracy. Such practical changes cannot take place without demanding an educational re-formation to meet them, and without leading men to ask what ideas and ideals are implicit in these social changes, and what revisions they require of the ideas and ideals which are inherited from older and unlike cultures.

2. THE CRITICAL FUNCTION OF PHILOSOPHY

Philosophy is inherently criticism, having its distinctive position among various modes of criticism in its generality; a criticism of criticisms, as it were. Criticism is discriminating judgment, careful appraisal, and judgment is appropriately termed criticism wherever the subject-matter of discrimination concerns goods or values. Possession and enjoyment of goods passes insensibly and inevitably into appraisal. First and immature experience is content simply to enjoy. But a brief course in experience enforces reflection; it requires but brief time to teach that some things sweet in the having are bitter in after-taste and in what they lead to. Primitive innocence does not last. Enjoyment ceases to be a datum and becomes a problem. As a problem, it implies intelligent inquiry into the conditions and consequences of a value-object; that is, criticism. If values were as plentiful as huckleberries, and if the huckleberry-patch were always at hand, the passage of appreciation into criticism would be a senseless procedure. If one thing tired or bored us, we should have only to turn to another. But values are as unstable as the forms of clouds. The things that possess them are exposed to all the contingencies of existence, and they are indifferent to our likings and tastes.

When criticism and the critical attitude are legitimately distinguished from appreciation and taste, we are in the presence of one case of the constant rhythm of "perchings and fights" (to borrow James' terms), characteristic of alternate emphasis upon the immediate and mediate, the consummatory and instrumental, phases of all conscious experience. If we are misled into ignoring the omnipresence in all observations and ideas of this rhythm, it is largely because, under the influence of formal theories, we attach too elaborate and too remote a signification to "appreciation" and "criticism." Values of some sort or other are not traits of rare and festal occasions; they occur whenever any object is welcomed and lingered over; whenever it arouses aversion and protest; even though the lingering be but momentary and the aversion a passing glance toward something else.

Similarly, criticism is not a matter of formal treatises, published articles, or taking up important matters for consideration in a serious way. It occurs whenever a moment is devoted to looking to see what sort of value is present; whenever instead of accepting a value-object wholeheartedly, being rapt by it, we raise even a shadow of a question about its worth, or modify our sense of it by even a passing estimate of its probable future. It is well upon the whole that we use the terms "appreciation" and "criticism" honorifically, to designate conspicuous instances. But it is fatal to any understanding of them to fail to note that formally emphatic instances are of exactly the same nature as rhythmic alternation between slight agreeable acceptances, annoyed rejections and passing questionings and estimates, which make up the entire course of our waking experience, whether in revery, in controlled inquiry or in deliberate management of affairs.

Criticism is judgment, ideally as well as etymologically. Understanding of judgment is therefore the first condition for theory about the nature of criticism. Perceptions supply judgment with its material, whether the judgments pertain to physical nature, to politics or biography. The subject-matter of perception is the only thing that makes the difference in the judgments which ensue. Control of the subject-matter of perception for ensuring proper data for judgment is the key to the enormous distinction between the judgments the savage passes on natural events and that of a Newton or an Einstein.

It cannot be safely assumed at the outset that judgment is an act of intelligence performed upon the matter of direct perception in the interest of a more adequate perception. For judgment has also a legalistic meaning and import, as in Shakespeare's phrase, "a critic, nay, a night watchman." Following the signification supplied by the practice of the law, a judge, a critic, is one who pronounces an authoritative sentence.

The judge—in the judicial sense—occupies a seat of social authority. His sentence determines the fate of an individual, perhaps of a cause, and upon occasion it settles the legitimacy of future courses of action. Desire for authority (and desire to be looked up to) animates the human breast. Much of our existence is keyed to the note of praise and blame, exculpation and disapproval. Hence there has emerged in theory, reflecting a widespread tendency in practice, a disposition to erect criticism into something "judicial." One cannot read widely in the out-givings of this school of criticism without seeing that much of it is of the compensatory type—the fact which has given rise to the gibe that critics are those who have failed in creation. Much criticism of the legalistic sort proceeds from subconscious self-distrust and a consequent appeal to authority for protection. Perception is obstructed and cut short by memory of an influential rule, and by the substitution of precedent and prestige for direct experience. Desire for authoritative standing leads the critic to speak as if he were attorney for established principles having unquestionable sovereignty.

Unfortunately such activities have infected the very conception of criticism. Judgment that is final, that settles a matter, is more congenial to unregenerate human nature than is the judgment that is a development in thought of a deeply realized perception. The original adequate experience is not easy to attain; its achievement is a test of native sensitiveness and of experience matured through wide contacts. A judgment as an act of controlled inquiry demands a rich background and a disciplined insight. It is much easier to "tell" people what they should believe than to discriminate and unify. And an audience that is itself habituated to being told, rather than schooled in thoughtful inquiry, likes to be told.

Judicial decision can be made only on the basis of general rules supposed to be applicable to all cases. The harm done by particular instances of judicial sentence, as particular, is much less serious than the net result in developing the notion that antecedent authoritative standards and precedents are at hand by which to judge.

The very meaning of an important new movement in any phase of life is that it expresses something new in human experience, some new mode of interaction of the live creature with his surroundings, and hence the release of powers previously cramped or inert. The manifestations of the movement therefore cannot be judged but only misjudged unless the critic is sensitive first of all to "meaning and life." He is otherwise helpless in the presence of the emergence of experience that has a distinctively new character. Every professional person is subject to the influence of custom and inertia, and has to protect himself from its influences by a deliberate openness to life itself. The judicial critic erects the very things that are the dangers of his calling into a principle and norm.

The blundering ineptness of much that calls itself judicial criticism has called out a reaction to the opposite extreme. The protest takes the form of "impressionist" criticism. It is in effect, if not in words, a denial that criticism in the sense of judgment is possible, and an assertion that judgment should be replaced by statement of the responses of feeling and imagery the object of value evokes. In theory, though not always in practice, such criticism reacts from the standardized "objectivity" of ready-made rules and precedents to the chaos of a subjectivity that lacks objective control, and would, if logically followed out, result in a medley of irrelevancies—and sometimes does.

Were it not for the blunders made by the judicial critic, blunders that proceed from the theory he holds, the reaction of the impressionist theory would hardly have been called forth. Because the former set up false notions of objective values and objective standards, it was made easy for the impressionist critic to deny there are objective values at all. Because the former has virtually adopted a conception of standards that is of an external nature, derived from use of standards developed for practical ends, and legally defined, the latter has assumed there are no criteria of any sort. In its precise signification, a "standard" is unambiguous. It is a quantitative measure. The yard as a standard of length, the gallon as a standard of liquid capacity, are as precise as legal definitions can make them. The standard of liquid measure for Great Britain was defined, for example, by an act of Parliament in 1825. It is a container holding ten pounds avoirdupois of distilled water, weighed in air with the barometer at thirty inches and the Fahrenheit thermometer at sixty-two degrees.

There are three characteristics of a standard. It is a particular physical thing existing under specified physical conditions; it is *not* a value. The yard is a yard-stick, and the meter is a bar deposited in Paris. In the second place, standards are measures of definite things, of lengths, weights, capacities. The things measured are not values, although it is of great social value to be able to measure them, since the properties of things in the way of size, volume, weight, are important for commercial exchange. Finally, as standards of measure, standards define things with respect to *quantity*. To be able to measure quantities is a great aid to further judgments, but it is not itself a mode of judgment. The standard, being an external and public thing, is applied *physically*. The yard-stick is physically laid down upon the things measured to determine their length.

When, therefore, the word "standard" is used with respect to judgment of value objects, nothing but confusion results, unless the radical difference in the meaning now given standard from that of standards of measurement is noted. The critic is really judging, not measuring physical fact. He is concerned with something individual, not comparative—as is all measurement. His subject-matter is qualitative, not quantitative. There is no external and public thing, defined by law to be the same for all transactions, that can be physically applied. The child who can use a yard-stick can measure as well as the most experienced and mature person, if he can handle the stick, since measuring is not judgment but is a physical operation performed for the sake of determining value in exchange or in behalf of some further physical operation—as a carpenter measures the boards with which he builds. The same cannot be said of judgment of the value of an idea or the value of any objects.

Yet it does not follow because of absence of a uniform and publicly determined external object, that objective criticism of value-objects is impossible. What follows is that criticism is judgment; that like every judgment it involves a venture, a hypothetical element; that it is directed to qualities which are nevertheless qualities of an *object*; and that it is concerned with an individual object, not with making comparisons by means of an external preestablished rule between different things. The critic, because of the element of venture, reveals himself in his criticisms. He wanders into another field and confuses values when he departs from the object he is judging. Nowhere are comparisons so odious as in fine art.

Criticism is judgment. The material out of which judgment grows is the work, the object, but it is this object as it enters into the experience of the critic by interaction with his own sensitivity and his knowledge and funded store from past experiences. As to their content, therefore, judgments will vary with the concrete material that evokes them and that must sustain them if criticism is pertinent and valid. Nevertheless, judgments have a common form because they all have certain functions to perform. These functions are discrimination and unification. Judgment has to evoke a clearer consciousness of constituent parts and to discover how consistently these parts are related to form a whole. Theory gives the names of analysis and synthesis to the execution of these functions.

They cannot be separated from each other, because analysis is disclosure of part as parts of a whole; of details and particulars as belonging to total situation, a universe of discourse. This operation is the opposite of picking to pieces or of dissection, even when something of the latter sort is required in order to make judgment possible. No rules can be laid for the performance of so delicate an act as determination of the significant parts of a whole, and of their respective places and weights in the whole. This is the reason, perhaps, why scholarly dissertations upon literature are so often merely scholastic enumerations of minutiae, and so-called criticisms of paintings are of the order of analyses of handwriting by experts.

Analytic judgment is a test of the mind of the critic, since mind, as organization into perceptions of meanings derived from past intercourse with objects, is the organ of discrimination. Hence the safeguard of the critic is a consuming informed interest. I say "consuming" because without natural sensitivity connected with an intense liking for certain subject-matters, a critic, having even a wide range of learning, will be so cold that he will remain on the outside. Yet, unless affection is informed with the insight that is the product of a rich and full experience, judgment will be one-sided or will not rise above the level of gushy sentimentalism. Learning must be the fuel of warmth of interest.

The difference between genuine, valid good and a counterfeit, specious good is unreal, or it is a difference consequent upon reflection, or criticism, and the significant point is that this difference is equivalent to that made by discovery of relationships, of conditions and consequences. With this conclusion are bound up two other propositions: Of immediate values as such, values which occur and which are possessed and enjoyed, there is no theory at all; they just occur, are enjoyed, possessed; and that is all. The moment we begin to discourse about these values, to define and generalize, to make distinctions in kinds, we are passing beyond value-objects themselves; we are entering, even if only blindly, upon an inquiry into causal antecedents and causative consequents, with a view to appraising the "real," that is the eventual, goodness of the thing in question. We are criticizing, not for its own sake, but for the sake of instituting and perpetuating more enduring and extensive values.

The other proposition is that philosophy is and can be nothing but this critical operation and function become aware of itself and its implications, pursued deliberately and systematically. It starts from actual situations of belief, conduct and appreciative perception which are characterized by immediate qualities of good and bad, and from the modes of critical judgment current at any given time in all the regions of value; these are its data, its subject-matter. These values, criticisms, and critical methods it subjects to further criticism as comprehensive and consistent as possible. The function is to regulate the further appreciation of goods and bads; to give greater freedom and security in those acts of direct selection, appropriation, identification and of rejection, elimination, destruction which enstate and which exclude objects of belief, conduct and contemplation.

Philosophic discourse partakes both of scientific and literary discourse. Like literature, it is a comment on nature and life in the interest of a more intense and just appreciation of the meanings present in experience. Its business is reportorial and transcriptive only in the sense in which the drama and poetry have that office. Its primary concern is to clarify, liberate and extend the goods which inhere in the naturally generated functions of experience. It has no call to create a world of "reality" *de nova,* nor to delve into secrets of Being hidden from common-sense and science. It has no stock of information or body of knowledge peculiarly its own; if it does not always become ridiculous when it sets up as a rival of science, it is only because a particular philosopher happens to be also, as a human being, a prophetic man of science. Its business is to accept and to utilize for a purpose the best available knowledge of its own time and place. And this purpose is criticism of beliefs, institutions, customs, policies with respect to their bearing upon good. This does not mean their bearing upon *the* good, as something itself attained and formulated in philosophy. For as philosophy has no private source of knowledge or of methods for attaining truth, so it has no private access to good. As it accepts knowledge of facts and principles from those competent in inquiry and discovery, so it accepts the goods that are diffused in human experience. It has no Mosaic nor Pauline authority of revelation entrusted to it. But it has the authority of intelligence, of criticism of these common and natural goods.

At this point, it departs from the arts of literary discourse. They have a freer office to perform—to perpetuate, enhance and vivify in imagination the natural goods; all things are forgiven to him who succeeds. But philosophic criticism has a stricter task, with a greater measure of responsibility to what lies outside its own products. It has to appraise values by taking cognizance of their causes and consequences; only by this straight and narrow path may it contribute to expansion and emancipation of values. For this reason the conclusions of science about matter-of-fact efficiencies of nature are its indispensable instruments. If its eventual concern is to render goods more coherent, more secure and more significant in appreciation, its road is the subject-matter of natural existence as science discovers and depicts it.

Philosophy, defined as a logic, makes no pretense to be an account of a closed and finished universe. Its business is not to secure or guarantee any particular reality or value. *Per contra,* it gets the significance of a method. The right relationship and adjustment of the various typical phases of experience to one another is a problem felt in every department of life. Intellectual rectification and control of these adjustments cannot fail to reflect itself in an added clearness and security on the practical side. It may be that general logic cannot become an instrument in the immediate direction of the activities of science or art or industry; but it is of value in criticizing and organizing tools of immediate research. It also has direct significance in the valuation for social or life-purposes of results achieved in particular branches. Much of the immediate business of life is badly done because we do not know the genesis and outcome of the work that occupies us. The manner and degree of appropriation of the goods achieved in various departments of social interest and vocation are partial and faulty because we are not clear as to the due rights and responsibilities of one function of experience in reference to others.

The value of research for social progress; the bearing of psychology upon educational procedure; the mutual relations of fine and industrial art; the question of the extent and nature of specialization in science in comparison with the claims of applied science; the adjustment of religious aspirations to scientific statements; the justification of a refined culture for a few in face of economic insufficiency for the mass, the relation of organization to individuality—such are a few of the many social questions whose answer depends upon the possession and use of a general logic of experience as a method of inquiry and interpretation. I do not say that headway cannot be made in such questions apart from the method indicated: a logic of experience. But unless we have a critical and assured view of the juncture in which and with reference to which a given attitude or interest arises, unless we know the service it is thereby called upon to perform, and hence the organs or methods by which it best functions in that service, our progress is impeded and irregular.

We take a part for a whole, a means for an end; or we attack wholesale some interest because it interferes with the deified sway of the one we have selected as ultimate. A clear and comprehensive consensus of social conviction and a consequent concentrated and economical direction of effort are assured only as there is some way of locating the position and role of each typical interest and occupation. The domain of opinion is one of conflict; its rule is arbitrary and costly. Only intellectual method affords a substitute for opinion. A general logic of experience alone can do for social qualities and aims what the natural sciences after centuries of struggle are doing for activity in the physical realm.

This does not mean that systems of philosophy which have attempted to state the nature of thought and of reality at large, apart from limits of particular situations in the movement of experience, have been worthless—though it does mean that their industry has been somewhat misapplied. The unfolding of metaphysical theory has made large contributions to positive evaluations of the typical situations and relationships of experience—even when its conscious intention has been quite otherwise. Every system of philosophy is itself a mode of reflection; consequently (if our main contention be true), it too has been evoked out of specific social antecedents, and has had its use as a response to them. It has effected something in modifying the situation within which it found its origin. It may not have solved the problem which it consciously put itself; in many cases we may freely admit that the question put has been found afterward to be so wrongly put as to be insoluble. Yet exactly the same thing is true, in precisely the same sense, in the history of science. For this reason, if for no other, it is impossible for the scientific man to cast the first stone at the philosopher.

The progress of science in any branch continually brings with it a realization that problems in their previous form of statement are insoluble because put in terms of unreal conditions; because the real conditions have been mixed up with mental artifacts or misconstructions. Every science is continually learning that its supposed solutions are only apparent because the "solution" solves, not the actual problem, but one which has been made up. But the very putting of the question, the very giving of the wrong answer, induces modification of existing intellectual habits, standpoints, and aims. Wrestling with the problem, there is evolution of new technique to control inquiry, there is search for new facts, institution of new types of experimentation; there is gain in the methodic control of experience.

And all this is progress. It is only the worn-out cynic, the devitalized sensualist, and the fanatical dogmatist who interpret the continuous change of science as proving that, since each successive statement is wrong, the whole record is error and folly; and that the present truth is only the error not yet found out. Such draw the moral of caring naught for all these things, or of flying to some external authority which will deliver once for all the fixed and unchangeable truth. But historic philosophy even in its aberrant forms has proved a factor in the valuation of experience; it has brought problems to light, it has provoked intellectual conflicts without which values are only nominal; even through its would-be absolutistic isolations it has secured recognition of mutual dependencies and reciprocal reinforcements. Yet if it can define its work more clearly, it can concentrate its energy upon its own characteristic problem: the genesis and functioning in experience of various typical interests and occupations with reference to one another.

Because intelligence is critical method applied to goods of belief, appreciation and conduct, so as to construct freer and more secure goods, turning assent and assertion into free communication of shareable meanings, turning feeling into ordered and liberal sense, turning reaction into response, it is the reasonable object of our deepest faith and loyalty, the stay and support of all reasonable hopes. To utter such a statement is not to indulge in romantic idealization. It is not to assert that intelligence will ever dominate the course of events; it is not even to imply that it will save from ruin and destruction. The issue is one of choice, and choice is always a question of alternatives.

What the method of intelligence, thoughtful valuation will accomplish, if once it be tried, is for the result of trial to determine. Since it is relative to the intersection in existence of hazard and rule, of contingency and order, faith in a wholesale and final triumph is fantastic. But some procedure has to be tried; for life is itself a sequence of trials. Carelessness and routine, Olympian aloofness, secluded contemplation are themselves choices. To claim that intelligence is a better method than its alternatives, authority, imitation, caprice and ignorance, prejudice and passion, is hardly an excessive claim. These procedures have been tried and have worked their will. The result is not such as to make it clear that the method of intelligence, the use of science in criticizing and recreating the casual goods of nature into intentional and conclusive goods of art, the union of knowledge and values in production, is not worth trying. There may be those to whom it is treason to think of philosophy as the critical method of developing methods of criticism. But this conception of philosophy also waits to be tried, and the trial which shall approve or condemn lies in the eventual issue. The import of such knowledge as we have acquired and such experience as has been quickened by thought is to evoke and justify the trial.

Speculative

Speculative Philosophy*

A. N. WHITEHEAD

1

Speculative Philosophy is the endeavour to frame a coherent, logical, necessary system of general ideas in terms of which every element of our experience can be interpreted. By this notion of "interpretation" I mean that everything of which we are conscious, as enjoyed, perceived, willed, or thought, shall have the character of a particular instance of the general scheme. Thus the philosophical scheme should be coherent, logical, and, in respect to its interpretation, applicable and adequate. Here "applicable" means that some items of experience are thus interpretable, and "adequate" means that there are no items incapable of such interpretation.

"Coherence," as here employed, means that the fundamental ideas, in terms of which the scheme is developed, presuppose each other so that in isolation they are meaningless. This requirement does not mean that they are definable in terms of each other; it means that what is indefinable in one such notion cannot be abstracted from its relevance to the other notions. It is the ideal of speculative philosophy that its fundamental notions shall not seem capable of abstraction from each other. In other words, it is presupposed that no entity can be conceived in complete

*Reprinted with the permission of The Macmillan Company from A. N. Whitehead, *Process and Reality* (New York: Harper and Brothers, 1960), pp. 4–26.

abstraction from the system of the universe, and that it is the business of speculative philosophy to exhibit this truth. This character is its coherence.

The term "logical" has its ordinary meaning, including "logical" consistency, or lack of contradiction, the definition of constructs in logical terms, the exemplification of general logical notions in specific instances, and the principles of inference. It will be observed that logical notions must themselves find their places in the scheme of philosophic notions.

It will also be noticed that this ideal of speculative philosophy has its rational side and its empirical side. The rational side is expressed by the terms "coherent" and "logical." The empirical side is expressed by the terms "applicable" and "adequate." But the two sides are bound together by clearing away an ambiguity which remains in the previous explanation of the term "adequate." The adequacy of the scheme over every item does not mean adequacy over such items as happen to have been considered. It means that the texture of observed experience, as illustrating the philosophic scheme, is such that all related experience must exhibit the same texture. Thus the philosophic scheme should be "necessary," in the sense of bearing in itself its own warrant of universality throughout all experience, provided that we confine ourselves to that which communicates with immediate matter of fact. But what does not so communicate is unknowable, and the unknowable is unknown[1]; and so this universality defined by "communication" can suffice.

This doctrine of necessity in universality means that there is an essence to the universe which forbids relationships beyond itself, as a violation of its rationality. Speculative philosophy seeks that essence.

2

Philosophers can never hope finally to formulate these metaphysical first principles. Weakness of insight and deficiencies of language stand in the way inexorably. Words and phrases must be stretched towards a generality foreign to their ordinary usage; and however such elements of language be stabilized as technicalities, they remain metaphors mutely appealing for an imaginative leap.

There is no first principle which is in itself unknowable, not to be captured by a flash of insight. But, putting aside the difficulties of language, deficiency in imaginative penetration forbids progress in any form other than that of an asymptotic approach to a scheme of principles, only definable in terms of the ideal which they should satisfy.

[1]This doctrine is a paradox. Indulging in a species of false modesty, "cautious" philosophers undertake its definition.

The difficulty has its seat in the empirical side of philosophy. Our *datum* is the actual world, including ourselves; and this actual world spreads itself for observation in the guise of the topic of our immediate experience. The elucidation of immediate experience is the sole justification for any thought; and the starting point for thought is the analytic observation of components of this experience. But we are not conscious of any clear-cut complete analysis of immediate experience, in terms of the various details which comprise its definiteness. We habitually observe by the method of difference. Sometimes we see an elephant, and sometimes we do not. The result is that an elephant, when present, is noticed. Facility of observation depends on the fact that the object observed is important when present, and sometimes is absent.

The metaphysical first principles can never fail of exemplification. We can never catch the actual world taking a holiday from their sway. Thus, for the discovery of metaphysics, the method of pinning down thought to the strict systematization of detailed discrimination, already effected by antecedent observation, breaks down. This collapse of the method of rigid empiricism is not confined to metaphysics. It occurs whenever we seek the larger generalities. In natural science this rigid method is the Baconian method of induction, a method which, if consistently pursued, would have left science where it found it. What Bacon omitted was the play of a free imagination, controlled by the requirements of coherence and logic. The true method of discovery is like the flight of an aeroplane. It starts from the ground of particular observation; it makes a flight in the thin air of imaginative generalization; and it again lands for renewed observation rendered acute by rational interpretation. The reason for the success of this method of imaginative rationalization is that, when the method of difference fails, factors which are constantly present may yet be observed under the influence of imaginative thought. Such thought supplies the differences which the direct observation lacks. It can even play with inconsistency; and can thus throw light on the consistent, and persistent, elements in experience by comparison with what in imagination is inconsistent with them. The negative judgment is the peak of mentality. But the conditions for the success of imaginative construction must be rigidly adhered to. In the first place, this construction must have its origin in the generalization of particular factors discerned in particular topics of human interest; for example, in physics, or in physiology, or in psychology, or in aesthetics, or in ethical beliefs, or in sociology, or in languages conceived as storehouses of human experience. In this way the prime requisite, that anyhow there shall be some important application, is secured. The success of the imaginative experiment is always to be tested by the applicability of its results beyond the restricted locus from which it originated. In default of such extended application, a generalization started from physics, for example, remains merely an alternative expression of notions applicable to physics. The partially successful philosophic generalization will, if derived from physics, find applications in fields of experience beyond physics. It will enlighten observation in those remote fields, so that general principles can be discerned as in process of illustration, which in the absence of the imaginative generalization are obscured by their persistent exemplification.

Thus the first requisite is to proceed by the method of generalization so that certainly there is some application; and the test of some success is application beyond the immediate origin. In other words, some synoptic vision has been gained.

In this description of philosophic method, the term "philosophic generalization" has meant "the utilization of specific notions, applying to a restricted group of facts, for the divination of the generic notions which apply to all facts."

In its use of this method natural science has shown a curious mixture of rationalism and irrationalism. Its prevalent tone of thought has been ardently rationalistic within its own borders, and dogmatically irrational beyond those borders. In practice such an attitude tends to become a dogmatic denial that there are any factors in the world not fully expressible in terms of its own primary notions devoid of further generalization. Such a denial is the self-denial of thought.

The second condition for the success of imaginative construction is unflinching pursuit of the two rationalistic ideals, coherence and logical perfection.

Logical perfection does not here require any detailed explanation. An example of its importance is afforded by the role of mathematics in the restricted field of natural science. The history of mathematics exhibits the generalization of special notions observed in particular instances. In any branches of mathematics, the notions presuppose each other. It is a remarkable characteristic of the history of thought that branches of mathematics developed under the pure imaginative impulse, thus controlled, finally receive their important application. Time may be wanted. Conic sections had to wait for eighteen hundred years. In more recent years, the theory of probability, the theory of tensors, the theory of matrices are cases in point.

The requirement of coherence is the great preservative of rationalistic sanity. But the validity of its criticism is not always admitted. If we consider philosophical controversies, we shall find that disputants tend to require coherence from their adversaries, and to grant dispensations to themselves. It has been remarked that a system of philosophy is never refuted; it is only abandoned. The reason is that logical contradictions, except as temporary slips of the mind—plentiful, though temporary—are the most gratuitous of errors; and usually they are trivial. Thus, after criticism, systems do not exhibit mere illogicalities. They suffer from inadequacy and incoherence. Failure to include some obvious elements of experience in the scope of the system is met by boldly denying the facts. Also while a philosophical system retains any charm of novelty, it enjoys a plenary indulgence for its failures in coherence. But after a system has acquired orthodoxy, and is taught with authority, it receives a sharper criticism. Its denials and its incoherences are found intolerable, and a reaction sets in.

Incoherence is the arbitrary disconnection of first principles. In modern philosophy Descartes' two kinds of substance, corporeal and mental, illustrate incoherence. There is, in Descartes' philosophy, no reason why there should not be a one-substance world, only corporeal, or a one-substance world, only mental. According to Descartes, a substantial individual "requires nothing but itself in order to exist." Thus this system makes a virtue of its incoherence. But on the other hand, the facts seem connected, while Descartes' system does not; for example, in the treatment of the body-mind problem. The Cartesian system obviously says something that is true. But its notions are too abstract to penetrate into the nature of things.

The attraction of Spinoza's philosophy lies in its modification of Descartes' position into greater coherence. He starts with one substance, *causa sui,* and considers its essential attributes and its individualized modes, i.e. the *"affectiones substantiae."* The gap in the system is the arbitrary introduction of the "modes." And yet, a multiplicity of modes is a fixed requisite, if the scheme is to retain any direct relevance to the many occasions in the experienced world.

The philosophy of organism is closely allied to Spinoza's scheme of thought. But it differs by the abandonment of the subject-predicate forms of thought, so far as concerns the presupposition that this form is a direct embodiment of the most ultimate characterization of fact. The result is that the "substance-quality" concept is avoided; and that morphological description is replaced by description of dynamic process. Also Spinoza's "modes" now become the sheer actualities; so that, though analysis of them increases our understanding, it does not lead us to the discovery of any higher grade of reality. The coherence, which the system seeks to preserve, is the discovery that the process, or concrescence, of any one actual entity involves the other actual entities among its components. In this way the obvious solidarity of the world receives its explanation.

In all philosophic theory there is an ultimate which is actual in virtue of its accidents. It is only then capable of characterization through its accidental embodiments, and apart from these accidents is devoid of actuality.

In the philosophy of organism this ultimate is termed "creativity"; and God is its primordial, nontemporal accident. In monistic philosophies, Spinoza's or absolute idealism, this ultimate is God, who is also equivalently termed "The Absolute." In such monistic schemes, the ultimate is illegitimately allowed a final, "eminent" reality, beyond that ascribed to any of its accidents. In this general position the philosophy of organism seems to approximate more to some strains of Indian, or Chinese, thought, than to western Asiatic, or European, thought. One side makes process ultimate; the other side makes fact ultimate.

In its turn every philosophy will suffer a deposition. But the bundle of philosophic systems expresses a variety of general truths about the universe, awaiting co-ordination and assignment of their various spheres of validity. Such progress in co-ordination is provided by the advance of philosophy; and in this sense philosophy has advanced from Plato onwards. According to this account of the achievement of rationalism, the chief error in philosophy is overstatement. The aim at generalization is sound, but the estimate of success is exaggerated. There are two main forms of such overstatement. One form is what I have termed elsewhere,[2] the "fallacy of misplaced concreteness." This fallacy consists in neglecting the degree of abstraction involved when an actual entity is considered merely so far as it exemplifies certain categories of thought. There are aspects of actualities which are simply ignored so long as we restrict thought to these categories. Thus the success of a philosophy is to be measured by its comparative avoidance of this fallacy, when thought is restricted within its categories.

The other form of overstatement consists in a false estimate of logical procedure in respect to certainty, and in respect to premises. Philosophy has been haunted by the unfortunate notion that its method is dogmatically to indicate premises which are severally clear, distinct, and certain; and to erect upon those premises a deductive system of thought.

But the accurate expression of the final generalities is the goal of discussion and not its origin. Philosophy has been misled by the example of mathematics; and even in mathematics the statement of the ultimate logical principles is beset with difficulties, as yet insuperable.[3] The vertification of a rationalistic scheme is to be sought in its general success, and not in the peculiar certainty, or initial clarity, of its first principles. In this connection the misuse of the *ex absurdo* argument has to be noted; much philosophical reasoning is vitiated by it. The only logical conclusion to be drawn, when a contradiction issues from a train of reasoning, is that

[2]Cf. *Science and the Modern World*, Ch. III.

[3]Cf. *Principia Mathematica*, by Bertrand Russell and A. N. Whitehead, Vol. I, Introduction and Introduction to the Second Edition. These introductory discussions are practically due to Russell, and in the second edition wholly so.

at least one of the premises involved in the inference is false. It is rashly assumed without further question that the peccant premise can at once be located. In mathematics this assumption is often justified, and philosophers have been thereby misled. But in the absence of a well-defined categoreal scheme of entities, issuing in a satisfactory metaphysical system, every premise in a philosophical argument is under suspicion.

Philosophy will not regain its proper status until the gradual elaboration of categoreal schemes, definitely stated at each stage of progress, is recognized as its proper objective. There may be rival schemes, inconsistent among themselves; each with its own merits and its own failures. It will then be the purpose of research to conciliate the differences. Metaphysical categories are not dogmatic statements of the obvious; they are tentative formulations of the ultimate generalities.

If we consider any scheme of philosophic categories as one complex assertion, and apply to it the logician's alternative, true or false, the answer must be that the scheme is false. The same answer must be given to a like question respecting the existing formulated principles of any science.

The scheme is true with unformulated qualifications, exceptions, limitations, and new interpretations in terms of more general notions. We do not yet know how to recast the scheme into a logical truth. But the scheme is a matrix from which true propositions applicable to particular circumstances can be derived. We can at present only trust our trained instincts as to the discrimination of the circumstances in respect to which the scheme is valid.

The use of such a matrix is to argue from it boldly and with rigid logic. The scheme should therefore be stated with the utmost precision and definiteness, to allow of such argumentation. The conclusion of the argument should then be confronted with circumstances to which it should apply.

The primary advantage thus gained is that experience is not interrogated with the benumbing repression of common sense. The observation acquires an enhanced penetration by reason of the expectation evoked by the conclusion of the argument. The outcome from this procedure takes one of three forms: (i) the conclusion may agree with the observed facts; (ii) the conclusion may exhibit general agreement, with disagreement in detail; (iii) the conclusion may be in complete disagreement in the facts.

In the first case, the facts are known with more adequacy and the applicability of the system to the world has been elucidated. In the second case, criticisms of the observation of the facts and of the details of the scheme are both required. The history of thought shows that false interpretations of observed facts enter into the records of their observation.

Thus both theory, and received notions as to fact, are in doubt. In the third case a fundamental reorganization of theory is required either by way of limiting it to some special province, or by way of entire abandonment of its main categories of thought.

After the initial basis of a rational life, with a civilized language, has been laid, all productive thought has proceeded either by the poetic insight of artists, or by the imaginative elaboration of schemes of thought capable of utilization as logical premises. In some measure or other, progress is always a transcendence of what is obvious.

Rationalism never shakes off its status of an experimental adventure. The combined influences of mathematics and religion, which have so greatly contributed to the rise of philosophy, have also had the unfortunate effect of yoking it with static dogmatism. Rationalism is an adventure in the clarification of thought, progressive and never final. But it is an adventure in which even partial success has importance.

3

The field of a special science is confined to one genus of facts, in the sense that no statements are made respecting facts which lie outside that genus. The very circumstance that a science has naturally arisen concerning a set of facts secures that facts of that type have definite relations among themselves which are very obvious to all mankind. The common obviousness of things arises when their explicit apprehension carries immediate importance for purposes of survival, or of enjoyment—that is to say, for purposes of "being" and of "well-being." Elements in human experience, singled out in this way, are those elements concerning which language is copious and, within its limits, precise. The special sciences, therefore, deal with topics which lie open to easy inspection and are readily expressed by words.

The study of philosophy is a voyage towards the larger generalities. For this reason in the infancy of science, when the main stress lay in the discovery of the most general ideas usefully applicable to the subject-matter in question, philosophy was not sharply distinguished from science. To this day, a new science with any substantial novelty in its notions is considered to be in some way peculiarly philosophical. In their later stages, apart from occasional disturbances, most sciences accept without question the general notions in terms of which they develop. The main stress is laid on the adjustment and the direct verification of more special statements. In such periods scientists repudiate philosophy; Newton, justly satisfied with his physical principles, disclaimed metaphysics.

The fate of Newtonian physics warns us that there is a development in scientific first principles, and that their original forms can only be saved by interpretations of meaning and limitations of their field of application—interpretations and limitations unsuspected during the first period of successful employment. One chapter in the history of culture is concerned with the growth of generalities. In such a chapter it is seen that the older generalities, like the older hills, are worn down and diminished in height, surpassed by younger rivals.

Thus one aim of philosophy is to challenge the half-truths constituting the scientific first principles. The systematization of knowledge cannot be conducted in watertight compartments. All general truths condition each other; and the limits of their application cannot be adequately defined apart from their correlation by yet wider generalities. The criticism of principles must chiefly take the form of determining the proper meanings to be assigned to the fundamental notions of the various sciences, when these notions are considered in respect to their status relatively to each other. The determination of this status requires a generality transcending any special subject-matter.

If we may trust the Pythagorean tradition, the rise of European philosophy was largely promoted by the development of mathematics into a science of abstract generality. But in its subsequent development the method of philosophy has also been vitiated by the example of mathematics. The primary method of mathematics is deduction; the primary method of philosophy is descriptive generalization. Under the influence of mathematics, deduction has been foisted onto philosophy as its standard method, instead of taking its true place as an essential auxiliary mode of verification whereby to test the scope of generalities. This misapprehension of philosophic method has veiled the very considerable success of philosophy in providing generic notions which add lucidity to our apprehension of the facts of experience. The depositions of Plato, Aristotle, Thomas Aquinas, Descartes, Spinoza, Leibnitz, Locke, Berkeley, Hume, Kant, Hegel, merely mean that ideas which these men introduced into the philosophic tradition must be construed with limitations, adaptations, and inversions, either unknown to them, or even explicitly repudiated by them. A new idea introduces a new alternative; and we are not less indebted to a thinker when we adopt the alternative which he discarded. Philosophy never reverts to its old position after the shock of a great philosopher.

4

Every science must devise its own instruments. The tool required for philosophy is language. Thus philosophy redesigns language in the same way that, in a physical science, pre-existing appliances are redesigned. It is exactly at this point that the appeal to facts is a difficult operation. This appeal is not solely to the expression of the facts in current verbal statements. The adequacy of such sentences is the main question at issue. It is true that the general agreement of mankind as to experienced facts is best expressed in language. But the language of literature breaks down precisely at the task of expressing in explicit form the larger generalities— the very generalities which metaphysics seeks to express.

The point is that every proposition refers to a universe exhibiting some general systematic metaphysical character. Apart from this background, the separate entities which go to form the proposition, and the proposition as a whole, are without determinate character. Nothing has been defined, because every definite entity requires a systematic universe to supply its requisite status. Thus every proposition proposing a fact must, in its complete analysis, propose the general character of the universe required for that fact. There are no self-sustained facts, floating in nonentity. This doctrine, of the impossibility of tearing a proposition from its systematic context in the actual world, is a direct consequence of the fourth and the twentieth of the fundamental categoreal explanations which we shall be engaged in expanding and illustrating. A proposition can embody partial truth because it only demands a certain type of systematic environment, which is presupposed in its meaning. It does not refer to the universe in all its detail.

One practical aim of metaphysics is the accurate analysis of propositions; not merely of metaphysical propositions, but of quite ordinary propositions such as "There is beef for dinner today," and "Socrates is mortal." The one genus of facts which constitutes the field of some special science requires some common metaphysical presupposition respecting the universe. It is merely credulous to accept verbal phrases as adequate statements of propositions. The distinction between verbal phrases and complete propositions is one of the reasons why the logicians' rigid alternative, "true or false," is so largely irrelevant for the pursuit of knowledge.

The excessive trust in linguistic phrases has been the well-known reason vitiating so much of the philosophy and physics among the Greeks and among the mediaeval thinkers who continued the Greek traditions. For example John Stuart Mill writes: "They (the Greeks) had great difficulty in distinguishing between things which their language confounded, or in putting mentally together things which it distinguished; and could hardly combine the objects in nature, into any classes but those which were made for them by the popular phrases of their own country; or at least could not help fancying those classes to be natural, and all others arbitrary and artificial. Accordingly, scientific investigation among the Greek schools of speculation and their followers in the Middle Ages, was little more than a mere sifting and analysing of the notions attached to common language.

They thought that by determining the meaning of words they could become acquainted with facts."[4] Mill then proceeds to quote from Whewell[5] a paragraph illustrating the same weakness of Greek thought.

But neither Mill, nor Whewell, tracks this difficulty about language down to its sources. They both presuppose that language does enunciate well-defined propositions. This is quite untrue. Language is thoroughly indeterminate, by reason of the fact that every occurrence presupposes some systematic type of environment.

For example, the word "Socrates," referring to the philosopher, in one sentence may stand for an entity presupposing a more closely defined background than the word "Socrates," with the same reference, in another sentence. The word "mortal" affords an analogous possibility. A precise language must await a completed metaphysical knowledge.

The technical language of philosophy represents attempts of various schools of thought to obtain explicit expression of general ideas presupposed by the facts of experience. It follows that any novelty in metaphysical doctrines exhibits some measure of disagreement with statements of the facts to be found in current philosophical literature. The extent of disagreement measures the extent of metaphysical divergence. It is, therefore, no valid criticism on one metaphysical school to point out that its doctrines do not follow from the verbal expression of the facts accepted by another school. The whole contention is that the doctrines in question supply a closer approach to fully expressed propositions.

The truth itself is nothing else than how the composite natures of the organic actualities of the world obtain adequate representation in the divine nature. Such representations compose the "consequent nature" of God, which evolves in its relationship to the evolving world without derogation to the eternal completion of its primordial conceptual nature. In this way the "ontological principle" is maintained—since there can be no determinate truth, correlating impartially the partial experiences of many actual entities, apart from one actual entity to which it can be referred. The reaction of the temporal world on the nature of God is considered subsequently in Part V: it is there termed "the consequent nature of God."

Whatever is found in "practice" must lie within the scope of the metaphysical description. When the description fails to include the "practice," the metaphysics is inadequate and requires revision. There can be no appeal to practice to supplement metaphysics, so long as we remain contented with our metaphysical doctrines. Metaphysics is nothing but the description of the generalities which apply to all the details of practice.

---

[4]Cf. *Logic*, Book V, Ch. III.
[5]Cf. Whewell's *History of the Inductive Sciences*.

No metaphysical system can hope entirely to satisfy these pragmatic tests. At the best such a system will remain only an approximation to the general truths which are sought. In particular, there are no precisely stated axiomatic certainties from which to start. There is not even the language in which to frame them. The only possible procedure is to start from verbal expressions which, when taken by themselves with the current meaning of their words, are ill-defined and ambiguous. These are not premises to be immediately reasoned from apart from elucidation by further discussion; they are endeavours to state general principles which will be exemplified in the subsequent description of the facts of experience. This subsequent elaboration should elucidate the meanings to be assigned to the words and phrases employed. Such meanings are incapable of accurate apprehension apart from a correspondingly accurate apprehension of the metaphysical background which the universe provides for them. But no language can be anything but elliptical, requiring a leap of the imagination to understand its meaning in its relevance to immediate experience. The position of metaphysics in the development of culture cannot be understood without remembering that no verbal statement is the adequate expression of a proposition.

An old established metaphysical system gains a false air of adequate precision from the fact that its words and phrases have passed into current literature. Thus propositions expressed in its language are more easily correlated to our flitting intuitions into metaphysical truth. When we trust these verbal statements and argue as though they adequately analysed meaning, we are led into difficulties which take the shape of negations of what in practice is presupposed. But when they are proposed as first principles they assume an unmerited air of sober obviousness. Their defect is that the true propositions which they do express lose their fundamental character when subjected to adequate expression. For example consider the type of propositions such as "The grass is green," and "The whale is big." This subject-predicate form of statement seems so simple, leading straight to a metaphysical first principle; and yet in these examples it conceals such complex, diverse meanings.

5

It has been an objection to speculative philosophy that it is overambitious. Rationalism, it is admitted, is the method by which advance is made within the limits of particular sciences. It is, however, held that this limited success must not encourage attempts to frame ambitious schemes expressive of the general nature of things.

One alleged justification of this criticism is ill-success: European thought is represented as littered with metaphysical systems, abandoned and unreconciled.

Such an assertion tacitly fastens upon philosophy the old dogmatic test The same criterion would fasten ill-success upon science. We no more retain the physics of the seventeenth century than we do the Cartesian philosophy of that century. Yet within limits, both systems express important truths. Also we are beginning to understand the wider categories which define their limits of correct application. Of course, in that century, dogmatic views held sway; so that the validity both of the physical notions, and of the Cartesian notions, was misconceived. Mankind never quite knows what it is after. When we survey the history of thought, and likewise the history of practice, we find that one idea after another is tried out, its limitations defined, and its core of truth elicited. In application to the instinct for the intellectual adventures demanded by particular epochs, there is much truth in Augustine's rhetorical phrase, *Securus judicat orbis terrarum.* At the very least, men do what they can in the way of systematization, and in the event achieve something. The proper test is not that of finality, but of progress.

But the main objection, dating from the sixteenth century and receiving final expression from Francis Bacon, is the uselessness of philosophic speculation. The position taken by this objection is that we ought to describe detailed matter of fact, and elicit the laws with a generality strictly limited to the systematization of these described details. General interpretation, it is held, has no bearing upon this procedure; and thus any system of general interpretation, be it true or false, remains intrinsically barren. Unfortunately for this objection, there are no brute, self-contained matters of fact, capable of being understood apart from interpretation as an element in a system. Whenever we attempt to express the matter of immediate experience, we find that its understanding leads us beyond itself, to its contemporaries, to its past, to its future, and to the universals in terms of which its definiteness is exhibited. But such universals, by their very character of universality, embody the potentiality of other facts with variant types of definiteness. Thus the understanding of the immediate brute fact requires its metaphysical interpretation as an item in a world with some systematic relation to it. When thought comes upon the scene, it finds the interpretations as matters of practice. Philosophy does not initiate interpretations. Its search for a rationalistic scheme is the search for more adequate criticism, and for more adequate justification, of the interpretations which we perforce employ. Our habitual experience is a complex of failure and success in the enterprise of interpretation. If we desire a record of uninterpreted experience, we must ask a stone to record its autobiography. Every scientific memoir in its record of the "facts" is shot through and through with interpretation. The methodology of rational interpretation is the product of the fitful vagueness of consciousness. Elements which shine with immediate distinctness, in some circumstances, retire into penumbral shadow in other circumstances, and into black darkness on other occasions. And yet all occasions proclaim themselves as actualities within the flux of a solid world, demanding a unity of interpretation.

Philosophy is the self-correction by consciousness of its own initial excess of subjectivity. Each actual occasion contributes to the circumstances of its origin additional formative elements deepening its own peculiar individuality. Consciousness is only the last and greatest of such elements by which the selective character of the individual obscures the external totality from which it originates and which it embodies. An actual individual, of such higher grade, has truck with the totality of things by reason of its sheer actuality; but it has attained its individual depth of being by a selective emphasis limited to its own purposes. The task of philosophy is to recover the totality obscured by the selection. It replaces in rational experience what has been submerged in the higher sensitive experience and has been sunk yet deeper by the initial operations of consciousness itself. The selectiveness of individual experience is moral so far as it conforms to the balance of importance disclosed in the rational vision; and conversely the conversion of the intellectual insight into an emotional force corrects the sensitive experience in the direction of morality. The correction is in proportion to the rationality of the insight.

Morality of outlook is inseparably conjoined with generality of outlook. The antithesis between the general good and the individual interest can be abolished only when the individual is such that its interest is the general good, thus exemplifying the loss of the minor intensities in order to find them again with finer composition in a wider sweep of interest.

Philosophy frees itself from the taint of ineffectiveness by its close relations with religion and with science, natural and sociological. It attains its chief importance by fusing the two, namely, religion and science, into one rational scheme of thought. Religion should connect the rational generality of philosophy with the emotions and purposes springing out of existence in a particular society, in a particular epoch, and conditioned by particular antecedents. Religion is the translation of general ideas into particular thoughts, particular emotions, and particular purposes; it is directed to the end of stretching individual interest beyond its self-defeating particularity. Philosophy finds religion, and modifies it; and conversely religion is among the data of experience which philosophy must weave into its own scheme. Religion is an ultimate craving to infuse into the insistent particularity of emotion that non-temporal generality which primarily belongs to conceptual thought alone. In the higher organisms the differences of tempo between the mere emotions and the conceptual experiences produce a life-tedium, unless this supreme fusion has been effected. The two sides of the organism require a reconciliation in which emotional experiences illustrate a conceptual justification, and conceptual experiences find an emotional illustration.

This demand for an intellectual justification of brute experience has also been the motive power in the advance of European science. In this sense scientific interest is only a variant form of religious interest. Any survey of the scientific devotion to "truth," as an ideal, will confirm this statement. There is, however, a grave divergence between science and religion in respect to the phases of individual experience with which they are concerned. Religion is centered upon the harmony of rational thought with the sensitive reaction to the percepta from which experience originates. Science is concerned with the harmony of rational thought with the percepta themselves. When science deals with emotions, the emotions in question are percepta and not immediate passions—other people's emotion and not our own; at least our own in recollection, and not in immediacy. Religion deals with the formation of the experiencing subject; whereas science deals with the objects, which are the data forming the primary phase in this experience. The subject originates from, and amid, given conditions; science conciliates thought with this primary matter of fact; and religion conciliates the thought involved in the process with the sensitive reaction involved in that same process. The process is nothing else than the experiencing subject itself. In this explanation it is presumed that an experiencing subject is one occasion of sensitive reaction to an actual world. Science finds religious experiences among its percepta; and religion finds scientific concepts among the conceptual experiences to be fused with particular sensitive reactions.

The conclusion of this discussion is, first, the assertion of the old doctrine that breadth of thought reacting with intensity of sensitive experience stands as an ultimate claim of existence; secondly, the assertion that empirically the development of self-justifying thoughts has been achieved by the complex process of generalizing from particular topics, of imaginatively schematizing the generalizations, and finally by renewed comparison of the imagined scheme with the direct experience to which it should apply.

There is no justification for checking generalization at any particular stage. Each phase of generalization exhibits its own peculiar simplicities which stand out just at that stage, and at no other stage. There are simplicities connected with the motion of a bar of steel which are obscured if we refuse to abstract from the individual molecules; and there are certain simplicities concerning the behavior of men which are obscured if we refuse to abstract from the individual peculiarities of particular specimens. In the same way, there are certain general truths, about the actual things in the common world of activity, which will be obscured when attention is confined to some particular detailed mode of considering them. These general truths, involved in the meaning of every particular notion respecting the actions of things, are the subject matter for speculative philosophy.

Philosophy destroys its usefulness when it indulges in brilliant feats of explaining away. It is then trespassing with the wrong equipment upon the field of particular sciences. Its ultimate appeal is to the general consciousness of what in practice we experience. Whatever thread of presupposition characterizes social expression throughout the various epochs of rational society, must find its place in philosophic theory. Speculative boldness must be balanced by complete humility before logic, and before fact. It is a disease of philosophy when it is neither bold nor humble, but merely a reflection of the temperamental presuppositions of exceptional personalities.

Analogously, we do not trust any recasting of scientific theory depending upon a single performance of an aberrant experiment, unrepeated. The ultimate test is always widespread, recurrent experience; and the more general the rationalistic scheme, the more important is this final appeal.

The useful function of philosophy is to promote the most general systematization of civilized thought. There is a constant reaction between specialism and common sense. It is the part of the special sciences to modify common sense. Philosophy is the welding of imagination and common sense into a restraint upon specialists, and also into an enlargement of their imaginations. By providing the generic notions philosophy should make it easier to conceive the infinite variety of specific instances which rest unrealized in the womb of nature.

Existentialist

I and Thou *

MARTIN BUBER

To man the world is twofold, in accordance with his twofold attitude.

The attitude of man is twofold, in accordance with the twofold nature of the primary words which he speaks.

The primary words are not isolated words, but combined words.

The one primary word is the combination *I–Thou*.

The other primary word is the combination *I–It*; wherein, without a change in the primary word, one of the words *He* and *She* can replace *It*.

Hence the *I* of man is also twofold.

For the *I* of the primary word *I–Thou* is a different *I* from that of the primary word *I–It*.

Primary words do not signify things, but they intimate relations.

Primary words do not describe something that might exist independently of them, but being spoken they bring about existence.

Primary words are spoken from the being.

If *Thou* is said, the *I* of the combination *I–Thou* is said along with it.

If *It* is said, the *I* of the combination *I–It* is said along with it.

The primary word *I–Thou* can only be spoken with the whole being.

The primary word *I–It* can never be spoken with the whole being.

There is no *I* taken in itself, but only the *I* of the primary word *I–Thou* and the *I* of the primary word *I–It*.

*Reprinted with the permission of the original publishers, T. & T. Clark, and of Charles Scribner's Sons from Martin Buber, *I and Thou* (New York: Charles Scribner's Sons, 1958), pp. 3–6, 11–18, 22–23, 28–34.

When a man says *I* he refers to one or other of these. The *I* to which he refers is present when he says *I*. Further, when he says *Thou* or *It,* the *I* of one of the two primary words is present.

The existence of *I* and the speaking of *I* are one and the same thing.

When a primary word is spoken the speaker enters the word and takes his stand in it.

The life of human beings is not passed in the sphere of transitive verbs alone. It does not exist in virtue of activities alone which have some *thing* for their object.

I perceive something. I am sensible of something. I imagine something. I will something. I feel something. I think something. The life of human beings does not consist of all this and the like alone.

This and the like together establish the realm of *It.*

But the realm of *Thou* has a different basis.

When *Thou* is spoken, the speaker has no thing for his object. For where there is a thing there is another thing. Every *It* is bounded by others; *It* exists only through being bounded by others. But when *Thou* is spoken, there is no thing. *Thou* has no bounds.

When *Thou* is spoken, the speaker has no *thing*; he has indeed nothing. But he takes his stand in relation.

It is said that man experiences his world. What does that mean?

Man travels over the surface of things and experiences them. He extracts knowledge about their constitution from them: he wins an experience from them. He experiences what belongs to the things.

But the world is not presented to man by experiences alone. These present him only with a world composed of *It* and *He* and *She* and *It* again.

I experience something.—If we add "inner" to "outer" experiences, nothing in the situation is changed. We are merely following the uneternal division that springs from the lust of the human race to whittle away the secret of death. Inner things or outer things, what are they but things and things!

I experience something.—If we add "secret" to "open" experiences, nothing in the situation is changed. How self-confident is that wisdom which perceives a closed compartment in things, reserved for the initiate and manipulated only with the key. O secrecy without a secret! O accumulation of information! It, always It!

The man who experiences has not part in the world. For it is "in him" and not between him and the world that the experience arises.

The world has no part in the experience. It permits itself to be experienced, but has no concern in the matter. For it does nothing to the experience, and the experience does nothing to it.

As experience, the world belongs to the primary word *I–It*.
The primary word *I–Thou* establishes the world of relation.

The spheres in which the world of relation arises are three.
First, our life with nature. There the relation sways in gloom, beneath the level of speech. Creatures live and move over against us, but cannot come to us, and when we address them as *Thou,* our words cling to the threshold of speech.
Second, our life with men. There the relation is open and in the form of speech. We can give and accept the *Thou.*
Third, our life with spiritual beings. There the relation is clouded, yet it discloses itself; it does not use speech, yet begets it. We perceive no *Thou,* but none the less we feel we are addressed and we answer—forming, thinking, acting. We speak the primary word with our being, though we cannot utter *Thou* with our lips.
But with what right do we draw what lies outside speech into relation with the world of the primary word?
In every sphere in its own way, through each process of becoming that is present to us we look out toward the fringe of the eternal *Thou*; in each we are aware of a breath from the eternal *Thou*; in each *Thou* we address the eternal *Thou.*

The *Thou* meets me through grace—it is not found by seeking. But my speaking of the primary word to it is an act of my being, is indeed *the* act of my being.
The *Thou* meets me. But I step into direct relation with it. Hence the relation means being chosen and choosing, suffering and action in one; just as any action of the whole being, which means the suspension of all partial actions and consequently of all sensations of actions grounded only in their particular limitation, is bound to resemble suffering.
The primary word *I–Thou* can be spoken only with the whole being. Concentration and fusion into the whole being can never take place through my agency, nor can it ever take place without me. I become through my relation to the *Thou*; as I become *I,* I say *Thou.*
All real living is meeting.

The relation to the *Thou* is direct. No system of ideas, no foreknowledge, and no fancy intervene between *I* and *Thou.* The memory itself is transformed, as it plunges out of its isolation into the unity of the whole. No aim, no lust, and no anticipation intervene between *I* and *Thou*. Desire itself is transformed as it plunges out of its dream into the appearance. Every means is an obstacle. Only when every means has collapsed does the meeting come about.

In face of the directness of the relation everything indirect becomes irrelevant. It is also irrelevant if my *Thou* is already the *It* for other *I's* ("an object of general experience"), or can become so through the very accomplishment of this act of my being. For the real, though certainly swaying and swinging, boundary runs neither between experience and non-experience, nor between what is given and what is not given, nor yet between the world of being and the world of value; but cutting indifferently across all these provinces it lies between *Thou* and *It*, between the present and the object.

The present, and by that is meant not the point which indicates from time to time in our thought merely the conclusion of "finished" time, the mere appearance of a termination which is fixed and held, but the real, filled present, exists only in so far as actual presentness, meeting, and relation exist. The present arises only in virtue of the fact that the *Thou* becomes present.

The *I* of the primary word *I–It*, that is, the *I* faced by no *Thou*, but surrounded by a multitude of "contents," has no present, only the past. Put in another way, in so far as man rests satisfied with the things that he experiences and uses, he lives in the past, and his moment has no present content. He has nothing but objects. But objects subsist in time that has been.

The present is not fugitive and transient, but continually present and enduring. The object is not duration, but cessation, suspension, a breaking off and cutting clear and hardening, absence of relation and of present being.

True beings are lived in the present, the life of objects is in the past.

Appeal to a "world of ideas" as a third factor above this opposition will not do away with its essential twofold nature. For I speak of nothing else but the real man, of you and of me, of our life and of our world—not of an *I*, or a state of being, in itself alone. The real boundary for the actual man cuts right across the world of ideas as well.

To be sure, many a man who is satisfied with the experience and use of the world of things has raised over or about himself a structure of ideas, in which he finds refuge and repose from the oncome of nothingness. On the threshold he lays aside his inauspicious everyday dress, wraps himself in pure linen, and regales himself with the spectacle of primal being, or of necessary being; but his life has no part in it. To proclaim his ways may even fill him with well-being.

But the mankind of mere *It* that is imagined, postulated, and propagated by such a man has nothing in common with a living mankind where *Thou* may truly be spoken. The noblest fiction is a fetish, the loftiest fictitious sentiment is depraved. Ideas are no more enthroned above our heads than resident in them; they wander amongst us and accost us. The man who leaves the primary word unspoken is to be pitied; but the man who addresses instead these ideas with an abstraction or a password, as if it were their name, is contemptible.

In one of the three examples it is obvious that the direct relation includes an effect on what confronts me. In art the act of the being determines the situation in which the form becomes the work. Through the meeting that which confronts me is fulfilled, and enters the world of things, there to be endlessly active, endlessly to become *It,* but also endlessly to become *Thou* again, inspiring and blessing. It is "embodied"; its body emerges from the flow of the spaceless, timeless present on the shore of existence.

The significance of the effect is not so obvious in the relation with the *Thou* spoken to men. The act of the being which provides directness in this case is usually understood wrongly as being one of feeling. Feelings accompany the metaphysical and metapsychical fact of love, but they do not constitute it. The accompanying feelings can be of greatly differing kinds. The feeling of Jesus for the demoniac differs from his feeling for the beloved disciple; but the love is the one love. Feelings are "entertained"; love comes to pass. Feelings dwell in man; but man dwells in his love. That is no metaphor, but the actual truth. Love does not cling to the *I* in such a way as to have the *Thou* only for its "content," its object; but love is *between I* and *Thou*. The man who does not know this, with his very being know this, does not know love; even though he ascribes to it the feelings he lives through, experiences, enjoys, and expresses. Love ranges in its effect through the whole world. In the eyes of him who takes his stand in love, and gazes out of it, men are cut free from their entanglement in bustling activity. Good people and evil, wise and foolish, beautiful and ugly, become successively real to him; that is, set free they step forth in their singleness, and confront him as *Thou*. In a wonderful way, from time to time, exclusiveness arises—and so he can be effective, helping, healing, educating, raising up, saving. Love is responsibility of an *I* for a *Thou*. In this lies the likeness—impossible in any feeling whatsoever—of all who love, from the smallest to the greatest and from the blessedly protected man, whose life is rounded in that of a loved being, to him who is all his life nailed to the cross of the world, and who ventures to bring himself to the dreadful point—to love *all men.*

Let the significance of the effect in the third example, that of the creature and our contemplation of it, remain sunk in mystery. Believe in the simple magic of life, in service in the universe, and the meaning of that waiting, that alertness, that "craning of the neck" in creatures will dawn upon you. Every word would falsify; but look! round about you beings live their life, and to whatever point you turn you come upon being.

Relation is mutual. My *Thou* affects me, as I affect it. We are moulded by our pupils and built up by our works. The "bad" man, lightly touched by the holy primary word, becomes one who reveals. How we are educated by children and by animals! We live our lives inscrutably included with the streaming mutual life of the universe.

—You speak of love as though it were the only relation between men. But properly speaking, can you take it even only as an example, since there is such a thing as hate?

—So long as love is "blind," that is, so long as it does not see a *whole* being, it is not truly under the sway of the primary word of relation. Hate is by nature blind. Only a part of a being can be hated. He who sees a whole being and is compelled to reject it is no longer in the kingdom of hate, but is in that of human restriction of the power to say *Thou.* He finds himself unable to say the primary word to the other human being confronting him. This word consistently involves an affirmation of the being addressed. He is therefore compelled to reject either the other or himself. At this barrier the entering on a relation recognises its relativity, and only simultaneously with this will the barrier be raised.

Yet the man who straightforwardly hates is nearer to relation than the man without hate and love.

But this is the exalted melancholy of our fate, that every *Thou* in our world must become an *It.* It does not matter how exclusively the *Thou* was in the direct relation. As soon as the relation has been worked out or has been permeated with a means, the *Thou* becomes an object among objects—perhaps the chief, but still one of them, fixed in its size and its limits. In the work of art realization in one sense means loss of reality in another. Genuine contemplation is over in a short time; now the life in nature, that first unlocked itself to me in the mystery of mutual action, can again be described, taken to pieces, and classified—the meeting-point of manifold systems of laws. And love itself cannot persist in direct relation.

It endures, but in interchange of actual and potential being. The human being who was even now single and unconditioned, not something lying to hand, only present, not able to be experienced, only able to be fulfilled, has now become again a *He* or a *She,* a sum of qualities, a given quantity with a certain shape. Now I may take out from him again the color of his hair or of his speech or of his goodness. But so long as I can do this he is no more my *Thou* and cannot yet be my *Thou* again.

Every *Thou* in the world is by its nature fated to become a thing, or continually to re-enter into the condition of things. In objective speech it would be said that every thing in the world, either before or after becoming a thing, is able to appear to an *I* as its *Thou*. But objective speech snatches only at a fringe of real life.

The *It* is the eternal chrysalis, the *Thou* the eternal butterfly—except that situations do not always follow one another in clear succession, but often there is a happening profoundly twofold, confusedly entangled.

The fundamental difference between the two primary words comes to light in the spiritual history of primitive man. Already in the original relational event he speaks the primary word *I-Thou* in a natural way that precedes what may be termed visualization of forms—that is, before he has recognised himself as *I*. The primary word *I-It,* on the other hand, is made possible at all only by means of this recognition—by means, that is, of the separation of the *I*.

The first primary word can be resolved, certainly, into *I* and *Thou,* but it did not arise from their being set together; by its nature it precedes *I*. The second word arose from the setting together of *I* and *It*: by nature it comes after *I*.

In the primitive relational event, in virtue of its exclusiveness, the *I* is included. While, that is to say, there are in it, in accordance with its being, only the two partners, the man and that which confronts him, in their full actuality, and while the world becomes in it a dual system, the man, without yet perceiving the *I* itself, is already aware of that cosmic pathos of the *I*.

On the other hand the *I* is not yet included in the natural, actual event which is to pass over into the primary word *I-It,* into the experience with its relation to *I*. This actual event is the separation of the human body, as the bearer of its perceptions, from the world round about it. The body comes to know and to differentiate itself in its peculiarities; the differentiation, however, remains one of pure juxtaposition, and hence cannot have the character of the state in which *I* is implied.

But when the *I* of the relation has stepped forth and taken on separate existence, it also moves, strangely tenuous and reduced to merely functional activity, into the natural, actual event of the separation of the body from the world round about it, and awakens there the state in which *I* is properly active. Only now can the conscious act of the *I* take place. This act is the first form of the primary word *I-It,* of the experience in its relation to *I.* The *I* which stepped forth declares itself to be the bearer, and the world round about to be the object, of the perceptions. Of course, this happens in a "primitive" form and not in the form of a "theory of knowledge." But whenever the sentence "I see the tree" is so uttered that it no longer tells of a relation between the man—*I*—and the tree—*Thou,* but establishes the perception of the tree as object by the human consciousness, the barrier between subject and object has been set up. The primary word *I-It,* the word of separation, has been spoken.

Through the *Thou* a man becomes *I.* That which confronts him comes and disappears, relational events condense, then are scattered, and in the change consciousness of the unchanging partner, of the *I,* grows clear, and each time stronger. To be sure, it is still seen caught in the web of the relation with the *Thou,* as the increasingly distinguishable feature of that which reaches out to and yet is not the *Thou.* But it continually breaks through with more power, till a time comes when it bursts its bonds, and the *I* confronts itself for a moment, separated as though it were a *Thou*; as quickly to take possession of itself and from then on to enter into relations in consciousness of itself.

Only now can the other primary word be assembled. Hitherto the *Thou* of relation was continually fading away, but it did not thereby become an *It* for some *I,* an object of perception and experience without real connection—as it will henceforth become. It became rather an *It,* so to speak, for itself, an *It* disregarded at first, yet waiting to rise up in a new relational event. Further, the body maturing into a person was hitherto distinguished, as bearer of its perceptions and executor of its impulses, from the world round about. But this distinction was simply a juxtaposition brought about by its seeing its way in the situation, and not an absolute severance of *I* and its object. But now the separated *I* emerges, transformed. Shrunk from substance and fulness to a functional point, to a subject which experiences and uses, *I* approaches and takes possession of all *It* existing "in and for itself," and forms in conjunction with it the other primary word. The man who has become conscious of *I,* that is, the man who says *I-It,* stands before things, but not over against them in the flow of mutual action. Now with the magnifying glass of peering observation he bends over particulars and objectifies them, or with the fieldglass of remote inspection he objectifies them and arranges them as scenery, he isolates them in observation without any feeling of their exclusiveness, or he knits them into a scheme of observation without any feeling of universality. The feeling of exclusiveness he would be able to find only in relation, the feeling of universality only through it. Now for the first time he experiences things as sums of qualities. From each relational experience qualities belonging to the remembered *Thou* had certainly remained sunk in his memory; but now for the first time things are for him actually composed of their qualities. From the simple memory of the relation the man, dreaming or fashioning or thinking, according to his nature, enlarges the nucleus, the substance that showed itself in the *Thou* with power and gathered up in itself all qualities. But now also for the first time he sets things in space and time, in causal connection, each with its own place and appointed course, its measurability and conditioned nature.

The *Thou* appears, to be sure, in space, but in the exclusive situation of what is over against it, where everything else can be only the background out of which it emerges, not its boundary and measured limit. It appears, too, in time, but in that of the event which is fulfilled in itself: it is not lived as part of a continuous and organized sequence, but is lived in a "duration" whose purely intensive dimension is definable only in terms of itself. It appears, lastly, simultaneously as acting and as being acted upon—not, however, linked to a chain of causes, but, in its relation of mutual action with the *I,* as the beginning and the end of the event. This is part of the basic truth of the human world, that only *It* can be arranged in order. Only when things, from being our *Thou,* become our *It,* can they be co-ordinated. The *Thou* knows no system of co-ordination.

But now that we have come so far, it is necessary to set down the other part of the basic truth, without which this would be a useless fragment— namely, a world that is ordered is not the world-order. There are moments of silent depth in which you look on the world-order fully present. Then in its very flight the note will be heard; but the ordered world is its indistinguishable score. These moments are immortal, and most transitory of all; no content may be secured from them, but their power invades creation and the knowledge of man, beams of their power stream into the ordered world and dissolve it again and again. This happens in the history both of the individual and of the race.

To man the world is twofold, in accordance with his twofold attitude.

He perceives what exists round about him—simply things, and beings as things; and what happens round about him—simply events, and actions as events; things consisting of qualities, events of moments; things entered in the graph of place, events in that of time; things and events bounded by other things and events, measured by them, comparable with them: he perceives an ordered and detached world. It is to some extent a reliable world, having density and duration. Its organization can be surveyed and brought out again and again; gone over with closed eyes, and verified with open eyes. It is always there, next to your skin, if you look on it that way, cowering in your soul, if you prefer it so. It is your object, remains it as long as you wish, and remains a total stranger, within you and without. You perceive it, take it to yourself as the "truth," and it lets itself be taken; but it does not give itself to you. Only concerning it may you make yourself "understood" with others; it is ready, though attached to everyone in a different way, to be an object common to you all. But you cannot meet others in it. You cannot hold on to life without it, its reliability sustains you; but should you die in it, your grave would be in nothingness.

Or on the other hand, man meets what exists and becomes as what is over against him, always simply a *single* being and each thing simply as being. What exists is opened to him in happenings, and what happens affects him as what is. Nothing is present for him except this one being, but it implicates the whole world. Measure and comparison have disappeared; it lies with yourself how much of the immeasurable becomes reality for you. These meetings are not organized to make the world, but each is a sign of the world-order. They are not linked up with one another, but each assures you of your solidarity with the world. The world which appears to you in this way is unreliable, for it takes on a continually new appearance; you cannot hold it to its word. It has no density, for everything in it penetrates everything else; no duration, for it comes even when it is not summoned, and vanishes even when it is tightly held. It cannot be surveyed, and if you wish to make it capable of survey you lose it. It comes, and comes to bring *you* out; if it does not reach you, meet you, then it vanishes; but it comes back in another form. It is not outside you, it stirs in the depth of you; if you say "Soul of my soul" you have not said too much. But guard against wishing to remove it into your soul—for then you annihilate it. It is your present; only while you have it do you have the present. You can make it into an object for yourself, to experience and to use; you must continually do this—and as you do it you have no more present. Between you and it there is mutual giving: you say *Thou* to it and give yourself to it, it says *Thou* to you and gives itself to you. You cannot make yourself understood with others concerning it, you are alone with it. But it teaches you to meet others, and to hold your ground when you meet them. Through the graciousness of its comings and the solemn sadness of its goings it leads you away to the *Thou* in which the parallel lines of relations meet. It does not help to sustain you in life, it only helps you to glimpse eternity.

The world of *It* is set in the context of space and time.

The world of *Thou* is not set in the context of either of these.

The particular *Thou,* after the relational event has run its course, *is bound* to become an *It*.

The particular *It,* by entering the relational event, *may* become a *Thou.*

These are the two basic privileges of the world of *It.* They move man to look on the world of *It* as the world in which he has to live, and in which it is comfortable to live, as the world, indeed, which offers him all manner of incitements and excitements, activity and knowledge. In this chronicle of solid benefits the moments of the *Thou* appear as strange lyric and dramatic episodes, seductive and magical, but tearing us away to danger-ous extremes, loosening the well-tried context, leaving more questions than satisfaction behind them, shattering security—in short, uncanny mo-ments we can well dispense with. For since we are bound to leave them and go back into the "world," why not remain in it? Why not call to order what is over against us, and send it packing into the realm of objects? Why, if we find ourselves on occasion with no choice but to say *Thou* to father, wife, or comrade, not say *Thou* and mean *It*? To utter the sound *Thou* with the vocal organs is by no means the same as saying the uncanny primary word; more, it is harmless to whisper with the soul an amorous *Thou,* so long as nothing else in a serious way is meant but *experience* and *make use of.*

It is not possible to live in the bare present. Life would be quite consumed if precautions were not taken to subdue the present speedily and thoroughly. But it is possible to live in the bare past, indeed only in it may a life be organized. We only need to fill each moment with experien-cing and using, and it ceases to burn.

And in all the seriousness of truth, hear this: without *It* man cannot live. But he who lives with *It* alone is not a man.

FOR FURTHER READING

Barrett, William, and Henry D. Aiken (eds.). *Philosophy in the Twentieth Cen-tury.* 4 vols. New York: Random House, 1962. Parts II and IV.

General survey of contemporary philosophy. Parts II and IV are readings in analytic and existentialist thought. Introductions provide good background material for understanding these two movements in contemporary philosophy.

Brown, L. M. *General Philosophy in Education.* New York: McGraw-Hill, Inc., 1966.

An introduction to philosophy of education written by an analytic phi-losopher.

Buchler, Justus. *The Concept of Method.* New York: Columbia University Press, 1961.

An examination of the meaning of the concept "method" through an analysis of one definition of method (Chapter I) followed by a discussion of the methods of Bentham, Coleridge, and Descartes (Chapters II–VI). Buchler's own position is developed in the remaining chapters, the last two of which are a careful defense of the method of Dewey (Chapter XI), and a critique of the method of Whitehead (Chapter XII).

Collins, James. *The Existentialists.* Chicago: Henry Regnery Company, 1952.

A solid study of four existentialist thinkers, Sartre, Jaspers, Heidegger, and Marcel. Chapters I and VI are helpful background and thematic studies of existentialism.

Feigl, Herbert, and Wilfrid Sellars. *Readings in Philosophical Analysis.* New York: Appleton-Century-Crofts, Inc., 1949.

A collection of essays devoted to an examination of such topics as language, meaning, truth, confirmation, logic and mathematics, induction, ethics. The introduction is an excellent summary statement of the field of language analysis.

Frankena, William. *Three Historical Philosophies of Education.* Glenview, Illinois: Scott, Foresman and Company, 1965, Chapter 1.

A study of the educational philosophies of Aristotle, Kant, and Dewey. Chapter I is an excellent statement of the normative method.

Hook, Sidney. *Education for Modern Man.* New York: Alfred A. Knopf, 1966. Chapter 1.

A series of essays which are devoted to an examination of the ends, means, content of education and its relation to the social order. Chapter I is devoted to a discussion of the contemporary scene in education centering on a defense of Dewey's educational thought; the last section is a short statement and critique of the analytic method in relation to educational philosophy.

Israel, Scheffler. "Toward an Analytic Philosophy of Education," *Harvard Educational Review,* XXIV (Fall 1954), 223–230.

Kneller, George F. *Existentialism and Education,* New York: Philosophical Library, 1958.

A statement of major existentialist themes and their implications for education. A book which broke new ground for educational philosophy.

Neff, Frederick C. *Philosophy and American Education.* New York: The Center for Applied Research in Education, Inc., 1966. Chapter 5.

A survey of three American educational philosophies, idealism, realism, and pragmatism. The final chapter (V) is a study of the analytic and existentialist contributions to philosophy of education in America.

Reid, Louis A. *Philosophy and Education.* New York: Random House, 1965.

A general introduction to philosophy of education by a thinker sympathetic to the analytic movement. Chapter I is an excellent statement of philosophical method from an analytic viewpoint.

3

THE PHILOSOPHY
OF LEARNING

The philosophy of learning is a philosophical investigation of what is meant by the transmission of a society's culture from one group to another. When a society experiences conflicts within its culture, it begins to look inward and consider not only what ought to be transmitted but also what it means to transmit the culture. To see clearly the importance of examining learning when faced with cultural conflicts, one needs only to consider what Plato attempts to do in the *Republic*.

Faced with the slow erosion of the mythopoeic, religious basis of the Greek *polis,* Plato sought to reconstitute the *polis* by giving it a rational foundation. In the *Republic* he structured the legal, social, economic, political, religious, literary, and familial aspects of an ideal society. The cornerstone of this structure was a philosophy of education with an emphasis on a philosophy of learning. Recognizing that the process of socialization is crucial to establishing a stable, orderly, just society, Plato not only outlined an educational curriculm, the duties of the auxiliaries as overseers of that program and educational aims, but also investigated and developed a philosophy of learning on the basis of which the curriculum could be built and the aims of education made realistic. Throughout the *Republic* the emphasis is on education. The point is made that what a society can hope to be and what a curriculum must be in order to achieve that hope depend on its assumptions about the nature of learning. For if there is no justification for believing that persons can learn certain skills, information, patterns of behavior, and dispositions and achieve no understanding of the process of such acquisition, then it would be foolish to advocate those as the ends toward which persons ought to be educated. Indeed, if Plato had agreed with Protagoras' view of perception, it would have been foolish for Plato to advocate for his society that at least some members should have a knowledge of the good, the true, and the beautiful, and that such knowledge can be acquired by following the particular curriculum he laid out. It was only on the basis of a defensible philosophy of learning that Plato believed he could set out realistic educational goals and a curriculum adequate to their achievement. Though Plato's philosophical position is unacceptable to most contemporary educational philosophers, his insight that a philosophy of learning is central to society's transmission of its culture is sound. If, then, one's philosophy of learning significantly influences not only the kind of curriculum one ought to build but also that which society ought to transmit to its young, then a careful investigation of the philosophy of learning must be carried out.

The essentials of a philosophy of learning can be grasped by examining a conceptual map of the terrain. The major features of such a map can easily be described. First, the territory philosophy of learning is concerned about has well-defined boundaries. Traditionally any discussion of the nature of learning has been carried out under the heading of knowing and within the general philosophical discipline of epistemology. By considering whether or not this is acceptable, the boundaries of the philosophy of learning will be clear. Further, the map includes the elevations in the territory being explored. These elevations refer to the levels of discourse employed in the philosophical investigation of learning. Finally, major themes have been and are being discussed by persons interested in the philosophy of learning. These themes are usually stated in the form of questions and will be the central landmarks by reference to which one will be able to work one's way through the region of learning and to understand where each philosopher included in this chapter pitches his philosophical tent. An analysis of this map will begin with a consideration of the territory to be investigated.

The territory of the philosophy of learning can be recognized by examining, first, what is meant by the terms knowledge, knowing, and learning. Consider the following statements, "Johnny knows that the North won the war between the states," and "Johnny is learning American history." In the first statement the word "knows" signifies that Johnny has acquired some information about which he is certain. He has sufficient evidence to support his knowledge claim and thus confidently maintains that he is right. In the second statement "is learning" signifies that Johnny is *coming to know.* This means that Johnny is in the process of acquiring information which he can claim if he has sufficient evidence to support the knowledge claim. The emphasis of the word "learning" in the sentence above, however, is on the process of acquisition and not on acquired information. Granting this distinction between knowledge and learning, we can say that the area about which we are concerned in this chapter is the *process of coming to know*. It must not be assumed that only the process of coming to knowledge is of interest. On the contrary, the emphasis is on the process and one clearly can be in the process of acquiring skills, dispositions, understandings, values, cultural orientation as well as beliefs, knowledge, opinions. Indeed, one can acquire information or an understanding which is erroneous. From this point of view learning is a much broader subject than is knowing. One should not infer that questions regarding knowledge and knowing are of no interest to the educational philsopher. The scope of this chapter is limited to the philosophical investigation of the *acquisition* of knowledge. If a philosophical investigation of learning is dealing with a different subject matter than is a philosophical investigation of knowing, what is the relation of the philosophy of learning to epistemology?

This question can be dealt with by discussing what epistemology and philosophy of learning are attempting to do. One way to view the concerns of epistemology is to divide them into areas of normative epistemology and metaepistemology. Normative epistemology is concerned with making knowledge claims and attempting to defend them with evidence. An example of a normative epistemic statement is "Johnny has greater justification for believing P than Q." The phrase "has greater justification" indicates that this sentence is a normative epistemological sentence. One would be doing normative epistemology, for example, if one were to claim that what one knows through the senses is always accurate and to support this claim with evidence. Metaepistemology, on the other hand, has at least two purposes: to clarify the words and statements used in making normative epistemological statements and to examine the grounds on which normative epistemic statements can be reasonably supported. For example, epistemologists use such words as "a priori," "synthetic," "pragmatic," "tacit," and "necessary." One doing metaepistemology would attempt to clarify how these words are used by the normative epistemologist in order to clear the way for more defensible and accurate statements. An investigation of the grounds on which normative epistemological statements are made would raise such questions as why accept P as evidence rather than Q, are epistemic principles to be validated by appeal to other epistemological statements or to relevant data from sense experience or to authority. If the domain of epistemology can be divided into these two areas, what relation, if any, does the philosophy of learning have to them?

A philosophical investigation of learning involves making knowledge claims about the process of acquiring knowledge, skills, and understandings. In this sense the philosophy of learning is an example of normative epistemology. And to the extent that a philosophical study of learning would involve an examination of terms such as "acquire," "motivation," "learning," and "process" it would be an example of metaepistemology. It can be said then that the philosophy of learning is an epistemological study of the "process of coming to *P,*" or the "process of acquiring *P.*" Most of the authors in this chapter are doing a normative epistemological study of learning. Most engage in the analysis of terms and statements and thus can be said to be doing a metaepistemological study. None, however, are actively engaged in examining the grounds on which epistemological statements should be validated. The boundaries of our terrain, then, are these: the philosophy of learning has for its subject matter the process of acquiring and examines this subject matter with the discipline of epistemology. The language elevations of this territory must now be examined.

Philosophical investigations employ language to perform different functions, and these functions can be seen if one determines what the words and statements are intended to do. Generally there are three central ways in which language is used, and these ways can be called elevations. First, language is used on the common sense level. When persons talk about learning or any other topic in an everyday, unreflective, uncritical way, they are using language in a common sense fashion. Most of us believe that it is important for the young in society to acquire the skills, understandings, and information requisite to living useful and happy lives. When we talk about the importance of learning for living well, we usually do not stop to reflect about what we mean by "learning." We simply use the word to refer to something we experience without reflecting on it in a critical fashion. Words and sentences used in this manner are used in a common sense way. Any scientific or philosophical investigation refers in some way to the common experiences of people living in society and to the common sense way of talking about these experiences. When reflection begins on such experiences as "coming to know," the second level of language comes into view. This level or elevation of language can be called the scientific level. Language on this level is used in the description of phenomena, in stating hypotheses for interpreting data, and in justifying the hypotheses. Psychological theories about learning, such as those influenced by the stimulus-response or the cognitive-structure orientation, are employing language on the scientific level.

The third level of language is the philosophical level. Language on this level is used in the critical examination of the assumptions underlying both common sense understandings and scientific understandings. Regarding the common sense view of learning, for example, one could attempt to determine how words and statements are used in talking about the learning experience. One could also inquire into the assumptions on which the stimulus-response or the cognitive-structure orientations toward learning operate. Language on this level is used to uncover what is being assumed both on the common sense level and on the scientific level about the mind, the role of the learner in learning, the origin of learning, and the limits of learning and to critically evaluate the alternative answers. One could then proceed to criticize the assumptions underlying these views, to advance one's own theory, and to support that theory with evidence. If this were done, one would be doing normative epistemology in the area of learning. Or one could proceed to analyze the way words are used by psychologists and by normative epistemologists and to investigate the grounds on which any normative theory of learning could be justified. If one did that, one would be doing a metaepistemological investigation of learning. The boundaries of the territory of the philosophy of learning have been explored and the elevations of the terrain have been pointed out. The final step in the consideration of the map of the philosophy of learning is to find the major landmarks with reference to which one can find one's way through the territory.

Although many landmarks could be noted, five are among the most important and will be adequate to understand most of the territory. The landmarks consist of questions and supported answers to those questions. The five questions which we will consider are these: what is the origin of learning, what is the role of the mind in learning, what is the role of the learner in learning, what are the limitations of learning, and what is the role of society in learning? Answers to these questions tend to fall into polarities and mediating positions. The selections included in this chapter were chosen not only because they are representative of major philosophical traditions in the philosophy of learning but also because they are representative of highly influential approaches to the five questions. Let us turn to the first of these: "What is the origin of learning?"

An inquiry into the origin of learning is an attempt to determine how learning gets started. The genetic question about learning has been traditionally answered in two ways. The first is that the origin of learning is experience. John Locke, who was a leader in the British Empiricist School of Philosophy, was the first major exponent of this position. Locke contended that the mind is a *tabula rosa* before sensations are received by the sense organs. When sensations are received, the mind grasps them and relates them through laws of association and builds a picture of the external world. Whatever a person learns, he learns through sense experience. The polarity to this position is that learning originates in the reason. A philosopher who holds this position would ask a thoroughgoing empiricist such as Locke how a mind ignorant to begin with ever comes to know, that is, to learn. How does the mind know what to look for in sense experience in order to interpret it? Plato, for example, contended that the mind must be guided by some form of knowledge present to the mind before sense experience. He argued that although the ideas are in the mind before sense experience, they are not fully grasped by the knower until sense experience takes place. Sensation prods the mind to remember what had been given to it in the Elysian Fields before the mind was entombed in the body. Learning is a process of recollection. For Plato, then, learning originates in the ideas which are vaguely present to the mind before sensation and which guide the mind in its interpretation of sensation.

Though these are the two extremes among answers given to the question of the origin of learning, it must be clear that most philosophers including Plato and Locke would want to recognize the importance of both experience and reason in learning. Plato recognized that sense experience is vital to learning and Locke recognized that reason is vital in drawing inferences from our ideas. Kant argued that both are the origin of learning when he said that experience without concepts is blind and concepts without experience are empty. Regarding the other authors, it can be suggested that Dewey and Buber are in the empiricist camp; that Augustine and Hegel are in the rationalist camp; and that Cassirer and Polanyi along with Kant hold to mediating positions.

The second major question has been stated: "What is the role of the mind in learning?" The answers to this question range from what can be called formalism on the one hand and functionalism on the other. Those philosophers who could be placed in the formalist camp argue that the mind has an a priori structure native or necessary to it in terms of which the mind learns. All learning on the part of persons takes place within the limits of this structure. Hegel, for example, believed that the process of learning must be understood in terms of the structure of reason. Logically, the learning process is a rational, dialectical movement from thesis to antithesis to synthesis. Learning for Hegel is the dialectical movement of the mind from the natural soul (pure immediate experience of immediacy) through the subjective soul (an analytic differentiation within pure immediacy in which the self is differentiated from the not self and the not self is differentiated into parts), to absolute mind (a synthesis of the preceding stages of learning into a unified whole, a harmonious comprehensiveness). At the stage of synthesis or harmonious comprehensiveness the mind is fully self-conscious, rational, and free. Hegel submits that this dialectical process of coming to self-consciousness and freedom is a necessary process. One learns under no other conditions.

The philosophers who could be placed in the functionalist camp argue that the mind has no necessary and universal a priori structure on the basis of which experience is to be interpreted. For many of these thinkers the mind is a function of a physical organism and acquired through biological development and mutation. The mind may develop structures but they are not necessary and universal. It is conceivable that, given another environment, what we call the human organism could have developed in other directions. An exponent of this position is John Dewey. Heavily influenced by the evolutionary thought of Darwin, Dewey believes that experience is a form of nature and that the mind is nature grown intelligent. The human organism living in a social physical environment receives data and develops patterns of behavior in creative response to those data. Met with obstacles blocking habitual activity, the organism develops a reflective capacity to deal with those obstacles. Employing this capacity for critical reflection, the biological organism articulates the problem, considers alternative courses of action, and decides on that one which it believes will fully satisfy its needs. That course of action which works is to the situation what the right key is to a lock.

A mediating position on the question of the role of the mind in learning is that of Polanyi. Unwilling to go to either extreme of formalism or functionalism, Polanyi argues that learning is an active integration of experience performed in the search for knowledge. In the act of integrating experience with reference to an end, we integrate much of which we are aware but cannot tell, that is, we have not only focal knowledge but also tacit knowledge. For Polanyi the mind not only brings to learning both a capacity to integrate experience and a purpose to which it is committed, that of achieving knowledge, but also develops that capacity and realizes that purpose only as it deals with the total experience of the human organism. Kant, Plato, and Augustine are closer to the formalist position, while Locke would be more in agreement with the reactionist point of view. Cassirer and Buber are closer to a middle position, though neither would be in complete agreement with Polanyi.

The third question or landmark in the map of the philosophy of learning is this: "What is the role of the learner in acquiring knowledge?" Most of the authors in this chapter would contend that the learner is not a passive recipient of sense experience but is actively engaged in coming to knowledge. Dewey, for example, contends that the learner actively seeks meaning through solving the problems he faces by means of the logical method experimentalism. Motivating the learner on a rudimentary level of life would be a desire for pleasure and for avoiding pain, and on a high level of life would be the desire to achieve a realization of values in concrete situations. Plato believed that the learner, born of Penury and Plenty, desires fully to possess that which he only partially possesses. This desire is *eros*. Eros is that which explains why persons actively seek to recollect, to come to a state of knowing. Kant argues that the learner actively seeks to interpret, via the categories, the phenomena given through the senses. Polanyi, Hegel, and Augustine would also be in this camp.

Although Locke in parts of the *Essay* seemed to imply that the learner is active, the general drift of his work on learning and knowledge is that the learner is passive in learning. One who learns is passive until nudged externally by objects which cause the learner to have ideas and to organize them into knowledge. He might be compared to a billiard ball which is inert until it collides with another billiard ball, at which time it moves and continues moving as long as it is stimulated externally. Augustine would contend that the learner is passive in the acquiring of some kinds of knowledge and active in others. The learner is passive in its reception of divine light or illumination (the ideas). Once the illumination has taken place, the mind actively employs the ideas in making judgments about one's world. Cassirer would also be in between these two poles but for different reasons than Augustine. The learner along with all animals receives data and responds with behavior. However, in between the reception and the response, the human does some things animals do not do. He interprets the data through a symbolic process found only in humans. The learner taking in the data actively interprets the data and responds in the light of its symbolic interpretation. Buber views the learner as an actor and as a responder in the I-Thou encounter.

The fourth question raises the issue of the extent to which one can learn. What limitations, if any, are there on the learning process? There are two major answers to this question. The first is that the mind is able to pierce appearance and know reality. Plato, for example, would contend that the ideas which are grasped in the process of drawing them out through use are not merely ideas in our minds which allow us to interpret sense experience; they are also necessary, permanent, and eternal. This means that the ideas are reality. Augustine would generally agree with Plato, but would correct the theory of recollection by saying that the ideas are in the mind of God and are given to man by God in the act of creation. Nevertheless, when one's mind is illuminated by the ideas, one's mind is being illumined by God, which enables one to know to some degree the mind of God. Hegel contended that the way the individual mind works when operating correctly and the way reality works is the same. In knowing oneself, one gains a knowledge of the essential processes of reality.

The other position which is developed in dealing with the question of the limitations of learning is that the mind is limited to appearance and can never learn anything about reality. Kant, for example, believed that the mind is able to know or to learn no more than what it can say about possible experience. One can claim to know nothing about that of which we have no sense experience. This means that the learner is not able to go beyond phenomena. Cassirer's position is close to that of Kant's for much the same reasons. Dewey would deny that the learner can come to a knowledge of any Platonic kind of reality. He might, however, come to recognize the naturalistic ground of all experience and thus know this much about reality. In the selections by Buber and Polanyi neither investigate this question. Locke, if he were as consistent in his empiricism as was his radical follower David Hume, would not have believed that the learner can know matter, the self, and God. But Locke did hold for reasons not entirely consistent with his empirical doctrine that one can know reality.

The final question is this: "What is the place of society in learning?" The answers to this question range from those who believe that society is crucial to learning to those who believe that society plays only a small part in learning. Buber contends that the heart of learning is a dialogical relation between the individual learner and society, particularly his teacher. Only within this relation can a person be addressed by society, select from it, and grow toward communion and inner directedness. The learner in Cassirer's view is a cultural animal whose distinguishing characteristic is the capacity to symbolize. On the basis of this ability men acquire a symbolic system filled with the cultural meanings of the society in which they live. All a person can know he learns by the "interposition" of symbols, an "artificial medium," the language of society. Indeed, one's acquisition of knowledge is significantly influenced by the system of linguistic symbols one acquires from his society. Polanyi believes that learning is an active shaping of experience in the pursuit of knowledge. The experiences which one integrates come from the social and physical circumstances in which one lives. The lowest form of integration is perception and this could possibly take place with a physical environment alone. However, the higher forms of integration found in the sciences and art, for example, take place only in the context of society. Science cannot advance unless some views have been accepted by the scientific community and act as stabilizers for future exploration. For Hegel, the process of coming to understanding, to freedom, involves stages one of which is the subjective soul. At this level the learner differentiates himself from what he is not, such as other persons and the natural world. This differentiation is necessary for the soul to recognize itself and to proceed to freedom, self-consciousness, and full rationality. Learning could not proceed beyond the barest rudiments of knowledge without society. Dewey believes man to be an animal who has acquired through the evolutionary process abilities to relate not only to a physical environment but also to a social environment. Humans can learn apart from society, though they achieve their noblest values only in social relationships. The remaining writers in this chapter, Plato, Augustine, Locke, and Kant, do not come to grips with this question. They take it for granted, however, that learning involves persons using language in society.

Two final comments must be made about the authors who have been located on this map. The first comment is about the philosophical method they employ in their investigations of learning. All of the thinkers employ to some extent the analytic method. Each is concerned about the way words are used and what they mean. In their attempt to be clear, some analysis of the way language is used is needed. The normative method of advancing an hypothesis and marshalling evidence to support it is also employed by every writer. Each is developing, if not a complete theory of learning, at least a theory about some question raised in the philosophical inquiry of learning. The speculative method is used by some of the authors, particularly Plato, Augustine, Hegel, and possibly Dewey. Buber employs the existentialist method and is the only thinker who does so. Cassirer uses his own brand of the phenomenological method, but one must not confuse what each man is attempting to do. Buber describes the learning phenomena in the context of the I-Thou category, while Cassirer is attempting to determine what learning and knowing are by reading the structure of human culture. In his attempt to read that structure, Cassirer looks for the conditions for the possibility of human knowledge, learning, and culture.

Second, the philosophy of learning has implications for the aims of education. Plato's and Augustine's views will probably lead to a perennialist position while Locke's, Kant's, Hegel's, Polanyi's, and Buber's positions would no doubt suggest an essentialist posture toward cultural aims. The position of Dewey would clearly be adequate to progressivism and Cassirer's views could lead to reconstructionism. Except in the cases of Dewey and Polanyi no one of these philosophies of learning is sufficient to support any one of the positions on educational aims discussed in the next chapter. However, through a critical appraisal of the learning theories advanced in this chapter, it should be possible to begin working toward a philosophy of learning adequate to support defensible aims of education.

Insight and Recollection*
PLATO

HOW CAN A MIND IGNORANT TO
BEGIN WITH LEARN?

soc.   Then now, Theaetetus, take another view of the subject: you answered that knowledge is perception?

THEAET.   I did.

soc.   And if any one were to ask you: With what does a man see black and white colors? and with what does he hear high and low sounds?—you would say, if I am not mistaken, "With the eyes and with the ears."

THEAET.   I should.

soc.   The free use of words and phrases, rather than minute precision, is generally characteristic of a liberal education, and the opposite is pedantic; but sometimes precision is necessary, and I believe that the answer which you have just given is open to the charge of incorrectness; for which is more correct, to say that we see or hear with the eyes and with the ears, or through the eyes and through the ears.

THEAET.   I should say "through," Socrates, rather than "with."

soc.   Yes, my boy, for no one can suppose that in each of us, as in a sort of Trojan horse, there are perched a number of unconnected senses, which do not all meet in some one nature, the soul or whatever we please to call it, of which they are the instruments, and with which through them we perceive objects of sense.

THEAET.   I agree with you in that opinion.

soc.   The reason why I am thus precise is, because I want to know whether, when we perceive black and white through the eyes, and again, other qualities through other organs, we do not perceive them with one and the same part of ourselves; and whether, if you were asked, you could refer all such perceptions to the body. Perhaps, however, I had better allow you to answer for yourself and not interfere. Tell me, then, are not

---

*From *The Dialogues of Plato* trans. by Benjamin Jowett, 4th ed., 1953, revised by D. J. Allan and H. E. Dale, Vol. I (*Symposium, Meno, Phaedo*), Vol. II (*Republic*). Vol. III (*Theaetetus*) by permission of the Clarendon Press, Oxford.

the organs through which you perceive warm and hard and light and sweet, organs of the body?

THEAET.   Of the body, certainly.

soc.   And you would admit that what you perceive through one faculty you cannot perceive through another; the objects of hearing, for example, cannot be perceived through sight, or the objects of sight through hearing?

THEAET.   Of course not.

soc.   If you have any thought about both of them, this common perception cannot come to you, either through the one or the other organ?

THEAET.   It cannot.

soc.   How about sounds and colors: in the first place you may reflect that they both *exist*?

THEAET.   Yes.

soc.   And that either of them is different from the other, and the same with itself?

THEAT.   Certainly.

soc.   And that both are two and each of them one?

THEAET.   Yes.

soc.   You can further observe whether they are like or unlike one another?

THEAET.   I dare say.

soc.   But through what do you perceive all this about them? for neither through hearing nor yet through seeing can you apprehend that which they have in common. Let me give you an illustration of the point at issue: —If there were any meaning in asking whether sounds and colors are saline or not, you would be able to tell me what faculty would consider the question. It would not be sight or hearing, but some other.

THEAET.   Certainly; the faculty of taste.

soc.   Very good; and now tell me what is the power which discerns, not only in sensible objects, but in all things, universal properties, such as those which are called being and not-being, and those others about which we were just asking—what organs will you assign for the perception of these by the appropriate power in us?

THEAET.   You are thinking of being and not-being, likeness and unlikeness, sameness and difference, and also of unity and any other number which occurs in our judgment of objects. And evidently your question applies to odd and even numbers and other arithmetical conceptions— through what bodily organ the soul perceives them.

soc.   You follow me excellently, Theaetetus; that is precisely what I am asking.

THEAET.   Indeed, Socrates, I cannot answer; my only notion is, that these, unlike objects of sense, have no separate organ, but that the mind, by a power of her own, contemplates such common properties in all things.

soc.   You are a beauty, Theaetetus, and not ugly, as Theodorus was saying; for he who utters the beautiful is himself beautiful and good. And besides being beautiful, you have done me a kindness in releasing me from a very long discussion, if you believe that the soul views some things by herself and others through the bodily organs. For that was my own opinion, and I wanted you to agree with me.

THEAET.   Indeed, I do believe it.

soc.   And to which class would you refer being or essence; for this, of all our notions, is the most universal?

THEAET.   I should say, to that class which the soul aspires to know of herself.

soc.   And would you say this also of like and unlike, same and other?

THEAET.   Yes.

soc.   And would you say the same of the noble and base, and of good and evil?

THEAET.   These also I conceive to be among the chief instances of those relative terms whose nature the soul perceives by comparing in herself things past and present with the future.

soc.   Hold! does she not perceive the hardness of that which is hard by the touch, and the softness of that which is soft equally by the touch?

THEAET.   Yes.

soc.   But their *being*, I mean the fact that they are, and their opposition to one another, and the being (to repeat that term) of this opposition, the soul herself endeavors to decide for us by the review and comparison of them?

THEAET.   Certainly.

soc.   The simple sensations which reach the soul through the body are given at birth to men and animals by nature, but their reflections on the being and use of them are slowly and hardly gained, if they are ever gained, by education and long experience.

THEAET.   Assuredly.

soc.   And can a man attain truth who fails of attaining being?

THEAET.   Impossible.

soc.   And can he who misses the truth of anything, have a knowledge of that thing?

THEAET.   He cannot.

soc.   Then knowledge does not consist in impressions of sense, but in reasoning about them; in that only, and not in the mere impression, truth and being can be attained?

THEAET.   Apparently.

HOW CAN A MIND JUDGE?

MEN.   O Socrates, I used to be told, before I knew you, that you were always doubting yourself and making others doubt; and now you are casting your spells over me, and I am simply getting bewitched and enchanted, and am at my wits' end. And if I may venture to make a jest upon you, you seem to me both in your appearance and in your power over others to be very like the flat torpedo fish, who torpifies those who come near him and touch him, as you have now torpified me, I think. For my soul and my tongue are really torpid, and I do not know how to answer you; and though I have been delivered of an infinite variety of speeches about virtue before now, and to many persons—and very good speeches they were, as I thought—at this moment I cannot even say what virtue is. And I think that you are very wise in not voyaging and going away from home, for if you did in other places as you do in Athens, you would be cast into prison as a magician.

SOC.   You are a rogue, Meno, and had all but caught me.

MEN.   What do you mean, Socrates?

SOC.   I can tell why you made a simile about me.

MEN.   Why?

SOC.   In order that I might make another simile about you. For I know that all beautiful youths like to have similes made about them—as well they may, since beautiful images, I take it, are naturally evoked by beauty—but I shall not return the compliment. As to my being a torpedo, if the torpedo is itself torpid as well as the cause of torpidity in others, then indeed I am a torpedo, but not otherwise; for I perplex others, not because I am clear, but because I am utterly perplexed myself. And now I know not what virtue is, and you seem to be in the same case, although you did once perhaps know before you touched me. However, I have no objection to join with you in the inquiry.

MEN.   And how will you investigate, Socrates, that of which you know nothing at all? Where can you find a starting-point in the region of the unknown? And even if you happen to come full upon what you want, how will you ever know that this is the thing which you did not know?

SOC.   I know, Meno, what you mean; but just see what a tiresome dispute you are introducing. You argue that a man cannot inquire either about that which he knows, or about that which he does not know; for if he knows, he has no need to inquire; and if not, he cannot; for he does not know the very subject about which he is to inquire.[1]

[1]Cf. Arist. *Post. Anal.* I. i. 6.

MEN.   Well, Socrates, and is not the argument sound?

SOC.   I think not.

MEN.   Why not?

SOC.   I will tell you why: I have heard from certain men and women skilled in things divine that—

MEN.   What did they say?

SOC.   They spoke of a glorious truth, as I conceive.

MEN.   What is it? and who are they?

SOC.   Some of them are priests and priestesses, who have striven to learn how to give a reasonable account of the things with which they concern themselves: there are poets also, like Pindar, and the many others who are inspired. And they say—mark, now, and see whether their words are true—they say that the soul of man is immortal, and at one time has an end, which is termed dying, and at another time is born again, but is never destroyed. And the moral is, that a man ought to live always in perfect holiness. *"For in the ninth year Persephone sends the souls of those whom she has received the penalty of ancient crime back again from beneath into the light of the sun above, and these are they who become noble kings and mighty men and great in wisdom and are for ever called saintly heroes."* The soul, then, as being immortal and having been born again many times, and having seen all things that exist, whether in this world or in the world below, has knowledge of them all; and it is no wonder that she should be able to call to remembrance all that she ever knew about virtue, and about everything; for as all nature is akin, and the soul has learned all things, there is no difficulty in a man eliciting out of a single recollection all the rest—the process generally called "learning"—if he is strenuous and does not faint; for all inquiry and all learning is but recollection. And therefore we ought not to listen to this eristic argument about the impossibility of inquiry: for it will make us idle, and it is sweet to the sluggard; but the other doctrine will make us active and inquisitive.

. . .

Yes, said Cebes interposing, your favorite doctrine. Socrates, that our learning is simply recollection, if true, also necessarily implies a previous time in which we have learned that which we now recollect. But this would be impossible unless our soul had been somewhere before existing in this form of man; here then is another proof of the soul's immortality.

But tell me, Cebes, interrupted Simmias, what arguments are urged in favor of this doctrine of recollection. I am not very sure at the moment that I remember them.

One excellent proof, said Cebes, is afforded by questions. If you put a question to a person properly, he will give a true answer of himself, but how could he do this unless there were knowledge and a right account of the matter already in him? Again, this is most clearly shown when he is taken to a diagram or to anything of that sort.[2]

But if, said Socrates, you are still incredulous, Simmias, I would ask you whether you may not agree with me when you look at the matter in another way;—I mean, if you are still incredulous as to whether what is called learning is recollection?

Incredulous I am not, said Simmias; but I want to have this doctrine of recollection brought to my own recollection, and, from what Cebes has started to say, I am beginning to recollect and be convinced: but I should still like to hear you develop your own argument.

This is what I would say, he replied: —We should agree, if I am not mistaken, that what a man is to recollect he must have known at some previous time.

Very true.

And do we also agree that knowledge obtained in the way I am about to describe is recollection? I mean to ask, Whether a person who, having seen or heard or in any way perceived anything, knows not only that, but also thinks of something else which is the subject not of the same but of some other kind of knowledge, may not be fairly said to recollect that of which he thinks?

How do you mean?

I mean what I may illustrate by the following instance: —The knowledge of a lyre is not the same as the knowledge of a man?

Of course not.

And yet what is the feeling of lovers when they recognize a lyre, or a cloak, or anything else which the beloved has been in the habit of using? Do not they, from knowing the lyre, form in the mind's eye an image of the youth to whom the lyre belongs? And this is recollection. In like manner anyone who sees Simmias may often remember Cebes; and there are endless examples of the same thing.

Endless, indeed, replied Simmias.

And is not this sort of thing a kind of recollection—though the word is most commonly applied to a process of recovering that which has been already forgotten through time and inattention?

Very true, he said.

Well; and may you not also from seeing the picture of a horse or a lyre recollect a man? and from the picture of Simmias, you may be led to recollect Cebes?

True.

Or you may also be led to the recollection of Simmias himself?

Quite so.

[2]Cf. *Meno* 83 foll.

And in all these cases, the recollection may be derived from things either like or unlike?

It may be.

And when the recollection is derived from like things, then another consideration is sure to arise, which is—whether the likeness in any degree falls short or not of that which is recollected?

Certainly, he said.

Now consider this question. We affirm, do we not, that there is such a thing as equality, not of one piece of wood or stone or similar material thing with another, but that, over and above this, there is absolute equality? Shall we say so?

Say so, yes, replied Simmias, and swear to it, with all the confidence in life.

And do we know the nature of this absolute existence?

To be sure, he said.

And whence did we obtain our knowledge? Did we not see equalities of material things, such as pieces of wood and stones, and conceive from them the idea of an equality which is different from them? For you will acknowledge that there is a difference? Or look at the matter in another way: —Do not the same pieces of wood or stone appear to one man equal, and to another unequal?

That is certain.

But did pure equals ever appear to you unequal? or equality the same as inequality?

Never, Socrates.

Then these equal objects are not the same with the idea of equality?

I should say, clearly not, Socrates.

And yet from these equals, although differing from the idea of equality, you obtained the knowledge of that idea?

Very true, he said.

Which might be like, or might be unlike them?

Yes.

But that makes no difference: so long as from seeing one thing you conceive another, whether like or unlike, there must surely have been an act of recollection?

Very true.

But what would you say of equal portions of wood or other material equals? and what is the impression produced by them? Are they equals in the same sense in which absolute equality is equal? or do they fall short of this perfect equality in a measure?

Yes, he said, in a very great measure too.

And must we not allow, that when a man, looking at any object, reflects "the thing which I see aims at being like some other thing, but falls short of and cannot be like that other thing, and is inferior," he who so reflects must have had a previous knowledge of that to which the other, although similar, was inferior?

Certainly.

And has not this been our own case in the matter of equals and of absolute equality?

Precisely.

Then we must have known equality previously to the time when we first saw the material equals, and reflected that they all strive to attain absolute equality, but fall short of it?

Very true.

And we recognize also that we have only derived this conception of absolute equality, and can only derive it, from sight or touch, or from some other of the senses, which are all alike in this respect?

Yes, Socrates, for the purposes of the present argument, one of them is the same as the other.

From the senses then is derived the conception that all sensible equals aim at an absolute equality of which they fall short?

Yes.

Then before we began to see or hear or perceive in any way, we must have had a knowledge of absolute equality, or we could not have referred to that standard the equals which are derived from the senses?—for to that they all aspire, and of that they fall short.

No other inference can be drawn from the previous statements.

And did we not begin to see and hear and have the use of our other senses as soon as we were born?

Certainly.

Then we must have acquired the knowledge of equality at some previous time?

Yes.

That is to say, before we were born, I suppose?

It seems so.

And if we acquired this knowledge before we were born, and were born having the use of it, then we also knew before we were born and at the instant of birth not only the equal or the greater or the less, but all other such ideas; for we are not speaking only of equality, but of beauty, goodness, justice, holiness, and of all which we stamp with the name of absolute being in the dialectical process, both when we ask and when we answer questions. Of all this we affirm with certainty that we acquired the knowledge before birth?

We do.

But if, after having acquired, we have not on each occasion forgotten what we acquired, then we must always come into life having this knowledge, and shall have it always as long as life lasts—for knowing is the acquiring and retaining knowledge and not losing it. Is not the loss of knowledge, Simmias, just what we call forgetting?

Quite true, Socrates.

But if this knowledge which we acquired before birth was lost by us at birth, and if afterwards by the use of the senses we recovered what we previously knew, will not the process which we call learning be a recovering of knowledge which is natural to us, and may not this be rightly termed recollection?

Very true.

So much is clear—that when we perceive something, either by the help of sight, or hearing, or some other sense, that perception can lead us to think of some other thing like or unlike which is associated with it but has been forgotten. Whence, as I was saying, one of two alternatives follows: — either we all have this knowledge at birth, and continue to know through life; or, after birth, those who are said to learn only recollect, and learning is simply recollection.

Yes, that is quite true, Socrates.

And which alternative, Simmias, do you perfer? Have we the knowledge at our birth, or do we recollect afterwards things which we knew previously to our birth?

I cannot decide at the moment.

At any rate you can decide whether he who has knowledge will or will not be able to render an account of his knowledge? What do you say?

Certainly, he will.

But do you think that every man is able to give an account of the matters about which we were speaking a moment ago?

Would that they could, Socrates, but I much rather fear that tomorrow, at this time, there will no longer be anyone alive who is able to give an account of them such as ought to be given.

Then you are not of opinion, Simmias, that all men know these things?

Certainly not.

They are in process of recollecting that which they learned before?

Certainly.

But when did our souls acquire this knowledge?—clearly not since we were born as men?

Certainly not.

And therefore, previously?

Yes.

Then, Simmias, our souls must also have existed without bodies before they were in the form of man, and must have had intelligence.

Unless indeed you suppose, Socrates, that all such knowledge is given us at the very moment of birth; for this is the only time which remains.

Yes, my friend, but if so, when, pray, do we lose it? for it is not in us when we are born—that is admitted. Do we lose it at the moment of receiving it, or if not at what other time?

No, Socrates, I perceive that I was unconsciously talking nonsense.

Then may we not say, Simmias, that if there do exist these things of which we are always talking, absolute beauty and goodness, and all that class of realities; and if to this we refer all our sensations and with this compare them, finding the realities to be pre-existent and our own possession—then just as surely as these exist, so surely must our souls have existed before our birth? Otherwise our whole argument would be worthless. By an equal compulsion we must believe both that these realities exist, and that our souls existed before our birth; and if not the realities, then not the souls.

Yes, Socrates; I am convinced that there is precisely the same necessity for the one as for the other; and the argument finds a safe refuge in the position that the existence of the soul before birth cannot be separated from the existence of the reality of which you speak. For there is nothing which to my mind is so patent as that beauty, goodness, and the other realities of which you were just now speaking, exist in the fullest possible measure; and I am satisfied with the proof.

WHAT MOTIVATES THE LEARNER?

And now, taking my leave of you, I will rehearse a tale of love which I heard from Diotima of Mantinea,[3] a woman wise in this and many other kinds of knowledge, who in the days of old, when the Athenians offered sacrifice before the coming of the plague, delayed the disease ten years. She was my instructress in the art of love, and I shall try to repeat to you what she said to me, beginning with the propositions on which Agathon and I are agreed; I will do the best I can do without any help.[4] As you, Agathon, suggested,[5] it is proper to speak first of the being and nature of Love, and then of his works. (I think it will be easiest for me if in recounting my conversation with the wise woman I follow its actual course of question and answer.) First I said to her in nearly the same words which he used to me, that Love was a mighty god, and likewise fair; and she proved to me, as I proved to him, that by my own showing Love was neither fair nor good. "What do you mean, Diotima," I said, "is Love then evil and foul?" "Hush," she cried; "must that be foul which is not fair?" "Certainly," I said. "And is that which is not wise,

[3]Cf. *Alcibiades I.*
[4]Cf. *Gorg.* 505 e.
[5]*Supra,* 195 a.

ignorant? do you not see that there is a mean between wisdom and ignorance?" "And what may that be?" I said. "Right opinion," she replied; "which, as you know, being incapable of giving a reason, is not knowledge (for how can knowledge be devoid of reason?) nor again ignorance (for neither can ignorance attain the truth), but is clearly something which is a mean between ignorance and wisdom." "Quite true," I replied. "Do not then insist," she said, "that what is not fair is of necessity foul, or what is not good evil; or infer that because Love is not fair and good he is therefore foul and evil; for he is in a mean between them." "Well," I said, "Love is surely admitted by all to be a great god." "By those who know or by those who do not know?" "By all." "And how, Socrates," she said with a smile, "can Love be acknowledged to be a great god by those who say that he is not a god at all?" "And who are they?" I said. "You and I are two of them," she replied. "How can that be?" I said. "It is quite intelligible," she replied; "for you yourself would acknowledge that the gods are happy and fair—of course you would— would you dare to say that any god was not?" "Certainly not," I replied. "And you mean by the happy, those who are the possessors of things good and things fair?" "Yes." "And you admitted that Love, because he was in want, desires those good and fair things of which he is in want?" "Yes, I did." "But how can he be a god who has no portion in what is good and fair?" Impossible." "Then you see that you also deny the divinity of Love."

"What then is Love?" I asked; "Is he mortal?" "No." "What then?" "As in the former instance, he is neither mortal nor immortal, but in a mean between the two." "What is he, Diotima?" "He is a great spirit ($\delta\alpha\iota\mu\omega\nu$), and like all spirits he is intermediate between the divine and the mortal." "And what," I said, "is his power?" "He interprets between gods and men, conveying and taking across to the gods the prayers and sacrifices of men, and to men the commands of the gods and the benefits they return; he is the mediator who spans the chasm which divides them, and therefore by him the universe is bound together, and through him the arts of the prophet and the priest, their sacrifices and mysteries and charms, and all prophecy and incantation, find their way. For God mingles not with man; but through Love all the intercourse and converse of gods with men, whether they be awake or asleep, is carried on. The wisdom which understands this is spiritual; all other wisdom, such as that of arts and handicrafts, is mean and vulgar. Now these spirits or intermediate powers are many and diverse, and one of them is Love." "And who," I said, "was his father, and who his mother?" "The tale," she said, "will take time; nevertheless I will tell you. On the day when Aphrodite was born there was a feast of all the gods, among them the god Poros or Plenty, who is the son of Metis or Sagacity. When the feast was over, Penia or Poverty, as the manner is on such occasions, came about the doors to beg. Now Plenty, who was the worse for nectar (there was no wine in those days), went into the garden of Zeus and fell into a heavy sleep; and Poverty considering that for her there was no plenty, plotted to have a child by him, and accordingly she lay down at his side and conceived Love, who partly because he is naturally a lover of the beautiful, and because Aphrodite is herself beautiful, and also because he was begotten during her birthday feast, is her follower and attendant. And as his parentage is, so also are his fortunes. In the first place he is always poor, and anything but tender and fair, as the many imagine him; and he is rough and squalid, and has no shoes, nor a house to dwell in; on the bare earth exposed he lies under the open heaven, in the streets, or at the doors of houses, taking his rest; and like his mother he is always in distress. Like his father too, whom he also partly resembles, he is always plotting against the fair and good; he is bold, enterprising, strong, a mighty hunter, always weaving some intrigue or other, keen in the pursuit of wisdom, fertile in resources; a philosopher at all times, terrible as an enchanter, sorcerer, sophist. He is by nature neither mortal nor immortal, but alive and flourishing at one moment when he is in plenty, and dead at another moment in the same day, and again alive by reason of his father's nature. But that which is always flowing in is always flowing out, and so he is never in want and never in wealth; and, further, he is in a mean between ignorance and knowledge. The truth of the matter is this: No god is a philosopher or seeker after wisdom, for he is wise already; nor does any man who is wise seek after wisdom. Neither do the ignorant seek after wisdom; for herein is the evil of ignorance, that he who is neither a man of honor nor wise is nevertheless satisfied with himself: there is no desire when there is no feeling of want." "But who then, Diotima," I said, "are the lovers of wisdom, if they are neither the wise nor the foolish?" "A child may answer that question," she replied; "they are those who are in a mean between the two; Love is one of them. For wisdom is a most beautiful thing, and Love is of the beautiful; and therefore Love is also a philosopher or lover of wisdom, and being a lover of wisdom is in a mean between the wise and the ignorant. And of this, too, his birth is the cause; for his father is wealthy and wise, and his mother poor and foolish. Such, my dear Socrates, is the nature of the spirit Love. The error in your conception of him was very natural; from what you say yourself, I infer that it arose because you thought that Love is that which is loved, not that which loves; and for that reason, I think, Love appeared to you supremely beautiful. For the beloved is the truly beautiful, and delicate, and perfect, and blessed; but the active principle of love is of another nature, and is such as I have described."

I said: "O thou stranger woman, thou sayest well; but, assuming Love to be such as you say, what is the use of him to men?" "That, Socrates," she replied, "I will attempt to unfold: of his nature and birth I have already spoken; and you acknowledge that love is of the beautiful. But someone will say: What does it consist in, Socrates and Diotima?—or rather let me put the question more clearly, and ask: When a man loves the beautiful, what does his love desire?" I answered her, "That the beautiful may be his." "Still," she said, "The answer suggests a further question: What is given by the possession of beauty?" "To v hat you have asked," I replied, "I have no answer ready." "Then," she said, "let me put the word "good" in the place of the beautiful, and repeat the question once more: If he who loves loves the good, what is it then that he loves?" "The possession of the good." "And what does he gain who possesses the good?" "Happiness." I replied; "there is less difficulty in answering that question." "Yes," she said, "the happy are made happy by the acquisition of good things. Nor is there any need to ask why a man desires happiness; the answer is already final." "You are right," I said. "And is this wish and this desire common to all? and do all men always desire their own good, or only some men?—what say you?" "All men," I replied; "the desire is common to all." "Why, then," she rejoined, "are not all men, Socrates, said to love, but only some of them? whereas you say that all men are always loving the same things." "I myself wonder," I said, "why this is." "There is nothing to wonder at," she replied; "the reason is that one part of love is separated off and receives the name of the whole, but the other parts have other names." "Give an illustration," I said. She answered me as follows: "There is creative activity which, as you know, is complex and manifold. All that causes the passage of non-being into being is a "poesy" or creation, and the processes of all art are creative; and the masters of arts are all poets or creators." "Very true." "Still," she said, "you know that they are not called poets, but have other names; only that one portion of creative activity which is separated off from the rest, and is concerned with music and metre, is called by the name of the whole and is termed poetry, and they who possess poetry in this sense of the word are called poets." "Very true," I said. "And the same holds of love. For you may say generally that all desire of good and happiness is only the great and subtle power of love; but they who are drawn towards him by any other path, whether the path of money-making or gymnastics or philosophy, are not called lovers—the name of the whole is appropriated to those whose desire takes one form only—they alone are said to love, or to be lovers." "I dare say," I replied, "that you are right." "Yes," she added, "and you hear people say that lovers are seeking for their other half; but I say that they are seeking neither for the half of themselves, nor for the whole, unless the half or the whole be also a good; men will cut off their own hands and feet and cast them away, if they think them evil. They do not, I imagine, each cling to what is his own, unless perchance there be someone who calls what belongs to him the good, and what belongs to another the evil; for there is nothing which men love but the good. Is there anything?" "Certainly, I should say, that there is nothing." "Then," she said, "the simple truth is, that men love the good." "Yes," I said. "To which must be added that they love the possession of the good?" "Yes, that must be added." "And not only the possession, but the everlasting possession of the good?" "That must be added too." "Then love," she said, "may be described generally as the love of the everlasting possession of the good?" "That is most true."

"Then if this be always the nature of love, can you tell me further," she went on, "what is the manner of the pursuit? what are they doing who show all this eagerness and heat which is called love? and what is the object which they have in view? Answer me." "Nay, Diotima," I replied, "if I knew, I should not be wondering at your wisdom, neither should I come to learn from you about this very matter." "Well," she said, "I will teach you: —The object which they have in view is birth in beauty, whether of body or soul." "I do not understand you," I said; "the oracle requires an explanation." "I will make my meaning clearer," she replied. "I mean to say, that all men are bringing to the birth in their bodies and in their souls. There is a certain age at which human nature is desirous of procreation—procreation which must be in beauty and not in deformity. The union of man and woman is a procreation; it is a divine thing, for conception and generation are an immortal principle in the mortal creature, and in the inharmonious they can never be. But the deformed is inharmonious with all divinity, and the beautiful harmonious. Beauty, then, is the destiny or goddess of parturition who presides at birth, and therefore, when approaching beauty the procreating power is propitious, and expansive, and benign, and bears and produces fruit: at the sight of ugliness she frowns and contracts and has a sense of pain, and turns away, and shrivels up, and not without a pang refrains from procreation. And this is the reason why, when the hour of procreation comes, and the teeming nature is full, there is such a flutter and ecstasy about beauty whose approach is the alleviation of the bitter pain of travail. For love, Socrates, is not, as you imagine, the love of the beautiful only." "What then?" "The love of generation and of birth in beauty." "Yes," I said. "Yes, indeed," she replied. "But why of generation? Because to the mortal creature, generation is a sort of eternity and immortality, and if, as has been already admitted, love is of the everlasting possession of the good, all men will necessarily desire immortality together with good: whence it must follow that love is of immortality."

All this she taught me at various times when she spoke of love. And I remember her once saying to me, "What is the cause, Socrates, of love, and the attendant desire? See you not how all animals, birds as well as beasts, in their desire of procreation, are in agony when they take the infection of love, which begins with the desire of union and then passes to the care of offspring, on whose behalf the weakest are ready to battle against the strongest even to the uttermost, and to die for them, and will let themselves be tormented with hunger, or make any other sacrifice, in order to maintain their young. Man may be supposed to act thus from reason; but why should animals have these passionate feelings? Can you tell me why?" Again I replied that I did not know. She said to me: "And do you expect ever to become a master in the art of love, if you do not know this?" "But I have told you already, Diotima, that my ignorance is the reason why I come to you, for I am conscious that I want a teacher; tell me then the cause of this and of the other mysteries of love." "Marvel not," she said, "if you believe that love is of the immortal, as we have several times acknowledged; for here again, and on the same principle too, the mortal nature is seeking as far as is possible to be everlasting and immortal: and this is only to be attained by generation, because generation always leaves behind a new and different existence in the place of the old. Nay, even in the life of the same individual there is succession and not absolute uniformity: a man is called the same, and yet in the interval between youth and age, during which every animal is said to have life and identity, he is undergoing a perpetual process of loss and reparation—hair, flesh, bones, blood, and the whole body are always changing. Which is true not only of the body, but also of the soul, whose habits, tempers, opinions, desires, pleasures, pains, fears, never remain the same in any one of us, but are always coming and going. What is still more surprising, it is equally true of science; not only do some of the sciences come to life in our minds, and others die away, so that we are never the same in regard to them either: but the same fate happens to each of them individually. For what is implied in the word 'recollection,' but the departure of knowledge, which is ever being forgotten, and is renewed and preserved by recollection, and appears to be the same although in reality new, according to that law by which all mortal things are preserved, not absolutely the same, but by substitution, the old worn-out mortality leaving another new and similar existence behind—unlike the divine, which is wholly and eternally the same? And in this way, Socrates, the mortal body, or mortal anything, partakes of immortality; but the immortal in another way. Marvel not then at the love which all men have of their offspring; for that universal love and interest is for the sake of immortality."

WHAT IS THE OBJECT OF LEARNING?

I was astonished at her words, and said: "Is this really true, O most wise Diotima?" And she answered with all the authority of an accomplished sophist: "Of that, Socrates, you may be assured;—think only of the ambition of men, and you will wonder at the senselessness of their ways, unless you consider how they are stirred by the passionate love of fame. They are ready to run all risks, even greater than they would have run for their children, and to pour out money and undergo any sort of toil, and even to die, 'if so they leave an everlasting name.' Do you imagine that Alcestis would have died to save Admetus, or Achilles to avenge Patroclus, or your own Codrus in order to preserve the kingdom for his sons, if they had not imagined that the memory of their virtues, which still survives among us, would be immortal? Nay," she said, "I am persuaded that all men do all things, and the better they are the more they do them, in hope of the glorious fame of immortal virtue; for they desire the immortal.

"Those who are pregnant in the body only, betake themselves to women and beget children—this is the character of their love; their offspring, as they hope, will preserve their memory and give them the blessedness and immortality which they desire for all future time. But souls which are pregnant—for there certainly are men who are more creative in their souls than in their bodies, creative of that which is proper for the soul to conceive and bring forth: and if you ask me what are these conceptions, I answer, wisdom, and virtue in general—among such souls are all creative poets and all artists who are deserving of the name inventor. But the greatest and fairest sort of wisdom by far is that which is concerned with the ordering of states and families, and which is called temperance and justice. And he who in youth has the seed of these implanted in his soul, when he grows up and comes to maturity desires to beget and generate. He wanders about seeking beauty that he may get offspring—for from deformity he will beget nothing—and naturally embraces the beautiful rather than the deformed body; above all, when he finds a fair and noble and well-nurtured soul, he embraces the two in one person, and to such a one he is full of speech about virtue and the nature and pursuits of a good man, and he tries to educate him. At the touch and in the society of the beautiful which is ever present to his memory, even when absent, he brings forth that which he had conceived long before, and in company with him tends that which he brings forth; and they are married by a far nearer tie and have a closer friendship than those who beget mortal children, for the children who are their common offspring are fairer and more immortal. Who when he thinks of Homer and Hesiod and other great poets, would not rather have their children than ordinary human ones? Who would not emulate them in the creation of children such as theirs, which have preserved their memory and given them everlasting glory? Or who would not have such children as Lycurgus left behind him to be the saviors, not only of Lacedaemon, but of Hellas, as one may say? There is Solon, too, who is the revered father of Athenian laws; and many others there are in many other places, both among Hellenes and barbarians, who have given to the world many noble works, and have been the parents of virtue of every kind; and many temples have been raised in their honor for the sake of the children such as theirs; which were never raised in honor of anyone, for the sake of his mortal children.

"These are the lesser mysteries of love, into which even you, Socrates, may enter; to the greater and more hidden ones which are the crown of these, and to which, if you pursue them in a right spirit, they will lead, I know not whether you will be able to attain. But I will do my utmost to inform you, and do you follow if you can. For he who would proceed aright in this matter should begin in youth to seek the company of corporeal beauty; and first, if he be guided by his instructor aright to love one beautiful body only—out of that he should create fair thoughts; and soon he will of himself perceive that the beauty of one body is akin to the beauty of another; and then if beauty of form in general is his pursuit, how foolish would he be not to recognize that the beauty in every body is one and the same! And when he perceives this he will abate his violent love of the one, which he will despise and deem a small thing, and will become a steadfast lover of all beautiful bodies. In the next stage he will consider that the beauty of the soul is more precious than the beauty of the outward form; so that if a virtuous soul have but a little comeliness, he will be content to love and tend him, and will search out and bring to the birth thoughts which may improve the young, until he is compelled next to contemplate and see the beauty in institutions and laws, and to understand that the beauty of them all is of one family, and that personal beauty is a trifle; and after institutions his guide will lead him on to the sciences, in order that, beholding the wide region already occupied by beauty, he may cease to be like a servant in love with one beauty only, that of a particular youth or man or institution, himself a slave mean and narrow-minded; but drawing towards and contemplating the vast sea of beauty, he will create many fair and noble thoughts and discourses in boundless love of wisdom, until on that shore he grows and waxes strong, and at last the vision is revealed to him of a single science, which is the science of beauty everywhere. To this I will proceed; please to give me your very best attention:

"He who has been instructed thus far in the things of love, and who has learned to see the beautiful in due order and succession, when he comes toward the end will suddenly perceive a nature of wondrous beauty (and this, Socrates, is the final cause of all our former toils) —a nature which in the first place is everlasting, knowing not birth or death, growth or decay; secondly, not fair in one point of view and foul in another, or at one time or in one relation or at one place fair, at another time or in another relation or at another place foul, as if fair to some and foul to others, or in the likeness of a face or hands or any other part of the bodily frame, or in any form of speech or knowledge, or existing in any individual being, as for example, in a living creature, whether in heaven, or in earth, or anywhere else; but beauty absolute, separate, simple, and everlasting, which is imparted to the ever growing and perishing beauties of all other beautiful things, without itself suffering diminution, or increase, or any change. He who, ascending from these earthly things under the influence of true love, begins to perceive that beauty, is not far from the end. And the true order of going, or being led by another, to the things of love, is to begin from the beauties of earth and mount upwards for the sake of that other beauty, using these as steps only, and from one going on to two, and from two to all fair bodily forms, and from fair bodily forms to fair practices, and from fair practices to fair sciences, until from fair sciences he arrives at the science of which I have spoken, the science which has no other object than absolute beauty, and at last knows that which is beautiful by itself alone. This, my dear Socrates," said the stranger of Mantinea, "is that life above all others which man should live, in the contemplation of beauty absolute; a beauty which if you once beheld, you would see not to be after the measure of gold, and garments, and fair boys and youths, whose presence now entrances you; and you and many a one would be content to live seeing them only and conversing with them without meat or drink, if that were possible—you only want to look at them and to be with them. But what if a man had eyes to see the true beauty—the divine beauty, I mean, pure and clear and unalloyed, not infected with the pollutions of the flesh and all the colors and vanities of mortal life— thither looking, and holding converse with the true beauty simple and divine? Remember how in that communion only, beholding beauty with that by which it can be beheld, he will be enabled to bring forth, not images of beauty, but realities (for he has hold not of an image but of a reality), and bringing forth and nourishing true virtue will properly become the friend of God and be immortal, if mortal man may. Would that be an ignoble life?"

SUMMARY

And now, I said, let me show in a figure how far our nature is enlightened or unenlightened: —Behold! human beings housed in an underground cave, which has a long entrance open towards the light and as wide as the interior of the cave; here they have been from their childhood, and have their legs and necks chained, so that they cannot move and can only see before them, being prevented by the chains from turning round their heads. Above and behind them a fire is blazing at a distance, and between the fire and the prisoners there is a raised way; and you will see, if you look, a low wall built along the way, like the screen which marionette players have in front of them, over which they show the puppets.

I see.

And do you see, I said, men passing along the wall carrying all sorts of vessels, and statues and figures of animals made of wood and stone and various materials, which appear over the wall? While carrying their burdens, some of them, as you would expect, are talking, others silent.

You have shown me a strange image, and they are strange prisoners.

Like ourselves, I replied; for in the first place do you think they have seen anything of themselves, and of one another, except the shadows which the fire throws on the opposite wall of the cave?

How could they do so, he asked, if throughout their lives they were never allowed to move their heads?

And of the objects which are being carried in like manner they would only see the shadows?

Yes, he said.

And if they were able to converse with one another, would they not suppose that the things they saw were the real things?[6]

Very true.

And suppose further that the prison had an echo which came from the other side, would they not be sure to fancy when one of the passers-by spoke that the voice which they heard came from the passing shadow?

No question, he replied.

To them, I said, the truth would be literally nothing but the shadows of the images.

That is certain.

[6][Text uncertain: perhaps "that they would apply the name *real* to the things which they saw".]

And now look again, and see in what manner they would be released from their bonds, and cured of their error, whether the process would naturally be as follows. At first, when any of them is liberated and compelled suddenly to stand up and turn his neck round and walk and look towards the light, he will suffer sharp pains; the glare will distress him, and he will be unable to see the realities of which in his former state he had seen the shadows; and then conceive someone saying to him that what he saw before was an illusion, but that now, when he is approaching nearer to being and his eye is turned towards more real existence, he has a clearer vision,—what will be his reply? And you may further imagine that his instructor is pointing to the objects as they pass and requiring him to name them,—will he not be perplexed? Will he not fancy that the shadows which he formerly saw are truer than the objects which are now shown to him?

Far truer.

And if he is compelled to look straight at the light, will he not have a pain in his eyes which will make him turn away to take refuge in the objects of vision which he can see, and which he will conceive to be in reality clearer than the things which are now being shown to him?

True, he said.

And suppose once more, that he is reluctantly dragged up that steep and rugged ascent, and held fast until he is forced into the presence of the sun himself, is he not likely to be pained and irritated? When he approaches the light his eyes will be dazzled, and he will not be able to see anything at all of what are now called realities.

Not all in a moment, he said.

He will require to grow accustomed to the sight of the upper world. And first he will see the shadows best, next the reflections of men and other objects in the water, and then the objects themselves; and, when he turned to the heavenly bodies and the heaven itself, he would find it easier to gaze upon the light of the moon and the stars at night than to see the sun or the light of the sun by day?

Certainly.

Last of all he will be able to see the sun, not turning aside to the illusory reflections of him in the water, but gazing directly at him in his own proper place, and contemplating him as he is.

Certainly.

He will then proceed to argue that this is he who gives the seasons and the years, and is the guardian of all that is in the visible world, and in a certain way the cause of all things which he and his fellows have been accustomed to behold?

Clearly, he said, he would arrive at this conclusion after what he had seen.

And when he remembered his old habitation, and the wisdom of the cave and his fellow-prisoners, do you not suppose that he would felicitate himself on the change, and pity them?

Certainly, he would.

And if they were in the habit of conferring honors among themselves on those who were quickest to observe the passing shadows and to remark which of them went before and which followed after and which were together, and who were best able from these observations to divine the future, do you think that he would be eager for such honors and glories, or envy those who attained honor and sovereignty among those men? Would he not say with Homer,

"Better to be a serf, laboring for a landless master,"

and to endure anything, rather than think as they do and live after their manner?

Yes, he said, I think that he would consent to suffer anything rather than live in this miserable manner.

Imagine once more, I said, such a one coming down suddenly out of the sunlight, and being replaced in his old seat; would he not be certain to have his eyes full of darkness?

To be sure, he said.

And, if there were a contest, and he had to compete in measuring the shadows with the prisoners who had never moved out of the cave, while his sight was still weak, and before his eyes had become steady (and the time which would be needed to acquire this new habit of sight might be very considerable), would he not make himself ridiculous? Men would say of him that he had returned from the place above with his eyes ruined; and that it was better not even to think of ascending; and if anyone tried to loose another and lead him up to the light, let them only catch the offender, and they would put him to death.

Insight and Divine Illumination *
AUGUSTINE

CHAPTER IX. WHETHER ALL THINGS, AND ALSO THE COGNITION OF THEM, SHOULD BE PREFERRED TO THEIR SIGNS

AUG. Now then, I wish you to understand that things which are signified are more to be depended upon than signs. For whatever exists because of another must of necessity be inferior to that because of which it exists, unless you think otherwise.

AD. It seems to me that assent should not be given too hastily. For when we say *coenum* [filth], this noun, I think, is far superior to that which it signifies. What offends us when we hear it does not pertain to the sound of the word itself, since *coenum* [filth] is changed by a single letter from *coelum* [heaven]. But we do see what a great difference there is between the things signified by these nouns. Hence I should not attribute to this sign what we so loathe in the thing signified. So for this reason I consider the sign superior to the thing, for we hear the sign with greater complaisance than we perceive the thing by means of any sense.

AUG. Most watchful indeed. It is false, therefore, that all things are to be considered superior to their signs?

AD. It seems so.

AUG. Then tell me what plan you think they followed who gave a name to this vile and despicable thing [*coenum*: filth]. Do you approve of them or not?

AD. Indeed, how should I dare to approve or to disapprove, for I do not know what plan they followed?

AUG. At least you can determine what plan you follow when you utter the name.

AD. Clearly I can; for I wish to signify that which I think ought to be taught or reminded in order to teach or to remind him with whom I am speaking of the thing itself.

AUG. The teaching or reminding, or the being taught or being reminded, which you either express suitably by means of the name or which is expressed to you—ought that not to be held superior to the name itself?

*From Whitney J. Oates (ed.), *Basic Writings of Saint Augustine* (2 vols.; New York: Random House, 1948), I, 382–395 with the permission of the publisher.

AD.   I grant that the knowledge itself which results from the sign should be considered superior to the sign, but not for that reason, I think, the thing also.

AUG.   In this argument of ours, therefore, although it be false that all things ought to be considered superior to their signs, yet it is not false that everything which exists because of another is inferior to that because of which it exists. Surely, the cognition of filth because of which the noun [name] *filth* was determined ought to be considered superior to the noun itself which we found to be superior to filth itself. For the cognition is considered superior to the sign of which we spoke for the sole reason that it is proved conclusively that the sign exists because of the cognition and not the cognition because of the sign. Since, the example, when a certain glutton and servant of the belly, as the Apostle calls him,[1] said that he lived in order to eat, the temperate man who heard him chided him and said: "Would it not be better to eat in order to live?" This was clearly said in conformity with the rule that inferiors exist for the sake of superiors. And the Apostle was displeased only because the glutton's life should be of so little worth to him that he would have it degraded by the passion of gluttony as indicated by his saying that he lived for the sake of feasting. And this should be praised because the Apostle taught in these two distinctions that what ought to be done for the sake of something is that which should be subject to it, for it is understood that it is perferable to eat in order to live. Similarly you as well as other men who judge matters suitably would reply to a garrulous word-lover who said: "I teach in order to talk" with "Man, why not rather speak in order to teach?" For if these things are true, as you know they are, you truly see how much less words are to be esteemed than that for the sake of which we use words, since the use of words is superior to the words. For words exist in order that they may be used, and in addition we use them in order to teach. As teaching is superior to talking, in like degree speech is better than words. So of course doctrine is far superior to words. But I wish to hear whatever objections you have to offer.

AD.   I agree indeed that doctrine is superior to words. But whether the rule that everything which exists for the sake of something else is inferior to that for the sake of which it exists has no exceptions is more than I am able to say.

AUG.   We shall discuss that more conveniently and more thoroughly at another time. For the present what you have granted is enough to prove what I now wish. For you grant that the cognition of things is superior to the signs of things. Consequently, the cognition of things which are signified is to be preferred to the cognition of signs by means of which they are signified. Do you agree?

[1]Rom. xvi. 18

AD.   Did I admit that the cognition of things is superior to the cognition of signs, and not just to signs themselves? Then I fear that I am not in agreement with you on this point. For if *coenum* [filth], the noun [name], is better than the thing it signifies, then the cognition of the noun [name] ought also to be preferred to the cognition of the thing, although the noun itself be inferior to the cognition. Indeed there are four considerations involved: (1) the noun, (2) the thing, (3) the cognition of the noun, (4) the cognition of the thing. Since the first is more excellent than the second, why is not the third better than the fourth? But if it is not better, must it therefore be considered as inferior?

AUG.   I see that you have very admirably retained what you conceded and understood what you thought. But you understood, I think, that the three-syllable word *vitium* [vice] is better than that which it signifies, though the cognition of the noun itself is far inferior to the knowledge of vices. Granted that you thus arrange and consider the four distinctions: (1) noun, (2) thing, (3) cognition of noun, (4) cognition of thing, we correctly place the first before the second. For the noun placed in the verse where Persius says, [2] "But he is drunk with vice," not only does not vitiate the verse but adds a certain ornament. But when the thing itself which is signified by this noun [*vitium*] is in anything it does vitiate it. So thus we see that the third does not excel the fourth, but the fourth the third. For the cognition of the noun *vitium* [vice] exists for the sake of the cognition [knowledge] of vices.

AD.   Do you think that the cognition of vices is preferable even though it makes men more wretched? For among all the afflictions which man suffers, devised by the cruelty or cupidity of tyrants, this same Persius ranks first that torture which results when men are forced to acknowledge vices which they cannot avoid.

AUG.   Reasoning in this way, you can also deny that a knowledge [cognition] of virtues is preferable to the cognition of the word *virtue*. Because to see virtue but not to possess it is torture, and it was by this means that the satirist wished tyrants to be punished. [3]

AD.   May God avert such madness. Now I do see that knowledge [the cognitions themselves] by which learning instructs the soul is not to be held as culpable, but that those men are to be judged the most pitiable of all, as I think Persius judged them, who are infected by such a malady that there is no remedy for it.

AUG.   You understand quite well. But then of what real moment is the opinion of Persius, the satirist, since in problems of the sort before us we are not subject to the authority of satirists? Well, if in some way one

[2]*Satira*, 3. 33
[3]*Satira*, 3. 35–38

cognition is to be preferred to another, still that point is not easily explained just now. I am satisfied that it has been shown that the cognition of the thing which a sign signifies is more powerful than the sign itself, even if it is not superior to the cognition of a sign. Hence, let us discuss more thoroughly what the genus is of those things we said can be shown through themselves [*per se*] without signs, as speaking, walking, sitting, throwing, etc.

AD.   I recall now what you speak of.

CHAPTER X.   WHETHER CERTAIN THINGS CAN BE TAUGHT WITHOUT SIGNS. THINGS ARE NOT LEARNED THROUGH WORDS THEMSELVES

AUG.   Does it seem to you that anything which may be immediately done when one asks a question about it can be shown without a sign, or do you see some exception?

AD.   Running through the items of this whole genus time and again, I do not indeed find anything in it which can be taught without some sign, except perhaps speaking and also possibly teaching. For I see that whatever I do after his question in order that he may learn, the questioner does not learn from the thing itself which he desires to have shown him. For if I am asked what walking is when I am still, or doing something else, and if I, by walking immediately, try to teach without a sign what has been asked—all of which has been discussed earlier—then how shall I avoid having the asker think that walking consists in walking only so far as I walked? And if he did think that he would be misinformed, for if someone walked not so far or farther than I did the questioner would think that this individual had not walked. And what I have said about this one word will be true of all the others which we thought could be shown without a sign, except the ones we excluded (talking and teaching).

AUG.   I accept that, in truth; but does it not seem to you that speaking is one thing and teaching another?

AD.   Surely it does, for if they were the same, none would teach without speaking, and since we teach many things by means of signs which are not words, who can doubt there is a difference?

AUG.   Are teaching and signifying the same or do they differ in some way?

AD.   I think that they are the same.

AUG.   Is it not true that we signify in order to teach?

AD.   That is true.

AUG.   What if it be said that we teach in order to signify? Is the assertion not easily refuted by the former statement?

AD.   That is so.

AUG.   If then we signify that we may teach and do not teach in order to signify, teaching is one thing, signifying another.

AD.   That is true, nor did I answer correctly that both are the same.

AUG.   Now tell me if he who teaches what teaching is does it by signifying or in some other way.

AD.   I do not see that there is any other way.

AUG.   Therefore, what you said awhile ago is false, namely, that when someone asks what teaching is the thing itself can be taught without signs, since we see that not even this can be done without signifying. For you have granted that signifying is one thing, teaching another. And if, as it seems, they are different, and teaching is only by means of signifying, then teaching is not shown through itself [*per se*], as you thought. Consequently, nothing has yet been found which can be shown through itself except speaking which also signifies itself as well as other things. Yet since this is a sign also it is still not entirely clear what things can be taught without the aid of signs.

AD.   I have no reason for disagreeing with you.

AUG.   It has been proved, therefore, that nothing is taught without signs, and that cognition itself should be dearer to us than the signs by means of which we cognize, although all things which are signified cannot be greater than their signs.

AD.   It seems so.

AUG.   Do you recall by what great circumlocutions we at length reached this slight point? For since we began this interchange of words which has occupied us for some time, we have labored to discover the following three points: 1. whether anything can be taught without signs, 2. whether certain signs ought to be preferred to the things which they signify, 3. whether the cognition of things is superior to their signs. But there is a fourth point which I wish to know briefly from you, namely, whether you think that these points are so clear and distinct that you cannot doubt them.

AD.   I wish indeed to have arrived at certainty after such great doubts and complications, but your question disturbs me, although I do not know why, and keeps me from agreeing. For I see that you would not have asked me about this, if you did not have some objection to raise, and the problem is such a labyrinth that I am not able to explore it thoroughly or to answer with assurance, for I am disquieted lest something lie hidden in these windings which evades the keenness of my mind.

AUG.   I commend your hesitation. For it indicates a mind which is cautious and this is the greatest safeguard to equanimity. It is very difficult not to be perturbed when things we consider easily and readily provable are shaken by contrary arguments and, as it were, are wrenched from our hands. For just as it is proper to assent to things well explored and perused, so it is perilous to consider things known which are not known. Because there is a danger, when those things are often upset which we supposed would stand firmly and endure, lest we fall into such distrust and hatred of reason that it might seem that confidence in evident truth itself is not warranted.

But come, let us consider more diligently whether you think any of the points should be doubted. For consider, if someone unskilled in the art of bird-catching, which is done with reeds and bird-lime, should happen upon a fowler, carrying his instruments as he walked along though not fowling at the time, he would hasten to follow and in wonderment he would reflect and ask himself, as indeed he might, what the man's equipment meant. Now if the fowler, seeing himself watched, were to exhibit his art, and skilfully employ the reed, and then noting a little bird nearby, if he were to charm, approach, and capture it with his reed and hawk, would the fowler not teach his observer without the use of signification, but rather by means of the thing itself which the observer desired to know?

AD. I fear this observer of bird-catching is like the man whom I referred to above, who inquires about walking; for it does not seem that in this case the entire art of fowling is exhibited.

AUG. It is easy to free you from that worry. For I suggest that an observer might be intelligent enough to recognize the whole complexity of the art from what he saw. It is enough for our purpose if certain men can be taught without signs about some things, if indeed not about all things.

AD. To that I can add that if the learner be very intelligent he will know what walking is fully when it has been shown by a few steps.

AUG. That is agreeable. And I not only do not object, but I approve of your statement. For you see that the conclusion has been reached by both of us, namely, that some men can be taught things without signs, and that what we thought awhile back is false, that is, that there is nothing at all which can be shown without signs. For now of that sort, not one thing only or another, but thousands of things occur to the mind, which may be shown through themselves when no sign has been given. Why then do we hesitate, I pray you? For passing over the innumerable spectacles of men in every theater where things are shown through themselves without signs, surely the sun and this light bathing and clothing all things, the moon and the other stars, the lands and the seas, and all things which are generated in them without number, are all exhibited and shown through themselves by God and nature to those who perceive them.

If we consider this more carefully, then perhaps you may find that there is nothing which is learned by means of signs. For when a sign is given me, if it finds me not knowing of what thing it is a sign, it can teach me nothing, but if it finds me knowing the thing of which it is the sign, what do I learn from the sign? For the word does not show me the thing which it signifies when I read: *Et saraballae eorum non sunt immutatae*[4] (And their *saraballae* are not changed). For if head-coverings of some sort are called by this name [*saraballae*], when I have heard it have I learned either what a head is or what coverings are? I knew these before, and it is not when someone names them, but when they are seen by me that knowledge of them is achieved for me. And indeed when the two syllables "caput" [head] were first expressed to me, I knew as little what they meant as when I first heard or read *saraballae*. But when "caput" was repeated over and over, as I observed and noticed when it was said, I found it to be the word of a thing which was already well known to me by sight. Before I discovered this the word was only a sound to me, and I learned that it is a sign when I found out of what thing it is a sign; which thing, indeed, I had learned, as I said above, not through its signification but by the sight of it. Therefore that the sign is learned after the thing is cognized is rather more the case than that the thing itself is learned after the sign is given.

That you may understand this more exactly, let us suppose that we now hear for the first time the word "caput" [head], and not knowing whether it is merely a meaningless sound or whether something is signified, we ask what "caput" [head] is. (Remember we want to have knowledge of the sign itself and not of the thing which it signifies, which knowledge we certainly lack as long as we do not know of what it is a sign.) And if, when we inquire, the thing itself is shown us by means of pointing the finger, when we have seen the thing we learn the sign which we had only heard before without knowing it. Since, however, two factors are involved with the sign, namely, sound and signification, we surely perceive the sound not through the sign but through the vibration when the ear is struck, while we learn the signification when the thing itself is shown. For the pointing of the finger can signify only that towards which the finger is pointed, but it was pointed not at the sign but at the member which is called the head; consequently, I have not learned by means of the pointing what the thing is, for I knew that already, nor did I learn the sign in that way since the pointing was not directed at the sign. But I do not wish to place too much emphasis on the pointing of the finger, because it seems to me that it is rather a sign of the demonstration itself rather than of the things demonstrated; as in the case of the adverb *ecce* [behold], for we are accustomed to point the finger with this adverb lest one sign of demonstration be not enough. And if I can, I shall try to prove to you above all that we learn nothing through those signs which are termed

---

[4]Dan. iii. 94

words. For it is more correct, as I have said, that we learn the meaning of the word, that is, the signification which is hidden in the sound when the thing itself which it signifies has been cognized, than that we perceive the thing through such signification.

And what I have said about *head,* I should say, too, of *coverings* [clothes] and of innumerable other things. And though I already know these, yet *saraballae* I do not know in the least. If someone were to indicate them by gesture or sketch them for me or show me something to which they are similar, I do not say that he would not teach me (which I could maintain if I wished to speak a little more fully). But I do say what is quite relevant to the point being discussed, namely, that he would not have taught me by means of words. If someone, seeing these *saraballae* while I was near, should bring them to my attention, saying "Ecce saraballas" [Here are the head-coverings], I would learn something unknown, not through the words which were spoken, but through its appearance, by means of which I was made to know and to retain the meaning of the name. For when I learned the thing itself I was not indebted to the words of others but to my eyes; yet perhaps I accepted their words in order to attend, that is, in order that I might find what was to be seen.

CHAPTER XI.   WE DO NOT LEARN THROUGH THE WORDS WHICH SOUND OUTWARDLY, BUT THROUGH THE TRUTH WHICH TEACHES WITHIN US

To give them as much credit as possible, words possess only sufficient efficacy to remind us in order that we may seek things, but not to exhibit the things so that we may know them. He teaches me something, moreover, who presents to my eyes or to any other bodily sense or even to my mind itself those things which I wish to know. By means of words, therefore, we learn only words or rather the sound and vibration of words, for if those things which are not signs cannot be words, even though I have heard a word, I do not know that it is a word until I know what it signifies. So when things are known the cognition of the words is also accomplished, but by means of hearing words they are not learned. For we do not learn the words which we know, nor can we say that we learn those which we do not know unless their signification has been perceived; and this happens not by means of hearing words which are pronounced, but by means of a cognition of the things which are signified. For it is the truest reasoning and most correctly said that when words are uttered we either know already what they signify or we do not know; if we know, then we remember rather than learn, but if we do not know, then we do not even remember, though perhaps we are prompted to ask.

If you say this, we cannot know the head-coverings, the name of which is only a sound to us, unless we see them; and we cannot know the name itself more fully except by cognizing the things themselves. But we do accept the story of the boys, that they triumphed over the king and over the fires by faith and religion, that they sang praises to God, and that they won honor even from their very enemies. Has this been transmitted to us otherwise than by means of words? I answer that everything signified by these words was already in our knowledge. For I already grasp what three boys are, what furnace is, and fire, and a king, what unhurt by fire is, and every thing else signified by those words. But Ananias and Azarias and Misael are as unknown to me as *saraballae*; these names do not help me at all to know these men, nor can they help me. I confess, moreover, that I believe rather than know that the things written in those stories were done at that time as they have been written; and those whom we believe knew the difference between believing and knowing. For the Prophet says: "If ye will not believe, ye shall not understand."[5] Surely he would not have said that, had he not thought that believing and understanding are different. Therefore, what I understand I also believe, but I do not understand everything that I believe; for all which I understand I know, but I do not know all that I believe. But still I am not unmindful of the utility of believing many things which are not known. I include in this utility the story about the three youths. And though the majority of things must remain unknown to me, yet I do know what is the utility of believing.

But, referring now to all things which we understand, we consult, not the speaker who utters words, but the guardian truth within the mind itself, because we have perhaps been reminded by words to do so. Moreover, He who is consulted teaches; for He who is said to reside in the interior man is Christ,[6] that is, the unchangeable excellence of God and His everlasting wisdom, which every rational soul does indeed consult. But there is revealed to each one as much as he can apprehend through his will according as it is more perfect or less perfect. And if sometimes one is deceived this is not due to a defect in the truth which he has consulted any more than it is a defect of external light that the eyes of the body are often deceived; yet we confess that we consult this external light about visible things in order that it may show them to us in so far as we have the power to discern.

[5]Isa. vii. 9
[6]Eph. iii. 16, 17

CHAPTER XII.   CHRIST THE TRUTH TEACHES WITHIN

If we consult light concerning color and other things which we sense through the body; if we consult the elements of this world and those bodies which we sense; if we consult the senses themselves which the mind uses as interpreters in recognizing things of this sort; and if we also consult the interior truth by means of reason about things which are understood: what can be said to indicate that we learn anything by means of words beyond that sound which strikes the ear? For all things which we perceive are perceived either through a sense of the body or by means of the mind. We call the former sensibles, the latter intelligibles; or to speak in the manner of our authorities, the former are carnal, the latter spiritual. If we are questioned about sensibles, we answer if the things sensed are at hand, as when we are questioned while gazing at the new moon as to where or of what sort it is. If the one who questions does not see, he believes words, and often he does not believe; but he learns nothing unless he also sees what is mentioned. If he does learn, he learns by means of the things themselves and from his own senses, but not through the articulated words. For the same words are heard by the man who sees and by the man who does not see. But if a question is not about things immediately sensed, although it is about things which we have sensed in the past, in this case we speak not of things themselves but of images impressed by things on the mind and committed to memory. I do not in the least know how we can speak of these as true when we see that they are false, unless it is because we do not speak of what we see or what we sense, but of what we have seen or have sensed. Thus we carry these images in the recesses of the memory as documents of things sensed before. Contemplating these in the mind, we say nothing that is false if we speak with good conscience. But these documents are our own, and he who hears of them, if he has been in their presence and sensed them, learns nothing from my words, but rather remembers [and confirms] what is said through the images hidden in himself. But if he has not perceived the things which are spoken of, it is clear that he believes [or accepts on trust] rather than learns through the words.

Indeed when things are discussed which we perceive through the mind, that is, by means of intellect and reason, these are said to be things which we see immediately in that interior light of truth by virtue of which he himself who is called the interior man is illumined, and upon this depends his joy. But then our hearer, if he also himself sees those things with his inner and pure eye, knows that of which I speak by means of his own contemplation, but not through my words. Accordingly, even though I speak about true things, I still do not teach him who beholds the true things, for he is taught not through my words but by means of the things themselves which God reveals within the soul. Hence, if he is questioned, he can answer about these. What could be more absurd than to think that he is taught by means of my speaking, when even before I speak he can express those very things if questioned? Now, if it often happens that he who is questioned denies something, and is driven by other questions to affirm that which he denied, this happens because of a defect in his discrimination in so far as he cannot consult that light about the whole matter. He is advised to do it part by part when he is questioned by one step after another about those very parts of which the whole consists, which he is unable to grasp in its entirety. If he is guided in this case by the words of the questioner, still he does not accomplish the grasp of the whole by means of verbal instruction, but by means of questions put in such a way that he who is questioned is able to teach himself through his inner power according to the measure of his ability. An apt example is found in our recent procedure, for when I asked you whether anything can be taught by words, the question at first seemed absurd to you, because you did not have an inclusive view of the problem. Thus, it was suitable for me to formulate my questions in such a way that your powers might be brought under the direction of the inner teacher. Accordingly, I should say things which as I spoke you would admit to be true, of which you would be certain, and about which you would declare that you had knowledge. From what source would you learn these things? You would perhaps answer that I had taught them to you. To that I should reply: "What if I should say that I had seen a man flying?" Would my words carry the same certitude as if you should hear that wise men are superior to fools? You would immediately answer in the negative and assert that you do not believe the former statement, or if you do believe it, that you do not know it to be true, but that you do know the latter statement with great certainty. From this discussion you would understand clearly that you did not learn anything from me through words, neither about a man flying, of which you knew nothing though I did state it, nor about the relative worth of wise men and fools, which you did know quite well. If in addition you were also questioned about each word, you would state on oath that the latter is well known to you, while the former is not known. Then indeed you would admit all that you had denied, as you knew with clarity and certainty the things in which it consists. Whenever we say anything, either the hearer does not know whether what is said is false or true, or he knows that it is false, or he knows that it is true. In the first mode he will either believe (or accept in good confidence), or he will form an opinion, or he will hesitate; in the second mode he will resist the statement and reject it; in the third he merely confirms. In none of these three cases does the hearer learn anything from what is heard. For he who does not know about the thing after we have spoken, he who knows that what we said is false, and he who would be able upon being asked to state the same things without having heard them, are all three shown to have learned nothing through words.

CHAPTER XIII.   THE POWER OF WORDS DOES NOT EVEN REVEAL THE MIND OF THE SPEAKER

From what has been said it follows, therefore, that in the case of those things which are grasped by the mind, anyone who is unable to grasp them hears to no purpose the words of him who does discern them; though we may make an exception in regard to the fact that where such things are unknown there is a certain utility in believing them until they are known. On the other hand, whoever can discern those things which are grasped by the mind is inwardly a pupil of truth and outwardly a judge of the speaker, or rather of his statements. For often he knows what has been said, though the speaker himself does not know; as if, for example, someone who is a follower of Epicurus and so thinks that the soul is mortal, should recite the arguments on the soul's immortality expounded by men of greater wisdom. If someone who is versed in spiritual things hears the speaker state the argument for the immortality of the soul, he will judge that true things have been said, but the speaker does not know that they are true; for, to the contrary, he thinks that they are quite false. Can he be understood as teaching what he does not know? He does use, however, the very same words which one who understood would use.

Now, therefore, not even this is left to words, namely, that at any rate they express the mind of the speaker, since a speaker may indeed not know the things about which he speaks. Consider also lying and deceiving, and you will easily understand from both of them that words not only do not disclose the true intention of the mind, but that they may serve to conceal it. For I by no means doubt that by words truthful men try, and to some extent do contrive, to disclose their minds, which would be accomplished, as all agree, if liars were not allowed to speak. And yet we have had the experience both in ourselves and in others of words being expressed which were not about the thing being thought. It seems to me that this can happen in two ways: (1) either when something which has been committed to memory and often repeated is expressed by one who is preoccupied with other things, as often happens to us when we sing a hymn, (2) or when against our will we make a slip in speech, for in this case, too, signs are expressed which are not of the things which we have in mind. For indeed those who lie also think of the things which they express, so that, although we do not know whether they tell the truth, we do yet know that they have in mind what they are saying, if they do not do one of the two things cited above. If anyone contends that this only happens now and then, and is apparent when it happens, I do not object, though frequently it is not observed and has often deceived me.

But among these there is another genus of words, one which is very prevalent and the cause of countless disagreements and battles, namely, that which is involved when he who speaks signifies the thing which he is thinking, but for the most part only to himself and certain others, while he does not signify the same thing to the one to whom he speaks nor to some others. For should someone say in our presence that man is surpassed in manly power [*virtus*] by certain large animals, we should not be able to brook such a statement; and we should deny this false and repugnant assertion with vehemence, though perhaps the speaker meant by *manly power* bodily strength. He may have expressed by the word what he had in mind, neither lying, nor making a mistake about the thing, nor linking together memorized words while turning other things over in his mind, nor saying by a slip of the tongue what he did not intend to say. He merely calls the thing about which he was thinking by a name which is other than the one by which we call it. We should agree with him at once if we could read his mind and see directly the thought which he was unable to express by the words spoken and the statement made. They say that definition can cure this error, so that in this case, if the speaker were to define what virtue is, it would be clear that the controversy is not about the thing but about the word. Now I may grant that this is so, but how often is it possible to find good definers? And yet many things have been charged against the science of defining, which are not approved by me in all respects, but it is not suitable to discuss this at present.

I pass over the fact that we hear many things imperfectly and yet wrangle long and forcefully as if we had heard perfectly; for example, you were saying but some time ago that you heard that *piety* is signified by a certain Punic word which I had called *mercy,* and you had heard this from those who know the language well. But I objected and insisted that you had forgotten what you had heard, for you seemed to me to say "faith" rather than "piety," though you were sitting near me and the two words are by no means deceptive to the ear because of their similarity in sound. Yet for a long time I thought that you did not know what had been said to you, whereas it was I who did not know what you had said. If I had heard you well, it would not have seemed at all absurd to me that in

Punic *piety* and *mercy* are called by one word. These things happen now and then, but, as I said, we shall overlook them lest I seem to bring false witness against words because of the negligence of the hearer or even because of human deafness. The points enumerated above are more distressing where, though we speak the same language as the speaker and the words are clearly heard and are Latin, we still are not able to understand the speaker.

But witness: I now relent and admit that when words are perceived in the hearing of him to whom they are known, the hearer may rest assured that the speaker has thought about the things which they signify. But we are now asking if for that reason he learns whether the speaker has told the truth?

CHAPTER XIV.   CHRIST TEACHES WITHIN. MAN REMINDS BY MEANS OF WORDS SPOKEN OUTWARDLY

For do teachers profess that it is their thoughts which are perceived and grasped by the students, and not the sciences themselves which they convey through speaking? For who is so stupidly curious as to send his son to school in order that he may learn what the teacher thinks? But all those sciences which they profess to teach, and the science of virtue itself and wisdom, teachers explain through words. Then those who are called pupils consider within themselves whether what has been explained has been said truly; looking of course to that interior truth, according to the measure of which each is able. Thus they learn, and when the interior truth makes known to them that true things have been said, they applaud, but without knowing that instead of applauding teachers they are applauding learners, if indeed their teachers know what they are saying. But men are mistaken, so that they call those teachers who are not, merely because for the most part there is no delay between the time of speaking and the time of cognition. And since after the speaker has reminded them, the pupils quickly learn within, they think that they have been taught outwardly by him who prompts them.

But we shall, God willing, inquire at some other time about the utility of words, which if it is well considered is no mean matter. For the present I have warned you that we should not attribute more to words than is proper. So that now we may not only believe but also begin to understand that it has truly been written on divine authority that we are not to call anyone on earth our master because there is only one Master of all who is in heaven.[7] But what *in heaven* means He Himself will advertise to us by

[7]Matt. xxiii. 8-10

means of men, through signs and outwardly, so that we may by turning inwardly to Him be made wise; whom to know and to love is the blessed life which, though all claim to seek it, few indeed may rejoice that they have found. But now pray tell me what you think about this long disquisition of mine. For if you know that what I have said is true, then had you been questioned about each statement you would have said that you did know it. You see, therefore, from whom you have learned these matters. Surely, not from me to whom you would have given the correct answer if questioned. However, if you do not know that they are true, neither the inner man nor I have taught you; not I, because I can never teach; not the inner man, because you have it not yet in you to learn.

AD.   But I have learned through being reminded by your words that man is only prompted by words in order that he may learn, and it is apparent that only a very small measure of what a speaker thinks is expressed in his words. Moreover, when He spoke among the people He reminded us that we learn whether things are true from that one only whose habitation is within us, whom now, by His grace, I shall so love more ardently as I progress in understanding. Nevertheless, I am most grateful to you for the discussion which you delivered without breaking the thread of your thought, because it anticipated and dissolved all the objections which occurred to me, and nothing which was causing me disquietude has been overlooked by you, nor is there anything about which the inner oracle does not tell me what your words stated.

Of Human Understanding*

JOHN LOCKE

INTRODUCTION

1. *An enquiry into the understanding pleasant and useful.*   Since it is the *understanding* that sets man above the rest of sensible beings, and gives him all the advantage and dominion which he has over them, it is certainly a subject, even for its nobleness, worth our labor to enquire into. The understanding, like the eye, whilst it makes us see and perceive all other things, takes no notice of itself; and it requires art and pains to set it

*From John Locke, *An Essay Concerning Human Understanding*, edited and abridged by A. S. Pringle-Pattison (Oxford: Clarendon Press, 1956), Book I, Chap. 1, Book II, Chaps. 1, 2, 6, 7, 8, 23, 33, and Book IV, Chaps. 1, 3, 4. Reprinted with the permission of the Clarendon Press.

at a distance, and make it its own object. But whatever be the difficulties that lie in the way of this enquiry; whatever it be that keeps us so much in the dark to ourselves; sure I am that all the light we can let in upon our own minds, all the acquaintance we can make with our own understandings, will not only be very pleasant, but bring us great advantage in directing our thoughts in the search of other things.

2. *Design.* This, therefore, being my purpose, to enquire into the original, certainty, and extent of human Knowledge, together with the grounds and degrees of Belief, Opinion, and Assent, I shall not at present meddle with the physical consideration of the mind, or trouble myself to examine wherein its essence consists, or by what motions of our spirits, or alterations of our bodies, we come to have any sensation by our organs, or any ideas in our understandings; and whether those ideas do, in their information, any or all of them, depend on matter or no. These are speculations which, however curious and entertaining, I shall decline, as lying out of my way in the design I am now upon. It shall suffice to my present purpose, to consider the discerning faculties of a man as they are employed about the objects which they have to do with: and I shall imagine I have not wholly misemployed myself in the thoughts I shall have on this occasion, if, in this historical, plain method, I can give any account of the ways whereby our understandings come to attain those notions of things we have, and can set down any measures of the certainty of our knowledge, or the grounds of those persuasions which are to be found amongst men, so various, different, and wholly contradictory; and yet asserted somewhere or other with some assurance, and confidence, that he that shall take a view of the opinions of mankind, observe their opposition, and at the same time consider the fondness and devotion wherewith they are embraced, the resolution and eagerness wherewith they are maintained, may perhaps have reason to suspect that either there is no such thing as truth at all, or that mankind hath no sufficient means to attain a certain knowledge of it.

3. *Method.* It is therefore worth while to search out the *bounds* between Opinion and Knowledge, and examine by what measures, in things whereof we have no certain knowledge, we ought to regulate our assent, and moderate our persuasions. In order whereunto, I shall pursue this following method: —

First, I shall enquire into the *original* of those *ideas,* notions or whatever else you please to call them, which a man observes, and is conscious to himself he has in his mind; and the ways whereby the understanding comes to be furnished with them.

Secondly, I shall endeavor to show what *knowledge* the understanding hath by those *ideas,* and the certainty, evidence, and extent of it.

Thirdly, I shall make some enquiry into the nature and grounds of Faith or Opinion; whereby I mean that assent which we give to any proposition as true, of whose truth yet we have no certain knowledge: and here we shall have occasion to examine the reasons and degrees of *Assent.*

4. *Useful to know the extent of our comprehension.*   If by this enquiry into the nature of the understanding, I can discover the powers thereof, *how far* they reach, to what things they are in any degree proportionate, and where they fail us, I suppose it may be of use, to prevail with the busy mind of man to be more cautious in meddling with things exceeding its comprehension, to stop when it is at the utmost extent of its tether, and to sit down in a quiet ignorance of those things which, upon examination, are found to be beyond the reach of our capacities. We should not then perhaps be so forward, out of an affectation of an universal knowledge, to raise questions, and perplex ourselves and others with disputes about things to which our understandings are not suited, and of which we cannot frame in our minds any clear or distinct perceptions, or whereof (as it has, perhaps, too often happened) we have not any notions at all. If we can find out how far the understanding can extend its view, how far it has faculties to attain certainty, and in what cases it can only judge and guess, we may learn to content ourselves with what is attainable by us in this state.

OF IDEAS IN GENERAL AND THEIR ORIGINAL

1. *Idea is the object of thinking.*   Every man being conscious to himself that he thinks, and that which his mind is applied about whilst thinking being the ideas that are there, it is past doubt that men have in their minds several ideas, such as are those expressed by the words, "whiteness, hardness, sweetness, thinking, motion, man, elephant, army, drunkenness," and others. It is in the first place then to be enquired, How he comes by them?

2. *All ideas come from sensation or reflection.*   Let us then suppose the mind to be, as we say, white paper, void of all characters, without any ideas; how comes it to be furnished? Whence comes it by that vast store, which the busy and boundless fancy of man has painted on it with an almost endless variety? Whence has it all the materials of reason and knowledge? To this I answer, in one word, from EXPERIENCE; in that all our knowledge is founded, and from that it ultimately derives itself. Our observation, employed either about external sensible objects, or about the internal operations of our minds, perceived and reflected on by ourselves, is that which supplies our understandings with all the materials

of thinking. These two are the fountains of knowledge, from whence all the ideas we have, or can naturally have, do spring.

3. *The objects of sensation one source of ideas.*   First, our senses, conversant about particular sensible objects, do convey into the mind several distinct perceptions of things, according to those various ways wherein those objects do affect them; and thus we come by those *ideas* we have of yellow, white, heat, cold, soft, hard, bitter, sweet, and all those which we call sensible qualities; which when I say the senses convey into the mind, I mean, they from external objects convey into the mind what produces there those perceptions. This great source of most of the ideas we have, depending wholly upon our senses, and derived by them to the understanding, I call, SENSATION.

4. *The operations of our minds the other source of them.*   Secondly, the other fountain, from which experience furnisheth the understanding with ideas, is the perception of the operations of our own minds within us, as it is employed about the ideas it has got; which operations, when the soul comes to reflect on and consider, do furnish the understanding with another set of ideas which could not be had from things without: and such are perception, thinking, doubting, believing, reasoning, knowing, willing, and all the different actings of our own minds; which we being conscious of, and observing in ourselves, do from these receive into our understanding as distinct ideas, as we do from bodies affecting our senses. This source of ideas every man has wholly in himself: and though it be not sense, as having nothing to do with external objects, yet it is very like it, and might properly enough be called internal sense. But as I call the other Sensation, so I call this REFLECTION, the ideas it affords being such only as the mind gets by reflecting on its own operations within itself. By Reflection, then, in the following part of this discourse, I would be understood to mean that notice which the mind takes of its own operations, and the manner of them, by reason whereof there come to be ideas of these operations in the understanding. These two, I say, viz., external material things as the objects of Sensation, and the operations of our own minds within as the objects of Reflection, are, to me, the only originals from whence all our ideas take their beginnings. The term *operations* here, I use in a large sense, as comprehending not barely the actions of the mind about its ideas, but some sort of passions arising sometimes from them, such as is the satisfaction or uneasiness arising from any thought.

5. *All our ideas are of the one or the other of these.*   The understanding seems to me not to have the least glimmering of any ideas which it doth not receive from one of these two. *External objects* furnished the mind with the ideas of sensible qualities, which are all those different perceptions they produce in us; and *the mind* furnishes the understanding

with ideas of its own operations. These, when we have taken a full survey of them, and their several modes, combinations, and relations, we shall find to contain all our whole stock of ideas; and that we have nothing in our minds which did not come in one of these two ways. Let any one examine his own thoughts, and thoroughly search into his understanding, and then let him tell me, whether all the original ideas he has there, are any other than of the objects of his senses, or of the operations of his mind considered as objects of his reflection; and how great a mass of knowledge soever he imagines to be lodged there, he will, upon taking a strict view, see that he has not any idea in his mind but what one of these two have imprinted, though perhaps with infinite variety compounded and enlarged by the understanding, as we shall see hereafter.

6. *Observable in children.*   He that attentively considers the state of a child at his first coming into the world, will have little reason to think him stored with plenty of ideas that are to be the matter of his future knowledge. It is by degrees he comes to be furnished with them: and though the ideas of obvious and familiar qualities imprint themselves before the memory begins to keep a register of time and order, yet it is often so late before some unusual qualities come in the way, that there are few men that cannot recollect the beginning of their acquaintance with them: and if it were worth while, no doubt a child might be so ordered as to have but a very few even of the ordinary ideas till he were grown up to a man. But all that are born into the world being surrounded with bodies that perpetually and diversely affect them, variety of ideas, whether care be taken about it or no, are imprinted on the minds of children. Light and colors are busy and at hand everywhere when the eye is but open; sounds and some tangible qualities fail not to solicit their proper senses, and force an entrance to the mind; but yet I think it will be granted easily, that if a child were kept in a place where he never saw any other but black and white till he were a man, he would have no more ideas of scarlet or green, than he that from his childhood never tasted an oyster or a pineapple has of those particular relishes.

7. *Men are differently furnished with these according to the different objects they converse with.*   Men then come to be furnished with fewer or more simple ideas from without, according as the objects they converse with afford greater or less variety; and from the operations of their minds within, according as they more or less reflect on them. For, though he that contemplates the operations of his mind cannot but have plain and clear ideas of them; yet, unless he turn his thoughts that way, and considers them *attentively,* he will no more have clear and distinct ideas of all the operations of his mind, and all that may be observed therein, than he will have all the particular ideas of any landscape, or of the parts and motions of a

clock, who will not turn his eyes to it, and with attention heed all the parts of it. The picture or clock may be so placed, that they may come in his way every day; but yet he will have but a confused idea of all the parts they are made up of, till he applies himself with attention to consider them each in particular.

8. *Ideas of reflection later, because they need attention.* And hence we see the reason why it is pretty late before most children get ideas of the operations of their own minds; and some have not any very clear or perfect ideas of the greatest part of them all their lives. Because, though they pass there continually, yet, like floating visions, they make not deep impressions enough to leave in the mind clear, distinct, lasting ideas, till the understanding turns inwards upon itself, reflects on its own operations, and makes them the object of its own contemplation. Children, when they come first into it, are surrounded with a world of new things, which, by a constant solicitation of their senses, draw the mind constantly to them, forward to take notice of new, and apt to be delighted with the variety of changing objects. Thus the first years are usually employed and diverted in looking abroad. Men's business in them is to acquaint themselves with what is to be found without; and so, growing up in a constant attention to outward sensations, seldom make any considerable reflection on what passes within them till they come to be of riper years; and some scarce ever at all.

OF SIMPLE IDEAS

1. *Uncompounded appearances.* The better to understand the nature, manner, and extent of our knowledge, one thing is carefully to be observed concerning the ideas we have; and that is, that some of them are *simple,* and some *complex.*

Though the qualities that affect our senses are, in the things themselves, so united and blended that there is no separation, no distance between them; yet it is plain the ideas they produce in the mind enter by the senses simple and unmixed. For though the sight and touch often take in from the same object at the same time different ideas; as a man sees at once motion and color, the hand feels softness and warmth in the same piece of wax; yet the simple ideas thus united in the same subject are as perfectly distinct as those that come in by different senses. The coldness and hardness which a man feels in a piece of ice being as distinct ideas in the mind as the smell and whiteness of a lily, or as the taste of sugar and smell of a rose: and there is nothing can be plainer to a man than the clear and distinct perception he has of those simple ideas; which, being each in itself uncompounded, contains in it nothing but one uniform appearance or conception in the mind, and is not distinguishable into different ideas.

2. *The mind can neither make nor destroy them.*   These simple ideas, the materials of all our knowledge, are suggested and furnished to the mind only by those two ways above mentioned, viz., sensation and reflection. When the understanding is once stored with these simple ideas, it has the power to repeat, compare, and unite them, even to an almost infinite variety, and so can make at pleasure new complex ideas. But it is not in the power of the most exalted wit or enlarged understanding, by any quickness or variety of thought, to invent or frame one new simple idea in the mind, not taken in by the ways before mentioned; nor can any force of the understanding destroy those that are there. The dominion of man in this little world of his own understanding, being much-what the same as it is in the great world of visible things, wherein his power, however managed by art and skill, reaches no farther than to compound and divide the materials that are made to his hand, but can do nothing towards the making the least particle of new matter, or destroying one atom of what is already in being. The same inability will every one find in himself, who shall go about to fashion in his understanding any simple idea not received in by his senses from external objects, or by reflection from the operations of his own mind about them. I would have any one try to fancy any taste which had never affected his palate, or frame the idea of a scent he had never smelt; and when he can do this, I will also conclude, that a blind man hath ideas of colors, and a deaf man true distinct notions of sounds.

OF SIMPLE IDEAS OF REFLECTION

1. *Are the operations of the mind about its other ideas.*   The mind, receiving the ideas mentioned in the foregoing chapters from without, when it turns its view inward upon itself, and observes its own actions about those ideas it has, takes from thence other ideas, which are as capable to be the objects of its contemplation as any of those it received from foreign things.

2. *The idea of perception, and idea of willing, we have from reflection.*   The two great and principal actions of the mind, which are most frequently considered, and which are so frequent that every one that pleases may take notice of them in himself, are these two: *perception* or *thinking,* and *volition* or *willing.* The power of thinking is called the *Understanding,* and the power of volition is called the *Will;* and these two powers or abilities in the mind are denominated *faculties.* Of some of the

modes of these simple ideas of reflection, such as are *remembrance, discerning, reasoning, judging, knowledge, faith,* etc. I shall have occasion to speak hereafter.

OF SIMPLE IDEAS OF BOTH SENSATION AND REFLECTION

1. There be other simple ideas which convey themselves into the mind by all the ways of sensation and reflection; viz., *pleasure* or *delight,* and its opposite, *pain* or *uneasiness; power; existence; unity.*

2. *Pleasure and pain.* Delight or uneasiness, one or other of them, join themselves to almost all our ideas both of sensation and reflection; and there is scarce any affection of our senses from without, any retired thought of our mind within, which is not able to produce in us pleasure or pain. By pleasure and pain, I would be understood to signify whatsoever delights or molests us; whether it arises from the thoughts of our minds, or anything operating on our bodies. For whether we call it satisfaction, delight, pleasure, happiness, etc. on the one side, or uneasiness, trouble, pain, torment, anguish, misery, etc. on the other, they are still but different degrees of the same thing, and belong to the ideas of pleasure and pain, delight or uneasiness; which are the names I shall most commonly use for those two sorts of ideas.

3. The infinite wise Author of our being, to excite us to these actions of thinking and motion that we are capable of, has been pleased to join to several thoughts and several sensations a perception of delight. If this were wholly separated from all our outward sensations and inward thoughts, we should have no reason to prefer one thought or action to another, negligence to attention, or motion to rest. And so we should neither stir our bodies, nor employ our minds, but let our thoughts (if I may so call it) run adrift, without any direction or design; and suffer the ideas of our minds, like unregarded shadows, to make their appearances there as it happened, without attending to them. In which state man, however furnished with the faculties of understanding and will, would be a very idle, unactive creature, and pass his time only in a lazy, lethargic dream.

4. Pain has the same efficacy and use to set us on work that pleasure has, we being as ready to employ our faculties to avoid that, as to pursue this: only this is worth our consideration, that pain is often produced by the same objects and ideas that produce pleasure in us. Thus heat, that is very agreeable to us in one degree, by a little greater increase of it proves no ordinary torment; and the most pleasant of all sensible objects, light itself, if there be too much of it, if increased beyond a due proportion to our eyes, causes a very painful sensation. Which is wisely and favorably

so ordered by nature, that when any object does by the vehemency of its operation disorder the instruments of sensation, whose structures cannot but be very nice and delicate, we might by the pain be warned to withdraw before the organ be quite put out of order, and so be unfitted for its proper functions for the future.

7. *Existence and unity.*   Existence and unity are two other ideas that are suggested to the understanding by every object without, and every idea within. When ideas are in our minds, we consider them as being actually there, as well as we consider things to be actually without us: which is, that they exist, or have existence. And whatever we can consider as one thing, whether a real being or idea, suggests to the understanding the idea of unity.

8. *Power.*   Power also is another of those simple ideas which we receive from sensation and reflection. For, observing in ourselves that we do and can think, and that we can at pleasure move several parts of our bodies which were at rest, the effects also that natural bodies are able to produce in one another occurring every moment to our senses, we both these ways get the idea of power.

9. *Succession.*   Besides these there is another idea, which though suggested by our senses yet is more constantly offered us by what passes in our own minds; and that is the idea of succession. For if we look immediately into ourselves, and reflect on what is observable there, we shall find our ideas always, whilst we are awake or have any thought, passing in train, one going and another coming without intermission.

10. *Simple ideas the materials of all our knowledge.*   These, if they are not all, are at least (as I think) the most considerable of those simple ideas which the mind has, and out of which is made all its other knowledge: all which it receives only by the two forementioned ways of sensation and reflection.

Nor let any one think these too narrow bounds for the capacious mind of man to expatiate in, which takes its flight farther than the stars, and cannot be confined by the limits of the world. I grant all this, but desire any one to assign any simple idea which is not received from one of those inlets before mentioned, or any complex idea not made out of those simple ones.

Nor will it be so strange to think these few simple ideas sufficient to employ the quickest thought or largest capacity, and to furnish the materials of all that various knowledge and more various fancies and opinions of all mankind, if we consider how many words may be made out of the various composition of twenty-four letters; or if, going one step farther, we will but reflect on the variety of combinations may be made with barely one of the above-mentioned ideas, viz., number, whose stock is inexhaustible and truly infinite: and what a large and immense field doth extension alone afford the mathematicians?

SOME FARTHER CONSIDERATIONS CONCERNING OUR SIMPLE IDEAS

1. *Positive ideas from privative causes.*   Concerning the simple ideas of sensation it is to be considered, that whatsoever is so constituted in nature as to be able by affecting our senses to cause any perception in the mind, doth thereby produce in the understanding a simple idea; which, whatever be the external cause of it, when it comes to be taken notice of by our discerning faculty, it is by the mind looked on and considered there to be a real positive idea in the understanding, as much as any other whatsoever; though perhaps the cause of it be but a privation in the subject.

2. Thus the ideas of heat and cold, light and darkness, white and black, motion and rest, are equally clear and positive ideas in the mind; though perhaps some of the causes which produce them are barely privations in those subjects from whence our senses derive those ideas. These the understanding, in its view of them, considers all as distinct positive ideas without taking notice of the causes that produce them: which is an enquiry not belonging to the idea as it is in the understanding, but to the nature of the things existing without us. These are two very different things, and carefully to be distinguished; it being one thing to perceive and know the idea of white or black, and quite another to examine what kind of particles they must be, and how ranged in the superficies, to make any object appear white or black.

3. A painter or dyer who never enquired into their causes, hath the ideas of white and black and other colors as clearly, perfectly, and distinctly in his understanding, and perhaps more distinctly than the philosopher who hath busied himself in considering their natures, and thinks he knows how far either of them is in its cause positive or privative; and the idea of black is no less positive in his mind than that of white, however the cause of that color in the external object may be only a privation.

4. If it were the design of my present undertaking to enquire into the natural causes and manner of perception, I should offer this as a reason why a privative cause might, in some cases at least, produce a positive idea, viz., that all sensation being produced in us only by different degrees and modes of motion in our animal spirits, variously agitated by external objects, the abatement of any former motion must as necessarily produce a new sensation as the variation or increase of it; and so introduce a new

idea, which depends only on a different motion of the animal spirits in that organ.

5. But whether this be so or no I will not here determine, but appeal to every one's own experience, whether the shadow of a man, though it consists of nothing but the absence of light (and the more the absence of light is, the more discernible is the shadow), does not, when a man looks on it, cause as clear and positive an idea in his mind as a man himself, though covered over with clear sunshine. And the picture of shadow is a positive thing. Indeed, we have negative names, which stand not directly for positive ideas, but for their absence, such as *insipid, silence, nihil,* etc., which words denote positive ideas, v.g., *taste, sound, being,* with a signification of their absence.

6. And thus one may truly be said to see darkness. The privative causes I have here assigned of positive ideas are according to the common opinion; but in truth it will be hard to determine whether there be really any ideas from a privative cause, till it be determined whether rest be any more a privation than motion.

7. *Ideas in the mind, qualities in bodies.*   To discover the nature of our ideas the better, and to discourse of them intelligibly, it will be convenient to distinguish them, as they are ideas or perceptions in our minds, and as they are modifications of matter in the bodies that cause such perceptions in us; that so we may not think (as perhaps usually is done) that they are exactly the images and resemblances of something inherent in the subject: most of those of sensation being in the mind no more the likeness of something existing without us than the names that stand for them are the likeness of our ideas, which yet upon hearing they are apt to excite in us.

8. Whatsoever the mind perceives in itself, or is the immediate object of perception, thought, or understanding, that I call *idea;* and the power to produce any idea in our mind, I call *quality* of the subject wherein that power is. Thus a snowball having the power to produce in us the ideas of white, cold, and round, the powers to produce those ideas in us as they are in the snowball, I call qualities; and as they are sensations or perceptions in our understandings, I call them ideas; which ideas, if I speak of them sometimes as in the things themselves, I would be understood to mean those qualities in the objects which produce them in us.

9. *Primary qualities of bodies.* Qualities thus considered in bodies are, First, such as are utterly inseparable from the body, in what estate soever it be; such as, in all the alterations and changes it suffers, all the force can be used upon it, it constantly keeps; and such as sense constantly finds in every particle of matter which has bulk enough to be perceived, and the mind finds inseparable from every particle of matter, though less

than to make itself singly be perceived by our senses: v.g., take a grain of wheat, divide it into two parts, each part has still solidity, extension, figure, and mobility; divide it again, and it retains still the same qualities: and so divide it on, till the parts become insensible; they must retain still each of them all those qualities. [These I call *original* or *primary qualities* of body, which I think we may observe to produce simple ideas in us, viz., solidity, extension, figure, motion or rest, and number.

10. *Secondary qualities of bodies.*   Secondly, Such qualities, which in truth are nothing in the objects themselves, but powers to produce various sensations in us by their primary qualities, i. e., by the bulk, figure, texture, and motion of their insensible parts, as colors, sounds, tastes, etc.; these I call *secondary qualities.* To these might be added a third sort, which are allowed to be barely powers, though they are as much real qualities in the subject as those which I, to comply with the common way of speaking, call qualities, but, for distinction, secondary qualities. For the power in fire to produce a new color or consistence in wax or clay by its primary qualities, is as much a quality in fire as the power it has to produce in *me* a new idea or sensation of warmth or burning, which I felt not before, by the same primary qualities, viz., the bulk, texture, and motion of its insensible parts.]

11. *How primary qualities produce their ideas.*   The next thing to be considered is, how bodies produce ideas in us; and that is manifestly by impulse, the only way which we can conceive bodies operate in.

12. If, then, external objects be not united to our minds when they produce ideas in it, and yet we perceive these original qualities in such of them as singly fall under our senses, it is evident that some motion must be thence continued by our nerves or animal spirits, by some parts of our bodies, to the brains or the seat of sensation, there to produce in our minds the particular ideas we have of them. And since the extension, figure, number, and motion of bodies of an observable bigness, may be perceived at a distance by the sight, it is evident some singly imperceptible bodies must come from them to the eyes, and thereby convey to the brain some motion which produces these ideas which we have of them in us.

13. *How secondary.*   After the same manner that the ideas of these original qualities are produced in us, we may conceive that the ideas of secondary qualities are also produced, viz., by the operation of insensible particles on our senses. The different motions and figures, bulk and number of such particles, affecting the several organs of our senses, produce in us those different sensations which we have from the colors and smells of bodies; v. g., that a violet, by the impulse of such insensible particles of matter of peculiar figures and bulks, and in different degrees and modifications of their motions, causes the ideas of the blue color and

sweet scent of that flower to be produced in our minds. It being no more impossible to conceive that God should annex such ideas to such motions with which they have no similitude, than that he should annex the idea of pain to the motion of a piece of steel dividing our flesh, with which that idea hath no resemblance.

14. What I have said concerning colors and smells may be understood also of tastes and sounds, and other the like sensible qualities; which, whatever reality we by mistake attribute to them, are in truth nothing in the objects themselves, but powers to produce various sensations in us, and depend on those primary qualities, viz., bulk, figure, texture, and motion of parts, as I have said.

15. *Ideas of primary qualities are resemblances; of secondary, not.* From whence I think it is easy to draw this observation, that the ideas of primary qualities of bodies are resemblances of them, and their patterns do really exist in the bodies themselves; but the ideas produced in us by these secondary qualities have no resemblance of them at all. There is nothing like our ideas existing in the bodies themselves. They are, in the bodies we denominate from them, only a power to produce those sensations in us: and what is sweet, blue, or warm in idea, is but the certain bulk, figure, and motion of the insensible parts in the bodies themselves, which we call so.

16. Flame is denominated hot and light; snow, white and cold; and manna, white and sweet, from the ideas they produce in us. Which qualities are commonly thought to be the same in those bodies that those ideas are in us, the one the perfect resemblance of the other, as they are in a mirror; and it would by most men be judged very extravagant, if one should say otherwise. And yet he that will consider that the same fire that at one distance produces in us the sensation of warmth, does at a nearer approach produce in us the far different sensation of pain, ought to bethink himself what reason he has to say, that his idea of warmth which was produced in him by the fire, is actually in the fire, and his idea of pain which the same fire produced in him the same way is not in the fire. Why is whiteness and coldness in snow, and pain not, when it produces the one and the other idea in us, and can do neither, but by the bulk, figure, number, and motion of its solid parts?

17. The particular bulk, number, figure, and motion of the parts of fire or snow are really in them, whether any one's senses perceive them or no; and therefore they may be called *real qualities,* because they really exist in those bodies. But light, heat, whiteness, or coldness, are no more really in them than sickness or pain is in manna. Take away the sensation of them; let not the eyes see light or colors, nor the ears hear sounds; let the palate not taste, nor the nose smell; and all colors, tastes, orders, and

sounds, as they are such particular ideas, vanish and cease, and are reduced to their causes, i. e., bulk, figure, and motion of parts.

18. A piece of manna of a sensible bulk is able to produce in us the idea of a round or square figure; and, by being removed from one place to another, the idea of motion. This idea of motion represents it as it really is in the manna moving; a circle or square are the same, whether in idea or existence, in the mind or in the manna; and this, both motion and figure are really in the manna, whether we take notice of them or no; this everybody is ready to agree to. Besides, manna, by the bulk, figure, texture, and motion of its parts, has a power to produce the sensations of sickness, and sometimes of acute pains or gripings, in us. That these ideas of sickness and pain are not in the manna, but effects of its operations on us, and are nowhere when we feel them not: this also every one readily agrees to. And yet men are hardly to be brought to think that sweetness and whiteness are not really in manna, which are but the effects of the operations of manna by the motion, size, and figure of its particles on the eyes and palate: as the pain and sickness caused by manna are confessedly nothing but the effects of its operations on the stomach. Why the pain and sickness, ideas that are the effects of manna, should be thought to be nowhere when they are not felt; and yet the sweetness and whiteness, effects of the same manna on other parts of the body, by ways equally as unknown, should be thought to exist in the manna, when they are not seen nor tasted, would need some reason to explain.

19. Let us consider the red and white colors in porphyry: hinder light but from striking on it, and its colors vanish; it no longer produces any such ideas in us. Upon the return of light, it produces these appearances on us again. Can any one think any real alterations are made in the porphyry by the presence or absence of light, and that those ideas of whiteness and redness are really in porphyry in the light, when it is plain *it has no color in the dark?* It has indeed such a configuration of particles, both night and day, as are apt, by the rays of light rebounding from some parts of that hard stone, to produce in us the idea of redness, and from others the idea of whiteness: but whiteness or redness are not in it at any time, but such a texture that hath the power to produce such a sensation in us.

22. I have, in what just goes before, been engaged in physical enquiries a little farther than perhaps I intended. But it being necessary to make the nature of sensation a little understood, and to make the difference between the *qualities* in bodies and the *ideas* produced by then in the mind to be distinctly conceived, without which it were impossible to discourse intelligibly of them, I hope I shall be pardoned this little excursion into natural philosophy, it being necessary in our present enquiry to distinguish

the *primary* and *real* qualities of bodies, which are always in them (viz., solidity, extension, figure, number, and motion or rest, and are sometimes perceived by us, viz., when the bodies they are in are big enough singly to be discerned), from those *secondary* and *imputed* qualities, which are but the powers of several combinations of those discerned: whereby we also may come to know what ideas are, and what are not, resemblances of something really existing in the bodies we denominate from them.

23. *Three sorts of qualities in bodies.*   The qualities then that are in bodies, rightly considered, are of three sorts:

First, the bulk figure, number, situation, and motion or rest of their solid parts. Those are in them, whether we perceive them or no; and when they are of that size that we can discover them, we have by these an idea of the thing as it is in itself, as is plain in artificial things. These I call *primary qualities.*

Secondly, the power that is in any body, by reason of its insensible primary qualities, to operate after a peculiar manner on any of our senses, and thereby produce in *us* the different ideas of several colors, sounds, smells, tastes, etc. These are usually called *sensible qualities.*

Thirdly, the power that is in any body by reason of the particular constitution of its primary qualities, to make such a change in the bulk, figure, texture, and motion of another body, as to make it operate on our senses differently from what it did before. Thus the sun has a power to make wax white, and fire, to make lead fluid. These are usually called *powers.*

The first of these, as has been said, I think may be properly called real, original, or primary qualities, because they are in the things themselves, whether they are perceived or no: and upon their different modifications it is that the secondary qualities depend.

The other two are only powers to act differently upon other things, which powers result from the different modifications of those primary qualities.

24. *The first are resemblances; the second thought resemblances, but are not; the third neither are, nor are thought so.*   But though these two latter sorts of qualities are powers barely, and nothing but powers, relating to several other bodies, and resulting from the different modifications of the original qualities, yet they are generally otherwise thought of. V. g., the idea of heat or light which we receive by our eyes or touch from the sun, are commonly thought real qualities existing in the sun, and something more than mere powers in it. But when we consider the sun in reference to wax, which it melts or blanches, we look upon the whiteness and softness produced in the wax, not as qualities in the sun, but effects produced by powers in it: whereas, if rightly considered, these qualities of

light and warmth, which are perceptions in me when I am warmed or enlightened by the sun, are no otherwise in the sun than the changes made in the wax, when it is blanched or melted, are in the sun. They are all of them equally powers in the sun, depending on its primary qualities.

25. The reason why the one are ordinarily taken for real qualities, and the other only for bare powers, seems to be because the ideas we have of distinct colors, sounds, etc., containing nothing at all in them of bulk, figure, or motion, we are not apt to think them the effects of these primary qualities which appear not to our senses to operate in their production, and with which they have not any apparent congruity, or conceivable connection. Hence it is that we are so forward to imagine that those ideas are the resemblances of something really existing in the objects themselves. But, in the other case, in the operations of bodies changing the qualities one of another, we plainly discover that the quality produced hath commonly no resemblance with anything in the thing producing it; wherefore we look on it as a bare effect of power. [26.] The former, I think, may be called secondary qualities immediately perceivable, the latter secondary qualities mediately perceivable.

OF OUR COMPLEX IDEAS OF SUBSTANCES

1. *Ideas of substances, how made.*   The mind being, as I have declared, furnished with a great number of the simple ideas conveyed in by the senses, as they are found in exterior things, or by reflection on its own operations, takes notice also, that a certain number of these simple ideas go constantly together; which being presumed to belong to one thing, and words being suited to common apprehensions, and made use of for quick dispatch, are called, so united in one subject, by one name; which, by inadvertency, we are apt afterward to talk of and consider as one simple idea, which indeed is a complication of many ideas together: because, as I have said, not imagining how these simple ideas can subsist by themselves, we accustom ourselves to suppose some *substratum* wherein they do subsist, and from which they do result, which therefore we call *substance.*

2. *Idea of substance in general.*   So that if any one will examine himself concerning his notion of pure substance in general, he will find he has no other idea of it at all, but only a supposition of he knows not what support of such qualities which are capable of producing simple ideas in us; which qualities are commonly called accidents. If any one should be asked, what is the subject wherein color or weight inheres, he would have nothing to say, but the solid extended parts: and if he were demanded,

what is it that that solidity and extension inhere in, he would not be in a much better case than the Indian before mentioned, who saying that the world was supported by a great elephant, was asked, what the elephant rested on; to which his answer was, a great tortoise: but being again pressed to know what gave support to the broad-backed tortoise, replied, something, he knew not what. And thus here, as in all other cases where we use words without having clear and distinct ideas, we talk like children; who being questioned what such a thing is which they know not, readily give this satisfactory answer, that it is *something;* which in truth signifies no more, when so used, either by children or men, but that they know not what; and that the thing they pretend to know, and talk of, is what they have no distinct idea of at all, and so are perfectly ignorant of it, and in the dark. The idea, then, we have, to which we give the general name substance, being nothing but the supposed, but unknown, support of those qualities we find existing, which we imagine cannot subsist *sine re substante,* without something to support them, we call that support *substantia;* which, according to the true import of the word, is, in plain English, standing under, or upholding.

3. *Of the sorts of substances.*   An obscure and relative idea of substance in general being thus made, we come to have the ideas of *particular sorts* of substances, by collecting such combinations of simple ideas as are, by experience and observation of men's senses, taken notice of to exist together, and are therefore supposed to flow from the particular internal constitution or unknown essence of that substance. Thus we come to have the ideas of a man, horse, gold, water, etc., of which substances, whether any one has any other clear idea, farther than of certain simple ideas coexisting together, I appeal to every one's own experience. It is the ordinary qualities observable in iron or a diamond, put together, that make the true complex idea of those substances, which a smith or a jeweller commonly knows better than a philosopher; who, whatever substantial forms he may talk of, has no other idea of those substances than what is framed by a collection of those simple ideas which are to be found in them. Only we must take notice, that our complex ideas of substances, besides all these simple ideas they are made up of, have always the confused idea of something to which they belong and in which they subsist. And therefore, when we speak of any sort of substance, we say it is a thing having such or such qualities; as body is a thing that is extended, figured, and capable of motion; a spirit, a thing capable of thinking; and so hardness, friability, and power to draw iron, we say, are qualities to be found in a loadstone. These and the like fashions of speaking intimate that the substance is supposed always something besides the extension, figure, solidity, motion, thinking, or other observable ideas, though we know not what it is.

4. *No clear idea of substance in general.*   Hence, when we talk or think of any particular sort of corporeal substances, as horse, stone, etc., though the idea we have of either of them be but the complication or collection of those several simple ideas of sensible qualities which we use to find united in the thing called horse or stone; yet because we cannot conceive how they should subsist alone, nor one in another, we suppose them existing in, and supported by, some common subject; which support we denote by the name substance, though it be certain we have no clear or distinct idea of that thing we suppose a support.

5. *As clear an idea of spirit as body.*   The same happens concerning the operations of the mind, viz., thinking, reasoning, fearing, etc., which we concluding not to subsist of themselves, nor apprehending how they can belong to body, or be produced by it, we are apt to think these the actions of some other substance, which we call spirit; whereby yet it is evident, that having no other idea or notion of matter, but something wherein those many sensible qualities which affect our senses do subsist; by supposing a substance wherein thinking, knowing, doubting, and a power of moving, etc., do subsist; we have as clear a notion of the substance of spirit as we have of body; the one being supposed to be (without knowing what it is) the *substratum* to those simple ideas we have from without; and the other supposed (with a like ignorance of what it is) to be the *substratum* to those operations which we experiment in ourselves within. It is plain, then, that the idea of corporeal substance in matter is as remote from our conceptions and apprehensions as that of spiritual substance or spirit; and therefore, from our not having any notion of the substance of spirit, we can no more conclude its non-existence than we can, for the same reason, deny the existence of body: it being as rational to affirm there is no body, because we have no clear and distinct idea of the substance of matter, as to say there is no spirit, because we have no clear and distinct idea of the substance of a spirit.

6. *Of the sorts of substances.*   Whatever therefore be the secret and abstract nature of substance in general, all the ideas we have of particular distinct sorts of substances are nothing but several combinations of simple idea coexisting in such, though unknown, cause of their union, as makes the whole subsist of itself. It is by such combinations of simple ideas, and nothing else, that we represent particular sorts of substances to ourselves. Such are the ideas we have of their several species in our minds; and such only do we, by their specific names, signify to others, v. g., man, horse, sun, water, iron; upon hearing which words, every one who understands the language frames in his mind a combination of those several simple ideas which he has usually observed or fancied to exist together under that denomination; all which he supposes to rest in, and be, as it were,

adherent to, that unknown common subject, which inheres not in anything else. Though in the meantime it be manifest, and every one upon enquiry into his own thoughts will find, that he has no other idea of any substance but what he has barely of those sensible qualities, which he supposes to inhere, with a supposition of such a substratum, as gives, as it were, a support to those qualities or simple ideas, which he has observed to exist united together. Thus the idea of the sun, what is it but an aggregate of those simple several ideas, bright, hot, roundish, having a constant regular motion, at a certain distance from us, and perhaps some other? As he who thinks and discourses of the sun, has been more or less accurate in observing those sensible qualities, ideas, or properties, which are in that thing which he calls the sun.

7. *Powers a great part of our complex ideas of substances.* For he has the perfectest idea of any of the particular sorts of substances who has gathered and put together most of those simple ideas which do exist in it, among which are to be reckoned its active powers and passive capacities; which, though not simple ideas, yet in this respect, for brevity's sake, may conveniently enough be reckoned amongst them; v. g., we immediately by our senses perceive in fire its heat and color; which are, if rightly considered, nothing but powers in it to produce those ideas in us: we also by our senses perceive the color and brittleness of charcoal, whereby we come by the knowledge of another power in fire, which it has to change the color and consistency of wood. By the former, fire immediately, by the latter it mediately, discovers to us these several powers, which therefore we look upon to be a part of the qualities of fire, and so make them a part of the complex idea of it. For all those powers that we take cognizance of, terminating only in the alteration of some sensible qualities in those subjects on which they operate, and so making them exhibit to us new sensible ideas; therefore it is that I have reckoned these powers amongst the simple ideas which make the complex ones of the sorts of substances; though these powers, considered in themselves, are truly complex ideas.

8. *And why.* Nor are we to wonder that powers make a great part of our complex ideas of substances, since their secondary qualities are those which, in most of them, serve principally to distinguish substances one from another, and commonly make a considerable part of the complex idea of the several sorts of them. For our senses failing us in the discovery of the bulk, texture, and figure of the minute parts of bodies, on which their real constitutions and differences depend, we are fain to make use of their secondary qualities as the characteristical notes and marks whereby to frame ideas of them in our minds, and distinguish them one from another. All which secondary qualities, as has been shown, are nothing but bare powers. For the color and taste of opium are, as well as its

soporific or anodyne virtues, mere powers depending on its primary qualities, whereby it is fitted to produce different operations on different parts of our bodies.

9. *Three sorts of ideas make our complex ones of substances.* The ideas that make our complex ones of corporeal substances are of these three sorts. First, the ideas of the primary qualities of things which are discovered by our senses, and are in them even when we perceive them not: such are the bulk, figure, number, situation, and motion of the parts of bodies, which are really in them, whether we take notice of them or no. Secondly, the sensible secondary qualities which, depending on these, are nothing but the powers those substances have to produce several ideas in us by our senses; which ideas are not in the things themselves otherwise than as anything is in its cause. Thirdly, the aptness we consider in any substance to give or receive such alterations of primary qualities as that the substance so altered should produce in us different ideas from what it did before; these are called active and passive powers: all which powers, as far as we have any notice or notion of them, terminate only in sensible simple ideas. For whatever alteration a loadstone has the power to make in the minute particles of iron, we should have no notion of any power it had at all to operate on iron, did not its sensible motion discover it; and I doubt not but there are a thousand changes that bodies we daily handle have a power to cause in one another, which we never suspect, because they never appear in sensible effects.

10. *Powers make a great part of our complex ideas of substances.* Powers therefore justly make a great part of our complex ideas of substances. He that will examine his complex idea of gold, will find several of its ideas that make it up to be only powers: as the power of being melted, but of not spending itself in the fire, of being dissolved in *aqua regia*, are ideas as necessary to make up our complex idea of gold, as its color and weight: which, if duly considered, are also nothing but different powers. For to speak truly, yellowness is not actually in gold, but is a power in gold to produce that idea in us by our eyes when placed in a due light: and the heat which we cannot leave out of our idea of the sun, is no more really in the sun than the white color it introduces into wax.

11. *The now secondary qualities of bodies would disappear, if we could discover the primary ones of their minute parts.* Had we senses acute enough to discern the minute particles of bodies, and the real constitution on which their sensible qualities depend, I doubt not but they would produce quite different ideas in us, and that which is now the yellow color of gold would then disappear, and instead of it we should see an admirable texture of parts of a certain size and figure. This microscopes plainly discover to us; for what to our naked eyes produces a certain color

is, by thus augmenting the acuteness of our senses, discovered to be quite a different thing; and the thus altering, as it were, the proportion of the bulk of the minute parts of a colored object to our usual sight, produces different ideas from what it did before. Thus sand, or pounded glass, which is opaque and white to the naked eye, is pellucid in a microscope: Blood to the naked eye appears all red; but by a good microscope, wherein its lesser parts appear, shows only some few globules of red, swimming in a pellucid liquor; and how these red globules would appear, if glasses could be found that yet could magnify them one thousand or ten thousand times more, is uncertain.

12. *Our faculties of discovery suited to our state.*   The infinite wise Contriver of us and all things about us hath fitted our senses, faculties, and organs to the conveniences of life, and the business we have to do here. We are able by our senses to know and distinguish things, and to examine them so far as to apply them to our uses, and several ways to accommodate the exigencies of this life. We have insight enough into their admirable contrivances and wonderful effects to admire and magnify the wisdom, power, and goodness of their Author. Such a knowledge as this, which is suited to our present condition, we want not faculties to attain. But it appears not that God intended we should have a perfect, clear, and adequate knowledge of them: that perhaps is not in the comprehension of any finite being. We are furnished with faculties (dull and weak as they are) to discover enough in the creatures to lead us to the knowledge of the Creator, and the knowledge of our duty; and we are fitted well enough with abilities to provide for the conveniences of living: these are our business in this world. But were our senses altered, and made much quicker and acuter, the appearance and outward scheme of things would have quite another face to us; and I am apt to think, would be inconsistent with our being, or at least wellbeing, in this part of the universe which we inhabit. He that considers how little our constitution is able to bear a remove into parts of this air not much higher than that we commonly breathe in, will have reason to be satisfied that, in this globe of earth allotted for our mansion, the all-wise Architect has suited our organs and the bodies that are to affect them one to another. If our sense of hearing were but a thousand times quicker than it is, how would a perpetual noise distract us. And we should, in the quietest retirement, be less able to sleep or meditate than in the middle of a sea-fight. Nay, if that most instructive of our senses, seeing, were in any man a thousand or a hundred thousand times more acute than it is now by the best microscope, things several millions of times less than the smallest object of his sight now would then be visible to his naked eyes, and so he would come nearer the discovery of the texture and motion of the minute parts of corporeal things, and in many of them probably get ideas of their internal

constitutions: but then he would be in a quite different world from other people: nothing would appear the same to him and others: the visible ideas of everything would be different. So that I doubt whether he and the rest of men could discourse concerning the objects of sight, or have any communication about colors, their appearances being so wholly different. And perhaps such a quickness and tenderness of sight could not endure bright sunshine, or so much as open daylight; nor take in but a very small part of any object at once, and that too only at a very near distance. And if by the help of such microscopical eyes (if I may so call them) a man could penetrate farther than ordinary into the secret composition and radical texture of bodies, he would not make any great advantage by the change, if such an acute sight would not serve to conduct him to the market and exchange; if he could not see things he was to avoid at a convenient distance, nor distinguish things he had to do with by those sensible qualities others do. He that was sharp-sighted enough to see the configuration of the minute particles of the spring of a clock, and observe upon what peculiar structure and impulse its elastic motion depends, would no doubt discover something very admirable. But if eyes so framed could not view at once the hand, and the characters of the hour-plate, and thereby at a distance see what o'clock it was, their owner could not be much benefited by that acuteness; which, whilst it discovered the secret contrivance of the parts of the machine, made him lose its use.

. . .

14. *Complex ideas of substances.*   But to return to the matter in hand, the ideas we have of substances, and the ways we come by them: I say, Our *specific* ideas of substances are nothing else but a *collection of a certain number of simple ideas, considered as united in one thing.* These ideas of substances, though they are commonly called simple apprehensions, and the names of them simple terms; yet, in effect, are complex and compounded. Thus the idea which an Englishman signifies by the name swan is white color, long neck, red beak, black legs, and whole feet, and all these of a certain size, with a power of swimming in the water, and making a certain kind of noise; and perhaps to a man who has long observed those kind of birds, some other properties, which all terminate in sensible simple ideas, all united in one common subject.

15. *Idea of spiritual substances as clear as of bodily substances.*   Besides the complex ideas we have of material sensible substances, of which I have last spoken,—by the simple ideas we have taken from those operations of our own minds, which we experiment daily in ourselves, we are able to frame the *complex idea of an immaterial spirit.* For putting together the ideas of thinking and willing, or the power of moving or quieting corporeal motion, joined to substance, of which we have no

distinct idea, we have the idea of an immaterial spirit; and by putting together the ideas of coherent solid parts, and a power of being moved, joined with substance, of which likewise we have no positive idea, we have the idea of matter. The one is as clear and distinct an idea as the other: the idea of thinking and moving a body being as clear and distinct ideas as the ideas of extension, solidity, and being moved. For our idea of substance is equally obscure, or none at all, in both; it is but a supposed I know not what, to support those ideas we call accidents. [It is for want of reflection that we are apt to think that our senses show us nothing but material things. Every act of sensation, when duly considered, gives us an equal view of both parts of nature, the corporeal and spiritual. For whilst I know, by seeing or hearing, etc., that there is some corporeal being without me, the object of that sensation, I do more certainly know that there is some spiritual being within me that sees and hears. This I must be convinced cannot be the action of bare insensible matter, nor ever could be without an immaterial thinking being.]

16. *No idea of abstract substance.*   By the complex idea of extended, figured, colored, and all other sensible qualities which is all that we know of it, we are as far from the idea of the substance of body as if we knew nothing at all: nor, after all the acquaintance and familiarity which we imagine we have with matter, and the many qualities men assure themselves they perceive and know in bodies, will it, perhaps, upon examination be found, that they have any more or clearer primary ideas belonging to body than they have belonging to immaterial spirit.

17. *The cohesion of solid parts and impulse, the primary ideas of body.*   The primary ideas we have *peculiar to body,* as contradistinguished to spirit, are *the cohesion of solid,* and consequently separable *parts, and a power of communicating motion by impulse.* These, I think, are the original ideas proper and peculiar to body; for figure is but the consequence of finite extension.

18. *Thinking and motivity, the primary ideas of spirit.*   The ideas we have belonging and *peculiar to spirit* are *thinking,* and *will,* or a power of putting body into motion by thought, and, which is consequent to it, liberty. For as body cannot but communicate its motion by impulse to another body, which it meets with at rest; so the mind can put bodies into motion, or forbear to do so, as it pleases. The ideas of existence, duration, and mobility, are common to them both.

19. *Spirits capable of motion.*   There is no reason why it should be thought strange that I make mobility belong to spirit: for having no other idea of motion but change of distance with other beings that are considered as at rest, and finding that spirits as well as bodies cannot operate but where they are, and that spirits do operate at several times in several

places, I cannot but attribute change of place to all finite spirits; (for of the infinite Spirit I speak not here). For my soul, being a real being, as well as my body, is certainly as capable of changing distance with any other body or being as body itself, and so is capable of motion. And if a mathematician can consider a certain distance or a change of that distance between two points, one may certainly conceive a distance and a change of distance between two sp.rits; and so conceive their motion, their approach or removal, one from another.

20. Every one finds in himself, that his soul can think, will, and operate on his body, in the place where that is; but cannot operate on a body, or in a place, a hundred miles distant from it. Nobody can imagine, that his soul can think or move a body at Oxford, whilst he is at London; and cannot but know that, being united to his body, it constantly changes place all the whole journey between Oxford and London, as the coach or horse does that carries him; and I think may be said to be truly all that while in motion: or if that will not be allowed to afford us a clear idea enough of its motion, its being separated from the body in death, I think, will: for to consider it as going out of the body, or leaving it, and yet to have no idea of its motion, seems to me impossible.

21. If it be said by any one, that it cannot change place, because it hath none, for spirits are not *in loco,* but *ubi,* I suppose that way of talking will not now be of much weight to many, in an age that is not much disposed to admire, or suffer themselves to be deceived by such unintelligible ways of speaking. But if any one thinks there is any sense in that distinction, and that it is applicable to our present purpose, I desire him to put into intelligible English; and then from thence draw a reason to show, that immaterial spirits are not capable of motion. Indeed motion cannot be attributed to God; not because he is an immaterial, but because he is an infinite Spirit.

OF THE ASSOCIATION OF IDEAS

1. *Something unreasonable in most men.*   There is scarce any one that does not observe something that seems odd to him, and is in itself really extravagant, in the opinions, reasonings, and actions of other men. The least flaw of this kind, if at all different from his own, every one is quick-sighted enough to espy in another, and will by the authority of reason forwardly condemn, though he be guilty of much greater unreasonableness in his own tenets and conduct, which he never perceives, and will very hardly, if at all, be convinced of.

5. *From a wrong connection of ideas.*   Some of our ideas have a natural correspondence and connection one with another; it is the office

and excellency of our reason to trace these, and hold them together in that union and correspondence which is founded in their peculiar beings. Besides this, there is another connection of ideas wholly owing to chance or custom: ideas that in themselves are not at all of kin, come to be so united in some men's minds that it is very hard to separate them; they always keep in company, and the one no sooner at any time comes into the understanding, but its associate appears with it; and if they are more than two which are thus united, the whole gang, always inseparable, show themselves together.

6. *This connection how made.*   This strong combination of ideas, not allied by nature, the mind makes in itself either voluntarily or by chance; and hence it comes in different men to be very different, according to their different inclinations, educations, interests, etc. Custom settles habits of thinking in the understanding, as well as of determining in the will, and of motions in the body; all which seems to be but trains of motion in the animal spirits, which, once set agoing, continue in the same steps they have been used to, which, by often treading, are worn into a smooth path, and the motion in it becomes easy, and as it were natural. As far as we can comprehend thinking, thus ideas seem to be produced in our minds; or if they are not, this may serve to explain their following one another in an habitual train, when once they are put into that track, as well as it does to explain such motions of the body. A musician used to any tune will find that, let it but once begin in his head, the ideas of the several notes of it will follow one another orderly in his understanding, without any care or attention, as regularly as his fingers move orderly over the keys of the organ to play out the tune he has begun, though his unattentive thoughts be elsewhere a-wandering. Whether the natural cause of these ideas, as well as of that regular dancing of his fingers, be the motion of his animal spirits, I will not determine, how probable soever by this instance it appears to be so: but this may help us a little to conceive of intellectual habits, and of the tying together of ideas.

7. *Some antipathies an effect of it.*   That there are such associations of them made by custom in the minds of most men, I think nobody will question who has well considered himself or others; and to this, perhaps, might be justly attributed most of the sympathies and antipathies observable in men, which work as strongly, and produce as regular effects, as if they were natural, and are therefore called so, though they at first had no other original but the accidental connection of two ideas which either the strength of the first impression, or future indulgence so united, that they always afterwards kept company together in that man's mind, as if they were but one idea. I say, most of the antipathies, I do not say all; for

some of them are truly natural, depend upon our original constitution, and are born with us.

8. I mention this not out of any great necessity there is, in this present argument, to distinguish nicely between natural and acquired antipathies; but I take notice of it for another purpose, viz., that those who have children, or the charge of their education, would think it worth their while diligently to watch, and carefully to prevent the undue connection of ideas in the minds of young people. [9] This wrong connection in our minds of ideas, in themselves loose and independent one of another, is of so great force to set us awry in our actions, as well moral as natural, passions, reasonings, and notions themselves, that perhaps there is not any one thing that deserves more to be looked after.   [10] The ideas of goblins and sprites have really no more to do with darkness than light; yet let but a foolish maid inculcate these often on the mind of a child, and raise them there together, possibly he shall never be able to separate them again so long as he lives.

11. A man receives a sensible injury from another, thinks on the man and that action over and over, and by ruminating on them strongly or much in his mind, so cements those two ideas together, that he makes them almost one; never thinks on the man, but the pain and displeasure he suffered comes into his mind with it, so that he scarce distinguishes them, but has as much an aversion for the one as the other. Thus hatreds are often begotten from slight and almost innocent occasions, and quarrels propagated and continued in the world. [12] A man has suffered pain or sickness in any place; he saw his friend die in such a room. Though these have in nature nothing to do with one another, yet when the idea of the place occurs to his mind, it brings that of the pain and displeasure with it; he confounds them in his mind, and can as little bear the one as the other.

13. *Why time cures some disorders in the mind which reason cannot.*   When this combination is settled, and whilst it lasts, it is not in the power of reason to help us, and relieve us from the effects of it. Ideas in our minds, when they are there, will operate according to their natures and circumstances: and here we see the cause why time cures certain affections, which reason, though in the right and allowed to be so, has not power over. The death of a child, that was the daily delight of his mother's eyes and joy of her soul, rends from her heart the whole comfort of her life. Use the consolations of reason in this case, and you were as good preach ease to one on the rack. Till time has by disuse separated the sense of that enjoyment, and its loss, from the idea of the child returning to her memory, all representations, though never so reasonable, are in

vain; and therefore some in whom the union between these ideas is never dissolved, spend their lives in mourning, and carry an incurable sorrow to their graves.

15. Many children, imputing the pain they endured at school to their books they were corrected for, so join those ideas together that a book becomes their aversion, and they are never reconciled to the study and use of them all their lives after; and thus reading becomes a torment to them, which otherwise possibly they might have made the great pleasure of their lives. There are rooms convenient enough that some men cannot study in, and fashions of vessels which, though never so clean and commodious, they cannot drink out of, and that by reason of some accidental ideas which are annexed to them, and make them offensive; and who is there that hath not observed some man to flag at the appearance or in the company of some certain person not otherwise superior to him, but because having once on some occasion got the ascendant, the idea of authority and distance goes along with that of the person, and he that has been thus subjected is not able to separate them.

16. Instances of this kind are so plentiful everywhere, that if I add one more, it is only for the pleasant oddness of it. It is of a young gentleman, who having learnt to dance, and that to great perfection, there happened to stand an old trunk in the room where he learnt. The idea of this remarkable piece of household stuff had so mixed itself with the turns and steps of all his dances, that though in that chamber he could dance excellently well, yet it was only whilst that trunk was there, nor could he perform well in any other place, unless that or some such other trunk had its due position in the room. If this story shall be suspected to be dressed up with some comical circumstances a little beyond precise nature, I answer for myself, that I had it some years since from a very sober and worthy man, upon his own knowledge, as I report it; and I dare say there are very few inquisitive persons, who read this, who have not met with accounts, if not examples, of this nature, that may parallel, or at least justify this.

OF KNOWLEDGE IN GENERAL

1. *Our knowledge conversant about our ideas.*   Since the mind, in all its thoughts and reasonings, hath no other immediate object but its own ideas, which it alone does or can contemplate, it is evident that our knowledge is only conversant about them.

2. *Knowledge is the perception of the agreement or disagreement of two ideas.*   Knowledge then seems to me to be nothing but the perception

of the connection and agreement, or disagreement and repugnancy, of any of our ideas. In this alone it consists. Where this perception is, there is knowledge; and where it is not, there, though we may fancy, guess, or believe, yet we always come short of knowledge. For when we know that white is not black, what do we else but perceive that these two ideas do not agree? When we possess ourselves with the utmost security of the demonstration that the three angles of a triangle are equal to two right ones, what do we more but perceive, that equality to two right ones does necessarily agree to, and is inseparable from, the three angles of a triangle?

3. *This agreement fourfold.*   But to understand a little more distinctly wherein this agreement or disagreement consists, I think we may reduce it all to these four sorts: (1) *Identity,* or *diversity.* (2) *Relation.* (3) *Coexistence,* or *necessary connection.* (4) *Real existence.*

4. *First, Of identity or diversity.*   As to the first sort of agreement or disagreement, viz., *identity, or diversity.* It is the first act of the mind, when it has any sentiments or ideas at all, to perceive its ideas, and, so far as it perceives them to know each what it is, and thereby also to perceive their difference, and that one is not another. This is so absolutely necessary, that without it there could be no knowledge, no reasoning, no imagination, no distinct thoughts at all. By this the mind clearly and infallibly perceives each idea to agree with itself, and to be what it is; and all distinct ideas to disagree, i.e., the one not to be the other: and this it does without pains, labor, or deduction; but at first view, by its natural power of perception and distinction. And though men of art have reduced this into those general rules, *What is, is*; and, *It is impossible for the same thing to be and not to be,* for ready application in all cases wherein there may be occasion to reflect on it; yet it is certain that the first exercise of this faculty is about particular ideas. A man infallibly knows, as soon as ever he has them in his mind, that the ideas he calls white and round are the very ideas they are, and that they are not other ideas which he calls red or square. Nor can any maxim or proposition in the world make him know it clearer or surer than he did before, and without any such general rule. This then is the first agreement or disagreement which the mind perceives in its ideas; which it always perceives at first sight; and if there ever happen any doubt about it, it will always be found to be about the names, and not the ideas themselves, whose identity and diversity will always be perceived as soon and as clearly as the ideas themselves are, nor can it possibly be otherwise.

5. *Secondly, Relative.*   The next sort of agreement or disagreement the mind perceives in any of its ideas may, I think, be called *relative,* and is nothing but the perception of the *relation* between any two ideas, of

what kind soever, whether substances, modes, or any other. For, since all distinct ideas must eternally be known not to be the same, and so be universally and constantly denied one of another, there could be no room for any positive knowledge at all, if we could not perceive any relation between our ideas, and find out the agreement or disagreement they have one with another, in several ways the mind takes of comparing them.

6. *Thirdly, Of coexistence.*   The third sort of agreement or disagreement to be found in our ideas, which the perception of the mind is employed about, is *coexistence,* or *non-coexistence* in the same subject; and this belongs particularly to substances. Thus when we pronounce concerning gold that it is fixed, our knowledge of this truth amounts to no more but this, that fixedness, or a power to remain in the fire unconsumed, is an idea that always accompanies and is joined with that particular sort of yellowness, weight, fusibility, malleableness, and solubility in *aqua regia,* which make our complex idea, signified by the word gold.

7. *Fourthly, Of real existence.*   The fourth and last sort is that of *actual real existence* agreeing to any idea. Within these four sorts of agreement or disagreement is, I suppose, contained all the knowledge we have or are capable of; for all the enquiries that we can make concerning any of our ideas, all that we know or can affirm concerning any of them, is, that it is or is not the same with some other; that it does or does not always coexist with some other idea in the same subject; that it has this or that relation to some other idea; or that it has a real existence without the mind. Thus, "Blue is not yellow," is of identity. "Two triangles upon equal bases between two parallels are equal," is of relation. "Iron is susceptible of magnetical impressions," is of coexistence. "God is," is of real existence. Though identity and coexistence are truly nothing but relations, yet they are so peculiar ways of agreement or disagreement of our ideas, that they deserve well to be considered as distinct heads, and not under relation in general: since they are so different grounds of affirmation and negation, as will easily appear to any one who will but reflect on what is said in several places of this *Essay.* I should now proceed to examine the several degrees of our knowledge, but that it is necessary first to consider the different acceptations of the word *knowledge.*

8. *Knowledge actual or habitual.*   There are several ways wherein the mind is possessed of truth, each of which is called knowledge.

(1) There is *actual knowledge,* which is the present view the mind has of the agreement or disagreement of any of its ideas, or of the relation they have one to another.

(2) A man is said to know any proposition which having been once laid before his thoughts, he evidently perceived the agreement or disagree-

ment of the ideas whereof it consists; and so lodged it in his memory, that whenever that proposition comes again to be reflected on, he, without doubt or hesitation, embraces the right side, assents to and is certain of the truth of it. This, I think, one may call *habitual knowledge.* For our finite understandings being able to think clearly and distinctly but on one thing at once, if men had no knowledge of any more than what they actually thought on, he that knew most would know but one truth, that being all he was able to think on at one time.

OF THE EXTENT OF HUMAN KNOWLEDGE

1. Knowledge, as has been said, lying in the perception of the agreement or disagreement of any of our ideas, it follows from hence that,

First, No farther than we have ideas.   First, We can have knowledge no farther than we have ideas.

2. *Secondly, No farther than we can perceive their agreement or disagreement.*   Secondly, That we can have no knowledge farther than we can have *perception* of that agreement or disagreement: which perception being, (1) Either by *intuition,* or the immediate comparing any two ideas; or, (2) By *reason,* examining the agreement or disagreement of two ideas by the intervention of some others; or (3) By *sensation,* perceiving the existence of particular things; hence it also follows,

3. *Thirdly, Intuitive knowledge extends itself not to all the relations of all our ideas.*   Thirdly, that we cannot have an intuitive knowledge that shall extend itself to all our ideas, and all that we would know about them; because we cannot examine and perceive all the relations they have one to another by juxtaposition, or an immediate comparison one with another. Thus having the ideas of an obtuse and an acute angled triangle, both drawn from equal bases, and between parallels, I can by intuitive knowledge perceive the one not to be the other; but cannot that way know whether they be equal or no: because their agreement or disagreement in equality can never be perceived by an immediate comparing them; the difference of figure makes their parts incapable of an exact immediate application; and therefore there is need of some intervening quantities to measure them by, which is demonstration or rational knowledge.

4. *Fourthly, Nor demonstrative knowledge.*   Fourthly, It follows also, from what is above observed, that our rational knowledge cannot reach to the whole extent of our ideas. Because between two different ideas we would examine, we cannot always find such mediums as we can connect one to another with an intuitive knowledge, in all the parts of the deduction; and wherever that fails, we come short of knowledge and demonstration.

5. *Fifthly, Sensitive knowledge narrower than either.*   Fifthly, Sensitive knowledge, reaching no farther than the existence of things actually present to our senses, is yet much narrower than either of the former.

6. *Sixthly, Our knowledge therefore narrower than our ideas.*   From all which it is evident, that the extent of our knowledge comes not only short of the reality of things, but even of the extent of our own ideas. We have the ideas of a square, a circle, and equality: and yet, perhaps, shall never be able to find a circle equal to a square, and certainly know that it is so. We have the ideas of matter and thinking, but possibly shall never be able to know whether any mere material being thinks or no; it being impossible for us, by the contemplation of our own ideas without revelation, to discover whether Omnipotency has not given to some systems of matter, fitly disposed, a power to perceive and think, or else joined and fixed to matter, so disposed, a thinking immaterial substance: it being, in respect of our notions, not much more remote from our comprehension to conceive that God can, if he pleases, superadd to matter a faculty of thinking, than that he should superadd to it another substance with a faculty of thinking; since we know not wherein thinking consists, nor to what sort of substances the Almighty has been pleased to give that power, which cannot be in any created being, but merely by the good pleasure and bounty of the Creator. [For I see no contradiction in it, that the first eternal thinking Being or omnipotent Spirit should, if he pleased, give to certain systems of created senseless matter, put together as he thinks fit, some degrees of sense, perception, and thought: though, as I think I have proved (Bk. IV, ch. 10), it is no less than a contradiction to suppose matter (which is evidently in its own nature void of sense and thought) should be that eternal first thinking Being.] What certainty of knowledge can any one have that some perceptions, such as, v.g., pleasure and pain, should not be in some bodies themselves, after a certain manner modified and moved, as well as that they should be in an immaterial substance upon the motion of the parts of body? Body, as far as we can conceive, being able only to strike and affect body; and motion, according to the utmost reach of our ideas, being able to produce nothing but motion: so that when we allow it to produce pleasure or pain, or the idea of a color or sound, we are fain to quit our reason, go beyond our ideas, and attribute it wholly to the good pleasure of our Maker. For since we must allow he has annexed effects to motion, which we can no way conceive motion able to produce, what reason have we to conclude that he could not order them as well to be produced in a subject we cannot conceive capable of them, as well as in a subject we cannot conceive the motion of matter can any way operate upon? I say not this that I would any way lessen the belief of the soul's immateriality: I am not here speaking of

probability, but knowledge; and I think not only that it becomes the modesty of philosophy not to pronounce magisterially, where we want that evidence that can produce knowledge; but also, that it is of use to us to discern how far our knowledge does reach; for the state we are at present in, not being that of vision, we must, in many things, content ourselves with faith and probability: and in the present question about the immateriality of the soul, if our faculties cannot arrive at demonstrative certainty, we need not think it strange. All the great ends of morality and religion are well enough secured, without philosophical proofs of the soul's immateriality; since it is evident that he who made us at first begin to subsist here, sensible intelligent beings, and for several years continued us in such a state, can and will restore us to the like state of sensibility in another world, and make us capable there to receive the retribution he has designed to men according to their doings in this life. [And therefore it is not of such mighty necessity to determine one way or the other, as some, over zealous for or against the immateriality of the soul, have been forward to make the world believe. Who, either on the one side, indulging too much their thoughts immersed altogether in matter, can allow no existence to what is not material: or who, on the other side, finding not cogitation within the natural powers of matter, examined over and over again by the utmost intention of mind, have the confidence to conclude that Omnipotency itself cannot give perception and thought to a substance which has the modification of solidity. He that considers how hardly sensation is, in our thoughts, reconcilable to extended matter, or existence to anything that hath no extension at all, will confess that he is very *far* from certainly knowing what his soul is. It is a point which seems to me to be put out of the reach of our knowledge: and he who will give himself leave to consider freely, and look into the dark and intricate part of each hypothesis, will scarce find his reason able to determine him fixedly for or against the soul's materiality. Since on which side soever he views it, either as an unextended substance, or as a thinking extended matter, the difficulty to conceive either will, whilst either alone is in his thoughts, still drive him to the contrary side. An unfair way which some men take with themselves; who, because of the unconceivableness of something they find in one, throw themselves violently into the contrary hypothesis, though altogether as unintelligible to an unbiased understanding.

It is past controversy, that we have in us something that thinks; our very doubts about what it is confirm the certainty of its being, though we must content ourselves in the ignorance of what kind of being it is: and it is in vain to go about to be sceptical in this, as it is unreasonable in most other cases to be positive against the being of anything, because we cannot comprehend its nature. For I would fain know, what substance exists, that has not something in it which manifestly baffles our under-standings. Other spirits, who see and know the nature and inward consti-tution of things, how much must they exceed us in knowledge? To which if we add larger comprehension, which enables them at one glance to see the connection and agreement of very many ideas, and readily supplies to them the intermediate proofs, which we, by single and slow steps, and long poring in the dark, hardly at last find out, and are often ready to forget one before we have hunted out another, we may guess at some part of the happiness of superior ranks of spirits, who have a quicker and more penetrating sight, as well as a larger field of knowledge.] But, to return to the argument in hand: our knowledge, I say, is not only limited to the paucity and inperfections of the ideas we have, and which we employ it about, but even comes short of that too; but how far it reaches, let us now enquire.

OF THE REALITY OF OUR KNOWLEDGE

1. *Objection, Knowledge placed in ideas may be all bare vision.*   I doubt not but my reader by this time may be apt to think that I have been all this while only building a castle in the air; and be ready to say to me, "To what purpose all this stir? Knowledge, say you, is only the perception of the agreement or disagreement of our own ideas; but who knows what those ideas may be? If it be true, that all knowledge lies only in the perception of the agreement or disagreement of our own ideas, the visions of an enthusiast and the reasonings of a sober man will be equally certain. It is no matter how things are: so a man observe but the agreement of his own imaginations, and talk conformably, it is all truth, all certainty. That an harpy is not a centaur, is by this way as certain knowledge, and as much a truth, as that a square is not a circle.

"But of what use is all this fine *knowledge of men's own imaginations* to a man that enquires after the reality of things? It matters not what men's fancies are, it is the knowledge of things that is only to be prized: it is this alone gives a value to our reasonings, and preference to one man's knowledge over another's, that it is of things as they really are, and not of dreams and fancies."

2. *Answer, Not so, where ideas agree with things.*   To which I an-swer, That if our knowledge of our ideas terminate in them, and reach no farther, where there is something farther intended, our most serious thoughts will be of little more use than the reveries of a crazy brain; and the truths built thereon of no more weight than the discourses of a man who sees things clearly in a dream, and with great assurance utters them.

But I hope before I have done to make it evident that this way of certainty, by the knowledge of our own ideas, goes a little farther than bare imagination; and I believe it will appear, that all the certainty of general truths a man has lies in nothing else.

3. It is evident the mind knows not things immediately, but only by the intervention of the ideas it has of them. Our knowledge, therefore, is real only so far as there is a conformity between our ideas and the reality of things. But what shall be here the criterion? How shall the mind, when it perceives nothing but its own ideas, know that they agree with things themselves? This, though it seems not to want difficulty, yet I think there be two sorts of ideas that we may be assured agree with things.

4. *As, First, all simple ideas do.*   The first are simple ideas, which since the mind, as has been showed, can by no means make to itself, must necessarily be the product of things operating on the mind in a natural way, and producing therein those perceptions which by the wisdom and will of our Maker they are ordained and adapted to. From whence it follows, that simple ideas are not fictions of our fancies, but the natural and regular productions of things without us, really operating upon us; and so carry with them all the conformity which is intended, or which our state requires; for they represent to us things under those appearances which they are fitted to produce in us: whereby we are enabled to distinguish the sorts of particular substances, to discern the states they are in, and so to take them for our necessities, and apply them to our uses. And this conformity between our simple ideas and the existence of things is sufficient for real knowledge.

5. *Secondly, All complex ideas, except of substances.*   All our complex ideas except those of substances being archetypes of the mind's own making, not intended to be the copies of anything, nor referred to the existence of anything, as to their originals, cannot want any conformity necessary to real knowledge. So that we cannot but be infallibly certain, that all the knowledge we attain concerning these ideas is real, and reaches things themselves: because in all our thoughts, reasonings, and discourses of this kind, we intend things no farther than as they are conformable to our ideas. So that in these we cannot miss of a certain undoubted reality.

6. *Hence the reality of mathematical knowledge.*   I doubt not but it will be easily granted that the knowledge we have of mathematical truths, is not only certain but real knowledge, and not the bare empty vision of vain, insignificant chimeras of the brain; and yet if we will consider, we shall find that it is only of our own ideas. The mathematician considers the truth and properties belonging to a rectangle or circle only as they are in ideas in his own mind. For it is possible he never found either of them

existing mathematically, i.e., precisely true, in his life. But yet the knowledge he has of any truths or properties belonging to a circle, or any other mathematical figure, are nevertheless true and certain, even of real things existing: because real things are no farther concerned, nor intended to be meant by any such propositions, than as things really agree to those archetypes in his mind. Is it true of the idea of a triangle, that its three angles are equal to two right ones? It is true also of a triangle, wherever it really exists. Whatever other figure exists, that is not exactly answerable to that idea of a triangle in his mind, is not at all concerned in that proposition.

7. *And of moral.*   And hence it follows that moral knowledge is as capable of real certainty as mathematics. [8.] All the discourses of the mathematicians concern not the existence of any of those figures. In the same manner, the truth and certainty of moral discourses abstracts from the lives of men, and the existence of those virtues in the world, whereof they treat: nor are Tully's *Offices* less true, because there is nobody in the world that exactly practices his rules, and lives up to that pattern of a virtuous man which he has given us, and which existed nowhere when he writ but in idea.

11. *Ideas of substances have their archetypes without us.*

12. *So far as they agree with those, so far our knowledge concerning them is real.*

13. *In our enquiries about substances we must consider ideas, and not confine our thoughts to names or species supposed set out by names.*   If we confine not our thoughts and abstract ideas to names, as if there were or could be no other sorts of things than what known names had already determined, and as it were set out, we should think of things with greater freedom and less confusion than perhaps we do. It would possibly be thought a bold paradox, if not a very dangerous falsehood, if I should say that some changelings who have lived forty years together without any appearance of reason, are something between a man and a beast: which prejudice is founded upon nothing else but a false supposition that these two names, man and beast, stand for distinct species so set out by real essences, that there can come no other species between them; whereas, if we would not fancy that there were a certain number of these essences, wherein all things, as in moulds, were cast and formed, we should find that the idea of the shape, motion, and life of a man without reason is as much a distinct idea, and makes as much a distinct sort of things from man and beast, as the idea of the shape of an ass with reason would be different from either that of man or beast, and be a species of an animal between, or distinct from both.

14. But I am not so unacquainted with the zeal of some men, which enables them to spin consequences, and to see religion threatened, whenever any one ventures to quit their forms of speaking, as not to forsee what names such a proposition as this is like to be charged with: and without doubt it will be asked, If changelings are something between man and beast, what will become of them in the other world? To which I answer, It concerns me not to know or enquire. To their own Master they stand or fall. They are in the hands of a faithful Creator and a bountiful Father, who disposes not of his creatures according to our narrow thoughts or opinions, nor distinguishes them according to names and species of our contrivance. And we that know so little of this present world we are in may, I think, content ourselves without being peremptory in defining the different states which creatures shall come into when they go off this stage.   [15.] This or that outward make of our bodies no more carries with it the hope of an eternal duration, than the fashion of a man's suit gives him reasonable grounds to imagine it will never wear out.

How Is Pure Science of Nature Possible?*

IMMANUEL KANT

14. Nature is the existence of things, so far as it is determined according to universal laws. Should nature signify the existence of things in themselves, we could never know it either *a priori* or *a posteriori*. Not *a priori,* for how can we know what belongs to things in themselves, since this never can be done by the dissection of our concepts (in analytical propositions)? For I do not want to know what is contained in my concept of a thing (for that belongs to its logical essence), but what in the actuality of the thing is superadded to my concept and by which the thing itself is determined in its existence apart from the concept. My understanding and the conditions on which alone it can connect the determination of things in their existence do not prescribe any rule to things [in] themselves; these do not conform to my understanding, but it would have to conform itself to them; they would therefore have to be first given me in order to gather these determinations from them, wherefore they would not be known *a priori*.

*From Immanuel Kant, *Prolegomena to Any Future Metaphysics* with introduction by Lewis White Beck, copyright, 1950, by The Liberal Arts Press, Inc., reprinted by permission of the Liberal Arts Press Division of The Bobbs-Merrill Company, Inc.

But knowledge of the nature of things in themselves *a posteriori* would be equally impossible. For, if experience is to teach us laws to which the existence of things is subject, these laws, if they have reference to things in themselves, would have to hold them of necessity even outside our experience. But experience teaches us what exists and how it exists, but never that it must necessarily exist so and not otherwise. Experience therefore can never teach us the nature of things in themselves.

15.   We nevertheless actually possess a pure science of nature in which are propounded, *a priori* and with all the necessity requisite to apodictical propositions, laws to which nature is subject. I need only call to witness that propaedeutic of natural science which, under the title of the universal science of nature, precedes all physics (which is founded upon empirical principles). In it we have mathematics applied to appearances, and also merely discursive principles (or those derived from concepts), which constitute the philosophical part of the pure knowledge of nature. But there are several things in it which are not quite pure and independent of empirical sources, such as the concept of *motion,* that of *impenetrability* (upon which the empirical concept of matter rests), that of *inertia,* and many others, which prevent its being called a perfectly pure science of nature. Besides, it only refers to objects of the outer sense, and therefore does not give an example of a universal science of nature, in the strict sense, for such a science must bring nature in general, whether it regards the object of the outer or that of the inner sense (the object of physics as well as psychology), under universal laws. But among the principles of this universal physics there are a few which actually have the required universality; for instance, the propositions that "substance is permanent," that "every event is determined by a cause according to constant laws," etc. These are actually universal laws of nature, which hold completely *a priori.* There is then in fact a pure science of nature, and the question arises, *How is it possible?*

16.   The word *nature* assumes yet another meaning which defines the object, whereas in the former sense it only denotes the conformity to law of the determinations of the existence of things generally. If we consider it *materialiter,* "nature is the complex of all the objects of experience." And with this only are we now concerned, for anyhow things which can never be objects of experience, if they had to be known as to their nature, would oblige us to have recourse to concepts whose meaning could never be given *in concreto* (by any example of possible experience). Consequently we would have to form for ourselves a list of concepts of their nature, the reality whereof could never be determined. That is, we could never learn whether they actually referred to objects or were mere creations of

thought. The knowledge of what cannot be an object of experience would be hyperphysical, and with things hyperphysical we are here not concerned, but only with the knowledge of nature, the actuality of which can be confirmed by experience, though this knowledge is possible *a priori* and precedes all experience.

17.   The formal aspect of nature in this narrower sense is therefore the conformity to law of all the objects of experience and, so far as it is known *a priori,* their *necessary* conformity. But it has just been shown that the laws of nature can never be known *a priori* in objects so far as they are considered, not in reference to possible experience, but as things in themselves. And our inquiry here extends, not to things in themselves (the properties of which we pass by), but to things as objects of possible experience, and the complex of these is what we here properly designate as nature. And now I ask, when the possibility of knowledge of nature *a priori* is in question, whether it is better to arrange the problem thus: "How can we know *a priori* that things as objects of experience necessarily conform to law?" or thus: "How is it possible to know *a priori* the necessary conformity to law of experience itself as regards all its objects generally?"

Closely considered, the solution of the problem represented in either way amounts, with regard to the pure knowledge of nature (which is the point of the question at issue), entirely to the same thing. For the subjective laws, under which alone an empirical knowledge of things is possible, hold good of these things as objects of possible experience (not as things in themselves, which are not considered here). It is all the same whether I say: "A judgment of perception can never rank as experience without the law that, whenever an event is observed, it is always referred to some antecedent, which it follows according to a universal rule," or: "Everything of which experience teaches that it happens must have a cause."

It is, however, more suitable to choose the first formula. For we can *a priori* and prior to all given objects have a knowledge of those conditions on which alone experience of them is possible, but never of the laws to which things may in themselves be subject, without reference to possible experience. We cannot, therefore, study the nature of things *a priori* otherwise than by investigating the conditions and the universal (though subjective) laws, under which alone such a cognition as experience (as to mere form) is possible, and we determine accordingly the possibility of things as objects of experience. For if I should choose the second formula and seek the *a priori* conditions under which nature as an object of experience is possible, I might easily fall into error and fancy that I was speaking of nature as a thing in itself, and then move round in endless circles, in a vain search for laws concerning things of which nothing is given me.

Accordingly, we shall here be concerned with experience only and the universal conditions of its possibility, which are given *a priori.* Thence, we shall define nature as the whole object of all possible experience. I think it will be understood that I here do not mean the rules of the observation of a nature that is already given, for these already presuppose experience. Thus I do not mean how (through experience) we can study the laws of nature, for these would not then be laws *a priori* and would yield us no pure science of nature; but [I mean to ask] how the conditions *a priori* of the possibility of experience are at the same time the sources from which all universal laws of nature must be derived.

18.   In the first place we must state that, while all judgments of experience are empirical (that is, have their ground in immediate sense-perception), all empirical judgments are not judgments of experience; but, besides the empirical, and in general besides what is given to the sensuous intuition, special concepts must yet be superadded—concepts which have their origin wholly *a priori* in the pure understanding, and under which every perception must be first of all subsumed and then by their means changed into experience.

Empirical judgments, so far as they have objective validity, are *judgments of experience,* but those which are only subjectively valid I name mere *judgments of perception.* The latter require no pure concept of the understanding, but only the logical connection of perception in a thinking subject. But the former always require, besides the representation of the sensuous intuition, special *concepts originally begotten in the understanding,* which make possible the objective validity of the judgment of experience.

All our judgments are at first merely judgments of perception; they hold good only for us (that is, for our subject), and we do not till afterward give them a new reference (to an object) and desire that they shall always hold good for us and in the same way for everybody else; for when a judgment agrees with an object, all judgments concerning the same object must likewise agree among themselves, and thus the objective validity of the judgment of experience signifies nothing else than its necessary universal validity. And conversely when we have ground for considering a judgment as necessarily having universal validity (which never depends upon perception, but upon the pure concept of the understanding under which the perception is subsumed), we must consider that it is objective also—that is, that it expresses not merely a reference of our perception to a subject, but a characteristic of the object. For there would be no reason for the judgments of other men necessarily agreeing with mine if it were not the unity of the object to which they all refer and with which they accord; hence they must all agree with one another.

19. Therefore objective validity and necessary universality (for everybody) are equivalent terms, and though we do not know the object in itself, yet when we consider a judgment as universal, and hence necessary, we thereby understand it to have objective validity. By this judgment we know the object (though it remains unknown as it is in itself) by the universal and necessary connection of the given perceptions. As this is the case with all objects of sense, judgments of experience take their objective validity, not from the immediate knowledge of the object (which is impossible), but from the condition of universal validity of empirical judgments, which, as already said, never rests upon empirical or, in short, sensuous conditions, but upon a pure concept of the understanding. The object in itself always remains unknown; but when by the concept of the understanding the connection of the representations of the object, which it gives to our sensibility, is determined as universally valid, the object is determined by this relation, and the judgment is objective.

To illustrate the matter: when we say, "The room is warm, sugar sweet, and wormwood bitter,"[1] we have only subjectively valid judgments. I do not at all expect that I or any other person shall always find it as I now do; each of these sentences only expresses a relation of two sensations to the same subject, that is, myself, and that only in my present state of perception; consequently they are not valid of the object. Such are judgments of perception. Judgments of experience are of quite a different nature. What experience teaches me under certain circumstances, it must always teach me and everybody; and its validity is not limited to the subject nor to its state at a particular time. Hence I pronounce all such judgments objectively valid. For instance, when I say the air is elastic, this judgment is as yet a judgment of perception only; I do nothing but refer two of my sensations to each other. But if I would have it called a judgment of experience, I require this connection to stand under a condition which makes it universally valid. I desire therefore that I and

[1] I freely grant that these examples do not represent such judgments of perception as ever could become judgments of experience, even though a concept of the understanding were superadded, because they refer merely to feeling, which everybody knows to be merely subjective and which of course can never be attributed to the object, and consequently never become objective. I only wished to give here an example of a judgment that is merely subjectively valid, containing no ground for necessary universal validity and thereby for a relation to the object. An example of the judgments of perception which become judgments of experience by superadded concepts of the understanding will be given in the next note.

everybody else should always connect necessarily the same perceptions under the same circumstances.

20.   We must consequently analyze experience in general in order to see what is contained in this product of the senses and of the understanding, and how the judgment of experience itself is possible. The foundation is the intuition of which I become conscious, that is, perception (*perceptio*), which pertains merely to the senses. But in the next place, there is judging (which belongs only to the understanding). But this judging may be twofold: first, I may merely compare perceptions and connect them in a consciousness of my particular state; or, secondly, I may connect them in consciousness in general. The former judgment is merely a judgment of perception, and hence is of subjective validity only; it is merely a connection of perceptions in my mental state, without reference to the object. Hence it does not, as is commonly imagined, suffice for experience that perceptions are compared and connected in consciousness through judgment; thence arises no universal validity and necessity by virtue of which alone consciousness[2] can be objectively valid, that is, can be called experience.

Quite another judgment therefore is required before perception can become experience. The given intuition must be subsumed under a concept which determines the form of judging in general relatively to the intuition, connects empirical consciousness of intuition in consciousness in general, and thereby procures universal validity for empirical judgments. A concept of this nature is a pure *a priori* concept of the understanding, which does nothing but determine for an intuition the general way in which it can be used for judgments. Let the concept be that of cause; then it determines the intuition which is subsumed under it, for example, that of air, relative to judging in general—namely, the concept of air in respect to its expansion serves in the relation of antecedent to consequent in a hypothetical judgment. The concept of cause accordingly is a pure concept of the understanding, which is totally disparate from all possible perception and only serves to determine the representation subsumed under it, with respect to judging in general, and so to make a universally valid judgment possible.

Before, therefore, a judgment of perception can become a judgment of experience, it is requisite that the perception should be subsumed under some such concept of the understanding; for instance, air belongs under the concept of cause, which determines our judgment about it in respect to its expansion as hypothetical.[3] Thereby the expansion of the air is

---

[2][Or "judgment."—L.W.B.]

[3]As an easier example, we may take the following: "When the sun shines on the stone, it grows warm." This judgment, however often I and others may have perceived it, is a mere judgment of perception and contains no necessity; perceptions are only

represented, not as merely belonging to the perception of the air in my present state or in several states of mine, or in the perceptual state of others, but as belonging to it necessarily. The judgment, "Air is elastic," becomes universally valid and a judgment of experience only because certain judgments precede it which subsume the intuition of air under the concept of cause and effect; and they thereby determine the perceptions, not merely with respect to one another in me, but with respect to the form of judging in general (which is here hypothetical), and in this way they render the empirical judgment universally valid.

If all our synthetical judgments are analyzed so far as they are objectively valid, it will be found that they never consist of mere intuitions connected only (as is commonly believed) by comparison into a judgment; but that they would be impossible were not a pure concept of the understanding superadded to the concepts abstracted from intuition, under which concept these latter are subsumed and in this manner only combined into an objectively valid judgment. Even the judgments of pure mathematics in their simplest axioms are not exempt from this condition. The principle, "A straight line is the shortest distance between two points," presupposes that the line is subsumed under the concept of magnitude, which certainly is no mere intuition, but has its seat in the understanding alone and serves to determine the intuition (of the line) with regard to the judgments which may be made about it, in respect to their quantity, that is, to plurality (as *judicia plurativa*).[4] For under them it is understood that in a given intuition there is contained a plurality of homogeneous parts.

21.   To prove, then, the possibility of experience so far as it rests upon pure concepts of the understanding *a priori,* we must first represent what belongs to judging in general and the various functions of the understanding in a complete table. For the pure concepts of the understanding must run parallel to these functions, as such concepts are nothing more than concepts of intuitions in general, so far as these are determined by one or other of these functions of judging, in themselves, that is, necessarily and universally. Hereby also *a priori* principles of the possibility of all experi-

---

usually conjoined in this manner. But if I say, "The sun warms the stone," I add to the perception a concept of the understanding, namely, that of cause, which necessarily connects with the concept of sunshine that of heat, and the synthetical judgment becomes of necessity universally valid, namely, objective, and is converted from a perception into experience.

[4]This name seems preferable to the term *particularia,* which is used for these judgments in logic. For the latter implies the idea that they are not universal. But when I start from unity (in singular judgments) and so proceed to totality, I must not [even indirectly and negatively] imply any reference to totality. I think plurality merely without totality, and not the exception from totality. This is necessary if logical distinctions are to form the basis of the pure concepts of the understanding. However, logical usage need not be changed.

ence, as objectively valid empirical knowledge, will be precisely determined. For they are nothing but propositions which subsume all perception (under certain universal conditions of intuitions) under those pure concepts of the understanding.

LOGICAL TABLE OF JUDGMENTS

1

As to Quantity
Universal
Particular
Singular

2

As to Quality
Affirmative
Negative
Infinite

3

As to Relation
Categorical
Hypothetical
Disjunctive

4

As to Modality
Problematic
Assertoric
Apodictic

TRANSCENDENTAL TABLE OF THE CONCEPTS OF THE UNDERSTANDING

1

As to Quantity
Unity (Measure)
Plurality (Magnitude)
Totality (Whole)

2

As to Quality
Reality
Negation
Limitation

3

As to Relation
Substance
Cause
Community

4

As to Modality
Possibility
Existence
Necessity

PURE PHYSICAL[5] TABLE OF THE UNIVERSAL PRINCIPLES OF
THE SCIENCE OF NATURE

I	2
Axioms of Intuition	Anticipations of Perception

3	4
Analogies of Experience	Postulates of Empirical Thinking Generally

21a.   In order to comprise the whole matter in one idea, it is first necessary to remind the reader that we are discussing, not the origin of experience, but that which lies in experience. The former pertains to empirical psychology and would even then never be adequately explained without the latter, which belongs to the critique of knowledge, and particularly of the understanding.

Experience consists of intuitions, which belong to the sensibility, and of judgments, which are entirely a work of the understanding. But the judgments which the understanding forms solely from sensuous intuitions are far from being judgments of experience. For in the one case the judgment connects only the perceptions as they are given in sensuous intuition, while in the other the judgments must express what experience in general and not what the mere perception (which possesses only subjective validity) contains. The judgment of experience must therefore add to the sensuous intuition and its logical connection in a judgment (after it has been rendered universal by comparison) something that determines the synthetical judgment as necessary and therefore as universally valid. This can be nothing else than that concept which represents the intuition as determined in itself with regard to one form of judgment rather than another, namely, a concept of that synthetical unity of intuitions which can only be represented by a given logical function of judgments.

22.   The sum of the matter is this: the business of the senses is to intuit, that of the understanding is to think. But thinking is uniting representations in one consciousness. This union originates either merely

---

[5][Kant uses the term *physiological* in its etymological meaning as "pertaining to the science of physics," that is, nature in general, not as we use the term now as "pertaining to the function of the living body." Accordingly, it has been translated as *physical*.— Carus.]

relative to the subject and is accidental and subjective, or takes place absolutely and is necessary or objective. The union of representations in one consciousness is judgment. Thinking, therefore, is the same as judging or referring representations to judgments in general. Hence, judgments are either merely subjective, when representations are referred to a consciousness in one subject only and united in it, or objective, when they are united in consciousness in general, that is, necessarily. The logical functions of all judgments are but various modes of uniting representations in consciousness. But if they serve for concepts, they are concepts of the necessary union of representations in [any] consciousness, and so are principles of objectively valid judgments. This union in consciousness is either analytical, by identity, or synthetical, by the combination and addition of various representations one to another. Experience consists in the synthetical connection of phenomena (perceptions) in consciousness, so far as this connection is necessary. Hence the pure concepts of the understanding are those under which all perceptions must be subsumed ere they can serve for judgments of experience, in which the synthetical unity of the perceptions is represented as necessary and universally valid.[6]

23.   Judgments, when considered merely as the condition of the union of given representations in a consciousness, are rules. These rules, so far as they represent the union as necessary, are rules *a priori,* and, insofar as they cannot be deduced from higher rules, are principles. But in regard to the possibility of all experience, merely in relation to the form of thinking in it; no conditions of judgments of experience are higher than those which bring the appearances, according to the various form of their intuition, under pure concepts of the understanding, which render the empirical judgment objectively valid. These are therefore the *a priori* principles of possible experience.

The principles of possible experience are then at the same time universal laws of nature, which can be known *a priori.* And thus the problem of our second question, "How is the pure science of nature possible?" is solved. For the system which is required for the form of a science is to be

---

[6]But how does the proposition that judgments of experience contain necessity in the synthesis of perceptions agree with my statement so often before inculcated that experience as cognition *a posteriori* can afford contingent judgments only? When I say that experience teaches me something, I mean only the perception that lies in experience—for example, that heat always follows the shining of the sun on a stone; consequently the proposition of experience is always so far accidental. That this heat necessarily follows the shining of the sun is contained indeed in the judgment of experience (by means of the concept of cause), yet is a fact not learned by experience; for conversely, experience is first of all generated by this addition of the concept of the understanding (of cause) to perception. How perception attains this addition may be seen by referring in the *Critique* itself to the [first] section of the "Transcendental Faculty of Judgment."

met with in perfection here, because, beyond the above-mentioned formal conditions of all judgments in general (and hence of all rules in general) offered in logic, no others are possible, and these constitute a logical system. The concepts grounded thereupon, which contain the *a priori* conditions of all synthetical and necessary judgments, accordingly constitute a transcendental system. Finally the principles, by means of which all phenomena are subsumed under these concepts, constitute a physical system, that is, a system of nature, which precedes all empirical knowledge of nature, and makes it possible. It may in strictness be denominated the universal and pure science of nature.

24.   The first of the physical principles subsumes all phenomena, as intuitions in space and time, under the concept of quantity, and is thus a principle of the application of mathematics to experience. The second one subsumes the strictly empirical element, namely, sensation, which denotes the real in intuitions, not indeed directly under the concept of quantity, because sensation is not an intuition that *contains* either space or time, though it places the respective object corresponding to it in both. But still there is between reality (sense-representation) and the zero, or total void of intuition in time, a difference which has a quantity. For between every given degree of light and of darkness, between every degree of heat and of absolute cold, between every degree of weight and of absolute lightness, between every degree of occupancy space and of totally void space, diminishing degrees can be conceived, in the same manner as between consciousness and total unconsciousness (psychological darkness) ever-diminishing degrees obtain. Hence there is no perception that can prove an absolute absence; for instance, no psychological darkness that cannot be considered as consciousness which is only outbalanced by a stronger consciousness. This occurs in all cases of sensation, and so the understanding can anticipate even sensations, which constitute the peculiar quality of empirical representations (appearances), by means of the principle that they all have degree (and consequently that what is real in all appearance has degree). Here is the second application of mathematics (*mathesis intensorum*) to the science of nature.

25.   Anent the relation of appearances merely with a view to their existence, the determination of the relation is not mathematical but dynamical, and can never be objectively valid, consequently never fit for experience, if it does not come under *a priori* principles by which the empirical knowledge relative to appearances first becomes possible. Hence appearances must be subsumed under the concept of substance, which as a concept of a thing is the foundation of all determination of existence; or, secondly—so far as a succession is found among appearances, that is, an event—under the concept of an effect with reference to cause; or lastly—

so far as coexistence is to be known objectively, that is, by a judgment of experience—under the concept of community (action and reaction). Thus *a priori* principles form the basis of objectively valid, though empirical, judgments—that is, of the possibility of experience so far as it must connect objects as existing in nature. These principles are the real laws of nature, which may be termed "dynamical."

Finally knowledge of the agreement and connection, not only of appearances among themselves in experience, but of their relation to experience in general, belongs to the judgments of experience. This relation contains either their agreement with the formal conditions, which the understanding recognizes, or their coherence with the materials of the senses and of perception, or combines both into one concept. Consequently, their relation to experience in general entails possibility, actuality, and necessity, according to universal laws of nature. This would constitute the physical doctrine of method for distinguishing truth from hypotheses and for determining the limits of certainty of the latter.

26.   The third table of principles drawn by the critical method from the nature of the understanding itself shows an inherent perfection, which raises it far above every other table which has hitherto, though in vain, been tried or may yet be tried by analyzing the objects themselves dogmatically. It exhibits all synthetical *a priori* principles completely and according to one principle, namely, the faculty of judging in general, constituting the essence of experience as regards the understanding; so that we can be certain that there are no more such principles. This affords a satisfaction which can never be attained by the dogmatic method. Yet this is not all; there is a still greater merit in it.

We must carefully bear in mind the premise which shows the possibility of this cognition *a priori* and, at the same time, limits all such principles to a condition which must never be lost sight of if we desire it not to be misunderstood and extended in use beyond the original sense which the understanding attaches to it. This limit is that they contain nothing but the conditions of possible experience in general so far as it is subjected to laws *a priori*. Consequently, I do not say that things *in themselves* possess a magnitude; that their reality possesses a degree, their existence a connection of accidents in a substance, etc. This nobody can prove, because such a synthetical connection from mere concepts, without any reference to sensuous intuition on the one side or connection of it in a possible experience on the other, is absolutely impossible. The essential limitation of the concepts in these principles then is that all things *as objects of experience only* stand necessarily *a priori* under the aforementioned conditions.

Hence there follows, secondly, a specifically peculiar mode of proof of these principles; they are not directly referred to appearances and to their relation, but to the possibility of experience, of which appearances constitute the matter only, not the form. Thus they are referred to objectively and universally valid synthetical propositions, in which we distinguish judgments of experience from those of perception. This takes place because appearances, as mere intuitions *occupying a part of space and time,* come under the concept of quantity, which synthetically unites their multiplicity *a priori* according to rules. Again, insofar as the perception contains, besides intuition, sensation, and between the latter and nothing (that is, the total disappearance of sensation), there is an ever-decreasing transition, it is apparent that the real within appearances must have a degree, so far as it (namely, the sensation) *does not itself occupy any part of space or of time.*[7] Still the transition to this real from empty time or empty space is possible only in time. Consequently, although sensation, as the quality of empirical intuition specifically differentiating it from other sensations, can never be known *a priori,* yet it can, in a possible experience in general, as quantity of perception be intensively distinguished from every other similar perception. Hence the application of mathematics to nature, as regards the sensuous intuition by which nature is given to us, thus becomes possible and definite.

Above all, the reader must pay attention to the mode of proof of the principles which occur under the title of "analogies of experience." For these do not refer to the genesis of intuitions, as do the principles of applying mathematics to natural science in general, but to the connection of their existence in an experience; and this can be nothing but the determination of their existence in time according to necessary laws, under which alone the connection is objectively valid and thus becomes experience. The proof, therefore, does not turn on the synthetical unity in the connection of things in themselves, but merely of perceptions; and of these, not in regard to their matter, but to the determination of time and of the relation of their existence in it according to universal laws. If the empirical determination in relative time is indeed to be objectively valid

---

[7]Heat and light are in a small space just as large, as to degree, as in a large one; in like manner the internal representations, pain, consciousness generally, whether they last a short or a long time, need not vary as to the degree. Hence the quantity is here in a point and in a moment just as great as in any space or time, however great. Degrees are quantities not in intuition, but in mere sensation (or the quantity of the content [*Grundes*] of an intuition). Hence they can only be estimated quantitatively by the relation of 1 to 0, namely, by their capability of decreasing by infinite intermediate degrees to disappearance, or of increasing from naught through infinite gradations to a determinate sensation in a certain time. *Quantitas qualitatis est gradus.* "The quantity of quality is degree."

(that is, to be experience), these universal laws must contain the necessary determination of existence in time generally (namely, according to a rule of the understanding *a priori*).

As these are prolegomena I cannot here further descant on the subject, but my reader (who has probably been long accustomed to consider experience a mere empirical synthesis of perceptions, and hence has not considered that it goes much beyond them since it imparts to empirical judgments universal validity, and for that purpose requires a pure and *a priori* unity of the understanding) is recommended to pay special attention to this distinction of experience from a mere aggregate of perceptions and to judge the mode of proof from this point of view.

27.   Now we are prepared to remove Hume's doubt. He justly maintains that we cannot comprehend by reason the possibility of causality, that is, of the reference of the existence of one thing to the existence of another which is necessitated by the former. I add that we comprehend just as little the concept of subsistence, that is, the necessity that at the foundation of the existence of things there lies a subject which cannot itself be a predicate of any other thing; nay, we cannot even form a notion of the possibility of such a thing (though we can point out examples of its use in experience). The very same incomprehensibility affects the community of things, as we cannot comprehend how from the state of one thing an inference to the state of quite another thing beyond it, and *vice versa,* can be drawn, and how substances which have each their own separate existence should depend upon one another necessarily. But I am very far from holding these concepts to be derived merely from experience, and the necessity represented in them to be imaginary and a mere illusion produced in us by long habit. On the contrary, I have amply shown that they and the principles derived from them are firmly established *a priori* before all experience and have their undoubted objective value, though only with regard to experience.

28.   Although I have no notion of such a connection of things in themselves, how they can either exist as substances, or act as causes, or stand in community with others (as parts of a real whole), and I can just as little conceive such properties in appearances as such (because those concepts contain nothing that lies in the appearances, but only what the understanding alone must think), we have yet a concept of such a connection of representations in our understanding and in judgments generally. This concept is: that representations appear, in one sort of judgments, as subject in relation to predicates; in another, as ground in relation to consequent; and, in a third, as parts which constitute together a total possible cognition. Furthermore, we know *a priori* that without considering the representation of an object as determined in one or the

other of these respects, we can have no valid knowledge of the object; and, if we should occupy ourselves about the object in itself, there is not a single possible attribute by which I could know that it is determined under any of these aspects, that is, under the concept either of substance, or of cause, or (in relation to other substances) of community, for I have no concept of the possibility of such a connection of existence. But the question is not how things in themselves but how the empirical knowledge of things is determined, as regards the above aspects of judgments in general; that is, how things, as objects of experience, can and must be subsumed under these concepts of the understanding. And then it is clear that I completely comprehend, not only the possibility, but also the necessity, of subsuming all appearances under these concepts—that is, of using them for principles of the possibility of experience.

29.   In order to test Hume's problematical concept (his *crux meta-physicorum*), the concept of cause, we are first given *a priori,* by means of logic, the form of a conditional judgment in general; that is, we have one cognition given as antecedent and another as consequent. But it is possible that in perception we may meet with a rule of relation which runs thus: that a certain appearance is constantly followed by another (though not conversely); and this is a case for me to use the hypothetical judgment and, for instance, to say if the sun shines long enough upon a body it grows warm. Here there is indeed as yet no necessity of connection or concept of cause. But I proceed and say that, if this proposition, which is merely a subjective connection of perceptions, is to be a proposition of experience, it must be seen as necessary and universally valid. Such a proposition would be that the sun is by its light the cause of heat. The empirical rule is now considered as a law, and as valid, not merely of appearances but valid of them for the purposes of a possible experience which requires universal and therefore necessarily valid rules. I therefore easily comprehend the concept of cause, as a concept necessarily belonging to the mere form of experience, and its possibility as a synthetical union of perceptions in consciousness in general; but I do not at all comprehend the possibility of a thing in general as a cause, because the concept of cause denotes a condition not at all belonging to things, but to experience. For experience can be nothing but objectively valid knowledge of appearances and of their succession, only so far as the earlier can be conjoined with the later according to the rule of hypothetical judgments.

30.   Hence if even the pure concepts of the understanding are thought to go beyond objects of experience to things in themselves (*noumena*), they have no meaning whatever. They serve, as it were, only to decipher appearances, that we may be able to read them as experience. The

principles which arise from their reference to the sensible world only serve our understanding for empirical use. Beyond this they are arbitrary combinations without objective reality, and we can neither know their possibility *a priori* nor verify—or even render intelligible by any example—their reference to objects; because examples can only be borrowed from some possible experience, and consequently the objects of these concepts can be found nowhere but in a possible experience.

This complete (though to its originator unexpected) solution of Hume's problem rescues for the pure concepts of the understanding their *a priori* origin and for the universal laws of nature their validity as laws of the understanding, yet in such a way as to limit their use to experience, because their possibility depends solely on the reference of the understanding to experience, but with a completely reversed mode of connection which never occurred to Hume—they do not derive from experience, but experience derives from them.

This is, therefore, the result of all our foregoing inquiries: "All synthetical principles *a priori* are nothing more than principles of possible experience" and can never be referred to things in themselves, but to appearances as objects of experience. And hence pure mathematics as well as a pure science of nature can never be referred to anything more than mere appearances, and can only represent either that which makes experience in general possible, or else that which, as it is derived from these principles, must always be capable of being represented in some possible experience.

31.   And thus we have at last something definite upon which to depend in all metaphysical enterprises, which have hitherto, boldly enough but always blindly, attempted everything without discrimination. That the aim of their exertions should be so near struck neither the dogmatic thinkers nor those who, confident in their supposed sound common sense, started with concepts and principles of pure reason (which were legitimate and natural, but destined for mere empirical use) in quest of insights to which they neither knew nor could know any definite bounds, because they had never reflected nor were able to reflect on the nature or even on the possibility of such a pure understanding.

Many a naturalist of pure reason (by which I mean the man who believes he can decide in matters of metaphysics without any science) may pretend that he, long ago, by the prophetic spirit of his sound sense, not only suspected but knew and comprehended what is here propounded with so much ado, or, if he likes, with prolix and pedantic pomp: "that with all our reason we can never reach beyond the field of experience." But when he is questioned about his rational principles individually, he must grant that there are many of them which he has not taken from experience and which are therefore independent of it and valid *a priori*.

How then and on what grounds will he restrain both himself and the dogmatist, who makes use of these concepts and principles beyond all possible experience because they are recognized to be independent of it? And even he, this adept in sound sense, in spite of all his assumed and cheaply acquired wisdom, is not exempt from wandering inadvertently beyond objects of experience into the field of chimeras. He is often deeply enough involved in them; though, in announcing everything as mere probability, rational conjecture, or analogy, he gives by his popular language a color to his groundless pretensions.

32. Since the oldest days of philosophy, inquirers into pure reason have conceived, besides the things of sense, or appearances (*phenomena*), which make up the sensible world, certain beings of the understanding[8] (*noumena*), which should constitute an intelligible world. And as appearance and illusion were by those men identified (a thing which we may well excuse in an undeveloped epoch), actuality was only conceded to the beings of the understanding.

And we indeed, rightly considering objects of sense as mere appearances, confess thereby that they are based upon a thing in itself, though we know not this thing as it is in itself but only know its appearances, namely, the way in which our senses are affected by this unknown something. The understanding, therefore, by assuming appearances, grants the existence of things in themselves also; and to this extent we may say that the representation of such things as are the basis of appearances, consequently of mere beings of the understanding, is not only admissible but unavoidable.

Our critical deduction by no means excludes things of that sort (*noumena*), but rather limits the principles of the Aesthetic[9] to this, that they shall not extend to all things—as everything would then be turned into mere appearance—but that they shall hold good only of objects of possible experience. Hereby, then, beings of the understanding are granted, but with the inculcation of this rule which admits of no exception: that we neither know nor can know anything at all definite of these pure beings of the understanding, because our pure concepts of the understanding as well as our pure intuitions extend to nothing but objects of possible experience, consequently to mere things of sense; and as soon as we leave this sphere, these concepts retain no meaning whatever.

33.   There is indeed something seductive in our pure concepts of the understanding which tempts us to a transcendent use—a use which transcends all possible experience. Not only are our concepts of substance, of

---

[8][*Verstandeswesen.*]

[9][That is, the first part of the *Critique of Pure Reason*, establishing space and time as pure intuitions.—L.W.B.]

power, of action, of reality, and others, quite independent of experience, containing nothing of sense appearance, and so apparently applicable to things in themselves (*noumena*), but, what strengthens this conjecture, they contain a necessity of determination in themselves, which experience never attains. The concept of cause implies a rule according to which one state follows another necessarily; but experience can only show us that one state of things often or, at most, commonly follows another, and therefore affords neither strict universality nor necessity.

Hence the concepts of the understanding seem to have a deeper meaning and import than can be exhausted by their merely empirical use, and so the understanding inadvertently adds for itself to the house of experience a much more extensive wing, which it fills with nothing but beings of thought, without ever observing that it has transgressed with its otherwise legitimate concepts the bounds of their use.

34.   Two important and even indispensable, though very dry, investigations therefore became indispensable in the *Critique of Pure Reason* [namely, the chapters "The Schematism of the Pure Concepts of the Understanding" and "On the Ground of the Distinction of All Objects as Phenomena and Noumena."] In the former it is shown that the senses furnish, not the pure concepts of the understanding *in concreto,* but only the schema for their use, and that the object conformable to it occurs only in experience (as the product of the understanding from materials of the sensibility). In the latter it is shown that, although our pure concepts of the understanding and our principles are independent of experience, and despite the apparently greater sphere of their use, still nothing whatever can be thought by them beyond the field of experience, because they can do nothing but merely determine the logical form of the judgment relatively to given intuitions. But as there is no intuition at all beyond the field of the sensibility, these pure concepts, as they cannot possibly be exhibited *in concreto,* are void of all meaning; consequently all these *noumena,* together with their complex, the intelligible world,[10] are nothing but representation of a problem, of which the object in itself is possible but the solution, from the nature of our understanding, totally impossible. For our understanding is not a faculty of intuition, but of the connection of

---

[10]We speak of the "intelligible world," not (as the usual expression is) "intellectual world." For cognitions are intellectual through the understanding and refer to our world of sense also; but objects, in so far as they can be represented merely by the understanding, and to which none of our sensible intuitions can refer, are termed "intelligible." But as some possible intuition must correspond to every object, we would have to assume an understanding that intuits things immediately; but of such we have not the least notion, nor have we any notion of the *beings of the understanding* to which it should be applied.

given intuitions in one experience. Experience must therefore contain all the objects for our concepts; but beyond it no concepts have any significance, as there is no intuition that might offer them a foundation.

35. The imagination may perhaps be forgiven for occasional vagaries and for not keeping carefully within the limits of experience, since it gains life and vigor by such flights and since it is always easier to moderate its boldness than to stimulate its languor. But the understanding which ought to *think* can never be forgiven for indulging in vagaries; for we depend upon it alone for assistance to set bounds, when necessary, to the vagaries of the imagination.

But the understanding begins its aberrations very innocently and modestly. It first brings to light the elementary cognitions which inhere in it prior to all experience, but which yet must always have their application in experience. It gradually drops these limits—and what is there to prevent it, as it has quite freely derived its principles from itself? It then proceeds first to newly imagined powers in nature, then to beings outside nature— in short, to a world for whose construction the materials cannot be wanting, because fertile fiction furnishes them abundantly, and though not confirmed it is never refuted by experience. This is the reason that young thinkers are so partial to metaphysics constructed in a truly dogmatic manner, and often sacrifice to it their time and their talents, which might be otherwise better employed.

But there is no use in trying to moderate these fruitless endeavors of pure reason by all manner of cautions as to the difficulties of solving questions so occult, by complaints of the limits of our reason, and by degrading our assertions into mere conjectures. For if their impossibility is not distinctly shown, and reason's knowledge of itself does not become a true science, in which the field of its right use is distinguished, so to say, with geometrical certainty from that of its worthless and idle use, these fruitless efforts will never be wholly abandoned.

36. This question—the highest point that transcendental philosophy can ever reach, and to which, as its boundary and completion, it must proceed—really contains two questions.

First: How is nature in the material sense, that is, as to intuition, or considered as the totality of appearances, possible; how are space, time, and that which fills both—the object of sensation—possible generally? The answer is: By means of the constitution of our sensibility, according to which it is in its own way affected by objects which are in themselves unknown to it and totally distinct from those appearances. This answer is given in the *Critique* itself in the "Transcendental Aesthetic," and in these *Prolegomena* by the solution of the first general problem.

Secondly: How is nature possible in the formal sense, as the totality of the rules under which all appearances must come in order to be thought as connected in experience? The answer must be this: It is only possible by means of the constitution of our understanding, according to which all the above representations of the sensibility are necessarily referred to a consciousness, and by which the peculiar way in which we think (namely, by rules) and hence experience also are possible, but must be clearly distinguished from an insight into the objects in themselves. This answer is given in the *Critique* itself in the "Transcendental Logic" and in these *Prolegomena,* in the course of the solution of the second main problem.

But how this peculiar property of our sensibility itself is possible, or that of our understanding and of the apperception which is necessarily its basis and that of all thinking, cannot be further analyzed or answered, because it is of them that we are in need for all our answers and for all our thinking about objects.

There are many laws of nature which we can know only by means of experience; but conformity to law in the connection of appearances, that is, in nature in general, we cannot discover by any experience, because experience itself requires laws which are *a priori* at the basis of its possibility.

The possibility of experience in general is therefore at the same time the universal law of nature, and the principles of experience are the very laws of nature. For we know nature only as the totality of appearances, that is, of representations in us; and hence we can only derive the laws of their connection from the principles of their connection in us, that is, from the conditions of their necessary union in one consciousness which constitutes the possibility of experience.

Even the main proposition expounded throughout this section—that universal laws of nature can be known *a priori*—leads naturally to the proposition that the highest legislation of nature must lie in ourselves, that is, in our understanding; and that we must not seek the universal laws of nature in nature by means of experience, but conversely must seek nature, as to its universal conformity to law, in the conditions of the possibility of experience which lie in our sensibility and in our understanding. For how were it otherwise possible to know *a priori* these laws, as they are not rules of analytical knowledge but truly synthetical extensions of it?

Such a necessary agreement of the principles of possible experience with the laws of the possibility of nature can only proceed from one of two causes: either these laws are drawn from nature by means of experience, or conversely nature is derived from the laws of the possibility of experience in general and is quite the same as the mere universal conformity to law of the latter. The former is self-contradictory, for the universal laws of nature can and must be known *a priori* (that is, independently of all experience) and be the foundation of all empirical use of the understanding; the latter alternative therefore alone remains.[11]

But we must distinguish the empirical laws of nature which always presuppose particular perceptions, from the pure or universal laws of nature, which, without being based on particular perceptions, contain merely the conditions of their necessary union in experience. In relation to the latter, nature and possible experience are quite the same; and as the conformity to law in the latter depends upon the necessary connection of appearances in experience (without which we cannot know any object whatever in the sensible world), consequently upon the original laws of the understanding, it seems at first strange, but is not the less certain, to say: The understanding does not derive its laws (*a priori*) from, but prescribes them to, nature.

37. We shall illustrate this seemingly bold proposition by an example, which will show that laws which we discover in objects of sensuous intuition (especially when these laws are known as necessary) are commonly held by us to be such as have been placed there by the understanding, in spite of their being similar in all points to the laws of nature which we ascribe to experience.

38. If we consider the properties of the circle, by which this figure combines in itself so many arbitrary determinations of space in a universal rule, we cannot avoid attributing a constitution[12] to this geometrical thing. Two straight lines, for example, which intersect each other and the circle, howsoever they may be drawn, are always divided so that the rectangle constructed with the segments of the one is equal to that constructed with the segments of the other. The question now is: Does this law lie in the circle or in the understanding? That is, does this figure, independently of the understanding, contain in itself the ground of the law; or does the understanding, having constructed according to its concepts (of the equality of the radii) the figure itself, introduce into it this law of the chords intersecting in geometrical proportion? When we follow the proofs of this law, we soon perceive that it can only be derived from the condition on which the understanding founds the construction on this figure, namely, the concept of the equality of the radii. But if we enlarge

[11]Crusius alone thought of a compromise: that a spirit, who can neither err nor deceive, implanted these laws in us originally. But since false principles often intrude themselves, as indeed the very system of this man shows in not a few instances, we are involved in difficulties as to the use of such a principle in the absence of sure criteria to distinguish the genuine origin from the spurious, since we never can know certainly what the spirit of truth or the father of lies may have instilled into us.

[12][*Eine Natur.*]

this concept to pursue further the unity of various properties of geometrical figures under common laws and consider the circle as a conic section, which of course is subject to the same fundamental conditions of construction as other conic sections, we shall find that all the chords which intersect within the ellipse, parabola, and hyperbola always intersect so that the rectangles of their segments are not indeed equal but always bear a constant ratio to one another. If we proceed still farther to the fundamental teachings of physical astronomy, we find a physical law of reciprocal attraction applicable to all material nature, the rule of which is that it decreases inversely as the square of the distance from each attracting point, that is, as the spherical surfaces increase over which this force spreads, which law seems to be necessarily inherent in the very nature of things, and hence is usually propounded as knowable *a priori*. Simple as the sources of this law are, merely resting upon the relation of spherical surfaces of different radii, its consequences are so valuable with regard to the variety and simplicity of their agreement that not only are all possible orbits of the celestial bodies conic sections, but such a relation of these orbits to one another results that no other law of attraction than that of the inverse square of the distance can be imagined as fit for a cosmical system.

Here accordingly is nature, which rests upon laws that the understanding knows *a priori,* and chiefly from the universal principles of the determination of space. Now I ask: Do the laws of nature lie in space, and does the understanding learn them by merely endeavoring to find out the enormous wealth of meaning that lies in space; or do they inhere in the understanding and in the way in which it determines space according to the conditions of the synthetical unity in which its concepts are all centered?

Space is something so uniform and as to all particular properties so indeterminate that we should certainly not seek a store of laws of nature in it. Whereas that which determines space to assume the form of a circle, or the figures of a cone and a sphere, is the understanding, so far as it contains the ground of the unity of their constructions.

The mere universal form of intuition, called space, must therefore be the substratum of all intuitions determinable to particular objects; and in it, of course, the condition of the possibility and of the variety of these intuitions lies. But the unity of the objects is entirely determined by the understanding and on conditions which lie in its own nature; and thus the understanding is the origin of the universal order of nature, in that it comprehends all appearances under its own laws and thereby produces, in an *a priori* manner, experience (as to its form), by means of which whatever is to be known only by experience is necessarily subjected to its laws. For we are not concerned with the nature of things in themselves, which is independent of the conditions both of our sensibility and our understanding, but with nature as an object of possible experience; and in this case the understanding, since it makes experience possible, thereby insists that the sensuous world is either not an object of experience at all or that it is nature [namely, the existence of things determined according to universal laws][13]

[13][Cf. § 14, beginning.—Carus.]

Learning as Dialectical Growth*

G. W. F. HEGEL

INTRODUCTION

377

Know thyself is an absolute imperative to fulfill. It is the most concrete, the highest, and most difficult task which mind can set for itself.

Self-knowledge of the spirit intends to know its true essence; truth as it actually exists in and for itself. This spiritual truth becomes the objective content and value of the human soul.

This Mind or Spirit (Geist) is the concrete universal and substantial core of human existence. It is presupposed and blindly taken for granted by empirical psychology, which is mainly engaged in the study of individual weaknesses, inclinations, pecularities, passions and aberrations—the so-called folds of the heart.

378

Mind-spirit (Geist) unites its own essential unity with its equally essential many partial and individual manifestations.

Philosophy as self-knowledge must therefore heal the split between a non-appearing soul as rationalistic metaphysics had it (23) and a mass of empirical details without spiritual orientation.

Aristotle's work on the soul—the soul is immanent purposiveness (entelechy) giving directions to its organic life and visible embodiments—is

*From G. W. F. Hegel, *Encyclopedia of Philosophy*, translated and annotated by Gustav E. Mueller (New York: Wisdom Library, 1959), pp. 191–192, 197–198, 201–227, 234–235, 269–270. Reprinted with the permission of the publisher, Philosophical Library.

still the most excellent, even unique treatise of this problem. The essential purpose of the philosophy of the spirit must re-introduce dialectical concreteness into spiritual self-knowledge; this would again disclose the profound meaning of Aristotle's works. . . .

380

Implicit in its concrete nature is a difficulty peculiar to the contemplation of the spirit. The many levels within its development are stations in its own maturing of self-realization; they are retained, as lower levels functioning together with higher levels. This differentiates the soul from nature where earlier strata of its life are left behind and are visible in their externality: The general mechanism of mass-movements disregarding its qualitative individuation are conditions of the solar systems; it in turn is the condition of organizing elementary life in the earth; and the earth is the condition of organic life, with its sensibilities and sense-qualities corresponding to its sensibility.

As distinct from nature, spirit retains in its development its earlier levels and phases as essential moments, moods, mental states and determinations; at the same time, its lower and earlier functions anticipate and foreshadow higher potentialities. Sleep, for example, is potential awakening in which it is known as sleep. The higher functions are rooted in simple sentient experience, which in turn is seen as bare abstract beginning from the point of view of later and developed contents.

381

Concept—the identity of subject-object—exists in nature in external objectivity. When this self-alienation is broken through, Concept gains a subjective objectivity for itself. Nature then actualizes its potential truth in the self of the spirit. In turn, spirit recognizes in nature its own presupposition and finds its own dialectic reflected in its own analogies of itself. Concept thus wrests from nature its true identity with itself. The primacy of the spirit over nature—which precedes it in time—lies in this absolute negativity which overcomes its natural externality, transforming it into means of expression of itself. Only in this work can spirit overcome its immediacy and gain its subjective identity for itself. But further than that, it does not only make nature its object, it makes itself its own object; this subject-object is its own product wherein the Idea is actualized and becomes real for itself.

382

The identity of the spirit is also its own non-identity with anything given. This absolute negativity is its own freedom; it is the essence of the spirit (40).

Spirit is, therefore, that which is able to abstract itself not only from all external conditions but also from its own previous embodiments (42). It can endure and suffer the negation of its individual immediacy and nevertheless affirm its freedom and its identity with itself in all such painful negations. In consciousness the negativity of the finite is sorrow (Schmerz). It is through this sacrificial work and suffering that the spirit affirms its true infinity (48).

383

This spiritual universality is also its omnipresence in all members of the spiritual community (43). Spirit is the subject making itself its own object and thus is in and for itself. In this activity it reveals itself, shows forth what it is, what it has been, and what it can be. In the spirit, possibility and actuality (Wirklichkeit) coincide.

What spirit is, does, and can be when it produces itself is not an entity or "thing" (Etwas, 44-46). The spirit is its own product which is not external to or distinguishable from its activity as form and content are distinguishable in things. Forms and contents of the spirit both are its self-determination and are nothing apart from self-revelation.

384

Man as spirit presupposes nature as an independent objective world, but at the same time posits it as possibility for his own freedom. Spirit, further, finds its own Concept evidently reflected in nature and in the speculative sense transforms it into the image of its own free being. Spirit thus reveals the world and recreates it in and as its own being. Spirit affirms and gives to itself the certainty and truth of its freedom. The dialectic of Being prepared the truth of spirit and its freedom. The transition of the Origin into that which begins in it, is in the abstract logic of Being the ontological analogy of the self-revelation of spirit (41-42).

The Absolute is Spirit—this is its ultimate definition.

To find this definition and to comprehend its meaning and content is the absolute tendency motivating all true cultures and their philosophy. All religion and Science are concentrated on this point. This absolute tendency alone makes the history of the world comprehensible.

Words and representational images of the absolute spirit are found in early thought; the message of the Christian religion is to reveal God as spirit: God is a spirit and those who worship him should worship him in spirit and in truth (Hegel's favorite passage from the New Testament).

Philosophy must comprehend in its own medium the essential truth given in mythical object-imagery. This task cannot be fulfilled and the problem cannot be adequately solved unless philosophy moves in the element of the Concept which is its necessary form. These two sides, the absolute freedom of the spirit and the necessity of its form, are its objective content and its soul.

385

Spirit is self-development: As *subjective spirit* or *natural soul* it tends towards realizing its Concept. The soul realizes itself as a being which is in and for itself, which relates itself to itself. In overcoming its immediacy, it reaches out towards freedom and agreement with itself.

As *objective spirit* or *mind*, spirit finds its freedom in an objective and necessary moral world-order, which it has produced and in which it takes part. Its aim is to find itself in this order of a reality with which it is confronted (vorhanden).

The absolute spirit finds itself united with truth. It realizes its identity with all being which is both an objective subjectivity and a subjective objectivity. The absolute spirit is actualized in art, religion, and philosophy.

386

Philosophy of Spirit is divided into two major parts. The first—subjective spirit or soul and objective spirit or mind—deals with the finite in the infinite; the second—absolute spirit—with the infinite in the finite spirit.

Finite spirit rises through many levels of its activity until it reaches its true identity in the light of which its previous phases and ascending steps are known in their truth. Concurrently each finite station and level in this ascent of the spirit is an obstacle and dim light (Schein) which the spirit has created in and for itself, in order to pass beyond it, in its very retention of it.

In breaking through its own self-producing limitations and in appreciating and preserving them as such in its absolute totality, spirit liberates itself from them and thus reaches its Concept. This is its freedom.

As one and the same, spirit finds a given world and engenders itself in appropriating it, and emancipates itself in its finitude from its finitude. The unity of infinite and finite spirit, wherein each is both caught up and free in the other, is absolute spirit.

The greatest and toughest of all obstacles is the standpoint of *reason*. Clinging to the finite as if it were ultimate and to abstract fixations as if they were absolute, in its false modesty, reason thus tries to ward off the comprehensiveness of the spirit. In its extreme form, this stubborn insistence on metaphysical untruth is *evil*. Absolute spirit, however, eternal in and for itself, annihilates this annihilation of finite reason and makes vain this vanity.

THE NATURAL SOUL

307

The natural soul in its immediacy is immersed in the unconscious life of nature. In breaking this immediacy, it distinguishes itself from a self-opposed, a natural, living environment. This is the beginning and an analogy of what later will turn out to be a comprehensive subject-object, wherein the subject makes itself its own object or problem, and develops objectivity within itself.

The soul awakens to consciousness, consciousness awakens to self-consciousness, and self-consciousness becomes comprehensive when it participates in and unites itself to the world. Potentially the soul is this budding comprehension. Its ascent and development is thus to actualize for itself what it potentially is in itself. "One may just as well say: The soul is first merely objective and should become truly subjective; as to say the soul is first merely subjective and should become truly objective. On the one hand, objective contents are subjectively appropriated—empty abstract subjectivity is filled; on the other hand, general objective contents find their living organs, their conscious representatives." (X, 48)

308

In the soul, nature herself begins to overcome its externality in assembling and collecting natural instincts, appetites, functions in an indivisible, individual unity. In distinction from the unconscious elementary and organic-vegetative life, the natural soul is awake.

309 (389)

But as not yet conscious of itself, as self-conscious I am or spirit, the natural soul is still subconscious or asleep. The waking life of nature is the slumber of the spirit.

Lacking heaviness and all other sensuous qualities, the soul is non-physical or immaterial. As diffused throughout nature, it is the world-soul.

Even the highest spheres of particular activity and the most outstanding manifestations of spirit could not exist without this all-pervasive presence of this living substance or world-soul which remains their absolute precondition. Life is potentiality, lending itself to and in turn being shaped by all higher formations of life.

Physical qualities, perceived by the sensing functions of the soul, are in reality qualities of life. In appearance, wherein all life is individuated, they are objectified. In its physical appearance life is given to all individuals in the form of self-estrangement. Physical "matter," however, is not real in and for itself—it may be treated as if it could be observed in pure externality and in abstraction from cosmic life.

Even to the physicist of recent times, matter has become thinner and imponderable.

Reason has transformed the dialectical unity of the psycho-physical polarity into an abstract dualism of two independent entities: extended body and unextended soul. From this perspective the concrete dialectical interrelation between body and soul becomes a completely incomprehensible mystery. . . .

315

The immediate original division (Ur-teil!) of the natural soul is its rhythm of being asleep and of being awake. Alternative opposites of sleeping and waking are equally necessary conditions for the preservation of the natural soul.

316

The soul, in becoming aware of itself as alive and awake, distinguishes itself from its own indistinct subconscious substance as *this* individual unit of life.

The initial act of awakening is the condition of all activities of mind and spirit. Sleep is not only a rest or a relaxation from daily activities, but it is also a return from the workaday world of dispersion and details to the substantial power and reservoir of such activity.

317 (396)

As the individual wrests himself away from his unconscious background of cosmic life, he hands himself over to the natural course of changes which belong to being awake and being an individual for himself. The whole course of his growth and decay is determined by the ages of life in their natural sequence:

"*Birth* is the enormous qualitative leap from subconscious nature into potential human existence (X. 98).

In the *infant,* spirit is still wrapped up or enveloped in its potentiality; it is potentially human.

Childhood is the age of natural harmony and satisfaction with himself and with his environment. The child thrives on the feeling of love for its parents, and in the feeling to be loved by them.

The *youth* develops tensions: Subjective ideals, illusions of grandeur, ambitions to live up to worshipped heroes, the question of what he ought to become, are all in tension and conflict with his immediate singularity. He feels the conflict between an objective world and his unreadiness and immaturity for it. The dreams, which he has idealized, clash with the repeated experience of non-fulfillment. And this shock, in turn, drives him to seek compensation in his ideal dreams.

The mature *man* acknowledges the necessity and comprehensiveness of an objective moral world-order into which he has entered and taken his place. In his activity he participates in a common work and in a growing concern for inter-activities which he enriches and by which his worth is proved and approved. Actual presence and objective value fuse. He has made himself to be what he is in co-operation with others.

The *old man* gains the freedom from restricting interests and worries; he is above the turmoil of his present time, which has become external to him. His unity with the objective world-order is a contemplative accomplishment.

As *senile* his activity is shrinking; nature reduces him to passive habits and dull routines—the beginning of death.

In *death* natural life is victorious and cancels its own individual modification." (X. 95)

"This physiological evolution from cradle to grave (Entwicklung) should not be confused with the unfolding (Entfaltung) of spirit." (X. 96)

318

The soul is alive for itself; it is at once a closed system of its inner functions and open towards the outside: It at once feels itself in feeling the other. Its sensing, perceiving functions are interfused with what is sensed and perceived; and sensed qualities are immediately fused with feeling tones, such as agreeable or disagreeable. The inner sense is a sympathetic identification (Mitleben) of the soul with all its functions, appetites, and desires. Courage and wrath, thinking and professional occupations are immediately felt functions of the self. When they are looked at from the outside, they are located in the reproductive and sensitive systems of the organism—in the intestine, the breast, and the head.

319 (403)

The soul is in tension: On the one hand, it is a subjective center for itself and, on the other hand, it remains tied to a vast subconscious substantial life. I am a simple, bottomless pit sunk into an infinite abundance of possible or virtual experiences. The individual never knows how many experiences have been experienced and absorbed by him or how many he has forgotten. In abnormal states memories of things forgotten are sometimes brought back. As a unique subjective center of all its functions, the soul is a monad: It carves out of its experience the totality of a particular world-view in which it mirrors itself. As a living mirror of the universe, it is the actual and individual existence of the speculative Concept.

320 (405)

The natural subconscious life may prevail in the soul, as the mother prevails in the embryo. Dreams, prophecies, presentiments, telepathy, clairvoyance, somnambulism, hypnosis, and unconscious suggestions immediately felt—all those so-called occult facts are evidence for the immediate immersion of the soul in non-spatial, purely functional relationships with natural life. . . .

322

The soul—in order to become what it ought to be—must fight its immediacy, while also preserving it as subordinate potential for its conscious purposiveness. In working at itself, it proves its power of controlling (übergreifend), making use of its irrational immediacy.

323

This must not be misunderstood as if the soul should be hostile towards its organic life. This would be insanity in reverse: If the spirit fights against its natural organic existence, it remains negatively fascinated by it. Such a negative abstraction leads one to mistreat life as if it were an external object, blind fate, an overwhelming evil to be eradicated. Such a false spiritualism or *moralism* also is loss of concrete unity.

324

The true relation of the conscious and the unconscious self, then, is this: The soul preserves its unity in meeting itself in all of its subconscious functions. As concrete identity it is present for itself in its living organization (Leib). In waking up, it breaks through its immediacy; concurrently it preserves and uses its immediacy to serve purposes going beyond the immediate living. The organism thus belongs to the soul, as a musical instrument belongs to the artist, or as a predicate belongs to the logical subject of which it is a true expression.

325 (410)

The soul is working on itself and thus exists as an educational process. It gladly gets hold of and penetrates its natural powers; repetition of actions serving purposes brings about and establishes habits; habits accumulate in skills. The soul thus prepares itself and makes itself fit for its activity in the world. It retains acquired habits and skills as a second nature, having made them inward, remembered (erinnert) possessions with which it maintains its identity. It can give account of them and is accountable for them. The subject has produced its own second nature; at the same time the product of his own subjective activity is a self-created objective state of affairs.

The consciously, as well as unconsciously, produced subject-object is the beginning of freedom, wherein the soul is one and in agreement with itself; freedom is the supreme end. Habits that do not contribute towards this end but enslave the soul are *bad habits*; if they accumulate into dull repetitive patterns, they lead to death and are the beginning of death in life.

326 (411)

Language transfigures physical sounds into *signs* through which the soul communicates its presence and actuality to others. The same holds true for preverbal communication: Gestures and movements of the living body (Leib), laughing and weeping, the tone in which something is said, the physiognomic figures and body-types—are all instrumental signs which in turn are interpreted as expressions of the soul by others. Its actuality lies in the mutual interpretation and in the identity of its inner life with its voluntary or involuntary signs.

In the interpretation of signs, however, the differences between inner and outer must not be overlooked; for the dialectical identity of opposites, which is not immediate, must be remembered. Taken in its immediacy, appearance is always contingent and uncertain. Physiognomy, for example, is not an immediate knowledge of the soul, whose freedom transcends its momentary expressions; it may even use them to hide itself from the interpreter.

327 (412)

In consciously treating the physical as a sign of its freedom, the soul becomes *subjective spirit* and mind, the conscious "I am." Subjective thinking acts upon, opposes and relates itself to an external world which is transformed into an object of its thought and action. This conscious subjective spirit is a second and higher awakening of the soul; it now lives in a conscious subject-object relation to itself as well as to others.

SUBJECTIVE MIND

329 (413)

The subjective mind appears in every individual consciousness. "It begins to *struggle* with external objects, which struggle is a higher value than the naive unity of the natural soul with its subconscious cosmic life." (X. 258) The subjective mind is simultaneously aware and certain of its conscious self as well as of its natural soul which it now opposes to itself as its own object and material to be shaped. The "I am," thus, is one side of this relation and at the same time the whole relation; in being aware of myself as my own object I am self-reflection. In the world of nature *light* is an analogy to this: By manifesting itself it makes a visible world evident to sight.

330 (414)

And as light reveals darkness, so natural existence becomes for mind a dark region below its consciousness; this dialectic of light and dark, high and low, is absent in the animal soul.

331-332

There is a further conflict between subjective mind as a conscious being-for-itself and the object which it poses and presupposes as an alien, given thing.

In *Fichte* this is the perennial problem of how I should handle the Not-I. For him there is no dialectical unity with both as poles of the same process. They only *ought* to be united—which ought prevents them from ever being united. Fichte's error lies in the false initial assumption that the "I am" and the Not-I are absolute entities in their finitude and separation.

Any world-viewed is correlative to the world-view of the subjective mind in which and for which it is evident. A change in the former is, therefore, also a change in the latter. In characterizing its world, the subjective mind also characterizes its own standpoint.

The phenomenology of mind thus reveals the subjective mind as an ascent from lower to higher, or from immediate to mediated positions; this is the educational process of maturing. It is actual for us, the phenomenologists of the mind, but the subjective mind itself is aware only of each of its stations or phases. In belaboring or working at its object it is aware only of its correlation with it.

The reason why the concrete educational process is hidden from its subjective mind is its representational thinking. For itself it maintains its formal-logical identity in opposition to its object-images (Vorstellung).

333 (416)

The subjective mind is, therefore, finite and rational. Its self-certainty is identical with its uncertainty concerning its alien object.

It exists, however, also in truth and not merely in its certainties. Its truth is the concrete process of self-development through the self-criticism of all insufficient stations and limited standpoints. In exploding one certainty after another, it works uncomprehendingly towards its goal which is the truth. The certainty of itself is elevated to its truth.

"The subject must fill itself with objective content or value, and objective contents or values must gain subjective existence in it." (X. 261)

334 (417)

The main levels of the subjective individual mind toward the realization of its truth are: *Consciousness* of objects, consciousness of the *self*, and *comprehension* (Vernunft) in which the subjective mind knows itself as a totality determining all levels and phases of its conscious and self-conscious appearance as its own essential development.

335

Sensuous consciousness is correlated to its world as *immediate experience*. I am a singular momentary "this" individual to whom appear in rapid, flickering changes, various and sundry qualitative contents. They are immediately transfused with my feeling; they seem attractive, repulsive, and so on.

The manifold contents are *relative* to one another: What appears big or small, far or near, up or down, depends on its relation to other things or movements; and they are subjective as tied to and conditioned by the organs for experiencing them.

Universal categories present in the immediacy of consciousness and its experienced world are: The singular "this something," the "now" in relation to "earlier" and "later," and the "here" of location.

These categories of the sensuous consciousness are extremely abstract and poor; as such they are in sharp contrast to the infinite qualitative wealth of the empirically concrete or immediate experience.

As soon as the sensuous consciousness becomes aware of this contradiction and of the abstract emptiness of those categories in which it must express its standpoint—"everything is a singular this, here, now"—it has ceased to be an immediate sensuous consciousness.

338 (421)

The dialectic inherent in this standpoint of empirical consciousness is at once also the dialectic of its finite objects.

On the one hand, perceptual consciousness clings to an empirical manifold of things ultimately real; on the other hand, they are negated and are classed under general concepts, which are *not* empirical things. Further, scientific objects, on the one hand, are unified through their general predicates; on the other hand, they are not unified, but torn apart as if they consisted of general matters (for example, sweetness, quietness, hardness, are such general matters assembled in a piece of sugar); thus, they form aggregates without a real unity.

In this *mixture* of empirical things and general classes, perceptual consciousness tumbles about, now declaring one side and then again the other side to be essential. It constantly contradicts itself: On the one hand, finite objects are essential and their general predicates unessential; on the other hand, the general features are essential and the particular thing only a case or illustration of them.

339-340

For *reason* (Verstand) this self-contradiction is intolerable. It solves it by declaring preceptual, observable objects to be external appearances of their inner essential nature. It intends to replace the above mixture or composite by a genuine synthesis of universal logical forms—laws of nature—and given perceptual materials, determined by the laws of various abstract sciences.

"General laws of nature maintain their identity throughout the changes of observable events. An inner realm of laws quietly reigns in the turmoil of external appearances.

In such concepts as 'cause and effect' or 'energy and its manifestations,' reason postulates a necessary inner connection of outer appearances. For example, the laws of planetary systems are united by a necessary non-appearing or inner unity in which reason finds its own law confirmed in external experience.

Universal objective rational world-order is correlative to reason." (X. 269)

341

But reason does not comprehend what it has discovered. Its universal coherent or rational world-order is not identical with any one of its many laws; they are self-distinctions within a concrete ideal unity. Reason demands a complete, rational unity, but none of its natural laws fulfills this demand or postulate.

But a concrete unity, which makes such distinctions within itself, is no longer an object at all that can be kept over against the finite subject. The rational subject finds its own nature in the object, and the object behaves as if it were a subject. An absolute concrete unity distinguishes forms of unity within itself, which it both posits and transcends. The various laws of nature are partial unifications, which are real distinctions within the whole, without tearing this whole apart. The truth of reason, hence, of which reason is not aware, is nothing less than the speculative Concept: A subject which is absolutely objective, and an object which is absolutely subjective. . . . One, which distinguishes many forms of unity within itself, without losing its concrete dialectical identity in them.

"Reason is the highest level of object-thinking. Its false initial assumption of a subject thinking, on one side, and an object alien to it and thought about, on the other side, is an untenable contradiction. In the discovery of this contradiction, reason is driven beyond its standpoint to the concrete dialectical unity of opposites—in this case the unity of subject-object in the comprehensive self-consciousness of life.

In life, consciousness contemplates a process which develops its own essential distinctions as modifications of its own concrete identity. As such, life is its own final cause (Selbstzweck). It produces itself as a totality in which all self-produced functions are mutually serving one another to form a functional whole.

As aware of this dialectical living unity in its infinite self-differentiation, consciousness becomes self-consciousness. Self-consciousness is actual in the "I am" who knows itself objectively." (X. 272)

342

This living actuality in the subject-object is its Concept (Begriff). It is speculative because it mirrors in itself a cosmic life which also is a concrete universality and self-differentiation. "I have thus in one and the same consciousness myself and my world; I find myself in my world and I find my world in myself; world-itself—that which *is*—gives me my objectivity and finds in me its subjectivity. This "I am" is the unity of I and objectivity or Being. This unity is spirit (Geist). As immediate, it is not yet developed; it must become for itself what it is in itself and attain its freedom." (X. 273)

343

Life aware of itself is self-knowledge or Concept. It results from the dialectical negation of reason as object-thinking: or reason, in overcoming its finite contradiction of subject vs. object, becomes the comprehensive Concept.

344

Self-consciousness—I am relating myself to myself—not only overcomes object-consciousness; it also preserves it as a necessary level or aspect of its concrete unity with itself and with its world.

The previous movements in the ascent of the mind are now understood as characterizing self-knowledge: Sensuous consciousness, perceptual experience, scientific object-thinking are also—although not known to themselves—the attitudes which spirit, in its freedom, has produced and chosen so as to express stations of its own development.

SELF-CONSCIOUSNESS

345

The core of self-consciousness is its practical intentionality (Trieb) to actualize its potentiality, to *find* itself in *producing* itself.

346 (426)

Desire or appetite is the immediate form of this practical intentionality (Begierde). It practically denies the independence of sensuous objects: It uses, destroys, and consumes them for its own satisfaction. "It maintains itself by negating threatening negations of life." (X. 277) (For example, eating negates the threat of starvation.)

347

The essential destiny of finite objects is: To be corroded and changed. Since they have no intentionality, they cannot ward off this destiny or put up a fight against anything which dissolves them. The practical activity of the I who uses them is therefore not an external abuse, for such actions, conform to the very nature of finite objects. The practical subject, in its struggle with them, links itself to their externality and mortality.

348

This destructive desire or appetite seeks its self-satisfaction; it is selfishness. The negation of felt wants, which is the fulfillment of selfishness, is singular and momentary and must constantly be renewed. No selfish satisfaction is lasting.

349-350

In the destruction and use of given objects, which are helpless and selfless, the selfish subject beholds its own futility. The object is appropriated by a practical activity and thereby enters and becomes part of this subjective practical self; the subject, on the other hand, depends for its life on objects external to it. Its desire or appetite is determined and colored by the objects of desire by which it is externalized (entäussert).

351

Being dissatisfied with the futility and negativity of its immediate satisfactions, the subjective mind rises above them. The immediate identity with its appetitive nature being broken, this *dissatisfaction* with its immediate satisfactions is a new and *mediated satisfaction*. One strives to rise above his natural immediacy and asserts himself as a free agent.

352

The I, in conflict with its immediate practical existence (Dasein), is both individual and social. Every practical self is in the same situation, recognizing in the other the same problem which is in itself. The object of desire thus changes and becomes another I. Each I wants to be one with and *recognized* by another I; concurrently, each I remains an independent individual, an alien object for the other.

353

The life of the subjective mind thus becomes a *struggle for recognition*: On the one hand, each is an internal struggle to gain mastery over its immediate appetitive existence, prove his freedom to himself, and produce a feeling of self-respect (Selbstgefühl); on the other hand, each is an external struggle to convince the other that it is worthy of his respect and recognition.

354

This mutual struggle for recognition is mingled with the feeling of mistrust and uncertainty; it entails the dangerous risk, which every self-consciousness takes, when it dares to lay itself open to the other. If this life-and-death struggle (a colloquial expression) degenerates into a bloody fight in which one combatant is killed, the whole problem of recognition is missed; this is the raw elimination of the whole problem, which requires the preservation of immediate existence as a condition and sign of freedom.

355 (333)

The internal and external struggle of the self-conscious subjective mind is essentially a *struggle for freedom;* even though, in a complex historical situation, it permits the rise of masters and slaves. The subjection of the appetitive mind to serve the freedom of the higher self appears externally in dominion and servitude. Preferring immediate existence to freedom, the slave forfeits to be recognized as free; the master, in turn, is recognized as free, beholding in the slave the sign of his freedom.

Historically states arise in this group struggle for status. Factually, if a self-consciousness, absorbed in its immediate appetites, is to be elevated to a higher form of a common universal self-consciousness, this transition is unavoidable and relatively speaking justified. This historical start of political life is *merely* the external beginning in appearance; it is not the principle of a true state. For instance, "it is the limitation of ancient peoples that they have not recognized freedom as essential to every self-consciousness; that every man qua human is entitled to be free and to participate in a universal self-consciousness of all." (X. 286) *Mere might is never the ground of right.*

356

Independent masters and dependent slaves form a *community*. To preserve and protect the life of his workers becomes the concern of the master. Instead of an immediate destruction and consumption of singular objects of momentary appetites, objects are cultivated, preserved, and transformed by *work* in anticipation of a future which is the common concern of the whole community.

357 (435)

The servant learns to work. He acquires habits and skills. At the same time he disciplines himself. In forming objects, he also informs himself. In working together with others he overcomes his immediacy and is recognized in his excellence. In this process, the relation of dependence and independence is being reversed: The independent master becomes dependent on the skills and virtues of the servant.

"Having elevated himself over the selfish singularity of his natural will, the servant now ranks higher in value than the master, who merely beholds the shallow sign of his freedom in the servant. His lordship sinks to a mere formality.

Learning to obey another, in willing to give up selfish immediacy of appetites, is a necessary *origin of all true education.* No man who has not gone through this discipline, breaking his immediate egotism, can become free and worthy of command. The educator, on the other hand, works to make himself superfluous." (X. 288)

"The former master can only be free if the former slave is also free." (X. 290)

The fear of the lord is the beginning of wisdom. (Hegel's quotation from the Bible is witty—the "lord" has undergone a remarkable transformation!)

358

Subjective mind actualizes its universal self-consciousness in the reciprocal recognition of the freedom and independence of the other and itself.

This mutuality and interdependence of voluntary recognition and respect is the substance of all communities—be they friendship, love, family, state, or church. *All virtues* are rooted in it; they are vices—hollow honor, vainglory—in isolation and separation from their substance.

359

Comprehension (Vernunft), as existing in the subjective mind, is the concrete identity of its object-consciousness and its free self-consciousness.

360

In this correlation of the consciousness of object with the consciousness of self, each side mutually characterizes the other: The *world-viewed* characterizes the *world-view* in and for which it is evident.

361

Comprehension exists in and for itself in every mature individual. The *objective determinations* of the essential nature of things are known to be partly identical with the *subjective self-determinations* of thought.

362

The subjective mind has thus reached its truth in Comprehension. Subjective mind, which knows truth and through which truth knows itself, is *spirit* (Geist).

363

Spirit is the goal whereby the progression through the levels of the soul and subjective mind is known as progress and ascent. It is a movement towards, as well as within, spirit. Soul and mind are finite in every one of their stations: Soul is finite because it is immersed in natural life; consciousness is finite because it is correlated to finite objects of knowledge and desire. Spirit is the totality of all functions of soul and mind.

364

Spirit as immediate unity of the finite soul and of the finite mind is still finite itself; it is its task to work out and to discover its infinity. The immediate finitude of spirit is the necessary prerequisite or obstacle overcoming which it become for itself what it is in itself: Free spirit.

365

The spirit is progression in the consciousness of freedom towards its absolute self-fulfillment, leaving no opposites outside its totality. "The finite struggle of the spirit within and against its finitude is eternally willed and posited in the holy, blessed, absolute, and infinite spirit. The divine spirit is thus present in the human. The *infinite and eternal spirit* is completely *one with the non-absolute finite spirit,* which is forever distinguished from it as its own self-distinction." (X. 298)

366

The way of liberation is the development of the spirit as free *theoretical* intelligence, and free *practical* will. These are two inseparable poles within its complete process.

367

The struggle with theoretical and practical obstacles characterizes the whole sphere of finite subjective mind. "The theoretical function is no less an activity than the practical function (X. 305). It is therefore wrong to say that theory is passive or is only receiving given stuff, and that practice is active in producing works that did not exist before. Theory also produces such works as for example *language,* apart from which productivity nothing would be knowable; and practice also is determined by given contents which are dependent upon being known prior to acting upon them. Equally false is the preference for practical over theoretical activity, declaring intelligence to be conditional and will to be unconditional. Both are conditional and unconditional. Practical will meets the resistance of objects and of other wills with which it is joined in battle; whereas free intelligence, realizing its intentions in language, remains one with its utterance and accomplishes a contemplative life which is divine and blessed in itself." (X. 396) These fallacies are examples of the general failure of rationalistic metaphysics, which divides the mind into separate compartments; and of empiristic psychology which singles out and prefers one detail over another.

The whole ascent of the soul through mind and spirit is leading towards that *logic of truth* which is at the same time its *ontological basis.* If empiricism renounces this logical principle of understanding spirit, it remains confined to an indefinite manifold of details, to the untruth and illusions of the empirical natural soul, and to the peculiarities and idiosyncrasies of individuals.

368

Willing and knowing, *heart* and *head* are dialectically interdependent. In and for spirit, the will with its purposes and interests is one content of knowledge; and knowledge is a content freely willed and chosen by the will to truth. In willing the truth, will renounces itself; it is its own self-determination to abstract from its interests, in contemplating them. There is no reason without will and no will without reason. This dialectic of subjectivity is the *Concept* of finite spirit: The self is the power to cancel, preserve, and unite its own opposite functions as fluid moments of its process of activity.

Pure subjectivity is knowledge in and for itself; it is its own object, which remains at the same time internal to itself.

Spirit is thus subject-object in and for itself. In distinction from object thinking or consciousness (Wissen), the self-conscious comprehensive knowledge (Erkennen) is a higher level, because its objectivity is insepara-ble from its subjectivity; or subjectivity is objectively real in and for itself." (X. 312)

This corresponds to Aristotle's "Dynamis" and "Entelechy": The former is the living potentiality; the latter is the activity which actualizes the subject as a being in becoming for itself what it is in itself. . . .

ABSOLUTE SPIRIT

453

The soul in its immediacy is irrational (begrifflos). This is a necessary side of objective mind; in turn objective mind gains its absolute justifica-tion in the absolute spirit, not in itself. All finite movements of the spirit are stations on its way; absolute spirit lingers in each while pressing on to gain its real existence and freedom by leaving them behind. A chain of exploded systems marks the fiery path of the absolute spirit. The Concept of the absolute Idea in *Logic* is the ontological category, being actualized and achieving existence in existence in absolute spirit. In actuality, abso-lute spirit appears in the forms (Gestalten) of art, religion, and philoso-phy, all of which at their best are worthy of the Concept. In each of them, free and actual intelligence grasps its identity with the dialectical essence of the world; it exists not only as achievement of a past, but also as the presence of the eternal Now in an educational process of self-liberation and self-articulation (herausbildet).

454 (554)

The dialectical negation of single individuals in their living immediacy mediates their participation in the life of an objective whole; this necessary participation is identical with a free dedication. The ethical community rests on such sacrificial life of all its members. This life of sacrifice, is, further, the ethical root of philosophy. All worldly existence is posited by and in the Absolute; it is also sacrificed for the sake of the Absolute in its eternal life. Philosophical contemplation in thinking this through, participates in the sacrificial life of the Absolute; like the Absolute, it transcends the dialectical essence of nature as well as of finite mind.

Absolute spirit is the living and actual identity of the eternal being which *is what it is in itself*, but which also is its own eternal self-differentiation, eternally re-absorbed by itself. As this absolute knowledge, absolute spirit is this process *for itself*.

Religion represents this same process and this absolute knowledge in the medium of faith; on the one hand, faith begins in the feeling of the finite subject and is not found outside of it; on the other hand, God absolutely establishes himself in the community of faith as their absolute ground; the absolute spirit is evident to the spirit of the faithful.

In recent times this interplay of absoluteness and its corresponding subjective response has been minimized: One only refers to religion as subjective state of mind or as a piety immanent in feeling and as anthropological projection. In contrast to this subjectivism as well as to objectivistic dogmatism, philosophy comprehends a truly religious faith as a form of absolute truth (455, 553-555).

Experience, Reflective Thinking, and Education

JOHN DEWEY

1. CRITERIA OF EXPERIENCE*

If there is any truth in what has been said about the need of forming a theory of experience in order that education may be intelligently conducted upon the basis of experience, it is clear that the next thing in order in this discussion is to present the principles that are most significant in framing this theory. I shall not, therefore, apologize for engaging in a certain amount of philosophical analysis, which otherwise might be out of place. I may, however, reassure you to some degree by saying that this analysis is not an end in itself but is engaged in for the sake of obtaining criteria to be applied later in discussion of a number of concrete and, to most persons, more interesting issues.

I have already mentioned what I called the category of continuity, or the experiential continuum. This principle is involved, as I pointed out, in every attempt to discriminate between experiences that are worth while educationally and those that are not. It may seem superfluous to argue that this discrimination is necessary not only in criticizing the traditional type of education but also in initiating and conducting a different type. Nevertheless, it is advisable to pursue for a little while the idea that it is necessary. One may safely assume, I suppose, that one thing which has recommended the progressive movement is that it seems more in accord with the democratic ideal to which our people is committed than do the procedures of the traditional school, since the latter have so much of the autocratic about them. Another thing which has contributed to its favorable reception is that its methods are humane in comparison with the harshness so often attending the policies of the traditional school.

The question I would raise concerns why we prefer democratic and humane arrangements to those which are autocratic and harsh. And by "why," I mean the *reason* for preferring them, not just the *causes* which

*From John Dewey, *Experience and Education* (New York: Collier Books, 1963), pp. 33–60 by permission of The John Dewey Foundation.

lead us to the preference. One *cause* may be that we have been taught not only in the schools but by the press, the pulpit, the platform, and our laws and law-making bodies that democracy is the best of all social institutions. We may have so assimilated this idea from our surroundings that it has become an habitual part of our mental and moral make-up. But similar causes have led other persons in different surroundings to widely varying conclusions—to prefer fascism, for example. The cause for our preference is not the same thing as the reason why we *should* prefer it.

It is not my purpose here to go in detail into the reason. But I would ask a single question: Can we find any reason that does not ultimately come down to the belief that democratic social arrangements promote a better quality of human experience, one which is more widely accessible and enjoyed, than do non-democratic and anti-democratic forms of social life? Does not the principle of regard for individual freedom and for decency and kindliness of human relations come back in the end to the conviction that these things are tributary to a higher quality of experience on the part of a greater number than are methods of repression and coercion or force? Is it not the reason for our preference that we believe that mutual consultation and convictions reached through persuasion, make possible a better quality of experience than can otherwise be provided on any wide scale?

If the answer to these questions is in the affirmative (and personally I do not see how we can justify our preference for democracy and humanity on any other ground), the ultimate reason for hospitality to progressive education, because of its reliance upon and use of humane methods and its kinship to democracy, goes back to the fact that discrimination is made between the inherent values of different experiences. So I come back to the principle of continuity of experience as a criterion of discrimination.

At bottom, this principle rests upon the fact of habit, when *habit* is interpreted biologically. The basic characteristic of habit is that every experience enacted and undergone modifies the one who acts and undergoes, while this modification affects, whether we wish it or not, the quality of subsequent experiences. For it is a somewhat different person who enters into them. The principle of habit so understood obviously goes deeper than the ordinary conception of *a* habit as a more or less fixed way of doing things, although it includes the latter as one of its special cases. It covers the formation of attitudes, attitudes that are emotional and intellectual; it covers our basic sensitivities and ways of meeting and responding to all the conditions which we meet in living. From this point of view, the principle of continuity of experience means that every experience both takes up something from those which have gone before and modifies in some way the quality of those which come after. As the poet states it,

> . . . all experience is an arch wherethro'
> Gleams that untraveled world, whose margin fades
> For ever and for ever when I move.

So far, however, we have no ground for discrimination among experiences. For the principle is of universal application. There is *some* kind of continuity in every case. It is when we note the different forms in which continuity of experience operates that we get the basis of discriminating among experiences. I may illustrate what is meant by an objection which has been brought against an idea which I once put forth—namely, that the educative process can be identified with growth when that is understood in terms of the active participle, *growing*.

Growth, or growing as developing, not only physically but intellectually and morally, is one exemplification of the principle of continuity. The objection made is that growth might take many different directions: a man, for example, who starts out on a career of burglary may grow in that direction, and by practice may grow into a highly expert burglar. Hence it is argued that "growth" is not enough; we must also specify the direction in which growth takes place, the end towards which it tends. Before, however, we decide that the objection is conclusive we must analyze the case a little further.

That a man may grow in efficiency as a burglar, as a gangster, or as a corrupt politician, cannot be doubted. But from the standpoint of growth as education and education as growth the question is whether growth in this direction promotes or retards growth in general. Does this form of growth create conditions for further growth, or does it set up conditions that shut off the person who has grown in this particular direction from the occasions, stimuli, and opportunities for continuing growth in new directions? What is the effect of growth in a special direction upon the attitudes and habits which alone open up avenues for development in other lines? I shall leave you to answer these questions, saying simply that when and *only* when development in a particular line conduces to continuing growth does it answer to the criterion of education as growing. For the conception is one that must find universal and not specialized limited application.

I return now to the question of continuity as a criterion by which to discriminate between experiences which are educative and those which are mis-educative. As we have seen, there is some kind of continuity in any case since every experience affects for better or worse the attitudes which help decide the quality of further experiences, by setting up certain preference and aversion, and making it easier or harder to act for this or that end. Moreover, every experience influences in some degree the objective conditions under which further experiences are had. For example, a child who learns to speak has a new facility and new desire. But he has also widened the external conditions of subsequent learning. When he learns to read, he similarly opens up a new environment. If a person decides to become a teacher, lawyer, physician, or stockbroker, when he executes his intention he thereby necessarily determines to some extent the environment in which he will act in the future. He has rendered himself more sensitive and responsive to certain conditions, and relatively immune to those things about him that would have been stimuli if he had made another choice.

But, while the principle of continuity applies in some way in every case, the quality of the present experience influences the *way* in which the principle applies. We speak of spoiling a child and of the spoilt child. The effect of over-indulging a child is a continuing one. It sets up an attitude which operates as an automatic demand that persons and objects cater to his desires and caprices in the future. It makes him seek the kind of situation that will enable him to do what he feels like doing at the time. It renders him averse to and comparatively incompetent in situations which require effort and perseverance in overcoming obstacles. There is no paradox in the fact that the principle of the continuity of experience may operate so as to leave a person arrested on a low plane of development, in a way which limits later capacity for growth.

On the other hand, if an experience arouses curiosity, strengthens initiative, and sets up desires and purposes that are sufficiently intense to carry a person over dead places in the future, continuity works in a very different way. Every experience is a moving force. Its value can be judged only on the ground of what it moves toward and into. The greater maturity of experience which should belong to the adult as educator puts him in a position to evaluate each experience of the young in a way in which the one having the less mature experience cannot do. It is then the business of the educator to see in what direction an experience is heading. There is no point in his being more mature if, instead of using his greater insight to help organize the conditions of the experience of the immature, he throws away his insight. Failure to take the moving force of an experience into account so as to judge and direct it on the ground of what it is moving into means disloyalty to the principle of experience itself. The disloyalty operates in two directions. The educator is false to the understanding that he should have obtained from his own past experience. He is also unfaithful to the fact that all human experience is ultimately social: that it involves contact and communication. The mature person, to put it in moral terms, has no right to withhold from the young on given occasions whatever capacity for sympathetic understanding his own experience has given him.

No sooner, however, are such things said than there is a tendency to react to the other extreme and take what has been said as a plea for some sort of disguised imposition from outside. It is worth while, accordingly, to say something about the way in which the adult can exercise the wisdom his own wider experience gives him without imposing a merely external control. On one side, it is his business to be on the alert to see what attitudes and habitual tendencies are being created. In this direction he must, if he is an educator, be able to judge what attitudes are actually conducive to continued growth and what are detrimental. He must, in addition, have that sympathetic understanding of individuals as individuals which gives him an idea of what is actually going on in the minds of those who are learning. It is, among other things, the need for these abilities on the part of the parent and teacher which makes a system of education based upon living experience a more difficult affair to conduct successfully than it is to follow the patterns of traditional education.

But there is another aspect of the matter. Experience does not go on simply inside a person. It does go on there, for it influences the formation of attitudes of desire and purpose. But this is not the whole of the story. Every genuine experience has an active side which changes in some degree the objective conditions under which experiences are had. The difference between civilization and savagery, to take an example on a large scale, is found in the degree in which previous experiences have changed the objective conditions under which subsequent experiences take place. The existence of roads, of means of rapid movement and transportation, tools, implements, furniture, electric light and power, are illustrations. Destroy the external conditions of present civilized experience, and for a time our experience would relapse into that of barbaric peoples.

In a word, we live from birth to death in a world of persons and things which in large measure is what it is because of what has been done and transmitted from previous human activities. When this fact is ignored, experience is treated as if it were something which goes on exclusively inside an individual's body and mind. It ought not to be necessary to say that experience does not occur in a vacuum. There are sources outside an individual which give rise to experience. It is constantly fed from these springs. No one would question that a child in a slum tenement has a different experience from that of a child in a cultured home; that the country lad has a different kind of experience from the city boy, or a boy on the seashore one different from the lad who is brought up on inland prairies. Ordinarily we take such facts for granted as too commonplace to record. But when their educational import is recognized, they indicate the second way in which the educator can direct the experience of the young without engaging in imposition. A primary responsibility of educators is that they not only be aware of the general principle of the shaping of actual experience by environing conditions, but that they also recognize in the concrete what surroundings are conducive to having experiences that lead to growth. Above all, they should know how to utilize the surroundings, physical and social, that exist so as to extract from them all that they have to contribute to building up experiences that are worth while.

Traditional education did not have to face this problem; it could systematically dodge this responsibility. The school environment of desks, blackboards, a small school yard, was supposed to suffice. There was no demand that the teacher should become intimately acquainted with the conditions of the local community, physical, historical, economic, occupational, etc., in order to utilize them as educational resources. A system of education based upon the necessary connection of education with experience must, on the contrary, if faithful to its principle, take these things constantly into account. This tax upon the educator is another reason why progressive education is more difficult to carry on than was ever the traditional system.

It is possible to frame schemes of education that pretty systematically subordinate objective conditions to those which reside in the individuals being educated. This happens whenever the place and function of the teacher, of books, of apparatus and equipment, of everything which represents the products of the more mature experience of elders, is systematically subordinated to the immediate inclinations and feelings of the young. Every theory which assumes that importance can be attached to these objective factors only at the expense of imposing external control and of limiting the freedom of individuals rests finally upon the notion that experience is truly experience only when objective conditions are subordinated to what goes on within the individuals having the experience.

I do not mean that it is supposed that objective conditions can be shut out. It is recognized that they must enter in: so much concession is made to the inescapable fact that we live in a world of things and persons. But I think that observation of what goes on in some families and some schools would disclose that some parents and some teachers are acting upon the idea of *subordinating* objective conditions to internal ones. In that case, it is assumed not only that the latter are primary, which in one sense they are, but that just as they temporarily exist they fix the whole educational process.

Let me illustrate from the case of an infant. The needs of a baby for food, rest, and activity are certainly primary and decisive in one respect. Nourishment must be provided; provision must be made for comfortable sleep, and so on. But these facts do not mean that a parent shall feed the baby at any time when the baby is cross or irritable, that there shall not be a program of regular hours of feeding and sleeping, etc. The wise mother takes account of the needs of the infant but not in a way which dispenses with her own responsibility for regulating the objective conditions under which the needs are satisfied. And if she is a wise mother in this respect, she draws upon past experiences of experts as well as her own for the light that these shed upon what experiences are in general most conducive to the normal development of infants. Instead of these conditions being subordinated to the immediate internal condition of the baby, they are definitely ordered so that a particular kind of *interaction* with these immediate internal states may be brought about.

The word "interaction," which has just been used, expresses the second chief principle for interpreting an experience in its educational function and force. It assigns equal rights to both factors in experience—objective and internal conditions. Any normal experience is an interplay of these two sets of conditions. Taken together, or in their interaction, they form what we call a *situation*. The trouble with traditional education was not that it emphasized the external conditions that enter into the control of the experiences but that it paid so little attention to the internal factors which also decide what kind of experience is had. It violated the principle of interaction from one side. But this violation is no reason why the new education should violate the principle from the other side—except upon the basis of the extreme *Either-Or* educational philosophy which has been mentioned.

The illustration drawn from the need for regulation of the objective conditions of a baby's development indicates, first, that the parent has responsibility for arranging the conditions under which an infant's experience of food, sleep, etc., occurs, and, secondly, that the responsibility is fulfilled by utilizing the funded experience of the past, as this is represented, say, by the advice of competent physicians and others who have made a special study of normal physical growth. Does it limit the freedom of the mother when she uses the body of knowledge thus provided to regulate the objective conditions of nourishment and sleep? Or does the enlargement of her intelligence in fulfilling her parental function widen her freedom? Doubtless if a fetish were made of the advice and directions so that they came to be inflexible dictates to be followed under every possible condition, then restriction of freedom of both parent and child would occur. But this restriction would also be a limitation of the intelligence that is exercised in personal judgment.

In what respect does regulation of objective conditions limit the freedom of the baby? Some limitation is certainly placed upon its immediate movements and inclinations when it is put in its crib, at a time when it wants to continue playing, or does not get food at the moment it would like it, or when it isn't picked up and dandled when it cries for attention. Restriction also occurs when mother or nurse snatches a child away from an open fire into which it is about to fall. I shall have more to say later about freedom. Here it is enough to ask whether freedom is to be thought of and adjudged on the basis of relatively momentary incidents or whether its meaning is found in the continuity of developing experience.

The statement that individuals live in a world means, in the concrete, that they live in a series of situations. And when it is said that they live *in* these situations, the meaning of the word "in" is different from its meaning when it is said that pennies are "in" a pocket or paint is "in" a can. It means, once more, that interaction is going on between an individual and objects and other persons. The conceptions of *situation* and of *interaction* are inseparable from each other. An experience is always what it is because of a transaction taking place between an individual and what, at the time, constitutes his environment, whether the latter consists of persons with whom he is talking about some topic or event, the subject talked about being also a part of the situation; or the toys with which he is playing; the book he is reading (in which his environing conditions at the time may be England or ancient Greece or an imaginary region); or the materials of an experiment he is performing. The environment, in other words, is whatever conditions interact with personal needs, desires, purposes, and capacities to create the experience which is had. Even when a person builds a castle in the air he is interacting with the objects which he constructs in fancy.

The two principles of continuity and interaction are not separate from each other. They intercept and unite. They are, so to speak, the longitudinal and lateral aspects of experience. Different situations succeed one another. But because of the principle of continuity something is carried over from the earlier to the later ones. As an individual passes from one situation to another, his world, his environment, expands or contracts. He does not find himself living in another world but in a different part or aspect of one and the same world. What he has learned in the way of knowledge and skill in one situation becomes an instrument of understanding and dealing effectively with the situations which follow. The process goes on as long as life and learning continue. Otherwise the course of experience is disorderly, since the individual factor that enters into making an experience is split. A divided world, a world whose parts and aspects do not hang together, is at once a sign and a cause of a divided personality. When the splitting-up reaches a certain point we call the person insane. A fully integrated personality, on the other hand, exists only when successive experiences are integrated with one another. It can be built up only as a world of related objects is constructed.

Continuity and interaction in their active union with each other provide the measure of the educative significance and value of an experience. The immediate and direct concern of an educator is then with the situations in which interaction takes place. The individual, who enters as a factor into it, is what he is at a given time. It is the other factor, that of objective conditions, which lies to some extent within the possibility of regulation by the educator. As has already been noted, the phrase "objective conditions" covers a wide range. It includes what is done by the educator and the way in which it is done, not only words spoken but the tone of voice in which they are spoken. It includes equipment, books, apparatus, toys, games played. It includes the materials with which an individual interacts, and, most important of all, the total *social* set-up of the situations in which a person is engaged.

When it is said that the objective conditions are those which are within the power of the educator to regulate, it is meant, of course, that his ability to influence directly the experience of others and thereby the education they obtain places upon him the duty of determining that environment which will interact with the existing capacities and needs of those taught to create a worth-while experience. The trouble with traditional education was not that educators took upon themselves the responsibility for providing an environment. The trouble was that they did not consider the other factor in creating an experience; namely, the powers and purposes of those taught. It was assumed that a certain set of conditions was intrinsically desirable, apart from its ability to evoke a certain quality of response in individuals. This lack of mutual adaptation made the process of teaching and learning accidental. Those to whom the provided conditions were suitable managed to learn. Others got on as best they could. Responsibility for selecting objective conditions carries with it, then, the responsibility for understanding the needs and capacities of the individuals who are learning at a given time. It is not enough that certain materials and methods have proved effective with other individuals at other times. There must be a reason for thinking that they will function in generating an experience that has educative quality with particular individuals at a particular time.

It is no reflection upon the nutritive quality of beefsteak that it is not fed to infants. It is not an invidious reflection upon trigonometry that we do not teach it in the first or fifth grade of school. It is not the subject *per se* that is educative or that is conducive to growth. There is no subject that is in and of itself, or without regard to the stage of growth attained by the learner, such that inherent educational value can be attributed to it.

Failure to take into account adaptation to the needs and capacities of individuals was the source of the idea that certain subjects and certain methods are intrinsically cultural or intrinsically good for mental discipline. There is no such thing as educational value in the abstract. The notion that some subjects and methods and that acquaintance with certain facts and truths possess educational value in and of themselves is the reason why traditional education reduced the material of education so largely to a diet of predigested materials. According to this notion, it was enough to regulate the quantity and difficulty of the material provided, in a scheme of quantitative grading, from month to month and from year to year. Otherwise a pupil was expected to take it in the doses that were prescribed from without. If the pupil left it instead of taking it, if he engaged in physical truancy, or in the mental truancy of mind-wandering and finally built up an emotional revulsion against the subject, he was held to be at fault. No question was raised as to whether the trouble might not lie in the subject-matter or in the way in which it was offered. The principle of interaction makes it clear that failure of adaptation of material to needs and capacities of individuals may cause an experience to be non-educative quite as much as failure of an individual to adapt himself to the material.

The principle of continuity in its educational application means, nevertheless, that the future has to be taken into account at every stage of the educational process. This idea is easily misunderstood and is badly distorted in traditional education. Its assumption is, that by acquiring certain skills and by learning certain subjects which would be needed later (perhaps in college or perhaps in adult life) pupils are as a matter of course made ready for the needs and circumstances of the future. Now "preparation" is a treacherous idea. In a certain sense every experience should do something to prepare a person for later experiences of a deeper and more expansive quality. That is the very meaning of growth, continuity, reconstruction of experience. But it is a mistake to suppose that the mere acquisition of a certain amount of arithmetic, geography, history, etc., which is taught and studied because it may be useful at some time in the future, has this effect, and it is a mistake to suppose that acquisition of skills in reading and figuring will automatically constitute preparation for their right and effective use under conditions very unlike those in which they were acquired.

Almost everyone has had occasion to look back upon his school days and wonder what has become of the knowledge he was supposed to have amassed during his years of schooling, and why it is that the technical skills he acquired have to be learned over again in changed form in order to stand him in good stead. Indeed, he is lucky who does not find that in order to make progress, in order to go ahead intellectually, he does not have to unlearn much of what he learned in school. These questions cannot be disposed of by saying that the subjects were not actually learned, for they were learned at least sufficiently to enable a pupil to pass examinations in them. One trouble is that the subject-matter in question was learned in isolation; it was put, as it were, in a water-tight compartment. When the question is asked, then, what has become of it, where has it gone to, the right answer is that it is still there in the special compartment in which it was originally stowed away. If exactly the same conditions recurred as those under which it was acquired, it would also recur and be available. But it was segregated when it was acquired and hence is so disconnected from the rest of experience that it is not available under the actual conditions of life. It is contrary to the laws of experience that learning of this kind, no matter how thoroughly engrained at the time, should give genuine preparation.

Nor does failure in preparation end at this point. Perhaps the greatest of all pedagogical fallacies is the notion that a person learns only the particular thing he is studying at the time. Collateral learning in the way of formation of enduring attitudes, of likes and dislikes, may be and often is much more important than the spelling lesson or lesson in geography or history that is learned. For these attitudes are fundamentally what count in the future. The most important attitude that can be formed is that of desire to go on learning. If impetus in this direction is weakened instead of being intensified, something much more than mere lack of preparation takes place. The pupil is actually robbed of native capacities which otherwise would enable him to cope with the circumstances that he meets in the course of his life. We often see persons who have had little schooling and in whose case the absence of set schooling proves to be a positive asset. They have at least retained their native common sense and power of judgment, and its exercise in the actual conditions of living has given them the precious gift of ability to learn from the experiences they have. What avail is it to win prescribed amounts of information about geography and history, to win ability to read and write, if in the process the individual loses his own soul: loses his appreciation of things worth while, of the values to which these things are relative; if he loses desire to apply what he has learned and, above all, loses the ability to extract meaning from his future experiences as they occur?

What, then, is the true meaning of preparation in the educational scheme? In the first place, it means that a person, young or old, gets out of his present experience all that there is in it for him at the time in which he has it. When preparation is made the controlling end, then the potentialities of the present are sacrificed to a suppositious future. When this happens, the actual preparation for the future is missed or distorted. The ideal of using the present simply to get ready for the future contradicts itself. It omits, and even shuts out, the very conditions by which a person can be prepared for his future. We always live at the time we live and not at some other time, and only by extracting at each present time the full meaning of each present experience are we prepared for doing the same thing in the future. This is the only preparation which in the long run amounts to anything.

All this means that attentive care must be devoted to the conditions which give each present experience a worthwhile meaning. Instead of inferring that it doesn't make much difference what the present experience is as long as it is enjoyed, the conclusion is the exact opposite. Here is another matter where it is easy to react from one extreme to the other. Because traditional schools tended to sacrifice the present to a remote and more or less unknown future, therefore it comes to be believed that the educator has little responsibility for the kind of present experiences the young undergo. But the relation of the present and the future is not an *Either-Or* affair. The present affects the future anyway. The persons who should have some idea of the connection between the two are those who have achieved maturity. Accordingly, upon them devolves the responsibility for instituting the conditions for the kind of present experience which has a favorable effect upon the future. Education as growth or maturity should be an ever-present process.

2.   ANALYSIS OF REFLECTIVE THINKING*

I. FACTS AND IDEAS

When a situation arises containing a difficulty or perplexity, the person who finds himself in it may take one of a number of courses. He may dodge it, dropping the activity that brought it about, turning to something else. He may indulge in a flight of fancy, imagining himself powerful or wealthy, or in some other way in possession of the means that would enable him to deal with the difficulty. Or, finally, he may face the situation. In this case, he begins to reflect.

*From *How We Think*, by John Dewey, © 1933 by D. C. Heath and Company. Reprinted by permission.

Reflection Includes Observation

The moment he begins to reflect, he begins of necessity to observe in order to take stock of conditions. Some of these observations are made by direct use of the senses; others by recollecting observations previously made either by himself or by others. The person who had the engagement to keep, notes with his eyes his present location, recalls the place where he should arrive at one o'clock, and brings back to mind the means of transportation with which he is acquainted and their respective locations. In this way he gets as clear and distinct a recognition as possible of the nature of the situation with which he has to deal. Some of the conditions are obstacles and others are aids, resources. No matter whether these conditions come to him by direct perception or by memory, they form the '*facts* of the case.' They are the things that are *there,* that have to be reckoned with. Like all facts, they are stubborn. They cannot be got out of the way by magic just because they are disagreeable. It is no use to *wish* they did not exist or were different. They must be taken for just what they are. Hence observation and recollection must be used to the full so as not to glide over or to mistake important features. Until the habit of thinking is well formed, facing the situation to discover the facts requires an effort. For the mind tends to dislike what is unpleasant and so to sheer off from an adequate notice of that which is especially annoying.

Reflection Includes Suggestions

Along with noting the conditions that constitute the facts to be dealt with, suggestions arise of possible courses of action. Thus the person of our illustration thinks of surface cars, elevated trains, and the subway. These alternative suggestions compete with one another. By comparison he judges which alternative is best, which one is the more likely to give a satisfactory solution. The comparison takes place indirectly. The moment one thinks of a possible solution and holds it in suspense, he turns back to the facts. He has now a point of view that leads him to new observations and recollections and to a reconsideration of observations already made in order to test the worth of the suggested way out. Unless he uses the suggestion so as to guide to new observations instead of exercising suspended judgment, he accepts it as soon as it presents itself. Then he falls short of truly reflective thought. The newly noted facts may (and in any complex situation surely will) cause new suggestions to spring up. These become clews to further investigation of conditions. The results of this survey test and correct the proposed inference or suggest a new one. This continuous interaction of the facts disclosed by observation and of the suggested proposals of solution and the suggested methods of dealing with conditions goes on till some suggested solution meets all the conditions of the case and does not run counter to any discoverable feature of it.

Data and Ideas Are Correlative and Indispensable Factors in Reflection

A technical term for the observed facts is *data*. The data form the material that has to be interpreted, accounted for, explained; or, in the case of deliberation as to what to do or how to do it, to be managed and utilized. The suggested solutions for the difficulties disclosed by observation form *ideas*. Data (facts) and ideas (suggestions, possible solutions) thus form the two indispensable and correlative factors of all reflective activity. The two factors are carried on by means respectively of *observation* (in which for convenience is included memory of prior observations of similar cases) and *inference*. The latter runs beyond what is actually noted, beyond what is found, upon careful examination, to be actually present. It relates, therefore, to what is *possible*, rather than to what is actual. It proceeds by anticipation, supposition, conjecture, imagination. All foresight, prediction, planning, as well as theorizing and speculation, are characterized by excursion from the actual into the possible. Hence (as we have already seen) what is inferred demands a double test: first, the process of forming the idea or supposed solution is checked by constant cross reference to the conditions observed to be actually present; secondly, the idea *after* it is formed is tested by *acting* upon it, overtly if possible, otherwise in imagination. The consequences of this action confirm, modify, or refute the idea.

We shall illustrate what has been said by a simple case. Suppose you are walking where there is no regular path. As long as everything goes smoothly, you do not have to think about your walking; your already formed habit takes care of it. Suddenly you find a ditch in your way. You think you will jump it (supposition, plan); but to make sure, you survey it with your eyes (observation), and you find that it is pretty wide and that the bank on the other side is slippery (facts, data). You then wonder if the ditch may not be narrower somewhere else (idea), and you look up and down the stream (observation) to see how matters stand (test of idea by observation). You do not find any good place and so are thrown back upon forming a new plan. As you are casting about, you discover a log (fact again). You ask yourself whether you could not haul that to the ditch and get it across the ditch to use as a bridge (idea again). You judge that idea is worth trying, and so you get the log and manage to put it in place and walk across (test and confirmation by overt action).

If the situation were more complicated, thinking would of course be more elaborate. You can imagine a case in which making a raft, constructing a pontoon bridge, or making a dugout would be the ideas that would finally come to mind and have to be checked by reference to conditions of action (facts). Simple or complicated, relating to what to do in a practical predicament or what to infer in a scientific or philosophic problem, there will always be the two sides: the conditions to be accounted for, dealt with, and the ideas that are plans for dealing with them or are suppositions for interpreting and explaining the phenomena.

In predicting an eclipse, for example, a multitude of observed facts regarding position and movements of earth, sun, and moon, comes in on one side, while on the other side the ideas employed to predict and explain involve extensive mathematical calculations. In a philosophic problem, the facts or data may be remote and not susceptible of direct observation by the senses. But still there will be data, perhaps of science, or of morals, art, or the conclusions of past thinkers, that supply the subject matter to be dealt with and by which theories are checked. On the other side, there are the speculations that come to mind that lead to search for additional subject matter which will both develop the proposed theories as ideas and test their value. Mere facts or data are dead, as far as mind is concerned, unless they are used to suggest and test some idea, some way out of a difficulty. Ideas, on the other hand, are *mere* ideas, idle speculations, fantasies, dreams, unless they are used to guide new observations of, and reflections upon, actual situations, past, present, or future. Finally, they must be brought to some sort of check by actual given material or else remain ideas. Many ideas are of great value as material of poetry, fiction, or the drama, but not as the stuff of knowledge. However, ideas may be of intellectual use to a penetrating mind even when they do not find any immediate reference to actuality, provided they stay in the mind for use when new facts come to light.

II. THE ESSENTIAL FUNCTIONS OF REFLECTIVE ACTIVITY

We now have before us the material for the analysis of a complete act of reflective activity. In the preceding chapter we saw that the two limits of every unit of thinking are a perplexed, troubled, or confused situation at the beginning and a cleared-up, unified, resolved situation at the close. The first of these situations may be called *pre*-reflective. It sets the problem to be solved; out of it grows the question that reflection has to answer. In the final situation the doubt has been dispelled; the situation is *post*-reflective; there results a direct experience of mastery, satisfaction, enjoyment. Here, then, are the limits within which reflection falls.

Five Phases, or Aspects, of Reflective Thought

In between, as states of thinking, are (1) *suggestions,* in which the mind leaps forward to a possible solution; (2) an intellectualization of the difficulty or perplexity that has been *felt* (directly experienced) into a *problem* to be solved, a question for which the answer must be sought; (3) the use of one suggestion after another as a leading idea, or *hypothesis,* to initiate and guide observation and other operations in collection of factual material; (4) the mental elaboration of the idea or supposition as an idea or supposition (*reasoning,* in the sense in which reasoning is a part, not the whole, of inference); and (5) testing the hypothesis by overt or imaginative action.

We shall now take up the five phases, or functions, one by one.

The First Phase, Suggestion

The most 'natural' thing for anyone to do is to go ahead; that is to say, to *act* overtly. The disturbed and perplexed situation arrests such direct activity temporarily. The tendency to continue *acting* nevertheless persists. It is diverted and takes the form of an idea or a suggestion. The *idea* of what to do when we find ourselves 'in a hole' is a substitute for direct action. It is a vicarious, anticipatory way of acting, a kind of dramatic rehearsal. Were there only one suggestion popping up, we should undoubtedly adopt it at once. But where there are two or more, they collide with one another, maintain the state of suspense, and produce further inquiry. The first suggestion in the instance recently cited was to jump the ditch, but the perception of conditions inhibited that suggestion and led to the occurrence of other ideas.

Some inhibition of *direct* action is necessary to the condition of hesitation and delay that is essential to thinking. Thought is, as it were, conduct turned in upon itself and examining its purpose and its conditions, its resources, aids, and difficulties and obstacles.

The Second Phase, Intellectualization

We have already noted that it is artificial, so far as thinking is concerned, to start with a ready-made problem, a problem made out of whole cloth or arising out of a vacuum. In reality such a 'problem' is simply an assigned *task.* There is not at first a situation *and* a problem, much less just a problem and no situation. There is a troubled, perplexed, trying situation, where the difficulty is, as it were, spread throughout the entire situation, infecting it as a whole. If we knew just what the difficulty was and where it lay, the job of reflection would be much easier than it is. As the saying truly goes, a question well put is half answered. In fact, we know what the problem *exactly* is simultaneously with finding a way out and getting it resolved. Problem and solution stand out *completely* at the same time. Up to that point, our grasp of the problem has been more or less vague and tentative.

A blocked suggestion leads us to reinspect the conditions that confront us. Then our uneasiness, the shock of disturbed activity, gets stated in some degree on the basis of observed conditions, of objects. The width of the ditch, the slipperiness of the banks, not the mere presence of a ditch, is the trouble. The difficulty is getting located and defined; it is becoming a true problem, something intellectual, not just an annoyance at being held up in what we are doing. The person who is suddenly blocked and troubled in what he is doing by the thought of an engagement to keep at a time that is near and a place that is distant has the suggestion of getting there at once. But in order to carry this suggestion into effect, he has to find means of transportation. In order to find them he has to note his present position and its distance from the station, the present time, and the interval at his disposal. Thus the perplexity is more precisely located: just so much ground to cover, so much time to do it in.

The word 'problem' often seems too elaborate and dignified to denote what happens in minor cases of reflection. But in every case where reflective activity ensues, there is a process of *intellectualizing* what at first is merely an *emotional* quality of the whole situation. This conversion is effected by noting more definitely the conditions that constitute the trouble and cause the stoppage of action.

The Third Phase, the Guiding Idea, Hypothesis

The first suggestion occurs, spontaneously; it comes to mind automatically; it *springs* up; it "pops," as we have said, "into the mind"; it flashes upon us. There is no direct control of its occurrence; the idea just comes or it does not come; that is all that can be said. There is nothing *intellectual* about its occurrence. The intellectual element consists in *what we do with it,* how we use it, *after* its sudden occurrence as an idea. A controlled use of it is made possible by the state of affairs just described. In the degree in which we define the difficulty (which is effected by stating it in terms of objects), we get a better idea of the kind of solution that is needed. The facts or data set the problem before us, and insight into the problem corrects, modifies, expands the suggestion that originally occurred. In this fashion the suggestion becomes a definite supposition or, stated more technically, a *hypothesis*.

Take the case of a physician examining a patient or a mechanic inspecting a piece of complicated machinery that does not behave properly. There is something wrong, so much is sure. But how to remedy it cannot be told until it is known *what* is wrong. An untrained person is likely to make a wild guess—the suggestion—and then proceed to act upon it in a random way, hoping that by good luck the right thing will be hit upon. So some medicine that appears to have worked before or that a neighbor has recommended is tried. Or the person fusses, monkeys, with the machine, poking here and hammering there on the chance of making the right move. The trained person proceeds in a very different fashion. He *observes* with unusual care, using the methods, the techniques, that the experience of physicians and expert mechanics in general, those familiar with the structure of the organism or the machine, have shown to be helpful in detecting trouble.

The idea of the solution is thus controlled by the diagnosis that has been made. But if the case is at all complicated, the physician or mechanic does not foreclose further thought by assuming that the suggested method of remedy is certainly right. He proceeds to act upon it tentatively rather than decisively. That is, he treats it as a guiding idea, a working hypothesis, and is led by it to make more observations, to collect more facts, so as to see if the *new* material is what the hypothesis calls for. He reasons that *if* the disease is typhoid, *then* certain phenomena will be found; and he looks particularly to see if *just* these conditions are present. Thus both the first and second operations are brought under control; the sense of the problem becomes more adequate and refined and the suggestion ceases to be a *mere* possibility, becoming a *tested* and, if possible, a *measured* probability.

The Fourth Phase, Reasoning(*in the Narrower Sense*)

Observations pertain to what exists in nature. They constitute the facts, and these facts both regulate the formation of suggestions, ideas, hypotheses, and test their probable value as indications of solutions. The ideas, on the other hand, occur, as we say, in our heads, in our minds. They not only occur there, but are capable, as well, of great development there. Given a fertile suggestion occurring in an experienced, well-informed mind, that mind is capable of elaborating it until there results an idea that is quite different from the one with which the mind started.

For example, the idea of heat in the third instance in the earlier chapter was linked up with what the person already know about heat—in his case, its expansive force—and this in turn with the contractive tendency of cold, so that the idea of expansion could be used as an explanatory idea, though the mere idea of heat would not have been of any avail. Heat was quite directly suggested by the observed conditions; water was felt to be hot. But only a mind with some prior information about heat would have reasoned that heat meant expansion, and then used the idea of expansion as a working hypothesis. In more complex cases, there are long trains of reasoning in which one idea leads up to another idea known by previous test to be related to it. The stretch of links brought to light by reasoning depends, of course, upon the store of knowledge that the mind is already in possession of. And this depends not only upon the prior experience and special education of the individual who is carrying on the inquiry, but also upon the state of culture and science of the age and place. Reasoning helps extend knowledge, while at the same time it depends upon what is already known and upon the facilities that exist for communicating knowledge and making it a public, open resource.

A physician to-day can develop, by reasoning from his knowledge, the implications of the disease that symptoms suggest to him as probable in a way that would have been impossible even a generation ago; just as, on the other hand, he can carry his observation of symptoms much farther because of improvement in clinical instruments and the technique of their use.

Reasoning has the same effect upon a suggested solution that more intimate and extensive observation has upon the original trouble. Acceptance of a suggestion in its first form is prevented by looking into it more thoroughly. Conjectures that seem plausible at first sight are often found unfit or even absurd when their full consequences are traced out. Even when reasoning out the bearings of a supposition does not lead to its rejection, it develops the idea into a form in which it is more apposite to the problem. Only when, for example, the conjecture that a pole was an index pole had been thought out in its implications could its particular applicability to the case in hand be judged. Suggestions at first seemingly remote and wild are frequently so transformed by being elaborated into what follows from them as to become apt and fruitful. The development of an idea through reasoning helps supply intervening or intermediate terms which link together into a consistent whole elements that at first seemingly conflict with each other, some leading the mind to one inference and others to an opposed one.

Mathematics as Typical Reasoning. Mathematics affords the typical example of how far can be carried the operation of relating ideas to one another, without having to depend upon the observations of the senses. In geometry we start with a few simple conceptions, line, angle, parallel, surfaces formed by lines meeting, etc., and a few principles defining equalities. Knowing something about the equality of angles made by parallel lines when they intersect a straight line, and knowing, by definition, that a perpendicular to a straight line forms two right angles, by means of a combination of these ideas we readily determine that the sum of the interior angles of a triangle is equal to two right angles. By continuing to trace the implications of theorems already demonstrated, the whole subject of plane figures is finally elaborated. The manipulation of algebraic symbols so as to establish a series of equations and other mathematical functions affords an even more striking example of what can be accomplished by developing the relation of ideas to one another.

When the hypothesis indicated by a series of scientific observations and experiments can be stated in mathematical form, that idea can be transformed to almost any extent, until it assumes a form in which a problem can be dealt with most expeditiously and effectively. Much of the accomplishment of physical science depends upon an intervening mathematical elaboration of ideas. It is not the mere presence of measurements in quantitative form that yields scientific knowledge, but that particular kind of mathematical statement which can be developed by reasoning into other and more fruitful forms—a consideration which is fatal to the claim to scientific standing of many educational measurements merely because they have a quantitative form.

The Fifth Phase, Testing the Hypothesis by Action

The concluding phase is some kind of testing by overt action to give *experimental corroboration, or verification,* of the conjectural idea. Reasoning shows that *if* the *idea* be adopted, certain consequences follow. So far the conclusion is hypothetical or conditional. If when we look we find present all the conditions demanded by the theory, and if we find the characteristic traits called for by rival alternatives to be lacking, the tendency to believe, to accept, is almost irresistible. Sometimes direct observation furnishes corroboration, as in the case of the pole on the boat. In other cases, as in that of the bubbles, experiment is required; that is, *conditions are deliberately arranged in accord with the requirements of an idea or hypothesis to see whether the results theoretically indicated by the idea actually occur.* If it is found that the experimental results agree with the theoretical, or rationally deduced, results, and if there is reason to believe that *only* the conditions in question would yield such results, the confirmation is so strong as to induce a conclusion—at least until contrary facts shall indicate the advisability of its revision.

Of course, verification does not always follow. Sometimes consequences show failure to confirm instead of corroboration. The idea in question is refuted by the court of final appeal. But a great advantage of possession of the habit of reflective activity is that failure is not *mere* failure. It is instructive. The person who really thinks learns quite as much from his failures as from his successes. For a failure indicates to the person whose thinking has been involved in it, and who has not come to it by mere blind chance, what further observations should be made. It suggests to him what modifications should be introduced in the hypothesis upon which he has been operating. It either brings to light a new problem or helps to define and clarify the problem on which he has been engaged. Nothing shows the trained thinker better than the use he makes of his errors and mistakes. What merely annoys and discourages a person not accustomed to thinking, or what starts him out on a new course of aimless attack by mere cut-and-try methods, is a stimulus and a guide to the trained inquirer.

The Sequence of the Five Phases Is Not Fixed

The five phases, terminals, or functions of thought, that we have noted do not follow one another in a set order. On the contrary, each step in genuine thinking does something to perfect the formation of a suggestion and promote its change into a leading idea or directive hypothesis. It does something to promote the location and definition of the problem. Each improvement in the idea leads to new observations that yield new facts or data and help the mind judge more accurately the relevancy of facts already at hand. The elaboration of the hypothesis does not wait until the problem has been defined and adequate hypothesis has been arrived at; it may come in at any intermediate time. And as we have just seen, any particular overt test need not be final; it may be introductory to new observations and new suggestions, according to what happens in consequence of it.

There is, however, an important difference between test by overt action in practical deliberations and in scientific investigations. In the former the practical commitment involved in overt action is much more serious than in the latter. An astronomer or a chemist performs overt actions, but they are for the sake of knowledge; they serve to test and develop his conceptions and theories. In practical matters, the main result desired lies outside of knowledge. One of the great values of thinking, accordingly, is that it defers the commitment to action that is irretrievable, that, once made, cannot be revoked. Even in moral and other practical matters, therefore, a thoughtful person treats his overt deeds as experimental so far as possible; that is to say, while he cannot call them back and must stand their consequences, he gives alert attention to what they teach him about his conduct as well as to the non-intellectual consequences. He makes a problem out of consequences of conduct, looking into the causes from which they probably resulted, especially the causes that lie in his own habits and desires.

In conclusion, we point out that the five phases of reflection that have been described represent only in outline the indispensable traits of reflective thinking. In practice, two of them may telescope, some of them may be passed over hurriedly, and the burden of reaching a conclusion may fall mainly on a single phase, which will then require a seemingly disproportionate development. No set rules can be laid down on such matters. The way they are managed depends upon the intellectual tact and sensitiveness of the individual. When things have come out wrong, it is, however, a wise practice to review the methods by which the unwise decision was reached, and see where the misstep was made.

Culture, Symbolism, and Man *

ERNST CASSIRER

2

A CLUE TO THE NATURE OF MAN: THE SYMBOL

The biologist Johannes von Uexküll has written a book in which he undertakes a critical revision of the principles of biology. Biology, according to Uexküll, is a natural science which has to be developed by the usual empirical methods—the methods of observation and experimentation. Biological thought, on the other hand, does not belong to the same type as physical or chemical thought. Uexküll is a resolute champion of vitalism; he is a defender of the principle of the autonomy of life. Life is an ultimate and self-dependent reality. It cannot be described or explained in terms of physics or chemistry. From this point of view Uexküll evolves a new general scheme of biological research. As a philosopher he is an idealist or phenomenalist. But his phenomenalism is not based upon metaphysical or epistemological considerations; it is founded rather on empirical principles. As he points out, it would be a very naïve sort of dogmatism to assume that there exists an absolute reality of things which is the same for all living beings. Reality is not a unique and homogeneous thing; it is immensely diversified, having as many different schemes and patterns as there are different organisms. Every organism is, so to speak, a monadic being. It has a world of its own because it has an experience of its own. The phenomena that we find in the life of a certain biological species are not transferable to any other species. The experiences—and therefore the realities—of two different organisms are incommensurable

*Reprinted by permission of Yale University Press from *An Essay on Man*, by Ernst Cassirer, pp. 23-41. Copyright © 1944 by Yale University Press.

with one another. In the world of a fly, says Uexküll, we find only "fly things"; in the world of a sea urchin we find only "sea urchin things."

From this general presupposition Uexküll develops a very ingenious and original scheme of the biological world. Wishing to avoid all psychological interpretations, he follows an entirely objective or behavioristic method. The only clue to animal life, he maintains, is given us in the facts of comparative anatomy. If we know the anatomical structure of an animal species, we possess all the necessary data for reconstructing its special mode of experience. A careful study of the structure of the animal body, of the number, the quality, and the distribution of the various sense organs, and the conditions of the nervous system, gives us a perfect image of the inner and outer world of the organism. Uexküll began his investigations with a study of the lowest organisms; he extended them gradually to all the forms of organic life. In a certain sense he refuses to speak of lower or higher forms of life. Life is perfect everywhere; it is the same in the smallest as in the largest circle. Every organism, even the lowest, is not only in a vague sense adapted to (*angepasst*) but entirely fitted into (*eingepasst*) its environment. According to its anatomical structure it possesses a certain *Merknetz* and a certain *Wirknetz*—a receptor system and an effector system. Without the coöperation and equilibrium of these two systems the organism could not survive. The receptor system by which a biological species receives outward stimuli and the effector system by which it reacts to them are in all cases closely interwoven. They are links in one and the same chain which is described by Uexküll as the *functional circle* (*Funktionskreis*) of the animal.[1]

I cannot enter here upon a discussion of Uexküll's biological principles. I have merely referred to his concepts and terminology in order to pose a general question. Is it possible to make use of the scheme proposed by Uexküll for a description and characterization of the *human world*? Obviously this world forms no exception to those biological rules which govern the life of all the other organisms. Yet in the human world we find a new characteristic which appears to be the distinctive mark of human life. The functional circle of man is not only quantitively enlarged; it has also undergone a qualitative change. Man has, as it were, discovered a new method of adapting himself to his environment. Between the receptor system and the effector system, which are to be found in all animal species, we find in man a third link which we may describe as the *symbolic system*. This new acquisition transforms the whole of human life. As compared with the other animals man lives not merely in a broader reality; he lives, so to speak, in a new *dimension* of reality. There is an

[1]See Johannes von Uexküll, *Theoretische Biologie* (2d ed. Berlin, 1938); *Umwelt und Innenwelt der Tiere* (1909; 2d ed. Berlin, 1921).

unmistakable difference between organic reactions and human responses. In the first case a direct and immediate answer is given to an outward stimulus; in the second case the answer is delayed. It is interrupted and retarded by a slow and complicated process of thought. At first sight such a delay may appear to be a very questionable gain. Many philosophers have warned man against this pretended progress. "L'homme qui médite," says Rousseau, "est un animal dépravé": it is not an improvement but a deterioration of human nature to exceed the boundaries of organic life.

Yet there is no remedy against this reversal of the natural order. Man cannot escape from his own achievement. He cannot but adopt the conditions of his own life. No longer in a merely physical universe, man lives in a symbolic universe. Language, myth, art, and religion are parts of this universe. They are the varied threads which weave the symbolic net, the tangled web of human experience. All human progress in thought and experience refines upon and strengthens this net. No longer can man confront reality immediately; he cannot see it, as it were, face to face. Physical reality seems to recede in proportion as man's symbolic activity advances. Instead of dealing with the things themselves man is in a sense constantly conversing with himself. He has so enveloped himself in linguistic forms, in artistic images, in mythical symbols or religious rites that he cannot see or know anything except by the interposition of this artificial medium. His situation is the same in the theoretical as in the practical sphere. Even here man does not live in a world of hard facts, or according to his immediate needs and desires. He lives rather in the midst of imaginary emotions, in hopes and fears, in illusions and disillusions, in his fantasies and dreams. "What disturbs and alarms man," said Epictetus, "are not the things, but his opinions and fancies about the things."

From the point of view at which we have just arrived we may correct and enlarge the classical definition of man. In spite of all the efforts of modern irrationalism this definition of man as an *animal rationale* has not lost its force. Rationality is indeed an inherent feature of all human activities. Mythology itself is not simply a crude mass of superstitions or gross delusions. It is not merely chaotic, for it possesses a systematic or conceptual form.[2] But, on the other hand, it would be impossible to characterize the structure of myth as rational. Language has often been identified with reason, or with the very source of reason. But it is easy to see that this definition fails to cover the whole field. It is a *pars pro toto;* it offers us a part for the whole. For side by side with conceptual language there is an emotional language; side by side with logical or scientific language there is a language of poetic imagination. Primarily language

[2]See Cassirer, *Die Begriffsform im mythischen Denken* (Leipzig, 1921).

does not express thoughts or ideas, but feelings and affections. And even a religion "within the limits of pure reason" as conceived and worked out by Kant is no more than a mere abstraction. It conveys only the ideal shape, only the shadow, of what a genuine and concrete religious life is. The great thinkers who have defined man as an *animal rationale* were not empiricists, nor did they ever intend to give an empirical account of human nature. By this definition they were expressing rather a fundamental moral imperative. Reason is a very inadequate term with which to comprehend the forms of man's cultural life in all their richness and variety. But all these forms are symbolic forms. Hence, instead of defining man as an *animal rationale,* we should define him as an *animal symbolicum.* By so doing we can designate his specific difference, and we can understand the new way open to man—the way to civilization.

3

FROM ANIMAL REACTIONS TO HUMAN RESPONSES

By our definition of man as an *animal symbolicum* we have arrived at our first point of departure for further investigations. But it now becomes imperative that we develop this definition somewhat in order to give it greater precision. That symbolic thought and symbolic behavior are among the most characteristic features of human life, and that the whole progress of human culture is based on these conditions, is undeniable. But are we entitled to consider them as the special endowment of man to the exclusion of all other organic beings? Is not symbolism a principle which we may trace back to a much deeper source, and which has a much broader range of applicability? If we answer this question in the negative we must, as it seems, confess our ignorance concerning many fundamental questions which have perennially occupied the center of attention in the philosophy of human culture. The question of the *origin* of language, of art, of religion becomes unanswerable, and we are left with human culture as a given fact which remains in a sense isolated and, therefore, unintelligible.

It is understandable that scientists have always refused to accept such a solution. They have made great efforts to connect the fact of symbolism with other well-known and more elementary facts. The problem has been felt to be of paramount importance, but unfortunately it has very rarely been approached with an entirely open mind. From the first it has been obscured and confused by other questions which belong to a quite different realm of discourse. Instead of giving us an unbiased description and analysis of the phenomena themselves the discussion of this problem has been converted into a metaphysical dispute. It has become the bone of contention between the different metaphysical systems: between idealism and materialism, spiritualism and naturalism. For all these systems the question of symbolism has become a crucial problem, on which the future shape of science and metaphysics has seemed to hinge.

With this aspect of the problem we are not concerned here, having set for ourselves a much more modest and concrete task. We shall attempt to describe the symbolic attitude of man in a more accurate manner in order to be able to contradistinguish it from other modes of symbolic behavior found throughout the animal kingdom. That animals do not always react to stimuli in a direct way, that they are capable of an indirect reaction, is evidently beyond question. The well-known experiments of Pavlov provide us with a rich body of empirical evidence concerning the so-called representative stimuli. In the case of the anthropoid apes a very interesting experimental study by Wolfe has shown the effectiveness of "token rewards." The animals learned to respond to tokens as substitute for food rewards in the same way in which they responded to food itself.[3] According to Wolfe the results of varied and protracted training experiments have demonstrated that symbolic processes occur in the behavior of anthropoid apes. Robert M. Yerkes, who describes these experiments in his latest book, draws from them an important general conclusion.

That they [symbolic processes] are relatively rare and difficult to observe is evident. One may fairly continue to question their existence, but I suspect that they presently will be identified as antecedents of human symbolic processes. Thus we leave this subject at a most exciting stage of development, when discoveries of moment seem imminent.[4]

It would be premature to make any predictions with regard to the future development of this problem. The field must be left open for future investigations. The interpretation of the experimental facts, on the other hand, always depends on certain fundamental concepts which have to be clarified before the empirical material can bear its fruit. Modern psychology and psychobiology take this fact into account. It seems to me highly significant that nowadays it is not the philosophers but the empirical observers and investigators who appear to be taking the leading roles in solving this problem. The latter tell us that after all the problem is not merely an empirical one but to a great degree a logical one. George Révész has recently published a series of articles in which he starts off

[3]J. B. Wolfe, "Effectiveness of Token-rewards for Chimpanzees," Comparative Psychology Monographs, 12, No. 5.
[4]Robert M. Yerkes, Chimpanzees. A Laboratory Colony (New Haven, Yale University Press, 1943), p. 189.

with the proposition that the warmly debated question of so-called *animal language* cannot be solved on the basis of mere facts of animal psychology. Everyone who examines the different psychological theses and theories with an unbiased and critical mind must come at last to the conclusion that the problem cannot be cleared up by simply referring to forms of animal communication and to certain animal accomplishments which are gained by drill and training. All such accomplishments admit of the most contradictory interpretations. Hence it is necessary, first of all, to find a correct logical starting point, one which can lead us to a natural and sound interpretation of the empirical facts. This starting point is the *definition of speech* (*die Begriffsbestimmung der Sprache*).[5] But instead of giving a ready-made definition of speech, it would be better perhaps to proceed along tentative lines. Speech is not a simple and uniform phenomenon. It consists of different elements which, both biologically and systematically, are not on the same level. We must try to find the order and interrelationships of the constituent elements; we must, as it were, distinguish the various geological strata of speech. The first and most fundamental stratum is evidently the language of the emotions. A great portion of all human utterance still belongs to this stratum. But there is a form of speech that shows us quite a different type. Here the world is by no means a mere interjection; it is not an involuntary expression of feeling, but a part of a sentence which has a definite syntactical and logical structure.[6] It is true that even in highly developed, in theoretical language the connection with the first element is not entirely broken off. Scarcely a sentence can be found—except perhaps the pure formal sentences of mathematics—without a certain affective or emotional tinge.[7] Analogies and parallels to emotional language may be found in abundance in the animal world. As regards chimpanzees Wolfgang Koehler states that they achieve a considerable degree of expression by means of gesture. Rage, terror, despair, grief, pleading, desire, playfulness, and pleasure are readily expressed in this manner. Nevertheless one element, which is characteristic of and indispensable to all human language, is missing: we find no signs which have an objective reference or meaning. "It may be taken as positively proved," says Koehler,

> that their gamut of *phonetics* is entirely "subjective," and can only express emotions, never designate or describe objects. But they have so many

[5]G. Révész, "Die menschlichen Kommunikationsformen und die sogenannte Tiersprache," *Proceedings of the Netherlands Akademie van Wetenschappen*, XLIII (1940), Nos. 9, 10; XLIV (1941), No. 1.

[6]For the distinction between mere emotive utterances and "the normal type of communication of ideas that is speech," see the introductory remarks of Edward Sapir, *Language* (New York, Harcourt, Brace, 1921).

[7]For further details see Charles Bally, *Le langage et la vie* (Paris, 1936).

phonetic elements which are also common to human languages, that their lack of articulate speech cannot be ascribed to *secondary* (glosso-labial) limitations. Their gestures too, of face and body like their expression in sound, never designate or "describe" objects (Buhler).[8]

Here we touch upon the crucial point in our whole problem. The difference between *propositional language* and *emotional language* is the real landmark between the human and the animal world. All the theories and observations concerning animal language are wide of the mark if they fail to recognize this fundamental difference.[9] In all the literature of the subject there does not seem to be a single conclusive proof of the fact that any animal ever made the decisive step from subjective to objective, from affective to propositional language. Koehler insists emphatically that speech is definitely beyond the powers of anthropoid apes. He maintains that the lack of this invaluable technical aid and the great limitation of those very important components of thought, the so-called images, constitute the causes which prevent animals from ever achieving even the least beginnings of cultural development.[10] The same conclusion has been reached by Révész. Speech, he asserts, is an anthropological concept which accordingly should be entirely discarded from the study of animal psychology. If we proceed from a clear and precise definition of speech, all the other forms of utterances, which we also find in animals, are automatically eliminated.[11] Yerkes, who has studied the problem with special interest, speaks in a more positive tone. He is convinced that even with respect to language and symbolism there exists a close relationship between man and the anthropoid apes. "This suggests," he writes, "that we may have happened upon an early phylogenetic stage in the evolution of symbolic process. There is abundant evidence that various other types of sign process than the symbolic are of frequent occurrence and function effectively in the chimpanzee."[12] Yet all this remains definitely pre-linguistic. Even in the judgment of Yerkes all these functional expressions

[8]Wolfgang Koehler, "Zur Psychologie des Schimpansen," *Psychologische Forschung*, I (1921), 27. Cf. the English ed., *The Mentality of Apes* (New York, Harcourt, Brace, 1925), App., p. 317.

[9]An early attempt to make a sharp distinction between propositional and emotional language was made in the field of the psychopathology of language. The English neurologist Jackson introduced the term "propositional language" in order to account for some very interesting pathological phenomena. He found that many patients suffering from aphasia had by no means lost the use of speech but that they could not employ their words in an objective, propositional sense. Jackson's distinction proved to be very fruitful. It has played an important part in the further development of the psychopathology of language. For details see Cassirer, *Philosophie der symbolischen Formen*, III, chap. vi, 237–323.

[10]Koehler, *The Mentality of Apes*, p. 277.

[11]Révész, *op. cit.*, XLIII, Pt. II (1940), 33.

[12]Yerkes and Nissen, "Pre-linguistic Sign Behavior in Chimpanzee," *Science*, LXXXIX, 587.

are exceedingly rudimentary, simple, and of limited usefulness by comparison with human cognitive processes.[13] The genetic question is not to be confused here with the analytical and phenomenological question. The logical analysis of human speech always leads us to an element of prime importance which has no parallel in the animal world. The general theory of evolution in no sense stands in the way of the acknowledgment of this fact. Even in the field of the phenomena of organic nature we have learned that evolution does not exclude a sort of original creation. The fact of sudden mutation and of emergent evolution has to be admitted. Modern biology no longer speaks of evolution in terms of earlier Darwinism; nor does it explain the causes of evolution in the same way. We may readily admit that the anthropoid apes, in the development of certain symbolic processes, have made a significant forward step. But again we must insist that they did not reach the threshold of the human world. They entered, as it were, a blind alley.

For the sake of a clear statement of the problem we must carefully distinguish between *signs* and *symbols*. That we find rather complex systems of signs and signals in animal behavior seems to be an ascertained fact. We may even say that some animals, especially domesticated animals, are extremely susceptible to signs.[14] A dog will react to the slightest changes in the behavior of his master; he will even distinguish the expressions of a human face or the modulations of a human voice.[15] But it is a far cry from these phenomena to an understanding of symbolic and

[13]Yerkes, *Chimpanzees*, p. 189.

[14]This susceptibility has, for instance, been proved in the famous case of "clever Hans" which a few decades ago created something of a sensation among psychobiologists. Clever Hans was a horse which appeared to possess an astounding intelligence. He could even master rather complicated arithmetical problems, extract cube roots, and so on, stamping on the ground as many times as the solution of the problem required. A special committee of psychologists and other scientists was called on to investigate the case. It soon became clear that the animal reacted to certain involuntary movements of its owner. When the owner was absent or did not understand the question, the horse could not answer it.

[15]To illustrate this point I should like to mention another very revealing example. The psychobiologist, Dr. Pfungst, who had developed some new and interesting methods for the study of animal behavior, once told me that he had received a letter from a major about a curious problem. The major had a dog which accompanied him on his walks. Whenever the master got ready to go out the animal showed signs of great joy and excitement. But one day the major decided to try a little experiment. Pretending to go out, he put on his hat, took his cane, and made the customary preparations—without, however, any intention of going for a walk. To his great surprise the dog was not in the least deceived; he remained quietly in his corner. After a brief period of observation Dr. Pfungst was able to solve the mystery. In the major's room there was a desk with a drawer which contained some valuable and important documents. The major had formed the habit of rattling this drawer before leaving the house in order to make sure that it was safely locked. He did not do so the day he did not intend to go out. But for the dog this had become a signal, a necessary element of the walk-situation. Without this signal the dog did not react.

human speech. The famous experiments of Pavlov prove only that animals can easily be trained to react not merely to direct stimuli but to all sorts of mediate or representative stimuli. A bell, for example, may become a "sign for dinner," and an animal may be trained not to touch its food when this sign is absent. But from this we learn only that the experimenter, in this case, has succeeded in changing the food-situation of the animal. He has complicated this situation by voluntarily introducing into it a new element. All the phenomena which are commonly described as conditioned reflexes are not merely very far from but opposed to the essential character of human symbolic thought. Symbols—in the proper sense of this term—cannot be reduced to mere signals. Signals and symbols belong to two different universes of discourse: a signal is a part of the physical world of being; a symbol is a part of the human world of meaning. Signals are "operators"; symbols are "designators."[16] Signals, even when understood and used as such, have nevertheless a sort of physical or substantial being; symbols have only a functional value.

Bearing this distinction in mind, we can find an approach to one of the most controverted problems. The question of the *intelligence of animals* has always been one of the greatest puzzles of anthropological philosophy. Tremendous efforts, both of thought and observation, have been expended on answers to this question. But the ambiguity and vagueness of the very term "intelligence" has always stood in the way of a clear solution. How can we hope to answer a question whose import we do not understand? Metaphysicians and scientists, naturalists and theologians have used the word intelligence in varying and contradictory senses. Some psychologists and psychobiologists have flatly refused to speak of the intelligence of animals. In all animal behavior they saw only the play of a certain automatism. This thesis had behind it the authority of Descartes; yet it has been reasserted in modern psychology. "The animal," says E. L. Thorndike in his work on animal intelligence, "does not think one is like the other, nor does it, as is so often said, mistake one for the other. It does not think *about* it at all; it just thinks *it* . . . The idea that animals react to a particular and absolutely defined and realized sense-impression, and that a similar reaction to a sense-impression which varies from the first proves an association by similarity, is a myth."[17] Later and more exact observations led to a different conclusion. In the case of the higher animals it became clear that they were able to solve rather difficult problems and that these solutions were not brought about in a merely mechanical way, by trial and error. As Koehler points out, the most striking difference

[16]For the distinction between operators and designators see Charles Morris, "The Foundation of the Theory of Signs," *Encyclopedia of the Unified Sciences* (1938).

[17]Edward L. Thorndike, *Animal Intelligence* (New York, Macmillan, 1911), pp. 119 ff.

exists between a mere chance solution and a genuine solution, so that the one can easily be distinguished from the other. That at least some of the reactions of the higher animals are not merely a product of chance but guided by insight appears to be incontestable.[18] If by intelligence we understand either adjustment to the immediate environment or adaptive modification of environment, we must certainly ascribe to animals a comparatively highly developed intelligence. It must also be conceded that not all animal actions are governed by the presence of an immediate stimulus. The animal is capable of all sorts of detours in its reactions. It may learn not only to use implements but even to invent tools for its purposes. Hence some psychobiologists do not hesitate to speak of a creative or constructive imagination in animals.[19] But neither this intelligence nor this imagination is of the specifically human type. In short, we may say that the animal possesses a practical imagination and intelligence whereas man alone has developed a new form: a *symbolic imagination and intelligence.*

Moreover, in the mental development of the individual mind the transition from one form to the other—from a merely practical attitude to a symbolic attitude—is evident. But here this step is the final result of a slow and continuous process. By the usual methods of psychological observation it is not easy to distinguish the individual stages of this complicated process. There is, however, another way to obtain full insight into the general character and paramount importance of this transition. Nature itself has here, so to speak, made an experiment capable of throwing unexpected light upon the point in question. We have the classical cases of Laura Bridgman and Helen Keller, two blind deaf-mute children, who by means of special methods learned to speak. Although both cases are well known and have often been treated in psychological literature,[20] I must nevertheless remind the reader of them once more because they contain perhaps the best illustration of the general problem with which we are here concerned. Mrs. Sullivan, the teacher of Helen Keller, has recorded the exact date on which the child really began to understand the meaning and function of human language. I quote her own words:

> I must write you a line this morning because something very important has happened. Helen has taken the second great step in her education. She

---

[18]See Koehler, *op. cit.*, chap. vii, " 'Chance' and 'Imitation.' "

[19]See R. M. and A. W. Yerkes, *The Great Apes* (New Haven, Yale University Press, 1929), pp. 368 ff., 520 ff.

[20]For Laura Bridgman see Maud Howe and Florence Howe Hall, *Laura Bridgman* (Boston, 1903); Mary Swift Lamson, *Life and Education of Laura Dewey Bridgman* (Boston, 1881); Wilhelm Jerusalem, *Laura Bridgman. Erziehung einer Taubstumm-Blinden* (Berlin, 1905).

has learned that *everything has a name, and that the manual alphabet is the key to everything she wants to know.*

. . . This morning, while she was washing, she wanted to know the name for "water." When she wants to know the name of anything, she points to it and pats my hand. I spelled "w-a-t-e-r" and thought no more about it until after breakfast. . . . [Later on] we went out to the pump house, and I made Helen hold her mug under the spout while I pumped. As the cold water gushed forth, filling the mug, I spelled "w-a-t-e-r" in Helen's free hand. The word coming so close upon the sensation of cold water rushing over her hand seemed to startle her. She dropped the mug and stood as one transfixed. A new light came into her face. She spelled "water" several times. Then she dropped on the ground and asked for its name and pointed to the pump and the trellis and suddenly turning round she asked for my name. I spelled "teacher." All the way back to the house she was highly excited, and learned the name of every object she touched, so that in a few hours she had added thirty new words to her vocabulary. The next morning she got up like a radiant fairy. She has flitted from object to object, asking the name of everything and kissing me for very gladness. . . . Everything must have a name now. Wherever we go, she asks eagerly for the names of things she has not learned at home. She is anxious for her friends to spell, and eager to teach the letters to everyone she meets. She drops the signs and pantomime she used before, as soon as she has words to supply their place, and the acquirement of a new word affords her the liveliest pleasure. And we notice that her face grows more expressive each day.[21]

The decisive step leading from the use of signs and pantomime to the use of words, that is, of symbols, could scarcely be described in a more striking manner. What was the child's real discovery at this moment? Helen Keller had previously learned to combine a certain thing or event with a certain sign of the manual alphabet. A fixed association had been established between these things and certain tactile impressions. But a series of such associations, even if they are repeated and amplified, still does not imply an understanding of what human speech is and means. In order to arrive at such an understanding the child had to make a new and much more significant discovery. It had to understand that *everything has a name*—that the symbolic function is not restricted to particular cases but is a principle of *universal* applicability which encompasses the whole field of human thought. In the case of Helen Keller this discovery came as a sudden shock. She was a girl seven years of age who, with the exception of defects in the use of certain sense organs, was in an excellent state of health and possessed of a highly developed mind. By the neglect of her education she had been very much retarded. Then, suddenly, the crucial

[21]See Helen Keller, *The Story of My Life* (New York, Doubleday, Page & Co., 1902, 1903), Supplementary Account of Helen Keller's Life and Education, pp. 315 ff.

development takes place. It works like an intellectual revolution. The child begins to see the world in a new light. It has learned the use of words not merely as mechanical signs or signals but as an entirely new instrument of thought. A new horizon is opened up, and henceforth the child will roam at will in this incomparably wider and freer area.

The same can be shown in the case of Laura Bridgman, though hers is a less spectacular story. Both in mental ability and in intellectual development Laura Bridgman was greatly inferior to Helen Keller. Her life and education do not contain the same dramatic elements we find in Helen Keller. Yet in both cases the same typical elements are present. After Laura Bridgman had learned the use of the finger-alphabet she, too, suddenly reached the point at which she began to understand the symbolism of human speech. In this respect we find a surprising parallelism between the two cases. "I shall never forget." writes Miss Drew, one of the first teachers of Laura Bridgman, "the first meal taken after she appreciated the use of the finger-alphabet. Every article that she touched must have a name; and I was obliged to call some one to help me wait upon the other children, while she kept me busy in spelling the new words."[22]

The principle of symbolism, with its universality, validity, and general applicability, is the magic word, the Open Sesame! giving access to the specifically human world, to the world of human culture. Once man is in possession of this magic key further progress is assured. Such progress is evidently not obstructed or made impossible by any lack in the sense material. The case of Helen Keller, who reached a very high degree of mental development and intellectual culture, shows us clearly and irrefutably that a human being in the construction of his human world is not dependent upon the quality of his sense material. If the theories of sensationalism were right, if every idea were nothing but a faint copy of an original sense impression, then the condition of a blind, deaf, and dumb child would indeed be desperate. For it would be deprived of the very sources of human knowledge; it would be, as it were, an exile from reality. But if we study Helen Keller's autobiography we are at once aware that this is untrue, and at the same time we understand why it is untrue. Human culture derives its specific character and its intellectual and moral values, not from the material of which it consists, but from its form, its architectural structure. And this form may be expressed in any sense material. Vocal language has a very great technical advantage over tactile language; but the technical defects of the latter do not destroy its essential use. The free development of symbolic thought and symbolic

[22]See Mary Swift Lamson, *Life and Education of Laura Dewey Bridgman, the Deaf, Dumb, and Blind Girl* (Boston, Houghton, Mifflin Co., 1881), pp. 7 ff.

expression is not obstructed by the use of tactile signs in the place of vocal ones. If the child has succeeded in grasping the meaning of human language, it does not matter in which particular material this meaning is accessible to it. As the case of Helen Keller proves, man can construct his symbolic world out of the poorest and scantiest materials. The thing of vital importance is not the individual bricks and stones but their general *function* as architectural form. In the realm of speech it is their general symbolic function which vivifies the material signs and "makes them speak." Without this vivifying principle the human world would indeed remain deaf and mute. With this principle, even the world of a deaf, dumb, and blind child can become incomparably broader and richer than the world of the most highly developed animal.

Universal applicability, owing to the fact that everything has a name, is one of the greatest prerogatives of human symbolism. But it is not the only one. There is still another characteristic of symbols which accompanies and complements this one, and forms its necessary correlate. A symbol is not only universal but extremely variable. I can express the same meaning in various languages; and even within the limits of a single language a certain thought or idea may be expressed in quite different terms. A sign or signal is related to the thing to which it refers in a fixed and unique way. Any one concrete and individual sign refers to a certain individual thing. In Pavlov's experiments the dogs could easily be trained to reach for food only upon being given special signs; they would not eat until they heard a particular sound which could be chosen at the discretion of the experimenter. But this bears no analogy, as it has often been interpreted, to human symbolism; on the contrary, it is in opposition to symbolism. A genuine human symbol is characterized not by its uniformity but by its versatility. It is not rigid or inflexible but mobile. It is true that the full *awareness* of this mobility seems to be a rather late achievement in man's intellectual and cultural development. In primitive mentality this awareness is very seldom attained. Here the symbol is still regarded as a property of the thing like other physical properties. In mythical thought the name of a god is an integral part of the nature of the god. If I do not call the god by his right name, then the spell or prayer becomes ineffective. The same holds good for symbolic actions. A religious rite, a sacrifice, must always be performed in the same invariable way and in the same order if it is to have its effect.[23] Children are often greatly confused when they first learn that not every name of an object is a "proper name," that the same thing may have quite different names in different languages. They tend to think that a thing "is" what it is called. But this only a first step. Every normal child will learn very soon that it

[23]For further details see Cassirer, *Sprache und Mythos* (Leipzig, 1925).

can use various symbols to express the same wish or thought. For this variability and mobility there is apparently no parallel in the animal world.[24] Long before Laura Bridgman had learned to speak, she had developed a very curious mode of expression, a language of her own. This language did not consist of articulated sounds but only of various noises, which are described as "emotional noises." She was in the habit of uttering these sounds in the presence of certain persons. Thus they became entirely individualized; every person in her environment was greeted by a special noise. "Whenever she met unexpectedly an acquaintance," writes Dr. Lieber, "I found that she repeatedly uttered the word for that person before she began to speak. It was the utterance of pleasurable recognition."[25] But when by means of the finger alphabet the child had grasped the meaning of human language the case was altered. Now the sound really became a name: and this name was not bound to an individual person but could be changed if the circumstances seemed to require it. One day, for instance, Laura Bridgman had a letter from her former teacher, Miss Drew, who, in the meantime, by her marriage had become a Mrs. Morton. In this letter she was invited to visit her teacher. This gave her great pleasure, but she found fault with Miss Drew because she had signed the letter with her old name instead of using the name of her husband. She even said that now she must find another noise for her teacher, as the one for Drew must not be the same as that for Morton.[26] It is clear that the former "noises" have here undergone an important and very interesting change in meaning. They are no longer special utterances, inseparable from a particular concrete situation. They have become abstract names. For the new name invented by the child did not designate a new individual but the same individual in a new relationship.

Another important aspect of our general problem now emerges—the problem of the *dependence of relational thought upon symbolic thought.* Without a complex system of symbols relational thought cannot arise at all, much less reach its full development. It would not be correct to say that the mere *awareness* of relations presupposes an intellectual act, an act of logical or abstract thought. Such an awareness is necessary even in elementary acts of perception. The sensationalist theories used to describe perception as a mosaic of simple sense data. Thinkers of this persuasion constantly overlooked the fact that sensation itself is by no means a mere aggregate or bundle of isolated impressions. Modern Gestalt psychology has corrected this view. It has shown that the very simplest perceptual processes imply fundamental structural elements, certain patterns or confi-

[24]For this problem see W. M. Urban, *Language and Reality*, Pt. I, iii, 95 ff.
[25]See Francis Lieber, "A Paper on the Vocal Sounds of Laura Bridgman," *Smithsonian Contributions to Knowledge*, II, Art. 2, p. 27.
[26]See Mary Swift Lamson, *op. cit.*, p. 84.

gurations. This principle holds both for the human and the animal world. Even in comparatively low stages of animal life the presence of these structural elements—especially of spatial and optical structures—has been experimentally proved.[27] The mere awareness of relations cannot, therefore, be regarded as a specific feature of human consciousness. We do find, however, in man a special type of relational thought which has no parallel in the animal world. In man an ability to isolate relations—to consider them in their abstract meaning—has developed. In order to grasp this meaning man is no longer dependent upon concrete sense data, upon visual, auditory, tactile, kinesthetic data. He considers these relations "in themselves"— αὐτὸ καθ' αὐτό, as Plato said. Geometry is the classic example of this turning point in man's intellectual life. Even in elementary geometry we are not bound to the apprehension of concrete individual figures. We are not concerned with physical things or perceptual objects, for we are studying universal spatial relations for whose expression we have an adequate symbolism. Without the preliminary step of human language such an achievement would not be possible. In all the tests which have been made of the processes of abstraction or generalization in animals, this point has become evident. Koehler succeeded in showing the ability of chimpanzees to respond to the *relation* between two or more objects instead of to a particular object. Confronted by two food-containing boxes, the chimpanzee by reason of previous general training would constantly choose the larger—even though the particular object selected might in a previous experiment have been rejected as the smaller of the pair. Similar capacity to respond to the nearer object, the brighter, the bluer, rather than to a particular box was demonstrated. Koehler's results were confirmed and extended by later experiments. It could be shown that the higher animals are capable of what has been called the "isolation of perceptual factors." They have the potentiality for singling out a particular perceptual quality of the experimental situation and reacting accordingly. In this sense animals are able to abstract color from size and shape or shape from size and color. In some experiments made by Mrs. Kohts a chimpanzee was able to select from a collection of objects varying extremely in visual qualities those which had some one quality in common; it could, for instance, pick out all objects of a given color and place them in a receiving box. These examples seem to prove that the higher animals are capable of that process which Hume in his theory of knowledge terms making a "*distinction of reason.*"[28] But all the experimenters engaged in

[27]See Wolfgang Koehler, "Optische Untersuchungen am Schimpansen und am Haushuhn; Nachweis einfacher Strukturfunktionen beim Schimpansen und beim Haushuhn," *Abhandlungen der Berliner Akademie der Wissenschaften* (1915, 1918).

[28]Hume's theory of the "distinction of reason" is explained in his *Treatise of Human Nature*, Pt. I, sec. 7 (London, Green and Grose, 1874), I, 332 ff.

these investigations have also emphasized the rarity, the rudimentariness, and the imperfection of these processes. Even after they have learned to single out a particular quality and to reach toward this, animals are liable to all sorts of curious mistakes.[29] If there are certain traces of a *distinctio rationis* in the animal world, they are, as it were, nipped in the bud. They cannot develop because they do not possess that invaluable and indeed indispensable aid of human speech, of a system of symbols.

The first thinker to have clear insight into this problem was Herder. He spoke as a philosopher of humanity who wished to pose the question in entirely "human" terms. Rejecting the metaphysical or theological thesis of a supernatural or divine origin of language, Herder begins with a critical revision of the question itself. Speech is not an object, a physical thing for which we may seek a natural or a supernatural cause. It is a process, a general function of the human mind. Psychologically we cannot describe this process in the terminology which was used by all the psychological schools of the eighteenth century. According to Herder speech is not an artificial creation of reason, nor is it to be accounted for by a special mechanism of associations. In his own attempt to set forth the nature of language Herder lays the whole stress upon what he calls "*reflection.*" Reflection or reflective thought is the ability of man to single out from the whole undiscriminated mass of the stream of floating sensuous phenomena certain fixed elements in order to isolate them and to concentrate attention upon them.

> Man evinces reflection when the power of his soul acts so freely that it can segregate from the whole ocean of sensation surging through all his senses *one* wave, as it were; and that it can stay this wave, draw attention to it, and be aware of this attention. He evinces reflection when from the whole wavering dream of images rushing through his senses he can collect himself into a moment of waking, dwell on *one* image spontaneously, observe it clearly and more quietly, and abstract characteristics showing him that *this* and no other is the object. Thus he evinces reflection when he can not only perceive all the qualities vividly or clearly but when he can *recognize* one or several of them as distinctive qualities. . . . Now by what means did this recognition come about? Through a characteristic which he had to abstract, and which, as an element of consciousness, presented itself clearly. Well then, let us exclaim: Eureka! This initial character of consciousness was the language of the soul. With this, human language is created.[30]

This has more the appearance of a poetical portrait than of a logical analysis of human speech. Herder's theory of the origin of language remained entirely speculative. It did not proceed from a general theory of

---

[29]Examples are given by Yerkes in *Chimpanzees*, pp. 103 ff.

[30]Herder, *Über den Ursprung der Sprache* (1772) "Werke," ed. Suphan, V, 34 ff.

knowledge, nor from an observation of empirical facts. It was based on his ideal of humanity and on his profound intuition of the character and development of human culture. Nevertheless it contains logical and psychological elements of the most valuable sort. All the processes of generalization or abstraction in animals that have been investigated and described with accuracy[31] clearly lack the distinctive mark emphasized by Herder. Later on, however, Herder's view found a rather unexpected clarification and confirmation from a quite different quarter. Recent research in the field of the *psychopathology of language* has led to the conclusion that the loss, or severe impairment, of speech caused by brain injury is never an isolated phenomenon. Such a defect alters the whole character of human behavior. Patients suffering from aphasia or other kindred diseases have not only lost the use of words but have undergone corresponding changes in personality. Such changes are scarcely observable in their outward behavior, for here they tend to act in a perfectly normal manner. They can perform the tasks of everyday life; some of them even develop considerable skill in all tests of this sort. But they are at a complete loss as soon as the solution of the problem requires any specific theoretical or reflective activity. They are no longer able to think in general concepts or categories. Having lost their grip on universals, they stick to the immediate facts, to concrete situations. Such patients are unable to perform any task which can be executed only by means of a comprehension of the abstract.[32] All this is highly significant, for it shows us to what degree that type of thought which Herder called reflective is dependent on symbolic thought. Without symbolism the life of man would be like that of the prisoners in the cave of Plato's famous simile. Man's life would be confined within the limits of his biological needs and his practical interests; it could find no access to the "ideal world" which is opened to him from different sides by religion, art, philosophy, science.

[31]See, for instance, the remarks of R. M. Yerkes about "generalized responses" in the chimpanzee, *op. cit.*, pp. 130 ff.

[32]A detailed and highly interesting account of these phenomena will be found in various publications of K. Goldstein and A. Gelb. Goldstein has given a general survey of his theoretical views in *Human Nature in the Light of Psychopathology*, the William James Lectures delivered at Harvard University, 1937–38 (Cambridge, Mass., Harvard University Press, 1940). I have discussed the question from a general philosophical point of view in *Philosophie der symbolischen Formen*, III, vi, 237–323.

Tacit Knowing*

MICHAEL POLANYI

Some of you may know that I turned to philosophy as an afterthought to my career as a scientist. I would like to tell you what I was after in making this change, for it will also explain the general task to which my present lecture should introduce us.

I first met questions of philosophy when I came up against the Soviet ideology under Stalin which denied justification to the pursuit of science. I remember a conversation I had with Bukharin in Moscow in 1935. Though he was heading toward his fall and execution three years later, he was still a leading theoretician of the Communist party. When I asked him about the pursuit of pure science in Soviet Russia, he said that pure science was a morbid symptom of a class society; under socialism the conception of science pursued for its own sake would disappear, for the interests of scientists would spontaneously turn to problems of the current Five-Year Plan.

I was struck by the fact that this denial of the very existence of independent scientific thought came from a socialist theory which derived its tremendous persuasive power from its claim to scientific certainty. The scientific outlook appeared to have produced a mechanical conception of man and history in which there was no place for science itself. This conception denied altogether any intrinsic power to thought and thus denied also any grounds for claiming freedom of thought.

I saw also that this self-immolation of the mind was actuated by powerful moral motives. The mechanical course of history was to bring universal justice. Scientific skepticism would trust only material necessity for achieving universal brotherhood. Skepticism and utopianism had thus fused into a new skeptical fanaticism.

It seemed to me then that our whole civilization was pervaded by the dissonance of an extreme critical lucidity and an intense moral conscience, and that this combination had generated both our tight-lipped modern revolutions and the tormented self-doubt of modern man outside revolutionary movements. So I resolved to inquire into the roots of this condition.

My search has led me to a novel idea of human knowledge from which a harmonious view of thought and existence, rooted in the universe, seems to emerge.

I shall reconsider human knowledge by starting from the fact that *we can know more than we can tell.* This fact seems obvious enough; but it is not easy to say exactly what it means. Take an example. We know a person's face, and can recognize it among a thousand, indeed among a million. Yet we usually cannot tell how we recognize a face we know. So most of this knowledge cannot be put into words. But the police have recently introduced a method by which we can communicate much of this knowledge. They have made a large collection of pictures showing a variety of noses, mouths, and other features. From these the witness selects the particulars of the face he knows, and the pieces can then be put together to form a reasonably good likeness of the face. This may suggest that we can communicate, after all, our knowledge of a physiognomy, provided we are given adequate means for expressing ourselves. But the application of the police method does not change the fact that previous to it we did know more than we could tell at the time. Moreover, we can use the police method only be knowing how to match the features we remember with those in the collection, and we cannot tell how we do this. This very act of communication displays a knowledge that we cannot tell.

There are many other instances of the recognition of a characteristic physiognomy—some commonplace, others more technical—which have the same structure as the identification of a person. We recognize the moods of the human face, without being able to tell, except quite vaguely, by what signs we know it. At the universities great efforts are spent in practical classes to teach students to identify cases of diseases and specimens of rocks, of plants and animals. All descriptive sciences study physiognomies that cannot be fully described in words, nor even by pictures.

But can it not be argued, once more, that the possibility of teaching these appearances by practical exercises proves that we can tell our knowledge of them? The answer is that we can do so only by relying on the pupil's intelligent co-operation for catching the meaning of the demonstration. Indeed, any definition of a word denoting an external thing must ultimately rely on pointing at such a thing. This naming-cum-pointing is called "an ostensive definition"; and this philosophic expression conceals a gap to be bridged by an intelligent effort on the part of the person to whom we want to tell what the word means. Our message had left something behind that we could not tell, and its reception must rely on it that the person addressed will discover that which we have not been able to communicate.

Gestalt psychology has demonstrated that we may know a physiognomy by integrating our awareness of its particulars without being able to identify these particulars, and my analysis of knowledge is closely linked to this discovery of Gestalt psychology. But I shall attend to aspects of Gestalt which have been hitherto neglected. Gestalt psychology has assumed that perception of a physiognomy takes place through the spontaneous equilibration of its particulars impressed on the retina or on the brain. However, I am looking at Gestalt, on the contrary, as the outcome of an active shaping of experience performed in the pursuit of knowledge. This shaping or integrating I hold to be the great and indispensable tacit power by which all knowledge is discovered and, once discovered, is held to be true.

The structure of Gestalt is then recast into a logic of tacit thought, and this changes the range and perspective of the whole subject. The highest forms of integration loom largest now. These are manifested in the tacit power of scientific and artistic genius. The art of the expert diagnostician may be listed next, as a somewhat impoverished form of discovery, and we may put in the same class the performance of skills, whether artistic, athletic, or technical. We have here examples of knowing, both of a more intellectual and more practical kind; both the *"wissen"* and *"können"* of the Germans, or the "knowing what" and the "knowing how" of Gilbert Ryle. These two aspects of knowing have a similar structure and neither is ever present without the other. This is particularly clear in the art of diagnosing, which intimately combines skillful testing with expert observation. I shall always speak of "knowing," therefore, to cover both practical and theoretical knowledge. We can, accordingly, interpret the use of tools, of probes, and of pointers as further instances of the art of knowing, and may add to our list also the denotative use of language, as a kind of verbal pointing.

Perception, on which Gestalt psychology centered its attention, now appears as the most impoverished form of tacit knowing. As such it will be shown to form the bridge between the higher creative powers of man and the bodily processes which are prominent in the operations of perception.

Some recent psychological experiments have shown in isolation the principal mechanism by which knowledge is tacitly acquired. Many of you have heard of these experiments as revealing the diabolical machinery of hidden persuasion. Actually, they are but elementary demonstrations of the faculty by which we apprehend the relation between two events, both of which we know, but only one of which we can tell.

Following the example set by Lazarus and McCleary in 1949, psychologists call the exercise of this faculty a process of "subception."[1] These

---

[1] Lazarus, R. S., and McCleary, R. A., *Journal of Personality* (Vol. 18, 1949), p. 191, and *Psychological Review* (Vol. 58, 1951), p. 113. These results were called in question by Eriksen, C. W., *Psychological Review* (Vol. 63, 1956), p. 74 and defended by

authors presented a person with a large number of nonsense syllables, and after showing certain of the syllables, they administered an electric shock. Presently the person showed symptoms of anticipating the shock at the sight of "shock syllables"; yet, on questioning, he could not identify them. He had come to know when to expect a shock, but he could not tell what made him expect it. He had acquired a knowledge similar to that which we have when we know a person by signs which we cannot tell.

Another variant of this phenomenon was demonstrated by Eriksen and Kuethe in 1958.[2] They exposed a person to a shock whenever he happened to utter associations to certain "shock words." Presently, the person learned to forestall the shock by avoiding the utterance of such associa-

---

Lazarus, *Psychological Review* (Vol. 63, 1956), p. 343. But in a later paper surveying the whole field—*Psychological Review* (Vol. 67, 1960), p. 279—Eriksen confirmed the experiments of Lazarus and McCleary, and accepted them as evidence of subception.

I am relying on subception only as a confirmation of tacit knowing in an elementary form, capable of quantitative experimental demonstration. For me it is the mechanism underlying the formation of Gestalt, from which I first derived my conception of tacit knowing in *Personal Knowledge*. Strangely enough, the connection of subception with Gestalt has been hardly noticed by psychologists in the course of their controversies on the validity of subception. I could find only one place alluding to it, in a paper by Klein, George S., "On Subliminal Activation," *Journal of Nervous Mental Disorders* (Vol. 128, 1959), pp. 293—301. He observes: "It requires no experimental demonstration to say confidently that we are not aware of all the stimuli which we use in behavior."

I have said already basically in *Personal Knowledge* and have continued to emphasize since then, that it is a mistake to identify subsidiary awareness with unconscious or preconscious awareness, or with the Jamesian fringe of awareness. What makes an awareness subsidiary is the *function it fulfills;* it can have any degree of consciousness, so long as it functions as a clue to the object of our focal attention. Klein supports this by saying that subliminal activation is but a special case of *transient or incidental stimuli* of all kinds. It is not the subliminal status that matters but "the meanings and properties [a stimulus] acquires at the periphery of thought and action."

Eriksen and Kuethe, whose observation of not consciously identified avoidance I have quoted as a kind of subception, have called this avoidance a defense mechanism, thus affiliating it to Freudian conceptions. This practice is widespread and has caused *Psychological Abstracts* to divide the subject matter into subception and defense mechanism.

Yet another fragmentation of this matter occurred by taking due notice of Otto Pötzl's observations going back to 1917. A survey of his work and of that of his direct successors has appeared in *Psychological Issues* (Vol. II, No. 3, 1960) under the title "Preconscious Stimulation in Dreams, Associations, and Images" by Otto Pötzl, Rudolf Allers, and Jacob Teler, International Universities Press, New York 11, N.Y. An introduction to this monograph by Charles Fisner links these observations to recent studies and notes the present uncertainty about the status of stimuli of which we become conscious only in terms of their contribution to subsequent experience. "The matter needs to be settled," writes Fisher on p. 33, "because the issue of subliminality has important implications for theories of perception."

I believe that this matter has actually much wider implications and must be generally subsumed under the logical categories of tacit knowing.

[2] Eriksen, C. W., and Kuethe, J. L., "Avoidance Conditioning of Verbal Behavior Without Awareness: A Paradigm of Repression," *Journal of Abnormal and Social Psychology* (Vol. 53, 1956), pp. 203—09.

tions, but, on questioning, it appeared that he did not know he was doing this. Here the subject got to know a practical operation, but could not tell how he worked it. This kind of subception has the structure of a skill, for a skill combines elementary muscular acts which are not identifiable, according to relations that we cannot define.

These experiments show most clearly what is meant by saying that one can know more than one can tell. For the experimental arrangement wards off the suspicion of self-contradiction, which is not easy to dispel when anyone speaks of things he knows and cannot tell. This is prevented here by the division of roles between the subject and the observer. The experimenter observes that another person has a certain knowledge that he cannot tell, and so no one speaks of a knowledge he himself has and cannot tell.

We may carry forward, then, the following result. In both experiments that I have cited, subception was induced by electric shock. In the first series the subject was shocked after being shown certain nonsense syllables, and he learned to expect this event. In the second series he learned to suppress the uttering of certain associations, which would evoke the shock. In both cases the shock-producing particulars remained tacit. The subject could not identify them, yet he relied on his awareness of them for anticipating the electric shock.

Here we see the basic structure of tacit knowing. It always involves two things, or two kinds of things. We may call them the two terms of tacit knowing. In the experiments the shock syllables and shock associations formed the first term, and the electric shock which followed them was the second term. After the subject had learned to connect these two terms, the sight of the shock syllables evoked the expectation of a shock and the utterance of the shock associations was suppressed in order to avoid shock. Why did this connection remain tacit? It would seem that this was due to the fact that the subject was riveting his attention on the electric shock. He was relying on his awareness of the shock-producing particulars only in their bearing on the electric shock. We may say that he learned to rely on his awareness of these particulars for the purpose of attending to the electric shock.

Here we have the basic definition of the logical relation between the first and second term of a tacit knowledge. It combines two kinds of knowing. We know the electric shock, forming the second term, by attending to it, and hence the subject is *specifiably* known. But we know the shock-producing particulars only by relying on our own awareness of them for attending to something else, namely the electric shock, and hence our knowledge of them remains *tacit*. This is how we come to know these particulars, without becoming able to identify them. Such is the *functional relation* between the two terms of tacit knowing: *we know the first term only by relying on our awareness of it for attending to the second.*

In this book on freedom of the will, Austin Farrar has spoken at one point of *disattending from* certain things for attending to others. I shall adopt a variant of this usage by saying that in an act of tacit knowing we *attend from* something for attending *to* something else; namely, *from* the first term *to* the second term of the tacit relation. In many ways the first term of this relation will prove to be nearer to us, the second further away from us. Using the language of anatomy, we may call the first term *proximal*, and the second term *distal*. It is the proximal term, then, of which we have a knowledge that we may not be able to tell.

In the case of a human physiognomy, I would now say that we rely on our awareness of its features for attending to the characteristic appearance of a face. We are attending *from* the features *to* the face, and thus may be unable to specify the features. And I would say, likewise, that we are relying on our awareness of a combination of muscular acts for attending to the performance of a skill. We are attending *from* these elementary movements *to* the achievement of their joint purpose, and hence are usually unable to specify these elementary acts. We may call this the *functional structure* of tacit knowing.

But we may ask: does not the *appearance* of the experimental setting—composed of the nonsense syllables and the electric shocks—undergo some change when we learn to anticipate a shock at the sight of certain syllables? It does, and in a very subtle way. The expectation of a shock, which at first had been vague and unceasing, now becomes sharply fluctuating; it suddenly rises at some moments and drops between them. So we may say that even though we do not learn to recognize the shock syllables as distinct from other syllables, we do become aware of facing a shock syllable in terms of the apprehension it evokes in us. In other words, we are aware of seeing these syllables in terms of that on which we are focusing our attention, which is the probability of an electric shock. Applying this to the case of a physiognomy, we may say that we are aware of its features in terms of the physiognomy to which we are attending. In the exercise of a skill, we are aware of its several muscular moves in terms of the performance to which our attention is directed. We may say, in general, that we are aware of the proximal term of an act of tacit knowing in the appearance of its distal term; we are aware of that *from* which we are attending *to* another thing, in the *appearance* of that thing. We may call this the *phenomenal structure* of tacit knowing.

But there is a significance in the relation of the two terms of tacit knowing which combines its functional and phenomenal aspects. When the sight of certain syllables makes us expect an electric shock, we may say that they *signify* the approach of a shock. This is their *meaning* to us. We could say, therefore, that when shock syllables arouse an apprehension in us, without our being able to identify the syllables which arouse it, we know these syllables only in terms of their meaning. It is their meaning to which our attention is directed. It is in terms of their meaning that they enter into the appearance of that *to* which we are attending *from* them.

We could say, in this sense, that a characteristic physiognomy is the meaning of its features; which is, in fact, what we do say when a physiognomy expresses a particular mood. To identify a physiognomy would then amount to relying on our awareness of its features for attending to their joint meaning. This may sound far-fetched, because the meaning of the features is observed at the same spot where the features are situated, and hence it is difficult to separate mentally the features from their meaning. Yet, the fact remains that the two are distinct, since we may know a physiognomy without being able to specify its particulars.

To see more clearly the separation of a meaning from that which has this meaning, we may take the example of the use of a probe to explore a cavern, or the way a blind man feels his way by tapping with a stick. For here the separation of the two is wide, and we can also observe here the process by which this separation gradually takes place. Anyone using a probe for the first time will feel its impact against his fingers and palm. But as we learn to use a probe, or to use a stick for feeling our way, our awareness of its impact on our hand is transformed into a sense of its point touching the objects we are exploring. This is how an interpretative effort transposes meaningless feelings into meaningful ones, and places these at some distance from the original feeling. We become aware of the feelings in our hand in terms of their meaning located at the tip of the probe or stick to which we are attending. This is so also when we use a tool. We are attending to the meaning of its impact on our hands in terms of its effect on the things to which we are applying it. We may call this the *semantic aspect* of tacit knowing. All meaning tends to be displaced *away from ourselves,* and that is in fact my justification for using the terms "proximal" and "distal" to describe the first and second terms of tacit knowing.

From the three aspects of tacit knowing that I have defined so far—the functional, the phenomenal, and the semantic—we can deduce a fourth aspect, which tells us what tacit knowing is a knowledge of. This will represent its *ontological* aspect. Since tacit knowing establishes a meaningful relation between two terms, we may identify it with the *understanding* of the comprehensive entity which these two terms jointly constitute. Thus the proximal term represents the *particulars* of this entity, and we can say, accordingly, that we comprehend the entity by relying on our awareness of its particulars for attending to their joint meaning.

This analysis can be applied with interesting results to the case of visual perception. Physiologists long ago established that the way we see an object is determined by our awareness of certain efforts inside our body, efforts which we cannot feel in themselves. We are aware of these things going on inside our body in terms of the position, size, shape, and motion of an object, to which we are attending. In other words we are attending *from* these internal processes *to* the qualities of things outside. These qualities are what those internal processes *mean* to us. The transposition of bodily experiences into the perception of things outside may now appear, therefore, as an instance of the transposition of meaning away from us, which we have found to be present to some extent in all tacit knowing.

But it may be said that the feelings transposed by perception differ from those transposed by the use of tools or probes, by being hardly noticeable in themselves previous to their transposition. An answer to this—or at least part of an answer to it—is to be found in experiments extending subception to subliminal stimuli. Hefferline and collaborators have observed that when spontaneous muscular twitches, unfelt by the subject—but observable externally by a million-fold amplification of their action currents—were followed by the cessation of an unpleasant noise, the subject responded by increasing the frequency of the twitches and thus silencing the noise much of the time.[3] Tacit knowing is seen to operate here on an internal action that we are quite incapable of controlling or even feeling in itself. We become aware of our operation of it only in the silencing of a noise. This experimental result seems closely analogous to the process by which we become aware of subliminal processes inside our body in the perception of objects outside.

This view of perception, that it is an instance of the transposition of feelings which we found in the use of probes and in the process of

[3]Hefferline, Ralph F., Keenan, Brian, and Harford, Richard A., "Escape and Avoidance Conditioning in Human Subjects Without Their Observation of the Response," *Science* (Vol. 130, November 1959), pp. 1338—39. Hefferline, Ralph F., and Keenan, Brian, "Amplitude-Induction Gradient of a Small Human Operant in an Escape-Avoidance Situation," *Journal of the Experimental Analysis of Behavior* (Vol. 4, January 1961), pp. 41—43. Hefferline, Ralph F., and Perera, Thomas B., "Proprioceptive Discrimination of a Covert Operant Without Its Observation by the Subject," *Science* (Vol. 139, March 1963), pp. 834—35. Hefferline, Ralph F., and Keenan, Brian, "Amplitude-Induction Gradient of a Small Scale (Covert) Operant," *Journal of the Experimental Analysis of Behavior* (Vol. 6, July 1963), pp. 307—15. See also general conclusions in Hefferline, Ralph F., "Learning Theory and Clinical Psychology: An Eventual Symbiosis?" from *Experimental Foundations of Clinical Psychology,* ed. Arthur J. Bachrach (1962).

Note also that numerous Russian observations, reported by Razran, G., "The Observable Unconscious and the Inferable Conscious," *Psychological Review* (Vol. 68, 1961), p. 81, have established the conditioning of intestinal stimuli, having a similar covert character as Hefferline's muscular twitches.

subception, is borne out by the fact that the capacity to see external objects must be acquired, like the use of probes and the feats of subception, by a process of learning which can be laborious.

Modern philosophers have argued that perception does not involve projection, since we are not previously aware of the internal processes which we are supposed to have projected into the qualities of things perceived. But we have now established that projection of this very kind is present in various instances of tacit knowing. Moreover, the fact that we do not originally sense the internal processes in themselves now appears irrelevant. We may venture, therefore, to extend the scope of tacit knowing to include neural traces in the cortex of the nervous system. This would place events going on inside our brain on the same footing as the subliminal twitches operated by Hefferline's subjects.[4]

This brings us to the point at which I hinted when I first mentioned perception as an instance of tacit knowing. I said that by elucidating the way our bodily processes participate in our perceptions we will throw light on the bodily roots of all thought, including man's highest creative powers. Let me show this now.

Our body is the ultimate instrument of all our external knowledge, whether intellectual or practical. In all our waking moments we are *relying* on our awareness of contacts of our body with things outside for *attending* to these things. Our own body is the only thing in the world which we normally never experience as an object, but experience always in terms of the world to which we are attending from our body. It is by making this intelligent use of our body that we feel it to be our body, and not a thing outside.

I have described how we learn to feel the end of a tool or a probe hitting things outside. We may regard this as the transformation of the tool or probe into a sentient extension of our body, as Samuel Butler has said. But our awareness of our body for attending to things outside it suggests a wider generalization of the feeling we have of our body. Whenever we use certain things for attending *from* them to other things, in the way in which we always use our own body, these things change their appearance. They appear to us now in terms of the entities to which we are attending *from* them, just as we feel our body in terms of the things outside to which we are attending *from* our body. In this sense we can say that when we make a thing function as the proximal term of tacit knowing, we incorporate it in our body—or extend our body to include it—so that we come to dwell in it.

---

[4]Such a hypothesis does not explain how perceived sights, or any other state of consciousness, arise in conjunction with neural processes. It merely applies the principle that wherever some process in our body gives rise to consciousness in us, our tacit knowing of the process will make sense of it in terms of an experience to which we are attending.

The full range of this generalization can only be hinted at here. Indications of its scope may be seen by recalling that, at the turn of the last century, German thinkers postulated that indwelling, or empathy, is the proper means of knowing man and the humanities. I am referring particularly to Dilthey[5] and Lipps.[6] Dilthey taught that the mind of a person can be understood only by reliving its workings; and Lipps represented aesthetic appreciation as an entering into a work of art and thus dwelling in the mind of its creator. I think that Dilthey and Lipps described here a striking form of tacit knowing as applied to the understanding of man and of works of art, and that they were right in saying that this could be achieved only by indwelling. But my analysis of tacit knowing shows that they were mistaken in asserting that this sharply distinguished the humanities from the natural sciences. Indwelling, as derived from the structure of tacit knowing, is a far more precisely defined act than is empathy, and it underlies all observations, including all those described previously as indwelling.

We meet with another indication of the wide functions of indwelling when we find acceptance to moral teachings described as their *interiorization*. To interiorize is to identify ourselves with the teachings in question, by making them function as the proximal term of a tacit moral knowledge, as applied in practice. This establishes the tacit framework for our moral acts and judgments. And we can trace this kind of indwelling to logically similar acts in the practice of science. To rely on a theory for understanding nature is to interiorize it. For we are attending from the theory to things seen in its light, and are aware of the theory, while thus using it, in terms of the spectacle that it serves to explain. This is why mathematical theory can be learned only by practicing its application: its true knowledge lies in our ability to use it.

The identification of tacit knowing with indwelling involves a shift of emphasis in our conception of tacit knowing. We had envisaged tacit knowing in the first place as a way to know more than we can tell. We identified the two terms of tacit knowing, the proximal and the distal, and recognized the way we attend *from* the first *to* the second, thus achieving an integration of particulars to a coherent entity to which we are attending. Since we were not attending to the particulars in themselves, we could not identify them: but if we now regard the integration of particulars as an interiorization, it takes on a more positive character. It now becomes a means of making certain things function as the proximal terms of tacit knowing, so that instead of observing them in themselves, we may

[5]Dilthey, W., *Gesammelte Schriften* (Vol. VII, Leipzig and Berlin, 1914—36), pp. 213—16; [Translation by H. A. Hodges, *Wilhelm Dilthey* (New York, Oxford University Press, 1944), pp. 121—24].

[6]Lipps, T., *Asthetik* (Hamburg, 1903).

be aware of them in their bearing on the comprehensive entity which they constitute. It brings home to us that it is not by looking at things, but by dwelling in them, that we understood their joint meaning.

We can see now how an unbridled lucidity can destroy our understanding of complex matters. Scrutinize closely the particulars of a comprehensive entity and their meaning is effaced, our conception of the entity is destroyed. Such cases are well known. Repeat a word several times, attending carefully to the motion of your tongue and lips, and to the sound you make, and soon the word will sound hollow and eventually lose its meaning. By concentrating attention on his fingers, a pianist can temporarily paralyze his movement. We can make ourselves lose sight of a pattern or physiognomy by examining its several parts under sufficient magnification.

Admittedly, the destruction can be made good by interiorizing the particulars once more. The word uttered again in its proper context, the pianist's fingers used again with his mind on his music, the features of a physiognomy and the details of a pattern glanced at once more from a distance: they all come to life and recover their meaning and their comprehensive relationship.

But it is important to note that this recovery never brings back the original meaning. It may improve on it. Motion studies, which tend to paralyze a skill, will improve it when followed by practice. The meticulous dismembering of a text, which can kill its appreciation, can also supply material for a much deeper understanding of it. In these cases, the detailing of particulars, which by itself would destroy meaning, serves as a guide to their subsequent integration and thus establishes a more secure and more accurate meaning of them.

But the damage done by the specification of particulars may be irremediable. Meticulous detailing may obscure beyond recall a subject like history, literature, or philosophy. Speaking more generally, the belief that, since particulars are more tangible, their knowledge offers a true conception of things is fundamentally mistaken.

Of course, tacit reintegration of particulars is not the only way to recover their meaning, destroyed by focusing our attention on them. The destructive analysis of a comprehensive entity can be counteracted in many cases by explicitly stating the relation between its particulars. Where such explicit integration is feasible, it goes far beyond the range of tacit integration. Take the case of a machine. One can learn to use it skillfully, without knowing exactly how it works. But the engineer's understanding of its construction and operation goes much deeper. We possess a practical knowledge of our own body, but the physiologist's theoretical knowledge of it is far more revealing. The formal rules of prosody may deepen our understanding of so delicate a thing as a poem.

But my examples show clearly that, in general, an explicit integration cannot replace its tacit counterpart. The skill of a driver cannot be replaced by a thorough schooling in the theory of the motorcar; the knowledge I have of my own body differs altogether from the knowledge of its physiology; and the rules of rhyming and prosody do not tell me what a poem told me, without any knowledge of its rules.

We are approaching here a crucial question. The declared aim of modern science is to establish a strictly detached, objective knowledge. Any falling short of this ideal is accepted only as a temporary inperfection, which we must aim at eliminating. But suppose that tacit thought forms an indispensable part of all knowledge, then the ideal of eliminating all personal elements of knowledge would, in effect, aim at the destruction of all knowledge. The ideal of exact science would turn out to be fundamentally misleading and possibly a source of devastating fallacies.

I think I can show that the process of formalizing all knowledge to the exclusion of any tacit knowing is self-defeating. For, in order that we may formalize the relations that constitute a comprehensive entity, for example, the relations that constitute a frog, this entity, i.e., the frog, must be first identified informally by tacit knowing; and, indeed, the meaning of a mathematical theory of the frog lies in its continued bearing on this still tacitly known frog. Moreover, the act of bringing a mathematical theory to bear on its subject is itself a tacit integration of the kind we have recognized in the use of a denotative word for designating its object. And we have seen also that a true knowledge of a theory can be established only after it has been interiorized and extensively used to interpret experience. Therefore: a mathematical theory can be constructed only by relying on *prior* tacit knowing and can function as a theory only *within* an act of tacit knowing, which consists in our attending *from* it to the previously established experience on which it bears. Thus the ideal of a comprehensive mathematical theory of experience which would eliminate all tacit knowing is proved to be self-contradictory and logically unsound.

But I must not rest my case on such an abstract argument. Let me finish this lecture, therefore, by presenting you with a most striking concrete example of an experience that cannot possibly be represented by any exact theory. It is an experience within science itself: the experience of seeing a problem, as a scientist sees it in his pursuit of discovery.

It is a commonplace that all research must start from a problem. Research can be successful only if the problem is good; it can be original only if the problem is original. But how can one see a problem, any problem, let alone a good and original problem? For to see a problem is to see something that is hidden. It is to have an intimation of the coherence of hitherto not comprehended particulars. The problem is good if this intimation is true; it is original if no one else can see the possibilities of the comprehension that we are anticipating. To see a problem that will lead to a great discovery is not just to see something hidden, but to see something of which the rest of humanity cannot have even an inkling. All this is a commonplace; we take it for granted, without noticing the clash of self-contradiction entailed in it. Yet Plato has pointed out this contradiction in the *Meno;* He says that to search for the solution of a problem is an absurdity; for either you know what you are looking for, and then there is no problem; or you do not know what you are looking for, and then you cannot expect to find anything.

The solution which Plato offered for this paradox was that all discovery is a remembering of past lives. This explanation has hardly ever been accepted, but neither has any other solution been offered for avoiding the contradiction. So we are faced with the fact that, for two thousand years and more, humanity has progressed through the efforts of people solving difficult problems, while all the time it could be shown that to do this was either meaningless or impossible. We have here the classical case of Poe's *Purloined Letter,* of the momentous document lying casually in front of everybody, and hence overlooked by all. For the *Meno* shows conclusively that if all knowledge is explicit, i.e., capable of being clearly stated, then we cannot know a problem or look for its solution. And the *Meno* also shows, therefore, that if problems nevertheless exist, and discoveries can be made by solving them, we can know things, and important things, that we cannot tell.

The kind of tacit knowledge that solves the paradox of the *Meno* consists in the intimation of something hidden, which we may yet discover. There exists another important manifestation of these mental powers. We are often told that great scientific discoveries are marked by their fruitfulness; and this is true. But how can we recognize truth by its fruitfulness? Can we recognize that a statement is true by appreciating the wealth of its yet undiscovered consequences? This would of course be nonsensical, if we had to know explicitly what was yet undiscovered. But it makes sense if we admit that we can have a tacit foreknowledge of yet undiscovered things. This is indeed the kind of foreknowledge the Copernicans must have meant to affirm when they passionately maintained, against heavy pressure, during one hundred and forty years before Newton proved the point, that the heliocentric theory was not merely a convenient way of computing the paths of planets, but was really true.

It appears, then, that to know that a statement is true is to know more than we can tell and that hence, when a discovery solves a problem, it is itself fraught with further intimations of an indeterminate range, and that furthermore, when we accept the discovery as true, we commit ourselves to a belief in all these as yet undisclosed, perhaps as yet unthinkable, consequences.

Since we have no explicit knowledge of these unknown things, there can also be no explicit justification of a scientific truth. But as we can know a problem, and feel sure that it is pointing to something hidden behind it, we can be aware also of the hidden implications of a scientific discovery, and feel confident that they will prove right. We feel sure of this, because in contemplating the discovery we are looking at it not only in itself but, more significantly, as a clue to a reality of which it is a manifestation. The pursuit of discovery is conducted from the start in these terms; all the time we are guided by sensing the presence of a hidden reality toward which our clues are pointing; and the discovery which terminates and satisfies this pursuit is still sustained by the same vision. It claims to have made contact with reality: a reality which, being real, may yet reveal itself to future eyes in an indefinite range of unexpected manifestations.

We have here reached our main conclusions. Tacit knowing is shown to account (1) for a valid knowledge of a problem, (2) for the scientist's capacity to pursue it, guided by his sense of approaching its solution, and (3) for a valid anticipation of the yet indeterminate implications of the discovery arrived at in the end.

Such indeterminate commitments are necessarily involved in any act of knowing based on indwelling. For such an act relies on interiorizing particulars to which we are not attending and which, therefore, we may not be able to specify, and relies further on our attending from these unspecifiable particulars to a comprehensive entity connecting them in a way we cannot define. This kind of knowing solves the paradox of the *Meno* by making it possible for us to know something so indeterminate as a problem or a hunch, but when the use of this faculty turns out to be an indispensable element of all knowing, we are forced to conclude that all knowledge is of the same kind as the knowledge of a problem.

This is in fact our result. We must conclude that the paradigmatic case of scientific knowledge, in which all the faculties that are necessary for finding and holding scientific knowledge are fully developed, is the knowledge of an approaching discovery.

To hold such knowledge is an act deeply committed to the conviction that there is something there to be discovered. It is personal, in the sense of involving the personality of him who holds it, and also in the sense of being, as a rule, solitary; but there is no trace in it of self-indulgence. The discoverer is filled with a compelling sense of responsibility for the pursuit of a hidden truth, which demands his services for revealing it. His act of knowing exercises a personal judgment in relating evidence to an external reality, an aspect of which he is seeking to apprehend.

The anticipation of discovery, like discovery itself, may turn out to be a delusion. But it is futile to seek for strictly impersonal criteria of its validity, as positivistic philosophies of science have been trying to do for the past eighty years or so. To accept the pursuit of science as a reasonable and successful enterprise is to share the kind of commitments on which scientists enter by undertaking this enterprise. You cannot formalize the act of commitment, for you cannot express your commitment non-committally. To attempt this is to exercise the kind of lucidity which destroys its subject matter. Hence the failure of the positivist movement in the philosophy of science. The difficulty is to find a stable alternative to its ideal of objectivity. This is indeed the task for which the theory of tacit knowing should prepare us.

Learning and the Dialogical Relation *

MARTIN BUBER

"The development of the creative powers in the child" is the subject of this conference. As I come before you to introduce it I must not conceal from you for a single moment the fact that of the nine words in which it is expressed only the last three raise no question for me.

The child, not just the individual child, individual children, but the child, is certainly a reality. That in this hour, while we make a beginning with the "development of creative powers," across the whole extent of this planet new human beings are born who are characterized already and yet have still to be characterized—this is a myriad realities, but also one reality. In every hour the human race begins. We forget this too easily in face of the massive fact of past life, of so-called world-history, of the fact that each child is born with a given disposition of "world-historical" origin, that is, inherited from the riches of the whole human race, and that he is born into a given situation of "world-historical" origin, that is, produced from the riches of the world's events. This fact must not obscure the other no less important fact that in spite of everything, in this as in every hour, what has not been invades the structure of what is, with ten thousand countenances, of which not one has been seen before, with ten thousand souls still undeveloped but ready to develop—a creative event if ever there was one, newness rising up, primal potential might. This potentiality, streaming unconquered, however much of it is squandered, is

*From Martin Buber, *Between Man and Man,* trans. Ronald G. Smith (Boston: Beacon Press, 1955), pp. 83–103. Reprinted with the permission of the publisher. An Address to the Third International Educational Conference, Heidelberg, August 1925, whose subject was "The Development of the Creative Powers in the Child."

the reality *child*: this phenomenon of uniqueness, which is more than just begetting and birth, this grace of beginning again and ever again.

What greater care could we cherish or discuss than that this grace may not henceforth be squandered as before, that the might of newness may be preserved for renewal? Future history is not inscribed already by the pen of a causal law on a roll which merely awaits unrolling; its characters are stamped by the unforeseeable decisions of future generations. The part to be played in this by everyone alive to-day, by every adolescent and child, is immeasurable, and immeasurable is our part if we are educators. The deeds of the generations now approaching can illumine the grey face of the human world or plunge it in darkness. So, then, with education: if it at last rises up and exists indeed, it will be able to strengthen the light-spreading force in the hearts of the doers—how much it can do this cannot be guessed, but only learned in action.

The child is a reality; education must become a reality. But what does the "development of the creative powers" mean? Is *that* the reality of education? Must education become that in order to become a reality? Obviously those who arranged this session and gave it its theme think this is so. They obviously think that education has failed in its task till now because it has aimed at something different from this development of what is in the child, or has considered and promoted other powers in the child than the creative. And probably they are amazed that I question this objective, since I myself talk of the treasure of eternal possibility and of the task of unearthing it. So I must make clear that this treasure cannot be properly designated by the notion of "creative powers," nor its unearthing by the notion of "development."

Creation originally means only the divine summons to the life hidden in non-being. When Johann Georg Hamann and his contemporaries carried over this term metaphorically to the human capacity to give form, they marked a supreme peak of mankind, the genius for forming, as that in which man's imaging of God is authenticated in action. The metaphor has since been broadened; there was a time (not long ago) when "creative" meant almost the same as "of literary ability"; in face of this lowest condition of the word it is a real promotion for it to be understood, as it is here, quite generally as something dwelling to some extent in all men, in all children of men, and needing only the right cultivation. Art is then only the province in which a faculty of production, which is common to all, reaches completion. Everyone is elementally endowed with the basic powers of the arts, with that of drawing, for instance, or of music; these powers have to be developed, and the education of the whole person is to be built up on them as on the natural activity of the self.

We must not miss the importance of the reference which is the starting-point of this conception. It concerns a significant but hitherto not properly heeded phenomenon, which is certainly not given its right name here. I mean the existence of an autonomous instinct, which cannot be derived from others, whose appropriate name seems to me to be the "originator instinct." Man, the child of man, wants to make things. He does not merely find pleasure in seeing a form arise from material that presented itself as formless. What the child desires is its own share in this becoming of things: it wants to be the subject of this event of production. Nor is the instinct I am speaking of to be confused with the so-called instinct to busyness or activity which for that matter does not seem to me to exist at all (the child wants to set up or destroy, handle or hit, and so on, but never "busy himself"). What is important is that by one's own intensively experienced action something arises that was not there before. A good expression of this instinct is the way children of intellectual passion produce speech, in reality not as something they have taken over but with the headlong powers of utter newness: sound after sound tumbles out of them, rushing from the vibrating throat past the trembling lips into the world's air, and the whole of the little vital body vibrates and trembles, too, shaken by a bursting shower of selfhood. Or watch a boy fashioning some crude unrecognizable instrument for himself. Is he not astonished, terrified, at his own movement like the mighty inventors of prehistoric times? But it is also to be observed how even in the child's apparently "blind" lust for destruction his instinct of origination enters in and becomes dominant. Sometimes he begins to tear something up, for example, a sheet of paper, but soon he takes an interest in the form of the pieces, and it is not long before he tries—still by tearing—to produce definite forms.

It is important to recognize that the instinct of origination is autonomous and not derivatory. Modern psychologists are inclined to derive the multiform human soul from a single primal element—the "libido," the "will to power," and the like. But this is really only the generalization of certain degenerates in which a single instinct not merely dominates but also spreads parasitically through the others. They begin with the cases (in our time of inner loss of community and oppression the innumerable cases) where such a hypertrophy breeds the appearance of exclusiveness, they abstract rules from them, and apply them with the whole theoretical and practical questionableness of such applications. In opposition to these doctrines and methods, which impoverish the soul, we must continually point out that human inwardness is in origin a polyphony in which no voice can be "reduced" to another, and in which the unity cannot be grasped analytically, but only heard in the present harmony. One of the leading voices is the instinct of origination.

This instinct is therefore bound to be significant for the work of education as well. Here is an instinct which, no matter to what power it is raised, never becomes greed, because it is not directed to "having" but only to doing; which alone among the instincts can grow only to passion, not to lust; which alone among the instincts cannot lead its subject away to invade the realm of other lives. Here is pure gesture which does not snatch the world to itself, but expresses itself to the world. Should not the person's growth into form, so often dreamed of and lost, at last succeed from this starting-point? For here this precious quality may be unfolded and worked out unimpeded. Nor does the new experiment lack demonstration. The finest demonstration I know, that I have just got to know, is this Children's Choir led by the marvellous Bakule of Prague, with which our Conference opened. How under his leadership crippled creatures, seemingly condemned to lifelong idleness, have been released to a life of freely moving persons, rejoicing in their achievement, formable and forming, who know how to shape sights and sounds in multiform patterns and also how to sing out their risen souls wildly and gloriously; more, how a community of achievement, proclaimed in glance and response, has been welded together out of dull immured solitary creatures: all this seems to prove irrefutably not merely what fruitfulness but also what power, streaming through the whole constitution of man, the life or origination has.

But this very example, seen more deeply, shows us that the decisive influence is to be ascribed not to the release of an instinct but to the forces which meet the released instinct, namely, the educative forces. It depends on them, on their purity and fervor, their power of love and their discretion, into what connections the freed element enters and what becomes of it.

There are two forms, indispensable for the building of true human life, to which the originative instinct, left to itself, does not lead and cannot lead: to sharing in an undertaking and to entering into mutuality.

An individual achievement and an undertaking are two very different matters. To make a thing is mortal man's pride; but to be conditioned in a common job, with the unconscious humility of being a part, of participation and partaking, is the true food of earthly immortality. As soon as a man enters effectively into an undertaking, where he discovers and practises a community of work with other men, he ceases to follow the originative instinct alone.

Action leading to an individual achievement is a "one-sided" event. There is a force within the person, which goes out, impresses itself on the material, and the achievement arises objectively: the movement is over, it has run in one direction from the heart's dream into the world, and its course is finished. No matter how directly, as being approached and claimed, as perceiving and receiving, the artist experiences his dealings with the idea which he faces and which awaits embodiment, so long as he is engaged in his work spirit goes out from him and does not enter him, he replies to the world but he does not meet it any more. Nor can he foster mutuality with his work: even in the legend Pygmalion is an ironical figure.

Yes; as an originator man is solitary. He stands wholly without bonds in the echoing hall of his deeds. Nor can it help him to leave his solitariness that his achievement is received enthusiastically by the many. He does not know if it is accepted, if his sacrifice is accepted by the anonymous receiver. Only if someone grasps his hand not as a "creator" but as a fellow-creature lost in the world, to be his comrade or friend or lover beyond the arts, does he have an awareness and a share of mutuality. An education based only on the training of the instinct of origination would prepare a new human solitariness which would be the most painful of all.

The child, in putting things together, learns much that he can learn in no other way. In making some thing he gets to know its possibility, its origin and structure and connections, in a way he cannot learn by observation. But there is something else that is not learned in this way, and that is the viaticum of life. The being of the world as an object is learned from within, but not its being as a subject, its saying of *I* and *Thou*. What teaches us the saying of *Thou* is not the originative instinct but the instinct for communion.

This instinct is something greater than the believers in the "libido" realize: it is the longing for the world to become present to us as a person, which goes out to us as we to it, which chooses and recognizes us as we do it, which is confirmed in us as we in it. The child lying with half-closed eyes, waiting with tense soul for its mother to speak to it—the mystery of its will is not directed towards enjoying (or dominating) a person, or towards doing something of its own accord; but towards experiencing communion in face of the lonely night, which spreads beyond the window and threatens to invade.

But the release of powers should not be any more than a *presupposition* of education. In the end it is not the originative instinct alone which is meant by the "creative powers" that are to be "developed." These powers stand for human spontaneity. Real education is made possible—but is it also established?—by the realization that youthful spontaneity must not be suppressed but must be allowed to give what it can.

Let us take an example from the narrower sphere of the originative instinct—from the drawing-class. The teacher of the "compulsory" school of thought began with rules and current patterns. Now you knew what beauty was, and you had to copy it; and it was copied either in apathy or in despair. The teacher of the "free" school places on the table a twig of broom, say, in an earthenware jug, and makes the pupils draw it. Or he places it on the table, tells the pupils to look at it, removes it, and then makes them draw it. If the pupils are quite unsophisticated soon not a single drawing will look like another. Now the delicate, almost imperceptible and yet important influence begins—that of criticism and instruction. The children encounter a scale of values that, however unacademic it may be, is quite constant, a knowledge of good and evil that, however individualistic it may be, is quite unambiguous. The more unacademic this scale of values, and the more individualistic this knowledge, the more deeply do the children experience the encounter. In the former instance the preliminary declaration of what alone was right made for resignation or rebellion; but in the latter, where the pupil gains the realization only after he has ventured far out on the way to his achievement, his heart is drawn to reverence for the form, and educated.

This almost imperceptible, most delicate approach, the raising of a finger, perhaps, or a questioning glance, is the other half of what happens in education.

Modern educational theory, which is characterized by tendencies to freedom, misunderstands the meaning of this other half, just as the old theory, which, was characterized by the habit of authority, misunderstood the meaning of the first half. The symbol of the funnel is in course of being exchanged for that of the pump. I am reminded of the two camps in the doctrine of evolution, current in the seventeenth and eighteenth centuries, the animalculists, who believed that the whole germ was present in the spermatozoon, and the ovists who believed it was wholly present in the ovum. The theory of the development of powers in the child recalls, in its most extreme expressions, Swammerdam's "unfolding" of the "preformed" organism. But the growth of the spirit is no more an unfolding than that of the body. The dispositions which would be discovered in the soul of a new-born child—if the soul could in fact be analyzed—are nothing but capacities to receive and imagine the world. The world engenders the person in the individual. The world, that is the whole environment, nature and society, "educates" the human being: it draws out his powers, and makes him grasp and penetrate its objections. What we term education, conscious and willed, means *a selection by man of the effective world*: it means to give decisive effective power to a selection of the world which is concentrated and manifested in the educator. The relation in education is lifted out of the purposelessly streaming education by all things, and is marked off as purpose. In this way, through the educator, the world for the first time becomes the true subject of its effect.

There was a time, there were times, where there neither was nor needed to be any specific calling of educator or teacher. There was a master, a philosopher or a coppersmith, whose journeymen and apprentices lived with him and learned, by being allowed to share in it, what he had to teach them of his handwork or brainwork. But they also learned, without either their or his being concerned with it, they learned, without noticing that they did, the mystery of personal life: they received the spirit. Such a thing must still happen to some extent, where spirit and person exist, but it is expelled to the sphere of spirituality, of personality, and has become exceptional, it happens only "on the heights." Education as a purpose is bound to be summoned. We can as little return to the state of affairs that existed before there were schools as to that which existed before, say, technical science. But we can and must enter into the completeness of its growth to reality, into the perfect humanization of its reality. Our way is composed of losses that secretly become gains. Education has lost the paradise of pure instinctiveness and now consciously serves at the plough for the bread of life. It has been transformed; only in this transformation has it become visible.

Yet the master remains the model for the teacher. For if the educator of our day has to act consciously he must nevertheless do it "as though he did not." That raising of the finger, that questioning glance, are his genuine doing. Through him the selection of the effective world reaches the pupil. He fails the recipient when he presents this selection to him with a gesture of interference. It must be concentrated in him; and doing out of concentration has the appearance of rest. Interference divides the soul in his care into an obedient part and a rebellious part. But a hidden influence proceeding from his integrity has an integrating force.

The world, I said, has its influence as nature and as society on the child. He is educated by the elements, by air and light and the life of plants and animals, and he is educated by relationships. The true educator represents both; but he must be to the child as one of the elements.

The release of powers can be only a presupposition of education, nothing more. Put more generally, it is the nature of freedom to provide the place, but not the foundation as well, on which true life is raised. That is true both of inner, "moral" freedom and of outer freedom (which consists in not being hindered or limited). As the higher freedom, the soul's freedom of decision, signifies perhaps our highest moments but not a fraction of our substance, so the lower freedom, the freedom of development, signifies our capacity for growth but by no means our growth itself. This latter freedom is charged with importance as the actuality from which the work of education begins, but as its fundamental task it becomes absurd.

There is a tendency to understand this freedom, which may be termed evolutionary freedom, as at the opposite pole from compulsion, from being under a compulsion. But at the opposite pole from compulsion there stands not freedom but communion. Compulsion is a negative reality; communion is the positive reality; freedom is a possibility, possibility regained. At the opposite pole of being compelled by destiny or nature or men there does not stand being free of destiny or nature or men but to commune and to covenant with them. To do this, it is true that one must first have become independent; but this independence is a foot-bridge, not a dwelling-place. Freedom is the vibrating needle, the fruitful zero. Compulsion in education means disunion, it means humiliation and rebelliousness. Communion in education is just communion, it means being opened up and drawn in. Freedom in education is the possibility of communion; it cannot be dispensed with and it cannot be made use of in itself; without it nothing succeeds, but neither does anything succeed by means of it: it is the run before the jump, the tuning of the violin, the confirmation of that primal and mighty potentiality which it cannot even begin to actualize.

Freedom—I love its flashing face: it flashes forth from the darkness and dies away, but it has made the heart invulnerable. I am devoted to it, I am always ready to join in the fight for it, for the appearance of the flash, which lasts no longer than the eye is able to endure it, for the vibrating of the needle that was held down too long and was stiff. I give my left hand to the rebel and my right to the heretic: forward! But I do not trust them. They know how to die, but that is not enough. I love freedom, but I do not believe in it. How could one believe in it after looking in its face? It is the flash of a significance comprising all meanings, of a possibility comprising all potentiality. For it we fight, again and again, from of old, victorious and in vain.

It is easy to understand that in a time when the deterioration of all traditional bonds has made their legitimacy questionable, the tendency to freedom is exalted, the springboard is treated as the goal and a functional good as substantial good. Moreover, it is idle sentimentality to lament at great length that freedom is made the subject of experiments. Perhaps it is fitting for this time which has no compass that people should throw out their lives like a plummet to discover our bearings and the course we should set. But truly *their* lives! Such an experiment, when it is carried out, is a neck-breaking venture which cannot be disputed. But when it is talked about and talked around, in intellectual discussions and confessions and in the mutual pros and cons of their life's "problems," it is an abomination of disintegration. Those who stake themselves, as individuals or as a community, may leap and crash out into the swaying void where senses and sense fail, or through it and beyond into some kind of existence. But they must not make freedom into a theorem or a programme. To become free of a bond is destiny; one carries that like a cross, not like a cockade. Let us realize the true meaning of being free of a bond: it means that a quite personal responsibility takes the place of one shared with many generations. Life lived in freedom is personal responsibility or it is a pathetic farce.

I have pointed out the power which alone can give a content to empty freedom and a direction to swaying and spinning freedom. I believe in it, I trust those devoted to it.

This fragile life between birth and death can nevertheless be a fulfilment—if it is a dialogue. In our life and experience we are addressed; by thought and speech and action, by producing and by influencing we are able to answer. For the most part we do not listen to the address, or we break into it with chatter. But if the word comes to us and the answer proceeds from us then human life exists, though brokenly, in the world. The kindling of the response in that "spark" of the soul, the blazing up of the response, which occurs time and again, to the unexpectedly approaching speech, we term responsibility. We practice responsibility for that realm of life allotted and entrusted to us for which we are able to respond, that is, for which we have a relation of deeds which may count—in all our inadequacy—as a proper response. The extent to which a man, in the strength of the reality of the spark, can keep a traditional bond, a law, a direction, is the extent to which he is permitted to lean his responsibility on something (more than this is not vouchsafed to us, responsibility is not taken off our shoulders). As we "become free" this leaning on something is more and more denied to us, and our responsibility must become personal and solitary.

From this point of view education and its transformation in the hour of the crumbling of bonds are to be understood.

It is usual to contrast the principle of the "new" education as "Eros" with that of the "old" education as the "will to power."

In fact the one is as little a principle of education as the other. A principle of education, in a sense still to be clarified, can only be a basic relation which is fulfilled in education. But Eros and the will to power are alike passions of the soul for whose real elaboration a place is prepared elsewhere. Education can supply for them only an incidental realm and moreover one which sets a limit to their elaboration; nor can this limit be infringed without the realm itself being destroyed. The one can as little as the other constitute the educational attitude.

The "old" educator, in so far as he was an educator, was not "the man with a will to power," but he was the bearer of assured values which were strong in tradition. If the educator represents the world to the pupil, the "old" educator represented particularly the historical world, the past. He was the ambassador of history to this intruder, the "child"; he carried to him, as the Pope in the legend did to the prince of the Huns, the magic of the spiritual forces of history; he instilled values into the child or he drew the child into the values. The man who reduces this encounter between the cosmos of history and its eternally new chaos, between Zeus and Dionysus, to the formula of the "antagonism between fathers and sons," has never beheld it in his spirit. Zeus the Father does not stand for a generation but for a world, for the olympic, the formed world; the world of history faces a particular generation, which is the world of nature renewed again and again, always without history.

This situation of the old type of education is, however, easily used, or misused, by the individual's will to power, for this will is inflated by the authority of history. The will to power becomes convulsive and passes into fury, when the authority begins to decay, that is, when the magical validity of tradition disappears. Then the moment comes near when the teacher no longer faces the pupil as an ambassador but only as an individual, as a static atom to the whirling atom. Then no matter how much he imagines he is acting from the fulness of the objective spirit, in the reality of his life he is thrown back on himself, cast on his own resources, and hence filled with longing. Eros appears. And Eros finds employment in the new situation of education as the will to power did in the old situation. But Eros is not a bearer or the ground or the principle any more than the will to power was. He only claims to be that, in order not to be recognized as longing, as the stranger given refuge. And many believe it.

Nietzsche did not succeed in glorifying the will to power as much as Plato glorified Eros. But in our concern for the creature in this great time of concern, for both alike we have not to consider the myths of the philosophers but the actuality of present life. In entire opposition to any glorification we have to see that Eros—that is, not "love," but Eros the male and magnificent—whatever else may belong to him, necessarily includes this one thing, that he desires to enjoy men; and education, the peculiar essence bearing this name which is composed of no others, excludes precisely this desire. However mightily an educator is possessed and inspired by Eros, if he obeys him in the course of his educating then he stifles the growth of his blessings. It must be one or the other: either he takes on himself the tragedy of the person, and offers an unblemished daily sacrifice, or the fire enters his work and consumes it.

Eros is choice, choice made from an inclination. This is precisely what education is not. The man who is loving in Eros chooses the beloved, the modern educator finds his pupil there before him. From this unerotic situation the *greatness* of the modern educator is to be seen—and most clearly when he is a teacher. He enters the school-room for the first time, he sees them crouching at the desks, indiscriminately flung together, the misshapen and the well-proportioned, animal faces, empty faces, and noble faces in indiscriminate confusion, like the presence of the created universe; the glance of the educator accepts and receives them all. He is assuredly no descendant of the Greek gods, who kidnapped those they loved. But he seems to me to be a representative of the true God. For if God "forms the light and creates darkness," man is able to love both—to love light in itself, and darkness towards the light.

If this educator should ever believe that for the sake of education he has to practice selection and arrangement, then he will be guided by another criterion than that of inclination, however legitimate this may be in its own sphere; he will be guided by the recognition of values which is in his glance as an educator. But even then his selection remains suspended, under constant correction by the special humility of the educator for whom the life and particular being of all his pupils is the decisive factor to which his "hierarchic" recognition is subordinated. For in the manifold variety of the children the variety of creation is placed before him.

In education, then, there is a lofty asceticism: an asceticism which rejoices in the world, for the sake of the responsibility for a realm of life which is entrusted to us for our influence but not our interference—either by the will to power or by Eros. The spirit's service of life can be truly carried out only in the system of a reliable counterpoint—regulated by the laws of the different forms of relation—of giving and withholding oneself, intimacy and distance, which of course must not be controlled by reflection but must arise from the living tact of the natural and spiritual man. Every form of relation in which the spirit's service of life is realized has its special objectivity, its structure of proportions and limits which in no way resists the fervor of personal comprehension and penetration, though it does resist any confusion with the person's own spheres. If this structure and its resistance are not respected then a dilettantism will prevail which claims to be aristocratic, though in reality it is unsteady and feverish: to provide it with the most sacred names and attitudes will not help it past its inevitable consequence of disintegration. Consider, for example, the relation of doctor and patient. It is essential that this should be a real human relation experienced with the spirit by the one who is addressed; but as soon as the helper is touched by the desire—in however subtle a form—to dominate or to enjoy his patient, or to treat the latter's wish to be dominated or enjoyed by him other than as a wrong condition needing to be cured, the danger of a falsification arises, beside which all quackery appears peripheral.

The objectively ascetic character of the sphere of education must not, however, be misunderstood as being so separated from the instinct to power and from Eros that no bridge can be flung from them to it. I have already pointed out how very significant Eros can be to the educator without corroding his work. What matters here is the threshold and the transformation which takes place on it. It is not the church alone which has a testing threshold on which a man is transformed or becomes a lie. But in order to be able to carry out this ever renewed transition from sphere to sphere he must have carried it out once in a decisive fashion and taken up in himself the essence of education. How does this happen? There is an elemental experience which shatters at least the assurance of the erotic as well as the cratetic man, but sometimes does more, forcing its way at white-heat into the heart of the instinct and remolding it. A reversal of the single instinct takes place, which does not eliminate it but reverses its system of direction. Such a reversal can be effected by the elemental experience with which the real process of education begins and on which it is based. I call it experiencing the other side.

A man belabors another, who remains quite still. Then let us assume that the striker suddenly receives in his soul the blow which he strikes: the same blow; that he receives it as the other who remains still. For the space of a moment he experiences the situation from the other side. Reality imposes itself on him. What will he do? Either he will overwhelm the voice of the soul, or his impulse will be reversed.

A man caresses a woman, who lets herself be caressed. Then let us assume that he feels the contact from two sides—with the palm of his hand still, and also with the woman's skin. The twofold nature of the gesture, as one that takes place between two persons, thrills through the depth of enjoyment in his heart and stirs it. If he does not deafen his heart he will have—not to renounce the enjoyment but—to love.

I do not in the least mean that the man who has had such an experience would from then on have this two-sided sensation in every such meeting—that would perhaps destroy his instinct. But the one extreme experience makes the other person present to him for all time. A transfusion has taken place after which a mere elaboration of subjectivity is never again possible or tolerable to him.

Only an inclusive power is able to take the lead; only an inclusive Eros is love. Inclusiveness is the complete realization of the submissive person, the desired person, the "partner," not by the fancy but by the actuality of the being.

It would be wrong to identify what is meant here with the familiar but not very significant term "empathy." Empathy means, if anything, to glide with one's own feeling into the dynamic structure of an object, a pillar or a crystal or the branch of a tree, or even of an animal or a man, and as it were to trace it from within, understanding the formation and motoriality of the object with the perceptions of one's own muscles; it means to "transpose" oneself over there and in there. Thus it means the exclusion of one's own concreteness, the extinguishing of the actual situation of life, the absorption in pure aestheticism of the reality in which one participates. Inclusion is the opposite of this. It is the extension of one's own concreteness, the fulfilment of the actual situation of life, the complete presence of the reality in which one participates. Its elements are, first, a relation, of no matter what kind, between two persons, second, an event experienced by them in common, in which at least one of them actively participates, and, third, the fact that this one person, without forfeiting anything of the felt reality of his activity, at the same time lives through the common event from the standpoint of the other.

A relation between persons that is characterized in more or less degree by the element of inclusion may be termed a dialogical relation.

A dialogical relation will show itself also in genuine conversation, but it is not composed of this. Not only is the shared silence of two such persons a dialogue, but also their dialogical life continues, even when they are separated in space, as the continual potential presence of the one to the other, as an unexpressed intercourse. On the other hand, all conversation derives its genuineness only from the consciousness of the element of inclusion—even if this appears only abstractly as an "acknowledgement" of the actual being of the partner in the conversation; but this acknowledgement can be real and effective only when it springs from an experience of inclusion, of the other side.

The reversal of the will to power and of Eros means that relations characterized by these are made dialogical. For that very reason it means that the instinct enters into communion with the fellow-man and into responsibility for him as an allotted and entrusted realm of life.

The element of inclusion, with whose recognition this clarification begins, is the same as that which constitutes the relation in education.

The relation in education is one of pure dialogue.

I have referred to the child, lying with half-closed eyes waiting for his mother to speak to him. But many children do not need to wait, for they know that they are unceasingly addressed in a dialogue which never breaks off. In face of the lonely night which threatens to invade, they lie preserved and guarded, invulnerable, clad in the silver mail of trust.

Trust, trust in the world, because this human being exists—that is the most inward achievement of the relation in education. Because this human being exists, meaninglessness, however hard pressed you are by it, cannot be the real truth. Because this human being exists, in the darkness the light lies hidden, in fear salvation, and in the callousness of one's fellow-men the great Love.

Because this human being exists: therefore he must be really there, really facing the child, not merely there in spirit. He may not let himself be represented by a phantom: the death of the phantom would be a catastrophe for the child's pristine soul. He need possess none of the perfections which the child may dream he possesses; but he must be really there. In order to be and to remain truly present to the child he must have gathered the child's presence into his own store as one of the bearers of his communion with the world, one of the focuses of his responsibilities for the world. Of course he cannot be continually concerned with the child, either in thought or in deed, nor ought he to be. But if he has really gathered the child into his life then that subterranean dialogic, that steady potential presence of the one to the other is established and endures. Then there is reality *between* them, there is mutuality.

But this mutuality—that is what constitutes the peculiar nature of the relation in education—cannot be one of inclusion, although the true relation of the educator to the pupil is based on inclusion. No other relation draws its inner life like this one from the element of inclusion, but no other is in that regard like this, completely directed to one-sideness, so that if it loses one-sideness it loses essence.

We may distinguish three chief forms of the dialogical relation.

The first rests on an abstract but mutual experience of inclusion.

The clearest example of this is a disputation between two men, thoroughly different in nature and outlook and calling, where in an instant—as by the action of a messenger as anonymous as he is invisible—it happens that each is aware of the other's full legitimacy, wearing the insignia of necessity and of meaning. What an illumination! The truth, the strength of conviction, the "standpoint," or rather the circle of movement, of each of them, is in no way reduced by this. There is no "relativizing," but we may say that, in the sign of the limit, the essence of mortal recognition, fraught with primal destiny, is manifested to us. To recognize means for us creatures the fulfilment by each of us, in truth and responsibility, of his own relation to the Present Being, through our receiving all that is manifested of it and incorporating it into our own being, with all our force, faithfully, and open to the world and the spirit. In this way living truth arises and endures. We have become aware that it is with the other as with ourselves, and that what rules over us both is not a truth of recognition but the truth-of-existence and the existence-of-truth of the Present Being. In this way we have become able *to acknowledge*.

I have called this form abstract, not as though its basic experience lacked immediacy, but because it is related to man only as a spiritual person and is bound to leave out the full reality of his being and life. The other two forms proceed from the inclusion of this full reality.

Of these the first, the relation of education, is based on a concrete but one-sided experience of inclusion.

If education means to let a selection of the world affect a person through the medium of another person, then the one through whom this takes place, rather, who makes it take place through himself, is caught in a strange paradox. What is otherwise found only as grace, inlaid in the folds of life—the influencing of the lives of others with one's own life—becomes here a function and a law. But since the educator has to such an extent replaced the master, the danger has arisen that the new phenomenon, the will to educate, may degenerate into arbitrariness, and that the educator may carry out his selection and his influence from himself and his idea of the pupil, not from the pupil's own reality. One only needs to read, say, the accounts of Pestalozzi's teaching method to see how easily, even with the noblest teachers, arbitrary self-will is mixed up with will. This is almost always due to an interruption or a temporary flagging of the act of inclusion, which is not merely regulative for the realm of education, as for other realms, but is actually constitutive; so that the realm of education acquires its true and proper force from the constant return of this act and the constantly renewed connection with it. The man whose calling it is to influence the being of persons that can be determined, must experience this action of his (however much it may have assumed the form of non-action) ever anew from the other side. Without the action of his spirit being in any way weakened he must at the same time be over there, on the surface of that other spirit which is being acted upon—and not of some conceptual, contrived spirit, but all the time the wholly concrete spirit of this individual and unique being who is living and confronting him, and who stands with him in the common situation of "educating" and "being educated" (which is indeed one situation, only the other is at the other end of it). It is not enough for him to imagine the child's individuality, nor to experience him directly as a spiritual person and then to acknowledge him. Only when he catches himself "from over there," and feels how it affects one, how it affects this other human being, does he recognize the real limit, baptize his self-will in Reality and make it true will, and renew his paradoxical legitimacy. He is of all men the one for whom inclusion may and should change from an alarming and edifying event into an atmosphere.

But however intense the mutuality of giving and taking with which he is bound to his pupil, inclusion cannot be mutual in this case. He experiences the pupil's being educated, but the pupil cannot experience the educating of the educator. The educator stands at both ends of the common situation, the pupil only at one end. In the moment when the pupil is able to throw himself across and experience from over there, the educative relation would be burst asunder, or change into friendship.

We call friendship the third form of the dialogical relation, which is based on a concrete and mutual experience of inclusion. It is the true inclusion of one another by human souls.

The educator who practices the experience of the other side and stands firm in it, experiences two things together, first that he is limited by otherness, and second that he receives grace by being bound to the other. He feels from "over there" the acceptance and the rejection of what is approaching (that is, approaching from himself, the educator) —of course often only in a fugitive mood or an uncertain feeling; but this discloses the real need and absence of need in the soul. In the same way the foods a child likes and dislikes is a fact which does not, indeed, procure for the experienced person but certainly helps him to gain an insight into what substances the child's body needs. In learning from time to time what this human being needs and does not need at the moment, the educator is led to an ever deeper recognition of what the human being needs in order to grow. But he is also led to the recognition of what he, the "educator," is able and what he is unable to give of what is needed—and what he can give now, and what not yet. So the responsibility for this realm of life allotted and entrusted to him, the constant responsibility for this living soul, points him to that which seems impossible and yet is somehow granted to us—to self-education. But self-education, here as everywhere, cannot take place through one's being concerned with oneself but only through one's being concerned, knowing what it means, with the world. The forces of the world which the child needs for the building up of his substance must be chosen by the educator from the world and drawn into himself.

The education of men by men means the selection of the effective world by a person and in him. The educator gathers in the constructive forces of the world. He distinguishes, rejects, and confirms in himself, in his self which is filled with the world. The constructive forces are eternally the same: they are the world bound up in community, turned to God. The educator educates himself to be their vehicle.

Then is this the "principle" of education, its normal and fixed maxim?

No; it is only the *principium* of its reality, the beginning of its reality — wherever it begins.

There is not and never has been a norm and fixed maxim of education. What is called so was always the norm of a culture, of a society, a church, an epoch, to which education too, like all stirring and action of the spirit, was submissive, and which education translated into its language. In a formed age there is in truth no autonomy of education, but only in an age which is losing form. Only in it, in the disintegration of traditional bonds, in the spinning whirl of freedom, does personal responsibility arise which in the end can no longer lean with its burden of decision on any church or society or culture, but is lonely in face of Present Being.

In an age which is losing form the highly-praised "personalities," who know how to serve its fictitious forms and in their name to dominate the age, count in the truth of what is happening no more than those who lament the genuine forms of the past and are diligent to restore them. The ones who count are those persons who—though they may be of little renown—respond to and are responsible for the continuation of the living spirit, each in the active stillness of his sphere of work.

The question which is always being brought forward—"To where, to what, must we educate?"—misunderstands the situation. Only times which know a figure of general validity—the Christian, the gentleman, the citizen—know an answer to that question, not necessarily in words, but by pointing with the finger to the figure which rises clear in the air, out-topping all. The forming of this figure in all individuals, out of all materials, is the formation of a "culture." But when all figures are shattered, when no figure is able any more to dominate and shape the present human material, what is there left to form?

Nothing but the image of God.

That is the indefinable, only factual, direction of the responsible modern educator. This cannot be a theoretical answer to the question "To what?", but only, if at all, an answer carried out in deeds; an answer carried out by non-doing.

The educator is set now in the midst of the need which he experiences in inclusion, but only a bit deeper in it. He is set in the midst of the service, only a bit higher up, which he invokes without words; he is set in the *imitatio Dei absconditi sed non ignoti.*

When all "directions" fail there arises in the darkness over the abyss the one true direction of man, towards the creative Spirit, towards the Spirit of God brooding on the face of the waters, towards Him of whom we know not whence He comes and whither He goes.

That is man's true autonomy which no longer betrays, but responds.

Man, the creature, who forms and transforms the creation, cannot create. But he, each man, can expose himself and others to the creative Spirit. And he can call upon the Creator to save and perfect His image.

FOR FURTHER READING

Bruner, Jerome. *On Knowing: Essays for the Left Hand.* Cambridge: Harvard University Press, 1964.

Provocative and suggestive essays on learning by a Harvard psychologist. The third section of Part II is a critique of Dewey's learning theory.

Demos, Raphael. *The Philosophy of Plato.* New York: Charles Scribner's Sons, 1939. Chapter 15.

An outstanding work on Plato's thought. Chapters XI–XV and XIX are particularly enlightening regarding Plato's epistemology.

Dewey, John. *Experience and Nature.* La Salle, Illinois: The Open Court Publishing Company, 1958.

A thoroughgoing examination of method, knowing, values, mind, nature, and art. Sets the general framework in which Dewey's philosophy of learning must be understood.

Frankena, William. *Three Historical Philosophies of Education.* Glenview, Illinois: Scott, Foresman and Company, 1965. Chapters 3 and 4.

Explorations in the educational thought of Aristotle, Kant, and Dewey.

Gallagher, Kenneth. *The Philosophy of Knowledge.* New York: Sheed and Ward, 1964. Chapters 1, 2, 3.

An excellent introductory text in epistemology written from a phenomenological point of view. Discussions of perception (Chapters 4 and 5), truth (Chapter 10), and intersubjective knowledge (Chapter 11) are particularly significant from the viewpoint of the philosophy of learning.

Gilson, Etienne. *The Christian Philosophy of Saint Augustine.* Translated by L. E. M. Lynch. New York: Random House, 1960. Part I.

The best statement of Augustine's philosophy. Part I is devoted to Augustine's epistemology.

Hardie, Charles D. *Truth and Fallacy in Educational Theory.* New York: Teachers College, Columbia University, 1962.

The method of philosophical analysis is applied to various theories of education, particularly theories of learning. A critique of Dewey is given in Chapter III while a discussion of the foundations on which any theory of education must be built is carried out in Chapter IV.

Hill, Thomas E. *Contemporary Theories of Knowledge.* New York: The Ronald Press Company, 1961.

Studies in major epistemic theories of the twentieth century. An excellent discussion of Dewey's instrumentalism is found in Chapter II.

Mure, G. R. G. *An Introduction to Hegel.* Oxford: Clarendon Press, 1959.

A short lucid introduction to Hegel. Chapters VIII, X, XIV are particularly enlightening regarding Hegel's philosophy of learning.

Nettleship, Richard L. *The Theory of Education in Plato's Republic.* Oxford: Oxford University Press, 1961.

An excellent analysis of Plato's educational theory as developed in the *Republic.* Argues that the soul has educational needs which the state must meet in the educational program it sets up. Emphasis is on the development of the soul's capacities, on the process of coming to all that it can become.

Polanyi, Michael. *Personal Knowledge.* New York: Harper & Row, Publishers, 1964.

A full treatment of the themes suggestively treated in *The Tacit Dimension.* Difficult but rewarding.

Scheffler, Israel. *The Conditions of Knowledge.* Glenview, Illinois: Scott, Foresman and Company, 1965.

An investigation of epistemological problems from the perspective of educational tasks and goals. A language analysis approach.

———. "Philosophical Models of Teaching," *Harvard Educational Review,* Vol. 35, No. 2 (1965), 131–143.

An examination of three models of teaching: impression (Locke), insight (Plato and Augustine), and rule (Kant). The strengths and weaknesses of each is discussed.

Stumpf, Samuel. *Socrates to Sartre.* New York: McGraw-Hill Inc., 1966.

Readable and sound survey of Western philosophy. Solid background reading for the philosophical positions of most of the philosophers included in this anthology.

Vandenburg, Donald. "Experimentalism in the Anesthetic Society Existential Education," *Harvard Educational Review,* Vol. 32, No. 2 (1962), 155-187.

An articulation of an existential position through the means of Dewey's epistemology. In the final section careful attention is given to the implications of existentialism for teaching.

4

CULTURAL POSTURES AND EDUCATIONAL AIMS

ontemporary American culture is in the throes of change and conflict. Not only are we heirs of a centrifugal, disintegrating cultural
force, the analytic temperament, which has gained momentum since
the Renaissance, but also we in America have added to this heritage the
implications of heavy industrialization, mass communication, urbaniza-
tion, and a success orientation. The results of this heritage were spelled
out in the introduction to the first section as undue intellectual specialization and compartmentalization, social estrangement, a spiritual anxiety
over values, and an explosion in knowledge. These cultural phenomena
have awakened us from our cultural sleep and now we are seeking and
demanding of ourselves answers about the ends to which the young in our
society ought to be educated. What should be transmitted to them? It is
the case that they will learn something, and if we want to exercise rational
guidance and control over our society, our educational goals must be
outlined in a rational manner and defended with acceptable evidence.

Unfortunately questions about the aims of education are too often
answered with a list of character traits, moral obligations, and political
ideals which each individual ought to internalize, while no consideration is
given to the cultural context in which this list is to be lived out. The
difficulty with such a procedure can be seen by recognizing that it is
possible to construct a theoretically defensible group of obligations and
traits which are not optional in a particular culture at a particular time.
For example, the ideal of rugged individualism was a character trait
highly prized in the American West in the nineteenth century. One simply

had to be able to fend for oneself during those hectic and demanding years. Such a character trait could be defended by saying that each man has the inalienable rights of life, liberty, and property given to him by the Creator. If this is the case, then each person should be able to exercise absolute control over his property, life, and actions. However, since persons often disagree over rights to possessions, it seems best for them to enter into a contract with each other to guarantee the protection of everyone's rights. On the basis of this contract a government is formed to regulate interpersonal relationships and to protect the life, liberty, and property of each citizen. Though rugged individualism can be argued for in this Lockean and theoretically persuasive manner, it is not a live option in a day in which a high degree of conformity is needed in order to live and to earn a living. Few men work by themselves for themselves. They work in groups, in factories, in large businesses, in planned suburbs, and are under the constant influence of mass media. Hence, to stop a discussion of educational goals with traits and obligations viewed apart from the context in which those traits and obligations are to be lived out is to stop too soon.

Education as cultural transmission must eventually deal with the problem of deciding on culturally realistic traits and obligations to teach its young. But it must first come to grips with the central issue in any discussion of educational goals. Given contemporary American culture and its problems, what kind of attitude toward it ought to be transmitted to the young? How this problem is handled determines what the future American way of life will be. Such an attitude is more than a theoretical viewpoint objectively taken toward the way of life in which one participates. It is one's own way of life, one's own life stance, one's own cultural posture. Once one has taken a stance toward the culture in which he lives and consequently toward himself as an integral member of society, a context is established in which moral obligations and character traits find their cultural meaning. It is also on the basis of the particular cultural posture assumed by a society that it will articulate educational goals and select from the plethora of values within it those which it intends to transmit. If the crucial question about the aims of education concerns the best cultural posture to be transmitted, then what are the major alternatives? Theodore Brameld has suggested at least four cultural postures which may be taken by a society toward its way of life. They are perennialism, progressivism, reconstructionism, and essentialism. In order to understand the selections in this chapter, it is important to understand not only the central point each author is making but also the historical, intellectual background of each of the cultural postures.

When attempting to find meaning in a culture in conflict, the perennialist contends that society must return to those beliefs which were fundamental to the High Middle Ages. The problem of contemporary American culture is that ever since the thirteenth century Western culture has progressively disintegrated through a loss of orientation and a growing analytical temperament. What must be recaptured is a grasp of and a living out of metaphysical principles which are extracultural, spaceless, timeless, axiomatic, transhistorical. These ultimate principles provide an authority orientation toward man, nature, and God which contemporary Americans lack and in the light of which they should attempt to adjust their lives and institutions. In an age when men seek security and meaningfulness, the perennialist position is especially appealing. The appeal is based, however, not just on the religious overtones involved in the perennialist's position but on the strong basis it has in the history of Western culture.

The first major Western philosophical figure to contribute to the perennialist viewpoint was Plato. It was his belief that reality is a realm of necessary, immutable, and eternal forms, patterns, or ideas of which men ought to come to an understanding and in terms of which they ought to conduct their lives individually and corporately. The ideals which Plato rationally defended and understood to be ultimately real were those ideals which had permeated the life of Athens during its golden age, the middle and late fifth century B.C. In that period the ideals were expressed in mythopoeic language but they were the ideals of justice, harmony, moderation, truth, beauty, goodness. Plato believed that men living in Greece during the mid-fourth century B.C. could find meaning if they returned to those ideals of the golden age.

Aristotle disagreeing with Plato about the nature of reality contended that reality must be understood as formed-matter. There is not a realm of absolute permanence and a realm of absolute change which God has mixed together to create the world we experience, a realm of orderly change. On the contrary, permanence and change are mingled together in every object of our experience. Furthermore, all objects including humans are constantly in the process of becoming what they can and ought to become. If one is to understand objects such as humans, then one must attempt to understand the end to which they are moving, their natural end. Aristotle believed that humans are rational animals and have as their natural purpose the actualization of their physical and rational potentialities. This entails not only developing the physical dimension of the human life but also developing the rational dimension. To develop the rational dimension, a human must exercise both his practical reason in seeking the moderate path in every moral decision and his theoretical reason in contemplating the meaning of reality, the end toward which it is moving, the unmoved mover. Aristotle contends in such works as the *Politics* that men can achieve these natural and universal ends only in society, and by society he meant the *polis* as understood in the golden age of Greece. Aristotle lived during the Alexandrian period of Greek life and experienced the continued dislocation of Greek culture under the foreign influence of Macedonian rule. If he recognized any prospects for meaning coming from the cosmopolitanism of Alexander, he never mentioned it in any of his extant works. What he does advocate, however, is a return to the ideals of an earlier period and argues for those metaphysical principles and cultural ideals in a way quite distinct from Plato.

Plato and Aristotle formulated the metaphysical aspects of the perennialist position, but it was through the Christian minds of Augustine and Aquinas that Western culture has been continually influenced by the belief that in a crisis culture what men ought to do is to return to the ideals of the past. Augustine was heavily influenced by Plato as interpreted to him through the writings of Plotinus. His Christian Platonism was developed in response to the theological and political problems of the fifth century A.D. Rome, which had been the bastion of political stability and justice for over six hundred years, and was being beseiged by its perennial enemies from the North. Many Romans blamed the Christian religion for the sack of Rome in 410 A.D. by Alaric and the Visigoths. They complained that if the city gods had not been set aside by Constantine in 322 A.D., when he declared Christianity to be the official religion of Rome, then those gods would have saved their people. In 413 A.D. Augustine began writing his famous work, *The City of God*, in an effort to answer such charges. He argued that the ideals which had made Rome great in the days of the Republic were consistent with those of the Christian faith and if Romans had held to either their own ideals or to those of the Christians, they would not be experiencing the difficulties of war with the Germanic tribes. In this work and in others he employed Platonic metaphysics to express Christian meanings and developed a world view which called for men in times of cultural crisis to return to the ideals the Christian faith had always taught.

Aquinas was deeply influenced by the new philosophical works of Aristotle which the Arabian philosophers were making available to Western Europe in the thirteenth century A.D. Although Christendom had had Aristotle's *Organon* (logical works) for a long time, it did not have his metaphysical and natural science works. Challenged by these new ideas, Aquinas began to interpret Aristotle's works and to employ Aristotelian ideas in expressing the faith of the Church.

The period of Christian theological and metaphysical synthesis of the twelfth through the fourteenth centuries was the high point in the Church's thinking through to an understanding of man, nature, and God. The Schoolmen or Scholastics who effected this formulation were led by Thomas Aquinas. Thomas believed that God created an order which should glorify Him through seeking to become what He wanted it to become. In order to achieve this purpose, each strata in the chain of being must seek to realize its fullest potential. The end of man is to become what God created him to become, and society is the context in which this purposive activity takes place. If man is to realize his God-given purposes, then the institutions and conduct of society must be arranged to aid man's pilgrimage. When faced with conflicts in culture and a concern about the aims of education, a person espousing this position has a metaphysically, theologically, and ethically sound orientation on the basis of which he can respond responsibly and constructively. The perennialist position, as it has come down through Western culture to the twentieth century, has usually been stated in Thomistic or neo-Thomist terms such as those of Jacques Maritain. However, some contemporary educational philosophers such as Robert M. Hutchins state the perennialist position in terms closer to that of Aristotle.

The most sustained attack on perennialism and at the same time the most influential educational philosophy of the twentieth century is that of progressivism. The progressivist posture toward a culture in conflict is to remain curious, flexible, tolerant, and open-minded in an effort to effect modifications in the culture. His attitude is like a scientist who through adventurous exploration within an area of investigation considers the range of alternative hypotheses and gives them opportunity to prove their merit. Society should not attempt to return to the ideals of the prescientific High Middle Ages. Not only are there strong doubts about justifying knowledge claims about necessary, immutable, eternal principles but also the scientific method when applied to understanding society and how to live within it has opened up new and dependable ways of learning and effecting desirable changes. Brameld contends that the progressivist takes the "liberal road to culture" with his confidence in the native intelligence of each person living in society. Though this cultural posture is relatively new to Western culture, it has deep roots in the Western intellectual tradition.

The earliest contribution to progressivism is found in pre-Socratic philosophy. Heraclitus, a sixth century B.C. philosopher, in an attempt to determine the nature of *physis*, contended that whatever exists is changing. There is nothing stable in the universe but the law of change itself. Almost a hundred years later Protagoras worked out the epistemic implications of Heraclitus' metaphysical beliefs about reality. Truth is not fixed but is temporally and spatially relative to the perceiver. The next major contribution to progressivism came during the English Renaissance and was made by Francis Bacon. Bacon reacted strongly against the old traditional authority of Scholasticism and its deductive approach to finding new knowledge. He contended that one must go to the things themselves, the objects of public experience, and with the aid of the inductive method must seek to understand them. Before one can do this, however, one must rid oneself of idols which are hindrances to finding the truth. One must eliminate the idols or prejudices which come from the nature of the mind itself (idols of the tribe), the particular enculturation of the person (idols of the den), the culturally established meanings of words (idols of the market place), and the false theories and philosophies taught in the past (idols of the theatre). Once one has rooted out these idols and has begun to approach objects themselves with an open mind and using the inductive method, one can then begin to understand. In the political thought of John Locke, progressivism finds one of its most cherished principles. It is indebted to Locke for Locke's advocacy of political freedom from the authority of the throne or from any other absolutism and for his contribution to democracy. Immanuel Kant's contention that each individual is an end in himself and not a means only is incorporated into progressivism as one of its central tenets. Although the works of Dewey seem in direct opposition to the absolutism of Hegel, he and progressivism are indebted to Hegel for the emphasis on environmentalism and the belief that reality is changing in an orderly everadjusting manner. Charles Darwin's biological investigations and his belief in evolution from lower species to higher forms of life through natural selection heavily influenced Dewey and progressivism.

The most direct influence on progressivism was the thought of Charles Sanders Peirce and William James. Peirce through an analysis of language contends that words gain meaning from what they do, from their practical effects. Also Peirce believes that meaning is achieved in community through using words which can be translated into some kind of operation. This pragmatic position about language deeply influenced Dewey's own version of pragmatism. William James continued Peirce's emphasis on the pragmatic theory of meaning. James did not advance a creed or a particular content so much as he advanced a method. For each word and belief one ought to seek "practical cash-value." Meaning and truth are not static entities written in the heart of the universe. Rather truth happens to an idea; it is part of living; indeed, truth is made by successful living. Though progressivism is varied and deeply rooted in western intellectual history, it is a peculiarly American philosophy and receives its best statement in the thought of John Dewey.

A third posture toward a culture in conflict is that of reconstructionism. Brameld, who is one of the chief advocates of this position, contends that American culture is in a state of crisis. We ought to realize that we are in a transition period from civilization to what Kenneth Boulding calls postcivilization. If this is correct, then it must be recognized that there can be no appeal either to past social institutions for orientation or to the ideals of the High Middle Ages. On the contrary, what is needed amid the conflicts and shambles of Western civilization is a reconstruction of culture. By reconstruction is meant a radical rebuilding of the culture constructed on values hammered out using the best tools and information from the social and natural sciences. The reconstruction should take a creative rebuilding approach to the contemporary conflicts in culture.

The roots of reconstructionism are as deep as those of progressivism because the reconstructionist is a modified progressivist. While the progressivist emphasizes method almost to the exclusion of ends, the reconstructionist emphasizes the method and the ends toward which society ought to move. The reconstructionist believes that the social sciences ought to be employed in the attempt to understand the culture, what its problems are, what the society in consensus desires. He is heavily indebted to the anthropologist, the sociologist, the economist, the political scientist, and the psychologist for their varied approaches and understandings of man in society. At least, in the case of Brameld, Utopian thought has influenced the reconstructionist position. Utopian works such as Plato's *Republic*, More's *Utopia*, Bellamy's *Looking Backward* point to a reconstructed understanding of society and man's place in it. These writers contend that values, orientations, and institutions of society are not what they ought to be and consequently new values, institutions, and patterns of behavior must be found and articulated. Though the reconstructionist would accept the utopian writers' emphasis on cultural critique and on the importance of developing a new culture, he would reject the otherworldly tendency in most of these works. What must be done is to employ the projective technique of the utopian writer when he is carving out a new way of life and to ground this projection in the contours of human experience and on the techniques of the social sciences.

The final cultural posture one could take in an attempt to come to grips with a culture in conflict is essentialism. The essentialist contends that what is needed for our day are stabilizers to keep us on an even keel. These stabilizers come from the culture itself, its past and present traditions and institutions. Only the time-tested content, the orderly sequence, the inherited principles, the guided discipline essential to one's culture will give one a stable perspective from which to confront the problems of a crisis culture. The essentialist position need not be one of mere acceptance of the past in a culture. Rather, it can be a critical appraisal of the importance of continuity in society and of what must be done if meaning is to be found.

Essentialism is a cultural posture which has a long heritage in Western culture. One of the first contributors to essentialism was Plato. He believed that the fourth century Greeks ought to look into their own culture and find their institutional forms and values around which they could organize their lives and answer the problems they faced in a disintegrating culture. Of course, the central institution which Plato believed ought to be maintained and its values preserved is the *polis*. He argued that the ideals which ought to govern the *polis* are a realm of forms which are necessary, immutable. At this point one can see that Plato contributed to essentialism as well as perennialism. For him the principles which are basic to the *polis* are also the perennial ones. Indeed, from Plato through Aquinas essentialism was undergirded by a metaphysics which was indistinguishable from the perennialist position. Augustine, for example, though a perennialist in that he advocated going back to the ideals of early Rome and to the early Christian faith, believed that the ideals of the Roman people and of the Christian faith are embodied in the institutions of the Roman state and the Christian Church. In this sense Augustine contributed to the essentialist as well as to the perennialist position.

In the nineteenth century essentialism received its strongest statement in the work of Edmund Burke. Burke's position was born not of speculative metaphysics nor of scientific studies of society. Rather, he came to his views through active participation in the affairs of the English Parliament and in reaction to the American and French Revolutions. Burke believed that men are creatures of habit and find meaning and intelligibility in stable social institutions and in traditional beliefs. Any radical changes in society would sweep away these underpinnings. The French Revolution which brought about sweeping changes in the lives of Frenchmen Burke believed to be wrong. The new institutions established in the late 1790s were not based on the traditions of the French people. The effect of such changes was to uproot the people and to leave them to the whims of passion. On the other hand, the American Revolution, which was clearly based on political traditions deeply imbedded in English life, was not a radical cutting off from social institutions and beliefs and consequently was defensible.

One of the best reasoned arguments advanced by a contemporary essentialist or conservative is that made by Michael Polanyi. Polanyi does not develop his position from the position of an active politician such as a Burke or a Christian facing radical changes in society such as Augustine. After training in the natural sciences he became interested in sociology and then in philosophy, particularly in epistemology. The work of Polanyi may be more easily understood if one recognizes that he is deeply indebted to Gestalt psychology and its work in perception. Psychologists working within a Gestalt orientation contend that perception is to be explained as arising from the observer's actively organizing his cultural experience into wholes on the basis of principles brought to the learning situation. This means that in the mind's search for knowledge its point of departure is the culture in which the person lives. However, because the mind is constantly having new experiences and because of the mind's capacity for integrating those experiences, the mind may begin to explore beyond the authority structure of a society and create new values, new understandings. Taking his cue then from the work of Gestalt psychologists, Polanyi develops an epistemology the implication of which is a social and cultural conservatism.

In conclusion, a society whose culture is in conflict and which considers carefully the ends to which it wants to educate its young and possibly its adults must recognize that it is transmitting attitudes toward itself which have important implications for the kinds of goals it wants to achieve. Particular character traits find their meaning in the context of one's attitudes toward oneself and one's society. This attitude may be called cultural posture. The authors in this chapter are attempting to articulate four such stances and to suggest particular goals which these orientations imply.

Perennialism

Education at the Crossroads*
JACQUES MARITAIN

1. THE NATURE OF MAN AND EDUCATION

The Education of Man

The general title I have chosen is *Education at the Crossroads.* I might also have entitled these chapters *The Education of Man*, though such a title may unintentionally seem provocative: for many of our contemporaries know primitive man, or Western man, or the man of the Renaissance, or the man of the industrial era, or the criminal man, or the bourgeois man, or the working man, but they wonder what is meant when we speak of man.

Of course the job of education is not to shape the Platonist man-in-himself, but to shape a particular child belonging to a given nation, a given social environment, a given historical age. Yet before being a child of the twentieth century, an American-born or European-born child, a gifted or a retarded child, this child is a child of man. Before being a civilized man—at least I hope I am—and a Frenchman nurtured in Parisian intellectual circles, I am a man. If it is true, moreover, that our chief duty consists, according to the profound saying of the Greek poet,

Pindar, in *becoming who we are,* nothing is more important for each of us, or more difficult, than *to become a man.* Thus the chief task of education is above all to shape man, or to guide the evolving dynamism through which man forms himself as a man. That is why I might have taken for my title *The Education of Man.*

We shall not forget that the word education has a triple yet intermingled connotation, and refers either to any process whatsoever by means of which man is shaped and led toward fulfilment (education in its broadest sense), or to the task of formation which adults intentionally undertake with regard to youth, or, in its strictest sense, to the special task of schools and universities.

In the present chapter I shall discuss the aims of education. In the course of this discussion we are to meet and examine, by the way, some significant misconceptions regarding education—seven of them in all.

Man is not merely an animal of nature, like a skylark or a bear. He is also an animal of culture, whose race can subsist only within the development of society and civilization, he is a *historical* animal: hence the multiplicity of cultural or ethico-historical patterns into which man is diversified; hence, too, the essential importance of education. Due to the very fact that he is endowed with a knowing power which is unlimited and which nonetheless only advances step by step, man cannot progress in his own specific life, both intellectually and morally, without being helped by collective experience previously accumulated and preserved, and by a regular transmission of acquired knowledge. In order to reach self-determination, for which he is made, he needs discipline and tradition, which will both weigh heavily on him and strengthen him so as to enable him to struggle against them—which will enrich that very tradition—and the enriched tradition will make possible new struggles, and so forth.

The First Misconception: a Disregard of Ends

Education is an art, and an especially difficult one. Yet it belongs by its nature to the sphere of ethics and practical wisdom. Education is an *ethical* art (or rather a practical wisdom in which a determinate art is embodied). Now every art is a dynamic trend toward an object to be achieved, which is the aim of this art. There is no art without ends, art's very vitality is the energy with which it tends toward its end, without stopping at any intermediary step.

Here we see from the outset the two most general misconceptions against which education must guard itself. The first misconception is a lack or disregard of ends. If means are liked and cultivated for the sake of their own perfection, and not as means alone, to that very extent they cease to lead to the end, and art loses its practicality; its vital efficiency is replaced by a process of infinite multiplication, each means developing and spreading for its own sake. This supremacy of means over end and the consequent collapse of all sure purpose and real efficiency seem to be the main reproach to contemporary education. The means are not bad. On the contrary, they are generally much better than those of the old pedagogy. The misfortune is precisely that they are so good that we lose sight of the end. Hence the surprising weakness of education today, which proceeds from our attachment to the very perfection of our modern educational means and methods and our failure to bend them toward the end. The child is so well tested and observed, his needs so well detailed, his psychology so clearly cut out, the methods for making it easy for him everywhere so perfected, that the end of all these commendable improvements runs the risk of being forgotten or disregarded. Thus modern medicine is often hampered by the very excellence of its means: for instance, when a doctor makes the examination of the patient's reactions so perfectly and carefully in his laboratory that he forgets the cure; in the meantime the patient may die, for having been too well tended, or rather analyzed. The scientific improvement of the pedagogical means and methods is in itself outstanding progress. But the more it takes on importance, the more it requires a parallel strengthening of practical wisdom and of the dynamic trend toward the goal.

The Second Misconception: False Ideas concerning the End

The second general error or misconception of education does not consist of an actual dearth of appreciation of the end but false or incomplete ideas concerning the nature of this end. The educational task is both greater and more mysterious and, in a sense, humbler than many imagine. If the aim of education is the helping and guiding of man toward his own human achievement, education cannot escape the problems and entanglements of philosophy, for it supposes by its very nature a philosophy of man, and from the outset it is obliged to answer the question: "What is man?" which the philosophical sphinx is asking.

The Scientific and the Philosophical-Religious Idea of Man

I should like to observe at this point that, definitely speaking, there are only two classes or categories of notions concerning man which play fair, so to speak: the purely scientific idea of man and the philosophical-religious one. According to its genuine methodological type, the scientific idea of man, like every idea recast by strictly experimental science, gets rid as far as possible of any ontological content, so that it may be entirely verifiable in sense-experience. On this point the most recent theorists of science, the neopositivists of the school of Vienna, are quite right. The purely scientific idea of man tends only to link together measurable and observable data taken as such, and is determined from the very start not to consider anything like being or essence, not to answer any question like: Is there a soul or isn't there? Does the spirit exist or only matter? Is there freedom or determinism? Purpose or chance? Value or simple fact? For such questions are out of the realm of science. The purely scientific idea of man is, and must be, a phenomenalized idea without reference to ultimate reality.

The philosophical-religious idea of man, on the contrary, is an ontological idea. It is not entirely verifiable in sense-experience, though it possesses criteria and proofs of its own, and it deals with the essential and intrinsic, though not visible or tangible characters, and with the intelligible density of that being which we call man.

Now it is obvious that the purely scientific idea of man can provide us with invaluable and ever-growing information concerning the means and tools of education, but by itself it can neither primarily found nor primarily guide education, for education needs primarily to know what man *is*, what is the nature of man and the scale of values it essentially involves; and the purely scientific idea of man, because it ignores "being-as-such," does not know such things, but only what emerges from the human being in the realm of sense observation and measurement. Young Tom, Dick, or Harry, who are the subjects of education, are not only a set of physical, biological, and psychological phenomena, the knowledge of which is moreover thoroughly needed and necessary; they are the children of man—this very name "man" designating for the common sense of parents, educators, and society the same ontological mystery as is recognized in the rational knowledge of philosophers and theologians.

It should be pointed out that if we tried to build education on the single pattern of the scientific idea of man and carry it out accordingly, we could only do so by distorting or warping this idea: for we should have to ask what is the nature and destiny of man, and we should be pressing the only idea at our disposal, that is the scientific one, for an answer to our question. Then we would try, contrary to its type, to draw from it a kind of metaphysics. From the logical point of view, we would have a spurious metaphysics disguised as science and yet deprived of any really philosophical insight; and from the practical point of view, we would have a denial or misconception of those very realities and values without which education loses all human sense or becomes the training of an animal for the utility of the state.

Thus the fact remains that the complete and integral idea of man which is the prerequisite of education can only be a philosophical and religious idea of man. I say philosophical, because this idea pertains to the nature or essence of man; I say religious, because of the existential status of this human nature in relation to God and the special gifts and trials and vocation involved.

The Christian Idea of Man

There are many forms of the philosophical and religious idea of man. When I state that the education of man, in order to be completely well grounded, must be based upon the Christian idea of man, it is because I think that this idea of man is the true one, not because I see our civilization actually permeated with this idea. Yet, for all that, the man of our civilization *is* the Christian man, more or less secularized. Consequently we may accept this idea as a common basis and imply that it is to be agreed upon by the common consciousness in our civilized countries, except among those who adhere to utterly opposite outlooks, like materialistic metaphysics, positivism, or skepticism—I am not speaking here of Fascist and racist creeds, which do not belong at all in the civilized world.

Now such a kind of agreement is all that any doctrine in moral philosophy can be expected to have, for none can pretend actually to obtain the literal universal assent of all minds—not because of any weakness in objective proof but because of the weakness inherent in human minds.

There does exist, indeed, among the diverse great metaphysical outlooks, if they recognize the dignity of the spirit, and among the diverse forms of Christian creeds, or even of religious creeds in general, if they recognize the divine destiny of man, a community of analogy as concerns practical attitudes and the realm of action, which makes possible a genuine human cooperation. In a Judeo-Greco-Christian civilization like ours, this community of analogy, which extends from the most orthodox religious forms of thought to the mere humanistic ones, makes it possible for a Christian philosophy of education, if it is well founded and rationally developed, to play an inspiring part in the concert, even for those who do not share in the creed of its supporters. Be it added, by the way, that the term concert, which I just used, seems rather euphemistic with regard to our "modern philosophies of education," whose discordant voices have been so valuably studied in Professor Brubacher's book.[1]

[1]Cf. John S. Brubacher, *Modern Philosophies of Education* (New York and London, 1939).

In answer to our question, then, "What is man?" we may give the Greek, Jewish, and Christian idea of man: man as an animal endowed with reason, whose supreme dignity is in the intellect; and man as a free individual in personal relation with God, whose supreme righteousness consists in voluntarily obeying the law of God; and man as a sinful and wounded creature called to divine life and to the freedom of grace, whose supreme perfection consists of love.

Human Personality

From the philosophical point of view alone the main concept to be stressed here is the concept of human personality. Man is a person, who holds himself in hand by his intelligence and his will. He does not merely exist as a physical being. There is in him a richer and nobler existence; he has spiritual superexistence through knowledge and love. He is thus, in some way, a whole, not merely a part; he is a universe unto himself, a microcosm in which the great universe in its entirety can be encompassed through knowledge. And through love he can give himself freely to beings who are to him, as it were, other selves; and for this relationship no equivalent can be found in the physical world.

If we seek the prime root of all this, we are led to the acknowledgment of the full philosophical reality of that concept of the soul, so variegated in its connotations, which Aristotle described as the first principle of life in any organism and viewed as endowed with supramaterial intellect in man, and which Christianity revealed as the dwelling place of God and as made for eternal life. In the flesh and bones of man there exists a soul which is a spirit and which has a greater value than the whole physical universe. Dependent though he may be upon the slightest accidents of matter, the human person exists by virtue of the existence of his soul, which dominates time and death. It is the spirit which is the root of personality.

The notion of personality thus involves that of wholeness and independence. To say that a man is a person is to say that in the depth of his being he is more a whole than a part and more independent than servile. It is this mystery of our nature which religious thought designates when it says that the person is the image of God. A person possesses absolute dignity because he is in direct relationship with the realm of being, truth, goodness, and beauty, and with God, and it is only with these that he can arrive at his complete fulfillment. His spiritual fatherland consists of the entire order of things which have absolute value, and which reflect, in some manner, a divine Absolute superior to the world and which have a power of attraction toward this Absolute.

Personality and Individualty

Now it should be pointed out that personality is only one aspect or one pole of the human being. The other pole is—to speak the Aristotelian language—individuality, whose prime root is matter. The same man, the same entire man who is, in one sense, a person or a whole made independent by his spiritual soul, is also, in another sense, a material individual, a fragment of a species, a part of the physical universe, a single dot in the immense network of forces and influences, cosmic, ethnic, historic, whose laws we must obey. His very humanity is the humanity of an animal, living by sense and instinct as well as by reason. Thus man is "a horizon in which two worlds meet." Here we face that classical distinction between the *ego* and the *self* which both Hindu and Christian philosophies have emphasized, though with quite diverse connotations. I shall come back to this thought later on.

I should like to observe now that a kind of animal training, which deals with psychophysical habits, conditioned reflexes, sense-memorization, etc., undoubtedly plays its part in education: it refers to material individuality, or to what is not specifically human in man. But education is not animal training. The education of man is a human awakening.

Thus what is of most importance in educators themselves is a respect for the soul as well as for the body of the child, the sense of his innermost essence and his internal resources, and a sort of sacred and loving attention to his mysterious identity, which is a hidden thing that no techniques can reach. And what matters most in the educational enterprise is a perpetual appeal to intelligence and free will in the young. Such an appeal, fittingly proportioned to age and circumstances, can and should begin with the first educational steps. Each field of training, each school activity—physical training as well as elementary reading or the rudiments of childhood etiquette and morals—can be intrinsically improved and can outstrip its own immediate practical value through being *humanized* in this way by understanding. Nothing should be required of the child without an explanation and without making sure that the child has understood.

2. CONCERNING THE AIMS OF EDUCATION

We may now define in a more precise manner the aim of education. It is to guide man in the evolving dynamism through which he shapes himself as a human person—armed with knowledge, strength of judgment, and moral virtues—while at the same time conveying to him the spiritual heritage of the nation and the civilization in which he is involved, and preserving in this way the century-old achievements of generations. The utilitarian aspect of education—which enables the youth to get a job and make a living—must surely not be disregarded, for the children of man are not made for aristocratic leisure. But this practical aim is best provided by the general human capacities developed. And the ulterior specialized training which may be required must never imperil the essential aim of education.

Now in order to get a complete idea of the aim of education, it is necessary to take into closer consideration the human person and his deep natural aspirations.

The Conquest of Internal Freedom

The chief aspirations of a person are aspirations to freedom—I do not mean that freedom which is free will and which is a gift of nature in each of us, I mean that freedom which is spontaneity, expansion, or autonomy, and which we have to gain through constant effort and struggle. And what is the more profound and essential form of such a desire? It is the desire for inner and spiritual freedom. In this sense Greek philosophy, especially Aristotle, spoke of the independence which is granted to men by intellect and wisdom as the perfection of the human being. And the Gospel was to lift up human perfection to a higher level—a truly divine one—by stating that it consists of the perfection of love and, as St. Paul put it, of the freedom of those who are moved by the divine Spirit. In any case it is by the activities that the philosophers call "immanent"—because they perfect the very subject which exerts them, and are within it the supreme activities of internal achievement and superabundance—that the full freedom of independence is won. Thus the prime goal of education is the conquest of internal and spiritual freedom to be achieved by the individual person, or, in other words, his liberation through knowledge and wisdom, good will, and love.

At this point we must observe that the freedom of which we are speaking is not a mere unfolding of potentialities without any object to be grasped, or a mere movement for the sake of movement, without aim or objective to be attained. It is sheer nonsense to offer such a movement to man as constituting his glory. A movement without aim is just running around in circles and getting nowhere. The aim, here on earth, will always be grasped in a partial and imperfect manner, and in this sense, indeed, the movement is to be pursued without end. Yet the aim will somehow be grasped, even though partially. Moreover the spiritual activities of the human being are *intentional* activities, they tend by nature toward an object, an objective aim, which will measure and rule them, not materially and by means of bondage, but spiritually and by means of liberty, for the object of knowledge or of love is internalized by the activity itself of the intelligence and the will, and becomes within them the very fire of their perfect spontaneity. Truth—which does not depend on us but on *what is*—truth is not a set of ready-made formulas to be passively recorded, so as to have the mind closed and enclosed by them. Truth is an infinite realm—as infinite as being—whose wholeness transcends infinitely our powers of perception, and each fragment of which must be grasped through vital and purified internal activity. This conquest of being, this progressive attainment of new truths, or the progressive realization of the ever-growing and ever-renewed significance of truths already attained, opens and enlarges our mind and life, and really situates them in freedom and autonomy. And speaking of will and love rather than knowledge, no one is freer, or more independent, than the one who gives himself for a cause or a real being worthy of the gift.

The Third Misconception: Pragmatism

Here we find ourselves confronted with the inappropriateness of the pragmatic overemphasis in education—a third error or misconception that we meet on our path. Many things are excellent in the emphasis on action and "praxis," for life consists of action. But action and praxis aim at an object, a determining end without which they lose direction and vitality. And life exists, too, for an end which makes it worthy of being lived. Contemplation and self-perfection, in which human life aspires to flower forth, escape the purview of the pragmatic mind.

It is an unfortunate mistake to define human thought as an organ of response to the actual stimuli and situations of the environment, that is to say, to define it in terms of animal knowledge and reaction, for such a definition exactly covers the way of "thinking" proper only to animals without reason. On the contrary, it is because every human idea, to have a meaning, must attain in some measure (be it even in the symbols of a mathematical interpretation of phenomena), what things *are* or consist of unto themselves; it is because human thought is an instrument or rather a vital energy of knowledge or spiritual intuition (I don't mean "knowledge about," I mean "knowledge into"); it is because thinking begins, not only with difficulties but with *insights,* and ends up in insights which are made true by rational proving or experimental verifying, not by pragmatic sanction, that human thought is able to illumine experience, to realize desires which are human because they are rooted in the prime desire for unlimited good, and to dominate, control, and refashion the world. At the beginning of human action, insofar as it is human, there is truth, grasped or believed to be grasped for the sake of truth. Without trust in truth, there is no human effectiveness. Such is, to my mind, the chief criticism to be made of the pragmatic and instrumentalist theory of knowledge.

In the field of education, this pragmatic theory of knowledge, passing from philosophy to upbringing, can hardly produce in the youth anything but a scholarly skepticism equipped with the best techniques of mental training and the best scientific methods, which will be unnaturally used against the very grain of intelligence, so as to cause minds to distrust the very idea of truth and wisdom, and to give up any hope of inner dynamic unity.[2] Moreoever, by dint of insisting that in order to teach John mathematics it is more important to know John than to know mathematics—which is true enough in one sense—the teacher will so perfectly succeed in knowing John that John will never succeed in knowing mathematics. Modern pedagogy has made invaluable progress in stressing the necessity of carefully analyzing and fixing its gaze on the human subject. The wrong begins when *the object to be taught* and *the primacy of the object* are forgotten, and when the cult of the means—not to an end, but without an end—only ends up in a psychological worship of the subject.

The Social Potentialities of the Person

I have spoken of the aspiration of the human person to freedom, and, first of all, to inner and spiritual freedom. The second essential form of this desire is the desire for freedom externally manifested, and this freedom is linked to social life and lies at its very root. For society is "natural" to man in terms not only of animal or instinctive nature but of human nature, that is, of reason and freedom. If man is a naturally political animal, this is so in the sense that society, required by nature, is achieved through free consent, and because the human person demands the communications of social life through the openness and generosity proper to intelligence and love as well as through the needs of a human individual born naked and destitute. Thus it is that social life tends to emancipate man from the bondage of material nature. It subordinates the individual to the common good, but always in order that the common good flow back upon the individuals, and that they enjoy that freedom of expansion or independence which is insured by the economic guarantees of labor and ownership, political rights, civil virtues, and the cultivation of the mind.

As a result, it is obvious that man's education must be concerned with the social group and prepare him to play his part in it. Shaping man to lead a normal, useful and cooperative life in the community, or guiding

---

[2]The "four cults"—skepticism, presentism, scientism, anti-intellectualism—listed by Dr. Hutchins (*Education for Freedom* [1943], p. 35–36) are but offsprings of pragmatism's domination over education.

the development of the human person in the social sphere, awakening and strengthening both his sense of freedom and his sense of obligation and responsibility, is an essential aim. But it is not the primary, it is the secondary essential aim. The ultimate end of education concerns the human person in his personal life and spiritual progress, not in his relationship to the social environment. Moreover, with regard to the secondary aim itself of which I am speaking, we must never forget that personal freedom itself is as the core of social life, and that a human society is veritably a group of human freedoms which accept obedience and self-sacrifice and a common law for the general welfare, in order to enable each of these freedoms to reach in everyone a truly human fulfillment. The man and the group are intermingled with each other and they surpass each other in different respects. Man finds himself by subordinating himself to the group, and the group attains its goal only by serving man and by realizing that man has secrets which escape the group and a vocation which is not included in the group.

The Fourth Misconception: Sociologism

Here we are confronted with a fourth error of misconception akin to the third one, which derives the supreme rule and standard of education from social conditioning. The essence of education does not consist in adapting a potential citizen to the conditions and interactions of social life, but first in *making a man,* and by this very fact in preparing a citizen. Not only is it nonsense to oppose education for the person and education for the commonwealth, but the latter supposes the former as a prerequisite, and in return the former is impossible without the latter, for one does not make a man except in the bosom of social ties where there is an awakening of civic understanding and civic virtues.

The old education is to be reproached for its abstract and bookish individualism. To have made education more experiential, closer to concrete life and permeated with social concerns from the very start is an achievement of which modern education is justly proud. Yet in order to reach completion such a necessary reform must understand, too, that to be a good citizen and a man of civilization what matters above all is the inner center, the living source of personal conscience in which originate idealism and generosity, the sense of law and the sense of friendship, respect for others, but at the same time deep-rooted independence with regard to common opinion. We must also understand that without abstract insight and intellectual enlightenment the more striking experiences are of no use to man, like beautiful colors in darkness; that the best way not to be bookish is to avoid textbooks as a plague, even textbooks in experientialism, but to read books, I mean to read them avidly; and to understand also that, in a more general way, the pursuit of concrete life becomes a decoy if it scatters the attention of man or child among practical trifles, psychotechnical recipes, and the infinity of utilitarian activities, while disregarding the genuine concrete life of the intellect and the soul. The sense of concrete reality is made blunt by utilitarianism; it develops and flowers forth through those activities which are all the more needed by human life since they are not at the service of any practical utility, because they are in themselves, freedom, fruit, and joy. Unfortunate is a youth who does not know the pleasure of the spirit and is not exalted in the joy of knowing and the joy of beauty, and enthusiasm for ideas, and quickening experience in the first love, delight and luxury of wisdom and poetry. Boredom and weariness with human affairs will come early enough indeed; to deal with them is the job of the grown-up.

To discuss the matter in a more specific manner, I should like to make the following observations: that conception which makes education itself a constantly renewed experiment, starting from the pupil s present purposes and developing in one way or another according to the success of his problem-solving activity with regard to these purposes and to new purposes arising from broadened experience in unforeseen directions, such a pragmatist conception has its own merits when it comes to the necessity of adapting educational methods to the natural interests of the pupil. But what are the standards for judging the purposes and values thus successively emerging in the pupil's mind? If the teacher himself has no general aim, nor final values to which all this process is related; if education itself is to grow "in whatever direction a novelly emerging future renders most feasible";[3] in other words, if the pragmatist theory requires a perpetual experimental reconstruction of the ends of the educator himself (and not only of the experience of the pupil), then it teaches educational recipes but gets away from any real art of education: for an education which does not have any goal of its own and tends only to growth itself without "end beyond further growth"[4] is no more an art of architecture which would not have any idea of what is to be built, and would only tend to the growth of the construction in whatever direction a new addition of materials is feasible. In nature itself, biological growth is nothing but a morphological process, or the progressive acquisition of a definite form. And finally the pragmatist theory can only subordinate and enslave education to the trends which may develop in collective life and society, for in the last analysis the aims newly arising in such a "reconstruction of ends" will only be determined by the precarious factors of the environment to be controlled and the values made at each moment predominant by given social conditions or tendencies by the state.

[3]Brubacher, *op. cit.*, p. 329.
[4]*Ibid.*

The element of truth which must be preserved in the conception I have just discussed, is the fact that the final end of education—the fulfillment of man as a human person—is infinitely higher and broader than the aim of architectural art or even the aim of medical art, for it deals with our very freedom and spirit, whose boundless potentialities can be led to full human stature only by means of constant creative renewal. As a result, the vital spontaneity of the one to be educated plays a major part in the progress toward this final end, as well as the steady widening of the pupil's experience; and the need for constantly renewed adaptation of methods, means, and approaches is much greater in educational art than in any art dealing only with some material achievement.

The Fifth Misconception: Intellectualism

With regard to the powers of the human soul I should like now to indicate as briefly as possible two other errors which oppose one another and which come from overemphasis: intellectualism, the fifth error or misconception on our list; the other, voluntarism.

Intellectualism takes on two principal forms: a certain form of intellectualism seeks the supreme achievements of education in sheer dialectical or rhetorical skill—such was the case of classical pedagogy, especially in the bourgeois era, in which education was a privilege of privileged classes.

Another form of intellectualism, a modern one, gives up universal values and insists upon the working and experiential functions of intelligence. It seeks the supreme achievements of education in scientific and technical specialization. Now specialization is more and more needed by the technical organization of modern life, yet it should be compensated for by a more vigorous general training, especially during youth. If we remember that the animal is a specialist, and a perfect one, all of its knowing-power being fixed upon a single task to be done, we ought to conclude that an educational program which would only aim at forming specialists ever more perfect in ever more specialized fields, and unable to pass judgment on any matter that goes beyond their specialized competence, would lead indeed to a progressive animalization of the human mind and life. Finally, as the life of bees consists of producing honey, the real life of man would consist of producing in a perfectly pigeonholed manner economic values and scientific discoveries, while some cheap pleasure or social entertainment would occupy leisure time, and a vague religious feeling, without any content of thought and reality, would make existence a little less flat, perhaps a little more dramatic and stimulating, like a happy dream. The overwhelming cult of specialization dehumanizes man's life.

Fortunately, nowhere in the world has any educational system been set up solely on this basis. Yet there exists everywhere a trend toward such a conception of education, following a more or less conscious materialistic philosophy of life. This represents a great peril for the democracies, because the democratic ideal more than any other requires faith in and the development of spiritual energies—a field which is over and above any specialization—and because a complete division of the human mind and activities into specialized compartments would make impossible the very "government of the people, by the people, and for the people." How could the common man be capable of judging about the good of the people if he felt able to pass judgment only in the field of his own specialized vocational competence? Political activity and political judgment would become the exclusive job of specialized experts in the matter— a kind of state technocracy which does not open particularly felicitous perspectives either for the good of the people or for liberty. As for education—complemented by some imperative vocational guidance—it would become the regular process of differentiation of the bees in the human beehive. In reality, the democratic way of life demands primarily liberal education for all and a general humanistic development throughout society. Even as to industrial achievements, man's free ingenuity strengthened by an education which liberates and broadens the mind is of as great import as technical specialization, for out of these free resources of human intelligence there arises, in managers and workers, the power of adapting themselves to new circumstances and mastering them.

The Sixth Misconception: Voluntarism

Voluntarism, also has two principal forms. In reaction against the first form of intellectualism, a voluntarist trend, developed since the time of Schopenhauer, has contributed to upset the internal order of human nature, by making intelligence subservient to the will and by appealing to the virtue of irrational forces. Accordingly, education was intended to concentrate either on the will which was to be disciplined according to some national pattern or on the free expansion of nature and natural potentialities. The merit of the best and wisest forms of voluntarism in the educational field[5] has been to call attention again to the essential importance of the voluntary functions, disregarded by intellectualist pedagogy, and to the primacy of morality, virtue, and generosity in the upbringing of man. For the main point is surely to be a good man rather than to be a learned man. As Rabelais put it, science without conscience is the ruin of

[5] I am thinking for instance of the work of F. W. Foerster, whose influence has been great in many European pedagogical circles.

the soul. Such was the ideal but in actual fact the pedagogic achievements of voluntarism have been strangely disappointing, at least from the point of view of the good. From the point of view of evil, they have had plenty of success—I mean in the effectiveness of Nazi training, schools, and youth organizations, in smashing all sense of truth in human minds and in perverting the very function of language and morally devastating the youth and making the intellect only an organ of the technical equipment of the state.

For the voluntarist trend in education combines very well with technical training. We find such a combination not only in the totalitarian corruption of education but elsewhere also, and there to some good purpose. As we see it in democratic countries, this peculiar form of educational voluntarism may be described as an effort to compensate for the inconveniences of the second form of intellectualism—overspecialized technical training—by what is known as education of will, education of feeling, formation of character, etc. Yet the misfortune is that this commendable effort has yielded, as a rule, the same disappointing result of which I spoke a moment ago.[6] Character is something easily warped or debased, difficult to shape. All the pedagogical hammering of nails into the shoe doesn't make the shoe more comfortable to the foot. The methods which change the school into a hospital for refitting and vitalizing the wills, suggesting altruistic behavior or infusing good citizenship, may be well conceived and psychologically suitable, but they are for the most part dishearteningly ineffective.

We believe that intelligence is in and by itself nobler than the will of man, for its activity is more immaterial and universal. But we believe also that, in regard to the things or the very objects on which this activity bears, it is better to will and love the good than simply to know it. Moreover it is through man's will, when it is good, not through his intelligence, be it ever so perfect, that man is made good and right. A similar intermingling of roles is to be found in education, taken in its broadest sense. The upbringing of the human being must lead both intelligence and will toward achievement, and the shaping of the will is throughout more important to man than the shaping of the intellect. Yet, whereas the educational system of schools and colleges succeeds as a rule

[6]Voluntarism does not succeed in forming and strengthening the will, but it succeeds in deforming and weakening the intellect, by the very fact that it exaggerates the province of the will in thought itself, so as to make everything a matter of one's will to believe. It has been pointed out in this connection that "just as in the realm of politics, the primacy of will identifies authority with force, so in the realm of thought the primacy of will reduces everything to arbitrary opinions or academic conventions. There are no first truths, but only postulates, demands of the will that something be taken for granted. In some sense, all knowledge rests on acts of faith, though the only principle of such faith is one's private predilections." Mortimer J. Adler, "Liberalism and Liberal Education," *The Educational Record*, July, 1939, pp. 435–436.

in equipping man's intellect for knowledge, it seems to be missing its main achievement, the equipping of man's will. What an infelicity!

3. THE PARADOXES OF EDUCATION

The Seventh Misconception: Everything Can Be Learned

We are here confronted with some paradoxical aspects of education. The main paradox can be formulated as follows: what is most important in education is not the job of education, and still less that of learning. Here we face an error terribly current in the modern world—the seventh error or misconception on our list—which boils down to the belief that everything can be learned. Greek sophists, too, believed that everything, even virtue, could be gotten by means of learning and discussing the matter. It is not true that everything can be learned, and that youth must earnestly expect from colleges not only courses in cooking, housekeeping, nursing, advertising, cosmetology,[7] moneymaking, and getting married, but also—why not?—courses on the scientific means of acquiring creative genius in art or science, or of consoling those who weep, or of being a man of generosity.

The teaching of morality, with regard to its intellectual bases, should occupy a great place in school and college education. Yet that right appreciation of practical cases which the ancients called *prudentia,* and which is an inner vital power of judgment developed in the mind and backed up by well-directed will, cannot be replaced by any learning whatsoever. Nor can experience, which is an incommunicable fruit of suffering and memory, and through which the shaping of man is achieved, be taught by any school or any courses. There are courses in philosophy, but no courses in wisdom; wisdom is gained through spiritual experience, and as for practical wisdom, as Aristotle put it, the experience of old men is both as undemonstrable and illuminating as the first principles of understanding. Moreover, is there anything of greater import in the education of man than that which is of the greatest import for man and human life? For man and human life there is indeed nothing greater than intuition and love. Not every love is right, nor every intuition well directed or conceptualized, yet if either intuition or love exists in any hidden corner, life and the flame of life are there, and a bit of heaven in a promise. Yet neither intuition nor love is a matter of training and learning, they are gift and freedom. In spite of all that, education should be

---

[7] "I attacked vocationalism, and the University of California announced a course in cosmetology, saying 'The profession of beautician is the fastest growing in this state.' " Robert M. Hutchins, *Education for Freedom* (Louisiana State University Press, 1943), p. 19.

primarily concerned with them[8]. . . With regard to love, which is the soul of moral life, the whole problem of morality is involved, and I shall be able only to touch upon it occasionally.

The Educational and Extra-educational Spheres

Another paradox deals with what may be called the educational and extra-educational spheres. By educational spheres I mean those collective entities which have always been recognized as especially committed to educational training: namely the family, the school, the state, and the Church. Here the surprising thing is that on the one hand the family, which is the first and fundamental educational sphere, grounded in nature, performs its educational task while not infrequently making the child a victim of psychological traumatisms, or of the bad example, ignorance, or prejudice of the adult; and that on the other hand the school, whose special and vocational function is education, performs its educational task while not infrequently making the youth a victim of stupefying overwork or disintegrating chaotic specialization, and often extinguishing the fire of natural gifts and defrauding the thirst of natural intelligence by dint of pseudo-knowledge. The solution is surely not to get rid of the family or of the school, but to endeavor to make them more aware and more worthy of their call, to acknowledge not only the necessity of mutual help but also the inevitability of a reciprocal tension between the one and the other, and to recognize, too, that from the very start, I say from childhood on, man's condition is to suffer from and defend himself against the most worthy and indispensable supporters whom material nature has provided for his life, and thus to grow amidst and through conflict, if only energy, love, and good will quicken his heart.

Yet what is perhaps most paradoxical is that the extra-educational sphere—that is, the entire field of human activity, particularly everyday work and pain, hard experiences in friendship and love, social customs, law (which is a "pedagogue," according to St. Paul), the common wisdom embodied in the behavior of the people, the inspiring radiance of art and poetry, the penetrating influence of religious feasts and liturgy—all this extra-educational sphere exerts on man an action which is more important in the achievement of his education than education itself. Finally the

---

[8]"Education ought to teach us how to be in love always and what to be in love with. The great things of history have been done by the great lovers, by the saints and men of science and artists; and the problem of civilization is to give every man a chance of being a saint, a man of science, or an artist. But this problem cannot be attempted, much less solved, unless men desire to be saints, men of science, and artists, and if they are to desire that continuously and consciously, they must be taught what it means to be these things." Sir Arthur Clutton-Brock, *The Ultimate Belief* (New York, 1916), p. 123. Quoted by John U. Nef, *The United States and Civilization* (Chicago, 1942), p. 265.

all-important factor is a transcendent one, that call of the hero which Henri Bergson so insistently emphasized, and which passes through the whole structure of social habits and moral regulations as a vitalizing aspiration toward the infinite Love which is the source of being. The saints and the martyrs are the true educators of mankind.

The Educational System with Regard to the Formation of the Will and the Dignity of the Intellect

We may now come back to the intermingling of intelligence and will of which I spoke earlier. We must here stress some characteristics of school and college education which are often insufficiently taken into account. School and college education is only a part of education. It pertains only to the beginnings and the completed *preparation* of the upbringing of man, and no illusion is more harmful than to try to push back into the microcosm of school education the entire process of shaping the human being, as if the system of schools and universities were a big factory through the back door of which the young child enters like a raw material, and from the front door of which the youth in his brilliant twenties will go out as a successfully manufactured man. Our education goes on until our death. Further, even in this preparatory field, school education itself has only a partial task, and this task is primarily concerned with knowledge and intelligence.

Teaching's domain is the domain of truth—I mean speculative as well as practical truth. The only dominating influence in the school and the college must be that of truth, and of the intelligible realities whose illuminating power obtains by its own virtue, not by virtue of the human authority of the master's say-so, the assent of an "open mind," intending to pronounce one way or another "according to the worth of evidence." No doubt the child's "open mind" is still unarmed, and unable to judge "according to the worth of evidence"; the child must believe his teacher. But from the very start the teacher must respect in the child the dignity of the mind, must appeal to the child's power of understanding, and conceive of his own effort as preparing a human mind to think for itself. The one who does not yet know must believe a master, but only in order to know, and maybe to reject at this very moment the opinions of the master; and he believes him provisionally, only because of the truth which the teacher is supposed to convey.

Thus it is chiefly through the instrumentality of intelligence and truth that the school and the college may affect the powers of desire, will, and love in the youth, and help him gain control of his tendential dynamism. Moral education plays an essential part in school and college education, and this part must be more and more emphasized. But it is essentially and above all by way of knowledge and teaching that school education must perform this moral task, that is to say, not by exercising and giving rectitude to the will—nor by merely illuminating and giving rectitude to speculative reason—but by illuminating and giving rectitude to practical reason. The forgetting of this distinction between *will* and *practical reason* explains the above-mentioned failure of school pedagogy in its attempts to "educate the will."

Now as concerns the will itself, and the so-called "education of the will" or character-building (let us say, more accurately, with regard to the attainment of moral virtues and spiritual freedom), the specific task of school education amounts essentially to the two following points: first, the teacher must be solidly instructed in and deeply aware of the psychology of the child, less in order to form the latter's will and feelings than in order to avoid deforming or wounding them by pedagogical blunders to which unfortunately adults seem naturally inclined (here all of the modern psychological research may afford great help). Second, school and school life have to do, in an especially important manner, with what I would suggest calling "premoral" training, a point which deals not with morality strictly speaking, but with the preparation and first tilling of the soil thereof.[9] Yet the main duty in the educational spheres of the school as well as of the state is not to shape the will and directly to develop moral virtues in the youth, but to enlighten and strengthen reason; so it is that an indirect influence is exerted on the will, by a sound equipment of knowledge and a sound development of the powers of thinking.

Thus the paradox of which I have spoken at such length comes to a solution: what is most important in the upbringing of man, that is, the uprightness of the will and the attainment of spiritual freedom, as well as the achievement of a sound relationship with society, is truly the main objective of education in its broadest sense. Concerning *direct* action on the will and the shaping of character, this objective chiefly depends on educational spheres other than school and college education—not to speak of the role which the extra-educational sphere plays in this matter. On the contrary, concerning *indirect* action on the will and the character, school and college education provides a basis and necessary preparation for the main objective in question by concentrating on knowledge and the intellect, not on the will and direct moral training, and by keeping sight, above all, of the development and uprightness of speculative and practical reason. School and college education has indeed its own world, which essentially consists of the dignity and achievements of knowledge and the intellect, that is, of the human being's root faculty. And of this world itself that knowledge which is wisdom is the ultimate goal.

[9]The system of city schools as known in this country and tried here and there in Europe has proved particularly fruitful for such premoral training.

Progressivism

Changed Conceptions of the Ideal and the Real*
JOHN DEWEY

It has been noted that human experience is made human through the existence of associations and recollections, which are strained through the mesh of imagination so as to suit the demands of the emotions. A life that is humanly interesting is, short of the results of discipline, a life in which the tedium of vacant leisure is filled with images that excite and satisfy. It is in this sense that poetry preceded prose in human experience, religion antedated science, and ornamental and decorative art while it could not take the place of utility early reached a development out of proportion to the practical arts. In order to give contentment and delight, in order to feed present emotion and give the stream of conscious life intensity and color, the suggestions which spring from past experiences are worked over so as to smooth out their unpleasantnesses and enhance their enjoyableness. Some psychologists claim that there is what they call a natural tendency to obliviscence of the disagreeable—that men turn from the unpleasant in thought and recollection as they do from the obnoxious in action. Every serious-minded person knows that a large part of the effort required in moral discipline consists in the courage needed to acknowledge the unpleasant consequences of one's past and present acts. We squirm, dodge, evade, disguise, cover up, find excuses and palliations—anything to render the mental scene less uncongenial. In short, the tendency of

*Reprinted with the permission of Beacon Press from *Reconstruction in Philosophy*, by John Dewey, pp. 103–126, 129–131. Enlarged Edition copyright 1948 by Beacon Press.

spontaneous suggestion is to idealize experience, to give it in consciousness qualities which it does not have in actuality. Time and memory are true artists; they remould reality nearer to the heart's desire.

As imagination becomes freer and less controlled by concrete actualities, the idealizing tendency takes further flights unrestrained by the rein of the prosaic world. The things most emphasized in imagination as it reshapes experience are things which are absent in reality. In the degree in which life is placid and easy, imagination is sluggish and bovine. In the degree in which life is uneasy and troubled, fancy is stirred to frame pictures of a contrary state of things. By reading the characteristic features of any man's castles in the air you can make a shrewd guess as to his underlying desires which are frustrated. What is difficulty and disappointment in real life becomes conspicuous achievement and triumph in revery; what is negative in fact will be positive in the image drawn by fancy; what is vexation in conduct will be compensated for in high relief in idealizing imagination.

These considerations apply beyond mere personal psychology. They are decisive for one of the most marked traits of classic philosophy: —its conception of an ultimate supreme Reality which is essentially ideal in nature. Historians have more than once drawn an instructive parallel between the developed Olympian Pantheon of Greek religion and the Ideal Realm of Platonic philosophy. The gods, whatever their origin and original traits, became idealized projections of the selected and matured achievements which the Greeks admired among their mortal selves. The gods were like mortals, but mortals living only the lives which men would wish to live, with power intensified, beauty perfected, and wisdom ripened. When Aristotle criticized the theory of Ideas of his master, Plato, by saying that the Ideas were after all only things of sense eternalized, he pointed out in effect the parallelism of philosophy with religion and art to which allusion has just been made. And save for matters of merely technical import, is it not possible to say of Aristotle's Forms just what he said of Plato's Ideas? What are they, these Forms and Essences which so profoundly influenced for centuries the course of science and theology, save the objects of ordinary experience with their blemishes removed, their imperfections eliminated, their lacks rounded out, their suggestions and hints fulfilled? What are they in short but the objects of familiar life divinized because reshaped by the idealizing imagination to meet the demands of desire in just those respects in which actual experience is disappointing?

That Plato, and Aristotle in somewhat different fashion, and Plotinus and Marcus Aurelius and Saint Thomas Aquinas, and Spinoza and Hegel all taught that Ultimate Reality is either perfectly Ideal and Rational in nature, or else has absolute ideality and rationality as its necessary attribute, are facts well known to the student of philosophy. They need no exposition here. But it is worth pointing out that these great systematic philosophies defined perfect Ideality in conceptions that express the opposite of those things which make life unsatisfactory and troublesome. What is the chief source of the complaint of poet and moralist with the goods, the values and satisfactions of experience? Rarely is the complaint that such things do not exist; it is that although existing they are momentary, transient, fleeting. They do not stay; at worst they come only to annoy and tease with their hurried and disappearing taste of what might be; at best they come only to inspire and instruct with a passing hint of truer reality. This commonplace of the poet and moralist as to the impermanence not only of sensuous enjoyment, but of fame and civic achievements was profoundly reflected upon by philosophers, especially by Plato and Aristotle. The results of their thinking have been wrought into the very fabric of western ideas. Time, change, movement are signs that what the Greeks called Non-Being somehow infect true Being. The phraseology is now strange, but many a modern who ridicules the conception of Non-Being repeats the same thought under the name of the Finite or Imperfect.

Wherever there is change, there is instability, and instability is proof of something the matter, of absence, deficiency, incompleteness. These are the ideas common to the connection between change, becoming and perishing, and Non-Being, finitude and imperfection. Hence complete and true Reality must be changeless, unalterable, so full of Being that it always and forever maintains itself in fixed rest and repose. As Bradley, the most dialectically ingenious Absolutist of our own day, expresses the doctrine "Nothing that is perfectly real moves." And while Plato took, comparatively speaking, a pessimistic view of change as mere lapse and Aristotle a complacent view of it as tendency to realization, yet Aristotle doubted no more than Plato that the fully realized reality, the divine and ultimate, is changeless. Though it is called Activity or Energy, the Activity knew no change, the energy did nothing. It was the activity of an army forever marking time and never going anywhere.

From this contrast of the permanent with the transient arise other features which mark off the Ultimate Reality from the imperfect realities of practical life. Where there is change, there is of necessity numerical plurality, multiplicity, and from variety comes opposition, strife. Change is alteration, or "othering" and this means diversity. Diversity means division, and division means two sides and their conflict. The world which is transient *must* be a world of discord, for in lacking stability it lacks the government of unity. Did unity completely rule, these would remain an unchanging totality. What alters has parts and partialities which, not recognizing the rule of unity, assert themselves independently and make life a scene of contention and discord. Ultimate and true Being on the other hand, since it is changeless is Total, All-Comprehensive and One. Since it is One, it knows only harmony, and therefore enjoys complete and eternal Good. It *is* Perfection.

Degrees of knowledge and truth correspond with degrees of reality point by point. The higher and more complete the Reality the truer and more important the knowledge that refers to it. Since the world of becoming, of origins and perishings, is deficient in true Being, it cannot be known in the best sense. To know it means to neglect its flux and alteration and discover some permanent form which limits the processes that alter in time. The acorn undergoes a series of changes; these are knowable only in reference to the fixed form of the oak which is the same in the entire oak species in spite of the numerical diversity of trees. Moreover, this form limits the flux of growth at both ends, the acorn coming from the oak as well as passing into it. Where such unifying and limiting eternal forms cannot be detected, there is mere aimless variation and fluctuation, and knowledge is out of the question. On the other hand, as objects are approached in which there is no movement at all, knowledge becomes really demonstrative, certain, perfect—truth pure and unalloyed. The heavens can be more truly known than the earth, God the unmoved mover than the heavens.

From this fact follows the superiority of contemplative to practical knowledge, of pure theoretical speculation to experimentation, and to any kind of knowing that depends upon changes in things or that induces change in them. Pure knowing is pure beholding, viewing, noting. It is complete in itself. It looks for nothing beyond itself; it lacks nothing and hence has no aim or purpose. It is most emphatically its own excuse for being. Indeed, pure contemplative knowing is so much the most truly self-enclosed and self-sufficient thing in the universe that it is the highest and indeed the only attribute that can be ascribed to God, the Highest Being in the scale of Being. Man himself is divine in the rare moments when he attains to purely self-sufficient theoretical insight.

In contrast with such knowing, the so-called knowing of the artisan is base. He has to bring about changes in things, in wood and stone, and this fact is of itself evidence that his material is deficient in Being. What condemns his knowledge even more is the fact that it is not disinterestedly for its own sake. It has reference to results to be attained, food, clothing, shelter, etc. It is concerned with things that perish, the body and its needs. It thus has an ulterior aim, and one which itself testifies to imperfection. For want, desire, affection of every sort, indicate lack. Where there is need and desire—as in the case of all practical knowledge and activity—

there is incompleteness and insufficiency. While civic or political and moral knowledge rank higher than do the conceptions of the artisan, yet intrinsically considered they are a low and untrue type. Moral and political action is practical; that is, it implies needs and effort to satisfy them. It has an end beyond itself. Moreover, the very fact of association shows lack of self-sufficiency; it shows dependence upon others. Pure knowing is alone solitary, and capable of being carried on in complete, self-sufficing independence.

In short, the measure of the worth of knowledge according to Aristotle, whose views are here summarized, is the degree in which it is purely contemplative. The highest degree is attained in knowing ultimate Ideal Being, pure Mind. This is Ideal, the Form of Forms, because it has no lacks, no needs, and experiences no change or variety. It has no desires because in it all desires are consummated. Since it is perfect Being, it is perfect Mind and perfect Bliss;—the acme of rationality and ideality. One point more and the argument is completed. The kind of knowing that concerns itself with this ultimate reality (which is also ultimate ideality) is philosophy. Philosophy is therefore the last and highest term in pure contemplation. Whatever may be said for any other kind of knowledge, philosophy is self-enclosed. It has nothing to do beyond itself; it has no aim or purpose or function—except to be philosophy—that is, pure, self-sufficing beholding of ultimate reality. There is of course such a thing as philosophic *study* which falls short of this perfection. Where there is learning, there is change and becoming. But the function of study and learning of philosophy is, as Plato put it, to convert the eye of the soul from dwelling contentedly upon the images of things, upon the inferior realities that are born and that decay, and to lead it to the intuition of supernal and eternal Being. Thus the mind of the knower is transformed. It becomes assimilated to what it knows.

Through a variety of channels, especially Neo-Platonism and St. Augustine, these ideas found their way into Christian theology; and great scholastic thinkers taught that the end of man is to know True Being, that knowledge is contemplative, that True Being is pure Immaterial Mind, and to know it is Bliss and Salvation. While this knowledge cannot be achieved in this stage of life nor without supernatural aid, yet so far as it is accomplished it assimilates the human mind to the divine essence and so constitutes salvation. Through this taking over of the conception of knowledge as Contemplative into the dominant religion of Europe, multitudes were affected who were totally innocent of theoretical philosophy. There was bequeathed to generations of thinkers as an unquestioned axiom the idea that knowledge is intrinsically a mere beholding or viewing of reality—the spectator conception of knowledge. So deeply engrained was this idea that it prevailed for centuries after the actual progress of science had demonstrated that knowledge is power to transform the world, and centuries after the practice of effective knowledge had adopted the method of experimentation.

Let us turn abruptly from this conception of the measure of true knowledge and the nature of true philosophy to the existing practice of knowledge. Nowadays if a man, say a physicist or chemist, wants to know something, the last thing he does is merely to contemplate. He does not look in however earnest and prolonged a way upon the object expecting that thereby he will detect its fixed and characteristic form. He does not expect any amount of such aloof scrutiny to reveal to him any secrets. He proceeds to *do* something, to bring some energy to bear upon the substance to see how it reacts; he places it under unusual conditions in order to induce some change. While the astronomer cannot change the remote stars, even he no longer merely gazes. If he cannot change the stars themselves, he can at least by lens and prism change their light as it reaches the earth; he can lay traps for discovering changes which would otherwise escape notice. Instead of taking an antagonistic attitude toward change and denying it to the stars because of their divinity and perfection, he is on constant and alert watch to find some change through which he can form an inference as to the formation of stars and systems of stars.

Change in short is no longer looked upon as a fall from grace, as a lapse from reality or a sign of imperfection of Being. Modern science no longer tries to find some fixed form or essence behind each process of change. Rather, the experimental method tries to break down apparent fixities and to induce changes. The form that remains unchanged to sense, the form of seed or tree, is regarded not as the key to knowledge of the thing, but as a wall, an obstruction to be broken down. Consequently the scientific man experiments with this and that agency applied to this and that condition until something begins to happen; until there is, as we say, something doing. He assumes that there is change going on all the time, that there is movement within each thing in seeming repose; and that since the process is veiled from perception the way to know it is to bring the thing into novel circumstances until change becomes evident. In short, the thing which is to be accepted and paid heed to is not what is originally given but that which emerges after the thing has been set under a great variety of circumstances in order to see how it behaves.

Now this marks a much more general change in the human attitude than perhaps appears at first sight. It signifies nothing less than that the world or any part of it as it presents itself at a given time is accepted or acquiesced in only as *material* for change. It is accepted precisely as the carpenter, say, accepts things as he finds them. If he took them as things to be observed and noted for their own sake, he never would be a carpenter. He would observe, describe, record the structures, forms and changes which things exhibit to him, and leave the matter there. If perchance some of the changes going on should present him with a shelter, so much the better. But what makes the carpenter a *builder* is the fact that he notes things not just as objects in themselves, but with reference to what he wants to do to them and with them; to the end he has in mind. Fitness to effect certain special changes that he wishes to see accomplished is what concerns him in the wood and stones and iron which he observes. His attention is directed to the changes they undergo and the changes they make other things undergo so that he may select that combination of changes which will yield him his desired result. It is only by these processes of active manipulation of things in order to realize his purpose that he discovers what the properties of things are. If he foregoes his own purpose and in the name of a meek and humble subscription to things as they "really are" refuses to bend things as they "are" to his own purpose, he not only never achieves his purpose but he never learns what the things themselves are. They *are* what they can do and what can be done with them,—things that can be found by deliberate trying.

The outcome of this idea of the right way to know is a profound modification in man's attitude toward the natural world. Under differing social conditions, the older or classic conception sometimes bred resignation and submission; sometimes contempt and desire to escape; sometimes, notably in the case of the Greeks, a keen esthetic curiosity which showed itself in acute noting of all the traits of given objects. In fact, the whole conception of knowledge as beholding and noting is fundamentally an idea connected with esthetic enjoyment and appreciation where the environment is beautiful and life is serene, and with esthetic repulsion and depreciation where life is troubled, nature morose and hard. But in the degree in which the active conception of knowledge prevails, and the environment is regarded as something that has to be changed in order to be truly known, men are imbued with courage, with what may almost be termed an aggressive attitude toward nature. The latter becomes plastic, something to be subjected to human uses. The moral disposition toward change is deeply modified. This loses its pathos, it ceases to be haunted with melancholy through suggesting only decay and loss. Change becomes significant of new possibilities and ends to be attained; it becomes prophetic of a better future. Change is associated with progress rather than with lapse and fall. Since changes are going on anyway, the great thing is to learn enough about them so that we will be able to lay hold of them and turn them in the direction of our desires. Conditions and events are neither to be fled from nor passively acquiesced in; they are to be utilized and directed. They are either obstacles to our ends or else means for their accomplishment. In a profound sense knowing ceases to be contemplative and becomes practical.

Unfortunately men, educated men, cultivated men in particular, are still so dominated by the older conception of an aloof and self-sufficing reason and knowledge that they refuse to perceive the import of this doctrine. They think they are sustaining the cause of impartial, thorough-going and disinterested reflection when they maintain the traditional philosophy of intellectualism—that is, of knowing as something self-sufficing and self-enclosed. But in truth, historic intellectualism, the spectator view of knowledge, is a purely compensatory doctrine which men of an intellectual turn have built up to console themselves for the actual and social impotency of the calling of thought to which they are devoted. Forbidden by conditions and held back by lack of courage from making their knowledge a factor in the determination of the course of events, they have sought a refuge of complacency in the notion that knowing is something too sublime to be contaminated by contact with things of change and practice. They have transformed knowing into a morally irresponsible estheticism. The true import of the doctrine of the operative or practical character of knowing, of intelligence, is objective. It means that the structures and objects which science and philosophy set up in contrast to the things and events of concrete daily experience do not constitute a realm apart in which rational contemplation may rest satisfied; it means that they represent the selected obstacles, material means and ideal methods of giving direction to that change which is bound to occur anyway.

This change of human disposition toward the world does not mean that man ceases to have ideals, or ceases to be primarily a creature of the imagination. But it does signify a radical change in the character and function of the ideal realm which man shapes for himself. In the classic philosophy, the ideal world is essentially a haven in which man finds rest from the storms of life; it is an asylum in which he takes refuge from the troubles of existence with the calm assurance that it alone is supremely real. When the belief that knowledge is active and operative takes hold of men, the ideal realm is no longer something aloof and separate; it is rather that collection of imagined possibilities that stimulates men to new efforts and realizations. It still remains true that the troubles which men undergo are the forces that lead them to project pictures of a better state of things. But the picture of the better is shaped so that it may become an instrumentality of action, while in the classic view the Idea belongs ready-made in a noumenal world. Hence, it is only an object of personal aspiration or consolation, while to the modern, an idea is a suggestion of something to be done or of a way of doing.

An illustration will, perhaps, make the difference clear. Distance is an obstacle, a source of trouble. It separates friends and prevents intercourse. It isolates, and makes contact and mutual understanding difficult. This state of affairs provokes discontent and restlessness; it excites the imagination to construct pictures of a state of things where human intercourse is not injuriously affected by space. Now there are two ways out. One way is to pass from a mere dream of some heavenly realm in which distance is abolished and by some magic all friends are in perpetual transparent communication, to pass, I say, from some idle castle-building to philosophic reflection. Space, distance, it will then be argued, is merely phenomenal; or, in a more modern version, subjective. It is not, metaphysically speaking, real. Hence the obstruction and trouble it gives is not after all "real" in the metaphysical sense of reality. Pure minds, pure spirits, do not live in a space world; for them distance is not. Their relationships in the true world are not in any way affected by special considerations. Their intercommunication is direct, fluent, unobstructed.

Does the illustration involve a caricature of ways of philosophizing with which we are all familiar? But if it is not an absurd caricature, does it not suggest that much of what philosophies have taught about the ideal and noumenal or superiorly real world, is after all, only casting a dream into an elaborate dialectic form through the use of a speciously scientific terminology? Practically, the difficulty, the trouble, remains. Practically, however it may be "metaphysically," space is still real: —it acts in a definite objectionable way. Again, man dreams of some better state of things. From troublesome fact he takes refuge in fantasy. But this time, the refuge does not remain a permanent and remote asylum.

The idea becomes a standpoint from which to examine existing occurrences and to see if there is not among them something which gives a hint of how communication at a distance can be effected, something to be utilized as a medium of speech at long range. The suggestion or fancy though still ideal is treated as a possibility capable of realization *in* the concrete natural world, not as a superior reality apart from that world. As such, it becomes a platform from which to scrutinize natural events. Observed from the point of view of this possibility, things disclose properties hitherto undetected. In the light of these ascertainments, the idea of some agency for speech at a distance becomes less vague and floating: it takes on positive form. This action and reaction goes on. The possibility or idea is employed as a method for observing actual existence; and in the light of what is discovered the possibility takes on concrete existence. It becomes less of a mere idea, a fancy, a wished-for possibility, and more of an actual fact. Invention proceeds, and at last we have the telegraph, the telephone, first through wires, and then with no artificial medium. The concrete environment is transformed in the desired direction; it is idealized in fact and not merely in fancy. The ideal is realized through its own use as a tool or method of inspection, experimentation, selection and combination of concrete natural operations.

Let us pause to take stock of results. The division of the world into two kinds of Being, one superior, accessible only to reason and ideal in nature, the other inferior, material, changeable, empirical, accessible to sense-observation, turns inevitably into the idea that knowledge is contemplative in nature. It assumes a contrast between theory and practice which was all to the disadvantage of the latter. But in the actual course of the development of science, a tremendous change has come about. When the practice of knowledge ceased to be dialectical and became experimental, knowing became preoccupied with changes and the test of knowledge became the ability to bring about certain changes. Knowing, for the experimental sciences, means a certain kind of intelligently conducted doing; it ceases to be contemplative and becomes in a true sense practical. Now this implies that philosophy, unless it is to undergo a complete break with the authorized spirit of science, must also alter its nature. It must assume a practical nature; it must become operative and experimental. And we have pointed out what an enormous change this transformation of philosophy entails in the two conceptions which have played the greatest role in historic philosophizing—the conceptions of the "real" and "ideal" respectively. The former ceases to be something ready-made and final; it becomes that which has to be accepted as the material of change, as the obstructions and the means of certain specific desired changes. The ideal and rational also ceased to be a separate ready-made world incapable of being used as a lever to transform the actual empirical world, a mere asylum from empirical deficiencies. They represent intelligently thought-out possibilities *of* the existent world which may be used as methods for making over and improving it.

Philosophically speaking, this is the great difference involved in the change from knowledge and philosophy as contemplative to operative. The change does not mean the lowering in dignity of philosophy from a lofty plane to one of gross utilitarianism. It signifies that the prime function of philosophy is that of rationalizing the *possibilities* of experience, especially collective human experience. The scope of this change may be realized by considering how far we are from accomplishing it. In spite of inventions which enable men to use the energies of nature for their purposes, we are still far from habitually treating knowledge as the method of active control of nature and of experience. We tend to think of it after the model of a spectator viewing a finished picture rather than after that of the artist producing the painting. Thus there arise all the questions of epistemology with which the technical student of philosophy is so familiar, and which have made modern philosophy in especial so remote from the understanding of the everyday person and from the results and processes of science. For these questions all spring from the assumption of a merely beholding mind on one side and a foreign and remote object to be viewed and noted on the other. They ask how a mind and world, subject and object, so separate and independent can by any possibility come into such relationship to each other as to make true knowledge possible. If knowing were habitually conceived of as active and operative, after the analogy of experiment guided by hypothesis, or of invention guided by the imagination of some possibility, it is not too much to say that the first effect would be to emancipate philosophy from all the epistemological puzzles which now perplex it. For these all arise from a conception of the relation of mind and world, subject and object, in knowing, which assumes that to know is to seize upon what is already in existence.

Modern philosophic thought has been so preoccupied with these puzzles of epistemology and the disputes between realist and idealist, between phenomenalist and absolutist, that many students are at a loss to know what would be left for philosophy if there were removed both the metaphysical task of distinguishing between the noumenal and phenomenal worlds and the epistemological task of telling how a separate subject can know an independent object. But would not the elimination of these traditional problems permit philosophy to devote itself to a more fruitful and more needed task? Would it not encourage philosophy to face the great social and moral defects and troubles from which humanity suffers, to concentrate its attention upon clearing up the causes and exact nature of these evils and upon developing a clear idea of better social possibilities; in short upon projecting an idea or ideal which, instead of expressing the notion of another world or some far-away unrealizable goal, would be used as a method of understanding and rectifying specific social ills?

This is a vague statement. But note in the first place that such a conception of the proper province of philosophy where it is released from vain metaphysics and idle epistemology is in line with the origin of philosophy sketched in the first hour. And in the second place, note how contemporary society, the world over, is in need of more general and fundamental enlightenment and guidance than it now possesses. I have tried to show that a radical change of the conception of knowledge from contemplative to active is the inevitable result of the way in which inquiry and invention are now conducted. But in claiming this, it must also be conceded, or rather asserted, that so far the change has influenced for the most part only the more technical side of human life. The sciences have created new industrial arts. Man's physical command of natural energies has been indefinitely multiplied. There is control of the sources of material wealth and prosperity. What would once have been miracles are now daily performed with steam and coal and electricity and air, and with the human body. But there are few persons optimistic enough to declare that any similar command of the forces which control man's social and moral welfare has been achieved.

Where is the moral progress that corresponds to our economic accomplishments? The latter is the direct fruit of the revolution that has been wrought in physical science. But where is there a corresponding human science and art? Not only has the improvement in the method of knowing remained so far mainly limited to technical and economic matters, but this progress has brought with it serious new moral disturbances. I need only cite the late war, the problem of capital and labor, the relation of economic classes, the fact that while the new science has achieved wonders in medicine and surgery, it has also produced and spread occasions for diseases and weaknesses. These considerations indicate to us how undeveloped are our politics, how crude and primitive our education, how passive and inert our morals. The causes remain which brought philosophy into existence as an attempt to find an intelligent substitute for blind custom and blind impulse as guides to life and conduct. The attempt has not been successfully accomplished. Is there not reason for believing that the release of philosophy from its burden of sterile metaphysics and sterile epistemology instead of depriving philosophy of problems and subject-matter would open a way to questions of the most perplexing and the most significant sort?

. . .

Yet the most obvious conclusion would seem to be the impotency and the harmfulness of any and every ideal that is proclaimed wholesale and in the abstract, that is, as something in itself apart from the detailed concrete existences whose moving possibilities it embodies. The true moral would seem to lie in enforcing the tragedy of that idealism which believes in a spiritual world which exists in and by itself, and the tragic need for the most realistic study of forces and consequences, a study conducted in a more scientifically accurate and complete manner than that of the professed *Real-politik*. For it is not truly realistic or scientific to take short views, to sacrifice the future to immediate pressure, to ignore facts and forces that are disagreeable and to magnify the enduring quality of whatever falls in with immediate desire. It is false that the evils of the situation arise from absence of ideals; they spring from wrong ideals. And these wrong ideals have in turn their foundation in the absence in social matters of that methodic, systematic, impartial, critical, searching inquiry into "real" and operative conditions which we call science and which has brought man in the technical realm to the command of physical energies.

Philosophy, let it be repeated, cannot "solve" the problem of the relation of the ideal and the real. That is the standing problem of life. But it can at least lighten the burden of humanity in dealing with the problem by emancipating mankind from the errors which philosophy has itself fostered—the existence of conditions which are real apart from their movement into something new and different, and the existence of ideals, spirit and reason independent of the possibilities of the material and physical. For as long as humanity is committed to this radically false bias, it will walk forward with blinded eyes and bound limbs. And philosophy can effect, if it will, something more than this negative task. It can make it easier for mankind to take the right steps in action by making it clear that a sympathetic and integral intelligence brought to bear upon the observation and understanding of concrete social events and forces, can form ideals, that is aims, which shall not be either illusions or mere emotional compensations.

Reconstructionism

Education for the Emerging Age

THEODORE BRAMELD

1. CULTURAL CRITIQUE*

One of the ironies of the Decade Since Hiroshima is that American education—and, I fear, education in much of the world—has not only failed to come to grips with unprecedented problems and tasks but has, if anything, receded from the level it had reached by the early 1940's.

In making this assertion I am aware of the need to qualify. In certain respects there has been progress. One example is the momentous decision of the United States Supreme Court outlawing segregated public schools— a decision that still remains to be implemented in largest part, yet is easily the most important interpretation of educational rights that the Court has made. Another sign of progress is the fact that larger sums are being spent for education today than ever before. Perhaps still more important, in long range, is the operation of the first permanent, internationally sponsored agency concerned with education on a world scale: United Nations Educational, Scientific and Cultural Organization (UNESCO). Nor should we overlook the salutary public concern with education as a democratic responsibility, as demonstrated in the White House Conference last year.

*From *The Humanist*, Copyright 1957, by the American Humanist Association, 125 El Camino del Mar, San Francisco, California, 94121. Reprinted by permission.

Nevertheless, such assets are offset by deficits. The more familiar ones may merely be summarized: the appalling shortage of teachers, equipment and buildings; the fresh inroads of sectarian religious pressure groups upon the public schools; the high rate of functional illiteracy—that is, the inability to use symbols meaningfully; the ignorance and indifference of millions of "educated" citizens concerning political and other crucial issues; the intimidations suffered by uncounted numbers of teachers victimized by Cold War hysteria; and finally, the spread of anti-intellectualism—of contempt for those rational processes typified by scientific method, philosophic analysis, and logical deliberation.

While each of these deficits could be documented at length, I wish to pass on to another that—besides being less often discussed—supports my opening statement in a still more fundamental sense. Education has retreated from the position it had reached by the early 1940's in that the theory which undergirds its practice has become increasingly sympathetic to what may be called the "new conservatism"—that is, to traditional canons of belief that are, in my judgment, outmoded as guides to the revolutionary age which, for better or worse, we have already entered.

I

The simplest way to support this contention is to look back upon the past decade of public discussion of education, and to recall the voices that have attracted widest attention. For the most part, these voices have attacked the schools for failure to teach "the three R's," for lack of discipline, for disregard of scholarship, and for encouragement of "radical" if not "subversive" attitudes. Often the scapegoat has been something ambiguously called "progressive education"—a witches' brew of iniquitous ideas concocted originally by John Dewey, kept to the boiling point by William H. Kilpatrick, ladled out to innocent teachers by professional hackmen in schools of education, and finally swallowed by generations of children whose brains and spirits are thereby permanently addled.

I have resorted to caricature in order to highpoint an opinion widespread among citizens. For example, the books dealing with educational theory and policy that have been most prominently reviewed in general magazines during recent years have seldom been those sympathetic to the experimentalist-progressivist philosophy which is the key to progressive education. Rather, with few exceptions, they have been books expressing views bitterly hostile both to that philosophy and to the kind of modern schools that result from its consistent application. They have been books that repudiate the scientific and naturalistic thought of such philosophers as Dewey, and that beseech us to accept some classical—if not metaphysical and pre-scientific—doctrine. Therefore their own thought is derived ultimately from ways of life and philosophical systems prevailing in earlier centuries of Western civilization.

While the more competent of these books pay their respects to Dewey and to experimentalism, and all of them of course declare their admiration for science, nevertheless the main impact of their arguments has been to the contrary. Not only do they arouse doubts and confusion about the most original and influential theory in American educational history. They also persuade innumerable citizens—and even many teachers—that such practices in the schools as functional methods of learning to read, first-hand community experience, democratic participation in curriculum planning and school administration, should be thrown on the rubbish-heap and supplanted by their own preferred forms of tradition-grounded theory and practice.

II

These generalizations may be exemplified by the widely disseminated views of the late Gordon Keith Chalmers, president of Kenyon College. One of his last articles, "The Purpose of Learning," is especially revealing as it was the only treatment of educational philosophy included in the issue on "Higher Education Under Stress" of the *Annals* of the American Academy of Political and Social Science. In this article, as in his book, *The Republic and the Person,* Mr. Chalmers seemed so troubled about education that one might suppose, were one unfamiliar with the premises of his discussion, that here indeed was a daring advocate of change in a new direction. "Where," he asked, "shall we find the new philosophy of education so desperately demanded by our country and our times . . .?" He apparently believed that he himself was offering a "radical redirection for American education." When, however, one correctly defines "radical" as connoting a thoroughgoing departure from historically familiar patterns of belief and practice in favor of patterns not hitherto known or experienced, Mr. Chalmers' "radical redirection" proves to be nothing of the sort. In his own words, it "must be based clearly on the classic understanding of the dual nature of man, which characterizes not only Christianity but Greek tragedy, Roman law, and historic Hebrew and ancient Indian thought." Careful inspection of his educational proposals bears out this statement. He would retreat to beliefs and practices that are classical indeed.

Such proposals are unlikely to have anything concrete to say about the burning educational and cultural issues of our day—the attack upon academic freedom, for example, or the implications for learning of such cataclysmic discoveries as atomic energy. Rather, like most neoconservatives, Mr. Chalmers thought that education can solve the great problems of life only by a spiritual and intellectual rejuvenation of the individual "person." And the "person," though described in somewhat different terms by other proponents of his position, turns out to be nothing so much as a twentieth-century prototype of traditional man governed by "right Reason"—the ideal of Renaissance and post-Renaissance aristocratic humanism.

Mr. Chalmers' approach to education was an important and earnest way of reacting, culturally as well as philosophically, to the crisis of our age. But it was a way of reacting that is easily accounted for. As Arnold Toynbee and other philosophers of history have shown, every great crisis in the affairs of men has produced more or less similar types of "solution" by entrenched minorities. In periods of tension and bewilderment, it is perhaps more typical than otherwise for educators, like citizens at large, to react at first shock by listening wistfully to voices that would dissolve their troubles by restoring nostalgic patterns of truth, value, and reality.

III

The recent appeal of traditional patterns is also due in part to the ineffectiveness with which other philosophies and programs have responded to our period of challenge. The experimentalist-progressivist philosophy, particularly, though it has held its own remarkably well since the early 1940's when it was still the dominant educational outlook, has for perhaps twenty years contributed little that can be said to enrich the original formulations of Dewey himself. The fact that the Progressive Education Association ceased to exist in 1955, after some thirty years of immense influence, is surely due largely to its failure to pioneer any longer. Moreover, there is considerable validity in the common criticism that many schools of education have been guilty of superficial and distorted application of the experimentalist-progressivist philosophy to learning and teaching.

Still more fundamentally, this philosophy, which underlies so much of our modern education, is itself gravely deficient in its capacity to cope with the issues generated by a period of history profoundly altered from that of the first quarter of our century, when it was developed to maturity. Elsewhere I have tried to analyze this deficiency. Here I may only point out that the essential weakness should be diagnosed not only in philosophic but in cultural terms; the experimentalist-progressivist outlook expresses the mood, the values and the practices of a culture *in transition* between two greatly different eras of modern history.

The first era may be bounded roughly by the fifteenth and late nineteenth centuries. It was during these centuries that industrialism, nationalism, capitalist democracy, and individualistic liberalism all achieved maturity. The second era has by no means fully emerged. Indeed, perhaps it may not emerge fully at all before civilization is degraded or even destroyed. Nevertheless, the second era is already more and more recognizable in potential design. And it is likely to be distinguished from all earlier eras by at least these fundamental features: a largely automatic, integrated technology powered increasingly by atomic energy; a world population sufficiently educated to regulate its own growth according to available resources; a publicly planned and directed system of distribution of these resources so that physical and spiritual deprivation due to inequitable distribution of goods is eliminated; and an *enforceable* international government under democratic and, as far as possible, decentralized control.

To argue the same point differently, the experimentalist-progressivist philosophy is transitional in its basic character in the same way that twentieth-century liberalism (as distinct from the original individualistic liberalism of John Locke) is transitional. Both tend to emphasize the qualities of open-mindedness, of social and political exploration, of regard for "all sides of the question"—above all, of experimental methodology as the key to progress. Both stress the interaction of individual and community, but neither wishes to consider one as, say, the moral criterion of the other. Likewise, both emphasize the reciprocity of means and ends, but both characteristically focus upon means—upon "how we think" (the title of a famous Dewey volume), upon hypothesis rather than solution, upon tolerance rather than conviction, upon process rather than product. Finally, both are critical of the first great era of Western culture: they condemn the evils generated by ruthless industrialism, nationalism, and laissez-faire capitalism. Indeed, their main concern, educationally as well as culturally, has been to alleviate these evils by a more socially responsible and more intelligently directed program.

But neither experimentalism-progressivism nor recent liberalism seems able or willing to go much further than this. Being concerned with the virtues of culture as transition more than with the directions or aims of this transition, each hesitates to commit itself to, or even appraise carefully, the imperatives I have described as potential to the second era. Instead, a characteristic reaction is to label them "utopian" or to condemn them as "dogmatic" without taking the trouble to distinguish between the illegitimacy of dogma and the legitimacy of conviction about these imperatives. In rejecting the desirability of planned designs for the future, experimentalism-progressivism, like typical liberalism, remains in a state of pendulum-like tension between polar values—between individual and community, between means and ends. It prefers to stress the fluid and dynamic experience that has been indigenous to the period of American life which it has so skillfully symbolized.

When neoconservatives attack Dewey's philosophy for glorifying the value of growth for the sake of further growth as the highest measure of good education, they are, then, touching a sensitive nerve. But they cannot, on their own assumptions, account either for the cultural roots of this value or for the emerging values of the second era. They can only suggest that the way to correct an over-emphasis upon process, methodology, and growth is to regress toward traditional standards that are termed "radical" only at the penalty of historic and semantic confusion.

IV

It should now be apparent that the kind of educational philosophy and program required for the second (though still potential) era of modern history cannot be satisfied by the orthodox formulations of the experimentalists-progressivists any more than by the genteel and wishful formulations of the neoconservatives. While the needed philosophy may learn much from both—and especially from the former—it should aim to remove their deficiencies and to reconstruct the principles, methods and contents of education. That the undertaking is tremendous, and that no one person or group can accomplish it alone, is evident. Particularly is it tremendous because the required formulation should be interdisciplinary throughout; not only should it utilize the best available knowledge from philosophy and education, but it should incorporate the most significant new research of the physical, biological and social sciences, and the new creations of every art from literature to architecture. Thus, if it crystallizes at all, it will prove to be vastly more than a formal philosophy of education. It will also be a philosophy of culture, with education conceived as the chief agency through which problems of every kind are attacked, and practices, institutions and values commensurate with the demands of the emerging age are developed and tested.

The primary conviction that should govern every phase of the proposed philosophy is that humanity is now caught in the throes of a planetary transformation. The interweaving characteristics of this transformation are many—scientific, religious, economic, political, esthetic, psychological. Without doubt, the most graphic and monstrous symbol is atomic energy, the consequences of which for good or evil are still far from predictable. No one can guarantee that it will not be utilized to degrade—if not to destroy—human civilization as we have known it. No one can assure us, either, that competing nations will not continue to blunder on for perhaps a very long time—threatening, cajoling, bluffing, fumbling as they now do, yet fearing to release the power stored in their dreadful arsenals because of the reprisals that would surely result. Thus, in epitomizing earlier the salient features of the second modern era toward which experimentalism-progressivism is transitional, I did not say that such an era *will* ever occur. No one knows whether it ever will or not. I described it as a potential design of what the future could be like, and I implied that it is also what it should be like if we reject the alternatives of degradation, destruction, or chronic trepidation.

The point is crucial for educational theory. For, in addition to recognizing the paramount importance of scientific and empirical means, the proposed theory insists upon the equal importance of strong conviction about desirable ends. I wish, therefore, to underscore the argument that the most vulnerable spot in public education, especially as it is influenced by experimentalism-progressivism, is that it has not clearly or unequivocally focused upon either the content or meaning of these ends. Like the American culture of which it is the ideological ally, it has been much more concerned to delineate an effective methodology of intelligent practice than to formulate the goals for which that methodology is indispensable. And while traditional theorists, neoconservative and others, are likewise disturbed by this inadequacy in the philosophy they oppose, they seek to counteract it primarily by restoring a doctrine of ends and purposes adapted to the earlier era of post-medieval culture but entirely unsuitable to the era that should now emerge.

2. Social Consensus*

If you and I say that we regard as immoral the exploitations, discriminations, and segregations suffered by Negroes or Jews or Mexican-Americans, *why* most basically do we? Clearly, many others do not, for which they also must have reasons. Clearly, too, we should be able to show to ourselves and others why we support the kind of human order where exploitations, discriminations, and segregations would completely disappear; and where, instead, people of all colors, nationalities, and religions enjoy the same rights, privileges, and opportunities at every time and every place.

To fall back upon the doctrine of innate rights or Scholastic reasoning which "proves" that equality is a first principle, is little if any improvement over the kind of "lip service" which progressivists themselves offer to "the dignity of man."

An alternative is to begin with no preconceived statement of values, but to inquire of ourselves what we are most eagerly striving for. Even little children are capable of probing into their own drives, needs, and wants, and of answering in their own terms. Surely then it is not impractical for older students and adults to do so. Without at first going beyond our own experience, we can, if we try, articulate at least certain of our own deepest desires, and by communicating these we can refine our meanings to ourselves.

Moreover, as we continue moving from the physiological to the psychological levels, we can call upon the sciences of man to help us in our search. Psychology is essential, and if we turn to experts like Kurt Lewin, who have approached human nature from the viewpoint of its dynamic, patterned quality, we find support for an approach to ourselves as, first of all, "goal-seeking animals." Psychology, however, is by no means enough—until, at least, it is fused with the sciences of man in his relations with other men: economics, politics, sociology, and anthropology are especially fundamental. From W. I. Thomas we find support for the desire we have for security, new experiences, response, and recognition. From Robert S. Lynd we are more able to recognize the nature of our "cravings" even for such seemingly elusive satisfactions as "a natural tempo and rhythm" or a "sense of fairly immediate meaning." From social psychiatrists like Karen Horney we sense more clearly that often our frustrations are, at bottom, blockages in the way of goal-seeking and goal-winning, which derive not merely (as Freud would have it) from suppression of the id, but from the confusions and scarcities of a disintegrating culture.

The task of approaching the problem of values inductively is further complicated, however, by the question: "Who are *we*?" More specifically in terms of intercultural relations, one of the most common and most potent of arguments against, say, racial equalitarianism is that great numbers of people in the world simply do not have this range of drives and wants which you and I—of the educated minority—may concede that we have. Granting, for example, that sexual satisfaction is virtually a universal want, how can it possibly be argued that the want of recognition or fairly immediate meaning is universal? And if it cannot be proved that our pattern of goal-seeking is common to others, are we not trying to impose that pattern upon dissimilar people?

In answer to these questions, it is necessary to admit frankly that neither religion nor science has established once and for all the precise number or order or quality of wants among diverse peoples. Indeed, since the whole history of human beings and of the cultures within which they live proves the pliability of goal-seeking proclivities, we must concede that such establishment is, in any case, impossible. All that can be shown, at the most, is about four important facts concerning who *we* are—whether a merely sophisticated minority, or a reasonably large majority of the races and nations of the world.

First, then, science, especially anthropology, again assists enormously in showing that, among all our differences, we do possess a striking number of similar wants and of similarly organized efforts to satisfy them.

Second, these common denominators, however few in different periods of history, tend to multiply today as acculturation and assimilation accelerate through the impact of communication and transportation. In other words, as more and more people learn more and more about one another, they come closer to a minimum pattern of similar wants. Such a pattern is temporal and cultural, not eternal or metaphysical, to be sure. But that is all we can properly expect.

Third, the equally evident fact that disagreement about wants is still widespread by no means proves that this disagreement is insoluble. Rather, all it may prove is that civilization has failed to provide facilities by which agreement might be achieved. If, for example, Jeeter Lester of *Tobacco Road* seems satisfied with a diet of turnips, does this mean that here is in fact his entire goal of food satisfaction? Or does it simply mean that he has never learned enough either about the meaning of adequate diet, or of the possibility of winning such a diet for himself and his children, to know what he actually wants? By the same token, can the Negro hater be right in his contention that shiftlessness is more satisfying to Negroes than initiative and neatness, so long as he does everything in his power to prevent fair testing of the latter alternative?

Fourth, and following more or less directly from the above three points, the assertion that *our* wants and their satisfaction are therefore also *common* wants claims no more than that they are, or probably could be, those of the *majority*. No matter how seemingly universal a want may be, some individual or group may deny its presence—a denial resulting either from an insistence that the majority simply has failed to recognize its own goal-seeking interests accurately at some point, or from the sheer stubbornness or fanaticism of some individual or group. In either case, there is no way, so long as the democratic process functions in value formulation, by which the dissenting minority can or should be coerced into agreement. In fact, the minority may conceivably be right. If, as we assume, wants are empirical, and we learn and relearn about them continuously, then we of the majority may need to be convinced that a meaning we previously attached to a certain want has been quite fallacious. But even if the minority is wrong, and it is denying agreement from ulterior motives, we shall have to admit there is no way of finally *proving* it wrong. The subjective element in all human wants makes it possible for anyone to deny the existence of any particular want simply by insisting that he has no such experience as the majority has.

We come, then, to the inference that *the final criterion of intercultural values is the social consensus that can be attained about them.* This criterion, as implied, has at least three essential steps in its complete application: (*a*) maximum presentation of evidence (especially of science, but also of art, history, religion, and all other spheres of human achievement) about what people want; (*b*) maximum communication of that evidence—a worldwide process which, of course, increases the exactitude of the evidence itself; and (*c*) maximum agreement among the widest possible range of people that, upon the basis of this evidence and communication, these are indeed the wants we most deeply seek to satisfy.

3.   ENDS

In this decade* another war has been fought—a war which uniquely demonstrated at least three tremendous facts: first, that the world is capable of producing and distributing through integrated direction on a scale inconceivable even to the most optimistic heralds of the steam engine—that it now possesses such natural and synthetic resources, such skills and knowledge, as could, were they but rationally utilized, literally wipe poverty and disease from the earth's surface; second, that the hitherto separate parts of this same earth are no longer separate—that through technological achievements all nations, all races, all cultures are brought into face-to-face proximity from which there is no escape except annihilation; and third, that such annihilation is itself now only too terrible a practicality—a practicality which can be prevented, if at all, only as those who have the most to lose by atomic war (and they are most of the people) awaken in time to the grim peril which confronts them.

These facts are familiar. Yet the heavy responsibility they place upon education is by no means so familiar. We are confronted with the need not only to re-examine the import of what we have been doing but of redetermining what we should do. And what we should do is connoted by

*1940–1950 (Editor)

the quotation from Koestler: *it is to determine whether and, if so, how we may mobilize our competences for the supreme imperative of bridging the chasm which now divides common understanding from the technological and other objective developments of our historic period.* To put it differently, our first imperative is to make as certain as cooperative intelligence, dexterity, and courage are capable of making certain that the human masses of the earth will learn in time to channel the giant energies, to train the giant machines, of this mid-century in behalf of common interests—and thus in behalf of peace, abundance, dynamic cultural evolution, happiness. In short, education in its comprehensive sense should become the co-partner of politics—the politics of comprehending and implementing popular government on a world-wide scale. The philosophy of education thereby becomes primarily concerned with the foundations upon which this co-partnership functions.

The aim of these considerations . . . is again the central one of bridge building: of providing a continuous and trustworthy span between the two shores of common enlightenment and objective social achievement. The blueprint of such a span may be considered around at least five buttresses. These may be called, respectively, an adequate theory of human nature; an adequate theory of social forces; an adequate theory of the state; an adequate theory of government; and an adequate theory of normative commitment. Each of these is connected with the others by the two great cables of an adequate theory of education and of politics.

I

Of all five philosophic buttresses, the first, concerning human nature, is thus far the most satisfactory in its present stage of formulation. By both anticipating and utilizing the investigations of modern experimental psychology, philosophers of a naturalistic and organismic preference have been converging for at least two generations toward the guiding hypothesis that human beings are best characterized in terms of a complex, dynamic fusion of drives. This hypothesis, to which the gestalt, functional, behaviorist, Freudian, and other psychologies have all contributed richly, has now reached sufficient crystallization for us confidently to declare that educational method could and should become transformed—transformed in so far, that is to say, as child development, emotional-intellectual growth, and other vital aspects of learning-as-living in their more individualized emphases are properly concerned.

In the perspective of our theme, this fruitful approach to human nature has both its positive and negative aspects. Positively, it supports the prime political assumption of democracy that people of every race, nationality, religion, or social status are sufficiently alike in their basic structures, energies, potential abilities, to reach a vastly higher level of competence, self-reliance, and achievement than social opportunity has thus far typically offered. Or, still more relevantly, the capacities of human beings for appreciating the requisites of complete self-government are now proving to be, not merely a pleasant sentiment, but a demonstrable expectation— an expectation supported even by scientific recognition that the desire for self-government, as one form of participation, is itself a basic drive of man. The problem for us thus becomes one of charging these capacities with the kind of educational energy which no longer conceals or warps economic and similar meanings, but rather reveals and translates them into democratic institutions consistent with such meanings.

Negatively, however, the contemporary theory of human dynamics has largely failed to cope with just this problem of translation. For the most part it has neither asked nor answered forthrightly the crucial question of what kind of humane order is essential so that human potentialities may flower to the maximum. In the degree of its concentration upon the psychological aspects of education to the neglect of the sociological, we venture the severe criticism that recent educational theory becomes thus far an irresponsible theory. It has not clearly recognized—rather it has evaded—the direct and logical consequence of its own priceless contribution; namely, the double necessity at once to destroy and to create social arrangements according to whether these frustrate or release for satisfaction the wants of the largest possible majority of men.

II

The need of a second buttress, an adequate theory of social forces, follows in part from the first. In order that human nature may reach the heights of fulfillment of which we now know it is capable, we are required not only to reconstruct institutional patterns but to analyze, utilize, or paralyze, as the case may be, those forces in our culture which accelerate or retard such reconstruction.

Here educational theory thus far has been woefully weak, so weak that we can scarcely point to a single outstanding educational contribution even remotely comparable to those bearing upon human nature. Take this instance: one of the most seminal, if not the single most seminal, of American contributors to a theory of social forces is still scarcely known to the teachers of our public schools, or perhaps even to most of us who teach these teachers. We refer, of course, to Thorstein Veblen.

To the extent that such a theory becomes adequate, it will surely recognize, for example, the potency of the unrational in all kinds of group relationships. It will diagnose and measure the stubborn ethnocentric allegiances and intergroup conflicts incipiently or overtly manifested in virtually all racial, national, religious clusterings. It will face head-on the flamboyant issue of the struggle between economic classes in all its subtle as well as obtuse forms. It will acquaint citizens, young and old, with the surreptitious and devious exertions of the forces which shape public opinion. It will ask and seek to answer the persistent question of how the still largely latent, yet also tremendous and constructive, power of the common peoples may be released and directed through democratic means in behalf of the building of a world-wide democratic culture.

III

A theory of the state, the third foundation required by our blueprint, has likewise been anticipated. The unrational factor in social forces, to take one instance, is demonstrated only too tragically by the pressures exerted by one state against another—pressures which, when resisted too heavily by counterpressures, generate war.

Yet it is this very power potential in the state which requires equally realistic appraisal by educational theory. Aside from the complicated question of whether supreme coercive power is not the prime differentiating quality of statehood, it is difficult any longer to deny that no state is actually a state which cannot authorize and enforce obedience to its own mandates. Such authorization and enforcement may, to be sure, assume a variety of organizational forms. Thus in an autocracy or oligarchy power is exercised over, rather than by, majorities—a kind of exercise which, under other guises, still characterizes too many modern states. Supreme coercive power need not and certainly should not, however, be of this kind: rather a compelling requirement of which education should be cognizant today is to guarantee that such power is exercised in behalf of and exclusively for the widest obtainable compass of peoples on an *international* plane. In short, a theory of the state appropriate to the revolutionary conditions thrust upon us by the dubious alliance of economics, militarism, and natural science needs to embrace the coercive powers of separate states by a still more coercive power—a supremely enforceable power over all states. It is not too much to insist, if life itself remains precious to men, that international sovereignty is the first item on civilization's agenda for survival.

It follows that a philosophy of education integrated with a philosophy of the state will also include a defensible conception of the relations of parts to the whole. Within America, the demand is, of course, that of establishing a functional association between the "pluralism" of localities, states, and regions, on the one hand, and the "monism" of the nation, on the other hand. Again, however, this demand is by no means confined to America alone: a far more urgent imperative, we reiterate, is for a whole never yet achieved in history—a *world* which is whole.

At least one other familiar, though important, constituent should be added to our third buttress. This is the theory of the positive welfare state of public service as a much more urgent approach to our closely knit industrial culture than the negative state of our *laissez-faire* past. The state, in other words, has a growing number of constructive duties to perform in behalf of popular well-being; and it is one of education's cutting edges to analyze these duties as exactly as possible. Thus, to select a particularly controversial illustration, education, instead of assuming as a matter of course that federal direction of the schools must be rejected a priori as contrary to the whole tradition of local autonomy, should scrupulously consider the case for such direction. In the same way that the service state now begins, even in America, to recognize its national obligations to the unemployed, the sick, or the aged, and to establish standards appropriate to human welfare, so it should begin also to recognize such obligations and standards in the education of all citizens. The core issue here is not federal *versus* local control: it is whether federal control can be more efficient and more effective at the same time that it is indisputably responsible to the majority. To learn how to provide wide two-way traffic lanes between centralized authority and decentralized administration, according to principles roughly analogous to those which the Tennessee Valley Authority has already experimentally provided, is another of education's high priority tasks.

IV

The fourth great theoretical need is an adequate theory of government. If the state be differentiated in terms of supreme coercive power, governments are the refined instruments and expressions of that power. For our own age the problem, we have urged, is to guarantee for the first time in history a government which *in action* is therefore completely the organization and agent of the widest possible range of common interests—in brief, an unqualifiedly *democratic* government.

The complexity of this problem has also been glossed over by some educational theorists. They have failed to appreciate that in a world of deep-seated conflict self-government is not necessarily identifiable with some abstract government of all or for all. Indeed, any dialectical definition of "majority" implies the polar fact of a minority whose own interests, or at least whose interpretation of such interests, differ from the majority's. Hence, we need here to perceive that the final import of majority rule for our period, if not for all periods, is to express and guarantee the largest obtainable consensus upon the largest quantity and richest quality of interests among the earth's peoples at any given time—a consensus springing always from the drives of human nature, individually and socially, and producing institutional arrangements, especially of the service state and government, through which those drives may be released.

Meanwhile, minority dissent consists of two main types. There is the dissent of those who, because of some heavy stake in traditional structures, exert every effort to thwart the will of the majority. They are likely to be, in our generation, the same forces of contraction which engineer the steam-shovels of public opinion to dig the void deeper. Second, there is the minority which dissents, not so much because it disagrees with the central aims of the majority, as because it is unconvinced of a particular means to their attainment and thus may prefer an alternative means. The importance of the service performed by this second type of minority can scarcely be overstressed: so long as judgments of the majority are not sanctified as absolutes they will continue to need salutary critiques of their own fallibility.

Another aspect of almost equal importance to an adequate theory of government is that of the proper role of democratic leadership. In light of the principles considered thus far, this role is a double one. On one side, democratic leaders carry out majority-formulated policies by expertly translating these into the specifics of legislative operation, executive application, judicial interpretation, a process during which leaders aim in every possible way to maintain close communication with their constituents to whom they are at every step responsible. On the other side, leaders are equally articulators and suggesters, that is to say, "pointers" who continually help people to perceive more exactly, more generously, their own best interests. Here is a role so suitable also to the democratic teacher that he himself becomes, in this sense, a democratic leader.

V

Fifth, a philosophy of education-as-politics should embrace an adequate theory of normative commitment.

Let us return for a moment to an earlier remark to the effect that educational theory, especially of one influential type, emphasizes methodology to such an extent as to squeeze all other considerations to minute proportions. That this, too, is a form of commitment has often been pointed out; indeed, certain of its most eloquent spokesmen are at times evangelistic in their fervent glorification of the scientific method as the be-all and end-all of democracy itself. As others, however, have also pointed out, such commitment is paradoxical. Since one of its most passionate beliefs is that we must at all cost avoid any sort of philosophy which gives itself too wholeheartedly to precise, future-oriented goals, therefore its own professed concern with ends somehow seems to dissolve usually into some renewed formulation of scientific means.

This avoidance, though it springs from a legitimate hostility to dogmatism and indoctrination, is no longer tenable. Actually, if we view educational philosophy in the setting of the history of ideas, we find that from Plato onward the attempt to interpret an age philosophically has been, and properly, the attempt to incorporate in one sweeping panorama both the necessary means and dominant ends of that age. In this respect, if no other, we would plead for a revivification of the great tradition of philosophy—a tradition which, applied to current education, would suggest that one pressing obligation is to construct *both* a potent methodology of social transformation and grand-scale designs for the future order.

Please do not misunderstand. This is no plea for a retrogression to the metaphysical systems of either ancient or modern history. We are asserting, rather, that men stand today in a unique intellectual position to build a theory of cultural commitment which is in complete accord with the canons of naturalism, empiricism, and of experimental method. More exactly, the theory now needed might be named one of "defensible partiality"—partiality to crystallized ends which fuse at every point with the deepest cravings of the largest possible majority; at the same time, ends steadily exposed to the bright light of maximum evidence, of continuous public inspection, of a free flow of communication. Unlike the ends of dogmatic doctrine, therefore, they are defensible in the way that outcomes of scientific investigation are defensible. Yet they are also definite and strong in the way that convictions should be definite and strong.

In our present setting, the need then is for commitment, first of all, to the end of that kind of world order where all such creations of man's inventive genius as atomic energy are brought under completely public control. Such an end, delineated into the specifics of human experience, requires the utmost cooperation of every department of learning: of politics, certainly, but likewise of all the social sciences; of physics, but likewise of all the natural sciences; of education, but likewise of all great religions and arts. The service that philosophy should render here becomes comparable in our time to that of such critical periods of both danger and promise as the fifth century B.C., or the seventeenth A.D.: the paramount service of viewing and testing the ends of life as a whole, of audacious and cosmic vision.

Essentialism

A Society of Explorers

MICHAEL POLANYI

We must ask whether intellectual powers, grounded in tacit knowing and descended from evolutionary emergence, can exercise the kind of responsible judgment which we must claim if we are to attribute a moral sense to man. Could, in fact, my rebuttal of exactitude as the ideal of science open the way toward a theory re-establishing the justification of moral standards?

Let me take my bearings once more from the questions which formed my point of departure. I told you how I was struck by the theory that prevailed for a considerable time under Stalin in Soviet Russia, which denied the justification of science as a pursuit of knowledge for its own sake. I said that this violent self-immolation of the mind was actuated by moral motives, and that a similar fusion of unprecedented critical lucidity and intensified moral passions pervades our whole civilization, inflaming or paralyzing both reason and morality.

The story has often been told how scientific rationalism has impaired moral beliefs, first by shattering their religious sanctions and then by questioning their logical grounds; but the usual account does not explain the state of the modern mind.

It is true that the Enlightenment weakened ecclesiastical authority and that modern positivism has denied justification to all transcendent values.

*From *The Tacit Dimension* by Michael Polanyi. Copyright © 1966 by Michael Polanyi. Reprinted by permission of Doubleday & Company, Inc. and by Routledge and Kegan Paul, Ltd.

But I do not think that the discredit which the ideal of exact scientific knowledge had cast on the grounds of moral convictions would by itself have much damaged these convictions. The self-destructive tendencies of the modern mind arose only when the influence of scientific skepticism was combined with a fervor that swept modern man in the very opposite direction. Only when a new passion for moral progress was fused with modern scientific skepticism did the typical state of the modern mind emerge.

The new social aspirations had their origins in Christianity, but they were evoked by the attacks on Christianity. It was only when the philosophy of Enlightenment had weakened the intellectual authority of the Christian churches that Christian aspirations spilled over into man's secular thoughts, and vastly intensified our moral demands on society. The shattering of ecclesiastical control may have been morally damaging in the long run, but its early effect was to raise the standards of social morality.

What is more, scientific skepticism smoothly cooperated at first with the new passions for social betterment. By battling against established authority, skepticism cleared the way for political freedom and humanitarian reforms. Throughout the nineteenth century, scientific rationalism inspired social and moral changes that have improved almost every human relationship, both private and public, throughout Western civilization. Indeed, ever since the French Revolution, and up to our own days, scientific rationalism has been a major influence toward intellectual, moral, and social progress.

Where, then, is the fateful conflict between the moral skepticism of science and the unprecedented moral demands of modern man?

Throughout the very period during which they were so beneficently combined, we can trace the rising undercurrent of their joint destructive influence, and this current finally surfaced and eventually became dominant in the last fifty years. Both scientific skepticism and moral perfectionism had for some time been growing more radical and more irreconcilable, and more deeply ingrained in our thought; and eventually they fused into various unions, each of which embodied a dangerous internal contradiction.

These hybrids of skepticism and perfectionism fall into two classes, one personal, the other political.

The first kind of hybrid can be represented by modern existentialism. Scientific detachment, it says, presents us with a world of bare facts. There is nothing there to justify authority or tradition. These facts are there; for the rest, man's choice is unrestricted. You might expect moral perfectionism to be shocked by this teaching. But no, it rejoices in it. For modern existentialism uses moral skepticism to blast the morality of the existing society as artificial, ideological, hypocritical.

Moral skepticism and moral perfectionism thus combine to discredit all explicit expressions of morality. We have, then, moral passions filled with contempt for their own ideals. And once they shun their own ideals, moral passions can express themselves only in anti-moralism. Professions of absolute self-assertion, gratuitous crime and perversity, self-hatred and despair, remain as the only defenses against a searing self-suspicion of bad faith. Modern existentialists recognize the Marquis de Sade as the earliest moralist of this kind. Dostoyevsky's Stavrogin in *The Possessed* is its classic representation in terms of fiction. Its theory was perhaps first outlined by Nietzsche in *The Genealogy of Morals*. Rimbaud's *Une Saison en Enfer* was its first major epiphany. Modern literature is replete with its professions.

The conception of morality established by this movement eliminates the distinction between good and evil, and it is pointless therefore to express opposition to it by moral reprobation.

The unprecedented critical lucidity of modern man is fused here with his equally unprecedented moral demands and produces an angry absolute individualism. But adjacent to this, the same fusion produces political teachings which sanction the total suppression of the individual. Scientific skepticism and moral perfectionism join forces then in a movement denouncing any appeal to moral ideals as futile and dishonest. Its perfectionism demands a total transformation of society; but this utopian project is not allowed to declare itself. It conceals its moral motives by embodying them in a struggle for power, believed to bring about automatically the aims of utopia. It blindly accepts for this belief the scientific testimony of Marxism. Marxism embodies the boundless moral aspirations of modern man in a theory which protects his ideals from skeptical doubt by denying the reality of moral motives in public life. The power of Marxism lies in uniting the two contradictory forces of the modern mind into a single political doctrine. Thus originated a world-embracing idea, in which moral doubt is frenzied by moral fury and moral fury is armed by scientific nihilism.

Bukharin, explaining urbanely, in the spring of 1935, that scientific truth would no longer be pursued for its own sake under socialism, completed the wheel full circle. Embodied in a scientifically sanctioned political power, moral perfectionism had no place left for truth. Bukharin confirmed this three years later when, facing death, he bore false witness against himself. For to tell the truth would have been to condemn the Revolution, which was unthinkable.

It may appear extravagant to hope that these self-destructive forces may be harmonized by reconsidering the way we know things. If I still believe that a reconsideration of knowledge may be effective today, it is because for some time past, a revulsion has been noticeable against the ideas which brought us to our present state. Both inside and outside the Soviet empire, men are getting weary of ideas sprung from a combination of skepticism and perfectionism. It may be worth trying to go back to our foundations and seek to lay them anew, more truly.

I have prepared for this in certain respects. All I have said implied my repudiation of the grounds on which the absolute intellectual self-determination of man was proclaimed by the great philosophic movement engendered by the Enlightenment. For to acknowledge tacit thought as an indispensable element of all knowing and as the ultimate mental power by which all explicit knowledge is endowed with meaning, is to deny the possibility that each succeeding generation, let alone each member of it, should critically test all the teachings in which it is brought up. Statements explicitly derived from identifiable premises can be critically tested by examining their premises and the process of inference which led to them. But if we know a great deal that we *cannot tell,* and if even that which we know and *can* tell is accepted by us as true only in view of its bearing on a reality beyond it, a reality which may yet manifest itself in the future in an indeterminate range of unsuspected results; if indeed we recognize a great discovery, or else a great personality, as *most real,* owing to the wider range of its yet unknown future manifestations: then the idea of knowledge based on wholly identifiable grounds collapses, and we must conclude that the transmission of knowledge from one generation to the other must be predominantly tacit.

We have seen that tacit knowledge dwells in our awareness of particulars while bearing on an entity which the particulars jointly constitute. In order to share this indwelling, the pupil must presume that a teaching which appears meaningless to start with has in fact a meaning which can be discovered by hitting on the same kind of indwelling as the teacher is practicing. Such an effort is based on accepting the teacher's authority.

Think of the amazing deployment of the infant mind. It is spurred by a blaze of confidence, surmising the hidden meaning of speech and adult behavior. This is how it grasps their meaning. And each new step can be achieved only by entrusting oneself to this extent to a teacher or leader. St. Augustine observed this, when he taught: "Unless you believe, you shall not understand."

It appears then that traditionalism, which requires us to believe before we know, and in order that we may know, is based on a deeper insight into the nature of knowledge and of the communication of knowledge than is a scientific rationalism that would permit us to believe only explicit statements based on tangible data and derived from these by a formal inference, open to repeated testing.

But I am not reasserting traditionalism for the purpose of supporting dogma. To argue, as I do, that confidence in authority is indispensable for the transmission of any human culture is not to demand submission to religious authority. I admit that my reaffirmation of traditionalism might have a bearing on religious thought, but I want to set this aside here. Modern man's critical incisiveness must be reconciled with his unlimited moral demands, first of all, on secular grounds. The enfeebled authority of revealed religion cannot achieve this reconciliation; it may rather hope to be revived by its achievement.

I will not resist in any way the momentum of the French Revolution. I accept its dynamism. But I believe that the new self-determination of man can be saved from destroying itself only by recognizing its own limits in an authoritative traditional framework which upholds it. Tom Paine could proclaim the right of each generation to determine its institutions anew, since the range of his demands was in fact very modest. He unquestioningly accepted the continuity of culture and of the order of private property as the framework of self-determination. Today the ideas of Tom Paine can be saved from self-destruction only by a conscious reaffirmation of traditional continuity. Paine's ideal of unlimited gradual progress can be saved from destruction by revolution only by the kind of traditionalism taught by Paine's opponent, Edmund Burke.

· · ·

Let me display the inescapable need for a traditional framework first in one example of great modern endeavor, which may then serve as a paradigm for other intellectual and moral progress in a free, dynamic society. My example will be the pursuit of the natural sciences. This may be surprising, for modern science was founded through the violent rejection of authority. Throughout the formative centuries of modern science, the revolt against authority was its battle cry: it was sounded by Bacon and Descartes, and by the founders of the Royal Society in their device, *Nullius in Verba*. What these men said was true and important at the time, but once the adversaries they fought had been defeated, the repudiation of all authority or tradition by science became a misleading slogan.[1]

The popular conception of science teaches that science is a collection of observable facts, which anybody can verify for himself. We have seen that this is not true in the case of expert knowledge, as in diagnosing a disease. But it is not true either in the physical sciences. In the first place, you

[1]My ideas about the traditional grounds of science, the organization of scientific pursuits, and the cultivation of originality go back to *Science, Faith and Society*. They were partly developed earlier in the essays published in *The Logic of Liberty* and they formed later the basis for *Personal Knowledge*. More recent statements on this are in "Science: Academic and Industrial," 1961; "The Republic of Science," 1962; "The Potential Theory of Adsorption," 1963; "The Growth of Science in Society," 1966. See Related Bibliography.

cannot possibly get hold of the equipment for testing, for example, a statement of astronomy or of chemistry. And supposing you could somehow get the use of an observatory or a chemical laboratory, you would probably damage their instruments beyond repair before you ever made an observation. And even if you should succeed in carrying out an observation to check upon a statement of science and you found a result which contradicted it, you would rightly assume that you had made a mistake.

The acceptance of scientific statements by laymen is based on authority, and this is true to nearly the same extent for scientists using results from branches of science other than their own. Scientists must rely heavily for their facts on the authority of fellow scientists.

This authority is enforced in an even more personal manner in the control exercised by scientists over the channels through which contributions are submitted to all other scientists. Only offerings that are deemed sufficiently plausible are accepted for publication in scientific journals, and what is rejected will be ignored by science. Such decisions are based on fundamental convictions about the nature of things and about the method which is therefore likely to yield results of scientific merit. These beliefs and the art of scientific inquiry based on them are hardly codified: they are, in the main, tacitly implied in the traditional pursuit of scientific inquiry.

To show what I mean I shall recall an example of a claim lacking plausibility to the point of being absurd, which I picked up twenty-five years ago in a letter published by *Nature*. The author of this letter had observed that the average gestation period of different animals ranging from rabbits to cows was an integer multiple of the number π. The evidence he produced was ample, the agreement good. Yet the acceptance of this contribution by the journal was meant only as a joke. No amount of evidence would convince a modern biologist that gestation periods are equal to integer multiples of π. Our conception of the nature of things tells us that such a relationship is absurd, but cannot prescribe how one could prove this. Another, more technical, example from physics can be found in a paper by Lord Rayleigh, published in the *Proceedings of the Royal Society* in 1947. It described some fairly simple experiments which proved, in the author's opinion, that a hydrogen atom impinging on a metal wire could transmit to it energies ranging up to a hundred electron volts. Such an observation, if correct, would be far more revolutionary than the discovery of atomic fission by Otto Hahn in 1939. Yet when this paper appeared and I asked various physicists' opinions about it, they only shrugged their shoulders. They could not find fault with the experiment, yet they not only did not believe its results, but did not even think it worth while to consider what was wrong with it, let alone check up on it.

They just ignored it. Again ten years later some experiments were brought to my notice which accidently offered an explanation of Lord Rayleigh's findings. His results were apparently due to some hidden factors of no great interest, but which he could hardly have identified at the time. He should have ignored his observation, for he ought to have known that there must be something wrong with it.[2]

The rejection of implausible claims has often proved mistaken, but safety against this danger could be assured only at the cost of permitting journals to be swamped by nonsense.

There is another requirement to be sustained by the authority of scientific opinion over scientists. To form part of science, a statement of fact must be not only true, but also interesting, and more particularly, interesting to science. Reliability, exactitude, does count as a factor contributing to scientific merit, but it is not enough. Two further elements enter into the assessment of a contribution. One is the relation to the systematic structure of science, to correcting or expanding this structure. The other is quite independent of both the reliability and the systematic interest of a discovery, for it lies in its subject matter, in its subject as known before it was taken up by science: it consists of the intrinsic interest of the subject matter.

Thus the scientific interest—or scientific value—of a contribution is formed by three factors: its *exactitude,* its *systematic importance,* and the *intrinsic interest of its subject matter.* The proportion in which these factors enter into scientific value varies greatly over the several domains of science: deficiency in one may be balanced by excellence in another. The highest degree of exactitude and widest range of systematization are found in mathematical physics, and this compensates here for a lesser intrinsic interest of its inanimate subject. By contrast, we have, at the other end of the sciences, domains like zoology and botany which lack exactitude and have no systematic structure comparable in range to that of physics, but which make up for this deficiency by the far greater intrinsic interest in living things compared with inanimate matter. The body of scientific knowledge is what it is by virtue of the fact that referees are constantly engaged in eliminating contributions offered to science which lack an acceptable scientific value, as measured by the compounded coefficients of accuracy, systematic interest, and lay interest of subject matter. Science is shaped by these delicate valuations by scientific opinion.

We may wonder, then, how the conformity enforced by current judgments of plausibility can allow the appearance of any true originality. For

[2]Further particulars on the letter to *Nature* are to be found in *The Logic of Liberty*, p. 17. For Lord Rayleigh, see *The Logic of Liberty*, p. 12 and for the later development of Lord Rayleigh's story, see *Personal Knowledge*, p. 276.

it certainly does allow it: science presents a panorama of surprising developments. How can such surprises be produced on effectively dogmatic grounds?

We often hear of *surprising confirmations* of a theory. The discovery of America by Columbus was surprising confirmation of the earth's sphericity; the discovery of electron diffraction was a surprising confirmation of De Broglie's wave theory of matter; the discoveries of genetics brought surprising confirmations of the Mendelian principles of heredity. We have here the paradigm of all progress in science: discoveries are made by pursuing possibilities suggested by existing knowledge.

This applies also to radically novel discoveries. All the material on which Max Planck founded his quantum theory in 1900 was open to inspection by all other physicists. He alone saw inscribed in it a new order transforming the outlook of man. No other scientist had any inkling of this vision; it was more solitary even than Einstein's discoveries. Although many striking confirmations of it followed within a few years, so strange was Planck's idea that it took eleven years for quantum theory to gain final acceptance by leading physicists. As late as 1914, the controversy over quanta was still sufficiently alive to serve as a joke at a dinner party in the home of the great Walther Nernst in Berlin. A graduate student named Lindemann (who later became Lord Cherwell), said of a fellow student who had just married a rich girl, that he had hitherto been equipartitionist, but now believed in quanta. Yet in another thirty years, Planck's position in science was approaching that hitherto accorded only to Newton.

While science imposes an immense range of authoritative pronouncements, it not merely tolerates dissent in some particulars, but grants its highest encouragement to creative dissent. While the machinery of scientific institutions severely suppresses suggested contributions, because they contradict the currently accepted view about the nature of things, the same scientific authorities pay their highest homage to ideas which sharply modify these accepted views.

This apparent self-contradiction is resolved on the metaphysical grounds which underlie all our knowledge of the external world. The sight of a solid object indicates that it has both another side and a hidden interior, which we could explore; the sight of another person points at unlimited hidden workings of his mind and body. Perception has this inexhaustible profundity, because what we perceive is an aspect of reality, and aspects of reality are clues to boundless undisclosed, and perhaps yet unthinkable, experiences. This is what the existing body of scientific thought means to the productive scientist: he sees in it an aspect of reality which, as such, promises to be an inexhaustible source of new, promising problems. And his work bears this out; science continues to be fruitful—as

I said in my first lecture—because it offers an insight into the nature of reality.

This view of science merely recognizes what all scientists believe—that science offers us an aspect of reality, and may therefore manifest its truth inexhaustibly and often surprisingly in the future. Only in this belief can the scientist conceive problems, pursue inquiries, claim discoveries; this belief is the ground on which he teaches his students and exercises his authority over the public. And it is by transmitting this belief to succeeding generations that scientists grant their pupils independent grounds from which to start toward their own discoveries, possibly in opposition to their teachers.

The discovery of new facts may change the interest of established facts, and intellectual standards themselves are subject to change. Interest in spectroscopy was sharply renewed by Bohr's theory of atomic structure, and the novelty of its appeal also wrought a change in the standards of scientific beauty. No single achievement has equaled Planck's discovery of quantum theory in transforming the quality of intellectual satisfaction in mathematical physics. Such changes have been accompanied through the centuries by the belief that they offered a deeper understanding of reality. This testifies to a belief in the reality of scientific value. Only by holding this belief can the scientist direct his inquiries toward tasks promising scientific value. And only in this conviction can he inaugurate novel standards with universal intent. He can then also teach his students to respect current values and encourage them perhaps one day to deepen these values in the light of their own insights.

But a description of scientific procedure implies no justification of it. If I trust, as I do, that the metaphysical beliefs of scientists necessarily assure discipline and foster originality in science, I must declare these beliefs to be true. I do this. Yet this does not mean that I share all accepted beliefs of scientists about the nature of things. On the contrary, all my writings show that I dissent from large tracts of scientific views, particularly in psychology and sociology. But this leaves my beliefs about the nature of external scientific truth unaffected.

These metaphysical beliefs are not explicitly professed today by scientists, let alone by the general public. Modern science arose claiming to be grounded in experience and not on a metaphysics derived from first principles. My assertion that science can have discipline and originality only if it believes that the facts and values of science bear on a still unrevealed reality, stands in opposition to the current philosophic conception of scientific knowledge.

I have next to answer some curious questions. Research is pursued by thousands of independent scientists all over the planet, each of whom really knows only a tiny part of science. How do the results of these inquiries, each conducted largely in ignorance of the others' work, sustain the systematic unity of science? And how can many thousands of scientists, each of whom has a detailed knowledge of only a very small fraction of science, jointly impose equal standards on the whole range of vastly different sciences?

Today's system of science has grown from the system as it was a generation ago through advances which originated independently at a great number of points where the old system offered a chance for progress. Spread over the different fields of scientific knowledge, scientists were looking out for such points and each developed one. Each has studied the work of others on various promising points and also considered for his choice how he could best make use of his special gifts. Such a procedure achieves the greatest total progress possible in practice and best assures the systematic character of science at successive stages of its progress. Such is the work of self-co-ordination by mutual adjustment in science.

All institutions serving the advancement and dissemination of science rely on the supposition that a field of potential systematic progress exists, ready to be revealed by the independent initiative of individual scientists. It is in view of this belief that scientists are appointed for life to the pursuit of research and permanent subsidies are granted to them for this purpose. Many expensive buildings, pieces of equipment, journals, etc. are founded and maintained in this belief. It is the most general traditional belief which a novice joining the scientific community accepts in becoming a scientist.

This raises another, more intricate, question. How can we confidently speak of science as a systematic body of knowledge and assume that it is sufficiently reliable and interesting in all its branches as judged by the same standards of scientific merit? Can we possibly be assured that new contributions will be accepted in all areas by the same standards of plausibility and be rewarded by the same standards of beauty and originality? Unless contributions are accepted in different areas by substantially equal standards, a gross waste of resources might ensue. Can such a scandal be guarded against by transferring resources from areas where standards are currently lower, to points at which they are higher?

It might seem impossible to compare the complex scientific value of marginal contributions over such different areas as, for example, astronomy and medicine. Yet I believe this is in fact done, or at least is reasonably approached in practice. It is done by applying a principle that

I have not seen described elsewhere, although it is used in various fields; I would call it the *principle of mutual control.* It consists, in the present case, of the simple fact that scientists keep watch over each other. Each scientist is both subject to criticism by all others and encouraged by their appreciation of him. This is how *scientific opinion* is formed, which enforces scientific standards and regulates the distribution of professional opportunities. It is clear that only fellow scientists working in closely related fields are competent to exercise direct authority over each other; but their personal fields will form *chains of overlapping neighborhoods* extending over the entire range of science. It is enough that the standards of plausibility and worthwhileness be equal around every single point to keep them equal over all the sciences. Even those in the most widely separated branches of science will then rely on each other's results and support each other against any laymen seriously challenging their authority.

Such mutual control produces a mediated consensus between scientists even if they cannot understand more than a vague outline of each other's subjects. And this applies, of course, also to myself. All that I have said here about the workings of mutual adjustment and mutual authority is based on my own personal belief that the modes of intercourse I have observed in my part of science can be assumed to extend through all sciences.[3]

Mutual control applies also to those newly joining the scientific community at any particular point of its vast domain. They start their inquiries by joining the interplay of mutual co-ordination and at the same time taking their own part in the existing system of mutual control, and they do so in the belief that its current standards are essentially true and common throughout science. They trust the traditions fostered by this system of mutual control without much experience of it and at the same time claim an independent position from which they may reinterpret and possibly revolutionize this tradition.

The scientific community shows some hierarchical features, but these do not alter the fact that the authority of scientific opinion is exercised by the mutual control of independent scientists, far beyond the direct scope of any one of them. When we speak of science and its progress, or its history, or speak of the standards of science and call them "scientific," we

[3]I shall explain in a moment how mutual authority also governs other cultural fields. But I think it applies to further consensual activities of which the participants know only a small fragment. It suggests a way by which resources can be rationally distributed between any rival purposes that cannot be valued in terms of money. All cases of public expenditure serving collective interests are of this kind. This is, I believe, how the claims of a thousand government departments can be fairly rationally adjudicated, although no single person can know closely more than a tiny fraction of them.

refer to a thing we call "science" of which no one has ever known more than a tiny fragment. We have seen that the tradition of science induces its own renewal by bearing on a reality beyond experience; now we find likewise that each scientist's knowledge of his own neighborhood bears on the whole of science far beyond his own experience. This is how he controls the standards of science indirectly, on the same footing of independence as all others do, while submitting to their control of his own work in return.

Each exchange of mutual criticism is something of a tussle and may be a mortal struggle. New standards of plausibility and of scientific interest are thus initiated and eventually established. The movement will start in one field and gradually diffuse into all others. This is how science is steadily reshaped and yet its coherence maintained over all its fields. I myself am involved in such a predicament today through my dissent from some methods of current psychology and sociology. But I do not challenge thereby the existence of science as a coherent system of thought: I merely press for its reform in certain respects.

. . .

We have seen that the scientist can conceive problems and pursue their investigation only by believing in a hidden reality on which science bears. Now that I have shown further how scientific originality springs from scientific tradition and at the same time supersedes it, I can show how this process establishes the sense of personal responsibility which sustains the scientist's search.

There are two possible ways of viewing the progress made by the front line of scientific discoveries as it advances over a period of time. We may look upon such progress as the growth of thought in the minds of gifted people along the pathways of science. The frequent occurrence of simultaneous discoveries may appear to support this image. Even major discoveries, which fundamentally refashion our conception of nature, can be made simultaneously by a number of scientists at different places. Quantum mechanics was discovered in 1925 by three authors so independent of each other that they were thought at the time to have given mutually incompatible solutions to the problem. Thus seen, the growth of new ideas appears altogether predetermined. The mind of those making discoveries seems merely to offer a suitable soil for the proliferation of new ideas.

Yet, looking *forward* before the event, the act of discovery appears personal and indeterminate. It starts with the solitary intimations of a problem, of bits and pieces here and there which seem to offer clues to something hidden. They look like fragments of a yet unknown coherent whole. This tentative vision must turn into a personal obsession; for a problem that does not worry us is no problem: there is no drive in it, it does not exist. The obsession, which spurs and guides us, is about something that no one can tell: its content is undefinable, indeterminate, strictly personal. Indeed, the process by which it will be brought to light will be acknowledged as a discovery precisely because it could not have been achieved by any persistence in applying explicit rules to given facts. The true discoverer will be acclaimed for the daring feat of his imagination, which crossed uncharted seas of possible thought.

Thus the backward-looking picture of thought as using human brains as the passive soil of its proliferation proves false. Yet it does represent an aspect of the pursuit of science. Scientific progress seen after the event may be taken to represent the possibilities that were previously hidden and dimly anticipated in a problem. This does explain how different scientists may independently feel intimations of a particular potentiality, often sighting it by different clues and possibly discovering it in different terms.

Note that there is a widespread opinion that scientists hit on discoveries merely by trying everything as it happens to cross their minds. This opinion follows from an inability to recognize man's capacity for anticipating the approach of hidden truth. The scientist's surmises or hunches are the spurs and pointers of his search. They involve high stakes, as hazardous as their prospects are fascinating. The time and money, the prestige and self-confidence gambled away in disappointing guesses will soon exhaust a scientist's courage and standing. His gropings are weighty decisions.

Such are the responsible choices made in the course of scientific inquiry. The choices are made by the scientist: they are his acts, but what he pursues is not of his making; his acts stand under the judgment of the hidden reality he seeks to uncover. His vision of the problem, his obsession with it, and his final leap to discovery are all filled from beginning to end with an obligation to an external objective. In these intensely personal acts, therefore, there is no self-will. Originality is commanded at every stage by a sense of responsibility for advancing the growth of truth in men's minds. Its freedom is perfect service.

Many writers have observed, since Dewey taught it at the close of the last century, that, to some degree, we shape all knowledge in the way we know it. This appears to leave knowledge open to the whims of the observer. But the pursuit of science has shown us how even in the shaping of his own anticipations the knower is controlled by impersonal requirements. His acts are personal judgments exercised responsibly with a view to a reality with which he is seeking to establish contact. This holds for all seeking and finding of external truth.

There is no more positive justification than this for accepting science to be true. Attempts have been made to compensate for this apparent deficiency by reducing the claims of science. The uncertainty and transiency of science was emphasized and exaggerated for this purpose. Yet this is beside the point. The affirmation of a *probable* statement includes a judgment no less personal than an affirmation of its *certainty* would do. Any conclusion, be it given as a surmise or claimed as a certainty, represents a commitment of the person who arrives at it. No one can utter more than a responsible commitment of his own, and this completely fulfills the finding of the truth and the telling of it.

For the scientist, having relied throughout his inquiry on the presence of something real hidden out there, will justly rely on that external presence also for claiming the validity of the result that satisfies his quest. As he accepted throughout the discipline which the external pole of his endeavor imposed upon him, he expects that others—if similarly equipped—will also recognize the presence that guided him. By his own command, which bound him to the quest of reality, he will claim that his results are universally valid. Such is the universal intent of a scientific discovery.

I speak not of an *established* universality, but of a universal *intent*, for the scientist cannot know whether his claims will be accepted. They may prove false or, though true, may fail to carry conviction. He may even expect that his conclusions will prove unacceptable, and in any case their acceptance will not guarantee him their truth. To claim validity for a statement merely declares that it *ought* to be accepted by all. The affirmation of scientific truth has an obligatory character which it shares with other valuations, declared universal by our own respect for them.

I have spoken of the excitement of problems, of an obsession with hunches and visions that are indispensable spurs and pointers to discovery. But science is supposed to be dispassionate. There is indeed an idealization of this current today, which deems the scientist not only indifferent to the outcome of his surmises, but actually seeking their refutation.[4] This is not only contrary to experience, but logically inconceivable. The surmises of a working scientist are *born of the imagination*

[4]This view has been persuasively expressed by K.R. Popper, e.g. in the *Logic of Scientific Discovery* (New York, 1959), p. 279, as follows:

"But these marvellously imaginative and bold conjectures or 'anticipations' of ours are carefully and soberly controlled by systematic tests. Our method of research is not to defend them, in order to prove how right we were. On the contrary, we try to overthrow them. Using all the weapons of our logical, mathematical, and technical armory we try to prove that our anticipations were false—in order to put forward, in their stead, new unjustified and unjustifiable anticipations, new 'rash and premature prejudices,' as Bacon derisively called them."

seeking discovery. Such effort *risks* defeat but never *seeks* it; it is in fact his craving for success that makes the scientist take the risk of failure. There is no other way. Courts of law employ two separate lawyers to argue opposite pleas, because it is only by a passionate commitment to a particular view that the imagination can discover the evidence that supports it.

The creative thrust of the imagination is fed by various sources. The beauty of the anticipated discovery and the excitement of its solitary achievement contribute to it in the first place. The scientist also seeks professional success, and, if scientific opinion rewards merit rightly, ambition too will serve as a true spur to discovery.

The part of science for the renewal of which the scientist assumes responsibility is surrounded by a sea of information on which he must rely for his enterprise. The scientist may regard his selected field as his "calling," which necessarily includes his submission to the vast area of information and belief surrounding his selected field of inquiry. Each scientist's calling has a different geography. Each must try to choose a problem that is not larger or more difficult than he can master. His faculties would not be fully utilized if he applied them to a lesser task, and would be altogether wasted on a larger one. The degree of originality any particular scientist trusts himself to possess should thus determine the range which he will venture to tackle and hence also the range of information which he will unquestioningly accept. Goethe wrote that the master proves himself by his restraint—and the same holds for science.

. . .

My account of scientific discovery describes an existential choice. We start the pursuit of discovery by pouring ourselves into the subsidiary elements of a problem and we continue to spill ourselves into further clues as we advance further, so that we arrive at discovery fully committed to it as an aspect of reality. These choices create in us a new existence, which challenges others to transform themselves in its image. To this extent, then, "existence precedes essence," that is, it comes before the truth that we establish and make our own.

But does this show us that "man is his own beginning, author of all his values"? If originality in science is taken as an example of existential choice, these claims of Nietzsche's and Sartre's existentialism appear ill-conceived. The most daring innovations of science spring from a vast range of information which the scientist accepts unchallenged as a background to his problem. Even when he is led to modify the standards of scientific merit, current standards will be the basis of this reform. Science as a whole, as mediated by thousands of fellow scientists he has never heard about, he accepts unchallenged.

His quest transforms him by compelling him to make a sequence of choices. Does this mean that he is existentially choosing himself? In a sense it does; he does seek intellectual growth. But he does *not* sit back and choose at his pleasure a new existence. He strains his imagination to the utmost to find a path that might lead to a superior life of the mind. All his existential choices are made in response to a potential discovery; they consist in sensing and following a gradient of understanding which will lead to the expansion of his mental existence. Every step is an effort to meet an immediate necessity; his freedom is continuous service.

There is here no existential choice comprising the whole world and claiming responsibility for it. Such a choice would leave neither a center to which it could be responsible, nor a criterion by which it could be judged. This impossible responsibility, which is the source of the existentialist's sense of universal absurdity, now appears as an obvious self-contradiction.

At the opposite extreme, the theory of science taught under Stalin is equally erroneous. To declare that in a classless society the pursuit of science—the search marked by the names of Copernicus and Newton, of Harvey, Darwin, and Einstein—will spontaneously turn to the advancement of the next Five-Year Plan is simply ludicrous.

Yet this doctrine was not without grave consequences in Soviet Russia and not without influence in England. It was my attempt to vindicate the freedom of science against such teachings that made me realize the weakness of the strict empiricism which has dominated our conception of science throughout this century. I saw that this philosophy left science defenseless against the Soviet doctrine and this led me to decide that only on metaphysical grounds can we account for the intrinsic powers of human inventiveness. Here I met also the presuppositions of freedom in science.

But more insistent than the imposition of dialectical materialism on science was the subjection of literature and the arts to socialist realism, and of the very conception of truth, morality, and justice to partyism. These doctrines gained force around 1932 and have been substantially relaxed only since the Hungarian and Polish revolutions of 1956. They were to embody man's homeless ideals in an absolute submission to the Communist party.

I have countered the attempt at transforming science on such lines by offering solid grounds for its independence. This would now have to be expanded to all other major principles of man. I cannot attempt this here, but I shall outline—however sketchily—those foundations of science which broadly hold also for all other creative systems of the modern mind.

Scientific tradition derives its capacity for self-renewal from its belief in the presence of a hidden reality, of which current science is one aspect, while other aspects of it are to be revealed by future discoveries. Any tradition fostering the progress of thought must have this intention: to teach its current ideas as stages leading on to unknown truths which, when discovered, might dissent from the very teachings which engendered them. Such a tradition assures the independence of its followers by transmitting the conviction that thought has intrinsic powers, to be evoked in men's minds by intimations of hidden truths. It respects the individual for being capable of such response: for being able to see a problem not visible to others, and to explore it on his own responsibility. Such are the metaphysical grounds of intellectual life in a free, dynamic society: the principles which safeguard intellectual life in such a society. I call this a society of explorers.

In a society of explorers man is *in thought*. Man the explorer is placed in the midst of potential discoveries, which offer him the possibility of numberless problems. We have seen how scientists, scattered over the globe, respond to one vast field of potential thought, how each finds in it a congenial area to develop, and how the results then coordinate themselves to produce a systematic expansion of science. This is also how other kinds of thought have developed in our time. Our age has seen an unprecedented wealth of literary and artistic movements growing into coherence. The ideas of the Enlightenment bred scientism and romanticism in a multitude of connected forms; and since the turn of the eighteenth century legal and social reforms have humanized life in a hundred mutually related ways. This is also how the hybrid of absolute skepticism and perfectionism has engendered in the present century new movements of fiction, poetry, music, and painting—although admittedly this movement has brought forth at the same time the theories prefiguring modern fanaticisms, with all their tyrannies and cruelties.

The structure of authority exercised over a society of explorers is different from that to which a dogmatic society submits. Take once more the example of science. I have spoken of the principle of mutual control through which each scientist independently plays his part in maintaining scientific traditions over an immense domain of inquiry of which he knows virtually nothing. A society of explorers is controlled throughout by such mutually imposed authority. The pressure exercised by literary and artistic circles is notorious. They control access to public recognition much as scientific opinion controls it for science. Their professional opinion commands lay assent just as scientific opinion does. There are of course, differences: reliance on secondhand authority reaches less far in literature and art than in science, and divisions between rival opinions go deeper. In our society, ideas about morality are also actively cultivated by different circles of mutual appreciation, which are deeply divided against each other; and in politics these circles are deliberately organized as rivals.

But we need not go into all these variations; they are transcended by a test which proves that all such groups effectively foster the intrinsic power of thought. For these circles, these professional associations—some perhaps no more than coteries of mutual admiration—are feared and hated by modern totalitarian rulers. They are feared because in them man lives in thought—in thought over which the rulers have no power. They are feared more than are scientific associations, because the truth of literature and poetry, of history and political thought, of philosophy, morality, and legal principles, is more vital than the truth of science. This is why the independent cultivation of such truth has proved an intolerable menace to modern tyranny.

I have now roughly generalized the principles underlying the pursuit of science to include the cultivation of man's other ideals. The result shows how closely the growth of thought intrinsically limits our self-determination everywhere. Whether his calling lies in literature or art, or in moral and social reform, even the most revolutionary mind must choose as his calling a small area of responsibility, for the transformation of which he will rely on the surrounding world as its premises. Perfectionism, which would transform the whole of thought and the entire society, is a program of destruction, ending up at best in a world of pretense. The existentialist contempt for all values not chosen by ourselves, condemning them as bad faith, is likewise either empty or destructive.

There is another way of dealing with the claim to absolute self-determination and the demands of perfectionism. I could reject these inordinate endeavors by referring to the logic by which successive levels of reality are related to each other. All our higher principles must rely for their working on a lower level of reality and this necessarily sets limits to their scope, yet does not make them reducible to the terms of the lower level. This argument confutes the current cultural movement which questions the intrinsic powers of our ideals. There is not one higher principle of our minds that is not in danger of being falsely explained away by psychological or sociological analysis, by historical determinism, by mechanical models or computers; but this battle cannot be joined here on this wide front.

Nevertheless, I must say a word on these lines about the principal ideal of man which is at the core of his involvement in a combination of extreme skepticism and perfectionism, for I have specifically promised to find a place for moral principles safe from self-destruction by a claim to boundless self-determination. Take the demand for social and moral perfection and recognize the presence of successive levels of reality. Society, as an organization of power and profit, forms one level, while its moral principles lie on a level above it. The higher level is rooted in the lower one: moral progress can be achieved only within the medium of a society operating by the exercise of power and aiming at material advantages. We must accept the fact that any moral advances must be tainted by this social mechanism which alone can bring them about. To attempt to enforce absolute morality in society is therefore to indulge in fantasies that will only lead to untamed violence.

The problem of a balanced mind, secured against both critical and moral frenzy, has gained new and novel urgency through the liberating movement that has arisen in the Soviet empire since Stalin's death, a movement which gradually widened into the rebellion of leading young Communists in Hungary, in Poland, and eventually in Russia itself. The question now is whether this revulsion can generate a steady movement of free thought. When I listen to my Hungarian friends who took refuge in England after taking part in the revolution of 1956, when I read their account of their times as ardent Stalinists and of the change of heart they have undergone since then, I find that their hopes are basically the same as those which animated liberal thought at the turn of the last century. They are the hopes with which I was brought up as a child in Hungary. But the innocence with which I breathed in these ideals cannot be recovered. The revival of the liberal tradition can be assured only if we can establish it on a new, conscious understanding of its foundation, on grounds which will withstand modern self-doubt coupled with perfectionism.

With this in mind, let me add a few more touches to the cosmic background of the ideas which I have tried to develop in answer to the need of our time.

I have shown how man can exercise responsible judgment when faced with a problem. His decisions in casting around for a solution are necessarily indeterminate, in the sense that the solution of an unsolved problem is indeterminate; but his decisions are also responsible in being subject to the obligation to seek the predetermined solution of his problem. I have said that this is a commitment to the anticipation of a hidden reality, a commitment of the same kind as exemplified in the knowledge of scientific truth. Responsibility and truth are in fact but two aspects of such a commitment: the act of judgment is its personal pole and the independent reality on which it bears is its external pole.

Since a problem can be known only tacitly, our knowledge of it can be recognized as valid only by accepting the validity of tacit knowing; and the same applies to truth in its bearing on reality. Herein lies the importance of establishing the validity of tacit knowing. But we must yet consider the evolutionary antecedents of man's power to see a problem and solve it. I have identified the antecedents of problem-solving with the process of emergence. Therefore, if responsible human decisions are identical to problem-solving, we must expect to find that similar decisive powers are intrinsic to the process of emergence throughout the evolutionary innovations which we ascribe to emergence.

Such speculations are necessarily hazardous, but I feel more repelled by our timidity which would leave these matters to the scientists, who actually regard them as unsuited for investigation by science.

I have said that the laws of nature that are manifest in the inanimate domain fail in two respects to account for the rise of living beings: (1) they leave open the boundary conditions which in living beings are fixed according to operational principles not manifested in inanimate nature, and (2) they contain no reference to sentience, which is a characteristic condition of life in higher animals. It seems reasonable to assume that these two deficiencies are but aspects of a single principle that must be added to those of inanimate nature in order to account for living things. I have, of course, introduced this assumption already by identifying emergence with tacit knowing.

A closer definition of the missing principle can be attempted by considering how it could best form a transition from physics to the process governing the growth of thought in the mind of man. Inanimate nature is controlled by forces which draw matter toward stabler configurations. This is equally true in mechanics and thermodynamics and it applies also to open systems, like flames or flows. The forces generated by stabler potentialities may be held in check by various kinds of friction, which may be overcome by catalytic releasing agents. An explosion can be triggered by the spontaneous disintegration of a single molecule. Quantum mechanics has also established the conception of uncaused causes, subject, only to control by a field of probabilities. The decomposition of a radioactive atom may be an uncaused cause. Let us then carry forward these three characteristics of inanimate processes: (1) we see forces driving toward stabler potentialities; (2) catalysts or accidental releasers of friction-locked forces cause them to actualize these potentialities; and (3) such accidents may be uncaused events, subject only to probable tendencies.

Look now at the way innovations are achieved by the effort of human thought. This process too can be described as the actualization of certain potentialities. To see a problem and undertake its pursuit is to see a range of potentialities, believed to be accessible. Such heuristic tension appears to be generated in the alert mind, much as forces in physics are generated by the accessibility of stabler configurations. But this tension appears to be deliberate: it is a response striving to comprehend a solution believed to be predetermined. It makes choices that are hazardous but always controlled by the pursuit of their intention. These choices resemble quantum mechanical events in being uncaused and at the same time guided by a field that leaves them largely indeterminate. But discoveries differ from inanimate events in three ways: (1) the field evoking and guiding them is not that of a more stable configuration but of a problem; (2) their occurrence is not spontaneous but due to an effort toward the actualization of certain hidden potentialities; and (3) the uncaused action which evokes them is usually an imaginative thrust toward discovering these potentialities.

So far there is not much speculation involved in this analysis, and I believe there is also some firm support for generalizing it to the process of evolutionary innovations. My analysis of consecutive operational levels necessitates the assumption of a principle which works in the manner of an innovation achieved by tacit integration. The assumption that this process is evoked by the accessibility of the higher levels of stable meaning which it eventually achieves, seems compelling to me. The tension generated by such a higher potentiality might then be triggered into action either by accident or by the operation of first causes. It seems, furthermore, consonant with the conceptual framework of quantum mechanics on the one hand and of problem-solving on the other hand to assume that these creative releases are controlled, and yet never fully determined, by their potentialities. They may succeed or fail. And it seems reasonable to assume, then, on grounds of continuity, that this peculiar kind of indeterminacy is accompanied by the rise of consciousness.

The overall title I gave to these lectures was Man in Thought. I wanted to speak of the logical interrelation between living and thinking in man and to extend this interrelation by tracing the joint ancestry of man and thought, all the way back to their inanimate antecedents. I have introduced a large number of new principles, crowding them on top of each other. I could not resist the temptation of giving you a glance at ideas that have filled volumes, and perhaps may fill others. But I feel that, actually, all I have spoken of presents a single, fairly simple vision. This part of the universe, in which man has arisen, seems to be filled with a field of potentialities which evoke action. The action thus evoked in inanimate matter is rather poor, perhaps quite meaningless. But dead matter, matter that is both lifeless and deathless, takes on meaning by originating living things. With them a hazard enters the hitherto unerring universe: a hazard of life and death.

The field of new potential meanings was so rich that this enterprise, once started, swept on toward an infinite range of higher meanings, unceasingly pouring them into existence, for the better part of a billion years. Almost from the start, this evolutionary response to potential meaning had its counterpart in the behavior of the living things it brought forth. It seems that even protozoa have the faculty of learning; they respond to potential meaning. Rising stages of evolution produce more meaningful organisms, capable of ever more complex acts of understanding. In the last few thousand years human beings have enormously increased the range of comprehension by equipping our tacit powers with a cultural machinery of language and writing. Immersed in this cultural milieu, we now respond to a much increased range of potential thought.

It is the image of humanity immersed in potential thought that I find revealing for the problems of our day. It rids us of the absurdity of absolute self-determination, yet offers each of us the chance of creative originality, within the fragmentary area which circumscribes our calling. It provides us with the metaphysical grounds and the organizing principle of a Society of Explorers.

Yet the question remains whether this solution will satisfy us. Can we recognize the limitations it imposes on us? Must not such a fragmented society appear adrift, irresponsible, selfish, apparently chaotic? I have praised the freedom of a community where coherence is spontaneously established by self-co-ordination, authority is exercised by equals over each other, all tasks are set by each to himself. But where are they all going? Nobody knows; they are just piling up works soon to be forgotten.

I have tried to affiliate our creative endeavors to the organic evolution from which we have arisen. This cosmic emergence of meaning is inspiring. But its products were mainly plants and animals that could be satisfied with a brief existence. Men need a purpose which bears on eternity. Truth does that; our ideals do it; and this might be enough, if we could ever be satisfied with our manifest moral shortcomings and with a society which has such shortcomings fatally involved in its workings.

Perhaps this problem cannot be resolved on secular grounds alone. But its religious solution should become more feasible once religious faith is released from pressure by an absurd vision of the universe, and so there will open up instead a meaningful world which could resound to religion.

FOR FURTHER READING

Archambault, Reginald D. (ed.). *Philosophical Analysis and Education.* New York: The Humanities Press, 1965.

Essays by leading English philosophers of the analytic persuasion. Investigate educational theory, "education" and "teaching." Two essays are particularly relevant to this chapter. Perry analyzes the weaknesses of both traditional and progressive education, and calls for an examination of the issues arising from the educational contexts themselves. Peters develops an essentialist educational philosophy; he argues that education is "initiation."

Booth, Wayne C. (ed.). *The Knowledge Most Worth Having.* Chicago: University of Chicago Press, 1967.
    A series of essays dealing with the question of what all men should learn. Provocative, suggestive.

Brameld, Theodore. *Philosophies of Education in Cultural Perspective.* New York: Holt, Rinehart and Winston, Inc., 1955.
    An examination of three philosophies of education: perennialism, essentialism, and progressivism. Argues that the philosophical investigation of education must take place with full recognition of their cultural context.

————. *Toward a Reconstructed Philosophy of Education.* New York: Holt, Rinehart and Winston, Inc., 1956.
    A thoroughgoing development of the reconstructionist philosophy of education by its leading advocate.

Buber, Martin. *Between Man and Man.* Boston: Beacon Press. 1955. Chapter 4.
    A series of essays by the leading Jewish existentialist philosopher. Chapter 4 is a statement of educational aims. Complements the essay in Chapter 3 of this anthology.

Hook, Sidney. *Education for Modern Man.* New York: Alfred A. Knopf, 1966. Chapters 2, 4, 5, 6, 7.
    A series of essays many of which are devoted to educational goals. Written from the viewpoint of a philosopher sympathetic to Dewey's orientation.

Hutchins, Robert M. *The Conflict in Education.* New York: Harper & Row, Publishers, 1953.
    A critique of progressive education and a discussion of the basis of a liberal education. Perennialist in perspective.

————. *The Higher Learning in America.* New Haven: Yale University Press, 1936.
    Analyzes the socio-cultural context of American education, the dilemma educators in higher education face, and a perennialist philosophy and program for a university.

Maritain, Jacques. *The Education of Man.* Edited with an introduction by Donald and Idella Gallagher. Notre Dame: University of Notre Dame Press, 1967.
    A series of essays elaborating and working out some educational implications of a Christian theistic realism by a great Catholic thinker. Perennialist in orientation.

O'Conner. D. J. *An Introduction to the Philosophy of Education.* London: Routledge and Kegan Paul, 1957. Chapter 3.
    Chapter 3 is devoted to an examination of how, on what grounds, value judgments or judgments about ends can be justified.

Peters, R. S. *Ethics and Education.* Glenview, Illinois: Scott, Foresman and Company, 1967.

An analytic approach to the ethical foundations of education. Investigates uses of the term "education," theories of justification of educational goals, and such educational goals as equality, freedom, and respect for persons and fraternity.

Whitehead, A. N. *The Aims of Education* New York: The New American Library of World Literature, Inc., 1961.

A series of essays developing an essentialist educational philosophy. Among the subjects dealt with are goals for education, the rhythm of the developmental process of the learner and the place of freedom and discipline in that rhythm, technical education, and the function of universities.

Glossary

(*Note*: Terms included are restricted to those used in the selections which are unfamiliar and technical. However, those terms and phrases which are adequately defined in the selection in which they appear are not included. For additional help refer to *The Encyclopedia of Philosophy*. Edited by Paul Edwards. 8 vols. New York: The Macmillan Company and The Free Press, 1967. Also see *The Concise Encyclopedia of Western Philosophy and Philosophers*. Edited by J. O. Urmson. New York: Hawthorn Books, Inc., 1960; and the *Dictionary of Philosophy*. Edited by Dagobert D. Runes. Ames, Iowa: Littlefield, Adams and Company, 1958.)

A posteriori.   Used with reference to statements whose truth or falsity is determined by recourse to evidence from sensory experience. "It will rain tonight" is a statement which can be verified by appeal to empirical evidence.

A priori.   A term referring to statements whose truth or falsity is determined without recourse to evidence from sensory experience. Aristotle held, for example, that either A is B or A is not B (Law of Excluded Middle) is one of the laws fundamental to all reasoning and is not established on observational grounds.

Absolutism.   In metaphysics the infinite, the whole, the complete, the all-embracing unity in contrast to the finite, the partial, the incomplete, the fragmented world of experiences, feelings, thoughts. Used of Hegel and the Absolute Idealists.

Actual entity.   (Whitehead) A term which refers to the real things of which the universe is composed. An experiencing entity. Resembles Leibniz's monads. See *concresence*.

496

Actuality.   That state of affairs in which a thing has become all that it can become, has achieved its essence. Opposed to *potentiality* (q.v.).

Analysis.   The separation of anything into its parts. Considered by many philosophers to be one major aspect of philosophical method. Opposed to *synthesis* (q.v.).

Analytic judgment.   A judgment relating a subject to a predicate included in the meaning of the subject. For example, "A bachelor is an unmarried male."

Appearance.   Used by some epistemologists to mean that which is sensuously observed to be the case. In Plato it means an incomplete exhibition of the real. See *phenomena*.

Associationism.   A psychological theory that the mind is developed from discrete elements and that all mental life can be explained by the combination or separation of these elements according to the laws of association. The classical list of the laws of association (similarity, contrast, and contiguity) were given by Aristotle. Hume cited resemblance and contiguity as the sole laws of association.

Axiomatic method.   The method of taking a set of general statements (axioms) and deducing from them further statements (theorems). If it can be shown that the theorems can validly be inferred from the premises, then it can be said a proof has been given.

Behaviorism.   An American school of psychology limiting the study of humans and animals to their behavior. It rejects mentalistic concepts such as mind, consciousness, images. Pavlov gave the movement impetus with his concept of conditioned reflex. J. B. Watson founded American behaviorism through his formulation of a program for psychology.

Cartesianism.   A noun derived from the name of Rene Descartes referring to two principle doctrines of his philosophy: (1) the delineation of the physical world as extension in motion, and (2) the dichotomy of substances into thinking things (mind) and extended things (matter).

Category.   The condition for the possibility of a universe of discourse being what it is. Some metaphysicians would contend, for example, that without time or duration there would be nothing. Time would be a category for all possible realms of discourse.

Cognition.   Knowledge in its widest sense.

Concrescence.   (Whitehead) A term used to refer to the unifying of various experiences as the actual entity grows towards ends.

Cosmology.   The study of the origin and structure of the universe.

Deduction.   See *inference*.

Determinism.   Every event is caused by other events and comes about as a result of those events. Indeterminism has it that some events happen without being brought about by other events.

Dialectic. The critical analysis of concepts to determine their presuppositions, meanings, implications. Used by Hegel to mean the continuous progress of thought from thesis through antithesis to synthesis.

Eleatic school. Founded by Parmenides in the fifth century B.C. in the town of Elea in Southern Italy. Xenophanes was a forerunner of Parmenides' doctrine that reality is permanent and unchanging. Zeno and Melissus followed Parmenides and defended his teachings.

Empiricism. The view that the origin and source of all knowledge is experience and that the truth value of philosophical statements is determined by appeal to experiences. It denys that knowledge can be gained through such means as innate ideas, reason alone, and instinct.

Epistemology. A branch of philosophy which seeks to criticize the grounds on which knowledge claims are supported, to investigate the principles on which the truth of statements can be evaluated, to construct a rationale of those principles.

Essence. That which a thing is in and for itself, its power, its being.

Forms. See *ideas*.

Forms of the sensibilities. (Kant) The faculty by which sensations are received through *sensuous intuition* (q.v.) and structured under two forms: space and time.

Geist. (Hegel) German word for spirit, mind, intelligence.

Historicism. The view that to give the history of anything is to give a sufficient explanation of it. To understand a nation state one has only to determine its origin and development.

Idealism. Opposed to *materialism* (q.v.).

Ideas. (Plato) A realm of forms which along with change are the essential structural constituents of things. They are necessary, immutable and eternal.

Indeterminism. Opposed to *determinism* (q.v.).

Induction. See *inference*.

Inference. The reasoning process whereby conclusions are drawn either from general propositions (deductive) or from factual data (inductive). A psychological operation which is not to be confused with implications which is a logical operation. An inference is valid only when a genuine implicative relation holds between propositions. See *syllogism*.

Innate ideas. The philosophical doctrine that the mind possesses ideas native to itself and that on proper occasions experiences can cause these ideas to become self-evident.

Irrationalism. The philosophical position that the way to achieve a knowledge of reality is not through reason. Opposed to *rationalism* (q.v.)

Judgment.   Act of the mind asserting (affirming or deny) a predicate of a subject. Immanuel Kant distinguished judgments on the basis of their quality (affirmative, negative, infinite), quantity (universal, particular, singular), relation (categorical, hypothetical, disjunctive), and modality (problematic, assertoric, apodeictic).

Libido.   Used by Freud to mean both the raw physical aspect and the mental aspect of the sexual instinct. By mental aspect is meant the desire for sexual relations.

Logic.   The study of certain types of valid inference.

Materialism.   A metaphysical view that the ultimate nature of things is material overagainst idealism, the view that reality is mental or spiritual.

Metaphysics.   The systematic study of the nature and structure of reality. Ontology is sometimes equated with metaphysics. Sometimes ontology and cosmology are included within it.

Milesian school.   A school of philosophy founded in the sixth century B.C. and situated in the seaport town of Miletus on the shores of Ionia in Western Asia Minor. Its major figures were Thales, Anaximenes, and Anaximander.

Monism.   A metaphysical doctrine that the universe is numerically and/or qualitatively one. Hegel, for example, holds that the universe is One and that it is Spirit.

Myth.   A story symbolically conveying a truth. The creation stories of Genesis 1 and 2 convey in a symbolic manner the Biblical truth that the universe is dependent on Yahweh.

Necessary.   Cannot be other than it is.

Noumena.   (Kant) That which things are in themselves as opposed to that which they appear to be. Opposed to *phenomena* (q.v.).

Ontology.   The study of the nature of reality. See *metaphysics, cosmology.*

Opinion.   A statement for which one lacks evidence or because of insufficient evidence one is unable to claim that one knows.

Phenomena.   Things as they appear to the perceiver. This in contrast to things as they are in themselves. A doctrine held by Immanuel Kant. Opposed to *noumena* (q.v.).

Phenomenal cause.   An objective necessary connection between two events in the field of *phenomena* (q.v.). Given event A, event B necessarily follows.

Philosophes.   A group of seventeenth century French publicists who were interested in the application of the methodology of the natural sciences for interpreting the economic, social, political experiences of men. Through their publications these men sought to make available to men of the Enlightenment the new knowledge developed in the natural sciences.

Philosophy of organism.   Whitehead often referred to his position in these terms. He seems to mean that his thought centers on internally organic actual entities, their nature, and their relation to one another. See *actual entity* and *concrescence.*

Positivism.   The belief that reliable knowledge is attainable only through methods employed by the physical sciences. Logical Positivism holds that meaningful assertions can be made only in propositions verifiable (at least in principle) by empirical evidence. "Time is unreal," is a meaningless assertion; no empirical evidence can count for or against the truth of this proposition. "It is raining outside," is a meaningful statement; it is known what kind of evidence would count for and against the truth of this proposition.

Potentiality.   The capacity of a thing to pass from its present state to a different state. Opposed to *actuality* (q.v.).

Pragmatism.   Primarily a doctrine of meaning and truth. The meaningfulness of an idea or hypothesis is determined by its consequences. If it leads truly, it is true; if falsely, false.

Praxis.   An activity the goal of which is within itself. Opposed to poiesis, an activity the goal of which is to bring about a state of affairs distinct from itself.

Pure concepts of the understanding.   (Kant) *Categories* (q.v.) of the *understanding* (q.v.) deduced from the four kinds of *judgments* (q.v.). The necessary conditions under which the mind makes judgments about the objective world.

Pythagoreans.   A group of philosophers around Pythagoras who were concerned with the form and relations of things. They held that numbers are the ultimate principles which underlie the formal and relational structure of things. The Pythagorean association flourished in Crotona during the sixth century B.C.

Rationalism.   A traditional method of philosophy which holds that the truth or falsity of philosophical statements is determined in a deductive manner. Compare with *empiricism* (q.v.). Generally associated with Platonism and the Continental Rationalists, Descartes, Spinoza, Leibniz.

Scepticism.   A suspension of judgment based on the lack of compelling evidence in favor of one answer to a problem as overagainst all other answers.

Sensuous intuition.   (Kant) Perception. Reception of sensations of the objective world through the *forms of the sensibilities* (q.v.).

Sign.   That which invariably points to a particular thing beyond itself; usually tied to events in the physical world. For example, a dark cloud accompanied by thunder and lightning invariably points to a thunderstorm.

Stoicism.   A school of philosophy founded by Zeno (334–262 B.C.) in Athens distinguished by an ethical position the key to which is the doctrine that one ought to seek to control only that which is within one's power and to resign oneself to what is not under one's control.

Subception. Perception below the conscious level but nevertheless able to result in emotional reactions.

Substance. That on which all things depend for their existence and which depends only upon itself for its own existence. Attributed by different thinkers to God, Reality, the Absolute, Nature.

Syllogism. A form of deductive argument in which the truth of a third proposition (conclusion) necessarily follows if the truth of two other propositions (premises) is granted. For example: No philosophers are educators; all teachers are philosophers; therefore, no teachers are educators.

Symbol. Used to mean the same as a *sign* (q.v.). However, also used to mean that which has general or universal applicability and is not tied to physical events. For example, the lion is the symbol of courage.

Synopsis. A general, overall view of the whole.

Synthesis. The putting together of discrete elements in order to form a whole. Opposed to *analysis* (q.v.).

Synthetic judgment. A judgment relating a subject to a predicate not included in the meaning of the subject. For example, "The music sounds like a waltz."

Teleology. An interpretation of things by referring to their aims, goals, implicit purposes.

Truth. For Plato the kind of knowledge possessed when one grasps reality. Restricted by many contemporary philosophers to refer to a characteristic of propositions, namely, those that are true. Hence one says that a proposition is true (or false).

Understanding. That faculty of the mind by which unity is introduced into the manifold of ideas presented to it. A doctrine developed by Immanuel Kant in his *Critique of Pure Reason.*

Upanishads. A group of ancient Indian religious writings which form the basis of the Vedanta philosophy of Hindu thinkers.

Utilitarianism. The view that an act is right if it produces the greatest amount of good over evil, wrong if it does not. Mill and Bentham defined good as pleasure and evil as pain. G. E. Moore and Hastings Rashdall, who have been called "Ideal" utilitarians, assert that the good may be defined in other ways.

Wissenschaft. (German) Learning, knowledge, scholarship, science.

Biographical Notes

Augustine (353–430 A.D.) was born in Tagaste, North Africa, of a Christian mother and pagan father. Studied and taught rhetoric in Tagaste and Milan. Converted to Christianity under preaching of St. Ambrose, Bishop of Milan. Became Bishop of Hippo, in North Africa. Most famous among his writings are *On the Trinity, Confessions, The City of God.*

Daniel Bell (1919–   ) was educated at City College of New York and Columbia. He taught at the University of Chicago (1945–1948) before joining the faculty of Columbia in 1952. Previously Dr. Bell worked on the editorial staffs of *The New Leader* and *Fortune.* Among his published works are *History of Marxian Socialism in the United States, Work and Its Discontents, The Radical Right.*

Theodore Brameld (1904–   ) received his education at Ripon College and the University of Chicago. He has taught at Long Island University, Adelphi College, University of Minnesota, New York University, and is presently on the faculty at Boston University. Among his best known works are *Ends and Means in Education, A Midcentury Appraisal, Philosophies of Education in Cultural Perspective,* and *Toward a Reconstructed Philosophy of Education.*

Martin Buber (1878–1965) born in Vienna, was the foremost Jewish religious scholar and philosopher. He was a leading figure in the Zionist movement and became Professor of Social Philosophy at the Hebrew University, Jerusalem, in 1938. *I-Thou*, Buber's most important work, has been influential on philosophers and theologians for almost half a century.

Ernst Cassirer (1874–1945) was educated at the Universities of Berlin and Marburg and taught at the Universities of Berlin, Hamburg, Oxford, Yale, and Columbia. His major writings include *The Problem of Knowledge, The Philosophy of Symbolic Forms,* and *An Essay on Man.*

502

John Dewey (1859–1952) was born in Vermont, studied at University of Chicago, and taught at Chicago and Columbia. Foremost among his writings are *How We Think, Democracy in Education, Logic, The Theory of Inquiry,* and *Experience and Nature.*

George W. F. Hegel (1770–1831) was born in Stuttgart, studied at Tubingen, taught in Switzerland, Frankfort, Jena, Heidelberg, and Berlin. His most important works are *Logic, Encyclopedia of Philosophy,* and *Phenomenology of Spirit.*

Carl Jung (1875–1961) was educated at the University of Basel and attained the M.D. degree in 1900. For a time he was associated with Freud but in 1913 he broke with Freud and founded his own school, known as Analytical Psychology.

John Locke (1632–1704) studied medicine and philosophy at Oxford and was keenly influenced by Descartes. He served the Earl of Shaftesbury as tutor and secretary and later held many important public offices. Among his writings are *An Essay Concerning Human Understanding* and *Treatise of Civil Government.*

Immanuel Kant (1724–1804), born in Könisburg, Prussia, of a saddler and reared in pietistic surroundings, was educated at the University of Könisburg. In 1755 he received an appointment at the University and remained there until his death. Foremost among his writings are *The Critique of Pure Reason, The Critique of Practical Reason,* and *The Critique of Judgment.*

Herbert Marcuse (1898–   ) was born in Berlin and received his Ph.D. from the University of Freiburg in 1922. Since coming to the United States he has taught at Columbia, Harvard, and Brandeis and has worked for both the Office of Strategic Services and the State Department. Among his works are *Reason and Revolution* and *Eros and Civilization.*

Jacques Maritain (1882–) was reared in the liberal intellectual climate of Paris and educated at the University of Paris. He taught at the Institute Catholique, Columbia, and Princeton. Foremost among his works are *Man and the State, Rights of Man and Natural Law, Science and Wisdom,* and *Education at the Crossroads.*

Daniel J. O'Conner (1914–   ) is a member of the Department of Philosophy, University of Liverpool. He is also the author of *A Critical History of Western Philosophy.*

Talcott Parsons (1902–   ) Professor of Sociology at Harvard University was educated at Amherst, London School of Economics, and the University of Heidelberg. Before joining the Harvard faculty he taught economics at Amherst for one year. His major works include *Protestant Ethic and the Spirit of Capitalism, Toward a General Theory of Action,* and *Social Structure and Personality.*

Plato (427–347 B.C.), son of noble parents, pupil of Socrates, established the Academy in Athens, teacher of Aristotle. Major writings are in dialogue form among which *The Republic, The Symposium, Timaeus, Crito, Meno,* and *Phaedo* are famous.

Michael Polanyi (1891–) taught social studies and physical chemistry at the University of Manchester before he was elected to his present position as Senior Research Fellow at Merton College, Oxford. His major writings include *Science, Faith and Society, Personal Knowledge,* and *The Study of Man.*

Sartre (1905–) was educated at the École Normale Supérievre in Paris and at the Institute Français in Berlin. After teaching for a short time he devoted himself exclusively to his literary works. A popularizer of existentialism in short stories and plays, Sartre writes complex philosophical treatises, such as his highly technical *Being and Nothingness.* He is best known for his essay "Existentialism."

Melvin Seeman (1918–) was educated at Hopkins College and Ohio State. He is now Professor of Sociology in the Department of Sociology and Anthropology at the University of California, Los Angeles.

A. N. Whitehead (1861–1947) was educated at Trinity College in Cambridge, remained to teach mathematics for twenty-five years, and later taught at London and Harvard Universities. During his career at Harvard, Whitehead wrote his major metaphysical works: *Science and the Modern World, Process and Reality,* and *Adventures of Ideas.*

William H. Whyte (1917–) is a graduate of Princeton and has been assistant managing editor of *Fortune.* He is a writer and now resides in New York City. Among his major works are *Is Anybody Listening?* and *The Organization Man.*

Index

Index

5